ABOUT THE AUTHOR

Photo by John Marelli

Mike Mayo wrote the original *VideoHound's Horror Show*, along with *Video Premieres* and *War Films*. He also edited three volumes of the *DVD Guide*, and was the host of the nationally syndicated *Movie Show on Radio*, also called *Max and Mike on the Movies*. He has reviewed films for *The Washington Post* and *The Roanoke Times*. He is the author of *American Murder: Criminals, Crime and the Media* and the novel *Jimmy the Stick*. He lives in Chapel Hill, North Carolina.

ALSO FROM VISIBLE INK PRESS

Conspiracies and Secret Societies: The Complete Dossier, 2nd edition
by Brad Steiger and Sherry Hansen Steiger
ISBN: 978-1-57859-368-2

Hidden Realms, Lost Civilizations, and Beings from Other Worlds
by Jerome Clark
ISBN: 978-1-57859-175-6

Real Aliens, Space Beings, and Creatures from Other Worlds
by Brad Steiger and Sherry Hansen Steiger
ISBN: 978-1-57859-333-0

Real Ghosts, Restless Spirits, and Haunted Places, 2nd edition
by Brad Steiger
ISBN: 978-1-57859-401-6

Real Monsters, Gruesome Critters, and Beasts from the Darkside
by Brad Steiger
ISBN: 978-1-57859-220-3

Real Vampires, Night Stalkers, and Creatures from the Darkside
by Brad Steiger
ISBN: 978-1-57859-255-5

Real Zombies, the Living Dead, and Creatures of the Apocalypse
by Brad Steiger
ISBN: 978-1-57859-296-8

The Superhero Book: The Ultimate Encyclopedia of Comic-Book Icons and Hollywood Heroes
by Gina Misiroglu
ISBN: 978-1-57859-375-0

The Supervillain Book: The Evil Side of Comics and Hollywood
by Gina Misiroglu and Michael Eury
ISBN: 978-1-57859-178-7

The Vampire Book: The Encyclopedia of the Undead, 3rd edition
by J. Gordon Melton, PhD
ISBN: 978-1-57859-281-4

The Werewolf Book: The Encyclopedia of Shape-Shifting Beings, 2nd edition
by Brad Steiger
ISBN: 978-1-57859-367-5

The Witch Book: The Encyclopedia of Witchcraft, Wicca, and Neo-paganism
by Raymond Buckland
ISBN: 978-1-57859-114-5

Real Nightmares Series

Real Nightmares: True and Truly Scary Unexplained Phenomena (Book 1)
Kindle ISBN: 978-1-57859-398-9
ePub ISBN: 978-1-57859-400-9
PDF ISBN: 978-1-57859-399-6

Real Nightmares: True Unexplained Phenomena and Tales of the Unknown (Book 2)
Kindle ISBN: 978-1-57859-402-3
ePub ISBN: 978-1-57859-403-0
PDF ISBN: 978-1-57859-404-7

Real Nightmares: Things That Go Bump in the Night (Book 3)
Kindle ISBN: 978-1-57859-405-4
ePub ISBN: 978-1-57859-406-1
PDF ISBN: 978-1-57859-407-8

Real Nightmares: Things That Prowl and Growl in the Night (Book 4)
Kindle ISBN: 978-1-57859-408-5
ePub ISBN: 978-1-57859-409-2
PDF ISBN: 978-1-57859-410-8

Real Nightmares: Fiends That Want Your Blood (Book 5)
Kindle ISBN: 978-1-57859-411-5
ePub ISBN: 978-1-57859-412-2
PDF ISBN: 978-1-57859-413-9

Real Nightmares: Unexpected Visitors and Unwanted Guests (Book 6)
Kindle ISBN: 978-1-57859-414-6
ePub ISBN: 978-1-57859-415-3
PDF ISBN: 978-1-57859-416-0

Real Nightmares: Dark and Deadly Demons (Book 7)
Kindle ISBN: 978-1-57859-436-8
ePub ISBN: 978-1-57859-435-1
PDF ISBN: 978-1-57859-434-4

Real Nightmares: Phantoms, Apparitions and Ghosts (Book 8)
Kindle ISBN: 978-1-57859-439-9
ePub ISBN: 978-1-57859-438-2
PDF ISBN: 978-1-57859-437-5

Real Nightmares: Alien Strangers and Foreign Worlds (Book 9)
Kindle ISBN: 978-1-57859-442-9
ePub ISBN: 978-1-57859-441-2
PDF ISBN: 978-1-57859-440-5

Real Nightmares: Ghastly and Grisly Spooks (Book 10)
Kindle ISBN: 978-1-57859-445-0
ePub ISBN: 978-1-57859-444-3
PDF ISBN: 978-1-57859-443-6

Real Nightmares: Secret Schemes and Conspiring Cabals (Book 11)
Kindle ISBN: 978-1-57859-448-1
ePub ISBN: 978-1-57859-447-4
PDF ISBN: 978-1-57859-446-7

Real Nightmares: Freaks, Fiends and Evil Spirits (Book 12)
Kindle ISBN: 978-1-57859-451-1
ePub ISBN: 978-1-57859-450-4
PDF ISBN: 978-1-57859-449-8

Please visit us at visibleinkpress.com.

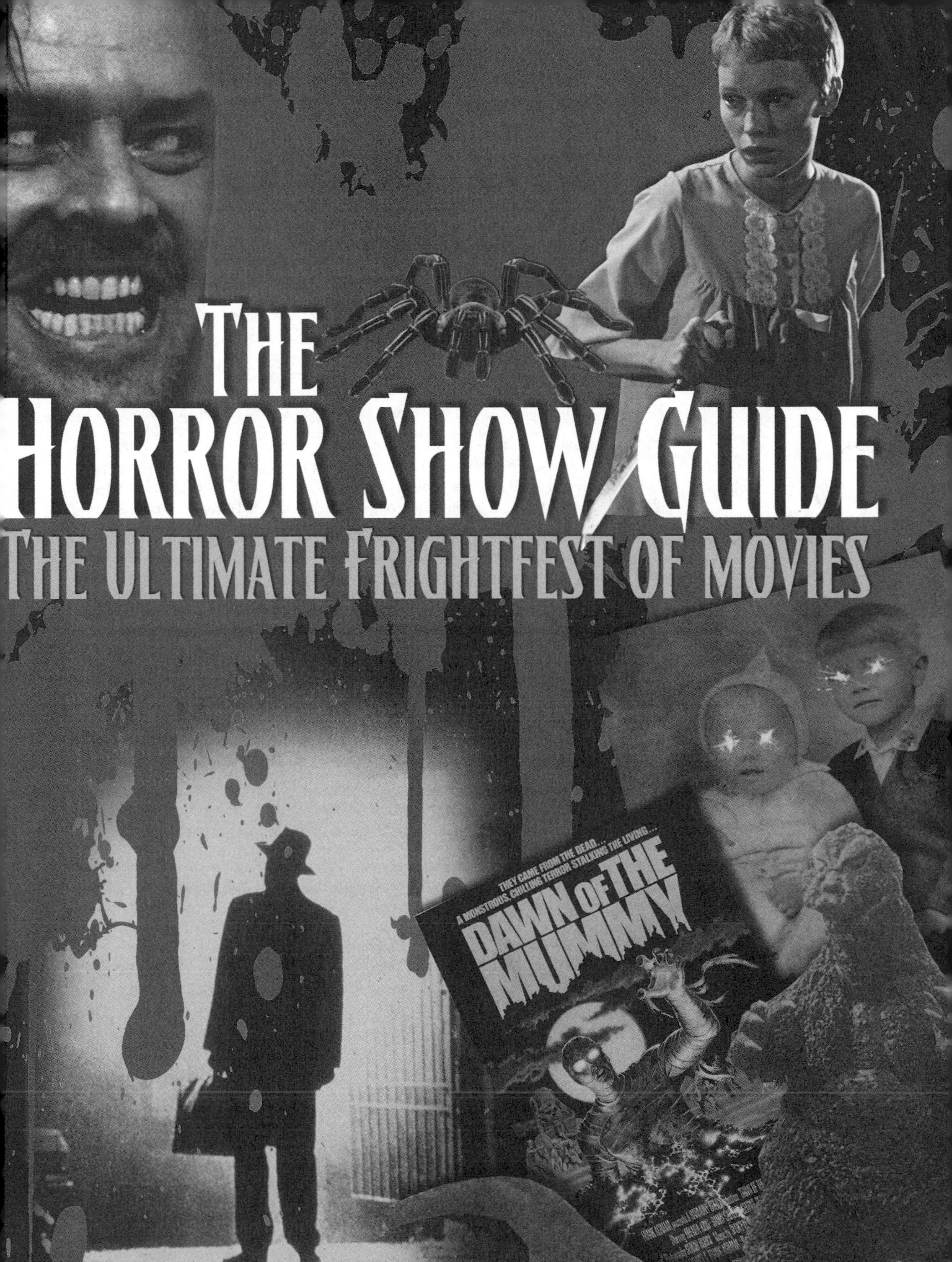
THE
HORROR SHOW GUIDE
THE ULTIMATE FRIGHTFEST OF MOVIES
THEY CAME FROM THE DEAD...
A MONSTROUS, CHILLING TERROR STALKING THE LIVING...
DAWN OF THE MUMMY

HORROR SHOW GUIDE
THE ULTIMATE FRIGHTFEST OF MOVIES

Visible Ink Press®
43311 Joy Rd., #414
Canton, MI 48187-2075
Visible Ink Press is a registered trademark of Visible Ink Press LLC.

Managing Editor: Kevin S. Hile
Art Director: Mary Claire Krzewinski
Typesetting: Marco Di Vita
Proofreaders: Chrystal Rosza and Sarah Trenz
Indexing: Larry Baker

Front cover images: Jack Nicholson in *The Shining* (Warner Bros./Kobal Collection), Mia Farrow in *Rosemary's Baby* (Paramount/The Kobal Collection), *The Woman in Black* (Hammer Film Productions/The Kobal Collection), *Godzilla* (Toho/The Kobal Collection), *The Exorcist* (Warner Bros./The Kobal Collection), *Dawn of the Mummy* (Harmony Gold/The Kobal Collection). Back cover image: Derek Graf in *Zombieland* (Pariah Films/The Kobal Collection). Other images: Shutterstock.

Library of Congress Cataloging-in-Publication Data

Mayo, Mike, 1948–
The horror show guide : the ultimate frightfest of movies / by Mike Mayo.
pages cm
Includes bibliographical references and index.
ISBN 978-1-57859-420-7 (pbk.: alk. paper)
1. Horror films—Catalogs. I. Title.
PN1995.9.H6M32465 2013
016.79143'6164—dc23

2012047065

Printed in the United States of America

10 9 8 7 6 5 4 3 2

CONTENTS

PHOTO CREDITS

KlickingKarl: 222.

The Kobal Collection: 4, 7, 11, 27, 30, 36, 52, 61, 68, 79, 89, 116, 124, 127, 131, 135, 145, 155, 158, 165, 172, 181, 199, 205, 208, 238, 257, 261, 271, 281, 299, 304, 309, 312, 318, 321, 338, 343, 347, 363, 369, 381, 385, 387.

PanzerschreckLeopard: 115.

Poco a poco: 287.

Shutterstock: 5, 34, 64, 66, 112, 120, 141, 148, 195, 248, 258, 289, 294, 358.

All other photos are in the public domain.

INTRODUCTION

They say that time flies but it also sneaks up on you.

When I wrote the first *VideoHound's Horror Show* in 1997, the film business in general and horror in particular were nothing like they are today. The changes, I discovered, were both obvious and subtle, aimed at a new generation of fans who have more experience, if not more sophisticated tastes. An update was needed. This book looks at the most important horror films that have been made in the last fifteen years and combines those reviews with the core pieces from the first book. The result is a mosaic of the horror film from 1910, when the *Edison Frankenstein* was released, until 2012's *Cabin in the Woods,* arranged alphabetically from *Abbott and Costello Meet Frankenstein* to *Zombieland.*

Looking back, the world of 1990s home entertainment seems downright primitive. DVD and HD were years away. VHS tapes were rented, not sold, and even small towns had one or more independently owned video stores. The Blockbuster and Hollywood chains were important, but they did not rule the business. Virtually nobody had broadband access to this new Internet thing. There was no reality TV.

The studios produced dozens of horror movies every year, mostly mid-budget productions with good scripts, casts, directors, and production values. In 1990 Kathy Bates won the Best Actress Oscar for *Misery*. A year later *The Silence of the Lambs* swept all of the major Academy Awards. At the other end of the spectrum, it was impossible for fans to find good copies of older, obscure horror movies. (In this context, "obscure" means European or Asian.) By the time I was working on the first book, horror had become a significant part of the home video business. That fact wasn't really recognized or talked about outside of the industry and growing groups of young fans.

Those were the moviegoers and videophiles who made Wes Craven's *Scream* trilogy a huge commercial hit, paving the way for more "meta" or self-referential horrors. Those films, and so many others made around the same time, were built on the idea that, despite their youth, viewers had a thorough understanding of the genre. These kids had already burned through the horror section of their local video store and were still hungry for more.

After talking and corresponding with a lot of them, I know that weekly gatherings in dens and basement rec rooms to watch horror movies were common everywhere. There was a strong *Mystery Science Theater 3000* component to those occasions, just as there had been a generation or so before, when kids gathered to watch weekend "fright night" broadcasts with the local horror host. Kids cracked jokes at the excesses and shortcomings of cheesy horror, but they still enjoyed it. And, sometimes, they were scared.

They were so familiar with the *Halloween* school of slasher horrors that the *Scream* films could enumerate the "rules." You'll die, for example, if you have sex, take a drink, use drugs or say that you'll be right back. Sequels always have higher body counts than the originals, with bloodier death scenes. By the third film in a series, all the rules were off and anyone can be killed. And in any horror film, the killer can be resurrected, no matter what has been done to him. After Craven set out those "rules" and they were memorized by literally millions of young fans, any horror film that aspired to be hip had to acknowledge them.

Inevitably, a certain sameness crept in, along with smirking irony, as horror became more self-referential and, inevitably, less seriously interested in scaring its viewers.

An equally large problem for horror and for movies in general has been a disturbing lack of originality and dependence on remakes and sequels. Those have been so numerous in the past fifteen years that we decided to change the arrangement of this book. Entries on series and remakes are grouped together by the primary word in the title—Amityville, Exorcist, Hellraiser—even when the titles break alphabetical order. Thus, *Hello, Mary Lou* is listed under *Prom Night, Leatherface* is included with *Texas,* etc. Cast and credits are listed in alphabetical order in a separate index at the end of this book.

For the fan, the consumer, the big technical change was DVDs. It transformed the home video market from a rental business to sales. Titles that had been priced at $50 to $60 on VHS tape were $15 to $20 on DVD. The medium was so successful that it spawned an interest in preservation and restoration of older titles.

When people began building libraries of their favorites, specialty labels and distributors searched the vaults for good prints and negatives of the wonderfully disreputable movies that had flourished in the 1970s. Titles that many fans had only heard of, or watched on murky tapes made from incomplete elements, were available in sparkling detail. In this edition, I have tried to address the changes between VHS and DVD versions wherever I could. I'm sure I missed some.

To write the first book, I watched a lot of movies on those low-def VHS tapes. I also saw them during their initial theatrical releases, in threadbare second-run theaters, drive-ins, projected on portable screens in college lecture halls, and in the best professional screening rooms. For this book, I used DVDs, pay-per-view on cable TV, more screening rooms, IMAX 3D, streaming video, and even a handheld device, something I could not imagined back in 1997.

Those technical changes in delivery systems were more than matched by changes in the content of horror.

The largest and most obvious of those is the rise of the zombie. Today's zombie has nothing to do with Haitian voodoo zombies. It comes straight from George Romero's 1968 *Night of the Living Dead,* though the word "zombie" is never used in the film. These "living dead" are exceptionally simple creatures, and the serious zombie film has simple rules that viewers came to understand instinctively.

The recently deceased suddenly rise to attack and eat the living. The cause is never supernatural. God and religion are seldom important aspects of the zombie film. The zombie plague is usually caused by a returning satellite, an experiment gone awry, the release of the wrong lab animal, something like that.

Zombies cannot run; they cannot speak. They stumble slowly and clumsily. They're not interested in sex. They moan and chew noisily. They can be killed only by decapitation or a bullet to the head.

The bite of the zombie, like the bite of the vampire, is fatal, and in both cases, the victim becomes one of the "undead."

Zombies congregate. There's always a lot of them.

Dan O'Bannon's *Return of the Living Dead* set out guidelines for more comic zombies. In his semi-sequel, zombies are intelligent, relatively nimble and they can speak. They prefer brains to other body parts. Virtually all zombie films feature graphic violence, cannibalism, and a little sex. (*Return* came out in 1985, two years after Michael Jackson's *Thriller*. They share a funky pop sensibility and both were extremely popular and influential.)

Both the serious and the comic zombie film led the way to a steady increase in the amount and explicitness of violence in horror films. The trend begun by Tom Savini's effects for Romero's *Dawn of the Dead,* most notable for the helicopter-blade-to-the-head shot, paved the way for more imaginative killings and mutilations from the '70s to the twenty-first century. Everything became even more "realistic" and detailed once computer-generated effects were introduced. It is not coincidental that the popularity of violent effects increased under the MPAA rating system that was inaugurated in the late 1960s. Reflecting the taste of the American public, the ratings board has always been tolerant of realistic violence. (More about that later.)

But what accounts for the popularity of the zombie film over other types of horror?

At first, it was, in part, a matter of availability. During the early days of the home video business, *Night of the Living Dead* was widely and mistakenly believed to be a public domain title. Thousands, perhaps millions, of bootleg tapes filled bargain bins in stores everywhere. Second rate copies sold for $5 to $10. While George Romero and the producers were screwed out of their investment, the film was gobbled up by countless young viewers, who absorbed its dark vision and the tenets of his zombie apocalypse.

Also, other independent filmmakers realized how effective and economical the zombie film could be. By following the formula that George Romero set out, almost anybody could cobble together a zombie picture. To make one, you need:

- Realistic locations, the more distressed and shopworn the better.
- Simple rotting-flesh makeup (dangling eyeballs optional).
- A dozen or so friends willing to spend several weekends wearing that makeup and tattered clothes.
- A story about a small group of people who fight against the zombie apocalypse.

If zombie films were inexpensive, "found footage" or fake documentary horrors virtually redefined "cheap." The trend began with the surprise hit of 1999, *The Blair Witch Project*. Clever marketing, much of it on the Internet, persuaded a large number of fans that the film showed real events and had been created from film and videotape that had been lost for years and only recently discovered. I remember the two guys who were sitting behind me at a matinée on the opening Friday. One of them really got into the film; the other scoffed throughout. When the lights came up at the end, the doubter said loudly, "You got me to take off work for *that*?"

Despite his reaction, *Blair Witch* was one of the most profitable low-budget movies ever made, and it demonstrated that visual sophistication and technical quality were not necessary. Audiences weaned on *America's Funniest Home Videos* and reality TV would accept a scratchy, poorly focused image and unintelligible sound if they were sufficiently engaged by the story. Many others tried to recreate that success, but no one really managed it until the *Paranormal Activity* franchise. These little films are even more parsimonious in production expenses and they have been stretched out to four installments so far.

When Hollywood attempted to mount more lavish productions, it often turned to the remake. In horror, it took the form of American versions of proven Asian hits. Beginning with *The Ring* and *The Grudge,* these were exceptionally well-crafted ghost stories with first-rate casts, restrained, imaginative special effects, and tremendous atmospherics built on ominous sounds and images of water. (*The Ring* also boasts one of the great third act shocks.) Most of the remakes that followed repeated those elements with considerably less success.

After that wave had passed, producers turned their greedy and unoriginal eyes to the great American horrors of the 1970s and '80s with remakes and reboots. In almost every case, the new films are much more expensive and technically polished. They also have a pasteurized quality that robs them of the frightening power generated by the groundbreaking originals. Note, for example, the slight but significant plot change in the remake of *Last House on the Left*. Though the 2009 film is more graphically and realistically violent than the original, it chickens out on a key point.

What else changed in horror after zombies, faux docs, and remakes?

"Rural" horror in the *Psycho/Deliverance* mode reappeared with dozens of variations on a plot that can be reduced to "A group of young people go off to a place in the country where they are attacked by an alien or a redneck or a zombie or a mutant."

While zombie and psycho killer stories have largely maintained their realistic or scientific basis, the religious/supernatural horror is represented by titles that usually include the words "exorcism," "possession," or "haunting." If those have not been as influential as their secular cousins, they tend to be carefully crafted, character-based stories heavy on contortionist effects. They are almost always profitable.

Grand Guignol made a brief, bloody return with "torture porn" in the *Saw* series, Eli Roth's *Hostel* films, and a few others.

In virtually all of those schools of horror, the rapid evolution of digital technology has made the depiction of monstrous creatures and human-on-human violence more realistic than they have ever been before, but that has not necessarily made them more believable or emotionally powerful. The super-slow-motion shot of a bullet entering and exiting flesh with each droplet of the blood spray rendered in crystalline clarity is, in its own way, as clearly unreal as a guy in a cheap rubber suit.

That graphic violence is part of the coarsening of entertainment in almost all forms, not just horror, but the genre has certainly been a testing ground.

The final, and probably the most important, change in horror has been the acceptance by the mainstream of horror's traditional characters and themes. Stephenie Meyers' *Twilight* series, both in print and on film, may not be true horror, but the works certainly appropriate key concepts and characters from classic horror and use them for new purposes.

With the exception of Lionsgate, the studios aren't interested in horror, or in any original dramas, really. The bulk of their money and creative energy is devoted to fantasy action blockbusters and animation. Everything else, including horror, suffers. But, as depressing as that thought may be, as long as people like Larry Fessenden, James Wan, and Guillermo del Toro horror movies, we have some reason to hope.

And a new generation of fans is ready to dive in.

So, as I've said before, step right up. Have a seat here on the sofa while I load this DVD and fire up the widescreen. The horror show is about to begin....

—Mike Mayo
Chapel Hill, NC
November, 2012

Because so many sequels, series and remakes have been produced in the past fifteen years, we have grouped reviews by the primary word in the title—*Amityville, Prom Night, Hellraiser,* etc.—rather than alphabetical order. Cast and credits are listed in strict alphabetical order in a separate appendix.

Abbott and Costello Meet ... Series (1948–1955)

In *Abbott and Costello Meet Frankenstein,* their first meeting with the studio's famous monsters, Bud Abbott and Lou Costello are railroad baggage clerks in Florida where strange crates arrive for the wax museum. Dracula (Bela Lugosi) wants to revive Frankenstein's monster (Glenn Strange) by giving him Lou's brain! Lawrence Talbot (Lon Chaney Jr.), a.k.a. The Wolfman, says no. It's all played for laughs, making this one of the better horror comedies, with the emphasis definitely on comedy. At one point, director Charles T. Barton allows the Count's reflection to show in a mirror! For shame! Still, some of the animated effects are pretty cool. By the time this lively romp was made, the monsters had passed their prime, and so they're figures of fun. That's fine for Bud and Lou, but for the creatures, familiarity breeds complacency.

As the clumsy title suggests, the second entry in the series, *Abbott and Costello Meet the Killer, Boris Karloff,* is hardly the finest hour for any of the key participants. Karloff is a conman to Bud and Lou's hotel employees. The comedy is played out on the studio's familiar sets. Compared to the duo's other teamings with Universal monsters, it's average or below, and wouldn't be included here if Karloff weren't in it.

In ... *Meet the Invisible Man,* Bud and Lou are newly graduated detectives who are hired by a boxer (Arthur Franz) to clear his name after being falsely accused of murder. Before they can do anything, he shoots up with Supertransparent Joy Juice. Yes, the plot is baldly lifted from *The Invisible Man Returns,* and some of the scenes are directly recycled, too, including those cute little hamsters in their leather harnesses. The special effects

Comedians Bud Abbott and Lou Costello met several monsters and spooks in their movies, including the Invisible Man.

make for a more comfortable fit with the popular comedians' style than many of their other outings with the Universal horror stars.

When they *Meet Dr. Jekyll and Mr. Hyde,* the boys are bumbling London Bobbies to Boris Karloff's Dr. Jekyll in a pedestrian entry in the comic series. The Hyde makeup, usually worn by stunt man Eddie Parker, is little more than a gorilla mask and the transformation effects are substandard. Karloff is completely comfortable with his limited role. Craig Stevens, TV's Peter Gunn, is the romantic lead. The suffragette chorus line routine will raise feminist hackles. Combining this particular horror story with comedy is handled more entertainingly by the various Warner Bros. cartoons starring Sylvester the Cat and Tweetie-Hyde.

The series comes to an end when the guys *Meet the Mummy.* By the time Universal made the film, the studio had produced five Mummy features and had paired the comedians with four other horror stars. The bloom was far off the rose. Still, the slapstick and pratfalls are quickly paced, and though there's comparatively little actual Mummy footage, a giant iguana does pop up briefly and inexplicably, and, yes, that's Richard Deacon as the high priest Semu.

Abominable Dr. Phibes, The (1971)
Dr. Phibes Rises Again (1972)

In Vincent Price's long and varied work in the field, this may be his most enjoyable role. As a vengeful 1920s mad doctor, he's droll and virtually silent. More important to the film, he's got a fine, funny script and excellent costars. Though Terry-Thomas, Hugh Griffith, and Joseph Cotten don't have as much to do, they contribute substantially. Add in grand sets, costumes, jazzy music, props, and even some fair scares amid the laughs. Robert Feust directs with a confident, wry tone and gives new meaning to the term "acid rain." Yes, that's Caroline Munro as the late Mrs. Phibes. Simply a delight for fans of Grand Guignol comedy.

The ostensible sequel, *Dr. Phibes Rises Again,* is really a baroque recreation of the original with humor that's even more tongue-in-cheek, if that's possible. (Sample dialogue: "I don't know about his body, but we should give his head a decent burial.") An introduction goes back over the key points of the first film wherein Phibes eludes capture by draining his blood and replacing it with embalming fluid. To rise again, he simply reverses the process. The new plot finds Phibes and Darius Biederbeck (Robert Quarry) heading for Egypt to discover the secret of eternal life at the Temple of Ibiskis. Amazingly, Quarry's flamboyance matches Price's. The presence of Hugh Griffith, Terry Thomas and, all too briefly, Beryl Reid helps, too. Fiona Lewis, Valli Kemp, and Caroline Munro provide delightful window dressing. The script is filled with visual and verbal wit seldom found in horror. It's difficult to maintain such a light tone without it disintegrating into frivolity. This one manages beautifully. With grand sets and props and literary references left and right, it's every bit as enjoyable as the original.

Abraham Lincoln: Vampire Hunter (2012)

Even those who are willing to accept the premise of the improbably popular novel may feel like they've been trampled into submission by the end of this adaptation. Could Abraham Lincoln's mother have been killed by a vampire? And might Lincoln (Benjamin Walker, who looks like Liam Neeson's kid brother) have sought revenge with a silver-tipped axe and then gone on to seek political office when he learned that the undead controlled the Southern slave trade? Writer Seth Grahame-Smith treats vampirism with the same frivolity—albeit bloody, graphic frivolity—that he brings to history. Both the decapitation-intensive action scenes and the period details are handled with heavy CGI effects, and the entire film has an almost hand-tinted ap-

A young Abe Lincoln slays vampires before becoming president of the United States in *Abraham Lincoln: Vampire Hunter.*

pearance. Character and plot particulars are sacrificed to a galloping pace.

Addams Family, The (1991) Addams Family Values, The (1993)

The original one-joke movie is short on plot, long on the delicious graveyard humor that Charles Addams created. The best moments are virtual recreations of magazine cartoons. A few scenes of manic action—a silly duel, a dance, a school play—seem out of step with the otherwise deliberately slow pace. Somehow, though, the relationship between Morticia (Anjelica Huston) and Gomez (Raul Julia) is so believably intense that it energizes the rest of the film. The rest of the casting, notably Christina Ricci as Wednesday and Christopher Lloyd as Uncle Fester, is equally inspired.

Remarkably, the sequel, *Addams Family Values,* is even better. As a killer blonde with the most basic instincts, Joan Cusack is a welcome addition to the ghoulish clan. She joins the family as a nanny for Gomez (Raul Julia) and Morticia's (Anjelica Huston) new son Pubert though her sights are really set on Uncle Fester (Christopher Lloyd). Young Christina Ricci almost steals the film from all of them. Even though the humor is based on grisly material, it's never offensive. As the title indicates, though, those who define "family values" narrowly will likely disagree. Paul Rudnick's script is stronger and funnier, and director Barry Sonnenfeld seems more comfortable with the material.

Addiction, The (1995)

Totally bummed out by pictures of My Lai and a walk down a tough inner city street, philosophy grad student Catherine (Lili Taylor) is set upon by a suave exotic vampire (Annabella Sciorra) in a slinky evening dress. Catherine's progress from neophyte to card-carrying undead is a slow dreamlike black-and-white exercise in contradiction. On one hand, vampirism is presented as a logical alternative to reading Kierkegaard and Sartre. In their worst moments—and there are far too many of these—the bloodsuckers sound like refugees from a particularly windy David Mamet play—talking, talking, talking about things the audience cares absolutely nothing about. The film is stylishly staged and photographed. Long stretches appear to be thoroughly humorless, but then they're punctuated by moments of violence so bizarre they can only be seen as low comedy. With the challenging and unpredictable Abel Ferrara, it's always hard to tell when he's being serious and when he's putting us on. Maybe those are the same.

Anjelica Huston played the part of Morticia in the movie versions of *The Addams Family*.

Afraid of the Dark (1991)

It would be unfair to reveal virtually any of the plot twists in this disturbing psychological horror story. It's told almost completely from the point of view of young Lucas (Ben Keyworth), a British boy who's first seen behind a pair of Coke-bottle-bottom glasses. Someone in his cozy urban neighborhood is slashing blind women with a straight razor. His own mother (Fanny Ardant) might be a victim. The real focus, though, is on Lucas as we slowly learn who and what he is. The source of the horror is childhood itself, what it's like to be small and inexperienced and powerless in a world made for larger beings. It's complex, challenging, and unconventional. Writer Mark Peploe's (*The Passenger, The Sheltering Sky, Little Buddha*) directorial debut is a small masterpiece.

After.life (2009)

Mad at her boyfriend (Justin Long) and generally unhappy, Anna (Christina Ricci) crashes her car and wakes up on a table in the basement of a funeral home. She wants to leave, but the proprietor, Mr. Deacon (Liam Neeson) says that she's dead and he's got the paperwork to prove it. Actually, she is between life and death and he can help her finish the transition. She is not persuaded. The creepy atmosphere is strong. Neeson's quiet severity is ideal for the role, and Anna is only a short step from Ricci's work as Wednesday Addams. Writer/director Agnieszka Wojtowicz-Vosloo handles the curious premise deftly.

Alice Sweet Alice (1976)

Though this psycho-horror is hyped as the debut of a very young Brooke Shields, she has a tiny role. The film is really a complex indictment of Catholicism. Director Alfred Soles' use of middle-class New Jersey locations recalls the better work of George Romero, and he fills the screen with realistic grotesques who are every bit as frightening as walking corpses. He and co-writer Rosemary Ritvo create an interconnected series of bizarre conflicts involving Alice (Paula Sheppard), her sister Karen (Shields), her extended family, community, and church in the early 1960s. The film's influence on various slasher films, particularly the Italians, of following decades is obvious. Despite a modest budget, it has aged better than many more expensive productions of the same era. The ending's terrific. (Alternate name: *Communion.*)

Alien (1979)
Aliens (1986)
Alien³ (1992)
Alien Resurrection (1997)

The seven-member crew of the space freighter *Nostromo* is awakened from artificial sleep when the ship's computer picks up a signal from a stormy planet. They investigate and the rest is horror history. Director Ridley Scott and writer Dan O'Bannon tell a deceptively simple and completely frightening story. The importance of the magnificent sets created by Ron Cobb and H.R. Geiger cannot be overemphasized. Geiger's "biomechanical" creature has influenced almost every screen monster that's come since. Cobb calls the interior of the *Nostromo* a "cross between an art deco dance hall and a World War II bomber." Combine all that with letter-perfect ensemble acting led by Sigourney Weaver's career-defining Ripley and the result is an unqualified masterpiece. None of the expensive sequels has approached its intensity.

In *Aliens,* James Cameron turns Scott's deliberately paced horror-suspense classic into a hard-charging action movie told at a roller-coaster pace. Space Marines go back to the original planet to rescue colonists and find an infestation of the H.R. Geiger's famous creations. Accompanying them, Ripley overcomes her fear, and ends things with a thrilling confrontation with the Queen Mother Alien. Fine performances all around, particularly from Lance Henriksen who gives his android character a subtle twist of mechanical weirdness.

Ripley (Sigourney Weaver) is menaced again by the horrific Geiger alien in *Alien³*.

Alien³, by far the weakest entry in the series, suffers from director David Fincher's rock-video approach to the subject. The studio went through several writers and directors and what emerged is a fairly unintelligible mess. It begins in standard fashion with Ripley crash landing her escape vehicle on a prison planet. Of course, the critter hitched a ride, too. But Fincher demonstrates such disdain for the basics of narrative storytelling that most viewers will probably watch the last third of the film wondering what the hell is going on. That's a perfect way to destroy any suspense the action might generate. The creature effects don't measure up to the others, either.

The fourth installment, *Alien: Resurrection,* finds that Ripley and the parasitic alien queen within her have been cloned on a medical research spaceship. The doctors think that they can contain and exploit the creature, etc. etc. You know where that part is going. Everything changes when the cargo ship *Betty* arrives, and writer Joss Whedon's fans realize that it's a prototype for *Serenity* and the *Firefly* TV series.

Alien Trespass (2009)

A DVD introduction presents this tongue-in-cheek parody as a "lost" masterpiece from 1957, hidden away in the vaults for all these years because of studio infighting. Like those '50s invasion pictures, this one is played out on inexpensive sets with low-fidelity special effects. It's also far too talky. On

The Top Seven Alien Invader Movies

The Arrival
Attack the Block
They Live
The Thing (1951)
Slither
Alien Trespass
The Blob

the night of the meteor shower over a little desert town, the usual suspects—scientist, his wife, cute waitress, teenagers parked on lover's lane, drunken desert rat and his dog—all see something crash to earth. The saucer holds a one-eyed monster that looks like a big carrot, and a spaceman in a shiny suit. What follows is campy and vampy but not quite enough.

Alligator (1980)
Alligator II: The Mutation (1991)

No-frills B-movie knows exactly what it is—a rip-off of *Jaws* complete with here-comes-the-monster music—and doesn't try to be anything else. Following the big-critter formula faithfully, John Sayles' script is based on the urban legend of a 'gator that was flushed down a toilet into metropolitan sewers where it grows to monstrous proportions. Robert Forster is the cop hunting the reptile; Robin Riker is the cute herpetologist who helps him; Dean Jagger is the evil millionaire behind it all; comic Jack Carter is the mayor of Chicago. Toward the end, when the beastie appears in full sunlight, the film becomes outright comedy and Sayles lets his politics show. Throughout, it's fast-moving and fun.

The only original element in *Alligator II: The Mutation* is professional wrestling. Beyond that dubious addition, the flick is a rehash of the above average original with Steve Railsback as the evil industrialist who dumps growth-enhancing chemicals into the sewers, Joseph Bologna as the police detective on the critter's trail, and Dee Wallace Stone as the scientist. They're abetted by a dozen or so equally stale stereotypes and some negligible monster effects.

Alone in the Dark (2005)

Uwe Boll borrows bits from *X-Files, Men in Black,* and *Aliens* in this adaptation of a video game. Comically lengthy introductory supertitles establish the vanished Abkani Indians who opened a gate between dimensions allowing in CGI critters called Zenoes. They're studied by the government's paranormal investigators, Bureau 713. Christian Slater is an ex-713 agent. Tara Reid is a brilliant anthropologist who helps him. The action scenes are elaborately choreographed and edited. The acting is wooden but given the stilted nature of the script and the general level of overall foolishness, it's hard to be too tough on anyone.

American Haunting, An (2005)

Underpowered period piece claims to be based on a true story. In Red River, Tennessee, 1817, John Bell (Donald Sutherland) is punished in church court for a land deal in which he cheated neighbor Kathe Batts (Gaye Brown). Some say she's a witch and straightaway, Bell's beloved daughter Betsy (Rachel Hurd-Wood) is attacked by an unseen entity in her bedroom. Most of the action involves people fighting against invisible ghosts and losing. Director Courtney Solomon tries to jazz things up with freewheeling camera movement. Graphic violence is kept to a minimum and the running time is a swift seventy-six minutes without the closing credits.

American Horror Story (2011)

Ambitious, multilayered, multipart television production actually manages to live up to its audacious title. It's an unusual work in that it was conceived as a twelve-part story that would arrive at a satisfying conclusion at the end of its single-season run. (The second season features some of the same cast members playing new characters in a different setting.) The troubled Harmon family—father Ben (Dylan McDermott), mother Vivien (Connie Britton), and their teenage daughter, Violet (Taissa Farmiga)—moves from Boston to a Los Angeles mansion that has been the site of several murders. Their neighbor Connie (Jessica Lange) is an aging actress who might have been created by Tennessee Williams on a really bad night. References to other horror films and to such real crimes as the Richard Speck and Black Dahlia murders appear throughout, along with some astonishing, monstrous creations. The result is every bit as imaginative, shocking, and frightening as any contemporary theatrical release, and more intelligent than most with an edge of bizarre humor.

American Nightmare (2002)

Occasionally amateurish low-budget Texas production benefits immeasurably from a terrific performance by Debbie Rochon as homicidal nurse Jane Toppan. (Yes, she's named for America's number one female serial killer.) The complicated plot revolves around her stalking a group of friends on Halloween, but it doesn't follow the familiar formula and leaves many significant details unresolved. The situation and the main character are cut from different cloth. The star is at her best.

American Psycho (2000)

Crazed adaptation of Brett Easton Ellis's controversial best-seller is a legitimate heir to *A Clockwork Orange* (and, for my money, more successful). It's a comedy of unimaginable excesses—excesses of food, drink, business cards, cosmetics, clothing, sex, furnishings, madness, and soaring pop soliloquies. Patrick Bateman (Christian Bale), a young master of the universe in 1980s New York, murders friends and strangers by night. The film begins as a relatively realistic portrait of city life among the rich and pretty, but it quickly floats farther and farther into its own fantastic realm. The tenuous balance of humor and horror is something that's seldom achieved. Credit writer/director Mary Harron and a bravura performance from the star. One of the greats. (Followed by a sequel in title only.)

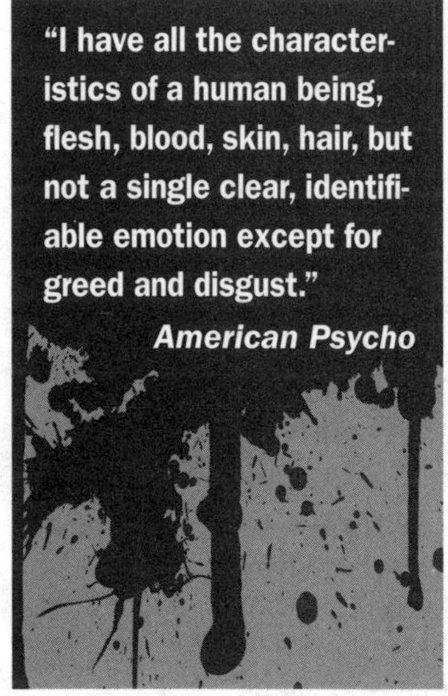

American Werewolf in London, An (1981)

John Landis' ambitious updating of *The Wolf Man* may be the most frightening combination of comedy and horror ever put on screen. Knocking around England, two American college kids, David (David Naughton) and Jack (Griffin Dunne), are attacked by a creature on the moor. Jack survives and his problems begin with a series of terrifying visions. Initially, Landis sets a friendly, leisurely pace and the first violent scenes are carefully shrouded in darkness. The really good scares in the middle are based on the characters, and particularly on Jack's state of mind, giving his terror a strongly sympathetic dimension. And that's the real appeal of good werewolf stories—the mix of revulsion and sympathy that the protagonist's situation produces. At the same time, waking up to find Jenny Agutter as your nurse makes you think that maybe a little case of lycanthropy wouldn't be so bad after all. The only flaw is a relatively weak ending.

American Werewolf in Paris, An (1997)

Semi-sequel begins with a meeting on the Eiffel Tower that's so preposterous the rest ought not to work at all, but somehow it does. Young tourist Andy (Tom Everett Scott) is immediately smitten by Seraphine (Julie Delpy), and soon learns that she's not like other French girls. The writers give credit to John Landis' *American Werewolf in London,* and they use some of the same plot devices but the tone is much lighter. The tragic aspects of the original, which came first in *The Wolf Man,* are absent. Instead, we've got good

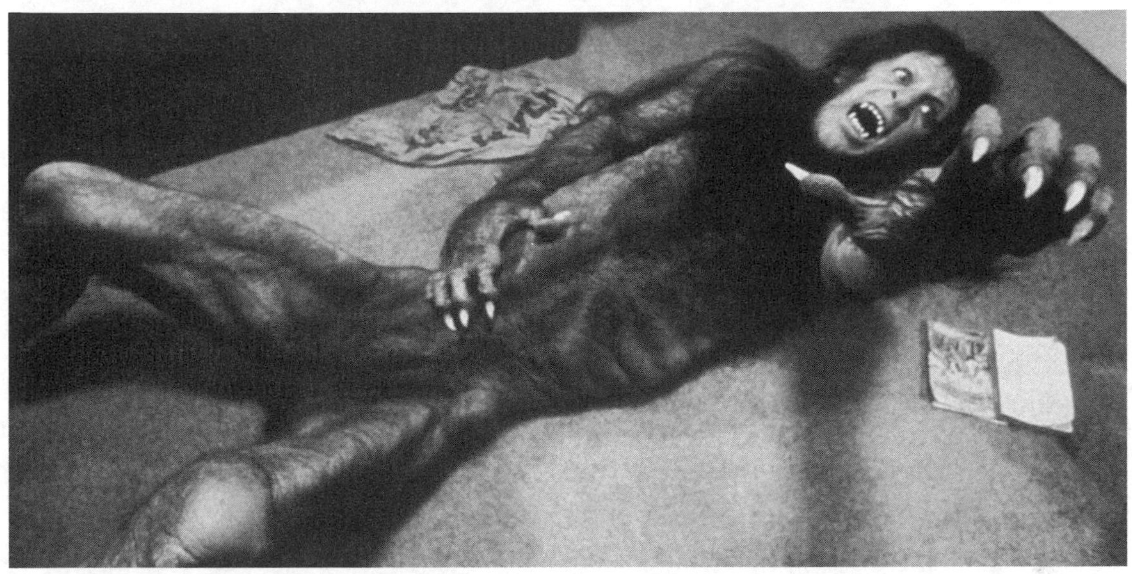

For a movie released in 1981, the special effects—especially the werewolf transformation scene—in *American Werewolf in London* are superb.

werewolves and bad werewolves. The pace is quick and director Anthony Waller's (*Mute Witness*) style is much more fluid. Even though Peter Lloyd's transformation and monster effects are more graphic, the film isn't as frightening as Landis'. That's Waller as the Metro driver.

Amityville Horror, The (1979, 2005)
Amityville II: The Possession (1982)
Amityville 3-D (1983)
Amityville 4: The Evil Escapes (1989)
Amityville Curse, The (1989)
Amityville 1992: It's about Time (1992)
Amityville: A New Generation (1993)
Amityville: Dollhouse (1996)

Stephen King argues that the success of the ridiculous *Amityville Horror* can be found in the lean economics of the 1970s—that people were able to identify with the plight of a young couple (James Brolin and Margot Kidder) who'd sunk everything they had into a Long Island house that turned out to be a lemon. So's the movie, but it has still turned the word "Amityville" into a franchise that's generated an impressive number of sequels and remakes. The plot is standard haunted house stuff with a weak ending and Rod Steiger on hand to chew the scenery as a priest. On the plus side, the house has a feeling of reality to it.

The first sequel, *Amityville II: The Possession,* finds Burt Young, in his usual obnoxious screen self, as the seedy patriarch of a family that buys the famous Long Island house. Child abuse, incest, arguments, shouting matches, telekinesis, possession, and the unspeakable horror of a damp basement are all visited upon them. Director Damiano Damini tries gamely to punch up the low-level suspense with a restlessly mobile camera. Filmed in Jersey City and Mexico City.

Like most 3s made in 3-D, *Amityville 3-D* looks muddy and dark on the conventional small screen, and without the dubious benefit of the optical effect of the third dimension, the in-your-face camerawork is pointless. So is the table-rapping plot which begins with a big green hairball. Why—beyond the obvious motivation of a paycheck—are such a talented cast and director wasting their time on drek like this? Yes, that is a young Meg Ryan.

Amityville 4: The Evil Escapes kicks off in high gear with the house attacking priests who come to exorcise it. According to the subtitle, the evil escapes through an electrical outlet and takes up residence in a particularly hideous lamp which then relocates to California. Many of the scares have to do with other appliances—from tea kettles to chainsaws and disposals—that turn themselves on. Stars Patty Duke and Jane Wyatt are spared the most embarrassing moments.

The Amityville Curse, the fifth installment in the title-only series, adds some intentional humor, but it's a wasted effort. Even judged by the low standards set by its predecessors, this one's a lackluster effort. It's about five adults who stay in a rundown house and are bothered by ghosts, dogs, tarantulas, a confessional in the basement, and that old favorite, the bathtub full of blood. Filmed in Canada, it's slow, pointless, and without scares.

Amityville: A New Generation transplants the questionable horrors of a Long Island single-family home and a middle-class family to a studio loft filled with boho artist types. It does not generate any significant increases on the scare-scale. This time, the source of the spooks or whatever is a mirror that a homeless guy claims is an old family heirloom. He gives it to photographer Keys (Ross Partridge) and terrible things happen to him and his pals. The young cast is blandly attractive.

The Top Nineteen Rural/Redneck Horrors

Attack of the Giant Leeches
Eaten Alive
Texas Chainsaw Massacre
House of 1,000 Corpses
Frailty
Hush Hush Sweet Charlotte
Wrong Turn
High Tension
I Spit on Your Grave
Storm Warning
Eden Lake
Tucker and Dale versus Evil
Bitter Feast
Cabin Fever
Cabin in the Woods
Wendigo
Pumpkinhead
Splinter
Frontier(s)

The same writers do better work with *Amityville 1992: It's about Time,* which, if truth-in-titling laws were enforced, would have been called "The Amityville Clock." Said timepiece is brought by Jake (Stephen Macht) from a house torn down for a tract development. Jake's an adman who's broken up with Andrea (Shawn Weatherly) but their relationship with each other and with his kids is complicated. Director Tony Randel also made one of the *Hellraiser* movies and displays more affinity for elaborate clockwork devices. Actually, this entry is the best in the weak series with top-notch production values and genuine scares, including a graphic dog attack.

In *The Amityville Dollhouse,* the economic premise of the original becomes 90s pop psychological stuff with two single parents (Robin Thomas and Starr Andreeff) bringing a "blended family" into an ugly new house in California. Some time before, another house burned on the site and the titular dollhouse (with the two funny little windows) has been left in a shed. Joshua Michael Stern's plot borrows freely from *Poltergeist* and *Pet Sematary* and contains some scary stuff involving wasps and an attempt at characterization. The rest is familiar special effects, capably done and arguably no worse than the original.

The original *Amityville Horror* was remade in 2005 with Ryan Reynolds and Melissa George in the leads. Made by the same producers who rehashed *Texas Chainsaw Massacre,* it employs some razzle-dazzle effects and editing, and shifts part of the focus to the original murders. That's certainly not to say it's any better than the so-so original.

Anaconda (1997)

Gonzo tongue-in-cheek take on *Creature From the Black Lagoon* is mildly enjoyable for all the wrong reasons. The snake itself is such a blatant special effect that it's not at all frightening and that's somehow part of the fun. Documentary filmmakers head up the Amazon to find the lost Shimmyshamba tribe. Director Terri Flores (Jennifer Lopez), cameraman Danny Rich (Ice Cube) and Dr. Cale (Eric Stoltz) are more or less in charge until they run into Paul Sarone (Jon Voight), a half-mad snake hunter. A few others fill out the cast, and experienced horror fans can predict the order in which they'll become anaconda snack-pacs. The critter itself is big enough to bolt down a Buick, but the main attraction is Jon Voight. He has a wonderful time playing a crazed villain with a psychotic Ricky Ricardo accent and a collection of grimacing facial expressions that bear no resemblance to any known human emotion.

Anatomy (2000)
Anatomy 2 (2003)

Medical student Paula Henning (Franka Potente) is accepted into a prestigious Heidelberg research program with the distinguished Prof. Grombek (Traugott Buhre). She's carrying on the family tradition of her grandfather, who's dying in the hospital he helped to build, and her father, with whom she disagrees on almost everything. When she arrives at the university, she finds that very creepy stuff is going on in the fancy new state-of-the-art anatomy lab. It's inventive and grotesque, with some of the most disgusting and lovingly photographed medical horror ever put on screen. If the ending isn't as strong as the beginning, the star is fine throughout.

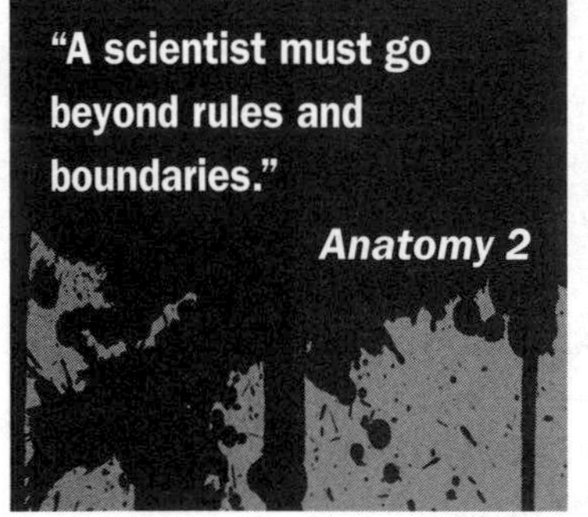

Anatomy 2 is an above-average sequel. It opens with an artily staged scene of self-mutilation. Joachim (Barnaby Metschurat) goes to Berlin to study medicine and falls in with a group of young students and doctors who work with the charismatic Dr. Müller-LaRousse (Herbert Knaup). Director Stefan Ruzowitzky works with new variations on the medical horrors of his first film. Production values are equally strong.

And Now the Screaming Starts (1973)

Handsome, slow-moving period piece begins with voice-over narration suggesting *Rebecca* but eventually becomes a town-with-a-secret Gothic as young bride Catherine (Stephanie Beacham) tries to learn what her husband Charles (Ian Ogilvy) is hiding at the Fengriffin estate. Director Roy Ward Baker overuses non-scary gimmicks—disembodied hand, face at the window, etc.—and bad music, but the story does have some suspense. Unfortunately, that suspense is overplayed and its revelation is less than compelling. The production is well acted throughout, with Peter Cushing bringing his customary grace to the proceedings.

Andy Warhol's Dracula (1974)

Tongue-in-cheek comedy opens with Dracula (Udo Kier) painting his hair—yes, painting—before a mirror in which he casts no reflection but can, presumably, see himself with vampire vision or something. His butler (Arno Juerging) persuades him to leave his castle and go to Italy where he can recharge his batteries with "wirgin" blood. He ends up on a nobleman's (Vittorio De Sica) estate where a Marxist stud-muffin servant (Joe Dallesandro) spouts rhetoric and makes the Count's quest much more difficult with the family's four daughters. The whole production is much more polished than the companion *Frankenstein,* and, until the last limb-lopping reel, it's not nearly as bloody either. The ensemble histrionics are wondrous to behold, and not one frame is meant to be taken seriously. Though Paul Morrissey is credited as director, some sources claim that the film was made by Antonio Margheriti.

Alternate names: *Andy Warhol's Young Dracula, Blood for Dracula, Dracula Cerca Sangue di Vergine e ... Mori de Sete, Dracula Vuole Vivere: Cerca Sangue de Vergina.*

Andy Warhol's Frankenstein (1973)

Infamous camp classic is still properly revolting. It's also slow, too talky, poorly acted and flat out ugly. The substandard production values don't look any better on video than they did on the big screen. The story revolves around the incestuous Baron (Udo Kier), his sister (Monique Van Vooren), her lover (Joe Dellesandro), and a couple of creations. Since the film was made for 3-D, lots of objects and bleeding organs are thrust toward the camera. The decapitation effects aren't going to scare anybody these days. For energy and imagination it compares poorly to *Rocky Horror,* which was made a year later. Though Warhol crony Morrissey is credited as director, many sources say that Italian Antonio Margheriti is responsible.

Alternate titles: *The Frankenstein Experiment, Up Frankenstein, The Devil and Dr. Frankenstein, Flesh for Frankenstein.*

Angel Heart (1987)

Some very scary stuff is undermined (at least partially) by an odd sense of humor. Tough '50s detective Harry Angel (Mickey Rourke) receives a call from the law firm of MacIntosh and Winesap. Not long after that, he tells us that he has a problem with chickens. We're supposed to take him seriously? What begins as *noir* moves into dreamy, nightmarish surrealism and becomes an exercise in style for director Alan Parker, sticking close to the source material, William Hjortsberg's fine novel, *Falling Angel.* Visually striking with Rourke at his seediest.

The Top Six Urban Horror Movies

Midnight Meat Train
Creep
Anatomy
Jacob's Ladder
The Grudge
Candyman

Apprentice to Murder (1988)

In Pennsylvania, 1928, John Reese (Donald Sutherland) is a faith healer and medicine man who mixes simple Christianity, mysticism, and potions. Billy Kelly (Chad Lowe) becomes his protégé, and at the same time meets Alice (Mia Sara), a bold, angelic young woman. Does Reese have supernatural powers, or is he a charlatan? When director R.L. Thomas tries to answer those questions, the action becomes choppy and fragmented. As long as it's focused on the three main characters and their setting, it's much more interesting. Give it an A for effort and a C for execution.

April Fool's Day (1986)
April Fool's Day (2008)

Is Muffy St. John (Deborah Foreman) the perky little cutie-pie she appears to be? Or is she a psycho who invites her college pals for a weekend getaway at her isolated island lodge so she can bump them off? They're all a bunch of blandly attractive white kids who look like they'd rather be on Melrose Place. How long does it take for them to start kicking the bucket? Not very. Do you care who's doing it or why? Nope, not a bit. Despite top grade studio production values, the whole thing is an ineffective repetition of the tired dead-teenager formula.

The twenty-first-century remake bears little resemblance to the plot of the tepid original. It does share a shiny gloss, but with even less substance, and again, the screen is filled with the kind of brittle, pretty, well-to-do characters that are usually seen in primetime soaps.

Arachnid (2001)

Throwback to '50s big-bug monster pictures is undone by uninspired writing and acting. A search party made of up scientists, military guys, and two babes heads off for a South Pacific island where a Stealth fighter crashed. They find a giant alien spider thingy. Locations are acceptable; effects less so. Some of the stuff involving webs will generate giggles instead of gasps. The ooky spider juice is better.

Arachnophobia (1990)

The Steven Spielberg production company puts its polished spin on a cracking good monster story. The critters in questions are the lethal offspring of a Venezuelan superspider who finds its way in a particularly gruesome manner to the little town of Camaina, California. That's also where the new doctor, Ross Jennings (Jeff Daniels) has just moved with his family. He's deathly afraid of spiders; his wife (Harley Jane Kozak) isn't. The clever script is built along familiar horror conventions. Director Frank Marshall lets things move a little too slowly, and at the key moment when he could really grab the audience, he lets go. But those are quibbles. Anyone who's at all arachnophobic—and who isn't?—will get serious creeps from the second half. The production may be too slick for the subject matter, but the film is still a real treat.

Army of Darkness

See Evil Dead, The

Arnold (1973)

In a bizarre wedding scene, Karen (Stella Stevens), an unapologetic gold digger, marries the title character (Norman Stuart), already a corpse, to get her hooks into his considerable estate. From that point on, this featherweight black horror spoof becomes even more outrageous with a series of creative murders. A stellar troupe of character actors does a fine job with saucy, offbeat material, particularly Stevens who has a touch for this kind of hard-to-define comedy. Recommended for her fans.

Arrival, The (1996)

Intense sci-fi horror is driven by the same paranoia that made *The X Files* such a hit, with some really creative special effects, good characters, and

THE TOP FIVE BAD BRAIN MOVIES

Brain that Wouldn't Die
Donovan's Brain
Fiend without a Face
Frankenstein
Young Frankenstein

an unpredictable story. Radio astronomer Zane Zaminski (Charlie Sheen) discovers a signal from another star and is immediately downsized by his boss Gordian (Ron Silver). At the same time, environmental researcher Ilana Green (Lindsay Crouse) can't believe some of the numbers she's seeing. In many respects writer-director David Twohy's first-contact story follows an established formula, but even its most familiar developments are handled with freshness, and no review should spoil the surprises. The well-chosen effects combine models, computer-generated creatures, some neat transformations, and a deeply frightening scene involving scorpions. It's one of the most uncomfortable moments in modern horror.

ART OF DYING (1991)

Wings Hauser is one of the best B-movie actors in the business and with this psycho-killer horror, he proves that he's not a bad director either. He stars as a Hollywood cop helping runaways. The most recent threat to these kids is insane would-be film director Werntz who stages reenactments of scenes from horror movies using real bullets and chainsaws. Though the violence is graphic, it's leavened by humor and it's not excessive. The performances are much better than you find in most B-movies, or most A-movies, for that matter. Kathleen Kinmont is very good as Hauser's mysterious girlfriend, but Mitch Hara, as the psycho's flamboyant assistant, steals this sleeper from everyone else.

ASHES AND FLAMES (1995)

Dreamlike independent production is a semi-plotless series of images and vignettes about death and madness, hence the title. The cast handles slow physical action and limited dialogue with deadpan lack of emotion. Imagine *Lost Highway* told in the black-and-white style of *Carnival of Souls.* Sam (Mark Schultz) is a man-child morgue attendant. Dahlia (Aisha Prigann) is a waitress. Her dead sister may be the connection between them, but nothing, not even the names, is certain. A strange heterophobia provides suspense of a sort, and it's also the source of considerable humor, possibly intentional. One character reduces the action to "the male specimen's problems with copulation" and that seems to be writer-director Anthony Kane's overriding concern. His screen is filled with phallic symbols, the most impressive among them being a thick firehose with a shiny nozzle. In the end, the vague surrealism may prove too arty for horror fans and not arty enough for cineastes. (Alternate title: *Phoenix.*)

Astronaut's Wife, The (1999)

Some sort of undefined disaster nearly killed Comm. Spencer Armacost (Johnny Depp) and Capt. Alex Streck (Nick Cassavetes) while they were working on a satellite outside the space shuttle. Back on Earth, a few people suspect that there's something wrong with the men. Mrs. Armacost (Charlize Theron) doesn't know what to think after she becomes pregnant. The pace is slow throughout; most big scenes are artfully composed and lit, and it all hinges on one of the most bizarre sex scenes ever committed to celluloid.

Asylum (1972)

Four inmates of a mental institution tell stories about themselves to a young doctor (Robert Powell). Barbara Parkins helps her lover kill his wife; Peter Cushing commissions a tailor to make a special suit; Charlotte Rampling is a woman with emotional problems and a murderous friend (Britt Eklund); Herbert Lom has created a homunculus of himself. A sense of humor helps the anthology, but an intrusive soundtrack incongruously taken from Dvorak's *New World Symphony* sets absolutely the wrong mood.

Attack of the Giant Leeches (1959)

It's poor white Florida swamp trash versus giant mutant worms in this early Roger Corman effort. (Roger's executive producer; his brother Gene is credited as producer.) The main attractions are perhaps the most comical rubber monster suits ever to grace a low-budget horror flick and Yvette Vickers, a blonde bombshell of the Mamie Van Doren school, as Liz, the wayward wife. Even for a black-and-white Corman quickie, it's pretty thin stuff but then, it doesn't claim to be anything more.

Attack of the Killer Tomatoes (1978)

Spoof of bad horror movies is arguably no funnier than its subject, but it's fine for the target audience—kids who like to watch adults acting silly. Most of the humor is pretty obvious, but some of the jokes are actually funny and nothing about the movie is mean-spirited. The monsters of the title are simply refugees from the produce department. There's no blood, sex, or rough language. According to at least one source, the helicopter crash is real—it certainly looks real—and the pilot was killed. The cult following that has developed—sequels, animated series, re-released "director's cut" on video—proves that indeed, there's no accounting for taste.

Attack the Block (2011)

The producers of *Shaun of the Dead* turn their sights on an alien invasion story with good results. These guys are dog-like black creatures with glow-in-the-dark blue teeth. They land in a London housing project one night while Moses (John Boyega) and his multi-racial gang of kids are mugging nurse Sam (Jodie Whittaker). In short order, the humans realize they'll have to work together against the beasts and an equally dangerous enemy, the local drug dealer. The action is more violent and the humor isn't as broad as it's been before. The CGI effects are relatively restrained, too, probably for budgetary reasons, but that's hardly a flaw. Like *Shaun,* this is a character-based action-comedy.

Audition (1999)

Despite a slow, talky middle section, this import delivers the goods with a fresh approach to domestic horror. Seven years after the death of his beloved wife, Aoyama (Ryo Ishibashi) is finally ready to remarry. He knows he wants a young woman who's obedient and has some musical abilities. How to find her? A fellow executive at his film company suggests they concoct a fake movie role and check out the girls who show up for the audition. That's where he meets the shy Asami (Eihi Shiina) who's just a little reminiscent of a young Audrey Hepburn. Even though some things don't add up on her resumé, he falls for her. Her reaction to him is even stronger. Without giving anything away, comparisons to Annie Wilkes in *Misery* are not out of place. But that film is an Oscar-winning studio production that stops short of certain excesses. This one is not nearly as restrained. Some viewers won't be able to watch the third act without hitting the fast-forward button.

Audrey Rose (1977)

All reincarnation stories tend to be a bit loopy. Even the most skeptical viewers accept that, but this one abuses the privilege, skipping off into the farthest regions of La-La Land. Anthony Hopkins persuades John Beck and Marsha Mason that their daughter has the soul of his daughter because that little girl died a few minutes before their girl was born. How does he know this? Psychics told him and he went to India to check it out. Throughout the action is either boring or silly. Blame Frank De Filitta. He wrote the novel and the script and he co-produced the film.

Awakening, The (1980)

A laborious introduction establishes the relationship between the mummy Kara and Margaret Corbeck (Stephanie Zimbalist). Margaret's dad Matthew (Charlton Heston) discovered Kara's tomb at the exact moment she—Margaret—was born. After that's sorted out, the pace becomes jerky and fragmented. Though a capable cast does good work, the plot is far too dependent on coincidence. The film is the second based on Bram Stoker's little-known novel, *Jewel of the Seven Stars.* (The first is *Jewel of the Mummy's Tomb.*) Director Mike Newell has had more success in the mainstream with *Four Weddings and a Funeral* and *Donnie Brasco.*

Awful Dr. Orlof, The (1962)

The prolific Spanish director Jesús Franco got his start with this hash of elements borrowed from Dr. Jekyll, Jack the Ripper, and Frankenstein. Trying to repair his daughter's scarred face, Dr. Orlof (Howard Vernon) and his blind assistant Morpho (Ricardo Valle, whose makeup looks weirdly like a cartoon of the young Dustin Hoffman) kidnap women and operate on them. The acting is alternately hammy and understated. The rest of the film is likewise uneven with some creepy images surrounded by clumsy clichés and overlong, talky scenes.

B

Bad Moon (1996)

Slick theatrical disappointment ought to fare better with fans on video. It's an inventive werewolf tale with a good twist—one of the main characters is a German Shepherd. That's Thor (Primo), who's owned by Marjorie (Mariel Hemingway) and her young son Brett (Mason Gamble). Marjorie invites her wayward brother Ted (Michael Pare) to stay at her Rocky Mountain home. Out in the Orient, Ted was bitten by a wolf creature. It doesn't take long for him and Thor to decide who's top dog, as it were. Director Eric Red sometimes shifts to a canine point of view with a slightly flattened, blurred image. The monster transformation effects aren't very good and they're not helped by the high polish of the whole production. A grittier, rougher look would have served the story better. Can't be compared to Mike Nichols' *Wolf* but worth a look.

Bad Seed, The (1956)

Hollywood's most famous "evil child" horror looks dated now. It's very much a filmed play that is too limited by conventions of the stage. Patty McCormack is Rhoda, the perfect little '50s girl whose model exterior hides a prepubescent sociopath. Nancy Kelly is the increasingly suspicious and fearful mother. Though those two have their moments, the rest of the cast seems to think they're still on Broadway, playing to the last row of the balcony. For a more moving and complex treatment of the same subject, see *The Other.* Ignore the embarrassing coda.

Bad Taste (1987)

Truth in titling! Director Peter Jackson's writing debut is virtually a student film—crude and grainy—with several confident directorial touches that preview what he'd do in *Heavenly Creatures* and *The Frighteners.* Carnivorous aliens take over a small town in rural New Zealand. "We've got a bunch of extraterrestrial psychopaths on our hands," says one of our silly heroes. The hit team sent to deal with them are comic figures. Their prolonged fight with the aliens is like a live action Road Runner cartoon with grotesquely exaggerated violence. Heads are split apart; brains are eaten, etc. Director Jackson also plays two of the leading roles and acts with himself in one remarkable cliff scene. It all ends with a nasty "born again" joke.

Banker, The (1989)

The title character, Spaulding Osbourne (Duncan Regehr), is a wealthy financier whose passions are primitive religions and *Snow White and the Seven Dwarfs.* The opening scene, strongly reminiscent of *Betty Blue,* is a stylish blend of eroticism and violence that sets the tone for the rest of this updating of Jack the Ripper. Robert Forster is the veteran cop with a rookie partner and an ex-girlfriend (Shanna Reed) who's a TV newswoman. These three walking clichés threaten to sink the story in predictability, but Osbourne gets crazier and crazier (and funnier) as the film goes along. You're never quite sure what he's going to do next and so the second half pulls away from the formula. Slick music video production values and a fast pace make it a potent guilty pleasure.

Basket Case (1982)
Basket Case 2 (1990)
Basket Case 3 (1992)

The first film is one of the all-time great low-budget horrors, an ingeniously twisted original in every respect. After a bloody suburban opening, the scene shifts to a grainy, squalid Times Square where Duane (Kevin Van Hentenryck) carries a large wicker basket. He talks to the basket; he feeds it hamburgers and hotdogs. Inside is Belial. He's the amazing creation of Kevin Haney and John Caglione who use stop motion animation and models to transform Belial into one of the most grotesque and believable monsters you'll ever see. Writer-director-editor Frank Henenlotter's plot is too outrageous for words, and the actors handle it masterfully. The combination of

The Top Twelve Nasty Bug Movies

Infestation
Cloverfield
The Mist
Beginning of the End
King Kong (2005)
Naked Lunch
The Nest
Them
Tarantula
Bite Me
Mimic
The Unborn

strong atmosphere and total unpredictability gives this one an overall weirdness that few horror films even attempt.

The disappointing sequel is a comparatively expensive production, but in this case, more is definitely less. Most of the action takes place on clean well-lighted sets with a glossy "Hollywood" look. The plot ignores key aspects of the first film. Until the conclusion, when Henenlotter does manage to twist some kinks into the action, the plot ambles along without focus or the raw craziness that drove the first film.

If the first sequel spoofed everything that was scary, sick, and wonderful in the original, the third installment is even weaker. It's a slender parody built around people in rubber masks and suits. The simple-minded plot about tolerance of differences and the unimportance of appearances would be preachy if it were meant to be taken seriously. It's not. Fans of the original should seek out Henenlotter's *Brain Damage*.

Beast Must Die, The (1974)

Curious werewolf tale based on a James Blish story (*There Shall Be No Darkness*) combines elements of *The Most Dangerous Game, Ten Little Indians,* and blaxploitation with a gimmick—the "werewolf break," which gives viewers thirty seconds near the end to come up with the identity of the wolfman (or wolfwoman). Multimillionaire Tom Newcliffe (Calvin Lockhart) invites houseguests—each with a nasty secret—for a weekend at his security-enhanced country estate, and claims that one of them is a monster. The mystery side of the story demands long passages of explanatory dialogue while the action side is often reduced to pointless motion. Peter Cushing stands out in the supporting cast. Lockhart's impressive in the lead. An archetypal '70s theme and score by Douglas Gamley is the finishing touch. (Alternate title: *Black Werewolf.*)

Beast of the Yellow Night (1971)

Drive-in classic from the Philippines combines a variation on the werewolf story and a sell-your-soul-to-the-devil angle. With the exception of familiar character actor Vic Diaz, as a plump cheerful Satan, the cast is stiff and seems uncomfortable with the fairly demanding dialogue. But for those who see the film as an exercise in nostalgia, that's more positive than negative. Despite the silly monster make up, complete with fright wig, this one's o.k.

Beast with Five Fingers (1946)

Despite a slow beginning and an uneven tone throughout, this is an intriguing horror based on flawed characters. At his mature creepiest, Peter Lorre is an astrologist who believes that his deceased employer's (Victor Francen) disembodied hand has escaped from the crypt. The acting ranges from J. Carrol Naish's delightfully stereotyped Italian police commisario to Robert Alda's silky conman and Charles Dingle's greedy heir. The hand effects by William McGann and H. Koenkamp are some of the best, far superior to the foolishness in Oliver Stone's *The Hand.* Director Robert Florey does fine black-and-white work and he gets a lot from Max Steiner's score.

Beast Within, The (1982)

Mid-budget combination of town-with-a-secret and werewolf plotlines puts the formulas through their paces well enough. A terrible assault takes place in Nioba, Mississippi, 1964. Seventeen years later, Eli (Ronny Cox) and Caroline (Bibi Besch) MacCleary go back there to find out what's wrong with their son Michael (Paul Clemens). The Southern Gothic elements have a gruff humor. A strong and slightly unusual setting—the deep South in winter—and a cast filled with seasoned character actors help considerably. The plot doesn't make as much sense as it might, but that's not a huge flaw. Careful viewers will catch a big continuity mistake in one kitchen scene before the gross-out stuff kicks in.

Beetlejuice (1988)

Perhaps Tim Burton's most imaginative combination of horror and comedy is also one of his most enjoyable. Alec Baldwin and Geena Davis are the recently deceased young couple who can't leave their beloved rural home and want to get rid of the shallow new inhabitants (Jeffrey Jones, Catherine O'Hara, and Winona Ryder). Michael Keaton is the title character, an ob-

Michael Keaton (left) is Beetlejuice, a supernatural being with a car salesman attitude who tries to take advantage of two confused spirits (Geena Davis and Alec Baldwin) who are new to the idea of being dead.

noxious supernatural used car salesman who offers to help. Burton's visual humor has never been stronger and it benefits immeasurably from Danny Elfman's score. As usual, Burton gets perfectly pitched performances from a well-cast troupe that includes Dick Cavett, Sally Kellerman, and Robert Goulet in key support. Of the witty effects, the sandworms, the dinner party, and the snake scene are the most impressive.

Before I Hang (1940)

In one way, this slow-moving talky thriller is as relevant as it ever was. It begins with Dr. Garth (Boris Karloff) on trial for physician-assisted-suicide. Later, with the help of Dr. Howard (Edward Van Sloan), he develops a miracle drug. It comes, of course, with a catch. Much of the "mad scientist" plot is downright silly, but Karloff's performance as an interesting, contradictory character is among his best. Otherwise, the stylized sets, lighting, and acting are very much a product of the time.

Beginning of the End (1957)

Archetypal big-bug horror begins with the couple making out in a parked car on lovers' lane and hits all of the familiar notes. We've got the Department of Agriculture scientist (Peter Graves) who's creating giant radioactive vegetables but never thought that locusts would chow down on his nuclear wheat. Then there's the glamour babe photo-journalist (Peggy Castle) who happens to be in the neighborhood when the first town is destroyed, and, of course, the khaki-clad troops who are helpless against the onslaught of the giant ravenous insects. The special effects are some of the least realistic you'll ever see. For a trip to memory lane, it's o.k. but not the best.

"Some time during the night, the town of Ludlow was completely demolished; the town's population, about 150 people, vanished."

Beginning of the End

Believers, The (1987)

Following the death of his wife, a police psychologist (Martin Sheen) moves from Minneapolis to New York City where he and his young son become the targets of a Santería cult that sacrifices children. Director John Schlesinger handles the potentially exploitative material with a sure hand. The script by Mark Frost—a frequent collaborator with David Lynch and a fine novelist in his own right—is built on carefully drawn, sympathetic characters and horrifying conflicts that move well beyond familiar formulas. The film shares some thematic elements with *Burn, Witch, Burn* and *Rosemary's Baby,* but don't make any direct comparisons. This sleeper's an original—one of the prolific director's best, but lesser-known efforts. Yes, that's Gary Farmer as one of the movers.

Below (2002)

Haunted house tale set on a submarine works well both as horror and a war movie. It's August, 1943, somewhere in the Atlantic when the *Tiger Shark* gets word that survivors in a lifeboat are nearby. Brice (Bruce Greenwood) orders that they be picked up even though a German destroyer is in the vicinity. From that beginning, writer/director David Twohy marches through a steady succession of revelations and surprises. The supernatural material—if that's what it is—is handled subtly. All the wonderful period sub stuff is done up in fine style with much more attention to detail than you see in most conventional war movies. If the '40s slang in the dialogue isn't authentic, it sure sounds good and Twohy and co-writers Lucas Sussman and Darren Aronofsky came up with some terrific talk. The boat's interior feels as authentic as *Das Boot,* and that's as good as it gets. This one's a genuine sleeper worthy of watching a second time with the DVD commentary track.

Beneath Still Waters (2005)

When the Spanish town of Marienbad was flooded by the DeBaria dam in 1965, some Satanists were trapped in a building and drowned. Or did they? This ham-fisted effort opens with the murder of a child. Many of the exteriors filmed on a lake are difficult to watch through the glaring reflections off the titular waters. The night scenes are far too murky, and the big orgiastic finish is unintentionally funny.

Beyond Re-Animator

See Re-Animator

Billy the Kid versus Dracula (1966)

The title is really more enjoyable than the execution of this mind-numbing genre-jumper. The title characters (Chuck Courtney and John Carradine) are both after the Barbie-esque Betty (Melinda Plowman). As an exercise in cheapjack '50s camp nostalgia, it's good for a few laughs, but nothing more. The bat effects, "transformations" (for want of a better word), and Carradine's pop-eyed hypnosis bit are the highlights ... or lowlights, depending.

Birds, The (1963)

Though incidents of avian attacks have been documented, Alfred Hitchcock has said that he views his most challenging horror film as "a speculation" with no connection to reality. In the book *Hitchcock Truffaut,* he says "With *the Birds* I made sure that the public would not be able to anticipate from one scene to another," and he certainly manages that. In the little town of Bodega Bay, flocks of birds inexplicably attack people. Non-lovebirds Mitch Brenner (Rod Taylor), an idealistic lawyer, and Melanie Daniels (Tippi Hedren), a flighty socialite, are inexorably drawn into and trapped by the situation. Reflecting the plot, all of the personal relationships defy cinematic conventions, and, more importantly, so does the ending. The big scenes—the attack on the restaurant, the schoolyard, the house, the escape—have been copied hundreds of times since. The film was a critical and commercial disappointment at the time, probably because the public that Hitchcock was trying to surprise was expecting another *Psycho.* Followed decades later by a poor TV sequel.

Our feathered friends go into freakish frenzies, attacking humans for apparently no reason in Alfred Hitchcock's *The Birds*.

Bite Me (2004)

Transformed by genetically altered marijuana, grotesque giant bugs infest a New Jersey strip joint. They multiply, mutate, and attack everybody—the dancers, the managers, the crooked feds, the exterminator—everybody. The effects are properly cheesy, sometimes reminiscent of those spooky insects from "The Zanti Misfits" on the old *Outer Limits* TV series. The pace zips right along and B-diva Misty Mundae is a natural, unaffected heroine who seems completely comfortable with the silly material. This is a movie you laugh with, not at.

Bitter Feast (2010)

Initially, it's difficult to get into this sharp, bloody comedy because the two main characters are so thoroughly and deliberately unsympathetic. Peter

Grey (James LeGros) is a thin-skinned egotistical New York celebrity chef. J.T. Franks (Joshua Leonard) is a thin-skinned egotistical New York restaurant critic who writes a withering review of Grey. Later, he finds himself an involuntary "guest" at Grey's isolated upstate farmhouse. The independent production makes a virtue of its limited budget with solid performances in the leads and key supporting roles, Amy Seimetz as the worried wife and Larry Fessenden as the detective she hires. The well-chosen locations and the sometimes harsh lighting are fine for the story. Stick with this one.

Black Cat, The (1934)

The collaboration of director Edgar G. Ulmer and stars Boris Karloff and Bela Lugosi in their first screen appearance together is the "suggestion" of a Poe story. It's also horror's forgotten masterpiece. The deceptively complex and elegant plot isn't particularly frightening by itself. Instead, the film should be appreciated for its look. In purely visual terms, the Bauhaus/art deco sets and costumes make this one of the most striking pictures ever made, regardless of genre. Boris Karloff and Bela Lugosi do some of their best work in quiet roles. It's quite clear throughout that the horrors being evoked are born in modern warfare. They're shown in architecture, image, and character. Ignore the off-putting, heavy classical score and comic relief.

Black Cat, The (1981)

Like so many Italian horrors, this one's a wacky, virtually plotless exercise in style—mediocre as it is—over substance. The titular feline is a harmless, altogether unthreatening creature, despite the filmmakers' best attempts to persuade us otherwise. Miles (the jut-jawed and always enjoyably hammy Patrick Magee) is a medium who hangs out in the cemetery of an English village. Jill (Mimsy Farmer) is a photographer. The aforementioned kitty is allegedly killing people. Yeah, right. On tape, the dark video transfer makes a hash of whatever director Lucio Fulci is trying to accomplish with his febrile camerawork. The Anchor Bay DVD corrects the visual flaws with an excellent image transfer. The cat is still less than terrifying.

Black Friday (1940)

Karloff and Lugosi's third teaming is more watchable than *The Raven,* but nowhere close to *The Black Cat.* The illogical plot has surgeon Karloff transplanting the brain of a gangster into the skull of his professor friend (Stanley Ridges) after a car accident. The good doctor then expects his pal to be

The Top Thirty-one Evil Doctor, Mad Scientist, and Maniacal Medico Movies

Awful Dr. Orloff
Brain Dead
Dr. Giggles
Coma
Hollow Man
Human Centipede [first sequence]
Human Centipede [full sequence]
Habitat
Invisible Man
Island of Dr. Moreau
Island of Lost Souls
Mad Doctor of Blood Island
Scalpel
Splice
The Surgeon
Tarantula
Vampire Bat
Frankenstein
Young Frankenstein
Abominable Dr. Phibes
Before I Hang
Black Friday
Blood Relations
Boxing Helena
Brain That Wouldn't Die
The Brood
Dr. Jekyll & Mr. Hyde
Gothika
Habitat
Night of the Comet
Species

himself, though he might remember where the gangster brain left a fortune in hidden loot. The use of spinning headlines to move the story along quickly becomes irritating, but Karloff's debonair performance overcomes a lot. Lugosi fares less well in a much smaller role as a rival gangster. The characters make no more sense than the plot which is a crazy riff on *Jekyll and Hyde.* It's somehow reminiscent of those Looney Tunes cartoons where Tweetie is transformed into a monstrous killer canary who terrifies poor Sylvester.

Black Heaven (2010)

Imagine a French combination of *Blue Velvet* and *The Vanishing* with a dash of *Rebel Without a Cause* for seasoning. The result certainly isn't pure horror, but it's so inventive and surprising and sexy that it earns a recommendation. It begins when Gaspard (Grégoire Leprince-Ringuet) and Marion (Pauline Etienne) find a cell phone that may belong to an exotic blonde (Louise Bourgoin). Out of a somewhat immature sense of playfulness, they try to find her, and become part of some twisted games involving suicide and on-line role playing. Whatever genre it belongs to, Gilles Marchand's film is fascinating.

Black Room, The (1935)

Period noir-ish yarn has nothing to do with *Frankenstein* in terms of plot, but the film is remarkably similar in other ways—sets, atmosphere, setting, the presence of Boris Karloff. He plays a dual role as an evil Baron and the good, foppish twin who, according to the family curse, will kill his older brother. The pace is swift and virtually all of the violence occurs off camera.

Black Sabbath (1963)

The venerable Boris Karloff introduces three short films and stars as a vampire in the last one. The pace is slow, and each tale contains at least one solid scare. Writer/director Mario Bava's horror is based on character and situation, not graphic visual effects. "The Drop of Water" comes from a Chekhov story about a nurse preparing a corpse. "The Telephone" has a contemporary—1960s—setting and makes incomplete sense. "Wurdalak," from a story by Alexei Tolstoy is creepily atmospheric with echoes of "The Monkey's Paw." It's the most substantial of the three and is complex enough to have been expanded to feature length.

Black Sunday (1960)

Despite some dated dialogue, the key images in Mario Bava's masterpiece have lost none of their power. The resurrected revenge-seeking witch plot is familiar, but it's spun out at a lively pace with attention to detail. The stunning Barbara Steele is the Russian witch in question, and her twin, a potential victim. Her initial execution is still a frightening moment. So is her rebirth, complete with scorpions. The inky black-and-white atmosphere, and the Gothic elements of the plot strongly influenced the generation of Hammer films that would follow. Bava would revisit the subject in the third section of *Black Sabbath.*

Black Swan (2010)

Nina (Natalie Portman) is a soloist with a classy New York ballet company. Obsessed with perfection, she has reason to believe that the company master (Vincent Cassell) is going to promote her in the upcoming season. But what about the free-spirited new dancer Lily (Mila Kunis)? The real competition is not between the two young women but inside Nina. Details of backstage life and practice ring true. So do the locations and the claustrophobic apartment Nina shares with her mother (Barbara Hershey). As the story unfolds, exactly what's real and what's imaginary becomes more and more difficult to discern and I'm not sure it's really that important in the end. Director Darren Aronofsky is deliberately unclear about clear details, including the finale. Ms. Portman deserves the Oscar she won. This one's the best of its kind since *Repulsion.*

Blade (1980)
Blade II (2002)
Blade: Trinity (2004)

Half-human, half-vampire Blade (Wesley Snipes) hunts vampires with shotguns, swords, a vintage Charger, and anything else he can find. The Marvel series is as much action as horror. The opening scene in a nightclub/slaughterhouse is a terrifically choreographed set piece. The violence is cartoonish and the whole thing goes on about twenty minutes too long.

Wesley Snipes starred as a kick-ass half-vampire in the "Blade" series.

Blade II relies on more elaborate and grotesque computer effects and less interesting fight scenes. Mutant vampires called Reapers are attacking regular vampires who enlist our hero in the fight. For me, the result is not as interesting as *Hellboy,* the next collaboration between director Guillermo del Toro and co-star Ron Perlman.

Blade: Trinity is my own favorite of the three. It's the most sophisticated visually and pyrotechnically. It's also got the most humor, and a strong supporting cast led by Ryan Reynolds, Jessica Biel, and Parker Posey.

Blade of the Ripper (1971)

Muddled slasher tale has to do with Julie Wardh (the lovely Edwige Fenech), an ambassador's wife, and her ex-lover (Ivan Rassimov) who may be a serial killer. Or is it her new beau (George Hilton) who's the bad guy? What about hubby (Alberto de Mendoza)? Most of the scares are retreaded Hitchcock, but as giallos go, this one is not the most nonsensical. In the early days of home video, various VHS editions suffered many flaws. They've been corrected on a DVD that faithfully recreates the riotous colors and soft garish look of the period clothes and décor, and the equally overblown score.

Blair Witch Project, The (1999) Book of Shadows: Blair Witch 2 (2000)

"In October of 1994," goes the introductory supertitle of this film, "three student filmmakers disappeared in the woods near Burkittsville, Maryland, while shooting a documentary. A year later their footage was found."

Back in the days when young people actually believed things they found on the Internet, many of them apparently thought that this ground-breaking, ultra-low-budget independent production was a documentary. Clever marketing created a large amount of pre-release interest, but the film became a huge commercial hit because viewers accepted the story of three filmmakers lost in the woods. Writer/directors Daniel Myrick and Eduardo Sánchez build tension nicely through such simple devices as twigs, string, and pebbles. The understated performances are effective, too, particularly Heather Donahue's. Her extreme close-up "I'm so scared" monologue comes across as absolutely authentic. Just as importantly, the film doesn't overstay its welcome. The seventy-seven-minute running time is just right. In the years since, other "found footage" horrors like *[REC]* and the *Paranormal Activity* series have mined the same rich vein of viewer credulity.

The fictional sequel attempts to build on the box office success of the first film. Supposedly, that popularity causes a massive influx of fans to the part of Maryland where the "events" took place. Four of those fans hire a semi-comic guide and head out on a "Blair Witch-Hunt" tour of the woods where they run into trouble. The studio added footage to director Joe Berlinger's work. The result is not impressive.

Bless the Child (2000)

Satanists under the leadership of self-help guru Eric Stark (Rufus Sewell) are out to get angelic little Cody (Holliston Coleman). Only Aunt Maggie (Kim

Basinger) and seminarian turned FBI agent Travis (Jimmy Smits), both constructed of low-grade cardboard, can save her. Pedophilic overtones give the story a nasty edge. The pompous religiosity, complete with sunlight streaming through stained glass and a chant-filled score, doesn't help either. In the end, it's not much different from the other religious-themed horrors of the late 1990s, but it's much more propagandistic.

Blessed (2004)

Low budget update of *Rosemary's Baby* is slow, talky, and overly familiar. New Yorkers Samantha (Heather Graham) and Craig (James Purefoy) head upstate to a shady fertility clinic for help in starting their family. They've hardly settled in before the obligatory ominous figure in the dark hoodie is lurking about. A game supporting cast, including David Hemmings in one of his last roles, can do little with the thin material.

Blob, The (1958, 1988)

A carnivorous glob of goo terrorizes a town in the classic 1958 horror flick *The Blob.*

Even if it didn't have a young "Steven" McQueen in the lead, this tongue-in-cheek gem would still be on the great '50s low-budget hit list. Carnivorous snot in a meteorite flashes above Lovers' Lane where Steve (McQueen) and Jane (Arneta Corseaut) are parked. The critter crashes into a farmer's field and grows to enormous size. The teens try to do all the right things but bone-headed adults pay no attention. Burt Bacharach's bouncy *Beware the Blob* theme sets exactly the right tone. The whole idea of combining *Rebel without a Cause* characters and a situation with a cheap monster from outer space plot is inspired. It was followed by a sequel, *Beware! The Blob.*

The 1988 remake is predictably pointless and overblown with a barfbag full of graphic effects. After a prolonged introduction of several characters who aren't going to be around very long, the titular creature crashes to earth and straightaway commences blobifying people. Brave young Brian (Kevin Dillon) and Meg (Shawnee Smith) try to warn everyone but the adults won't listen. Toward the end, when the Blob has achieved split-level dimensions, the special effects really aren't any better than they were in 1958.

Blood and Donuts (1995)

Director Holly Dale and writer Andrew Rai Berzins make full use of a limited budget in this enjoyable little Canadian comedy. Boya (Gordon Currie) is a Toronto vampire who's accidentally awakened after a twenty-five-year-long nap. Perhaps in need of a caffeine fix, he hangs out at a rundown coffee shop where Molly (Helene Clarkson) is a waitress. He's a romantic Byronic vampire who upsets a gangster's (David Cronenberg) plans to take over the neighborhood. Considering the current excesses of the genre, the action is relatively restrained. The main irritant is Justin Louis as Earl, the cabbie. While everyone else is playing it straight, he shamelessly gnaws on the scenery. Dale has come up with neat variations on familiar themes.

Blood and Roses (1961)

This version of the oft-told story makes less than complete sense, and the sight of Bardot wannabe Annette Vadim strolling about lazily in a wedding dress isn't nearly as frightening as it's intended to be (or needs to be). She's Carmilla Karnstein who's in love with her wealthy cousin Leopoldo (Mel Ferrer) who's about to marry Georgia (Elsa Martinelli). The romantic comedy aspects are particularly out of place and the film treats the whole issue of vampirism like an embarrassing relative it would rather not acknowledge. The performances are anemic. Apparently director Roger Vadim means for this to be taken as serious drama when it needs a strong shot of the cheesiness he brings to *Barbarella.*

Blood Beach (1980)

Modest, well-photographed little B-movie seems almost embarrassed by the silliness of its own plot. Something is living under the Santa Monica beach and sucking people and animals down into the sand. In the last reel, when the monster has to make an appearance, writer/director Jeffrey Bloom keeps it in shadow and makes no attempt to explain its presence. That's probably just as well. The film is more comfortable with kitschy beach scenes, slightly overexposed and in soft focus so that the light takes on an almost tangible quality. Those have nothing to do with the alleged story, but they're pretty to watch.

Blood Feast (1963)
Blood Feast 2: All U Can Eat (2002)

Reportedly filmed for less than $70,000 in Miami, the first splatter movie is really a camp comedy. The silly writing and non-professional acting are actually part of the film's weird appeal. By today's standards, the gore effects in the story of Egyptian caterer/killer Fuad Ramses (Mal Arnold) are tame. But in 1963, no one showed lopped limbs or scooped brains on the silver screen. Producer-director Herschell Gordon Lewis creates—in his own crude way—a pornography of violence. Like conventional pornography, it's about limits, about crossing lines that cannot be crossed. Because of that, the film has undeniable historical value as a milestone in the genre.

The curious 2002 sequel finds Fuad Ramses III (J.P. Dellahoussaye), reopening granddad's catering business. The film is every bit as cheaply made as the original. The sound is so bad that you often won't be able to understand a word, but so what? This is a movie about gore and exploitation, and in an era of "photo-realistic" computer effects, it's old-school crude.

Blood Freak (1972)

Remember what happened to Al Hedison in the original *The Fly*? Something similar befalls poor Hershell (Steve Hawkes), an Elvisian biker ... but with a turkey. He's the hero of this drive-in wonder made in Florida. He's also involved with two sisters, devout Christian Angel who gives impromptu Bible lessons to her depraved dope-toking sister Anne and anyone else who'll listen. Topping it all off is a seedy, chain-smoking, wheezing on-camera narrator who interrupts the action at regular intervals to read a script that might have been written by Ed Wood Jr. on a particularly festive day. It's a rambling meditation on faith, God, the nature of the universe, and health that ends with a coughing fit. Required viewing for connoisseurs of the bizarre. Everyone else can pass.

Blood of Dracula (1957)

Camp classic from 1957 is a perfect example of Mayo's First Rule of Horror—No film with a dance scene can be seriously frightening. This one has teen boarding-school debs spinning the platters and dancing with seat cushions, not to mention the "Puppy Love" production number. The other parts of the slow-moving snoozer involve pre-liberation feminism and risible vampire makeup, as the evil Miss Branding (Louise Lewis) taps into young

The Top Eight Bad Dads and Monstrous Moms Movies

The Stepfather (1987)
Frankenstein
Parents
Fido
Serial Mom
Carrie
Psycho
Friday the 13th

Nancy's (Sandra Harrison) inner sources of power and turns her into a monster. Recommended for viewing by large groups who are ready to laugh.

Blood of Dracula's Castle (1969)

Camp 1960s drive-in fare actually begins at Marineland, and then heads for the desert (or is the beach?) where Mr. and Mrs. Dracula (Alex D'Arcy and Paula Raymond) have their titular castle. Their servant John Carradine keeps a supply of nubile, young blood donors chained up in the basement. An escaped homicidal maniac (Robert Dix) and a hunchback (Ray Young) are part of the mix, too, when a young couple comes to visit the place. Director Al Adamson pushed the limits for graphic violence in those gentler times, but the whole film is still an ultra-low-budget effort of some historical and curiosity value but little else.

Blood on Satan's Claw (1971)

Is the devil loose in a seventeeth-century English village? Or are malicious teen-aged girls (a la *The Crucible*) up to something, or are high-spirited kids playing, or is something else going on? That's the curious beginning of a first-class historical horror. The large cast lacks individual definition and the story is sometimes too confused, particularly toward the end, but that's o.k. Director Piers Haggard creates a strong evocation of place and time with carefully chosen locations and a restrained use of effects. His work is comparable in style and subtlety to another unorthodox film of its time, *The Wicker Man.*

Blood Orgy of the She Devils (1972)

Fans of alternative cinema are the only audience for this grandly titled, wonderfully overacted goofiness. The story of witches, zombies, past lives, interpretive dance, the Indian spirit guide Taka-Waka, and "psychometrized" objects is told with the cheesy look and cheesy mindset of an early '70s Philippine exploitation flick but without the skin, the sex, or the gore. Instead, it's got unfettered imagination to burn with wacky plot twists that other movies never even imagine, much less attempt to show.

Blood Relations (1988)

In an unhappy Canadian household, even lies aren't what they seem. An egomaniacal surgeon (Jan Rubes) may have killed his wealthy wife. His unstable son (Kevin Hicks) hasn't forgiven him. The son's manipulative girlfriend (Lydie Denier) looks like the dead woman, and his dying grandfather (Ray Walston) may be the kinkiest of them all. The games they play with and against each other in a snow-covered mansion become creepier and creepier until they reach a wonderfully nasty Grand Guignol conclusion. One of the better sleepers.

Blood Salvage (1990)

Horror/comedy about organ transplants is cut from the same cloth as the cult classic *Motel Hell.* Jake (Danny Nelson) uses his tow-truck business as a front for an organ bank. He removes them from unwilling donors and sells them to unscrupulous doctors through middleman Ray Walston. Things are just dandy until Jake falls for April (Lori Birdsong), who's paralyzed from the waist down. Jake, a latter-day Victor Frankenstein in coveralls, decides to help her. Writing, acting, direction, and sense of place (rural Georgia) are several notches above average. The gross moments are played for laughs of the haunted house peeled-grapes-for-eyeballs variety. Also, the screen is filled with religious imagery and language that's somehow appropriate to this story of twisted love and sacrifice.

Blood Spattered Bride (1972)

Vincent Aranda mixes exploitation and fiery no-prisoners feminism in a strange evocative update of Sheridan LeFanu's *Carmila.* Troubled newlyweds (Simon Andrews and Mirabel Martin) go to his lonely, lavish provincial estate and eventually are joined by a vampiric ghost (Alexandra Bastedo), who has perhaps the weirdest introduction in the history of horror. Time has rendered some of the film's surrealistic touches and sexual notions dated and humorous. The somnambulant pace and striking locations have lost nothing, though. Simon Andrews' portrayal of the nameless self-centered husband is piggishly perfect. In theatrical release, the violent ending was severely re-edited. The unrated version is shocking. Of the three adaptations of the novel (the others are Roger Vadim's *Blood and Roses* and *The Vampire Lovers*), this is by far the best. The clichéd use of a body double is a flaw.

Blood Ties (1991)

Cult fav director Jim McBride makes this Fox-TV pilot a combination of *The Lost Boys* and *Melrose Place.* A young man goes to Los Angeles to stay with relatives after his family is murdered. Christian vigilantes led by Bo Hopkins are after him, too. Though Hopkins' people think of the boys kinfolk as "the undead," they prefer to be called "Carpathian-Americans." While some keep to the old traditions, others, including our hero Harry (Patrick Bauchau), think "it's time we came out of the coffin." But uncle Eli (Salvator Xuereb) warns that if they go public, that's "when the pogroms begin." The rest involves conflicts between the elders and the young Carpathian-Americans who live in loft apartments, ride motorcycles, and engage in sexy dance numbers. McBride has fun with well-worn horror movie themes, tinkering with the conventions of the genre, and indulging in some timely social humor.

BloodRayne (2005)

Adaptation of a videogame stays true to its roots in pace and the inventiveness of some of the effects. In a vaguely medieval/renaissance world, Rayne (Kristanna Loken) is a "dhamphir," half human, half vampire. It all looks like a thrift store version of *Underworld* without the guns. As a group, the supporting cast is afflicted with the worst collection of wigs and hairdos you'll ever see. For all the swordplay and spurting blood, the action scenes are slow and studied. Followed by sequels.

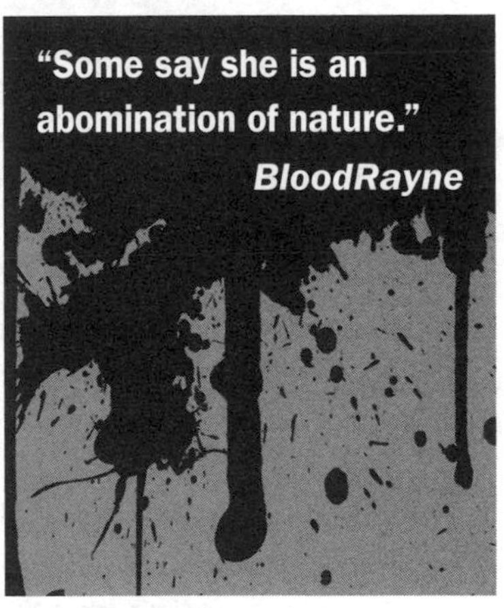

"Some say she is an abomination of nature."
BloodRayne

Bloodsuckers (1971)

Offbeat vampire tale opens with the spires of Oxford but quickly goes to Greece where Richard Fountain (Patrick Mower), a Don with a future, is seduced by Chrises (Imogen Hassell). Their drug orgy scene is really funny. When his pals, led by Patrick MacNee, try to bring him back, their search turns into several long chase scenes. Between those, the film often resorts to voice-over narration to keep things moving. That may partially explain why director Robert Hartford-Davis had his name removed from the credits. Both the alternate title, *Incense for the Damned* and the title of the novel it's based on, *Doctors Wear Scarlet,* are more appropriate. Much of the acting is fine and the exotic settings are well utilized. Writer Julian More doesn't so much equate vampirism with drug use and sexual obsession as to intermix the three. The ending is unfortunate.

Bloodsucking Nazi Zombies (1982)

The title will warm the heart of any horror fan, but the execution doesn't live up to it. Aside from some brightly lit desert scenes, the film is so dark and hard to make out that it's virtually unwatchable. The story has to do with a World War II treasure hidden at an oasis where the titular characters are still hanging around. The zombie makeup is so lame that it makes the slow travelogue scenes look good. The obvious inspirations are George Romero's *Living Dead* movies and Amando de Ossorio's *Blind Dead,* but this doesn't measure up.

Boccaccio '70 (1962)

This anthology was so scandalous when it was released in the United States in 1962 that it played only at a few drive-ins, "art houses," and college campuses. Though relatively few people saw these short Italian films, two images from them were burned into the public consciousness. The first is Sophia Loren in lacy underwear; the second is Anita Ekberg as the giant temptress who steps off of a billboard in Federico Fellini's "The Temptation of Dr. Antonio." The doctor (Peppino De Fellipo) is a blue-nosed prude; she's his sweetest nightmare come to monstrous life. The sight of this huge buxom goddess striding through miniature sets like a blonde Godzilla is indescribable and altogether wonderful.

Body Snatcher, The (1945)

Classy horror begins on an incongruously bright note with the sunny streets of Edinburgh, 1831, and Gray (Boris Karloff), the friendly cabman. But the story moves slowly into darker, more complex moral ground. Gray is a grave robber. His client, Dr. MacFarlane (Henry Daniell) is having an affair. The script, reportedly rewritten by producer Val Lewton under the name Carlos Keith from Philip MacDonald's original, is about degrees of responsibility, and evil acts committed for the greater good. Director Robert Wise handles it masterfully, using sound to suggest violence and shadows to hide it. Karloff's sparkling performance is one of his most engaging, and it's a solid counterpoint to Daniell's long slow boil. In Karloff's career, all roles pale in comparison to Frankenstein's Monster, but the wily Gray is a strong second. The film's style may have fallen out of fashion, but it's still a masterpiece.

Body Snatchers (1993)

See Invasion of the Body Snatchers

Bones (2001)

Director Ernest Dickerson brings the sensibility and look of '70s blaxploitation to an urban ghost story. Back in those days of stacked heels and pimpmobiles, Jimmy Bones (Snoop Dogg) refused to allow crack to be sold in his 'hood. A generation later, his spirit arises when four young people decide to turn his old home into a nightclub. Dickerson's strong aggressive visuals, including some unexpected and effective humor, are really more interesting than the story.

Boogens, The (1981)

In the years between its short theatrical release and its belated appearance on home video, this wonderful little low-budget horror developed a cult reputation. It's really nothing more than a torpidly slow variation on the dead-teenager formula, but it's still fun for fans of alternative cinema. Why? Because the title creatures are so silly. When they finally show up, having boogenized most of the cast, they look like large, toothy, tentacled frogs that have been squashed. Maybe that's why they live in abandoned Colorado mine shafts, but nothing about them is explained. Why bother?

Boogeyman, The (2005)

As a child, Tim (Barry Watson) watched something come out of his bedroom closet one night and attack his father. Of course, everyone believes that the man simply abandoned his family, but years later, Tim is still plagued by night terrors when he has to return home. The plot takes several head-scratching turns, and Watson is not a particularly engaging protagonist. The scene where he fights with his closet defies description. The film is similar in some ways to *Dead Silence* and *Darkness Falls.*

Book of Shadows: Blair Witch 2

See Blair Witch Project

Borderland (2007)

More than any of the remakes and sequels, Zev Berman's film is the legitimate successor to the original *Texas Chainsaw Massacre.* Based about as much as it needs to be on real events, it's the story of three graduating high school seniors who decide to sow oats in Mexico. They run across a gang of drug smugglers who believe that human sacrifice imbues them with magical powers. If our heroes are a bit too conventionally handsome, they are believable, likeable characters and they capture that moment of being young and irresponsible. More impressive are Damián Alcázar as a deeply wounded cop, Sean Astin in a demented cameo, and, particularly, Marco Bacuzzi, who looks like a Satanic Michael Berryman. The horrifying violence is about as graphic as you'll see, and the setting is sweatily realistic.

"Imagine a land, if you will, where a man can be a man. A land where he can indulge in all those animal urges.... A land where he can ride the demon!"

Borderland

Boxing Helena (1993)

David Lynch's daughter Jennifer makes a credible debut with a grim little black comedy about sex, dismemberment, and power. For assorted Oedipal reasons, Dr. Cavanaugh (Julian Sands) is obsessed by the mercurial Helena (Sherilyn Fenn). When fate, or something, brings her to his isolated mansion, he makes the best of it, even if he has to resort to drastic measures to make her stay. Ms. Lynch contends that her plot is a metaphor for love and that has some validity. She does sustain a surreal, dreamlike mood with an ending that's as loopy as the rest. The unrated version differs only slightly from the theatrical release.

Brain Damage (1988)

Frank Henenlotter's second low-budget feature about a boy and his pet monster is a visceral antidrug horror/comedy that's almost as good as *Basketcase.* The critter is a grotesque, intelligent parasite that feeds on brains (human or animal) and is capable of injecting its host with a highly addictive hallucinogen. This thing is called Aylmer, or Elmer, and in one of the film's strangest moments, it launches into an a cappella version of the old Glenn Miller favorite, "Elmer's Tune." Aylmer comes into the possession of young Brian (Rick Herbst), and, as it begins to gain control of him, Aylmer argues that it's all right to kill people, as long as Brian isn't directly involved. Or, as he puts it, "Part of my talent, Brian, is to spare you any unpleasantness."

There's plenty of unpleasantness to be spared. The violence is graphic, outlandish, and comic. A strong sexual element, again reminiscent of *Basketcase,* is played mostly for laughs. Beyond the Grand Guignol horror, *Brain Damage* has some serious things to say about addiction, about how it changes a person, and about how it can kill or hurt others. For Henenlotter's fans, it's a must-see.

Brain Dead (1990)

Dr. Martin (Bill Pullman) is deeply involved with theoretical brain research until his unctuous, avaricious pal Reston (Bill Paxton) persuades him to do a little primary work on Halsey (Bud Cort), a madman who knows some things that the Eunice corporation needs. A "kinder, gentler lobotomy" may be in order. As Dr. Martin becomes more deeply involved, he shares Halsey's paranoid schizophrenia. Veteran writer Charles Beaumont's script is a sharp, intelligent, hallucinatory comedy. Combine it with two terrific performances from the Bills, and savvy direction by Adam Simon, making the most of a modest budget. Beaumont, responsible for many of the best *Twilight Zone* episodes, brings the same fascinating unpredictability. Before it's over, the film becomes a multilayered examination of madness.

Brain That Wouldn't Die, The (1962)

This obscure little '50s schlocker deserves a place in the Alternative Hall of Fame (or Shame). Though writer/director Joseph Green never reaches the heights that Ed Wood Jr. achieved, it's not for lack of trying. After a painfully slow, uneventful introduction and an off-camera car crash, a mad scientist (Herb Evers) keeps his decapitated fiancé Janey's (Virginia Leith) head alive on a tray in his lab. He tenderly advises the noggin, "Sleep, my darling, rest and grow stronger," and then sets out to strip clubs and modeling agencies to find a suitable body for reattachment. Yes, this mad scientist is also a lounge lizard! Janey, meanwhile, has gone a little nutso—and who could blame her?—psychically contacting the creature who lives in the closet. But the film really belongs to Leslie Davis as the henchman Kurt. He and Janey engage in such long philosophical conversations you'd think they're Vladimir and Estragon waiting for Godot, not the closet creature. None of that—bizarre as it is—can prepare the viewer for Kurt's death. It is a full two minutes and forty-five seconds of rabid, unfettered scenery chewing that must be seen to be appreciated.

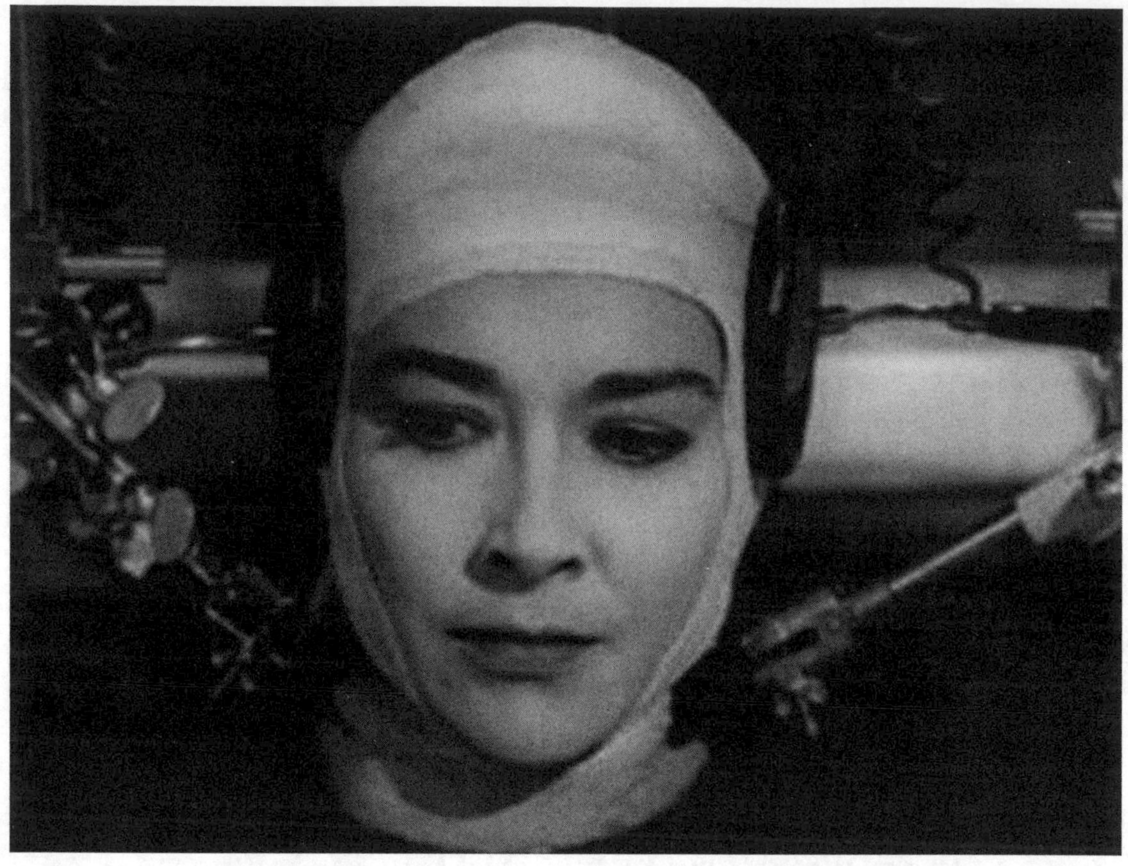

In the hokey *Brain That Wouldn't Die*, actress Virginia Leith sticks her head up through a hole in a table.

Bram Stoker's Burial of the Rats (1995)

Ruthless, sword-fighting lesbian feminist rat-worshippers in black leather thong bikinis kidnap aspiring young author Bram Stoker (Kevin Alber) and this wacky horror spoof is off and running. Madeleine (Maria Ford) and her pals serve the Queen of Vermin (Adrienne Barbeau) whose aim is to unseat the male power structure of the village of St. Cecile—just as soon as her minions finish their topless modern dance routine. The Russian American made-for-cable production is a throwback to Britain's Hammer Films with the same look and a cheekier attitude toward its "classic" horror source.

Bram Stoker's Dracula

See Dracula

Breed, The (2006)

Babes in bikinis versus genetically enhanced attack dogs on an island. O.K., there are some guys involved, too, but Michelle Rodriguez and her stunt double Lee-Anne Liebenberg are the focus of most of the action. The dogs are frightening, particularly when they've been feeding and their heads are covered with blood. The characters are slightly less irritating than they often are in the subgenre of Young People Go Off to a Remote Place Where They Are Attacked by Mutants/Rednecks/Aliens/Whatever.

Bride of Chucky

See Child's Play

Bride of Frankenstein (1935)

Though James Whale's sequel is considered superior to his original by many critics, it is at best an uneven film filled with dated humor. (The introduction remains a particular embarrassment.) Yes, it's much more polished and Whale's direction is more confident. Yes, Boris Karloff's interpretation of the Monster is more complex and nuanced. Yes, the Bride (Elsa Lancaster) is created in the mother-of-all lab scenes. But the famous sequence at the Hermit's cabin is so brilliantly spoofed by Mel Brooks, Peter Boyle, and Gene Hackman in *Young Frankenstein* that it's almost impossible to watch it now without unintentional laughter. Flaws notwithstanding, this is one of horror's finer, but not finest moments.

Bride of Re-Animator

See Re-Animator

Bride of the Monster (1955)

Though *Plan 9 from Outer Space* is Ed Wood Jr.'s alternative masterpiece, this one is arguably more inept. Made famous in Tim Burton's *Ed Wood,* it's a silly exercise notable for Bela Lugosi's final starring appearance—he died during the filming of *Plan 9*—and the ridiculous immobile octopus monster with which several "victims" pretend to struggle. Even Wood's fans—and I am one—must admit that he could be boring with long, pointless scenes that

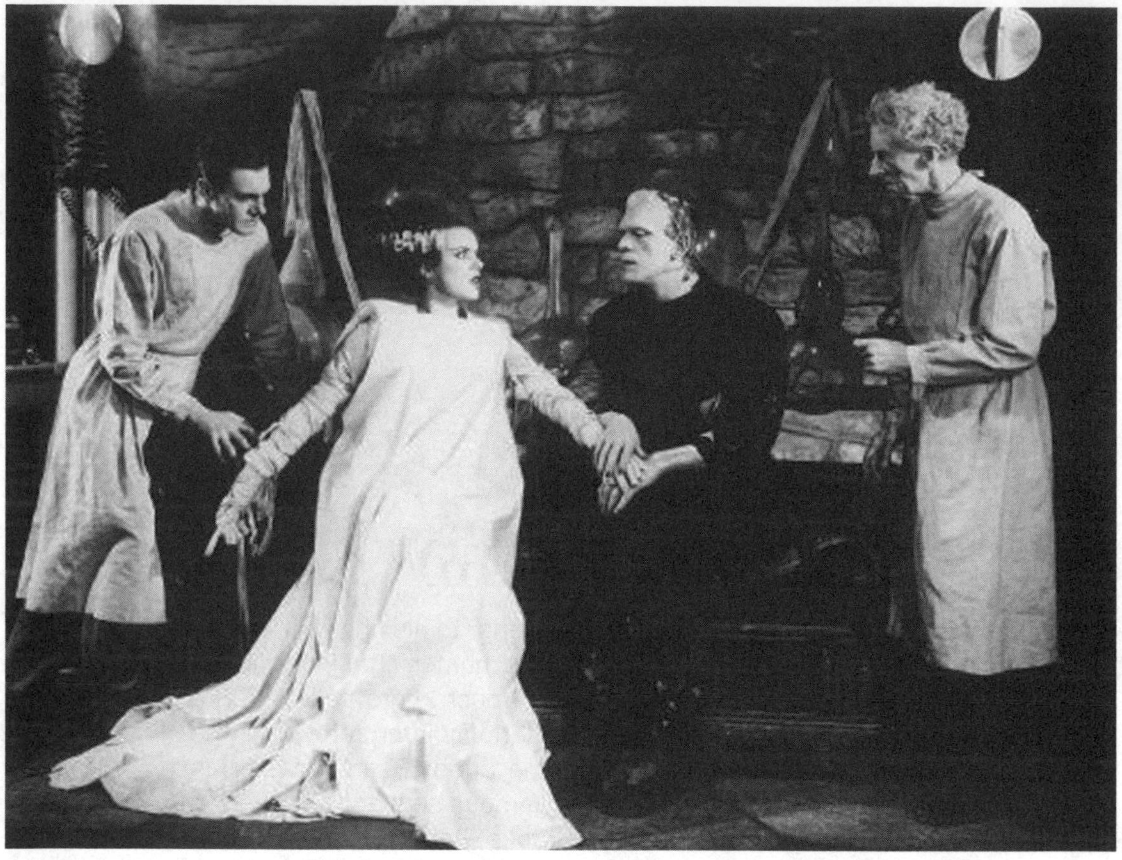

Elsa Lancaster gets to ham it up as Frankenstein's bride.

are neither funny, suspenseful, nor goofy. They're just slow and lifeless, and *Bride* has far too many of them.

Bride with White Hair (1993)
Bride with White Hair II (1994)

Supernatural epic is one of the most lavish and ambitious Hong Kong imports. It's a magical tale of warring clans, one led by Ye Hong (Leslie Cheung who looks a lot like Johnny Depp), the young warrior prince who falls in love with his enemy Wolf Girl (Brigette Lin Ching-Hsia). Their story mixes operatic overstatement with soaring Shakespearian plot turns and real emotional depth. Director Ronny Yu works with a large cast on unbelievably evocative sets. The action scenes employ flying effects and highly stylized fights and swordplay. The stunt work owes more to dance than to conventional martial arts films.

The absolutely wonderful sequel is simpler than the original, as the white-haired witch continues her revenge against the eight clans. A straightforward rescue-of-the-kidnapped-bride plot provides the basis for a no-holds-barred battle of the sexes fought on a cosmic scale—men against women, youth against elders, love against anger. Blood flies; passions soar; the Bride's white hair can now behead her enemies. The story works with the stuff of myth and fairy tales which is also the stuff of horror with the thematic compass needle closer to true north. Even viewers who are not familiar with the conventions of Chinese film will appreciate the power of these images and the epic scope of the story. Brigitte Lin Ching-Hsia and Leslie Cheung repeat their roles, but most of the action is handled by young cast members. As the fearless Moon, Christy Chung easily steals the film.

Brides of Dracula (1960)

Despite the absence of Christopher Lee—there is no character named Dracula in the film and no one gets married, either—the whole production has the studio's famous high gloss and the story is carefully written. Key elements of the script would be recycled many times in other films. This may be Peter Cushing's finest portrayal of Van Helsing. Here he's an active, energetic protagonist. As the lovely, young teacher Marianne and the evil Baron, Yvonne Monlaur and David Peel bear a disquieting resemblance to Barbie and Ken. The other characters are clever variations on familiar stereotypes with a proper amount of humor. The conclusion is especially suspenseful. One of Hammer's best.

Brood, The (1979)

For straightforward horror, this may be David Cronenberg's best. It's controlled, carefully focused, imaginative, and frightening. Cronenberg works with possibly repressed memories of childhood abuse as the basis for his horror, more than a decade before the subjects would become part of popular culture. Flamboyantly mad Nola (Samantha Eggar) is under the care of Dr. Raglan (Oliver Reed), possibly a charlatan, at his "Institute of Psychoplasmics." Her ex-husband Frank (Art Hindle) fears that she's abusing their little girl during their visits. The first big scene is a remarkable set piece in a kitchen where an unseen something goes to work. The scares are so unusual that any synopsis would spoil them. The only flaws are a visually weak scene explaining the physical nature of the evil involved, and a score that borrows too heavily from *Psycho.* Like many of Cronenberg's other films, it's about insanity taking on a physical manifestation.

Brotherhood of Satan (1971)

Actors L.Q. Jones and Alvy Moore produced this laborious, low-budget town-with-a-secret tale. Dan (Charles Bateman), Nicky (Ahna Capri), and Dan's young daughter are trapped by mysterious and largely unexplained forces in a remote hamlet where adults are being killed and the survivors are insane. The whole thing has an Ed Woodsian quality of enthusiastic incoherence that's irritating and endearing in about equal measures. Veteran character actor Strother Martin (who worked with Jones in *The Wild Bunch*) attacks the material with gusto.

Brotherhood of the Wolf (2001)

Your basic eighteenth-century political conspiracy/martial arts/horror/special effects epic is told with the sensibility of a spaghetti Western. It's based on a legend about a Bigfoot-like creature that attacks people in provincial France. Enter the naturalist/adventurer Grégoire de Fronsac (Samuel Le Bihan) and his companion and bodyguard Mani (Marc Dacascos). The fights are elaborately choreographed. The whole thing is wonderfully entertaining, well photographed, and bawdy at the right times. I prefer the more expressive French language track on the DVD. English is also available. Director Christophe Gans' comments on the deleted scenes are instructive on narrative momentum and editing. He also admits the influence of Hammer films. If it all gets a little silly by the end, that's just fine.

Bucket of Blood (1959)

Roger Corman says that he was trying to make "a horror-type film with a hip cutting edge" and he got it. This low-budget marvel, actually a companion piece to the original *Little Shop of Horrors,* was filmed in five days. Walter Paisley (Dick Miller) is the coffee-shop busboy who becomes an overnight sensation with the realistic statues he makes of his inadvertent murder victims. The high points are Julian Burton's Allan Ginzbergian poem-performance art, and Miller's transformation into a card-carrying boho beatnik. Remade as the altogether inferior *Death Artist.*

A busboy played by Dick Miller becomes famous making statues out of corpses in 1959's *Bucket of Blood.*

Buffy the Vampire Slayer (1992)

"Don't you get it? I don't want to be the Chosen One! I don't want to spend the rest of my life chasing after vampires. All I want to do is graduate from high school, go to Europe, marry Christian Slater and die!" That's how Buffy (Kristy Swanson) explains things when Donald Sutherland tries to persuade her that she's the only person who can save Southern California from an infestation of the undead. The *Clueless* humor is dated and overly broad, and the situation has been used far too often in recent years. Even so, this one works because Kristy Swanson turns in such a bright, sexy performance. The fact that in her prom dress, she looks like a young Grace Kelly doesn't hurt, either, and she gets considerable help from five athletic stunt doubles. For comparative purposes, this one's somewhat better than *The Lost Boys,* not as good as the original *Fright Night.* It's also the basis for the popular TV series.

While the television version starring Sarah Michelle Gellar was more popular, the movie *Buffy the Vampire Slayer* features a sexy performance by vampire killer Kristy Swanson.

Bug, The (1975)

An earthquake brings huge electrically charged cockroaches from the center of the earth to the surface. These bugs eat carbon, create sparks by rubbing their legs together, and ignite their own gas. Yes, *Firefarter* might be a more appropriate title, and this too serious, too slow production from the usually reliable producer William Castle needs all the help it can get. The uninvolving plot doesn't measure up to the insect effects or to Bradford Dillman's extremely mad scientist. The gonzo second half is better than the first. Though most guides and the videotape and DVD box copy list the title as *Bug,* on the film, it's *The Bug.*

Buried Alive (2005)

Disaster done on the cheap is not a pretty sight but it can be a funny sight and this one is funny, at least some of the time. Greedy developer Stewart

(Jay Pickett) cuts corners on his new condos and fakes geologic reports. Things then go badly when they start blasting at Diamondback Ridge. Landslides, high tension lines snapping, rooms turning upside down, angry rattlers, etc. Production values are on a par with '80s made-for-TV fare. The CGI effects and backgrounds are marginally more realistic than some matte paintings but not as good as the best. Characters never rise above their stereotypes, but a sense of humor helps.

Burn, Witch, Burn! (1962)

Two of horror's best screenwriters, Richard Matheson and Charles Beaumont, adapt one of the field's best novelist's best works—Fritz Leiber's *Conjure Wife*—with satisfying results. Despite the stupefying title, this is a keenly observed exploration of contemporary witchcraft. It's set on a college campus where the faculty wives know a lot more about the petty academic turf wars than their allegedly smarter husbands. Professor Norman Taylor (Peter Wyngarde) is in line for a big promotion. His wife Tanzie (Janet Blair) is sure that her spells and charms are responsible. The costumes, acting style, and attitudes are a cinematic primer on late '50s sexual conflicts and identities. Stereotypes of male rationality and feminine intuition are sharpened to wicked points. (In manner, dress, look, and bearing, Wyngarde is presented as an unmistakably phallic character.) Though the conflicts are a little slow to develop, the story becomes really involving about half way through and maintains that suspense until a terrific ending.

Burning, The (1981)

Summer campers play a mean prank on caretaker Cropsy (Lou David). Five years later ... oh, come on, you don't need to be told anything about the plot. A little "T," a little "A," a lot of Tom Savini's bloody effects. The kids look and act more like real adolescents than they usually do in stalker-slasher flicks. Yes, that's an incredibly young Jason Alexander under a full head of hair, and, in a much smaller role, Holly Hunter. More importantly, the film is the debut for Miramax founders Bob and Harvey Weinstein, who share various production and writing credits.

Cabin Fever (2002)

Dedicated horror fans will spot little bits from *Pumpkinhead, Evil Dead, Texas Chainsaw Massacre, Night of the Living Dead,* and even *Piranha* in director Eli Roth's sure-handed debut. The college-kids-go-out-into-the-woods plot is nothing special but it's handled with wit and the entire cast seems to have understood exactly what they were trying to do from the scares to the laughs to the gratuitous sex. Followed by a sequel.

Cabin in the Woods, The (2012)

Stop me if you've heard this one: Five young people head off into the boonies for fun and whatever, and they run into something nasty. From that standard-issue premise, Joss Whedon and Drew Goddard craft a wonderfully inventive tale that needs no further synopsis. The characters are well drawn and sympathetic. Veteran character actor Richard Jenkins almost steals the show. The plot wanders so far afield that even the most dedicated fan will be surprised and most will be delighted. Even if the film is built with familiar materials, the final result is a true original.

Cabinet of Dr. Caligari (1920)

Younger viewers will probably have trouble appreciating this early and extraordinarily influential film. With its painted-flat sets, exaggerated acting, and cartoonish costumes, it's as much a work of the nineteenth century as the

Released in 1920, *Cabinet of Dr. Caligari* had an early influence on the horror genre.

twentieth. And Cesar, the Somnambulist (Conrad Veidt), can be dismissed as a guy with a funny walk and too much eye makeup. The slowly paced, grainy images are perhaps the first use of narrative film as waking dream. Along with the original *Nosferatu* and *Vampyre, Caligari* played a large part in the creation of the landscape of the horror film.

Call of Cthulhu, The (2005)

If a filmmaker of the silent era had decided to adapt a Lovecraft story for the screen, he might well have come up with something like this labor of love. Director Andrew Leman and the H.P. Lovecraft Historical Society use black-and-white film, pasty makeup, intertitle cards, overly dramatic acting, and the best special effects that cardboard and glitter can provide. The fast-moving story involves madness, ancient lore, and a sea voyage to remote islands. The short film may be meant only for Lovecraft's most devoted fans but it's still a successful exercise in style.

Candyman (1992)
Candyman: Farewell to the Flesh (1995)

On one level, this contradictory horror is a basic gore-fest. At the same time, it's visually sophisticated and well acted with a score by noted minimalist composer Philip Glass. More often than not, the two sides work well together. The title character (Tony Todd) is an urban legend who dwells in Cabrini Green, the notorious Chicago housing project. Graduate student Helen Lyle (Virginia Madsen) leaves the groves of academe to do some dangerous primary research into the myth. Writer-director Bernard Rose indulges his music-video taste for fast cutting in some key scenes. For the most part, though, he plays straight with the viewer and creates a palpable atmosphere of fear and dread. The conclusion is risky.

Candyman: Farewell to the Flesh, a totally unnecessary sequel, repeats the original plot in New Orleans with the same gimmick. If anyone looks into a mirror and says the name "Candyman" five times, a towering hook-handed black man will appear and eviscerate the speaker. Guess what happens about every fifteen minutes. Two large flaws sink the film before it has a chance. First, Clive Barker's story demands that in any potentially dangerous situation, the characters involved must do the most stupid thing possible. Second, director Bill Condon lets the action ooze along at a tedious pace. Almost all of the scares come from the hook-through-the-guts routine, which isn't even very disgusting after the third or fourth time, or generic spooky stuff—one character creeping up on another, a flapping crow, swarming bees, etc. Followed by a third.

Cape Fear (1991)

In *Taxi Driver,* Robert De Niro and Martin Scorsese make Travis Bickle a human monster who finds redemption. In Max Cady, they find a much more powerful monster who is angry evil incarnate. Judged by any standard, he's one of the most frightening creations of 1990s horror. From the ultraviolent "date" with Ileana Douglas to Juliette Lewis' infamous thumb-sucking scene (one of the screen's truly sick inventions) to the bloody kitchen, the horrible moments just keep on coming. Admittedly, the filmmakers may be slumming, but they also give the manipulative story a strong moral dimension. In the end, they mean to scare you, and they certainly do. In spades. That's why this is a horror film while the 1961 Robert Mitchum-Gregory Peck version is suspense. Elmer Bernstein's score is based on Bernard Herrmann's work for the original. Director of photography Freddie Francis directed several British horror films.

A pale figure with dark eyes (Herk Harvey) haunts a car crash survivor in Herk Harvey's *Carnival of Souls.*

Captivity (2007)

Roland Joffé has directed such diverse films as *The Mission* and *The Scarlet Letter.* How did he come to make this piece of lesser torture porn? Jennifer Tree (Elisha Cuthbert) is a New York supermodel who is easily kidnapped and held in a chamber of horrors. The plot, cooked up by B-movie veteran Larry Cohen, is a variation on *Private Obsession* with the emphasis on sadism and violence instead of sex. As the story unfolds, one key revelation is easy to predict. The big finish does contain some surprises, but they seem forced. The running time is listed on the DVD is eighty-five minutes, but it's only seventy-seven minutes at the closing credits.

Carnival of Souls (1962, 1998)

A car runs off a bridge and into a deep river. One young woman (Candace Hilligoss) walks out of the water, apparently unharmed. She tries to resume her life as if nothing has happened, taking a job as a church organist in another town. At first, everything appears to be normal and dull, but then she has visions of a pale figure with dark eyes. Over the course of the film, her sense of reality steadily erodes as a dreamlike atmosphere of eeriness grows stronger. Without resorting to any of the overt tricks that have become the common currency of horror films since, writer/producer/director/actor Herk Harvey delivers the chills found in a really good episode of *The Twilight Zone.* It's easy to read deeper meanings into the plot—alienation, a descent into madness, the role of young women in a changing society—but that's not really Harvey's point. He wants to tell a good scary story that begins and ends as a mystery, without verbal explanations for the striking black-and-white images. He also presents a surprisingly realistic and detailed portrait of everyday life in the United States in the early 1960s. George Romero has said that he had it in mind when he made *The Night of the Living Dead.*

The 1998 *Wes Craven Presents* remake retains a few elements of the original story, and then overuses the it's-a-dream-no-it's-real-no-it's-a-dream device familiar to fans of the *Elm Street* series. Larry Miller is scary as a murderous clown.

Carnosaur (1992)
Carnosaur 2 (1995)
Carnosaur 3: Primal Species (1996)

The title sequence—disgusting stuff apparently filmed in a real poultry processing plant—sets the tone for your basic mad scientist plot with several environmental twists. Out in the Nevada desert, Dr. Jane Tiptree (Diane Ladd) has created some nasty unseen critters who attack chickens, then make their way up the food chain. If the dinosaur effects created by John Buechler and Magical Media Industries aren't as realistic and convincing as Spielberg's Jurassic monsters, they're not bad at all. In fact, they're much more believable than you normally find in more expensive productions. Writer/director Adam Simon has a wicked sense of humor that gets consistently stronger and more crazed as the movie goes along. Toward the end, it becomes downright Strangelovian. Fans should seek out his other work, *Brain Dead* and *Body Chemistry 2.*

The real inspiration for the 1995 sequel isn't *The Lost World* but James Cameron's *Aliens.* The mutant-chicken dinosaurs from the first film are back and looking for more human Happy Meals in a super-secret government installation that's about to blow up. Tick, tick, tick. Overall, the acting is better than average and the dialogue has that gritty quality that makes

Cameron's early work so much fun. Director Louis Morneau keeps things moving quickly enough that the plot lapses and less-than-stellar special effects aren't fatal.

Carnosaur 3: Primal Species comes up with fresh situations for their low-budget saurians. This time out, the government-created critters are hijacked by terrorists. Col. Higgins (Scott Valentine) leads the crack (but extremely small) military unit that's sent to get them back. Dr. Hodges (Janet Gunn) is the glamorous dinosaur expert. The basic military-academic conflict is lifted from Howard Hawks' *The Thing.* Even though the setting is your basic empty-warehouse industrial park, the whole film is arguably no sillier or more poorly plotted than *Jurassic Park: The Lost World,* but with much less impressive effects.

Carpenter, The (1988)

The scenes of gory horror are the weakest parts of this stylish Canadian production. Some of the humor is overstated, too. Otherwise, it's a sleeper of the Stephen King school with a tongue-in-cheek "all men are pigs" attitude. The film begins with a frighteningly realistic depiction of a mental breakdown. After it, Alice (Lynne Adams) and Martin (Pierce Lenoir) move to a big rural house as it's being renovated. The carpenter (Wings Hauser) is a mysterious figure who may be supernatural, or he may be a creation of Alice's imagination, or perhaps the officious Martin is up to something. For most of the running time, director David Wellington maintains that tension and uses the house to create a spooky, dreamlike atmosphere. Hauser, one of the better actors in the business, is in top form and so is Adams.

Carrie (1976)

Brian DePalma's adaptation of Stephen King's first published novel is one of the most influential horrors of the 1970s. The opening locker room scene so powerfully lays out the terrors of adolescence—physical, emotional, and social terrors—that the whole film plays itself out at a much higher level. Sissy Spacek's performance is so believably vulnerable and winning that it makes up for a lot later when the action shifts weakly to her fellow students' machinations. (Both she and Piper Laurie as her mother received richly deserved Academy Award nominations.) The famous pig blood scene is an extended (but mechanical) Hitchcock moment, and a key musical theme is baldly lifted from *Psycho.* Unfortunately, the cheap "surprise" finish has been copied countless times since, by DePalma among others. The film was also the base for a notoriously short-lived Broadway musical flop and its twenty-first-century revival.

High school students learn the hard way why you should not torment a girl with psychic abilities in Brian DePalma's adaptation of Stephen King's *Carrie*.

Carriers (2009)

A zombie movie without zombies presents a depopulated post-apocalypse America where four young people are driving across the desert. The plague that has killed virtually everyone is highly contagious. The sick spread the infection with their breath or a touch, and there is no cure. The filmmakers try to handle the premise realistically but some details make no sense. If this world is so lawless and dangerous, why do our protagonists have only one pistol? The unsympathetic characters are a larger problem. The lead, Chris Pine's Brian, is an obnoxious jerkwad.

Case 39 (2009)

Social worker Emily Jenkins' (Renée Zellweger) thirty-ninth case is Lilith Sullivan (Jordelle Furland), a young girl who's terrified of her parents. After a few silly scares, the film settles in on the question: Is she being abused or is she the child of Satan? The answer is fairly predictable, but the scenes of violence against the little girl are all too disturbing and realistic. Performances are above average, too, particularly Ms. Furland and Ian McShane as a sympathetic cop.

Cat and the Canary, The (1927, 1939, 1978)

The story of a large group of people who are brought together at some remote luxurious location—usually on a dark and stormy night—and then are bumped off in inventive ways has been told many times. This is one of the more enjoyable and lively. A breathless title card in the silent 1927 film sets the scene, "On a lonely, pine-clad hill overlooking the Hudson, stood the grotesque mansion of an eccentric millionaire...." Director Paul Leni uses a restlessly mobile camera to inject life into this adaptation of a play about the reading of a will twenty years after the death of the aforementioned eccentric millionaire. The story is as much comedy as horror with verbal and

The Cat and the Canary is an early version of the horror device of inviting a group of people to a spooky mansion, where they get bumped off one by one.

slapstick humor provided mostly by Creighton Hale, a lightweight Harold Lloyd–type leading man. Leni also distorts images and plays with extreme closeups and superimposed images. As a result, the style is much more enjoyable than the substance.

The main attractions of the 1939 film are stars Bob Hope, as a radio actor, and his co-star Paulette Goddard, at her youthful, sexy best. They're supported by a capable cast. The scares come from a spooky hand reaching out from sliding panels, revolving bookcases, hidden passageways in walls, and the like. Standard stuff for a formula picture of the time.

The 1978 version boasts dry wit ("Between the Bolsheviks on one side and the Democrats on the other, the world will become unrecognizable") and a solid British ensemble cast led by Wendy Hiller. The setting is Glencliffe Manor, 1934; the reason is the reading of the will.

Cat People (1942, 1982)

Producer Val Lewton and director Jacques Tourneur are famous for suggesting everything and showing nothing. It's an approach that's won critical praise but horror fans have always been divided. Today's younger viewers are likely to be impatient with the talky, stodgy script that's notably lacking in action. But the film does work well in the important moments—the famous stalking scene, for example, is superbly put together without a wasted frame—and the crisp black-and-white looks great. Irina (Simone Simon) is the mysterious Serbian woman that the clueless Oliver (Kent Smith) falls for. Their relationship is simply too coy and ill-defined for horror or for straight drama. Perhaps the constraints of the time kept the film from dealing honestly with its sexual subject and so the approach is oblique. It becomes blatant only in such odd touches as the design of a swimming suit. (Followed by the non-horror *Curse of the Cat People.*)

A poster for the 1942 original version of *Cat People* that starred Simone Simon.

Paul Schrader takes a decidedly different tack with his excellent remake. It may be the most sexually charged film in all horror. Where the original is based on an ill-defined idea of original sin through female rebellion against male authority, this one works with more overt themes—incest, bestiality—all boiling down to the basic conservative Christian notion that sex is evil. Not that the film believes or promotes that. The keys are a feral, innocent, seductive performance by Nastassja Kinski and much more threatening work from Malcolm McDowell as her brother; a spooky, hypnotic score by Giorgio Moroder; and the genteel seediness of the New Orleans setting. Schrader carefully quotes the original without really turning his film into a remake. It's on the long side, but not indulgent.

Cat's Eye (1985)

A smart grey tabby connects three Stephen King tales. In the first, James Woods takes drastic measures to quit smoking. Then Robert Hays and Kenneth McMillan are involved in a vertiginous bet, and finally Drew Barrymore is menaced by a monstrous troll. The second installment is the strongest, though the troll effects by Carlo Rimbaldi are the highpoint. Director Lewis Teague gets fine performances from his felines; he's less successful with Drew Barrymore and Candy Clark.

James Woods plays a man taking desperate measures to quit smoking in one of the tales from *Cat's Eye.*

Cave, The (2005)

Big-budget equivalent of *The Descent* (released the same year) focuses on a team of hot-shot divers who explore a newly-discovered Carpathian cavern and find themselves under attack by grotesque beasties. The main problem is tissue-thin, clichéd characters who do little to inspire any empathy. And because the image is so clear and the effects so realistic and the lighting so precise, the cave never seems claustrophobically real either. The semi-vampiric creatures are all right.

Cemetery Man (1994)

Before he caught on with the moviegoing public in *My Best Friend's Wedding,* Rupert Everett attracted a large following among horror fans with this Italian philosophical comedy of the grotesque. He plays Francesco Delamorte, groundskeeper at the Buffalora cemetery where the dead have suddenly and for no reason begun to come back seven days after they're interred. Why? Delamorte doesn't know and doesn't care. It's just his job to keep 'em in place. In fact, he's so blasé about the whole thing he hasn't even bothered to tell the authorities because there'd be too many forms to fill out. At least that's how he sees it at first, but the situation soon complicates itself in unusual ways. For example, a voluptuous woman (Anna Falchi) appears as several characters, living and dead, to tempt Delamorte. The plot doesn't follow other horror conventions, either. Director Michele Soavi is more interested in an exaggerated autumnal atmosphere and Delamorte's delicious spiritual malaise. "The living dead and the dying living are all the same," he says, "cut from the same cloth." That's only the beginning of the nasty comments he has about today's trendily necrophilic youth culture. Balanced against that—and complementing it—is Delamorte's comic assistant Nagi (François Hadji-Lazaro) whose rotund body, bald head, and childish enthusiasms are clearly inspired by Curly of the Three Stooges. Other obvious influences come from Fellini and Sam Raimi. The violence is excessive and graphic; that's part of Soavi's point and it's not meant to be taken seriously.

Chain Letter (2010)

A wonderfully sick visual joke opens a slasher tale that eventually dissolves into the laboriously paced torture porn of *Seven* and *Saw.* The senseless plot revolves around an email that teenagers must forward to their friends lest they suffer a violent death. The production has an expensive but overly busy look, and the body of the work doesn't come close to the introduction.

Changeling, The (1980)

After the death of his wife and daughter, composer John Russell (George C. Scott) rents a spooky mansion in Seattle. He tries to resume his life but finds that the place is haunted by the loud ghost of a child. Overt scares are secondary to an understated, old-fashioned approach. The classy cast includes Melvyn Douglas as a senator and Jean Marsh, all too briefly, as the deceased wife. Comparisons to *Ghost Story* are not out of place, though this one is probably too deliberate for some. The film is beautifully photographed and the music is well integrated into the plot.

Chasing Sleep (2000)

If a restrained David Lynch made a variation on *Repulsion,* he might come up with something like this dark, sometimes surreal horror. Troubled, possibly insane, barefoot college professor Ed Saxon (Jeff Daniels) calls the police when his wife fails to come home, and waits there for news. Almost all of the action takes place within that tiny, dank house with its spotty plumbing, ominous groans, and decaying ceiling. Is it real or a manifestation of Ed's instability? Even the daylight scenes have a 3:00 A.M. feeling. This one's certainly not to all tastes, but a strong ensemble led by Daniels' performance, if nothing else, will stay with you.

Children of the Corn (1984)
Children of the Corn II: The Final Sacrifice (1992)
Children of the Corn III: Urban Harvest (1995)
Children of the Corn: The Gathering (1996)

So-so adaptation of a fair Stephen King story has been the basis for several so-so sequels. Go figure. The first film begins with a familiar premise—

Many of bestselling author Stephen King's novels have been adapted to film, including *Children of the Corn, Carrie, It, The Shining,* and *Misery,* among others.

city couple (Peter Horton and Linda Hamilton) stop in remote rural town and find it deserted. What happened to the inhabitants? Where did they go? Director Fritz Kiersch does a fair job of establishing his eerie atmosphere. He doesn't fare as well with a cast of child actors who are either shrill, exaggerated monsters or overly cute moppets. They can't handle writer George Goldsmith's stilted biblical language and they shouldn't have been expected to. When the big critter finally shows up—a scene which King describes in two sentences—he doesn't work too well, either.

The first sequel is a hapless little snoozer that appears to have been a local production made somewhere in the Midwest with a few professional actors in the leads and enthusiastic semipros filling out the cast. Expect no surprises in the connect-the-dots script or the not-very-special effects. It's just a boring little horror sequel that has virtually nothing to do with King's original story. At their best, low-budget horror movies are unpredictable and bizarre. This sequel is tedious and ordinary.

The whole idea of vaguely Amish boys practicing Voodoo is too ridiculous for words, but it's the premise of *III: Urban Harvest,* a nutty sequel that's far removed from the source material. Two farm boys, Eli (Daniel Cerny, who looks like a young Sal Mineo) and his older brother Joshua (Ron Melendez), are sent to Chicago foster parents where evil Eli conjures up monstrous corn critters in the vacant lot next door. Most of the scares are accomplished through the familiar dream-reality switch. Some of the effects by Screaming Mad George are o.k.; others are laughable. Nothing new.

Amazingly, the fourth film, subtitled *The Gathering,* is the best in the lackluster series and a good film in its own right. Retaining Stephen King's original rural setting and villain (sort of), it really has nothing to do with the other three entries. Grace (a terrific Naomi Watts) goes back to her Nebraska hometown to take care of her ailing mother (Karen Black). Immediately, she and Doc (William Windom) are in the middle of an epidemic of an inexplicable juvenile fever. A few too many scares rely on the it's-not-real-it's-a-dream bit that's been so overused lately, but others come from the editing and the situation, and they're knockouts. The best moments involve real fears—dealing with a frail parent or a sick child. Despite some other flaws, director Greg Spence makes a fine debut. He has gone on to produce well-respected television work including *Generation Kill* and *Game of Thrones.* The *Corn* series has continued as DVD premieres.

Child's Play (1988)
Child's Play 2 (1990)
Child's Play 3 (1991)
Bride of Chucky (1998)
Seed of Chucky (2004)

Though the box art and premise make the first film look like a formula studio production, it's really much better. At death, the spirit of mad killer Charles Lee Ray (Brad Dourif) is transported into a Good Guys doll named Chucky. A young boy (Alex Vincent), his mother (Catherine Hicks), and a Chicago police detective (Chris Sarandon) come to realize the truth, but not before the deranged toy has run amok. The writing is well above average with inventive plotting and attention to character. The toy effects and Chicago locations are fine, too. Add in grim humor and an ending that just won't quit and you've got one of the best of the late 1980s.

The first sequel actually begins well with a nice Chucky "reconstruction" scene, and young Andy (Alex Vincent) being taken in by foster parents (Jenny Agutter and Gerrit Graham) while his mom's under psychiatric observation. Unfortunately, the plot quickly collapses into all-too-familiar routines with clearly telegraphed scares. The Universal studio has a long history of franchising its most popular horror characters, and this one maintains the original's high production values and attention to detail, but not originality.

The subtitle of *3* could be "Chucky Goes to Military School" and the characters are now mostly teenagers. The programmed scares haven't changed, neither have the slick production values or the doll effects. They're the same combination of blood and plastic. Even for fans of the character, life is too short to watch such crappy sequels, and the series has limped on into the current century.

Bride of Chucky boasts a snappy script and Jennifer Tilly constantly threatening to burst out of her tight little black dress. Still carrying a torch for Charles Lee Ray (Dourif), she uses a copy of *Voodoo for Dummies* to revive his spirit in the famous doll. The jokes wear thin before it's over.

One of the creepier "scary doll" horror series features the deranged, murderous Chucky.

The fun returns in *Seed of Chucky,* arguably the most successful of all the sequels. Directed by Don Mancini, who has written all of the films in the series, it's a pure comedy, a sort of "meta" *Scream* of animatronics. A *Psycho* homage introduces Glen (voice of Billy Boyd), the child of Chucky and Tiffany, who finds his way to Hollywood where they're making another movie. Jennifer Tilly, playing a very funny version of herself, is on hand, too. She's hoping to step up from these cheap horrors and land a part in the new Biblical epic to be made by Redman (also playing himself). The humor is aimed squarely at fans.

Chinese Ghost Story, A (1987)

Once you get past the cultural differences—and there are a lot of them to get past—you find the familiar classic horror structure. Two young lovers—Ning Tsai-shen (Leslie Cheung) and Nieh Hsiao-tsing (Joey Wong)—confront an evil force and are guided by an older man, Yen (Ng Ma), a grumpy Taoist swordsman. The special effects range from crawling, desiccated corpses to a giant tongue with considerable acrobatic martial arts. Director Ching Sui

Tung mixes the spooky supernatural atmosphere of a ruined temple with lyrical romanticism and some lively camerawork. In one shot, the camera appears to zoom right down a screaming man's throat. Along with John Woo's thrillers, this is one of the films that brought Honk Kong to the attention of an international audience.

Christine (1983)

Under John Carpenter's usual competent direction, Stephen King's automotive horror is engaging and well made, but not particularly frightening. Bookish teen Arnie (Keith Gordon) becomes the proud owner of a '58 Chrysler that's bad to the bone, and is changed by it. Dennis (John Stockwell) is his friend and protector; Leigh (Alexandra Paul) falls for the transformed Arnie. The effects are terrific, but the best part of King's novel is his understanding of teenagers and their changeable relationships. That's precisely the side of the story that's left out.

Christmas Carol, A (1984)

George C. Scott is one of the screen's finest Scrooges, both the famous "Bah, Humbug!" character and his changed or reborn self. Director Clive Donner creates an almost palpable sense of place with the historic town of Shrewsbury, England. Filled with snow and coal smoke, it captures that potent combination of horror and character revelation that makes the story so effective. Where most Christmas tales tend to be sweet and loving, Donner follows Dickens' lead and takes a more frightening path. Whatever else it may be, this is a ghost story, with Frank Finlay, Edward Woodward, and Susannah York as the spirits. All in all, a first-rate dramatization of one of the most popular works in the English language. Highly recommended.

C.H.U.D. (1984)
C.H.U.D. II: Bud the CHUD (1989)

Two of Hollywood's favorite political causes—homelessness and toxic waste—combine to create a so-so variation on a standard monster story. John Heard is a photographer and Daniel Stern is an activist who team up to convince corrupt officials to tell the truth about a series of disappearances. The makeup effects are good and director Douglas Cheek wisely keeps his monsters out of full sight most of the time. Watch for John Goodman and Jay Thomas briefly at the end.

The featherweight comic sequel really owes more to *Weekend at Bernie's* than to the original. It attempts to turn generic living-dead stuff into slapstick with government-created zombies attacking suburbia. The presence of dozens of familiar faces from primetime TV makes the whole thing look like a really bad sitcom. The material would be offensive if weren't so lame.

Church, The (1989)

Considering how crazed Italian films have been recently, this Dario Argento-Michele Soavi collaboration is downright restrained. Medieval Teutonic knights massacre peasants said to be Satanists and bury them in a mass grave. Centuries later, a huge church has been built on the site. A curious librarian (Tomas Arana) thinks all cathedrals hold secrets and means to unlock them. Lotte (Asia Argento) is a caretaker's daughter there. The story begins well with some surprising visuals and intense images. Unfortunately, director Soavi and co-writers Argento and Franco Ferrini lose sight of their main characters and shift the focus in the second half to a group of largely unknown strangers who are dispatched straightaway. Much of the music is inspired by Philip Glass.

Climax, The (1944)

Doctor Hohner (Boris Karloff) of the Royal Opera mourns his lost love Marselina (June Vincent), or so all of Vienna thinks. Ten years before, in a possessive rage, he strangled her. When young Angela (Susanna Foster) arrives to reprise the role that made Marselina famous, the doctor's bad thoughts come back. The film was inspired by the box office success of the studio's remake of *Phantom of the Opera* and is easily as enjoyable as the Claude Rains film. It's a Technicolor production that features one of Karloff's better understated performances. As the young romantic lead, Turhan Bey isn't bad, either. Judicious use of the fast-forward button makes the arias and musical numbers much easier to take.

Closure (2007)

Irritatingly hard to read credits presented in a distressed type face set the stage for an arty British variation on *I Spit On Your Grave.* London executive Alice Comfort (Gillian Anderson) impulsively invites young security system installer Adam (Danny Dyer) to accompany her to a lavish country party. Late at night on the way back, they are attacked by rapacious rubes. A month later, Alice stumbles across the identity of one of them. Throughout, the plotting veers between the unrealistic and the convenient with no stops in between. In the hands of another filmmaker, it might have been exploitation, but director Dan Reed favors dimly under-illuminated extreme close-ups, so it's difficult to tell exactly what's going on in key scenes. At the end, though, when Alice exacts her revenge, you see what you need to see.

The Top Five Evil Doll Movies

Dead Silence
Saw
Child's Play
Seed of Chucky
Devil Doll (1964)

Cloverfield (2008)

Alternately frustrating and intriguing "found footage" monster picture begins with a supertitle stating that the film came from "the area formerly known as Central Park." What follows is a disjointed story of several often indistinguishable, attractive young people. They come together for a going-away party in downtown New York. It's interrupted by explosions somewhere close and TV news reports of something happening in the harbor. Before long, landmarks are being destroyed and the streets of the city are filled with billowing clouds of dust and smoke. Appropriation of those sounds and images of 9/11 for shallow escapism is troubling. The rest of the story follows the structure of H.G. Wells's *War of the Worlds* with a filmmaker managing to be on hand for key moments of an attack by an impressively realized big nasty critter. But the "realistic" technique makes it difficult to work up much involvement with the characters or even to understand what's happening.

Club Dread (2004)

Loosely wrapped horror spoof understands the conventions of the genre as well as the *Scary Movie* and *Scream* franchises. Members of the Broken Lizard comedy troupe play staffers at a hedonistic tropical resort run by past-his-prime singer Coconut Pete (Bill Paxton). Pete's a singer whose big hit, "Pina Coladaburg," was written seven years before "Margaritaville." Everything's wonderful until a machete-wielding slasher starts knocking people off. The girls are sexy, the guys are goofy, the effects are funny, and you gotta love the ending.

Cobra Woman (1944)

Technically, this camp masterpiece isn't part of the genre but several of the most famous names in Universal's horror stable, including producer George Wagner and director Robert Siodmak, are involved. Maria Montez is the simple South Seas island village girl who's kidnapped by Lon Chaney Jr. on the

Actor Edgar Barrier plays Martok, a cobra priest in 1944's *Cobra Woman.*

day of her wedding and taken to the island of the Cobra People where her evil twin rules. Jon Hall sets out to bring her back. The bizarre material—complete with erupting volcano, incredible costumes, and dance numbers that must be seen to be believed—is given an unusually lush Technicolor treatment.

Cold Sweat (1994)

Dark, tongue-in-cheek humor lifts this crime thriller/ghost story above the expected levels of either genre. The main players are a hitman (Ben Cross) haunted by the ghost of a recent victim, a financially strapped businessman (Dave Thomas), his faithless wife (Shannon Tweed), and their drug dealer (Adam Baldwin). The plot follows a familiar course for about an hour and then comes thoroughly unhinged in the last act. Like so many Canadian productions, the film has a bleak look. It won't be to all tastes, but horror fans in the mood for something quirky ought to give it a try.

Collector, The (2009)

Arkin (Josh Stewart) is a handyman working on the house of a well-to-do family. It's clear from the outset that he's troubled. Are all of the spiders and bugs that he sees real, or are they products of his imagination? From that promising beginning, the story slips into some of the most implausible torture porn ever put on film. No surprise there, co-writer/director Marcus Dunstan has also worked on scripts in the *Saw* and *Feast* series. Much of the action takes place inside the dimly lit house at night, and it's difficult to follow, most noticeably when Dunstan sends his camera soaring up to the ceiling. Stewart is very good. A sequel—*The Collection*—has been made.

Color Me Blood Red (1965)

Goremeister H.G. Lewis's 1964 answer to Roger Corman's *Bucket of Blood* isn't as snappy or as sophisticated. (This is, of course, the only context in which *Bucket of Blood* could ever be called sophisticated.) Adam Sorg (Don Joseph) decides that he prefers blood to oils or tempera for the reds in his paintings, so he murders for art supplies. Obviously, Adam's a man ahead of his time. Today he'd get a grant and be pilloried by Republicans. It's all extremely silly with gore effects, faux hip humor, and several pointless scenes on water bicycles.

Colour from the Dark (2008)

Based on the Lovecraft story that inspired *Die, Monster, Die,* this often perplexing Italian production is somber, moody, and challenging. It's set in 1943 near the end of the war on two small hardscrabble farms. Something strange is going on there, but the shifting atmosphere is more important than conventional narrative. Relationships among the main characters are revealed slowly. They're often presented in confusingly similar dress and appearance, and so the viewer is often unsure about both what's happening and who is involved. Throughout, images of growth, decay, and madness are punctuated by sudden bloody violence. Debbie Rochon's performance is perhaps her best.

Coma (1978)

When a friend goes into a coma, Dr. Susan Wheeler (Genevieve Bujold) becomes interested in the idea of being alive and dead at the same time. She looks into her hospital's records and finds that it's happening there more than it should. Writer/director Michael Crichton bases his horror on the all-too real world of the hospital. He doesn't need monsters or gallons of blood. The sight of ominous figures in green scrubs, medical machines, and tile walls are enough to scare the pants off most viewers. Once the setting has been established, he doesn't need to do much more. The only real flaw is an overreliance on loud music at key moments.

Comedy of Terrors (1963)

Unscrupulous undertaker Trumbull (Vincent Price) has twenty-four hours to come up with the back rent for Mr. Black (Basil Rathbone). After an unfunny screaming match with his wife (Joyce Jameson), he and his partner Gilly (Peter Lorre) set out to scare up new business. The pace picks up with a corpse that refuses to rest in peace. Not surprisingly, the tone owes more to the other American-International releases of the day and to the overall spirit of experimentation of the mid-1960s than to director Jacques Tourneur's better known work. Though Boris Karloff has little to do as the doddering father-in-law, it's fun to see these four stars on screen together.

Company of Wolves (1984)

Fans will be either infuriated or entranced by Angela Carter's atmospheric tale. It contains elements of horror, but its real subject is myth—fantasy, fairy tale, nursery rhyme, and archetype all mixed and layered in a dreamlike structure with repeated images, phrases, and stories taking the place of the conventional well-made plot. Grandmother (Angela Lansbury) makes a red cloak for Rosaleen (Sarah Patterson) and fills her head with cautionary tales. But Rosaleen is making the awkward, halting transition from girl to woman and does not accept everything she hears. The setting—a foggy, nightmare combination of Disney's *Snow White* forest and Kong's Skull Island—is inseparable from the action. Like the film, it's the world of a child's fantasy seen through adult eyes.

Conqueror Worm, The (1968)

The England of 1645 is torn apart by civil war and a widespread witch hunt paranoia. Matthew Hopkins (Vincent Price) leads the faithful, torturing confessions out of the accused for a price. Young Sarah (Hilary Dwyer) catches his eye. She's the fiancé of Richard (Ian Ogilvy), a soldier in Cromwell's army. Director Michael Reeves handles Hopkins' character carefully, presenting him as a conman who, to a degree, believes his own con. (The real Hopkins was involved with the prosecution and execution of more than sixty women, and was himself hanged as a sorcerer in 1647.) The pace is a bit too deliberate, but it effectively creates suspense. Though the American title comes from Poe, the film is really closer in spirit and appearance to the contemporaneous Hammer films. Also, for the times when it was made, the sexual and violent aspects of the film are groundbreakingly frank. Reeves died soon after the film was finished.

Contagion (2011)

A highly virulent strain of flu develops in China and is brought to America by businesswoman Beth Emhoff (Gwyneth Paltrow). Her husband (Matt Damon) is unaffected, while doctors (Laurence Fishburne, Kate Winslet) at the Centers for Disease Control work to create a vaccine. As the lethal infection spreads, a malicious blogger (Jude Law) exploits the situation. For the most part, the characters act believably, and the story plays out with chilling, all too plausible realism. Coughs and hands touching doorknobs become as frightening as any monster. The only major flaw is one subplot involving a noble doctor played by Marion Cotillard. Cliff Martinez provides a spare, off-putting score.

Count Dracula (1970)

Complete disappointment. Given a fine cast and an apparently adequate budget, director Jesús Franco delivers perhaps the most anemic and dispirited version of the story ever put on screen. In one short scene, Christopher Lee plays the Count as a megalomaniacal Magyar, but for the rest of his screentime, he's a pedestrian figure. Klaus Kinski's Renfield is more interesting, but not much. All of the characters are adrift in dark, deep sets. Franco's use of zoom focus has seldom been more irritating, and his attempt to use stuffed animals for scares is the final insult. It will make you appreciate the Hammer Dracula films.

Count Yorga, Vampire (1970)
Return of Count Yorga (1971)

Should a European vampire relocate to trendy Los Angeles, might he not set up shop as a spiritualist? That's what Yorga (Robert Quarry) does in a nicely handled horror that's also a postcard of the late 1960s. The script and the acting are more polished than the production values, but the location work is typical of the time. Quarry is properly seductive and regal, though his harem of converts and a wardrobe that only a Vegas lounge lizard could love are more humorous than they once were. If the sight of an aristocratic vampire riding in a VW minibus is odd, the whole effort is more successful than the Hammer attempts to bring Dracula into the present.

The uneven but more polished sequel, *Return of Count Yorga,* begins with a spooky vampires-erupting-from-the-grave scene. It's followed by an attack on a house taken from *Night of the Living Dead.* The scene also recalls the Manson family's Tate-LaBianco murders that were still fresh in the public mind when the film was made. Quarry is an imposing European vampire who seems totally out of place in the tackiness of early 1970s California. Mariette Hartley is an attractive, mostly passive heroine, but too much of the action is frantic, pointless running down dark hallways and stairs. Look for Craig T. Nelson in a small supporting role as a cop.

Countess Dracula (1971)

Ingrid Pitt solidified her reputation as one of horror's sexiest stars with her second feature. Loosely based on legends of Countess Elizabeth Bathory, it's about a Hungarian widow (Pitt) who must bathe in the blood of virgins to retain her youth and her young beau (Sandor Eles). Compared to conventional vampire stories focused on a male figure, it's a fresh approach. Director Peter Sasdy also made the relatively unknown *Taste the Blood of Dracula* and *Hands of the Ripper* around the same time. Any horror fan who hasn't discovered these three is in for a treat.

Craft, The (1996)

Sleeper hit that might have been pure exploitation is a keenly observed, well-acted story of four teenage girls. The supernatural elements are handled with restraint, and it's not until the big grossout conclusion that the special effects really kick in. Troubled Sarah (Robin Tunney) finds it hard to fit in at her new L.A. school. Three girls who are ostracized from the rest of the students offer friendship. With her nose ring and attitude, Nancy (Fairuza Balk) is the group's leader. Bonnie (Neve Campbell) has serious self-image problems, and Rochelle (Rachel True) is the target of racist taunts. The three have formed a frivolous coven that's all talk and silliness, but they think that having a fourth member will allow them to call up the elements or whatever. The script by Peter Filardi (*Flatliners*) and director Andrew Fleming treats magic almost as an extension of emotion. Beyond the incantations and rituals, these four girls are expressing the real fears and desires of their age—to be pretty, to be accepted, to get back at the guy who's been mean to you. Favorable comparisons to *Carrie* aren't out of place.

Crash (1996)

Renowned writer and critic Anthony Boucher reportedly asked a colleague his opinion of a new novel. The man dismissed it as pornography. Still curious, Boucher pressed on and asked, "But is it good pornography?" He might have been inquiring about *Crash* and the answer would be, yes, it's good porn; slickly made and perversely enjoyable for fans of director David Cronenberg. In many ways, the film is a companion piece to his *Dead Ringers.* Both are horror films of disturbing originality. James Spader and Deborah Unger play a kinky Canadian couple who become sexually fixated on the injured victims of automobile accidents. Holly Hunter introduces them to this peculiar subculture, and Elias Koteas becomes their guide through it. That journey is essentially a series of sex scenes that emphasize broken bones, stitches, scar tissue, braces, and crutches. Cronenberg is a fine creepy director, and the first scenes are shocking. With graphic sexual material, though, acts that are at first surprising eventually become silly and finally banal. Of course, individual viewers will disagree about where those grada-

THE TOP TEN (+) BAD HAIR DAYS

The Hand
Underworld series
BloodRayne
The Hanging Woman
I Dismember Mama
Rasputin the Mad Monk
Subspecies series
eXistenZ
Jennifer's Body
Almost anything with Brad Dourif

tions occur. Throughout, only the characters' sexual sides are revealed, and those don't really change much. As a group, they begin and end with the same slack-faced expressions of jaded desire and sated fulfillment.

CRAVING, THE (1981)

Though it's not meant to be funny, Paul Naschy's tale of reincarnated monsters is so wild and wooly that it's best appreciated as a comedy. Wolfman Valdemar (Naschy) is brought back to life with Elizabeth Bathory (Silvia Aquilar). He's the good monster (sort of); she's the villain. The plot whips vampirism, grave robbing, sex, and other stuff into a semi-coherent sepulchral stew. For those unfamiliar with Naschy, think of a Spaghetti Western version of *Dark Shadows.*

CRAWLING HAND, THE (1963)

In many ways, this is nothing more than a low-budget, black-and-white teen horror from the early 1960s with a particularly loony premise. Mild mannered student Paul (Peter Breck) turns into a raccoon-eyed homicidal zombie after he and his Swedish girlfriend Marte (Sirry Steffen) find the hand of an astronaut on the beach. With Gilligan's Skipper Alan Hale as the sheriff and The Rivingtons' "The Bird Is the Word" on the soundtrack, the comic side is complete. But toward the end, Brock comes up with one brief moment that perfectly expresses the whole teen-angst appeal of horror to young audiences when Paul desperately tries to explain what's happening to Marte: "There are times when I'm all right and then I'm not, and then … then when I'm myself and I'm not and the periods when I'm myself are getting shorter and shorter. Do you understand?" "No." "Then don't try! I gotta get outta here. Leave me alone!"

Crazies, The (1973, 2010)

George Romero's third film is an anti-military story about a bacteriological weapon named Trixie that gets loose, causing people to go berserk, in rural western Pennsylvania. The Army attempts to contain both the actual and PR damage. Remember that the film was made around the same time that the Air Force killed a flock of sheep and tried to cover it up. The references to the Vietnam War are less than subtle. Like most of Romero's work, it's rough in technical terms—harsh colors, mostly no-name cast, shot on location—but emotionally effective. In some ways, this one can be seen as a link between *Night of the Living Dead* and *Dawn of the Dead.*

The 2010 remake is predictably much more polished, carefully constructed, and expensive. Timothy Olyphant is the sheriff of a small Iowa town suddenly beset by a plague that makes the residents uncontrollably violent. Radha Mitchell is his pregnant wife, a doctor. The emphasis here is as much on the zombie-like creatures as it is on the government conspiracy. Acting, direction, and writing are first rate. Overall, this is a remake that actually adds something to the original. Recommended.

Creature from the Black Lagoon (1954)
Revenge of the Creature (1955)
Creature Walks among Us, The (1956)

The Gill Man is certainly the most memorable guy-in-a-rubber-fish-suit monster to come out of the 1950s. That subgenre of horror is inherently lightweight, so why has this example remained so popular? It's simple. Sex. The white bathing suit scene with Julie Adams is as sensual and suggestive as Hollywood got in those days. (So that's what synchronized swimming is all about.) Beyond that indelible moment, the rubber fish suit is pretty good. The simple plot moves quickly and, somehow, that backlot Amazon set is believable. Joseph Gershenson's brassy score set the tone for the whole era. Originally filmed in 3-D.

The insipid sequel, *Revenge of the Creature,* largely ignores the elements that made the original so good. The Gill Man spends most of the running time chained to the bottom of a tank at Marineland pining away for flashy ichthyology grad student Lori Nelson. (Yes, Mr. G still has a thing for bleached blondes.) As an example of '50s kitsch nostalgia, it earns full marks; as a horror film, it's a joke. Yes, that's a young Clint Eastwood as the comic lab assistant.

The Gill Man's third outing, *The Creature Walks among Us,* is more boats, blondes, and bubbles as a quartet of doctors—and one curvy wife (Leigh Snowden)—sail into the Everglades to fetch everyone's favorite fish monster and then to surgically alter him. No, not that way; these guys want to "bring a new species into existence!" After a lot of pseudoscientific gobbledegook, they strap on the air tanks and catch him. The black-and-white photography is crystalline, both underwater and above. Though this one's more enjoyable than the second, it doesn't equal the original and it can't live up to that great title. The way the story is set up, you're rooting for the Creature all the way. The racial overtones of his eventual appearance in "human" form are unmistakable. The action's relatively slow until the conclusion when Gill finally decides to kick ass and take names. Enjoy the movie as a period piece, and, of course, check out that great monster suit.

One of the classics of the genre, *Creature from the Black Lagoon* features a man in an obvious rubber suit, but it still works, and audiences often end up rooting for the Creature.

Creep (2004)

In London, party girl Kate (Franka Potente) misses the last train and finds herself trapped in a locked subway station. A potential rapist turns out to be the least of her problems. The monster of the title remains hidden for a time, and writer/director Christopher Smith (*Severance*) reveals the game slowly. Some abrupt transitions keep the audience off balance, and some important questions are only partially answered. Those are not flaws. Excellent performances, quirky humor, and a fast pace earn a solid recommendation. It's similar to *Midnight Meat Train* but, in the end, much more successful.

Creepers

See Phenomena

Creeping Flesh, The (1973)

Perhaps Cushing and Lee's most underrated work together is a complicated psychological tale that can be viewed as either supernatural horror or delusion. In 1893 Emmanuel Hildman (Peter Cushing) is an archeologist who's just found the "missing link" which in turn is the source of a phallic fossil. Emmanuel's half-brother James (Christopher Lee) runs a mental asylum. Emmanuel is obsessively overprotective of his daughter Penelope (Lorna Heilbron) and that's the real source of the story. However it's interpreted, this is a film about patriarchal power and the inability of men to understand women. Though the setting and casting make it look like a Hammer production, it's much more intricate and indirect. Also, despite the PG rating, the film contains a strong scene of sexual assault.

Creepshow (1982)
Creepshow 2 (1987)

Stephen King and George Romero pay affectionate and gory tribute to E.C. Comics with these five short films. With its use of split screens, animated frames, bright primary colors, live action that fades into and out of comic art, and even ads between the episodes, the collection is a true cinematic comic book. The best ones are "The Crate," with Adrienne Barbeau as a brassy shrew, and "Creeping Up on You," with E.G. Marshall as a cheerfully wicked millionaire. King himself plays "Jordy." Fans of blood-soaked silliness won't be disappointed.

Creepshow 2 is second-tier material from King and screenwriter Romero. All three stories lack interesting twists, depending instead on good production values and middling effects. The first, with George Kennedy and Dorothy Lamour as shopkeepers, is about a vengeance-seeking wooden Indian. The second puts four teenagers in the path of a lake-dwelling blob. In the third, a socialite (Lois Chiles) tries to run away from responsibility. None are as good as the better episodes of the first, or King's *Cat's Eye* either. (King appears briefly as a truck driver in the last part.)

Cronos (1993)

Guillermo del Toro's elegant, haunting horror film is completely unlike any that have been produced in this country for years. It's reminiscent of David Cronenberg's early work, though del Toro's use of special effects is much more limited. Where Cronenberg might have exploded a human head on screen, del

Toro will use a glittering golden needle with fiendish delight. The bejeweled Cronos Device is a fourteenth-century alchemist's invention that confers immortality upon the owner—immortality with a price. In present-day Mexico City, it falls into the possession of Jesus Gris (Federico Luppi), an aging antiques dealer who's devoted to his young granddaughter Aurora (Tamara Shanath). De la Guardia (Claudio Brook), a crippled and corrupt millionaire, owns the instruction manual for the gizmo and, along with his mercurial nephew (Ron Perlman), has been searching for it for years. The quirky humor has a strong Felliniesque edge, and compared to American horror movies, the pace is almost stately. There are also some genuinely tender moments, to go along with those that are utterly revolting. Writer/director Toro tells the story through a series of slow, vivid nightmare images. More importantly, he got a winning performance from his star. Federico Luppi is the kind of actor that audiences warm to instantly, and so the film is much more involving than it sounds. Some of the scenes between him and Tamara Shanath are really touching.

The Top Seven Motels-You-Absolutely-Do-Not-Want-to-Visit Movies

Identity
John Carpenter's Vampires
Tourist Trap
Twentynine Palms
Vacancy
Psycho
The Forsaken

Cropsey (2009)

The title of this documentary comes from an imaginary character who's the subject of campfire tales in the Hudson River Valley. His real-life equivalent may have been responsible for a series of disappearances and murders on Staten Island in the 1980s. They occurred close to the Willowbrook State School for the mentally ill, an abandoned facility that is every bit as frightening as any fictional setting. The main focus is on Jennifer Schweiger who disappeared in 1987, and Andre Rand, the homeless man who was accused of her murder. Filmmakers Barbara Brancaccio and Joshua Zeman appear on camera frequently, but they maintain a careful neutrality throughout. The people they talk to, and who refuse to talk to them, are a fascinating bizarre group. In the end, the film is about the horror stories we tell ourselves, and in its refusal to accept any easy conclusions, it has real staying power. Comparisons to *Paradise Lost: The Child Murders at Robin Hood Hills* are not out of place.

Crow, The (1994)
Crow, The: City of Angels (1996)

In an unnamed, decaying inner city on Devil's Night (an excuse for arson before Halloween), Eric Draven (Brandon Lee) and his fiancé Shelly (Sofia Shinas) are murdered by four thugs. One year later, Eric rises out of the grave, literally, for revenge. Our young narrator Sarah (Rochelle Davis) explains that his love was so strong that a crow has brought him back to this world for revenge. The main villain is a Byronic gangster, Top Dollar (Michael Wincott) who lives incestuously with his half-sister Myca (Bai Ling). Eric's only ally is an honest beat cop named Albrecht (Ernie Hudson). The script, by David Schow and John Shirley from James O'Barr's comic book and strip, distills the story down to its basic elements, borrowing freely from the works of Poe and a hardcore rock sensibility. Virtually all of the action takes place at night on rainy streets or in grimy interiors. Director Alex Proyas fills the screen with shiny blacks, deep grays, and red highlights. That dampens the film's violence while heightening the mood. The accidental death of Lee while making the film underscores its dark themes of resurrection and revenge.

"Avoid suspicion. Manipulate your friends. Eliminate your enemies."
Cry_Wolf

Like most sequels, *The Crow: City of Angels* slavishly rehashes the most popular elements of the original. That calls for lots of inky dark atmosphere, violent special effects, and pop nihilism. The rest is nothing more than a second-rate revenge flick with a plot that lacks any complexity, and characters who have no personalities. Press notes explain that Sarah (Mia Kirschner) is a grown-up version of the character who was a child in the first film, though that's never explained on screen. Writer David Goyer tosses enough gimmicks to keep the action moving, but the script lacks the poetic flourishes that add so much to the first film. Director Tim Pope relies on computer-generated effects and models to keep the action lively in a strictly visual sense.

Cry of the Banshee (1970)

Oona (Elizabeth Bergner), a clichéd and vaguely silly sixteenth-century witch, vows vengeance on Lord Edward Whitman (Vincent Price) after his men attack and kill more of her people. Roderick (Patrick Mower) is her instrument. Compared to other witchcraft films of the era, this one is better than *Mark of the Devil,* but not nearly as complex as *The Conqueror Worm.* Also, it's not nearly as much fun as director Gordon Hessler's *Scream and Scream Again.* Hugh Griffith has a nice cameo as a gravedigger. If he's not at his best, Price is still fine.

Cry_Wolf (2005)

From the first scene—terrified girl running through the woods at night—to the setting—prep school for spoiled rich kids—this one is pretty much standard-issue. The plot involves a crazily complex prank about an imaginary serial killer, and the whole thing is almost as self-aware and "meta" as the *Scream* movies. Throughout, the pace is quick but the image is muddy.

Cube (1997)

Several people find themselves trapped in a structure of large interconnected cubes made of metal and glass. They don't know how they got there or what they have to do to get out. Some of the cubes are booby-trapped with inventively lethal and bloody devices. The severe limitations of the premise aren't a problem. The sets and effects are neat. The problem is the characters. They're not particularly interesting or sympathetic and so I never really cared about what happened to them. Followed by two sequels.

Curse of Frankenstein

See Frankenstein

Curse of the Demon (1957)

Word has it that producers forced director Jacques Tourneur to include explicit shots of the fire demon in his adaptation of M.R. James' great story "Casting the Runes." Though most critics decry the monster, I think this carefully made psychological horror needs those explicit moments. (Besides, hokey as the demon may be, it scared the hell out of me when I was ten years old.) Dana Andrews is excellent as the skeptical scientist who refuses to believe that Karswell (Niall MacGinnis) leads a cult of English Satanists. The film's central conceit—the audience understands how important a slip of paper is while the hero treats it as a trifle—builds a unique suspense that's hard to describe. MacGinnis, perhaps more familiar to American audiences as Zeus in Ray Harryhausen's *Jason and the Argonauts,* steals the film. The DVD edition contains both the original ninety-five-minute British release titled *Night of the Demon* and the shorter American version.

Curse of the Komodo (2004)

The story, the bad acting, and the simple special effects could have come straight from any 1950s big lizard drive-in flick. Army experiments gone wrong on a Pacific island result in giant, mutant carnivorous Komodos with poison slime. Trapped with them are busty babes and guys with guns. It's a typically cheap and efficient entry from B-movie veteran Jim Wynorski under his Jay Andrews pseudonym.

Curse of the Werewolf (1961)

One of Hammer's most successful horrors is second only to *The Wolfman* in its exploration of the subject. It's actually more serious in some ways and more carefully constructed. Writer-producer Anthony Hinds (whose script is based on Guy Endore's novel *Werewolf of Paris*) and director Terence Fisher see the cause of lycanthropy as human depravity, embodied in a corrupt aristocrat (Anthony Dawson). Shape-changing Leon (Oliver Reed) is the product of a series of atrocities that turn him into a genuinely tragic figure. The ambitious story is played out on a larger scale than most of the studio's efforts, and though the political element is strong, it never overpowers the personal. Religious themes are important, too. Reed, who does not appear until the midpoint, turns in a near flawless performance. Hinds reworks the material, not quite as successfully, in *Legend of the Werewolf.*

Cursed (2005)

Unusual misfire from veterans Kevin Williamson and Wes Craven is basically a slapstick werewolf comedy. Brother and sister Jimmy (Jesse Eisenberg) and Ellie (Christina Ricci) are injured in a car accident that involves some sort of beast. Soon enough, they're experiencing strange symptoms and other people are meeting extremely violent deaths. Are they responsible or is someone else the real shape shifter? A few of the genre-related jokes work but Eisenberg's familiar twitchy, whiney insecurity wears thin, and the filmmakers do not pay strict attention to all of the traditional rules. Transformation effects are acceptable. According to several sources, the production was plagued with problems leading to significant script and cast changes.

D

Dagon (2001)

Four Americans are on a yacht off the Spanish fishing village of Imboca when they're hit by a sudden storm. Paul (Ezra Godden) and Barbara (Raquel Merono) go ashore for help and find themselves threatened at every turn by the misshapen locals and mostly unseen sea monsters. The action moves quickly enough, but it's poorly acted and never develops any sense of place or reality. Fans hoping that director Stuart Gordon would recreate the wonders of his earlier Lovecraft adaptation, *Re-Animator,* will be disappointed.

Damien: Omen II

See The Omen

Dario Argento's Trauma (1993)

Argento rounds up his usual suspects—the beautiful teen heroine; the threatening institution, the Farraday Clinic; the psychic (Piper Laurie); the serial killer, this one called the Headhunter (who uses a mechanical decapitator); spooky empty houses; the hurricane of wind and rain effects—and whips them into his usual fevered hash. Compared to other Argento Grand Guignols, the story of two young protagonists (his daughter Asia Argento and Christopher Rydell) seeking the identity of the killer as they're stalked by him (or her) makes moderately more sense than *Tenebrae* and *Phenomena,* perhaps creditable to co-writer T.E.D. Klein. That relative coherence along with good Minnesota locations make this perhaps Argento's most accessible film for American audiences.

The Top Fifteen More or Less "Based on a True Story" Horrors

The Haunting in Connecticut
M
Maniac
Primeval
Serpent and the Rainbow
The Strangers
From Hell
American Haunting
Dead Ringers
Deranged
Exorcism of Emily Rose
The Exorcist
Wolf Creek
Henry: Portrait of a Serial Killer
Rogue

Dark, The (1993)

A creepy creepy premise, an overdeveloped sense of humor, and a deep streak of humanism make this a sleeper. The main characters are a half-mad ex-FBI agent (Brion James), a doctor (Stephen McHattie) on a mission, a sympathetic waitress (Cynthia Belliveau), an understanding gravedigger (Jaimz Woolvett), and the monstrous creature who lives under the cemetery and eats bodies. Robert C. Cooper's script follows the rules for the genre and gives fans what they want to see. But it goes a step farther and gives all of the characters—including the monster—more depth than you usually see in the genre. It's the kind of understanding that's found in stories like *Frankenstein* and *The Hunchback of Notre Dame,* but few others. By the way, the film has nothing to do with the identically titled 1979 release.

Dark, The (2005)

A family is coming apart. Dad (Sean Bean) has moved into a house in Wales near the dramatic and dangerous cliffs overlooking the ocean. Mother (Maria Bello) and daughter (Sophie Stuckey) get lost before they arrive for a visit, and there's something they don't want to talk about. After a few phony scares, a ghost story of sorts emerges. Though the acting is excellent and the effects are restrained, the setting is more impressive than the sometimes unfocused plot. It's not at all exploitative, but a lot of terrible stuff involves children.

Dark Angel: The Ascent (1994)

Director Linda Hassani makes a memorable debut with a horror film of humor, imagination, intelligence and, perhaps even wisdom. In the fire and brimstone hell of Hieronymus Bosch, the souls of sinners suffer eternal pain and fallen angels rule. Some of them still worship God even though they have been banished from his presence. These, after all, are rebellious angels, and none more than Veronica (Angela Featherstone) who dreams of the world above. Then she learns of an unguarded cavern that leads to the surface. Up she pops, buck naked, from a manhole cover in the middle of an unnamed city where things are just as nasty and dangerous as they are back home. Matthew Bright's script borrows bits from such diverse sources as *Splash, Death Wish,* and *The Exorcist,* but it's neither derivative nor predictable. Even the most jaded horror fan will be surprised by some of the twists. Fuzzbee Morse's score steals blatantly and effectively from Bernard Herrmann. Any fan who hasn't seen this one yet is in for a treat.

Dark City (1998)

In its initial theatrical release, this noir-ish horror/sci-fi mindbender was compared to *The Matrix* for its depiction of an alternate reality. It stands on its own just fine, and rewards repeated viewings. The action takes place in a city of perpetual night. An amnesiac (Rufus Sewell) wakes up in a bathtub in a hotel room with a dead woman. He suspects that he may be a murderer. A twitchy doctor (Kiefer Sutherland) is also involved and so are some chittering guys (and one scary kid) in black leather coats, reminiscent of the Cenobites from the *Hellraiser* movies. The director's cut is probably preferable to the first DVD release, but in either version, it's a personal favorite.

Dark Half, The (1993)

Stephen King's relationship with his nom de plume Richard Bachman provides the basis for this variation on Jekyll and Hyde. When serious novelist Thad Beaumont (Timothy Hutton) tries to kill off George Stark, the name he uses for violent potboilers, Stark appears in the flesh (Hutton again). As the greasy-haired George, Hutton looks like he's about to morph into David Keith, but he's still good in both roles. He gets excellent support from Amy Madigan, as his wife, and Michael Rooker, as the local sheriff. As always, writer-director George Romero's cluttered middle-class world adds a strong note of realism to the fantastic story. He also gives new meaning to the term "pencil neck." Perhaps the film is a little too long, but the ending justifies the length.

Dark Mirror (2007)

Some extremely inventive photography is much more interesting than the run-of-the-mill haunted house tale. Well, make that haunted bungalow (2 bedroom, 1 bath). That's what Deb (Lisa Vidal) and her husband Jim (David Chisum) find when they move to Los Angeles from Seattle. Turns out that a semi-famous painter and his family disappeared from the place years ago. Before they have even finished unpacking, the clichéd hooded figure is hanging around on the sidewalk. The script has its clumsy moments, and it arrives at a nutty ending, but it clocks in at a swift seventy-nine minutes, and the inventive visuals alone rate a qualified recommendation.

Dark Secret of Harvest Home (1978)

In some ways, both Tom Tryon's novel and this made-for-TV adaptation can be seen as answers to *Rosemary's Baby.* The story is about the urban Constantin family (David Ackroyd, Rosanna Arquette, Joanna Miles) who move to the idyllic, rural hamlet of Harvest Home. It's ruled by Widow Fortune (Bette Davis). The pace is slow and the conclusion is strong. This is Bette Davis' last major horror role and one of her best. Not yet available on DVD.

Dark Shadows (2012)

Tim Burton and Johnny Depp take a curiously jokey, scattershot approach to their adaptation of the supernatural TV soap opera. They retain the premise of Barnabas Collins (Depp with whiteface and finger extensions) being turned into a vampire in the eighteenth century by the witch Angelique (Eva Green, who commandeers the show). Entombed until 1972, Barnabas escapes to reunite with his true love Victoria/Josette (Bella Heathcote). The elaborate sets and special effects, and the swooping camera movement, are totally out of keeping with the original. The ironic use of sugary pop songs and kitschy period details don't add much when the tone veers more than once from comic to kinky. Look for Christopher Lee in a cameo as a fisherman, as well as blink-and-you'll-miss-them appearances by Jonathan Frid, Kathryn Leigh Scott, David Selby, and Lara Parker from the original series.

Dark Water (2005)

Comparisons to *The Ring* are inevitable. Both are remakes of Japanese horror stories about single moms facing difficulties that are both real and supernatural. Dahlia (Jennifer Connelly) is newly separated and looking for an apartment

Johnny Depp stars as Barnabas Collins in the 2012 movie version of the classic horror television drama *Dark Shadows*.

she can afford for her and her young daughter. She finds it on Roosevelt Island, though the place looks like East Berlin in the darkest days of the Cold War. As the garrulous real estate agent (John C. Reilly) puts it, the complex was built in the "brutalist" style. That includes really bad plumbing and ghostly neighbors. The strong New York setting is complemented by realistic details of divorce and custody hearings and excellent performances from the supporting cast.

Darkman (1990)
Darkman II: The Return of Durant (1995)
Die, Darkman, Die (1996)

Writer/director Sam Raimi goes back to the Universal horror heroes of the 1930s for Dr. Peyton Westlake (Liam Neeson), "the man trapped inside the beast." He's a brilliant scientist on the verge of a huge discovery when the evil Durant (Larry Drake) tries to kill him, turning Westlake into a tortured, physically repulsive monster of great strength and uncontrollable rages. Raimi borrows bits from *The Invisible Man, The Wolf Man,* and even *Phantom of the Opera.* The plot zooms along at pace familiar to fans of his *Evil Dead* films, and it's punctuated with moments of crystal-clear detail. Topping off the inspired cast is Frances McDormand as a smart heroine. Danny Elfman's "cornball" score adds immeasurably.

The Top Four Absolutely-Not-Based-on-a-True-Story

Paranormal Activity series
Blair Witch Project
Book of Shadows: Blair Witch 2
Amityville Horror

"I choose to live on as a creature of the shadows—as Darkman!" So proclaims brilliant scientist Peyton Westlake in *Darkman II: The Return of Durant.* Evil villain Durant (Larry Drake) has chosen to live on, too, even though he was turned to toast in the helicopter crash at the end of the first film. But villains that good are hard to come by, so he miraculously survived and has been in the traditional cinematic coma. Meanwhile, Westlake (Arnold Vosloo ably taking over for Liam Neeson) is still working on a formula for synthetic skin. Director-cinematographer Bradford May captures the energy, black humor, and comic book spirit of Sam Raimi's original, but this one lacks that extra spark, polish, and attention to small details that mark the best of Raimi's work.

Third installment, *Die, Darkman, Die,* adds new characters and conflicts to the premise. Dr. Westlake (Vosloo) is still searching for a formula for synthetic skin. The stuff he's got is temporary but it does allow him to look briefly like anyone else including new bad guy, drug dealer Peter Rooker (Jeff Fahey, who has a grand time). Under Bradford May's direction, the pace is crisp and the action has a deliciously nasty edge with beheadings and self-administered spinal surgery.

Darkness (2002)

Variation on a haunted house tale begins on a promising note but quickly devolves into allegedly scary, low whispery sounds punctuated by loud whooshes and thunder and rain. Things are not going well for an American family recently relocated to Spain. Dad (Iain Glen) is flipping out, little brother (Stefan Enquist) is suddenly afraid of the dark, and teenaged Regina (Anna Paquin) doesn't know what to do. It all involves an eclipse that occurs every forty years and unspeakable acts in the past. The ending makes less than perfect sense, and the whole thing feels like some important explanatory scenes were left on the cutting room floor.

Darkness Falls (2003)

Modest little chiller never really rises above its nutty premise. Years ago in the little town of Darkness Falls, Matilda Dixon, who loved children, was falsely accused of murdering two of them and was executed. Now her ghost comes back to take the last baby tooth of every kid who lives there, and she kills anyone who wakes up and sees her. Kyle (Chaney Kley) managed to escape but Matilda got his mother. Twelve years later, he is a very troubled adult who returns to his hometown. The plot has a strong Stephen King quality, but it's loosely stitched together, and too many of the scares are based on flashlights waving around in the dark and nasty, growly noises.

Daughters of Darkness (1971)

Without question, this is the most erotic lesbian vampire movie ever made. *The Hunger* pales in comparison. The opening shots establish a honeymooning couple, Stefan (John Karlen) and Valerie (Danielle Ouimet), married only a few hours, but already being divided by dishonesty and tension. After an unplanned stop at a huge, empty seaside hotel, they meet the Countess (Delphine Seyrig) and her secretary Ilona (Andrea Rau), glamorous women languid as cats. The level of sexual uncertainty among the quartet rises steadily and largely without the expected conventions. The film is beautifully written and acted on a curiously conversational level. The filmmakers approach their subject from the edges. For example, they delay the introduction of key characters and information, and they use color, pace, and camera angles to keep the viewer off balance.

Dawn of the Dead

See Night of the Living Dead

Day of the Beast (1995)

Alex de la Iglesia combines savage humor with social commentary. Father Angel (Álex Argulo), a self-effacing priest, deciphers a Biblical code that tells him when and where Satan is returning to earth. To stop the Evil One from taking over, he decides that he must commit enough sins to get close when the act occurs. Breaking commandments left and right, he heads off to Madrid and straightaway meets José (Santiago Segura), a long-haired biker working in a record store who knows exactly where the local Satanic metal group will be performing. Filling out the trio is Prof. Cavan (Armando De Razza), a television psychic who doesn't believe any of the baloney that his adoring audience accepts unconditionally. At the same time, a shadowy group of urban terrorists (or are they Satanists?) commit random acts of horrible violence. Once our three heroes overcome their differences and go to work, the film becomes a sort of Marx Brothers version of *The Exorcist.* De la Iglesia shares Sam Raimi's rambunctious, maniacal energy and he keeps viewers guessing throughout. The ending is particularly offbeat.

Day of the Dead

See Night of the Living Dead

Daybreakers (2009)

In 2019, vampires have become the dominant species (if *species* is the right term) and run all governments and corporations. Society operates much as did before, but they don't go out much in the daytime. The problem is that they're running out of human food. Vampire hematologist Edward Dalton (Ethan Hawke) is working on an artificial blood substitute with, so far, disastrous results. He's contacted by the resistance to help with a cure for vampirism. This handsome Australian production hits all the right notes. Computer effects are used to tell a complicated, well-imagined story. Along with *30 Days of Night,* it's one of the best of the recent crop.

"Humans were offered a chance to assimilate but they refused. Therefore, they are enemies of the state ... and will be captured ... for blood supply."
Daybreakers

Dead Alive (1992)

Peter Jackson's gore-fest comedy begins with a parody of *Raiders of the Lost Ark,* then shifts gears and slams into gross-out mode. The stomach-churning starts when Lionel's (Timothy Baine) mother (Elizabeth Moody) eats her own ear and it gets much, much worse. She was bitten, you see, by a Sumatran Rat-monkey, causing no end of problems for Lionel and his beloved Paquita (Diana Penalver) in New Zealand, 1957. Like *Evil Dead* and *Re-Animator,* the film establishes an unhinged internal logic, then, having set its grotesque wheels in motion, it charges forward relentlessly breaking new boundaries of bad taste wherever it goes. The slapstick guts and gore are so excessive that they are no longer disgusting. Required viewing for fans of the strong stuff.

Dead and Buried (1981)

Anyone unfamiliar with this largely unknown shocker is in for a real treat. It's one of the best sleepers around, filled with jolts and surprises. James Farentino is the sheriff of Potters Bluff, a New England seaside town where bizarre events are taking place, and seem, somehow to involve his sweet wife (Melody Anderson) and the garrulous undertaker/coroner (Jack Albertson). The script by Ronald Shusett and Dan O'Bannon combines a series of genuinely horrifying images with macabre humor and a cold, fog-shrouded atmosphere. Look for Robert Englund and Barry Corbin as townsfolk, and Tim Burton's ex-squeeze Lisa Marie as a hitchhiker.

Dead Man's Eyes (1944) / Pillow of Death (1945)

Overlapping love triangles are the basis of this poorly plotted horror-mystery. They're composed of an artist (Lon Chaney Jr.), his fiancé (Jean Parker), his model (Acquanetta), the model's beau (Paul Kelly), and the fiancé's ex-boyfriend (George Meeker). Cornea transplants are the gimmick. The story is too talky and built on conventions that work well on radio, but not on the screen. The costumes are cooler than the characters. Acquanetta is out of her depth even in these shallow dramatic waters. The second half of the double feature, *Pillow of Death,* is much more enjoyable. It's unusually sharp with crabby humor and a tighter plot. Lawyer Chaney is accused of murdering his wife by a bunch of goony psychics. The story works through all of your basic haunted house conventions with some decent twists. Solid performances throughout.

Dead Ringers (1988)

David Cronenberg forgoes graphic special effects for much darker psychological horrors, and makes perhaps his most accomplished and frightening film. Loosely based on truth, it's the story of twin gynecologists Bev and Elliot Mantle (both Jeremy Irons) and their relationship to an actress, Claire Niveau (Genevieve Bujold). The source of the tension is a single identity split into two bodies, but what sets this one apart is its lack of a sympathetic protagonist. There's no hero to root for and no heroine to be placed in danger. In their place is a slowly thickening atmosphere of fear that's underlined by glossy, stylized sets and pervasive religious imagery. Cronenberg's fans will also catch the reference to *Scanners.* One of the best.

Dead Silence (2007)

Director James Wan continues to work with the dolls and dummies featured in *Saw.* Newlywed Jamie (Ryan Kwanten) receives a mysterious package containing a ventriloquist's dummy that makes Chucky look like a Cabbage Patch Kid. It leads him back to his hometown where he discovers secrets long hidden, etc. Plot and characters are less important than the dreamlike look and texture and some neat visual tricks. Wan is a superb craftsman who has yet to make his best work. The film is dedicated to Gregg Hoffman, producer of the original *Saw* who died before his time in 2005.

Dead Snow (2009)

These freeze-dried Nazi zombies are not your usual shambling, stupid undead. They're fast and well organized. They also follow orders and attack a group of medical students who pick the wrong Norwegian mountain cabin for their Easter vacation. If the cast is unknown to American audiences, horror fans will find a smart, strikingly photographed comedy filled with all the guts, gore, and nastiness they could possibly want. The protagonists have some depth and definition, and the action takes very strange turns. Fans of *Severance,* take notice of this exceptionally well made sleeper.

Dead Weight (2012)

Despite an occasionally meandering pace and a flashback structure that's initially confusing, this Wisconsin independent production actually attempts something different and original with the zombie formula. As some sort of virus breaks out in American cities, slacker Charlie (Joe Belknap), who's in Toledo, and his girlfriend Samantha (Mary Lindberg), who's in Minneapolis, agree that they'll meet in Wausau. What follows is fairly realistic as Charlie walks across a desolate autumn/winter rural landscape, meeting and losing companions along the way. Filmmakers Adam Bartlett and John Pata rigorously avoid clichés throughout and the characters behave believably, given the circumstances. Violence is appropriate to the story without excess. A solid sleeper worth seeking out.

Dead Zone, The (1983)

David Cronenberg's thoughtful adaptation of Stephen King's novel is one of the best for both, though in many ways, it's not typical of either. John Smith (Christopher Walken) comes out of a five-year coma to find that he has unwanted psychic powers. Though Walken has gone on to create characters of much more flamboyant weirdness, this is one of the early defining roles. In Herbert Lom's long career of character parts, Dr. Weizak may be his best. Martin Sheen's chest-thumping politico is a maniacal villain. Such key details as a murderer's bedroom that reflects his madness are carefully chosen, and a suicide is about as frightening as any put on film. Cronenberg's work has gone in different directions, but echoes of this one can be seen in *The Dark Half* and other King films and fiction.

Deadly Blessing (1981)

After Martha's (Maren Jensen) husband is killed, she finds herself alone in a rural "Hittite" community. These are not the Hittites of ancient history, but vaguely Amish folk who are obsessed by fear of the "Incubus." Even so, Ernest Borgnine and Michael Berryman are believably threatening. Some of the spider stuff involving a young Sharon Stone works well and so does the infamous snake scene. If director Wes Craven doesn't reach the imaginative commercial success that he realizes with the *Elm Street* series, he creates legitimate tension. Though he doesn't hold much back in the last reel, the overt violence is kept to a minimum, making this one of his better efforts.

Deadly Friend (1986)

Paul (Matthew Laborteaux) is a boy genius who invents an artificial intelligence robot, and does a little brain surgery on the side. Both skills come in handy when his pretty next door neighbor Sam (Kristy Swanson) is hurt by her abusive father. The second half is a variation on *Frankenstein* concerning a creator's responsibility to his creation. The movie has such good intentions and good ideas that you wish it were better. The robot shouldn't be so cute; the story should be less dependent on stereotypes. It's aimed at a young audience, but kids can recognize formulas, too. Fans of director Wes Craven's *Elm Street* series will find some similarities, but they may be surprised at the film's human side.

Death Bed (2002)

Low-budget, low-voltage exploitation boasts "Stuart Gordon Presents" as part of the title but any resemblance to his brilliant *Re-Animator* is coincidental. Newlyweds Karen (Tanya Dempsey) and Jerry (Brave Matthews) find an old brass bed in their new apartment and are soon having black-and-white visions of a Prohibition-era murder. The cast is small; the sets are simple, and several often-repeated shots give the short film a padded feeling.

Death by Invitation (1971)

Early '70s rarity is worth seeking out for fans of the bizarre. The tired story is about a Colonial-era witch (Shelby Levington) who is reincarnated and seeks vengeance on the ancestors of her killer (Aaron Phillips). The opening scenes are balanced between incoherence and boredom. That part ends with an inspired monologue about militant, female-chauvinist, lesbian Indians. That, in turn, is matched later by a eulogy taken from the Book of Job. Though writer-director Ken Friedman has an invisible budget, the grainy black-and-white photography recalls *Carnival of Blood.* Some of the soundtrack could have come from a pinball game; other parts are acid-laced Muzak. Altogether indescribable.

Deep Rising (1998)

Standard big-budget studio action flick posits a bunch of guys with bulging biceps and large automatic weapons setting out to sea on Captain Finnegan's (Treat Williams) speedboat. Though he doesn't know it, they mean to knock over a luxury liner. Instead, they find that a nasty sea monster has beaten them to it. Some of the bloody makeup effects are inventive and so are the bits involving giant carnivorous tentacles. Wes Studi is a fine villain, too. In the end, though, like most action movies, this one is about stuff blowing up.

Demon Hunter (1965)

Bizarre Ed-Woodsian Georgia production is a hidden treasure for fans of alternative cinema. Bestoink Dooley (George Ellis) is an overweight, lank-haired, Jimmy Olsen-wannabe reporter who looks like a burlesque comedian with his spats, funny derby, and a big rose in his lapel. Given an opportunity to write his first story, he heads out in an old MG to find the monster of Blood Mountain, which turns out to be a guy in a goofy half-suit with a tail on each hip. The soundtrack could have been lifted from 1950s Muzak. The voice dubbing is unlike anything you've ever heard and it's matched by the beehive hair-dos, courtesy of the Decatur University of Cosmetology. The action swings back and forth between silliness and boring inanity. Not available on DVD. (Alternate title: *The Legend of Blood Mountain.*)

Demon in My View (1991)

Anthony Perkins plays another variation on his archetypal serial killer, Norman Bates, in his last big-screen role. Arthur Johnson (Perkins) has lived for more than twenty years in an aging London apartment. He stays on while other tenants come and go, and when the pressures of memory become too great, he strangles young women. Writer-director Petra Haffter does a fine job of adapting Ruth Rendell's novel to the screen and revealing the inner workings of Arthur's fevered psyche. She also captures the dangerous, complex moral texture of Rendell's fiction. Almost all of the violence and physical action is suggested or shown quickly. The most frightening moment—and it's a real skin crawler—involves nothing more threatening than a safety pin. Even so, this is one of the spookiest psychological horror films since the original *The Vanishing.*

Demon Seed (1977)

Rosemary's Baby meets Microsoft in an eerie cyber-sexual horror. Fritz Weaver has perfected artificial intelligence in his computer Proteus IV. It's hooked up to his house via another computer named Joshua. After the workaholic Weaver separates from his wife Julie Christie, she's alone with the machines. Proteus decides he wants a son. Director Donald Cammell tries to show Proteus' thought processes through electronic optical effects, not through the narrative line of the film, so the pace is slow and hard to follow at first. Once the "seduction" begins, the tension picks up considerably.

Demons of the Mind (1972)

Hammer's offbeat psychological horror can be seen as a companion piece to *The Wicker Man* and *The Blood on Satan's Claw,* both made around the same time. It's about a sexually troubled, nineteenth-century Baron (Paul Jones) who has decided that his teen-aged children (Gillian Hills and Shane Briant) are insane and must be kept locked up in his mansion. The family's problems are reflected in the local population where someone is stalking young women. Director Peter Sykes isn't as straightforward as he could be, particularly early on, but his atmospherics are strong. The medical details are as horrifying as anything else in the film. By today's standards of sexual frankness, the premise may be hard to appreciate.

Deranged (1974)

Midwestern Gothic Grand Guignol is based on the horrors of famous serial killer Ed Gein. Roberts Blossom is spookily good as Ezra, the childlike murderer who tells his unbelieving neighbors what he means to do. Directors Jeff Gillian and Alan Ormsby and makeup master Tom Savini mix graphic gore—scooping brains out of a skull with a spoon—with indescribable humor. They also make Ezra's bleak pre-psychotic life absolutely real and depressing. The dirt cheap sets and props are somehow appropriate to the story, and the filmmakers stay closer to their source material than any of the other films Gein inspired, *Psycho, Texas Chainsaw Massacre,* and part of *Silence of the Lambs.* On VHS, the feature is followed by the short 1981 documentary, *Ed Gein: American Maniac.* Producer and narrator Richard Sarno uses magazine and newspaper articles, audio clips and fuzzy video to tell the story of Gein's crimes and arrest. He attempts to separate fact from conjecture and that's often difficult. The details described there are even sicker than any fictionalized versions and will tell you more than you really want to know. The hard-to-find DVD reportedly does not contain the second film.

Descent, The (2005)

After an inventive, disquieting prologue, a group of adventurous female friends gather to explore a cave in the mountains of North Carolina. The main characters are Sarah (Shauna Macdonald) and Juno (Natalie Mendoza). Though this is a monster movie, it generates much of its suspense from the setting. Director Neil Marshall makes the underground world all too believably claustrophobic. The watery cavern is as scary as the nasty critters who show up about an hour in. Some of the human complications are not as effective and Marshall overuses one flashback device. Even so, this works well enough. The unrated version comes to a different ending than the theatrical release. Followed by a sequel.

Devil (2010)

Five people are in an elevator in a Philadelphia office building when it gets stuck between floors. A security guard (Jacob Vargas) realizes that one of the occupants is Satan. Actually, he sees a fuzzy image of Old Scratch on a closed circuit camera, and then proves his presence with the infallible jelly-side-down test. From that giddy premise, a finely inventive, consistently surprising, and swiftly paced story unfolds. Equal credit goes to producer M. Night Shyamalan for the story, Brian Nelson for the screenplay, director John Erick Dowdle, and director of photography Tak Fujimoto.

Devil Doll (1936)

Though Tod Browning is best known for *Dracula* and *Freaks,* this is his most wonderfully maniacal work. Lavond (brilliantly played by Lionel Barrymore, at times in drag) is an escaped convict out for vengeance against the traitorous ex-partners who framed him. His means are miniature creatures and people manufactured by the mad bug-eyed Melita (Rafaela Ottiano, who appears to be closely related to Elsa Lancaster's Bride of Frankenstein). The second half is less bizarre and more sentimental than the first, but the film is still a sleeper that deserves a much larger audience.

Frank Lawton plays Toto, fiancé to Maureen O'Sullivan's Lorraine, the daugher of an escaped convict (Lionel Barrymore) out for revenge in *Devil Doll.*

Devil Doll (1964)

Entertaining if largely unknown black-and-white British horror revolves around the adversarial relationship between the Great Vorelli (Bryant Haliday) and his dummy, Hugo. The devilish hypnotist-ventriloquist is up to no good, particularly where wealthy London socialite Maryann Horn (Yvonne Romain) is concerned. The simple effects work well, and though Ms. Romaine's performance lacks complexity, the film generates some sexual tension.

Devil Rides Out, The (1968)

Many consider this to be Hammer's finest achievement and I agree, though I'd hate to choose between it and *Curse of the Werewolf.* If the film isn't as well known in the United States as the studio's various series featuring Dracula, Frankenstein, and the Mummy, it's a solid witchcraft tale written by Richard Matheson. In 1925, the Duc de Richleau (Christopher Lee), a "good" warlock, and the evil Mocata (Charles Gray) battle each other over Richleau's friend Simon (Patrick Mower). Some of the effects are a little dated now, but director Terence Fisher builds suspense through a stately pace. Add in the usual excellent sets and a fleet of vintage cars. Lee's performance is one of his strongest in a conventionally heroic role.

Devil's Advocate, The (1997)

Kevin Lomax (Keanu Reeves) is the best defense lawyer in Gainesville, Florida, when the wealthy and powerful John Milton (Al Pacino) invites the young man to join his international practice in New York. At first, Lomax and his wife Mary Ann (Charlize Theron) are seduced by high life in the Big Apple, but beyond the work pressure, other more frightening problems present themselves. Is Milton really Satan or is something else going on? Taylor Hackford directs with some flashy visual tricks—the first "morphing" scare is genuinely creepy—and he plays the humorous angles for all they're worth. Reeves' limitations, including an atrocious Southern accent, are glaring, but Pacino compensates with a charming, serpentine performance. Add in top drawer production values, some relative subtle biblical quotes, and good support from Jeffrey Jones and Judith Ivey.

Devil's Backbone, The (2001)

In the middle of the Spanish Civil War, young Carlos (Fernando Tielve) is deposited at an orphanage with a huge unexploded bomb embedded in the courtyard. The place also has a ghost, a treasure, and extremely complicated relationships among the staff. Guillermo del Toro tells a handsomely photographed Gothic ghost story. The young actors are fine but del Toro regular Federico Luppi is terrific, as usual. Del Toro has said that the film is a companion piece to *Pan's Labyrinth.* They are variations on the same story of magic or fantasy set against horrifying violence that is far too real. Each is superb.

"I think that the fairy tale in some form evolved into the horror tale, and it required that some sort of innocent figure at the center to gel, to continue living."

Guillermo del Toro on the commentary track of *The Devil's Backbone* DVD.

Devil's Rain, The (1975)

Contemporary horror-Western ought to be better than it is. It boasts an impressive cast doing fair work and a talented director. But the light touch that Robert Fuest displayed with the *Dr. Phibes* films is buried under a leaden pace. On tape, part of the problem is the image itself. The film was made in Todd-AO widescreen but the grubby pan-and-scan transfer effectively negates the power of the desert landscape. The Dark Sky DVD corrects that flaw with an accurate, if grainy image transfer. A lesser problem is the silly wicker cowboy hat that William Shatner wears. Ernest Borgnine is the bull-goose Satanist who demands a book from Ida Lupino and her son Shatner. Brother Tom Skerritt comes to the rescue. The melting effects at the end are impressive but too late.

Devil's Rejects, The (2005)

Rob Zombie has carved out a little corner of the horror market for himself. Call it low-rent redneck comic torture porn. The subject here, as it was in

House of 1,000 Corpses, is the Firefly family of psycho killers. They escape capture by Sheriff Wydell (William Forsythe) and kidnap another family. It's similar in look and feel to *Texas Chainsaw Massacre* and *The Hills Have Eyes.* If nothing else, Zombie stays true to that fevered vision. But as director he is overly enamored of extreme close-ups with his shaky handheld camera, harsh lighting, garish grainy colors, and enhanced natural sounds. He means to be intentionally unpleasant and he succeeds.

Dial Help (1988)

Over-the-top Italian production is one of the all-time alternative greats. Italian telephones are possessed by spirits and communicate with Jenny (Charlotte Lewis), an English model. The evil phones also sneak up on unsuspecting victims. Toward the end, director Ruggero Deodato creates one brilliant moment of slapstick supernatural eroticism when the telephones call Jenny and seduce her into putting on her sexiest underwear (including high heels). Then she writhes around in a tub full of sudsy green water while her phone serenades her with lush, soaring violin music. Must be seen to be appreciated.

Diary of the Dead

See Night of the Living Dead

Die, Monster, Die (1965)

Typical American-International Gothic is a bit underpowered and lacking in real scares compared to A-I's best. Steve Reinhart (Nick Adams) goes to rural England to visit his sweetie Susan (Suzan Farmer). The suspicious villagers won't tell him the way to her father's (Boris Karloff) estate. He finds it to be a blighted wasteland. The pace plods and Karloff has a relatively ineffectual role. The plot is based on H.P. Lovecraft's "The Color Out of Space" (also adapted as *The Curse* and *Colour From the Dark*). Overall, it's not as much cheesy fun as a comparable Lovecraft film of the time, *The Dunwich Horror.*

Disturbing Behavior (1998)

Mashup of elements from *The Faculty* and *The Stepford Wives* is colorful, lively, and drawn in broad strokes. Troubled teen Steve (James Marsden) moves with his family to Cradle Bay where the highly stratified high school students are ruled by the hair-trigger "Blue Ribbon" popular kids. The script doesn't vary a whit from the paranoid playbook, but the young cast is attractive and capable. And any movie that names two characters Newberry and Caldicott has the right sense of humor.

Dr. Giggles (1992)

Allegedly young characters lifted from a dead teenager slasher flick are transplanted to an escaped-lunatic plot. Dr. Rendell (Larry Drake) is said wacko who goes back to his hometown after the breakout to reopen his practice and kill the locals with medical devices, including a giant Band Aid. The jokes are grisly and grim. Director Manny Coto makes a limited budget look extravagant. Even though this one made its debut on video, it's solidly in the Universal tradition of slickly made, energetic horror. The good doctor deserves a place at the table with the Wolfman, Dracula, et al.

Dr. Jekyll and Mr. Hyde (1920, 1931, 1941)

John Barrymore is featured in this 1920 poster for *Dr. Jekyll and Mr. Hyde*.

Perhaps its simple-minded notions of women as frail vessels and men as depraved beasts have kept the silent 1920 version of the famous story from exerting much influence on the genre. By keeping the two sides of the character completely separate, the film never addresses the real conflict. To be fair, John Barrymore's vampiric Hyde has effective moments. In one brief shot, he creates the elongated face without makeup, and the appearance of Hyde in another scene as a huge spider is shocking. Curiously, the hideous character did not become an icon of early horror the way Lon Chaney Sr.'s Phantom or Max Schreck's Nosferatu did. Director John Robertson's primitive, uncinematic style has something to do with that. So does Barrymore's theatrical acting style.

Changes in filmmaking and acting styles have transformed some serious moments of the 1931 version into comedy. Despite those, modern audiences who give this one a try will find a lot to like. Fredric March, who won an Oscar for this film, and director Rouben Mamoulian see Jekyll as a saintly scientist who wants to be even saintlier. The transformation scenes actually aren't bad, though that can't be said of the Hyde makeup which, through no fault of its own, conjures up the image of Jerry Lewis. Miriam Hopkins is fine as the sexy floozie who brings out the beast in the Doc. The sets are wonderful and the visual symbolism plays itself out in both subtle and blatant ways. By the way, this is one of the few productions that uses the British pronunciation GEE-kul instead of JEK-ul. Most tapes and DVDs restore censored footage, thought to have been lost for years, including the infamous whipping scene.

The horror in Robert Louis Stevenson's famous story comes directly from the flawed quality of human nature. That's also what makes it so appealing to filmmakers and that side has never been stronger than it is in the 1941 Victor Fleming-Spencer Tracy version. Their Jekyll is more lusty and forthright, and Hyde is played virtually without makeup or big transformation scenes. Yes, the casting is odd. Of the leads, only Lana Turner, whose Beatrice is a bit too beatific, seems incongruous. Somehow, Ingrid Bergman is believable as a Cockney cupcake, even without the accent. The Oscar-winning black-and-white cinematography by Joseph Ruttenberg doesn't get any better. Fleming uses darkness and spiky shadows to depict emotional turmoil, and repeats key plot points and images of the 1931 film. In that "golden age," Hollywood really understood how stories work—how to balance character, setting, and conflict to build suspense. For my money, this is the best film version of the story.

Dr. Jekyll and Ms. Hyde (1995)

Like so many made-for-cable features, this one looks great; it's cast with attractive, funny characters; it's kinda sexy and it's as thin as dishwater. Richard Jacks (Tim Daly) is a chemist for a perfume company who reads Dr. Jekyll's notebooks and rediscovers "a gene for all human evil." When he swallows the formula, he becomes Helen Hyde (Sean Young) in so-so transformation scenes. The rest is really an abysmal sex farce with the male-female switches occurring at inopportune moments. Though the film pretends to deplore sexual stereotypes, the first thing Helen Hyde does is to max out Richard's credit cards.

Dr. Phibes Rises Again

See Abominable Dr. Phibes, The

Harry Beresford is Duke, an irrascible man who could possibly be the "Moon Killer" in 1932's *Doctor X.*

Doctor X (1932)

Dated, talky thriller is very much a filmed play. Still, to horror fans, it's well worth a look for its historical value if nothing else. For decades this early two-color Technicolor feature was lost until a print surfaced in the UCLA archives. From the opening outside of the Mott Street Morgue on a foggy pier to mad scientists' labs to the gloomy mansion where the third act takes place, the atmospheric sets look great. Dr. Xavier (Lionel Atwill) and his lovely daughter Joann (Fay Wray) help the cops in their search of the serial "Moon Killer." Though the excessive comic relief and expansive acting style—both spoofed in *Young Frankenstein*—preclude any real scares, the monster makeup at the end is pretty good. Beyond director Michael Curtiz's better known mainstream work (*Casablanca*), his horror films also include *Mystery of the Wax Museum* and *The Walking Dead.*

Dog Soldiers (2002)

After a moderately confusing introduction that jumps back and forth in time, a squad of British soldiers helicopters into the Scottish wilderness for war games. "I expect nothing less than gratuitous violence from the lot of you!" Sarge (Sean Pertwee) tells his men and that's what they get when it turns out that their enemy isn't other troops but werewolves. The physical action and gunplay are handled more confidently than the less-than-stellar werewolf effects. The filmmakers keep the action murkily dark for the most part, the better to mask the rigid-looking wolf heads. Solid ensemble acting and a bizarre sense of humor help considerably.

Dolores Claiborne (1995)

One of the best and most handsomely produced adaptations of Stephen King's work is powered by three excellent performances and unusual conflicts. Kathy Bates is Dolores, hard-bitten Maine woman accused of murdering her employer. Det. John Mackey (Christopher Plummer) is sure that she also killed her husband (David Strathairn) years before. Her troubled daughter Selena (Jennifer Jason Leigh) isn't sure what she believes when she comes back to the island where she grew up. Director Taylor Hackford turns the curious tale into his most satisfying work since *An Officer and a Gentleman.* Kathy Bates isn't as commanding as she was in *Misery,* but Dolores is a much more complex character. Curiously, the film never caught on in theaters, so it's a first-rate sleeper.

Donnie Darko (2001)

Imagine a *Twilight Zone* version of *American Beauty* with a dash of John Hughes teen spirit. Donnie (Jake Gyllenhaal) is a bright high school student who's troubled by dreams or fantasies concerning a nightmarish rabbit figure who orders him to commit odd destructive acts. That only begins to describe the knotty plot. Revelations of the seething underbelly of suburbia are hardly revelatory, but the leisurely paced, dreamlike atmosphere, imaginative casting, and smart script more than make up for that. The performances and the curious structure improve with a second viewing.

Donovan's Brain (1953)

Dr. Cory (Lew Ayres) has just successfully removed a monkey brain from its body and kept it alive in an aquarium when, as luck would have it, he gets

Nancy Reagan—then Nancy Davis, and seen here on the set with her husband and future president, Ronald Reagan—played Janice Cory in *Donovan's Brain.*

a human brain to play with. It belongs to corrupt millionaire Warren Donovan. Before long, it's growing and pulsating in its tank of brain juice, and it slowly begins to take psychic control of the increasingly mad doctor. The film isn't as blazingly crazed as the similar *Brain That Wouldn't Die,* but it has wonderfully unpredictable moments and pops right along at a zippy pace. Yes, that's future First Lady Nancy Reagan as the doc's adoring wife.

Don't Be Afraid of the Dark (2010)

Produced by Guillermo del Toro, this lavish remake of a 1973 TV movie may not be on a level with *Pan's Labyrinth* but it shares some of the same themes, and del Toro's sure touch with kids is matched by director Troy Nixie. Young Sally (Bailee Madison) resents being sent to live with her father (Guy Pearce) and his new girlfriend (Katie Holmes) in the spooky old Rhode Island mansion that they're restoring. Then she discovers the other residents. The sets and exteriors have a beautiful otherworldly quality reminiscent of the glory days of the Hollywood studio system. Performances are excellent throughout. The nasty creatures themselves are quasi-human little rat monkeys that come straight from nightmares.

Don't Look Back (2009)

Intelligent, complex European psychological horror is difficult to describe and completely involving. Jeanne (Sophie Marceau) is a writer and mother who's having difficulties with her work and her family. Her problems get much worse when the most ordinary things—a kitchen table, a husband (Andrea Di Stefano)—are inexplicably not what they have always been. Those changes are shown with subtle and unsettling special effects. Without giving the game away, comparisons to David Lynch are not out of order but not completely accurate or useful either. The story has a strong *Alice in Wonderland* quality, and I have to admit that I don't quite understand the conclusion either.

Don't Look Now (1973)

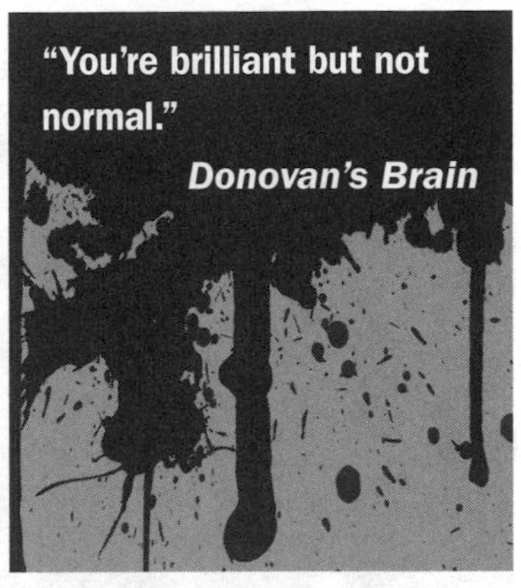

Nicholas Roeg's non-linear approach turns what might have been a dull and conventional mystery into a harrowing horror that defies classification. In both plot and construction, the film is a constant surprise. Nothing follows expected patterns. John (Donald Sutherland) is an art historian. He and his wife, Laura (Julie Christie), are in Venice working on a church restoration and getting over a devastating family loss. A series of murders have just begun and the two English sisters John and Laura meet claim to be psychic. Those elements, combined with an unusual use of color, transform the ordinary into the ominous with remarkable effectiveness. An intensely erotic love scene may be the part that most viewers remember. It's as unconventional as all other aspects of the film, including a shocking conclusion.

Dorian Gray (2009)

Orphan Dorian Gray (Ben Barnes) returns to Victorian London on the death of his wealthy grandfather. Straightaway, he comes under the influence of the wicked Lord Henry Wotton (Colin Firth) who introduces the young man to the fleshpots of White Chapel, and Basil Hallward (Ben Chaplin), the artist who paints his portrait. Shadowy, minimal sets are less than lavish but the sharp economical script is filled with aphorisms (Firth gets most of the best lines) and the effects used on the painting are well chosen and surprising. All in all, a fairly faithful adaptation of Oscar Wilde's novel.

Dracula (1931)
Dracula (Spanish language version) (1931)
Horror of Dracula (1958)
Bram Stoker's Dracula (1974)
Dracula (1979)
Bram Stoker's Dracula (1992)

The years have not been kind to the 1931 version of Bram Stoker's seminal story. All of its flaws are glaring—stagebound script, archaic acting style, the bobbing bats, opossums apparently meant to pass for big rats (and who knows

Bela Lugosi's portrayal of Count Dracula made the 1931 film the seminal vampire movie. Unfortunately, the actor would be typecast throughout his career.

what the armadillos are doing in a Transylvanian castle?)—but the strengths are undiminished: the backgrounds and sets, the atmosphere, and, of course, Bela Lugosi himself. Some aspects of his performance have been imitated and parodied so often that they've lost much of their power, and younger audiences will laugh at the accent and the theatrical posturing. To appreciate the film now, they should note how the various masculine-feminine conflicts are played out, with women depicted as weak-willed beings who must be protected by the male power structure and its symbol of authority—the cross.

The famous Spanish language version was made simultaneously with the Lugosi/Tod Browning film, on the same sets, at night with a Spanish-speaking cast. It shares the same flaws and strengths. By today's standards, the pace is slow but the film is so richly atmospheric—even more than the English version—that it's still a treat, particularly for those who know and love the English-language version. If Carlos Villarias lacks Bela Lugosi's presence, Lupita Tovar is a delightful (and sexy) heroine. The recently discovered print translates beautifully to video. Required viewing for the serious horror fan.

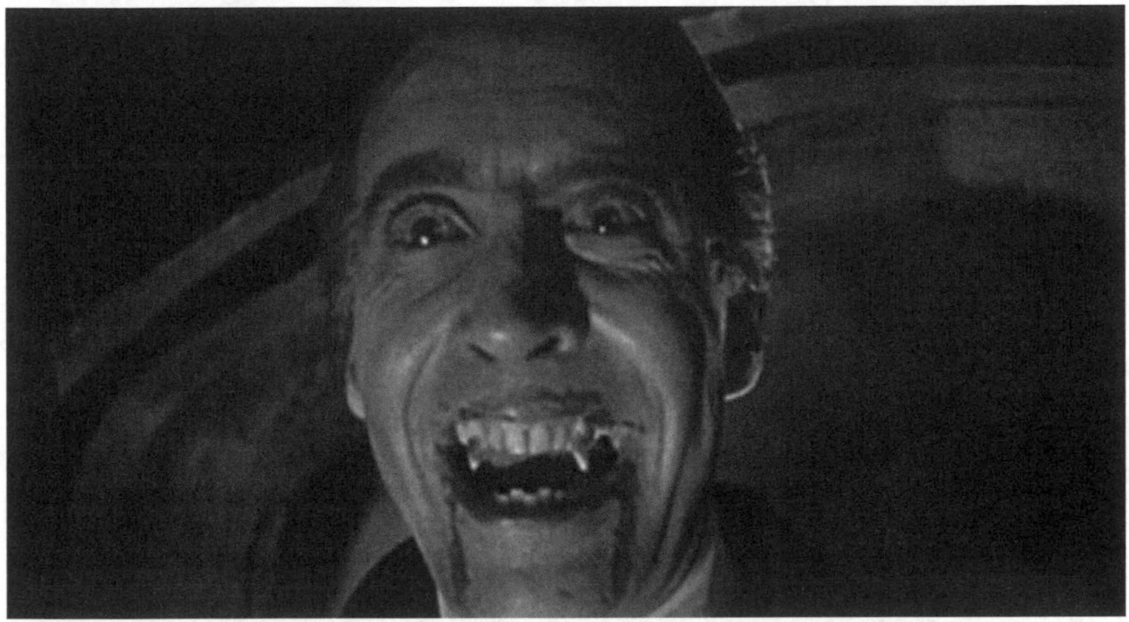

Christopher Lee assumed the cape and fangs in *Horror of Dracula.*

Hammer's adaptation of the novel, *Horror of Dracula,* opens with the spiral columns which would become a virtual signature for the studio. The shot is followed by blood spattering on a closed coffin, setting an appropriate mood. Screenwriter Jimmy Sangster's telling of the story owes more to Bram Stoker's novel than to the stage play which had launched Bela Lugosi's career. This one is also more streamlined and cinematic than earlier versions. But the real key to the film's enduring success is the teaming of Christopher Lee and Peter Cushing—horror's answer to Jack Lemmon and Walter Matthau—as the Count and Van Helsing. They play the roles with absolute conviction. Lee's interpretation of the familiar character is fresh and sexually charged; Cushing's Van Helsing is equally energetic. They complement each other well and make perfectly matched antagonists. The unsubtle message of many early Hammer films—men's domination of women and fear of female sexuality—is in full flower here.

In 1974, Dan Curtis, the man responsible for the original *Dark Shadows* series, produced an unusually fine version for television. If it pales beside Francis Ford Coppola's identically titled *Bram Stoker's Dracula,* it still gives horror fans what they want to see in the story. Richard Matheson's script is faithful to the source material and the supporting cast, including Simon Ward, Fiona Lewis, and Nigel Davenport, is first rate. You could do much worse.

Frank Langella's 1979 Dracula isn't as menacing as Lugosi's or as powerful as Lee's. He and director John Badham interpret the Count as a Gothic hero. We see him dancing, riding a black horse with his cape flowing in the breeze, emerging dramatically from the fog, and seated for dinner surrounded by thousands of candles. Stoker's plot has been compressed and altered considerably, downplaying Van Helsing (Laurence Olivier). This version is as much a romance as pure horror, and that's certainly a valid approach. Peter Murton's sets, particularly Carfax Abbey, and John Williams' lush score are both impressive.

With the exception of one backlot shot, director Francis Ford Coppola and photographer Michael Balhaus made their film on elaborate sets where they had full control of the frame. In almost every shot, something's going on beyond the simple narrative flow. On Coppola's densely layered, crowded screen, the background may contain an unusual twist to the action, or an odd arrangement of shapes. The simple act of stepping over a threshold may seem strange and hesitant because the action has been filmed backward, then run forward through the projector. The familiar plot is presented as a romantic love story taken to an operatic extreme. Gary Oldman is perhaps the most Byronic Dracula ever brought to the screen. Despite all the changes in makeup—many of them hideous and grotesque—he's handsome, exotic, dark, larger than life. Anthony Hopkins' Van Helsing is a masterful combination of eccentricity, authority, and almost Pythonesque humor. On a commentary track, Coppola, his son Roman who worked as special effects supervisor and second-unit director, and makeup supervisor Greg Cannon talk about their work and their intentions. They reveal how many of the special effects were accomplished. (Some of them are so simple, you'll be surprised at how easily you were tricked.) Coppola also explains why he gave the film such baroque depth. He's able to analyze his own creative processes as well as any director since Hitchcock.

Dracula 2000 (2000)
Dracula II: Ascension (2003)
Dracula III: Legacy (2005)

Thieves break into the heavily guarded Carfax Antiques in London and reanimate the Count (Gerard Butler). Abraham Van Helsing (Christopher Plummer) follows them to New Orleans where Mardi Gras is in progress. The formulaic big-budget production is energetic and kind of fun in a curious way. The main reason is Plummer who's able to deliver the silliest drivel with

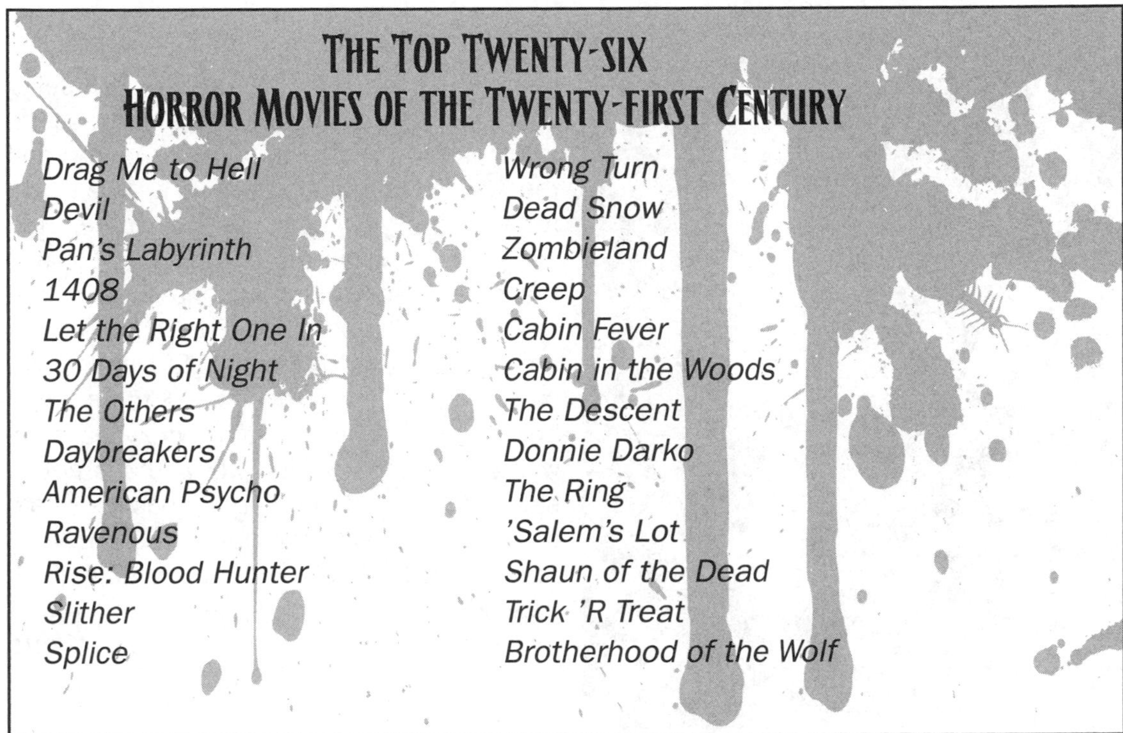

The Top Twenty-Six Horror Movies of the Twenty-First Century

Drag Me to Hell
Devil
Pan's Labyrinth
1408
Let the Right One In
30 Days of Night
The Others
Daybreakers
American Psycho
Ravenous
Rise: Blood Hunter
Slither
Splice
Wrong Turn
Dead Snow
Zombieland
Creep
Cabin Fever
Cabin in the Woods
The Descent
Donnie Darko
The Ring
'Salem's Lot
Shaun of the Dead
Trick 'R Treat
Brotherhood of the Wolf

some conviction and make it sound good. The big effects are all right, and the stuff involving leeches and eyeballs really is nasty.

The sequel, *Dracula II: Ascension* (2002), follows the formula by repeating key elements of the original with a less-than-stellar cast, so-so makeup and digital effects, and a limited sense of humor. Dr. Liz (Diane Neal) hopes to use vampire blood from the charred non-dead corpse of the title character (Stephen Billington) in the morgue to heal her Stephen Hawking-like boyfriend (Craig Sheffer). Other parties are interested, too.

In *Dracula III: Legacy,* the half-vampire warrior priest Uffizi (Jason Scott Lee) and Luke (Jason London), both from the second film, are still on the trail of the big guy (Rutger Hauer, this time). It leads them to NATO-occupied Romania. Typical for a Roman numeral III, this one is a solid step down from II, with a depressing Eastern European look and clumsy humor.

Dracula, A.D. 1972 (1972)

What an embarrassment! Christopher Lee and Peter Cushing manage to maintain their dignity in this ill-advised update, but just barely. They play the

Director and producer Mel Brooks spoofed the classic vampire film in 1995's *Dracula: Dead and Loving It.*

reconstituted Count and a Van Helsing descendent who are brought together by a bunch of dope-smoking, devil-worshipping London hippies. The opening party scene looks like an outtake from TV's *Laugh-In* and the resurrection that follows is just as weak. It's all brutally dated now—the clothes, the slang, the hair, the attitude, and particularly the soundtrack that might have been borrowed from *Starsky & Hutch.* The character and intent of the "traditional" Stoker vampire story simply don't translate well to an urban environment of noisy traffic, crowded sidewalks, and construction work. That's not to say that the contemporary bloodsucker tale can't work. See *Martin, Near Dark, The Night Stalker, The Lost Boys,* etc. But Hammer films depend on period atmosphere. Without that for support, Lee and Cushing's best efforts aren't enough.

Dracula: Dead and Loving It (1995)

To place this comedy within the spectrum of Mel Brooks' films, it's much better than *Robin Hood: Men In Tights,* but not nearly as good as his masterpiece, *Young Frankenstein.* Brooks—who produced, directed, cowrote, and starred—goes back to the original 1931 Lugosi film for most of his jokes, the plot, and even for the impressive sets. He also tosses in references to England's Hammer films and Francis Ford Coppola's baroque adaptation of Stoker's story. The result is fun for horror movie fans. Leslie Nielsen is actually fairly restrained as Dracula, particularly when he's sharing the screen with Peter MacNicol as the insect-eating Renfield. MacNicol does a terrific impersonation and parody of Dwight Frye. The humor is mostly physical with some bits involving grotesque spurts of blood. Even if Brooks' more outrageous sense of humor is missing here, his genuine affection for old movies still shows through.

Dracula, Prince of Darkness (1966)

The second film in Hammer's successful series begins with the ending of the first, wherein the good Count is reduced to a shoebox full of ashes. Flash forward ten years—about as long as it took the producers to coax Christopher Lee back into the cape. The rest follows one of the studio's favorite formulas with two couples innocently wandering into the monster's lair. An energetic abbot, Father Sandor (Andrew Kier) takes over the Van Helsing role as head vampire hunter. The best moments are the reconstitution and the imaginative ending. A grandly melodramatic score dates the film and the pace is slow by current standards, but it still stands up well to another viewing. The small cast is excellent. The women are classy and about as sexy as the 1965 screen would allow. Barbara Shelley's transformation from a proper Victorian lady into a red hot vampire mama who's ready to rumba in her negligee is a delight. Lee's silent performance is one of his strongest.

Dracula's Daughter (1936)

The sequel begins precisely at the end of the first film with Van Helsing (Edward Van Sloan) explaining to the cops how Dracula and Renfield happen to be dead. After that bit of business and some comic relief, Countess Marya (Gloria Holden) arrives to claim the body of her dad, and the film shifts to a slow pace and somber tone. She's a complex character who wants to be "normal" and thinks that psychiatrist Dr. Garth (Otto Kruger) can cure her. The film is at best half successful with dark, beautifully staged scenes balanced against some dated overacting. Both Holden and Marguerite Churchill as Janet, the doctor's secretary and fiancée, are given the full glamour treatment.

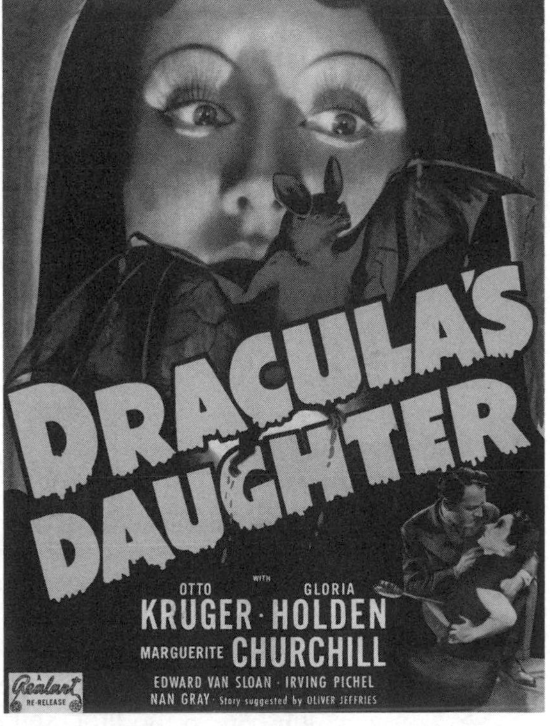

A poster for *Dracula's Daughter*.

Drag Me to Hell (2009)

Director Sam Raimi returns to his *Evil Dead* roots with a rousing witchcraft tale. Ambitious young bank executive Christine (Alison Lohman) is in line for a promotion but she's got to prove that she's tough enough. So when a disgusting old gypsy woman (Lorna Raver) asks for help with missed mortgage payments, Christine plays hardball and forecloses. The old lady promptly puts a curse on her. The afflictions that result make up the body of the film and they range from some really scary, nasty stuff to cartoonish excesses that Tex Avery would have appreciated. Production values are first rate. In short, this is what horror movies set out to be but so seldom are—fast, energetic, loud, unpredictable, violent, cheeky, and funny with grand effects that tell the story without overpowering it. And, finally, it's original, not a remake, not a sequel, not a "reboot," but an original.

Dragon Wars: D-War (2007)

Some really convoluted and repetitious exposition explains how ancient Korean dragons—the good Imoogi and the bad Buraki—both need the "gift of Yuh Yi Joo" to take over the world, or something to that effect. The plot really doesn't matter once they start fighting it out above and below contemporary Los Angeles. In their different forms, the richly detailed serpentine CGI giants are much more engaging and interesting than Transformers, even if they lack the personality of the original King Kong. Of the human characters, only the sagacious Jack (Robert Forster) makes much of an impression.

Dreamcatcher (2003)

Four middle-aged friends with varying psychic abilities go off for a hunting trip in the Maine woods where they run across an alien invasion and a half-mad army officer (Morgan Freeman) who's trying to stop it. In different incarnations, the creature is one of the most disgusting and disquieting since the original *Alien* hatchling burst onto the scene. The filmmakers translate Stephen King's novel to the screen faithfully. The "memory warehouse" scenes are very nice. But it all ends on a disappointing note with two gigantic computer-generated monsters duking it out.

Dressed to Kill (1980)

Brian DePalma's *Psycho* homage/imitation begins with a soapy shower scene that paves the way for the hundreds of erotic thrillers that have come since. DePalma, star Angie Dickinson, and her body double establish a new standard for mainstream films, and the scene heightens the sexual tension that's the basis for the film's horror. The real highpoint, though, is a brilliant, wordless eleven-minute museum scene that ends with a weird joke. After it, the film never completely recovers its balance. The second half isn't nearly as intense as the first, and in the finale, DePalma copies himself with the end of *Carrie*.

This is the last surviving truck used from the movie *Duel* that was not wrecked during filming.

Drive Angry (2011)

Somewhat above-average Nic Cage horror movie of the week is a pungent mix of humor, ultraviolence, hot babes, and muscle cars. The star mopes through his performance as John Milton who springs himself from hell in a vintage Riviera to save his little granddaughter from a demonic preacher (Billy Burke). Supporting performances are a lot of fun, particularly Amber Heard as a free-spirited waitress, and William Fichtner as The Accountant, Satan's long-suffering fixer. A prime guilty pleasure.

Duel (1971)

Steven Spielberg had the good sense (or the good luck) to find a terrific Richard Matheson script that dovetailed with his talents as a director for his feature debut. Suburbanite David Mann (Dennis Weaver) encounters an early case of road rage writ large when he runs afoul of a psycho Peterbilt tanker truck on a rural Southern California highway. At first, it appears to be a simple misunderstanding, the kind of situation most drivers have encountered. But, as the film progresses, the semi becomes a more real and threatening monster. Note how Spielberg uses real sounds on the soundtrack at first—road noise, wind, and AM radio—and then switches to a musical score indicating a significant increase in tension and conflict. Throughout, the truck

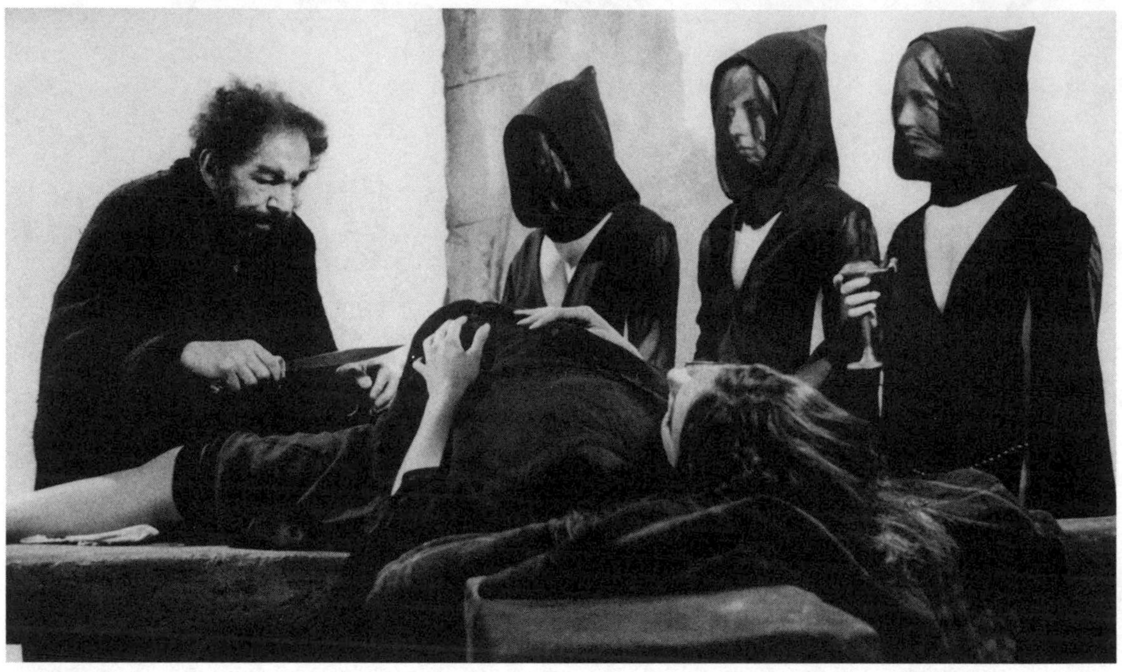
A warlock uses the *Necronomicon* to try and restore power to the Whatley family in *The Dunwich Horror.*

remains a believable threat because the filmmakers never resort to movie "magic" for its scares.

Dunwich Horror, The (1971)

Young warlock Wilbur Whatley (Dean Stockwell) steals a copy of the dreaded and powerful *Necronomicon* from the Miskatonic University Library and sets about to restore the Whatley family to its rightful place as rulers of the earth and the rest of the known universe. He's also got his eye on a cute co-ed (Sandra Dee). Stockwell is appropriately hammy; Dee is her inimitable blonde self, and they both get considerable help from Ed Begley and Sam Jaffe. The film is loosely based on an H. P. Lovecraft story with a strong influence of TV's *Dark Shadows.* It also foreshadows the fiction and films of Stephen King. Given the cast and the times, generational conflicts are important, too. Yes, that's Talia Coppola (Shire) as the nurse.

Dust Devil (1992)

Like Clive Barker's *Candyman,* this African import tries to tell a horror story with well developed characters in a realistic contemporary political context and an exotic setting. Chelsea Fields is running away from her abusive husband when she picks up hitchhiker Robert John Burke in the Namibian desert. She should have been tipped off by his ugly sideburns. He's the title character, a spiritual creature that is endlessly rejuvenated by ritual murder. But this demon kills only people who have reached spiritual despair—those who are about to commit suicide—and he even develops an emotional attachment to them. The only person who has any understanding of what he's doing is black policeman Zakes Mokae. Writer-director Richard Stanley tends to get too tricky and inventive for his own good toward the end, and at times the film threatens to become a Spaghetti Western. Still, it's a cut above average. Recommended.

Dylan Dog: Dead of Night (2011)

Just about everything that can go wrong in a movie goes wrong here. Brandon Routh is completely miscast as an allegedly tough private investigator who handles supernatural crimes in New Orleans. Everyone else in the cast is equally ill-considered and they all ham it up shamelessly. The humor is lame. The image is unpleasantly, muddily tinted and far too dark. The story has to do with murder and war among the Big Easy's werewolves, vampires, and zombies.

E

Earth versus the Spider (1958)

Despite so-so effects—accomplished through blown-up footage of a real spider, not stop-motion animation—this is one of the more enjoyable big-bug horrors. The script doesn't bother with explanations. No radiation or pollution causes a giant tarantula to crawl out of the Carlsbad Caverns; it just does. O.k.? The film's real purposes are revealed during the spider-attacks-the-town scene. Note the Civil Defense emblem on the rooftop siren. For those too young to remember, that siren was the sound we were expecting to hear right before the Russian missiles vaporized us. That's the real threat being addressed. Goofy dialogue helps, too. Upon first seeing the cavern, the sheriff notes, "What a place! Make a nice Elk's Hall." When old Jake ties a mattress to the roof of his car, he says, "I'm evacuatin'. That darn monster run me outta house'n'home."

Eaten Alive (1977)

Southern Gothic is as surreal, sick, and ultraviolent as director Tobe Hooper's previous feature, *The Texas Chainsaw Massacre.* In fact, some critics see it as a continuation with a stronger correlation between sex and violence. The setting's a swamp where innkeeper Judd (Neville Brand) feeds unlucky guests (and their puppies!) to his crocodile. The low-budget effort is notable for squalid yellow light, leisure suits, and the presence of such stars as an unhealthy-looking Carolyn Jones and Mel Ferrer. The croc effects are less disgusting than the human monsters of *TCM.* Southern viewers will pick up on Hooper's regional references. Recommended only for fans of the gamiest

Grand Guignol; those who "enjoy" seeing children attacked by rats, scythe-wielding maniacs, and giant reptiles. Brand is disturbingly good.

Director Tim Burton has created numerous quirky films such as *Edward Scissorhands, The Corpse Bride,* and *Ed Wood.*

Ed Wood (1994)

Despite its unorthodox subject matter, Tim Burton's bio-horror/comedy is a winning tale with genuine heart. Essentially, it's the true story of the first years of Ed Wood Jr.'s (Johnny Depp) Hollywood career, and his friendship with aging horror star Bela Lugosi (Martin Landau who won a well-deserved Oscar). Though opinions about Wood and his low-budget movies differ, two points are universally accepted. First, he was one of the worst directors ever to work behind a camera. Second, he was a terrific guy. That's what makes the movie so much fun. Depp is first rate and he gets fine support from Bill Murray, Jeffrey Jones, Sarah Jessica Parker, and Patricia Arquette. Crisp black-and-white photography makes the story less dependent on the whimsical atmosphere that underlies *Beetlejuice* and *Edward Scissorhands.* Here, Burton keeps the focus on the characters, not the sets or the special effects.

Eden Lake (2008)

British variation on American redneck-rural horror hits all the right buttons but somehow doesn't manage to rise above its formulaic structure. Steve (Michael Fassbender) and Jenny (Kelly Reilly) head out of the city to visit an idyllic lake. They encounter loutish lethal locals. Yes, the situation is thoroughly familiar but the characters have some depth and complexity, and the violence is handled realistically. Production values are above average, but this is still the kind of story that leaves a bad taste.

Edward Scissorhands (1990)

From the opening credits, it's clear that the whole story takes place within a cinematic snowglobe. Tim Burton's take on Pinocchio is a combination of fantasy, myth, fairy tale, and horror. It's also a sweet-natured companion piece to *Beetlejuice* that ought not to work at all, but does, splendidly. Vincent Price is the Inventor who creates Edward (Johnny Depp) but dies before he can give the boy human hands, leaving him with blades for fingers (Stan Winston created those effects). The Avon lady (Dianne Wiest) brings Edward down from his black hilltop castle to the pastel 'burbs below, where he falls in love with her daughter, Kim (Winona Ryder). The brief role, virtually a cameo, is a fitting coda to Price's career in the field. Danny Elfman's score is one of his best.

Eight Legged Freaks (2002)

The prodigal son (David Arquette) returns to the dusty little desert town of Prosperity, Arizona, only to find the place overrun by several species of angry giant spiders. A game cast handles the stereotyped characters well enough, and the CGI arachnids are certainly a step up from earlier efforts on the same theme (*Giant Spider Invasion, Kingdom of the Spiders*). A bouncy score and well placed tongue-in-cheek humor don't get in the way of the scares for those who are uncomfortable around creepy-crawlies.

"She fills her prey with digestive acid to liquefy the internal organs so she can drink it from the inside out while it's alive."
Eight Legged Freaks

Embrace of the Vampire (1995)

Virginal college student Charlotte (Alyssa Milano) is pursued by a vampire (Jeremy Kemp) who, for reasons never explained, needs her to recharge his batteries. Though the same plot device was used in the frantic *Andy Warhol's Dracula,* director Anne Goursaud handles it more seriously. She certainly knows how to steam things up, making this one of the more intense "erotic" horrors. Her approach ranges from bodice-ripper romanticism to *90210* stereotypes to artfully posed Gothic seduction. Forget about coherence or logic.

Emerald Jungle (1980)

Any movie that begins with blow-gun murders in midtown Manhattan and Niagara Falls at Christmas can't be all bad, and this one lives up to its exploitative promise. The thin story of a Jim Jones–type cult is full of gratuitous mondo touches—giant hooks pierced through skin, firewalking, animal slaughter, a mongoose-cobra fight, people eating lizard guts—along with conventional cannibalism and sex. Nasty exploitation that ought to be seen through a bug-spotted windshield on a hot summer night at the drive-in. (Alternate titles: *Eaten Alive by Cannibals* and *Eaten Alive.*)

End of Days (1999)

Imagine a combination of *The Omen, Rosemary's Baby,* and *The Terminator.* Yes, it's that screwy. This big-budget action-horror begins with some very nasty business involving a snake and a newborn baby, followed by demon beasties emerging from flaming New York sewers. On the eve of the millennium, a nameless priest (Gabriel Byrne) is possessed by Satan and goes looking for a date. It's up to tortured security guard Jericho Cane (Arnold Schwarzenegger) to keep Old Scratch from hooking up with Christine York (Robin Tunney) before the stroke of midnight, 2000. Stan Winston's creature effects are up to snuff, as always, but they're not as frightening as a Father with flammable urine. For over-the-top silliness, this one does what it needs to do.

End of the Line (2007)

It's the end of the world as we know it. Maybe. This ambitious low-budget Canadian effort focuses on characters who believe that the Rapture is upon us. Nurse Karen (Ilona Elkin) is on a late night subway train when the first signs appear, and things go bad quickly. Some of the acting is semi-professional but enthusiastic. Effects are acceptable but the film can't quite measure up to other more expensive public transportation-themed horrors like *Midnight Meat Train* and *Creep.*

Poster for *Eraserhead.*

Eraserhead (1977)

David Lynch's debut is not so much a conventional narrative as a series of disquieting yet hypnotic images played out slowly over a soundtrack of atonal rumbling bass notes and other heightened environmental sounds that are equally unsettling and annoying. The sound design is complemented by an often muddy black-and-white image. What plot there is revolves around the moon-faced Henry (John

The Top Seventeen Most Memorable Serial Killer Movies

Silence of the Lambs
Henry Portrait of a Serial Killer
The Untold Story
Scream
Manhunter
Red Dragon
Hannibal
Hannibal Rising
Deranged
Demon in my View
Feardotcom
From Hell
Henry Portrait of a Serial Killer
Jack's Back
Last Horror Movie
The Lodger
Luther the Geek

Nance), with the extreme hair-do that explains the title; his unhappy wife, Mary (Charlotte Stewart); and their disgusting newborn baby. It's a bizarre bawling creation that looks like a combination of E.T. and the chest-burster from *Alien.* Her nightmarish family and his strange neighbors fill out the dance card. You can see the roots of *Twin Peaks, Blue Velvet,* and *Mulholland Drive.*

Evil, The (1978)

Though it appears to be in the *Exorcist-Omen* school, this one is really more like *The Shining.* A group of researchers inadvertently let the devil himself loose, and then try to put him back where he belongs. With solid cast of character actors, the result is better than you might expect and the film does have some moments that are frightening and surprising. Since the plot depends on those surprises, the less said about it, the better.

Evil Dead, The (1981)
Evil Dead II: Dead by Dawn (1987)
Army of Darkness (1992)

Director Sam Raimi and actor Bruce Campbell produced this cult favorite in 1981, right when the "slasher" trend in horror movies was ending. The film was lumped in with that bad lot and had only a limited theatrical release. But when home video appeared a few years later, it found its audience and

Brains! Brains! An insatiable zombie prepares to munch cranium in *Evil Dead II.*

became a bona fide cult hit. The story involves a group of young people who go off to a cabin in the woods and accidentally read from the Sumerian *Book of the Dead,* calling up all sorts of murderous spirits. Raimi's inventive camerawork is the real star though. Like New Zealander Peter Jackson, his approach to violence is so extreme that it's comic.

Evil Dead II: Dead by Dawn is the rare sequel that's actually superior to the original in some senses. Sam Raimi creates a special effects tour de force using stop motion animation, prosthetics, reverse motion, and long dizzying tracking shots. Bruce Campbell (also a producer) being attacked by his own hand is a grand moment. The graphic violence is so removed from any reality that it has no emotional content and that heightens the film's strong humor.

The third installment, *Army of Darkness,* is a multi-genre parody of horror, action, sword-and-sorcery, and scifi where no convention is sacred. Everything is played for laughs. A brief introduction, including a cameo appearance by Bridget Fonda, explains how Ash (Bruce Campbell) came to be hurled back through time to the thirteenth century, along with a chainsaw, a sawed off 12 gauge, and a 1973 Olds Delta 88 to save the world from a host of the living dead. Imagine the physical violence of the Three Stooges combined with the absurdism of *Monty Python and the Holy Grail* and you'll see what Raimi is trying to do.

Evil of Frankenstein, The (1964)

Like all Hammer films—and most films of any genre or type—this one's no better than its script. As long an Anthony Hind's story sticks to the Baron (Peter Cushing) and his attempts to recreate his earlier work, the film is on firm ground with grand gizmo-intensive lab scenes and another strong performance by the star. But when it wanders afield with revisionist flashbacks to the Monster (Kiwi Kingston), a crude caricature of makeup man Jack Pierce's original, and such tired gimmicks as said Monster being preserved in a glacier (Please!), it's in trouble.

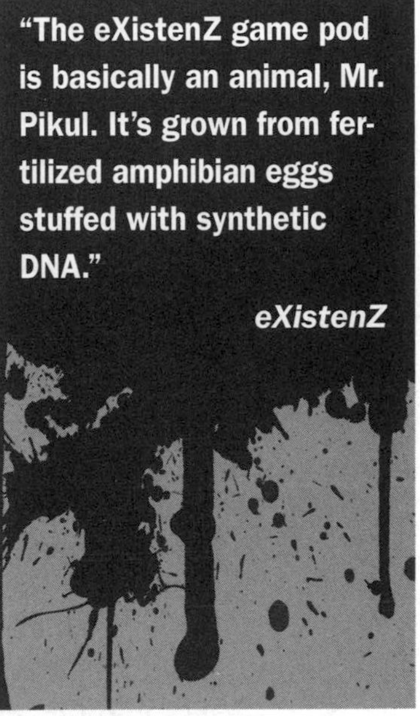

eXistenZ (1999)

Budgetary limitations are obvious in almost every frame of David Cronenberg's examination of the corruption of the flesh. Game designer Allegra Geller (Jennifer Jason Leigh) is testing her newest and most complex creation when she is attacked and flees with PR guy Ted Pikul (Jude Law). The bio-mechanical game devices, weapons, and umbilical connections are creepy, though they never rise to the levels of *Videodrome.* The action becomes more game-like as it goes on. In the end, it's more game-like than most films that are based on real games. In the years since he made this one, Cronenberg has moved into more mainstream work.

Exorcism of Emily Rose, The (2005)

Obersided winter's tale really works more as a courtroom drama than true horror, and it's not completely successful as either. Father Moore (Tom Wilkinson) is accused of negligent homicide after Emily (Jennifer Carpenter) dies while he is trying to drive out a demon. The church simply wants the whole affair to go away, hoping that he'll take a plea deal, and so hot-shot defense lawyer Erin Bruner (Laura Linney) is brought in to show him the way and the light. But the priest wants his story to be made public. Outside of the trial, the rural Gothic setting is strong. So are the performances, but much of the horror has to do with hokum about the significance of the time 3:00.

Exorcist, The (1973)
Exorcist II, The: The Heretic (1977)
Exorcist III, The (1990)
Exorcist, The: The Version You've Never Seen (2000)
Dominion (2004)
Exorcist, The: The Beginning (2005)

The big special effects—projectile pea soup, swiveling head—aren't particularly impressive any more. The important aspects still shine. Director William Friedkin's spare, no-frills style is as powerful as ever. He and writer/producer William Peter Blatty balance the supernatural elements with an almost documentary realism in the locations and personal relationships of the characters. They also wisely break unwritten "rules" by having important events take place off-camera. The performances and the rigorous religious aspects of the story also elevate the potentially ridiculous material. Unlike so many films in the genre, this one doesn't attempt to answer all its questions. The essential mystery remains. Stephen King has written that the source of the film's popularity lies in the generational conflicts of its time, and they are important, both explicitly and thematically.

In 2000, *The Exorcist: The Version You've Never Seen* was released in theaters. About ten minutes longer than the original cut, it adds a few more spectral images and the famous upside down "crab walk" scene. That moment is pretty strange, all right, particularly after it's been digitally scrubbed and massaged to hide the wires. For my money, though, the additions detract from the real strength of the film. That's the contrast between the reality of Father Karras' worries about his mother and the tightly focused, claustrophobic world that's created within the bedroom where the exorcism takes place. And, at 122 minutes, the film is already long; at 132, it's too long.

In the annals of horror, *The Exorcist II: The Heretic* (1977) can make a legitimate claim for worst major motion picture of all time. Admittedly, it's enjoyable as an alternative so-bad-it's-fun classic, but that's all. Fans of the original should never see it. Richard Burton plays a priest (and protégé of Max von Sydow's character) who's brought in to tidy things up with the teenaged Linda Blair. What is the most embarrassing moment? Could it be Burton telling his Cardinal (Paul Henreid) "I am not worthy"? Or the dual hypnosis machine that could have come straight from a bad sci-fi flick? How about the penthouse apartment made of polished steel? My own vote

The original *Exorcist* was groundbreaking, featuring great performances and excellent direction.

would go to Blair's "Lullaby of Broadway" softshoe routine which rivals Peter Boyle's "Putting on the Ritz" from *Young Frankenstein,* but that, of course, is meant to be funny.

In 1990, possibly trying to make up for the humiliation of *The Heretic,* writer-director William Peter Blatty turned his novel *Legion* into the talky serial killer-reincarnation-exorcism tale, *Exorcist III.* Taking over for Lee J. Cobb as a Jewish D.C. detective, George C. Scott has a fine time with some delicious dialogue. (His "carp" speech is a joy.) The problem is that there is far too much of that dialogue. Blatty manages to create a few interesting visuals, but the true scares are few. Virtually all of the violence and much of the important physical action takes place off camera. They're described, not shown. Yes, Fabio and Patrick Ewing appear briefly.

In 2004 and 2005, two "prequels" were produced: *Dominion* and *Exorcist: The Beginning.* Watching the two of them together is a bit like seeing a couple of the old Universal horrors from the 1940s back to back. You've got the same sets and many of the same actors in slightly different roles working their way through variations on one story. Here it's Father Merrin (Stellan Skarsgård, in the Max von Sydow role), retired from the priesthood after World War II and working as an archeologist in Africa. He's engaged to examine an ancient Christian temple that's just been found in the desert. The first film, *Dominion,* was developed by John Frankenheimer, but he fell ill (and died) and so it was turned over to Paul Schrader. He tells a fairly serious story about religious faith, reason, and the nature of evil. It actually works fairly well, but the studio disliked his work and hired director Renny Harlin to make a new film, *Exorcist: The Beginning.* It has the same premise, and rehashes the Linda Blair makeup effects that made the original film such a hit. This one is heavy on cartoonish CGI effects and turns the material into generic pulp.

Eye, The (2008)

Blind violinist Sydney Wells (Jessica Alba) receives a cornea transplant and as soon as the bandages come off, she's seeing stuff that's not there. Could it be that her new lenses are still getting signals from the previous owner? That's the gist of this big-budget studio remake of a 2002 Hong Kong film. Some of the computer-generated effects that are used to show the world according to Sydney are inventive. Most are clichés. No real scares.

F

Faculty, The (1998)

Rather than attempting yet another needless remake, writer Kevin Williamson and director Robert Rodriguez simply steal the best parts of *Invasion of the Body Snatchers*. The result is smart, funny, and nasty in all the right ways. Casey (Elijah Wood) is the first to notice that something strange is happening to the teachers and his fellow students at Herrington High. When he tries to explain to his parents that an alien invasion in happening, they want him tested for drugs. A few other kids, including the drug dealer (Josh Hartnett), the Goth girl (Clea DuVall), and the new girl (Laura Harris) join him in the resistance, but are they to be trusted? Much of the fun lies in the inventive casting of the supporting characters. When the big effects kick in toward the end, it loses some focus but that's not a serious flaw.

Fade to Black (1980)

Undervalued character study can almost be seen as a west coast *Taxi Driver* with Hollywood Blvd. standing in for the mean streets of New York. Toss in strong nods to *Targets* and *Whatever Happened to Baby Jane*. Eric Binford (Dennis Christopher) is a delivery boy who has trouble separating his encyclopedic knowledge of old movies with everyday reality. A young Marilyn wannabe (Linda Kerridge) further blurs his perceptual problems until Eric begins to take on his favorite screen identities—Dracula, the Mummy, Cody Jarrett from *White Heat*—to get even with an uncaring world. The attractions are Christopher's flamboyant but believable performance and dozens of clips and quotes from old films.

Fall of the House of Usher (1960)

Roger Corman's first adaptation of Edgar Allan Poe is creaky—literally. It's a three-character drama set in a mansion that is slowly and groaningly collapsing. Roderick Usher (Vincent Price) refuses to let his sister (Myrna Fahey) marry her fiancé (Mark Damon) because of an undefined "family curse." Price is excellent in one of his most restrained and quiet roles. Corman and writer Richard Matheson present the story as a product of Roderick's imagination and it certainly works that way.

Fascination (1979)

In 1916, well-to-do Frenchwomen (Franca Mai and Brigitte Lahaie) meet at a slaughterhouse to drink bull's blood for their health. They're up to something else, too. When a small-time thief (Jean-Marie Lemaire) who has betrayed his gang takes up refuge in their chateau, he thinks he's in charge. The first half is essentially soft-core exploitation that turns to fairly graphic violence in the second, with some interesting ideas about sexual power. Jean Rollin's work—one of his best—compares favorably to American low-budget work of the same era, though it would be better if Lemaire were able to project a stronger screen presence.

Feardotcom (2002)

Fervid combination of serial killer and ghost-in-the-machine plotlines works through dark murky visuals borrowed from *Seven.* People are dying after they visit a website. The investigating cop (Stephen Dorff) is helped by a disease control expert (Natascha McElhone) because the victims' symptoms seem to have come from a hemorrhagic virus, not a computer. Stephen Rea is a fine creepily unemotional psycho who prefigures Jigsaw in the *Saw* movies. The film can be seen as an early and relatively restrained example of torture porn. Bizarre images make up for a loopy, nonsensical plot up to a point. That point does not include the finish.

Fearless Vampire Killers; or, Pardon Me, but Your Teeth Are in My Neck (1967)

Taking another look at Hammer's *Kiss of the Vampire,* it's easy to see where Roman Polanski got most of the inspiration for his 1967 horror/comedy. Most video and DVD editions are a full-length "director's version" that doesn't ap-

Poster for *Fall of the House of Usher.*

pear to be noticeably different from the theatrical release. Longer doesn't necessarily mean better, either. Like the other stylish Hammer horrors of the period, the sets and costumes are lavish. So are the camerawork and acting. Today's audiences will find the pace a little slow and Polanski's humor sometimes forced. The film has its moments—Ferdy Mayne is an excellent vampire and Sharon Tate was a lovely heroine—but it's no *Young Frankenstein.* (Alternate title: *Dance of the Vampires.*)

Feast (2005)

Cheerfully mean-spirited little low-budget horror/comedy comes from the Project Greenlight reality TV series. With absolutely no explanation, four heavily fanged monsters set upon a poorly lit desert roadhouse bar. On-screen supertitles explain who the mostly unpleasant inhabitants of the joint are and estimate their life expectancy. Then the attack begins. The survivors first attempt to keep the nasties out. Then they try to escape. Throughout, the lighting and editing are used to conceal the guys-in-rubber-suits creatures and to keep the focus on the bloody violent effects. Followed by two sequels.

Fellini Satyricon (1969)

Federico Fellini's "free adaptation of the Petronius classic" is an autobiographical horror film of pre-Christian pagan decadence. It's an episodic journey through a surreal hell that's fetid, swollen, and about to burst. "What caused the decadence?" the film's Felliniesque poet asks. "Lust of money," he answers. But a literal reading of the plot—difficult if not impossible—means less than the images, and those are some of the strongest in a body of work filled with indelible images. The underground human hive destroyed by an earthquake, a huge seafaring barge in the snow, the temple of the hermaphrodite, the Minotaur's city. On one level, it's a journey from darkness to light in a world filled with grotesques, suicide, dismemberment, impotence, and fart jokes. Given the strength of the visuals, the film is best seen in a theater, not on DVD or tape. Though this hideous masterpiece has never been a commercial hit, it's one that people will be watching a hundred years from now.

Fido (2006)

Suburban satire shares some characteristics with the deeply twisted *Parents* and *Meet the Hollowheads.* A vaguely 1950s world of big cars and stay-at-home moms has survived a zombie plague caused by "space dust." The Zomcon company has perfected a domestication collar that turns flesh-eaters into trainable slaves. When a well-to-do family moves in next door, Helen Robinson (Carrie-Anne Moss) decided that her family must keep up and so she acquires one (Billy Connolly). He becomes friendly with her son Timmy (K'Sun Ray). Still, zombies will be zombies. Though it's not up there with *Shaun of the Dead* or *Zombieland,* the comedy has its moments.

Fiend without a Face (1958)

Something strange is happening at the Air Force Intercept Command in Manitoba, Canada. People's brains and spinal cords are being sucked out of their skulls. For most of the swift running time, these suckers are invisible but they do make disgusting slurpy sounds when they attack. When they finally show up, they're stop-motion critters that share a few characteristics with

William Castle's Tingler. Stock footage confuses B-47s and B-52s but that's a minor flaw. Black-and-white cinematography is excellent, and this is one of the most enjoyable of the '50s atomic monsters.

Final Destination (2000)
Final Destination 2 (2003)
Final Destination 3 (2006)
Final Destination 3D (2009)
Final Destination 5 (2011)

These gimmick films are based on a simple premise: a young person has a vision of immediate impending disaster and tells his or her friends about it, allowing them to escape. In the first film, it's a plane crash; in the second an automobile accident; in the third a roller coaster. Then for the rest of the running time, fate stalks the survivors, and viewers are treated to a series of elaborate Rube Goldberg setups with fatal conclusions. The original uses an airliner that explodes on takeoff and effectively plays on the nervousness any infrequent flier feels.

The first sequel, *Final Destination 2* (2003) takes more care in crafting knotty complications that aren't worked out until the final scene. To my taste, it's the best of the bunch.

By the third film, the kids have pretty much been reduced to caricature, but the production values, particularly at the amusement park with its fatal roller coaster, are solid. As black comedy, they're something of an acquired taste, but, for the first two films, at least, the humor is lively and inventive. After that installment, titling in the series becomes somewhat problematic.

The first three are simple enough, but the fourth is *The Final Destination in 3-D.* The addition of a third dimension to the story of a racetrack catastrophe doesn't keep it from feeling a bit stale.

Final Destination 5 (2011) apparently brings the series to a conclusion. The structure is identical to the others, and the inciting incident is the vertiginous collapse of a suspension bridge. Given the massive advances in computer effects, the violent deaths are presented in exact detail.

Firestarter (1984)

Stephen King's story of psychic powers, government spooks, and violent effects is comparable to the contemporaneous *The Fury,* but it's much more enjoyable. The difference is that veteran B-movie director Mark L. Lester (*Truck Stop Women*) understands the pulp roots of the material and doesn't try to make the film more than it is. He keeps the plot moving swiftly, but not at the expense of believably middle class protagonists. No matter what has happened since, Drew Barrymore certainly was a cute chubby-cheeked little rascal, even when she flames feds, turning them into shish kabobs in suits. George C. Scott and Martin Sheen are good villains, too.

Flatliners (1990)

Variation on *Frankenstein* posits four brilliant, attractive medical students searching for the secrets of death and life by experimenting on themselves. Working in a homemade lab, they artificially induce the stoppage of all bodily functions and then jump-start the "corpse." The horrific elements work well enough, particularly the scenes with grimier settings, but they're not really the point. These seekers-after-truth have great hair and clothes, and they live in cavernous apartments. Style is far more important than any substance.

Fly, The (1958)
Return of the Fly (1959)
Fly, The (1986)
Fly II, The (1989)

One of the most famous '50s horror movies is also one of the most lavish. The story of a scientist (David Hedison) whose teleportation experiment goes horribly awry is remembered for its makeup effects, still shocking despite massive advances in the field. More impressive today are the strong characters who react realistically to a fantastic situation, a complex script by James Clavell (who'd go on to write the best-selling novels *Shogun* and *Tai Pan*), and a really sumptuous production. Vincent Price is excellent in a serious dramatic role. The key emotional moments are genuinely poignant, and the "Help me, please, help me!" ending is one of the finest moments in all movies. Followed by two sequels and a strong remake.

Return of the Fly begins with the funeral of the original Fly's widow, with her brother-in-law Delambre (Vincent Price) and son Philippe (Brett Halsey) who has yet to learn the truth about dear old dad's experiments. Once he does, you know what's going to happen. The film isn't as expensively produced as the original. The cheesy pulp plot and makeup effects really owe more to the lower-budget Universal productions of the 1940s and the Amer-

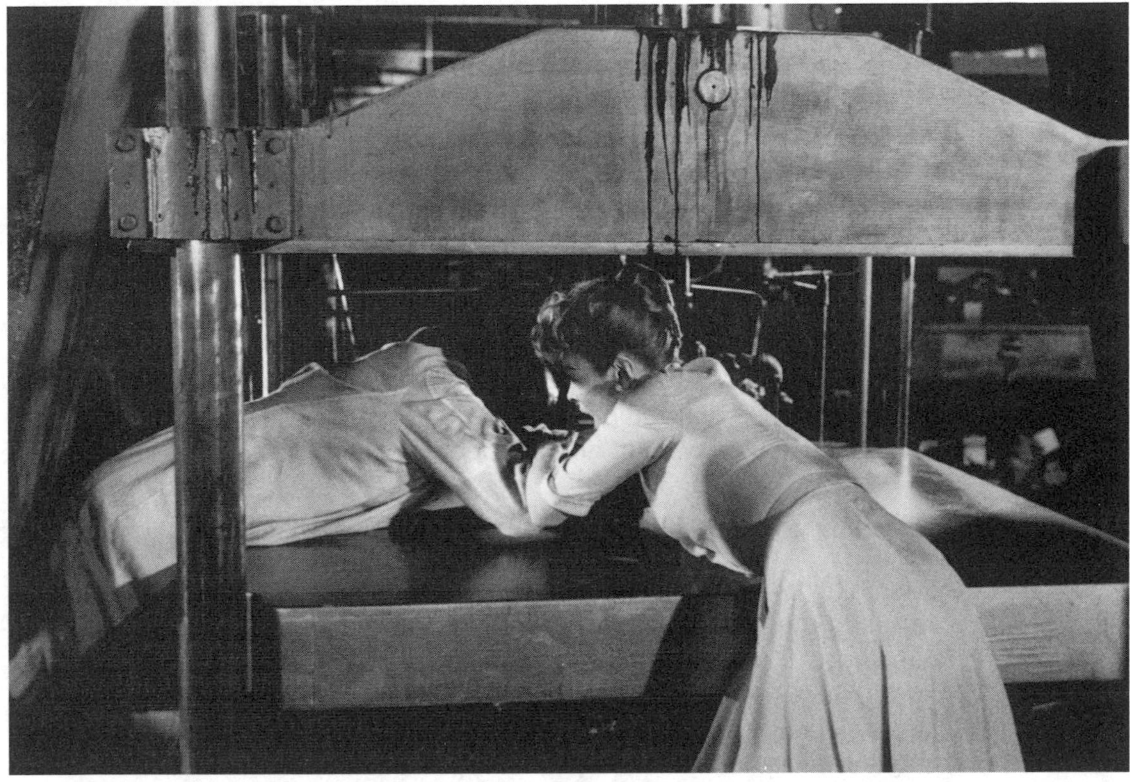

A desperate scientist ends it all after having his head replaced by that of an insect in 1958's *The Fly.*

ican International horrors of the 1950s. Price is at his most theatrical. This one's followed by a third, *Curse of the Fly.*

The 1986 remake of the first film is, if anything, better than the original. David Cronenberg and Jeff Goldblum take the fantastic premise (teleportation) and treat it matter-of-factly. As the scientist Seth Brundle, Goldblum mixes humor, horror, and pathos so effectively that his performance merits comparison to Boris Karloff in *Frankenstein.* As he is progressively transformed into something more and more monstrous, he becomes a creature that we still care about and sympathize with. The Oscar-winning effects may lose something in transition to the small screen, but that personal element is even stronger in the more intimate medium of home video.

The Fly II is one of those rare sequels that's actually pretty good. It begins with a harrowing birth scene and introduces Martin Brundle (Eric Stoltz), son of Seth, who has inherited his father's genetic changes. None of the scenes can top the gross-out stuff in the original, but the characters and situation are treated seriously and the story is original, not a rehash of the first.

Fog, The (1980, 2005)

An old sailor (John Houseman) sits with a group of wide-eyed kids around a campfire on a beach and tells them how a ship was wrecked by a false signal fire in the fog one hundred years before. If the fog ever returns, so will the sailors' ghosts, looking for revenge. They do, attacking the local radio dj (Adrienne Barbeau), a drunken priest (Hal Holbrook), a hitchhiker (Jamie Lee Curtis), and several others. No, the film isn't as taut as John Carpenter's previous effort, *Halloween,* but it's a fine spooky ghost story and that's all it means to be.

The 2005 remake, produced by Carpenter and his partner Debra Hill, is more polished and complicated than the original with bigger computer effects and deeper layers of hokum. Decidedly less enjoyable.

Forgotten One, The (1989)

Searching for inspiration, a widowed novelist (Terry O'Quinn) moves to Denver and buys an old Victorian house that's haunted by a fetching, mysterious ghost (Blair Parker). His neighbor (Kristie McNichol) helps him find answers. Admittedly, this one suffers from the logic problems that plague most supernatural stories, but beyond that, it's a spooky, sexy ghost movie. O'Quinn brings the same tightly wrapped unpredictability to this role that makes *The Stepfather* so memorable. Throughout, the formula aspects of the genre are kept to a minimum, and the special effects are atmospheric and effective. One of the best and least appreciated sleepers around.

Forsaken, The (2001)

Driving from Los Angeles to Miami, Sean (Kerr Smith) picks up hitchhiking Nick (Brendan Fehr) and they run afoul of a carload of traveling vampires. Though it doesn't come close to *Near Dark,* this western/road horror works well enough most of the time. The tone is uneven. Desert and mountain landscapes are handled properly, and the colorful characters are interesting, if some of them are so broadly drawn as to be parodies. The rules for vampirism and its transmission via "telegenetic" virus are complicated.

Four Flies on Grey Velvet (1971)

One of Dario Argento's lesser giallos is occasionally interesting and sometimes intentionally (I think) funny, but it's mostly incoherent. Drummer Roberto (Michael Brandon) is a charismatically challenged hero who's being shadowed by a guy in a hat. Said guy soon winds up dead as do many of Roberto's acquaintances. The killings are not concerned with reality or logic, and so it's difficult to care much about them one way or another, or even to pay much attention to the various cinematic touches that the director brings to bear. Morricone's score is one of his more dischordant.

1408 (2007)

Writer Mike Enslin (John Cusack) has pretty much given up on his once promising career as a novelist to crank out stories debunking haunted buildings. Then he receives a postcard daring him to spend the night in room 1408 at the Dolphin Hotel in New York. Intrigued when the manager (Samuel L. Jackson) refuses to accept a reservation, he presses the issue and the result is the best adaptation of a Stephen King hotel story since *The Shining.* Writers Matt Greenberg, Scott Alexander, and Larry Karaszewski and director Mikael Håfström know the tricks of the genre and stay one step ahead of viewers. Some of the visual effects are genuinely surprising, but the film finally works because the script is so smart and complicated, and the leads are so good.

Fragile (2005)

Nurse Amy (Calista Flockhart) arrives at Mercy Falls Children's Hospital on the Isle of Wight and realizes right away that something is amiss. The second floor has been locked up since the 1950s and something is scaring the kids at night. She has her own problems, too. The first half is fairly restrained. Some of the dialogue is unintelligible (the DVD has no subtitles) and important action is too dark to see. In terms of plot and style, comparisons to *The Others* are unavoidable and unfortunate. It's difficult to make a really good ghost story and this one comes up short.

Frailty (2001)

One of the great sleepers warrants comparison to *The Shining* and *Take Shelter* as a tale that carefully walks the fine line that divides insanity and horror. Single Dad Meiks (director Bill Paxton) awakens his two young sons one night and tells them that he has had a vision from God, and the three of them have been ordered to go forth and slay the demons that are trying to take over the earth. These demons have taken the form of their neighbors. They look just like regular people but, even so, they must be slaughtered. What are the kids to do, and what does any of it mean to FBI agent Doyle (Powers Boothe)? The place and the characters ring true, and the ending is terrific.

Frankenhooker (1990)

"Bioelectrotechnician" Jeffrey Franken's (James Lorinz) fiancée (Patty Mullen) is killed in a tragic lawn mower accident. But he manages to salvage a few key body parts. If he can just find donors for the rest, he's sure he can recreate her, so late one night he heads for Times Square. Like director Frank Henenlotter's overlooked *Brain Damage,* this one is strongly, even violently anti-drug. Though parts of the story are every bit as grotesque as his most famous cult hit *Basketcase,* they're exaggerated for a more comic effect. The real surprise here is Patty Mullen, an ex-*Penthouse* model who turns out to be an accomplished comedienne.

Frankenstein (1910)
Frankenstein (1931)
Curse of Frankenstein (1953)
Mary Shelley's Frankenstein (1994)

The first film version is the 1910 short produced by Thomas Edison. It calls itself "A Liberal Adaptation From Mrs. Shelley's Famous Story." In a mere nineteen minutes, with time left over for considerable arm flailing, it hits the high points—the mad scientist, the lab scene, the creature's birth, his creator's wedding, the confrontation. Even if the images are flickering and indistinct, the makeup that star Charles Ogle created for himself still has shock value and the film concludes with an odd visual twist.

James Whale's 1931 *Frankenstein* remains, justifiably, the most famous. The trappings—clothes, sets, makeup, acting—are all dated now, and the plot, based on a stage play has some glaring lapses that don't completely work on the screen. All of those will probably seem funny to young audiences. But when Boris Karloff makes his big entrance as the Monster, the laughter will stop. At heart, Whale's adaptation of the novel remains the model for most of the horror films that have followed. (It's also one of the most deceptively complex films ever made.) The mad scientist with his lab full of crackling electricity, the peasant mob, the stylized cemetery—they've all become instantly recognizable parts of the language of film. More importantly, so is the Monster, a combination of Jack Pierce's makeup and

Boris Karloff's genius as an actor. With his expressive hands, a face often filled with tortured confusion, and ungainly physical presence, he is one of horror's immortal figures. Many critics prefer the sequel, *Bride of Frankenstein,* to the original, but the films really should be seen as two parts of one story. Most tapes and DVDs include the famous "missing" scene at the lake, though a controversial line of dialogue—"Now I know what it feels like to be God!"—is still distorted.

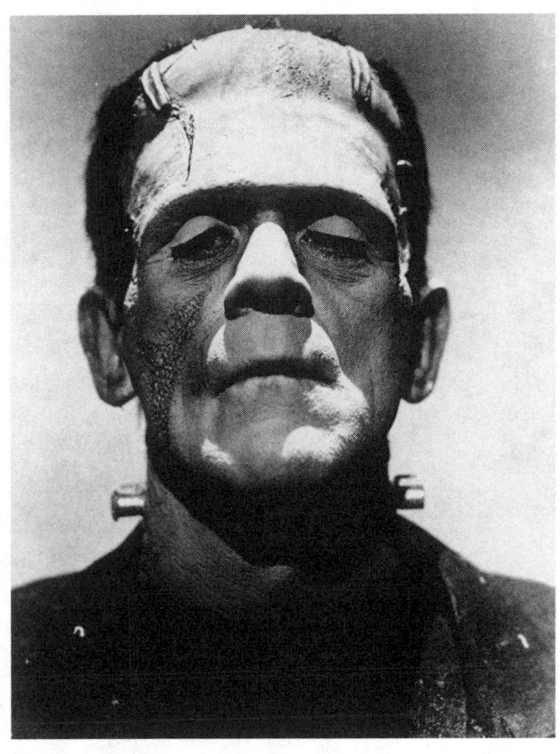
Boris Karloff in his Frankenstein's Monster make up.

Curse of Frankenstein, the Hammer organization's first foray into horror is one of its best—a fast-moving and fresh interpretation of the relationship between creator and creation. Peter Cushing is the brilliant young Baron who discovers the secret of life. Christopher Lee has a much smaller role as the Creature. (He and Cushing wouldn't really achieve equal footing until a year later with *The Horror of Dracula.*) Hazel Court, also familiar for her work in Roger Corman's low-budget movies, is the sexy Hammer heroine. Squeezing every penny out of a modest budget, the producers manage to create a credible mad scientist's laboratory. Cushing's approach to the role of Victor is more realistic and arrogant than Colin Clive's in 1931. Writer Jimmy Sangster compresses a complex literary work into a short, efficient screenplay with a neatly ironic ending. Terence Fisher's direction is equally economical. The humor is bleak, gory, and wry.

Director-star Kenneth Branagh's *Mary Shelley's Frankenstein* is a glorious mess of a movie—energetic to a fault, handsomely produced, and often visually astonishing. A stilted, creaky script by Steph Lady and Frank Darabont and an unbalanced pace lie at the heart of the film's problems. Victor's (Branagh) childhood and family life are laboriously detailed. The centerpiece lab scenes are real lulus involving assorted fluids, industrial-strength acupuncture, and a Rube Goldberg contraption that looks like an old-fashioned copper bathtub. The result is the Creature (Robert De Niro), scarred, innocent, frightened, and strong. Some of the early scenes are staged on huge but virtually empty sets that leave the viewer wondering where all the furniture is. In the middle section, where several important events take place, the pace is so hurried that the plot makes virtually no

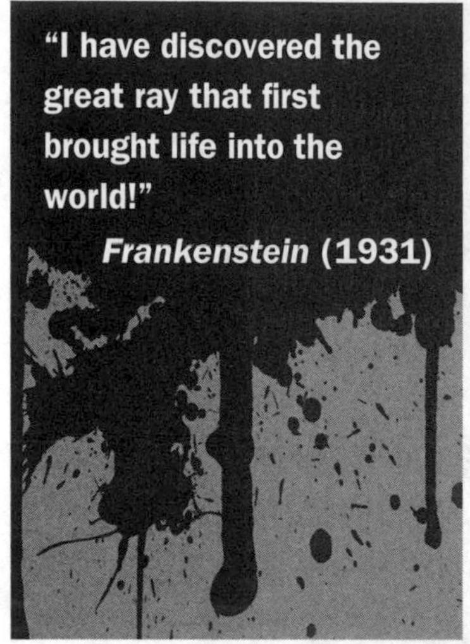

sense. As both actor and director, Branagh seems barely under control. He and Helena Bonham Carter might have found their characters on the cover of a paperback bodice-ripper. Co-producer Francis Ford Coppola was much more successful with a similar approach to *Bram Stoker's Dracula.*

Frankenstein Created Woman (1969)

Hammer's fourth take on the Frankenstein story is a departure from most sequels. The traditional mad scientist scenes with crackling electrodes and lightning are largely absent. In their place are less expensive "soul" translocations from one body to another. To satisfy horror fans, the film has an ongoing fascination with decapitation that begins with the first scene. Peter Cushing is a bit abrupt and curt as the Baron, leaving most of the dramatic work to his co-stars Susan Denberg, Robert Morris, and particularly Thorley Walters as a sidekick whose bumbling is reminiscent of Sherlock Holmes' Dr. Watson. The story has a warm, honestly emotional basis that's often lacking in horror. The plot moves away from the traditional structure of earlier Hammer films. It's more openly geared toward a younger audience, reflecting the changes that were going on in the mid-1960s.

Frankenstein Meets the Wolfman (1943)

Technically a sequel to *The Wolf Man,* this is the first Universal feature to bring two of the studio's monsters together. The formula worked well enough for a dozen or so lower-budget films that are entertaining enough, even if they don't approach the 1930s originals. Lawrence Talbot (Lon Chaney Jr.) is brought back by grave robbers and then cannot persuade anyone that he's a werewolf. Maleeva (Maria Ouspenskaya) persuades him to see Dr. Frankenstein. Instead, they find his creation. As the Monster, Bela Lugosi is a parody of Karloff, though that's not entirely his fault. His character is supposed to be blind, though prerelease cuts eliminated that information. Look for Dwight Frye in a cameo.

Frankenstein Must Be Destroyed (1969)

The fifth of Hammer's Frankenstein series was meant to be the final installment. There's a coldness to the sleek production—almost a bitterness—much stronger and more obvious than it had been two years before in *Frankenstein Created Woman.* Dapper in spats, Peter Cushing is "a mad and highly dangerous medical adventurer," as the clueless authorities put

Frankenstein castle in Darmstadt, Germany, supposedly gave Mary Shelley the inspiration to pen her novel.

it. He ruthlessly blackmails a young couple (Simon Ward and Veronica Carlson) into helping him with an oddly baroque scheme. They and the other supporting characters are colorful and well defined. In place of the conventional (and expensive) lab scenes, the monster business is accomplished through creative surgery. The simplicity of the early Hammer films has been replaced by strange plotting that includes a strong rape scene. The crazed final act is still emotionally moving.

Frankenstein Unbound (1990)

Curious sci-fi/horror (based on a Brian Aldiss novel) begins in Los Angeles, 2031, where Joseph Buchanan (John Hurt) invents a particle weapon that creates "time slips" which transport him and his computer-enhanced sports car to Switzerland, 1817, where he meets Victor Frankenstein (Raul Julia). Mary (Bridget Fonda) and Percy Shelley (Michael Hutchence) and Lord Byron (Jason Patric) are hanging around, too, though they take smaller supporting roles. It's every bit as screwy as it sounds but not as much fun. Roger Corman, behind the camera for the first time in twenty years, gives the film a glowing look that partially makes up for the thin period details. The special

A poster for the 1932 film *Freaks*.

effects are limited to lightshow stuff and forgettable monster makeup from Nick Brimble. In the end, the film is more interesting than good and that's unusual for Corman who usually works within a stronger narrative structure.

Freaks (1932)

After a lengthy and defensive on-screen written introduction, Tod Browning's curious little thriller literally rips into action. Trapeze artiste Cleo (Olga Baclanova) flirts with the midget Hans (Harry Earles) though she and her strongman lover Hercules (Henry Victor) are mocking the little man. When they learn that Hans is rich, she schemes to marry and murder him. Browning's none-too-subtle point is that humanity has nothing to do with appearance. While the "normal" people plot to kill, the Bearded Woman has a baby and the Siamese twins work through their marital and dating problems. In their fine book *Dark Carnival,* David Skal and Elias Savada write that the famously troubled production so shocked preview audiences that the studio cut almost a third of the running time. An attack on Cleopatra and Hercules was lost. Even so, the rainy conclusion is brilliant. But much of the acting, notably by Baclanova, is crazily overwrought and much of the dialogue is impossible to understand. A surprising amount of humor still shines through.

Freakshow (1995)

Anthology of short South Carolina horror films uses a carnival sideshow as a framing device. That's where two teens listen to scary stories told by Gunnar Hansen (without his "Leatherface" mask from *Texas Chainsaw Massacre*). They're fairly graphic tales about revenge, cannibalism, and such with a grisly sense of humor along the lines of the old E.C. Comics. The production values are a bit on the thin side and the pace is slow, but the films get better. "The Mummy" has a slight Poe quality and it stars Veronica Carlson, familiar to fans for her work in Hammer horror films of the 1960s, and still looking terrific. Co-director Paul Talbot is also responsible for *Hellblock 13.*

Friday the 13th (1980)
Friday the 13th Part II (1981)
Friday the 13th Part III (1982)
Friday the 13th: The Final Chapter (1984)
Friday the 13th: A New Beginning (1985)
Jason Lives: Friday the 13th Part VI (1986)
Friday the 13th Part VII: The New Blood (1988)
Friday the 13th Part VIII: Jason Takes Manhattan (1989)
Jason Goes to Hell: The Final Friday (1993)
Jason X (2001)
Freddy versus Jason (2003)
Friday the 13th (2009)

The first entry in one of the genre's most successful franchises is a long variation on that old campfire favorite, The Hook. Judged as a low-budget horror flick, it's not bad, and not particularly original, either. The plot and direction rip off *Halloween,* and the score rips off Bernard Herrmann. Tom Savini's bloody effects are well done and have been repeated many many times since. So has the story of camp counselors being preyed on by a slasher.

The series really doesn't get started until the second entry which establishes the ground rules. Like *Halloween*'s Michael Myers and all of the Universal studio monsters before him, Jason is an unstoppable monster of ill-defined superpowers. Shoot him, stab him, burn him, blow him up—it doesn't matter. Every time you're really and truly sure that he's dead, he pops back up for more. Sex is the trigger; violent death is the result. That's the ongoing message of the films.

Theatrically released in 3-D, *Part III* features objects being thrust toward the camera. The 3-D process also accounts for the picture's graininess on video and DVD. The film simply looks ugly. The producers daringly expand the original concept by having Jason kill middle-aged people along with teens, and the entry is notable for Jason's acquisition of his trademark hockey goalie's mask. Beyond that, it's the same old slash-o and arguably the worst of the series, though personally, I'd vote for *VIII* on that count.

It has long been my belief that the subtitle of the fourth entry , "the final chapter," carries with it an implied guarantee. At the very least, anyone who watches it has permission never to look at another installment. At best, the producers would have been prohibited from making any more sequels. All that this one really has to offer is a pubescent Corey Feldman. (The horror! The horror!) The intentionally comic elements are stronger, too.

And then there was the fifth, *A New Beginning.* The effects, the story, and the pace of the murders slavishly follow the pattern set in the earlier films. Relatively strong production values are the only virtue of this otherwise derivative effort.

Jason Lives the sixth installment, deserves some credit for a fresh start, albeit one borrowed from *Ghost of Frankenstein,* wherein Jason's batteries are recharged. But that introduction uses up all the energy in this pointless sequel to a sequel to a ...

Roman numeral VII, *The New Blood* is solidly in the tradition of the Universal ensemble horrors like *Frankenstein Meets the Wolfman* and *House of Dracula,* wherein all of the studio's fading monsters were brought together. It might have been called *Jason Meets Carrie,* with the hockey-masked cliché set against psychokenetic teen, Tina (Lar Park Lincoln). Given the excesses of the series, the violence is relatively tame, and the action never even pretends to make sense.

The next, *Jason Takes Manhattan* ought to have been subtitled *Jason Takes a Boat Ride* because Mr. Hockey Mask doesn't hit the Big Apple until

The masked Jason goes on the rampage over and over in movie after movie in the successful *Friday the 13th* franchise.

the last reel. Why? Because it costs less to shoot film on a passenger ship than in Times Square at night. The only other difference here is more overt sadism. Writer/director Rob Hedden often pauses for several seconds while the various victims scream before Jason stabs, crushes, electrocutes, decapitates, drowns, or spears them.

With *Jason Goes to Hell* the "Final Friday" subtitle is an outright falsehood. The original series had been more than played out by then and the film is nothing but ninety minutes of rote, repetitive violence, and after it, they put the hockey mask in cold storage for eight years.

CGI effects make the tenth entry, *Jason X,* the most visually sophisticated. It begins with a drugged out Jason awaiting "cryogenic suspension" until an officious bureaucrat (David Cronenberg!) orders tests to determine the source of his invulnerability. That leads to our boy and the comely Dr. Rowan (Lexa Doig) waking up in the year 2455 on a spaceship filled with young people who ... well, you know the drill.

The sets and important dream elements of the plot make *Freddy versus Jason* more Elm Street than Crystal Lake. Putting the two series characters on screen together dilutes their power and essentially turns them into comic figures. Despite some impressive moments—a fiery Jason striding

The Top Twelve Vampire Movies

30 Days of Night
Day breakers
Rise: Blood Hunter
Shadow of the Vampire
Vampire Circus
The Vampyres
Jugular Wine
Kiss of the Vampire
Martin
Near Dark
The Night Stalker
Nosferatu

through a cornfield, and a giant CGI caterpillar—the big showdown between the two is just silly. The fight choreography could have come from a professional wrestling bout.

The 2009 remake, *Friday the 13th,* essentially compresses the plots of the first three '80s films and rehashes the story with very slick production values. The plot calls for characters to wander off into the woods at night for foolish reasons. Tellingly, the title does not appear on the screen until the twenty-three minute mark. Much of the action in the last act is so dark you really can't tell what's happening or where people are.

Fright Night (1985)
Fright Night Part 2 (1988)
Fright Night (2011)

Perhaps the best of the 1980s vampires-in-the-'burbs flicks makes fine use of all the conventions of the sub-genre and combines them with first rate effects. Teenaged Charlie (William Ragsdale) can't persuade anyone that his new neighbor Jerry Dandridge (Chris Sarandon) is undead. His girlfriend Amy (Amanda Bearse) thinks Charlie's being a jerk. Making his debut, director Tom Holland treats his young characters more honestly than many "serious" filmmakers. The nightclub scene is a brilliant set piece, but note the neat smaller touches. Dandridge makes his entrance drinking a Bloody Mary. Before an attack he whistles an offhand bar of "Strangers In the Night." Stephen Geoffrey's Beavis & Butthead-inspired Evil Ed is terrific. So is Roddy McDowall as the hambone horror host, but the film belongs to Sarandon.

As the sequel begins, therapy has convinced Charlie (Ragsdale) that he really didn't fight a vampire in the first movie. But isn't someone moving another coffin into the horror host's (McDowell) building? As Regine, who puts the vamp back in vampire, Julie Carmen is good, but she's not nearly as impressive as Chris Sarandon in the original. Again, the inventive and often-changing monster effects are impressive. The tone is not. No matter how gruesome, vampires on roller skates are not frightening. Admittedly the film is as interested in laughs as it is in screams.

The 2011 remake of the original moves the setting to Las Vegas and tweaks the plot with dozens of pop culture references, a talented cast, and some nasty makeup effects. But everyone (except Christopher Mintz-Plasse) seems to be working a little too hard and so it lacks the cheesy fun of the first film.

Frighteners, The (1996)

Ghost meets *Re-Animator* as director Peter Jackson stirs wild special effects, laughs, swooping camerawork, scares, and a breakneck pace into a zesty mix. Psychic exterminator Frank Bannister (Michael J. Fox) is a conman with ESP. Working with his ghost pals Cyrus (Chi McBride), Stuart (Jim Fyfe), and the Judge (John Astin), Bannister "haunts" houses and then charges the owners to exorcise the spirits. Despite his powers, Bannister doesn't know what to do when a more malevolent spirit appears, killing innocent victims at random. Without giving too much away, the other key ingredients are a young woman (Trini Alvarado) who believes in Bannister, a paranoid FBI agent (an inspired Jeffrey Combs), a serial murderer (Jake Busey, son of Gary), and his possibly innocent accomplice (Dee Wallace Stone). Don't worry about the plot details in the script by Jackson and collaborator Fran Walsh. They're explained as fully as they need to be. The special effects deserve as much attention as the cast. Jackson uses some impressive computer-generated scenes to tell the story.

From Beyond (1986)

Reteaming of the director and stars of *Re-Animator* isn't as successful because it doesn't go as far. Very loosely based on another H.P. Lovecraft story, it involves interdimensional travel via the "Praetorius Resonator" which stimulates the pineal gland. To be sure, it has its moments and the film is funny, but star Barbara Crampton never gets the chance to top her infamous "head" scene. Too bad.

Writer and director Quentin Tarantino.

From Dusk 'til Dawn (1996)

Guilty-pleasure escape from the drive-in is so violent, bloody, and grimly funny that even the most devoted fans of low-budget horror may be surprised at how far it goes. Decapitations, amputations, and burning bodies are just the beginning. After a couple of graphic killings and a rape-murder that thankfully occurs offscreen, bank-robbers Seth (George Clooney) and Richard Gecko (writer Quentin Tarantino) kidnap a family (Harvey Keitel, Juliette Lewis, and Ernest Liu). They drive their RV across the border to a Mexican strip bar, the Titty Twister, which turns out to be full of vampires. Director Robert Rodriguez keeps the action zipping right along with a quirky visual humor that gives a cartoonish quality to the most graphic moments. Tarantino's script is much closer in tone and intention to his *True Romance.* The complexity of *Pulp Fiction* is notably absent. Keitel plays the only sympathetic adult protagonist with an easy grace that leaves his younger and flashier costars in the shadows.

From Hell (2001)

Disregarding its conjecture about motives and the Ripper's identity, and a protagonist (Johnny Depp) who's yet another psychic detective, the Hughes brothers' take on the first and most famous serial killer is a fine film that is accurate in the details of the crimes. The opening image of a tarry ball of opium being lit sets a properly dreamlike mood. For my money, the filmmakers strike the right balance in their depiction of the story's violence and a believably squalid Whitechapel, or at least as squalid as a big-budget Hollywood production can be.

Frontier(s) (2007)

It's not so much the quantity of the gory violence or the explicitness as it is the quality. Writer/director Xavier Gens steals the premise of *Texas Chainsaw Massacre* and steadily amps up the intensity. Four basically unlikeable young thieves, one (Karina Testa) pregnant, flee political riots in Paris for refuge in the country. They wind up at house where an aged Nazi (Jean-Pierre Jorris) has turned his grown children into murderous cannibals. Initially, Gens's shaky cam is off-putting but he settles down as the unhinged plot takes one bizarre turn after another. Clearly, it's not to all tastes. Fans of *Wrong Turn* and *High Tension* should take a look.

Funhouse, The (1981)

Tobe Hooper pays tribute to some of horror's best with this original and grimly funny tale. Fans will catch references to *Psycho, Halloween,* and, significantly, James Whale's *Frankenstein.* The premise traps four young people (Elizabeth Berridge, Cooper Huckabee, Largo Woodruff, and Miles Davis) in a carnival funhouse with a hideously deformed freak (Wayne Doba) and his father (Kevin Conway). But ... who are the good guys and who are the bad guys? That's the point of Larry Block's script. John Beal's music and makeup by Rick Baker and Craig Reardon add a lot. No, it's not as intense as *Chainsaw*—few movies are—but it does just about everything you could ask of a good fright flick.

Funny Games (1997, 2007)

Michael Haneke has made this nasty home invasion story twice, first in Austria and a decade later, in America. The identical stories revolve around a well-to-do couple and their son who drive out to their lake house and find themselves under attack by unlikely but ominous assailants. Haneke reworks the conventions of the genre by making his villains clean-cut, outwardly respectable types, just as Hitchcock did in *Psycho* and *Rope.* Both versions of the film are handsomely made with excellent photography and acting. To me, though, the end result is more depressing than frightening.

Fury, The (1978)

Wildly plotted mix of horror, cold war espionage, action, and psychic piffle never quite comes together as well as it ought. John Cassavetes creates a well-shaded villain, and Kirk Douglas is easily his equal as the hero. Youngsters Andrew Stevens and Amy Irving frown a lot and make ookey things happen with their brains. John Williams' music helps considerably, as it always does. Yes, that's Dennis Franz as Bob, proud owner of the new Caddy. You'll also see Daryl Hannah and James Belushi in small roles.

Galaxy of Terror (1981)

One demented scene has elevated this otherwise forgettable sci-fi/horror to true cult status. That moment comes when a ten-foot-long maggot monster attacks Technical Chief Dameia (Taaffe O'Connell), rips off all her clothes, and "licks" her to ecstasy or something to that effect. Director Bruce Clark is understandably vague on details here. The rest is a fairly witless rip-off of *Alien* and *Star Wars* with some interesting but often gory effects and a nonsensical script.

Gamera, Guardian of the Universe (1995)

This remake of an early Japanese giant city-stomper monster flick retains all the energy and humor of the original, and adds better special effects, acting, and production values including more expressive voice dubbing. Our hero is a big green flying turtle with a bad attitude and a desperate need for orthodontics. In this incarnation, the reason behind his resurrection isn't simple nuclear weapons but a veritable grab-bag of environmental issues from global warming to littering. Gamera appears at the same time as the Gaos show up. They're big flying creatures who eat people and poop all over the place. The movie is pure fun for kids and adults. Matt Greenfield takes particular care with the English language version, translating signs and headlines pertinent to the action.

The Top Eleven Big Bad Werewolves Movies

The Wolf Man (1941)
The Wolf Man (2010)
Werewolf of Washington
Wolf
Bad Moon
I Was a Teenage Werewolf
Curse of the Werewolf
Dog Soldiers
Ginger Snaps
The Howling
Silver Bullet

Gate, The (1986)
Gate II: The Trespassers (1990)

A clichéd but passable nightmare sequence introduces another hell-comes-to-suburbia story. When his parents leave young Glen (pudgy-cheeked, prepubescent Stephen Dorff) unsupervised for the weekend, he opens up a doorway to another dimension in the backyard and demons pour through. (And you thought things got crazy for Tom Cruise in *Risky Business*!) It all bears some similarity to *Scream,* though for a slightly younger audience, with a nod to Lovecraft's Chtulhu mythos. The stop-motion and animation effects are excellent.

In *Gate II: The Trespassers,* that doorway to another dimension is still there. Like people who leave their Christmas lights up all year, the folks in this neighborhood haven't done anything about this supernatural nuisance that lets in demons, devils, and stuff like that. It's just sitting there so teen Terrence (Louis Tripp) can sneak over and sacrifice a hamster to call up the forces of darkness. Any movie showing teenaged characters involved in animal sacrifice is dealing with dangerous material, but this one's so inept and formulaic that it's probably harmless.

Gathering, The (2003)

Mash-up contains elements of a religious historic conspiracy, Gothic horror, paranormal stuff, and town-with-a-secret tale. Soon after a buried first-century church is discovered near the village of Ashby Wake, amnesiac Cassie (Christina Ricci) shows up. Director Brian Gilbert overuses a few simple tricks for scares. Throughout, the writing and acting are pedestrian. British locations are used to good effect. The big surprise ending is really screwy.

Generation X-Tinct (1997)

Defying an ultra-low budget, filmmaker Michele Pacitto makes an impressive debut with a grim social satire. Set in suburbs, it's the story of Robert Tilton (Michael Passion), a true loser's loser, or, as his favorite bartender says, "a pathetic little chimp." Vain, self-pitying, manipulative, lazy, and none-too-bright, Robert is a blithe and obvious liar who deserves everything that happens to him. He's also a would-be psycho killer. In their quest for weed, he and his slacker pals entangle themselves in the lives of a no-nonsense drug dealer, a real estate salesman with the gonzo name Thunder Goldberg, and a hapless homicide detective. The plot is so quick and unpredictable that any synopsis would spoil the fun. And the film is fun, despite or perhaps because of the fact that all of the main characters are so unsympathetic. Writer-director-editor Pacitto has borrowed bits from *Pulp Fiction, Tree's Lounge,* and *True Romance* but he has created a genuine original. The film rolls right along from one unexpected jolt to another and finally to a dead right, downbeat ending. Some of the acting is amateurish; some of the props and sets won't stand up to close inspection. But so what? *Generation X-Tinct* is a tough, smart, risky movie aimed at audiences looking for substance with a difference.

Ghost Breakers, The (1940)

It's another dark and stormy night in New York. Radio gossip monger Larry Lawrence (Bob Hope) jumps out of the frying pan and into the fire when he offends a local mobster and stumbles into a conspiracy against Mary Carter (Paulette Goddard). She has just inherited Castillo Maldito on Black Island off the coast of Cuba, but someone is trying to drive her off. The last third takes place in the castle where all the traditional spooky elements of an "old dark house" tale are trotted out: secret passageways, hidden panels, zombies, ghosts, etc. Some viewers will have problems with the character of Alex (Willie Best), the stereotyped and subservient black family retainer. But it's really not fair to judge this light comedy too harshly by today's standards. No, the film is not particularly enlightened; it's just a product of its time.

Ghost Galleon

See Tombs of the Blind Dead

Ghost of Frankenstein (1942)

The fourth installment in the Universal series begins with the torch-bearing villagers attacking the Baron's castle, a scene usually reserved for the last reel. They blow up the joint, freeing the Monster (Lon Chaney Jr.) trapped in dried sulfur ... hunchbacked Ygor (Bela Lugosi) helps him out ... lightning strike to the neck bolts ... Dr. Ludwig (Cedric Hardwicke), the "second son of Frankenstein" ... You can fill in the rest of the blanks. Chaney actually acquits himself well and he's backed up by several members of the studio's stock troupe. Followed by *Frankenstein Meets the Wolfman.*

Ghost Rider (2007)

The soupy music is completely appropriate for a pulpish story that never strays from its roots as a second-tier comic book. As a boy, Johnny Blaze (Matt Long) sells his soul to Mephistopheles (Peter Fonda). He grows up to be Nic Cage, a motorcycle daredevil by day, Satanic bill collector by night. His head turns into a flaming skull and he rides on wheels of fire, etc. etc. It's all as silly as it can be, and so the effects are intentionally cartoonish. Followed by a sequel.

Ghost Ship (2002)

The opening credits written in flowing hot pink letters are backed up by music that might have introduced Rock Hudson and Doris Day. It sets up the opening scene of elegant people in evening wear dancing on the deck of a luxury cruise ship. All that leads to one of the all-time great mass gross-outs and a floating haunted house story. The crew of a salvage tug tries to figure out how a liner that disappeared in 1962 has shown up in the Bering Sea. Director Steve Beck (*Thirteen Ghosts*) and a good cast understand the pulp center of the material and handle it accordingly.

Ghost Story (1981)

Though it's generally dismissed by critics for the "stunt" casting of veterans Fred Astaire, Melvyn Douglas, John Houseman, and Douglas Fairbanks Jr., I'm partial to this unconventional story of old men remembering the worst thing that ever happened to them fifty years in the past, and its supernatural consequences in the present. Besides the presence of four canny pros and Alice Krige's complex, sexy performance, the evocation of small town New England in winter is so strong that it makes up for the flaws. Most of the literary recreations in Peter Straub's novel are missing.

Harold Ramis, Dan Aykroyd, and Bill Murray use bizarre plasma ray guns to battle a demigoddess from Hell in the original *Ghostbusters.*

Ghostbusters (1986)
Ghostbusters II (1989)

Admittedly, this big-budget spoof is more comedy than horror, but the special effects are so good and often so startling that it deserves inclusion here. First there's Sigourney Weaver's possession and transformation from classical musician to lust-crazed demon-babe and then there are Randall William Cook's terrific stop-motion animation creatures. Of course, Bill Murray and the giant Marshmallow Boy upstage them all, and the whole thing is a tongue-in-cheek romp. Worth another look on a rainy afternoon.

In the second film, a river of "psychomagnetheric" slime is running through an abandoned subway tunnel under First Avenue, and New York is suffering another supernatural psychic attack. Alas, the Ghostbusters were broken up after they were sued for all the damage they caused at the end of the original. The villainous Janosz Poha (Peter MacNichol), with a fractured accent and quirky performance, almost steals the film from the good guys, but Bill Murray's Venkman is still the center of attention. Even so, it's a sequel and lacks originality.

Ghosts of Mars (2001)

In 2176, the colonization of Mars is incomplete and people from Earth live in a sort of Wild West frontier that's run by women. Commander Braddock (Pam Grier) and Lt. Ballard (Natasha Henstridge) and their crew are ordered to bring in the notorious criminal "Desolation" Williams (Ice Cube) from the jail where he's being held in a remote mining town. They discover that native ghosts, or something, have turned the colonists into insane, zombie-like killers. Unfortunately, the disparate elements never come together in a satisfying mix. Minimalist sets don't help.

Ghoul, The (1934)

A dying Egyptologist (Boris Karloff) believes that the jewel of "Eternal Light" will bring him immortality if he's buried with it clasped in his hand. His squabbling heirs and an assortment of greedy colleagues would rather keep said gem in the realm of the living. Karloff's makeup and performance display hints of his work in *Frankenstein* and *The Mummy.* But the pace is slow and so this one is enjoyable now mostly for the cast and its historical value. It was lost for years until a Czech print was discovered and restored by the Museum of Modern Art and Janus Films.

Giant Spider Invasion (1975)

A meteorite crashes in rural Wisconsin, and, given the title, you can easily connect the rest of the dots in this formula effort. Notoriously bad special effects are the main attraction. The title critter may be the funniest ever to grace the screen. It bears a striking resemblance—particularly around the eyes—to Kermit the Frog, but it's clearly a Volkswagen. Best moment is the unforgettable spider-in-the-blender scene. A familiar "B" cast led by Steve Brodie, Alan Hale (the Skipper, whose first line is "Hi, little buddy!"), Barbara Hale (Della Street), and Bill Williams has a grand time.

Ginger Snaps (2000)
Ginger Snaps Back: The Beginning (2004)

Something is killing and mutilating pet dogs in the Canadian suburb of Baileys Down where Brigitte (Emily Perkins) and Ginger (Katharine Isabelle) live.

They're smart teenaged sisters with a Goth bent, "united against life as we know it," they say. Their school project is a series of gruesomely staged death photos they've taken of themselves. Then Ginger is bitten by the mysterious beast. Admittedly, the special effects are lacking, but they're much less important than the complex, difficult relationship between the two girls. Seldom have the physical and emotional changes of adolescence, as seen from a woman's point of view, been translated so effectively into the stuff of horror.

The curious prequel, *Ginger Snaps Back: The Beginning,* is set in 1815 where Brigitte and Ginger are lost deep in the Canadian woods. They arrive at Ft. Bailey to find it nearly deserted and under nightly attack by beasts. The werewolf makeup and effects are no better, and the sharp snark that seasons the first film is lacking.

The Top Seven Big Critter Movies

Trollhunter
Rodan
Mighty Peking Man
Anaconda
King Kong (1931, 2005)
Attack of the Giant Leeches
The Host

God Told Me To (1976)

Almost twenty years before the first episode of *The X Files* aired, Larry Cohen made the prototype. All the key elements of the series are there—alien abduction, religion, troubled cop who refuses to let go of the case, his suspect superiors, a powerful cabal, several bizarre inexplicable twists. A hymn-like theme (by Frank Cordell) sets the mood and it's followed by a stunning opening scene. NYPD detective Peter Nicholas (Tony LoBianco) discovers links between several apparently unrelated killings and becomes involved on the most personal level. Despite a relatively modest budget writer/producer/director Larry Cohen has created a richly complex film that makes extensive use of New York locations. The garish colors, quick pace and unpredictability are the stuff of a truly great B-movie. If you've missed it, find this off-kilter masterpiece. Two postscripts: That is the late Andy Kaufman as a policeman and the film is dedicated to the memory of composer Bernard Herrmann, so famous for his work with Alfred Hitchcock, Ray Harryhausen, and Cohen's own *It's Alive.*

Godsend (2004)

Paul (Greg Kinnear), Jessie (Rebecca Romjin), and their young son Adam (Cameron Bright) are the kind of ideal family found only in movies. Their happiness ends when the boy is killed. But Dr. Wells (Robert De Niro) shows up and offers them another chance. He claims that he can clone Adam from his remaining cells. Yes, it's illegal but what parent wouldn't break the law?

Man in rubber monster suit destroys a model city in *Godzilla: King of the Monsters.* Many Japanese monsters would follow in his considerable footsteps.

And, of course, there's a catch. From that plausible premise, the plot wanders in some screwy directions, and never really delivers. That said, Cameron Bright is one persuasively creepy kid.

Gojira (1954)
Godzilla: King of the Monsters (1956)
Godzilla (1998)

Most American audiences didn't see the original 1954 Japanese film until it was released on DVD. The 1956 American version, re-edited to include Raymond Burr as a reporter, tells the same story with a distinctly different tone. The original has a serious, elegiac tone largely missing in the second, shorter cut. In both, the Big G has been living happily at the bottom of the sea for millions of years until he's disturbed by experimental hydrogen bomb explosions that make him radioactive and really honk him off. He then rises up to tap dance on Tokyo. Unable to afford the time or expense of the stop-motion animation that created the original King Kong, the Japanese filmmakers used a man in a stiff, restrictive rubber suit, miniature city sets, and inventive sound effects for the famous roar. Despite the technical shortcomings, the film and the character have proved so popular that dozens of sequels co-starring even sillier giant monsters have followed.

The 1998 American remake moved the action to New York and used computer-generated effects to create a monster that's more "realistic" but no less ridiculous. And seeing the Big Apple reduced to smoking rubble has lost much of its appeal since the film was made.

The 1920 poster from the German film *The Golem*.

Golem, The (1920)

Dated conventions have robbed the film of many of its horrific qualities, though it remains one of the most ambitious productions of the silent era with impressive sets and a large cast. The inventive use of extreme camera angles is years ahead of its time. The story of a clay creature (played by co-director Paul Wegener) who's brought to life by a Rabbi to defend his community has strong political implications, and the subplots involving young lovers and the monster's emotions are still in use today. So is the central theme of a creator who loses control of his creation.

Gorgon, The (1964)

"Overshadowing the village of Vandorf stands the Castle Borski. From the turn of the century a monster from an ancient age came to live here. No living thing survived and the spectre of death hovered in waiting for her next victim." That foreword sets the tone for one of Hammer's most unclassifiable horrors. It's probably not best to ask why or how Megara (Prudence Hyman), sister of the Greek mythological monster Medusa, came to take up residence in Castle Borski. Just accept the fact and appreciate the intense autumnal Gothic atmosphere of the place. Peter Cushing plays a doctor who's part of a local effort to cover up the fact that people are being turned to stone. The role is out of the ordinary for him. Christopher Lee's visiting professor is the Van Helsing character.

Gothic (1986)

Ken Russell twists real historical and literary events into a wild psycho-sexual fantasy about Lord Byron (Gabriel Byrne), Percy Shelley (Julian Sands), his wife Mary (Natasha Richardson), and her step-sister Clair (Myriam Cyr) on a dark and stormy night. The film is filled with naked poets on the roof, women throwing fits and foaming at the mouth, bodies in bathtubs, laudanum and leeches, mucus and mud, perversions and phallic symbols, mechanical strippers and self-mutilation—the whole nine yards. Stephen Volks's script owes as much to Poe as it does to Mary Shelley. The same historical material provides the basis for *Haunted Summer.*

Gothika (2003)

Dr. Grey (Halle Berry) treats psychiatric patients at Woodward Penitentiary. After a lengthy prologue setting up a plethora of clues and possible plotlines, she finds herself accused of murder and incarcerated in the place. Inexplicable, possibly supernatural developments ensue. Insanity? Possession? Amnesia? Conspiracy? For a time, the *Jacob's Ladder* vibe and a cast filled with first-rate characters actors and Oscar nominees who don't act like they're slumming manage to overcome the sheer impossibility of it all, and the all too familiar dark-and-stormy-night trappings.

Graveyard Shift (1987)

Stephen Tsepses (Silvio Olivero) is a vampire who works as a New York cabbie. That's how he meets his prey, people who are about to die. He's a sympathetic sort who bites only people who want to be bitten. Enter Michelle (Helene Papas), a filmmaker with a host of problems. Though the action seems serious at first, director Gerard Ciccoritti is stylish to a fault, willing to sacrifice anything for flashy rock music visuals. The performances are well above average, and the film is one of the better exercises in undead romanticism.

Gremlins (1984)
Gremlins 2: The New Batch (1990)

The combination of executive producer Steven Spielberg's schmaltzy vision of smalltown life with monsters who are never quite as horrible as they ought to be just doesn't work. At first, the title critters are cute, little handpuppets, but if they're fed after midnight, they become grotesque creatures. Of course, our feckless hero Billy (Zach Galligan) does just that. Kids may be able to ignore the inherent contradictions in the film's two halves, but what will they make of the blackly humorous scene where Billy's girlfriend Kate (Phoebe Cates) explains why she hates Christmas?

In the superior sequel, the little critters from the original are even more insipid and obnoxious than they were before. But about midway through, everything changes and a streak of nasty humor makes this one better than the first film. Billy (Galligan) and Katie (Cates) now work in New York for Daniel Clamp (John Glover), a zillionaire of the Trump-Turner-Murdoch school. When the Gremlins multiply into reptilian multitudes, they take over his high-tech corporate headquarters in Manhattan. It's a target-rich environment, as they say, and the satiric jabs are right on target.

The Top Five Gigantic Lizard Movies

Godzilla
Curse of the Komodo
Dragon Wars: D-War
King Kong
Gamara

Grindhouse (2007)

Robert Rodriguez and Quentin Tarantino's affectionate homage to the cheap exploitation flicks of their youth is a very mixed bag. The theatrical release presented *Planet Terror* and *Deathproof* as a double feature, complete with trailers for then-fictional releases. The images were deliberately distressed with scratches, missing reels, and even a moment when the film appears to melt in the projector. Those of us who remember those days get a nice nostalgic buzz from the "Our Feature Presentation" intertitle with that wonderful music. As for the films, only Rodriguez's *Planet Terror* is true horror, a silly but complex comic zombie story. Tarantino's contribution is a disappointment. The story of serial killer stuntman Mike (Kurt Russell) ends with a magnificent chase sequence. But to get to it, you have to suffer through about an hour of tedious banal conversation. But, then, that's why your DVD player has a fast-forward button. That version is available on DVD. So are longer versions of each title.

Grudge, The (2004)

Takashi Shimizu's remake of his own Japanese film *Ju-On: The Grudge* certainly boasts American star power and all the elements that have become so familiar: creaky groaning sounds, images of drowning and water, a weird pale girl with hair hanging down in front of her face, and a weird pale little boy. Told in an interesting non-linear time scheme, the story begins with a suicide, and moves on to a small Tokyo house where American nurse (Sarah Michelle Gellar) is sent on her first job. A few shocking images punctuate the slowly paced action. The acting is very good, particularly by Ryo Ishibashi as a detective. Followed by a sequel.

Habitat (1997)

Despite a half-baked stereotyped premise and an uneven script, this off-beat sci-fi/eco-horror is really ambitious and more successful than not. In a near future when the ozone layer has disappeared, Hank Symes (Tchery Kayro), a renegade mad scientist who's madder than most, turns the interior of his house into a fertile Garden of Eden. It's a lush jungle in a sunblasted suburban wasteland where everything grows. His not-quite-so-mad wife, Clarissa (Alice Krige), thinks it's neat. Their teenaged son Andreas (Balthazar Getty) is horribly embarrassed. That conflict between the freaky parents and the kid who wants to fit in is the most interesting part of the film, along with the computer effects. The cardboard villains and the less than successful sets get in the way. Some of the one-with-nature dialogue comes off as bad Walt Whitman—"I swim with the plankton and frolic with the sperm!"—but the intentional comic touches are fine. Writer-director Rene Daalder also made *Massacre at Central High*.

Halloween (1978)
Halloween II (1981)
Halloween 3: Season of the Witch (1982)
Halloween 4: The Return of Michael Myers (1988)
Halloween 5: The Revenge of Michael Myers (1989)

Halloween: The Curse of Michael Myers (1995)
Halloween H20: Twenty Years Later (1998)
Halloween: Resurrection (2002)
Halloween (2007)
Halloween II (2009)

In 1978, John Carpenter made a "little" movie about three teenage girls and a madman, and changed the motion picture business. In terms of return on investment, *Halloween* quickly became the most profitable independent film ever made. Its influence on virtually every horror movie that's been made since then is incalculable. The implacable stalker who kills young people (usually while they're engaged in any sexual activity) has become a cliché, but Carpenter and Debra Hill—his co-writer, producer, and even co-director in some scenes—invented the character. The plot is simple and relentless. So is Carpenter's direction, and his famous score has become as iconic as anything by Bernard Herrmann or John Williams.

The earnest, uninspired sequel, *Halloween II,* is set directly after the original. Apparently unfazed by the second-story fall and the six slugs Dr. Loomis (Donald Pleasence) pumped into him at the end of the first film, Michael Myers wanders about collecting sharp instruments while Laurie (Jamie Lee Curtis) heads off to the hospital where most of the second half is set. Director Rick Rosenthal repeats the same scare gimmicks of the first film and they simply can't stand up to repetition. The various plot revelations actually diminish the raw power of Carpenter's original concept and put the series on a downward spiral that has continued.

Halloween III: Season of the Witch is a sequel in title only that has nothing to do with the others in the series. Instead it's a town-with-a-secret story that borrows freely from *Invasion of the Body Snatchers, Stepford Wives,* and even *Alien.* Dr. Challis (Tom Atkins) and Ellie (Stacey Nelkin) try to find out what happened to her father in the little town of Santa Mira. Yes, that's the home of the pod people, but something else is going on at the Silver Shamrock Novelty Co. there. Unfortunately, the script by director Tommy Lee Wallace works itself into a corner and can't find its way out. Reportedly, writer Nigel Kneale (*Quatermass and the Pit*) had his name removed. The effects are bloody and imaginative.

Eagle-eyed viewers of *Halloween 4: The Return of Michael Myers* will remember that at the end of "2," Michael Myers isn't merely dead, he's really

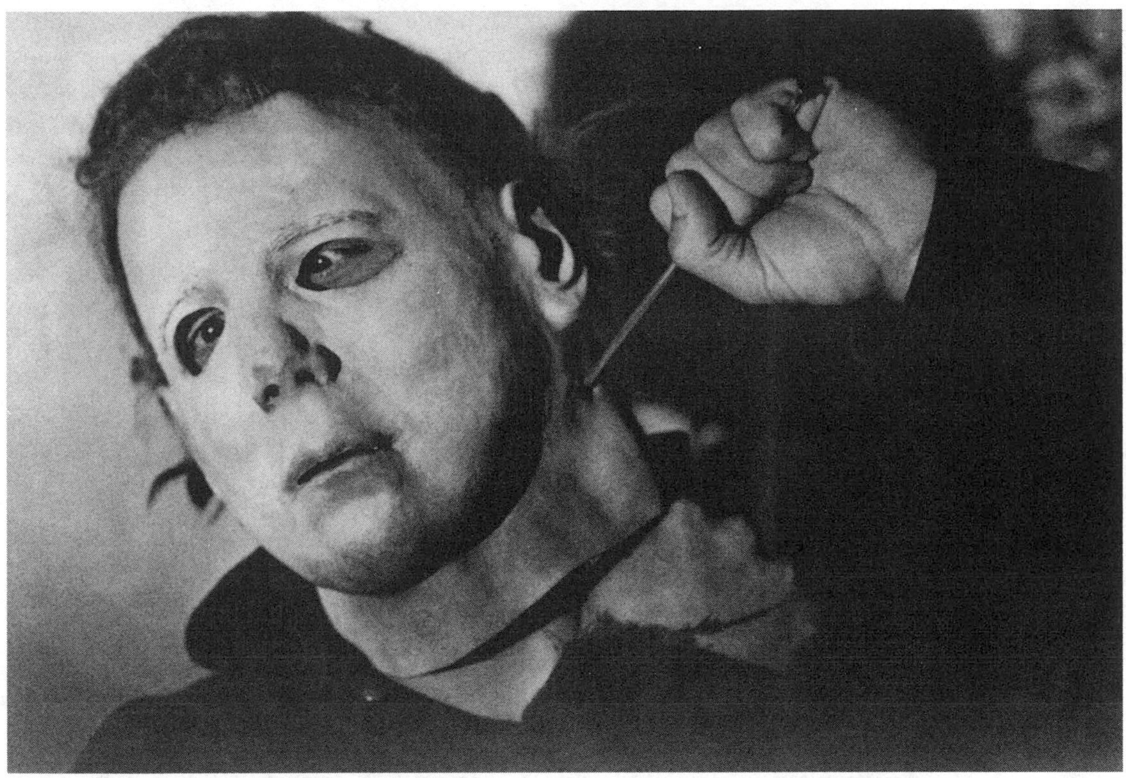

The original masked slasher flick, 1978's *Halloween* inspired the copycat *Friday the 13th* two years later.

most sincerely dead—morally, ethically, spiritually, physically, positively, absolutely, undeniably, and reliably DEAD. But, sensing a profit, studio executives decreed that he lives, hence this connect-the-dots installment. The plot contains nothing new but several scenes have the supernatural psychopath stalking a young child (Danielle Harris) and that's offensive.

At the time it was made, 1989, *Halloween 5: The Revenge of Michael Myers* set a low-water mark for the series. It has, of course, been eclipsed, but for overall lack of originality—not to mention contempt for its audience—this one remains hard to top. Beyond a few curious attempts to treat the material as comedy, the plot is the same old same old, presented with needlessly slick production values. Involving a psychic little girl (Michael Myers' niece) is inexcusable.

The film performed so poorly in theatrical release that six years passed before *Halloween 6: The Curse of Michael Myers* infected the multiplexes. It's a putrid little movie that opens with shots of pseudo-Satanic ritual where a blackrobed figure threatens a naked infant with a large knife. But after the

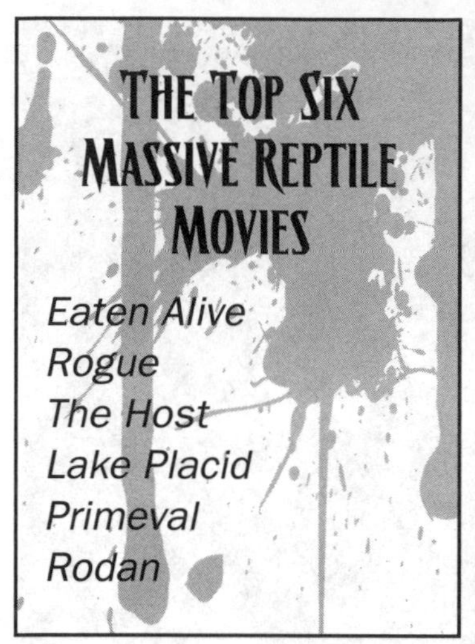

repugnant beginning, it quickly disintegrates into a virtually plotless series of predictable murders. The victims include an abusive father, his nearsighted wife, and an obnoxious radio talk show host. Veteran character actor Donald Pleasence returns as Dr. Loomis. This was his final role, completed just before he died.

The original series comes to a fine conclusion with *Halloween H20: Twenty Years Later*. Laurie Strode (Jamie Lee Curtis) has changed her name and runs a small private school in California when Michael Myers finds his way back. The young supporting cast is filled with now-familiar faces. The inclusion of Janet Leigh in a small role is inspired. Note the nice little music cue from Herrmann's *Psycho* score, and, yes, that's the same Ford from the film. It would have been a fine finish to the series, since once again, Michael is definitely kaput, but alas, it continued in 2002 with *Halloween: Resurrection*. The film begins with a flimsily cooked up reason for our boy to have survived the last film and eventually gets to its point of six students spending the night in the famous Haddonfield house on Halloween for an Internet reality show broadcast. You don't need to be psychic to see where it's going. The result is a solid step down from its overachieving predecessor.

In 2007, writer/director Rob Zombie remade the original film. It's much nastier in look, feel, and language, and goes into voluminous detail explaining how young Michael Myers came to be what he was. It proves, once again, that more can be less, much less. The film was so commercially successful that Zombie followed it with a predictably weak sequel, *Halloween 2,* three years later. More graphic hospital and medical details do not make the recycled story any better, or any scarier. Neither do a near record number of f-bombs.

Hand, The (1981)

Director Oliver Stone screws things up grandly with this abysmal exercise in psychological horror. After a troubled cartoonist (Michael Caine) loses his hand in an auto accident, his various marital, professional, and personal problems expand to monstrous proportions. Meanwhile, the missing appendage is crawling around and killing people. Is it real or is it his fevered imagination? By turns, the action is too literal and too abstract. Unlike's Stone's later work, the film lacks the stylistic flourishes or narrative drive to haul it over the long rough stretches. Yes, that's Stone as the one-handed tramp. Caine's haircut is more frightening than the silly effects.

Hands of Orloc, The (1960)

Concert pianist (Mel Ferrer) injured in an accident is given an executed murderer's hands and comes to believe that they have a mind of their own. The whole idea is more than a little silly and never rings true in a psychological sense, either. Yeah, it's the hands that make the respectable newlywed check into a seedy Marseilles hotel where he runs into an equally seedy Christopher Lee. Claude Bolling's jazzy score is more enjoyable. Some tapes are of less than perfect quality with scenes alternately muddy and bleached out.

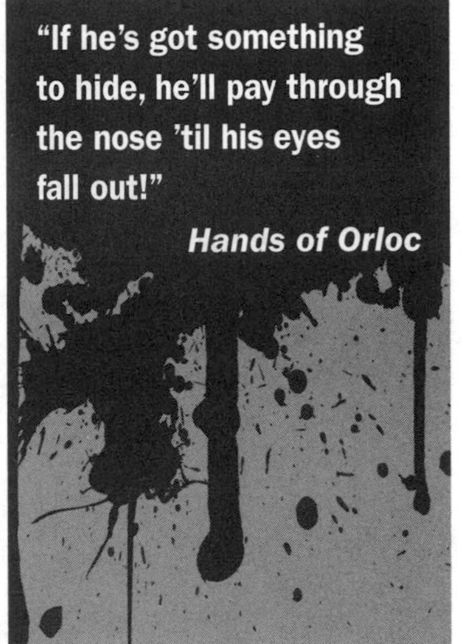

Hands of the Ripper (1971)

As a child, Anna (Angharad Rees) watches her father, Jack the Ripper, murder her mother. Not surprisingly then, she grows up to be a troubled, lethal young woman. Dr. Pritchard (Eric Porter), a pioneering Freudian psychoanalyst, wants to study and help her, though his motives are as much ambitious as altruistic. Director Peter Sasdy makes the violence an important and inventive aspect of the story, and he handles it with some facile camerawork. Writer L.W. Davidson also adds political and social dimensions to the believable characters. Though the cast is relatively unknown in this country, the acting is exemplary in both the leads and secondary characters. Hammer fans who have missed this sleeper are in for a treat.

Hanging Woman, The (1973)

Truly crazed Italian-Spanish production begins with a strong, rainy funeral scene that could have introduced a good Hammer film. Within minutes, the plot sails off to the farthest shores of exploitation with necrophilia, grave robbing, and the like. Serge (Stan Cooper, with an impressive early '70s helmet of blond hair) goes to a small town to collect an inheritance from his departed uncle, the Count. He also finds the seductive Countess (Dianik Zurakowska), Igor (Paul Naschy) the lecherous gravedigger, and humor beyond description. The hyperbolic plot twists are often ridiculous and always unpredictable. In many ways, the film can be seen as a precursor to the even more unhinged Italian "living dead" movies of the 1990s. Alternate titles: *Return of the Zombies; Beyond the Living Dead; La Orgia de los Muertos; Dracula, the Terror of the Living Dead; Orgy of the Dead; House of Terror.*

Hannibal (2001)

Of all the adaptations of Thomas Harris's Hannibal Lecter novels, Ridley Scott's is the most handsome. He and writers David Mamet and Steve Zaillian deftly translate a complex, wide-ranging, and darkly violent work into mainstream entertainment. The story contains so many extreme elements that Jodie Foster famously elected not to return to the role of Clarice Starling. Julianne Moore doesn't miss a step filling in. Villains Mason Verger (Gary Oldman) and Paul Krendler (Ray Liotta) are so monstrous that they turn Lecter into a relatively sympathetic protagonist. Anthony Hopkins wears the role like his most comfortable suit. If the third act doesn't go as far as Harris does in print, it's still surprisingly strong. Scott's DVD commentary is illuminating.

Hannibal Rising (2006)

For me, Thomas Harris's fourth Lecter novel and its adaptation are a bridge too far. When we know too much about a character as memorable as the doctor, he loses some of his mystery. Harris craftily and skillfully transformed him from the supporting figure in *Red Dragon* to the charismatic central figure of *Silence of the Lambs* to the hero of *Hannibal.* Filling in the details of his early life as a child caught up in the fighting on the European Eastern Front does him few favors. That said, Harris and director Peter Webber do spin a good, involved revenge yarn. Production values and performances are fine.

Harvest, The (1992)

Variations on a popular urban myth posit a middle class man on a trip who meets a sexy girl, gets drunk, and wakes up the next day minus a kidney or some other major organ. Charlie Pope (Miguel Ferrer) is a screenwriter who goes to Mexico to research a murder. Natalie (Leilani Sarelle Ferrer) is the very sexy girl he meets. If he's not completely successful with the resolution of that premise, director David Marconi gives the film a fever dream quality that carries it over the rough spots. Recommended.

Haunted (1995)

Handsome, classy ghost story harkens back to such atmospheric productions as *The Uninvited.* In 1928, professor and spiritualist debunker David

Ash (Aidan Quinn) goes to a country estate in answer to an old woman's cry for help. Something terrible is going on, she says. But, upon arriving, Ash is more interested in Christina (Kate Beckinsale), an uninhibited young woman who admires his book. Ash isn't so sure about her brother (Anthony Andrews) who claims, "We're all mad, you know." Based on James Herbert's novel, the script combines a nostalgic evocation of the period with various sexy undercurrents and a teasing attitude toward the supernatural. Director Lewis Gilbert (*Alfie, Educating Rita, Shirley Valentine*) handles it all with a sure hand throughout, and tosses in several surprises toward the end when many fans will think that they've got everything figured out.

Haunted Summer (1988)

Historical horror based on a real event tries to turn its famous characters—the great Romantic poets, Shelley and Byron, and Mary Shelley, author of *Frankenstein*—into real, flesh and blood human beings. The year is 1816 when all of them lived together for a time in Byron's Swiss villa. Shelley (Eric Stoltz) is fond of morphine cocktails, skinny-dipping, and spitballs. Byron (Philip Anglim) prefers smoking opium. He's also a sexual tyrant who carries on overlapping affairs with partners of both sexes. It's all just too too decadent. It's also too slow and oddly comic when it may not mean to be. If all of this seems more than a little familiar, it's because Ken Russell handled exactly the same material in his wonderfully weird horror-comedy *Gothic.*

Haunting, The (1963, 1999)

Director Robert Wise has a mixed track record in horror. *The Body Snatcher* is brilliant, while *Audrey Rose* is an embarrassment. Though this effort has been widely praised by mainstream critics, it remains seriously flawed. The story of psychics (Julie Harris and Claire Bloom) and a scientist (Richard Johnson) investigating a haunted house is famous for its restraint; there are no graphic visual scares. The same can't be said of the ponderous, oppressive music and the overstated dialogue. Some of the breathless acting has aged poorly, too. Though the film is based on Shirley Jackson's novel, it feels like a play with the claustrophobic house substituting for the proscenium. To be fair, the story is more effective and enjoyable if it's seen as a character study of a complex, emotionally damaged woman.

The 1999 remake is ponderous and heavy-handed. Cavernous sets and big computer effects dwarf an ensemble cast that never generates any screen chemistry. Owen Wilson's smart-alecky humor is particularly out of place.

Haunting in Connecticut, The (2009)

Lifting several pages from the *Amityville/Exorcist* playbook, this "based-on-a-true-story" haunted house take boasts first-rate production values and a fine cast including Virginia Madsen as a mother worried about her son (Kyle Gallner) who's struggling with cancer treatments. Beyond that, the scares contrast things that go bump in the night with large intimidating medical devices. This is the kind of film where people go wandering down dark creaky basement stairs in the middle of the night for no real reason, but wait ... that was just a dream.

Haunting of Molly Hartley, The (2008)

A blandly attractive cast and a low energy level do little to recommend this passionless possession tale. Our young heroine (Haley Bennett) hears whispery voices and experiences nose-bleeds when she enters a ritzy new private school. Why? Could it have anything to do with her mother's attempt to murder her, and mom's subsequent incarceration in a loony bin? Curiously, several important scenes take place on bathroom floors. Beyond a few pointless directorial flourishes, the scares are clichés.

He Knows You're Alone (1980)

Not content to rip off John Carpenter's plot for *Halloween,* the brazen makers of this by-the-numbers slasher flick also lift his music! Caitlin O'Heaney screams well and loudly in the lead. Scott Parker's script has a few bright moments that survive Armand Mastroianni's ham-fisted direction. In one key scene, he does everything but superimpose an arrow on the screen to call your attention to a missing knife. Fans of the genre will hoot with derision.

Heartless (2009)

Ambitious British import is equally concerned with characters and scares. Young Jamie (Jim Sturgess) is painfully shy because he has a large port wine birthmark on his face. One night in a rough neighborhood, he sees something that might be a monster. But writer-director Philip Ridley quickly shifts gears and the plot remains unpredictable throughout. Comparisons to *Urban Ghost Story* and *Attack the Block* are not out of place but they don't fully describe the film, either. Both script and the ensemble acting are excellent. Watch for Eddie Marsan in an important and slyly comic cameo.

Hell Night (1981)

Four college pledges, including Marti (Linda Blair), must spend the night in haunted Garth Manor for their initiation. Their friends mean to scare them but the ghostly murderer may still be alive. Cast, plot, and setting make this one a combination of *The Exorcist, Halloween,* and *Animal House.* Actually, the setting is strong and this is one of the better dead-teen flicks, coming as it does near the beginning of the cycle.

Hellboy (2004)
Hellboy II: The Golden Army (2008)

Guillermo del Toro's comedy/horror/action/fantasy stands right up there with *Ghostbusters.* Our crimson hero (Ron Perlman) is a demon whose relationship with his girlfriend Liz (Selma Blair) troubles him almost as much as his day job of saving the world from the forces of darkness. The trick with this kind of big-budget escapism is to keep all of the elements in balance and the filmmakers do. Naturally enough, the sequel lacks the freshness of the first film, but the CGI creatures, great and small, are properly disgusting, inventive, and ornate, and the humor may be a bit more pointed. In both, Perlman is able to give his character personality and believable emotions despite the heavy makeup.

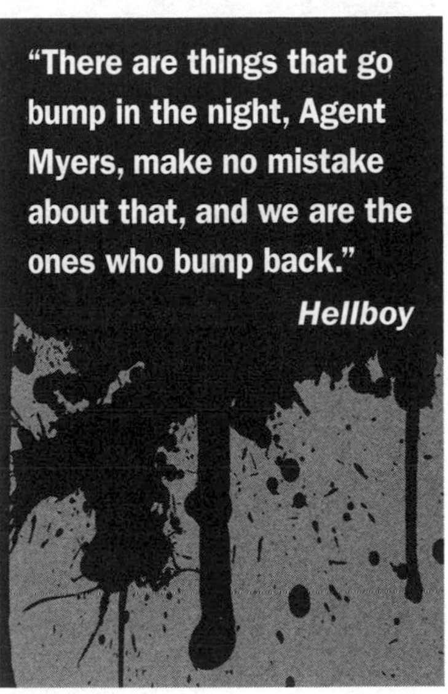

Hello, Mary Lou: Prom Night II

See Prom Night

Hellraiser (1987)
Hellbound: Hellraiser II (1988)
Hellraiser III: Hell on Earth (1992)

Author Clive Barker makes a credible directorial debut in this tale of ultimate pleasure and pain. Those come from the Cenobites, five creatures who are conjured up by an intricate puzzle box, and who descend upon a damaged family (Andrew Robinson, Clare Higgins, Ashley Laurence). Though the tricky story is bloody, it doesn't wallow in gore. Four of the Cenobites are genuinely

The Cenobite leader in author and director Clive Barker's *Hellraiser*.

frightening figures, but the fifth, and allegedly the most terrifying, is a guy who's got his head where his butt ought to be.

Following the rules for sequels, *Hellbound* amplifies the most popular elements of the first and omits the less-than-successful aspects. It can't replace the originality. Kirstie (Ashley Laurence) is recovering in a sanatorium. Her psychiatrist, Dr. Channard (creepily underplayed by Kenneth Cranham) knows more about her strange experiences than he should. Despite a preposterous plot and a weak ending, the film still has its moments, particularly for fans of Barker, who is executive producer.

The series follows a predictably smooth downward curve in originality and quality with *Hellraiser III.* Too-familiar exploding heads and rattling chains have replaced the Cenobites. When variations of them finally do show up, they're almost tongue-in-cheek (or at least camera-in-cheek). TV reporter Joey (Terry Ferrell) tracks down the story behind an emergency room death and eventually finds Pinhead (Doug Bradley). The film is fairly well acted, but like virtually all sequels these days, it over-relies on elaborate sets, slick visuals, and a conventional plot. Several more direct-to-video and DVD sequels have followed.

Henry: Portrait of a Serial Killer (1986)

John McNaughton's fact-based chiller is simply one of the most disturbing and frightening horror films anyone has ever made. Henry, (grimly underplayed by Michael Rooker) is an illiterate drifter who moves from job to job, and kills at random. Though Henry claims to have been abused as a child, that doesn't explain him. Neither does the sexual element that some of the murders contain. Killing is simply something he does without emotion or pleasure. McNaughton tells the story with a deliberately flat, documentary style: stark naturalistic lighting and acting, Midwest locations, grainy color, limited music. The film was rated X for violence and subject matter, but has been released on tape and DVD without a rating. It is definitely not for kids, and older audiences looking for titillating violence or elaborate effects will be disappointed. In terms of onscreen acts of violence, *Henry* contains only a tiny fraction of the average *Friday the 13th* or *Elm Street* flick. But this is a real nightmare and these suggested horrors—including an unexpected ending—are much more terrifying than graphic cinematic schlock. Followed by a lesser 1996 sequel.

Hide and Seek (2005)

Distraught over the death of his wife, Dr. David Calloway (Robert De Niro) moves from his palatial Park Avenue apartment to bucolic Woodland, NY, pop. 2,206. His young daughter Emily (Dakota Fanning) is silent and withdrawn until she meets an imaginary friend named Charlie. To describe any of the horrors that slowly ensue would give the game away, not that there's really much of a game to give away. The filmmakers were aiming at another *Sixth Sense* but this one's not in the same league. Lights go out at regular and predictable intervals. A larger problem is a cast of dark and not particularly interesting characters. The DVD proudly boasts "4 alternative endings." That tells me that considerable indecision was involved. Considering the cast, a disappointment.

Hideous Sun Demon (1959)

Archetypal monster-created-by-nuclear-radiation story begins with this ominous voiceover narration: "Immediately after the launching of U.S. satellites number one and number three into outer space, newspaper headlines across the country told the world of a new radiation hazard from the sun, far more deadly than cosmic rays. An obscure scientist, my colleague Dr. Gilbert MacKenna, had already discovered this danger from the sun. This is his story." The unlucky Gilbert (producer/director Robert Clarke) is exposed to a new isotope—pesky things, those isotopes—and comes to realize that every time he goes out in the sun, he turns into the title character and commits unspeakable acts. Does Gil put up the convertible top on his MG? Of course not.

High Tension (2003)

Alexandre Aja's first horror film begins as a French variation on the American "redneck" school with two pretty city girls (Cécile de France and Maïwann) driving out for a country vacation and running across a monstrous, hulking murderer (Philippe Nahon). (All three are excellent in offbeat roles.) The stripped down story is told with violence so graphic that it verges on the cartoonish, though other aspects have a strong naturalistic feel. But just

The Top Eight Big Monsters on Campus Movies

Burn Witch Burn
Sorority Row
House on Sorority Row
Monster on the Campus
Soul Survivors
The Hole
Suspiria
The Woods

when you think things have settled down, a wacky plot twist arrives out of nowhere. It's really so bizarre that it turns the whole film into a comedy of violence, slightly reminiscent of *American Psycho*.

Hills Have Eyes, The (1977, 2006)
Hills Have Eyes Part II, The (1985)
Hills Have Eyes II, The (2007)

Wes Craven's companion piece to *Texas Chainsaw Massacre* deals with subject matter that's actually more revolting, but it isn't presented with the same unrelenting intensity. Three generations of a Midwestern family head out into the desert in a station wagon towing a camper trailer (complete with air freshener) and run smack into a degenerate clan of subhuman cannibal savages. In the end, though, it's hard to say who is the more savage. That's Craven's unsubtle point, and for low-budget, violent exploitation it certainly delivers the goods. The villains are a full evolutionary step down from the drug dealers in his *Last House on the Left*.

Like most sequels, the 1985 film is a transparent attempt to milk a title for a few more bucks. Motorcycle-racing teens—who happen to have a drum of highly explosive "superfuel" in their bus—go back out into the desert. A couple of cannibals from the first film, including bald Michael Berryman, are still hanging around, etc. etc. More sophisticated production values are not necessarily an improvement. The whole thing lacks the raw reptilian manipulative power of the original.

The 2006 *Hills Have Eyes* follows the playbook for twenty-first-century remakes with a cast of conventionally attractive actors, slick photography, zippy editing, and more graphic violence. French director Alexandre Aja brings his smashmouth approach to grotesque action. It's probably one of the better entries in the spotty collection of twenty-first-century interpretations. That should not be considered a recommendation. Aja's original films are much better.

For a sequel to a remake, the 2007 *Hills Have Eyes II* is about what you'd expect. Two years later, the mutants are still hanging around in the desert. They attack soldiers who are setting up electronic monitoring equipment and then a group of green National Guard trainees. The film shares the burnt yellow color scheme of Aja's work. It has nothing to do with the 1985 sequel.

Hitcher, The (1986)

Cult favorite is a rare horror that makes a virtue of its low budget. Jim Halsey (C. Thomas Howell) is an innocent young man driving across a lonely desert highway where he picks up Ryder (Rutger Hauer), one of the most believably terrifying psychos ever to ooze onto the screen. Or is he something else? Eric Red's (*Near Dark*) script is properly vague. For a time. You don't want to know anything more about the plot. Director Robert Harmon sets the story against a sunblasted, dusty Western landscape. If he can't maintain complete intensity to the end, he comes close enough. Jazzman Mark Isham gives him a subdued haunted score to set the mood. This one would make a great triple-bill with *Nature of the Beast* and *Duel.* Followed by a sequel and a 2007 remake.

Hole, The (2001)

Liz (Thora Birch) stumbles, bloody and beaten, into a deserted but clearly expensive private school. The body of the film is her explanation of what happened to her and her friends (Keira Knightley, Desmond Harrington, and Daniel Brocklebank) to a police psychologist (Embeth Davidtz). It turns out to be a complicated, malleable story. Credit writers Guy Burt and Ben Court and director Nick Hamm with a new approach to the familiar "beautiful nasty rich kids" premise, a deft touch with violence, and for stopping on precisely the right note.

Hollow Man (2000)

Big-budget updating of *The Invisible Man* is a showcase for some spectacular computer effects. Brilliant young doctor Sebastian Caine (Kevin Bacon) and his team have just perfected a method to render a primate invisible and to return it to visibility. But they don't tell their Pentagon superiors. Why? Because the not-so-good doctor wants to test it on himself first. Of course, he goes just as mad as Claude Rains did in the original and in that regard, Bacon's cockiness is just right for the character. Director Paul Verhoeven emphasizes the most graphic and tawdry exploitation elements of the story. In the end, though, it all settles down to good old-fashioned explosions and fires in a gloriously pyrotechnic conclusion.

Horror Chamber of Dr. Faustus, The (1960)

It's difficult to overestimate the influence of Georges Franju's film, particularly on the European horrors of the 1960s and '70s. The story of a doctor—in this case played by Pierre Brasseur—trying to restore a young woman's beauty (Edith Scob) with the help of another woman (Alida Valli) is one that would be revisited often, particularly by Jesús Franco. Franju handles it much more subtly, though his explicit surgery scenes pave the way for the bloody excesses to come. The film bears some similarities to *Psycho* too, with an equally strong conclusion.

Horror Express (1972)

Spanish production is set in pre-revolutionary Russia. Imagine *The Thing* on the Trans-Siberian Express. Archeologist Christopher Lee has found a critter frozen in the ice and is taking it to England for study. Rival Peter Cushing is jealous and wants to find out what's happening, but said critter has no intention of going to England or anywhere else. Then toss in a mad monk and Telly Savalas as a crazed cossack. The railway setting works well, too, making this one classy fun with a slight satiric edge.

Horror Hotel (1960)

In an early role, Christopher Lee firmly establishes his horror credentials as Prof. Driscoll who sends young Nan Barlow (Venetia Stevenson) off for some primary research in Whitewood, Mass., where a witch was burned centuries before. George Baxt's script owes a bit to *Burn, Witch, Burn* and can be seen as a precursor to *Psycho.* With its lovely black-and-white photography and fog-shrouded atmosphere, the film really is a "lost" milestone of the 1960s. Its influence on such films as *Salem's Lot, Carnival of Souls,* and many of the Italian horrors of the '80s and '90s is not hard to spot.

Horror of Dracula

See Dracula

Christopher Lee (left) and Peter Cushing star in *Horror Express.*

Horror of Frankenstein (1970)

In one of Hammer's last variations on the famous tale, it's obvious that everyone involved was more interested in having fun with the material than in telling a serious story. This Victor Frankenstein (Ralph Bates) is an amoral libertine who blithely kills his father and then moves in with Dad's mistress (Kate O'Mara). When he gets around to his "experiments" he hires a comic body snatcher (Dennis Price) who steals the movie. The monster is played by David Prowse who went on to be Darth Vader in the *Star Wars* trilogy. Writer/director Jimmy Sangster is an old hand at this kind of material. It's enjoyable if you're in the mood for fairly heavy-handed gallows humor, particularly in the last reel. But it's far from Hammer's best work.

Host, The (2006)

An American military doctor in Korea orders that toxic chemicals be dumped down a sink that drains into the Han River. Four years later, a hungry beastie emerges from the water. The CGI creation looks like a giant tadpole with too many legs and teeth, and a prehensile tail. In its first attack, it snatches Hyun-seo (Ah-sung Ko), the plucky young daughter of the immature Gang-Du (Kang-ho Song). Before it's all over their entire extended family will search for the girl while attempting to evade the incompetent authorities. To American audiences, the Stoogian histrionics are funnier than they're meant to be. At least, I think that's the case. Some cultural differences are difficult to bridge, but they count for little against the agile critter and the inventive plotting.

Hostel (2005)
Hostel: Part II (2007)
Hostel: Part III (2011)

Two American college guys (Jay Hernandez and Derek Richardson) are bumming around Belgium with their new Icelandic pal (Eythor Gudjonsson). The cheap drugs are great but the girls aren't exactly what they're looking for. A questionable guy tells them of a place near Bratislava where the hot Euro-babes go crazy over foreigners. They head east and find that it's true. At first. By the time they learn the truth, they're in a world of excruciating pain. The real strength of Eli Roth's horror is in the resolution. Any number of films can set up grotesquely sadistic villains, only to fall back on clichés and easy scares in the third act. This one gets stronger all the way through.

The sequel continues directly from the end of the first film, going into more detail about the workings of the organization responsible for the horrors. The scene shifts to Italy with an homage to *Torso,* and introduces three young women. Though it's far superior to most movies that end with *II,* somehow it doesn't work as well as the first.

The series gets some of its mean mojo back in the third outing. Though the Las Vegas setting throws off a certain *Hangover* vibe, the film works through inventive reversals of audience expectations, leading to exceptionally weird moments, often seen from the victims' point of view.

Hour of the Wolf (1968)

Ingmar Bergman's foray into horror is an unconventional story that ignores conventional narrative structure for a more dreamlike surrealism. Johan Borg (Max von Sydow) and his wife (Liv Ullmann) live in a cottage on an isolated island. Their supposedly simple life is complicated by a gaggle of bizarre neighbors. Or are they ghosts? Visions? One is a Lugosi-like figure and the others are grotesques of various stripes. They constantly crowd and threaten Johan, making key scenes intensely claustrophobic. Sven Nykvist's black-and-white photography is striking, but despite the strength of the images and tightly wrapped performances from the leads, Bergman is very much an acquired taste.

House (1986)
House II: The Second Story (1987)

Roger Cobb (William Katt) is a horror novelist suffering writer's block. You'd think that inheriting the haunted house where he grew up would be just the thing for him, but no. Instead of inspiration, he gets some of the cheesiest Vietnam flashbacks ever put on film. A few of the effects have a little shock value, but that's about all. The attempts at humor undercut the horror and the story disintegrates in the last third, becoming a "lite" version of Sam Raimi's *Evil Dead* movies. The basic problem is that the house itself is too obviously a set. Followed by a sequel.

In the last scene of the slow sequel-in-name-only, our hero Jesse (Arye Gross) straps on his six-shooter, gets into a horse-drawn wagon, and rides off into the sunset with his best friend (Jonathan Stark), a sacrificial virgin (Devin Devasquez), a baby pterodactyl, and a critter that's a cross between a puppy and a caterpillar. Unfortunately, the road to that lunatic conclusion isn't much fun. The film follows no internal logic. Anything can happen at any time. The humor seems to be aimed at a pre-teen audience but the violence involves lots of blood and exploding heads. Why bother?

House of Dark Shadows (1970)

The first feature taken from the popular TV series isn't taken quite far enough. It hurriedly introduces a large cast of characters without fully explaining their relationships or the setting—all of which were familiar to viewers in the early 1970s—and then lets the story drag along at a lugubrious pace. That's part of the suspense of an episodic soap opera but it's completely wrong for a film. This one has also aged poorly with a raw, grainy look on video that compares poorly to the Hammer and Corman films of the same era. Barnabas Collins (Jonathan Frid) predates the "good" Byronic vampire popularized by Anne Rice. Here, he's revived in the present, finds a double of his lost love (Kathryn Leigh Scott), etc. etc. Once things get cranked up, they run more smoothly, but the movie is still too slow with an overwrought score that doesn't help.

House of Dracula (1945)

Sequel to *House of Frankenstein* brings Universal's most popular characters—Dracula (John Carradine), the Wolfman (Lon Chaney Jr.), Frankenstein's Monster (Glenn Strange)—back for a second ensemble effort. Nothing's particularly scary. In the opening shot, the strings holding up the bat are clearly visible. Dr. Edelman (Onslow Stevens) tries to "cure" the various monsters, until Drac puts his moves on the doc's glamorous nurse (Martha O'Donnell). Except for that bat, the production values and sets are up to the studio's standard, and it's fun to watch a veteran cast going through familiar paces.

House of Frankenstein (1944)

One dark and stormy night, Prof. Lampini's (George Zucco) Chamber of Horrors sideshow is passing by Newstadt Prison where Dr. Neiman (Boris Karloff) and his hunchback Daniel (J. Carrol Naish) escape. The fifth in Universal's series isn't the equal of the first three, but it's thoroughly enjoyable formula entertainment from a studio that knew exactly what it was doing. The story is divided into two halves, both moving rapidly and with a remarkable amount of physical action. The ice cave set (used a year before in *Frankenstein Meets the Wolfman*) is grand. John Carradine fits right in as Dracula. Once again, the Monster (Glenn Strange) and the Wolfman (Lon Chaney Jr.) have issues.

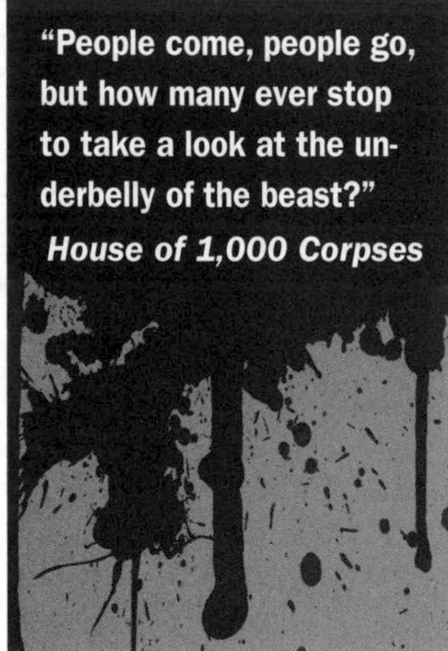

"People come, people go, but how many ever stop to take a look at the underbelly of the beast?"
House of 1,000 Corpses

House of 1,000 Corpses (2003)

Rob Zombie's directorial debut comes close to recreating the mood of psychotic dread established in the original *Texas Chainsaw Massacre*. It may be built of borrowed and stolen parts, but Zombie's film wanders much farther afield. There's nothing original about the premise—four naïve city kids encounter a family of backwoods sadists—but Zombie attacks it with enthusiasm, humor, and ingenuity. Just when you think he's going to settle into a well-worn groove, he angles off in another direction. That's most notable in the third act when the action gets really strange. Followed by a more conventional sequel, *The Devil's Rejects*.

House of the Dead (2003)

Five college students want to go to a big rave that's happening on an offshore island. They catch a ride with Capt. Kirk (yes!) (Jurgen Prochnow) on his fishing boat. Zombies ensue. The adaptation of a video game actually goes into first-person shooter mode from time to time. The rest is lots of shooting, slo-mo, and so-so zombie makeup.

Horror movie veteran Vincent Price goes mad after he is disfigured in a fire in *House of Wax*.

House of the Devil (2009)

Ti West's debut is engaging, original, and flawed. Desperate to raise rent money, college sophomore Samantha (a winning Jocelin Donohue) agrees to a suspicious babysitting job. She arrives at a creepy Addams-family style mansion where Mr. and Mrs. Ulman (Tom Noonan and Mary Woronov) explain that they've been less than completely truthful. West deftly sets up the place and the feeling that something's not quite right. He maintains a measured pace, too measured for some tastes. Throughout, the story seems somewhat underwritten, and details are sketchy in the big finish. Even so, this one is a promising beginning.

House of Wax (1953)

In its original theatrical release, this remake of *Mystery of the Wax Museum* was part of the 3D craze of the 1950s. In 2D, it's a variation on *Phantom*

The Top Eleven Most Appetizing Cannibal Movies

Terror at Red Wolf Inn
Ravenous
Silence of the Lambs
Hannibal
Motel Hell
Texas Chainsaw Massacre
Night of the Living Dead
Tombs of the Blind Dead
The Untold Story
Wrong Turn
Frontier(s)

of the Opera. A subdued Vincent Price is the sculptor who is disfigured in a fire and driven mad. His heavy, glopped-on monster makeup is nothing much. The real fun comes in the elaborate laboratory scenes, complete with what looks like a giant hot tub filled with bubbling hot Pepto-Bismol-pink wax.

House of Wax (2005)

Slowly paced town-with-a-secret horror saves most of the good stuff for the second half. Six friends on the way to a football game find themselves stranded in the little town of Ambrose looking for help. Instead they find Mrs. Trudy's World Famous House of Wax and unfriendly rednecks. The characters may be a bit more developed than the usual stereotypes, but only a bit and they're not particularly likable. Some humor helps, and the town itself is kind of neat. The big fiery finish has a surreal Daliesque quality. (The plot has nothing to do with the 1953 Vincent Price film.)

House on Haunted Hill (1958 & 1999) Return to House on Haunted Hill (2007)

Secret passages, the vat of acid in the basement, walking skeletons, ghosts in the hallway, even the proverbial dark and stormy night—they're all part of William Castle's good-natured collection of clichés. Eccentric millionaire Vincent Price offers a disparate group—test pilot, shop girl, columnist, doctor—$10,000 apiece to spend the night in a house where gruesome murders have been committed. You don't need three guesses to figure out the rest, and you get the feeling, right or wrong, that everybody had fun on the sets of Castle productions. Nobody had any illusions about art; this is unapologetic cinematic popcorn with lots of salt and butter. For those who don't know, Castle was affectionately spoofed in *Matinee.*

In the 1999 remake, Geoffrey Rush turns in an energetic, toothsome performance in the lead. The price for the sleepover has gone up to a million, and the action is much more graphic and bloody, particularly in the scenes set in Vannacutt's Asylum for the Criminally Insane where the doctors are worse than the patients. Both films revel in their cheesiness.

The sequel, *Return to House on Haunted Hill,* was made in Bulgaria and doesn't come close to either of the earlier films. The script is silly; the effects are so-so. At least it's short.

House on Sorority Row (1983)

Filmed near Baltimore, this tepid little time-waster came near the end of the first wave of "dead-teenager" movies and helped to send the genre into welcome oblivion for several years. Some of the sisters think that they've killed their strict housemother, but since they're about to throw a big party, they decide to chuck the old gal into the swimming pool and proceed as planned. Before long, sorority sisters are being stabbed, slashed, and gored, and writer-director Mark Rossman abandons any pretense at logic.

House on Straw Hill (1976)

Offbeat exploitation mixes inventive soft-core sex (some of it quite funny) with bloody psycho-revenge elements. The key characters are a successful novelist (Udo Kier), his girlfriend (Fiona Richmond), and his new secretary (Linda Hayden). Each has secrets to keep. A couple of rapacious rubes fill out the cast. Sources claim that censors cut thirty minutes from the running time which might account for the uncertain shifts in tone. Even so, this one deserves its cult following.

House that Vanished, The (1974)

Flighty English model Valerie (Andrea Allan) wanders out into the country with her beau Terry (Alex Leppard) on a foggy night. In a grim dark house, they witness a murder. The next day, it doesn't seem so real, but other questions remain. The rest is about half exploitation and half solid horror. A scruffy, realistically middle class milieu serves the story well and balances the Gothic aspects. Though she's not a particularly versatile actress, Andrea Allan is an attractive heroine. The most effective moments contain twisted echoes of *Psycho.* Director José Larraz takes a similarly evocative approach in his cult favorite, *Vampyres.*

Howling, The (1981)
Howling II: Your Sister Is a Werewolf (1985)
Howling III: The Marsupials (1987)
Howling IV: The Original Nightmare (1988)
Howling: New Moon Rising (1995)

Director Joe Dante and writer John Sayles have created one of the smartest and funniest werewolf movies ever, and Rob Bottin's makeup is the equal of their story. The film is a particular treat for horror fans because it's filled with jokes and appearances by some of the most familiar faces in the genre. (Yes, that's Roger Corman as the man fishing for change in the phone booth, and Sayles himself as the morgue attendant.) The plot successfully combines realistic contemporary horror—in the form of a serial murderer-rapist (Robert Picardo) who's fixated on a TV newswoman (Dee Wallace)—with semi-traditional lycanthropy. More importantly, the story has an emotional realism which is, admittedly, sometimes overplayed by Wallace. The conclusion is as strong as the rest, making this one required viewing. By the way, it has virtually nothing to do with the several sequels that have followed.

In the first of those, *The Howling II: Your Sister Is a Werewolf,* real and unintentional humor commingle to create a genuinely bizarre alternative classic. Christopher Lee appears to be justifiably embarrassed to find himself in this nonsense. Though Sybil Danning is only on-screen briefly and has to play her big love scene while sprouting fur, the producers make the most of her presence. They were so enamored of the moment where she rips her dress off that they repeat it not once, not twice, but ten—count 'em, ten—times during the closing credits.

Director Philippe Mora, also responsible for the semi-uproarious adaptation of Whitley Strieber's *Communion,* attempts to mix scares and laughs in *Howling III: The Marsupials,* but completely misses the sly humor of the original. Jerboa (Imogen Annesley) is a psychic Australian werewolf who leaves the country for the big city and immediately lands a role in a cheap horror flick. Curiously, a defecting Russian ballerina suffers a similar telepathic-lycanthropic condition. The writing, acting, and editing suggest that the humor is meant to be parody, but can a bad movie really spoof other bad movies? And even if it can, do you want to watch that?

The title of *Howling IV* is the only link to the original. The plot contains all the right ingredients for decent cheap thrills: novelist (Romy Windsor) recovering from nervous breakdown goes to the country to relax and hears strange animal noises at night. Why are the locals so strange? Is her husband part of their conspiracy? Is he fooling around with the sultry shopkeeper in town? Why is she having visions of a short nun? Alas, these goofy goings-on generate no suspense. The whole thing is almost saved by some really bad acting, but fans have seen better.

In the long and sorry history of multiple sequels, *Howling: New Moon Rising* may well be the most egregious and inexcusable. Redneck humor and amateur acting make the horror/comedy look (and sound) like the *Hee-Haw* version of *The Wolfman.* Australian writer-producer-star-director-editor and post production supervisor Clive Turner is the man responsible. When his characters aren't engaged in endless boring conversations or telling penis jokes, they're playing "Deep In the Heart of Texas" on their zippers or—worse yet!—line dancing. This is one of those rare movies that you watch with a growing sense of wonder as you tell yourself that it cannot possibly get any worse and then it does—over and over again. The negligible effects are a short step up from home movies. More low-budget sequels have followed.

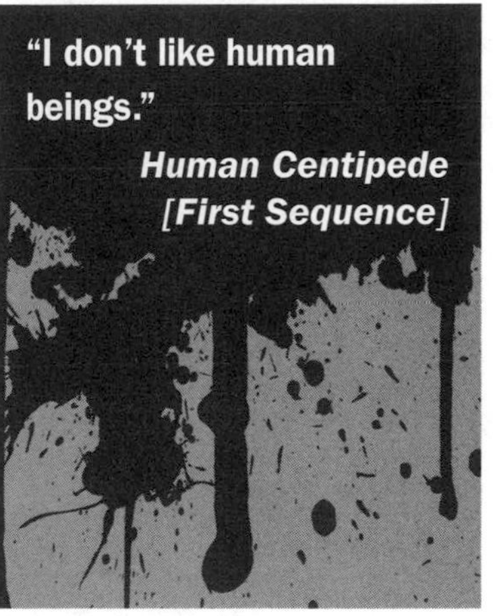

Human Centipede [First Sequence] (2009) Human Centipede [Full Sequence] (2011)

In the first film, mad doctor Heiter (Dieter Laser) kidnaps passers-by and subjects them to anatomical experiments. He hopes to attach a Japanese businessman and two American girls via their gastrointestinal tracts. In one extremely strange scene, he describes the operation with illustrations that make it look and sound like it comes from an Ikea catalog. Laser resembles a really creepy Udo Kier, and that certainly adds something, but the film has such a clinical detachment from its subject matter that it's more disgusting, in an intellectual sense, than frightening.

That is certainly not the case with the "meta" sequel, though it, too, is a comedy that's so bizarre viewers are not really meant to suspend disbelief. Where the first film is done in crisp pastel colors, the second is squalid black and white. The protagonist (Laurence R. Harvey) is a suety slob who is obsessed with the first film and wants to surpass it with twelve unwilling subjects. It's the gamiest of gamy humor. Personally, I find both to be so extreme that they're interesting curiosities but not effective horror.

Humanoids from the Deep (1980, 1997)

The 1980 original lives up to its title as one of the genuinely great drive-in exploitation flicks. In the first shots, veteran B-movie director Barbara Peeters establishes a strong Pacific Northwest locale, and then proceeds to tell an unembarrassed story of giant, mutant salmon monsters (i.e. guys in drippy, long-armed rubber suits created by Rob Bottin) whose accelerated evolutionary drive forces them out of the ocean and onto the shore to mate with human women! It ends with a grand nighttime attack on a waterfront fair.

In the 1997 remake, evil executives at the Canco fishery have been dumping a green growth hormone that looks like industrial-strength creme de menthe into the bay to increase their catch. Instead, they create giant mutant salmon monsters. Before you can say "Sushi!" guys in rubber suits are chowing down on beach parties and skinny dippers. This low-budget effort lacks the sense of place and unashamed cheesiness of the 1980 film, not to mention its originality. In their place is a too-ridiculous-for words sexual angle. A couple of o.k. explosions and flaming fishmen are all this one's got to offer. Find the first film.

Hunchback of Notre Dame, The (1923, 1939, 1957, 1982)

The first filmed version of Victor Hugo's enduring potboiler is really more a big-budget melodrama than true horror. It's dated, grainy, and overblown. Still, Lon Chaney Sr.'s makeup and athletic performance set early standards for the genre. More important, Chaney's Quasimodo is one of the earliest and more influential examples of the character whose monstrous appearance belies a sympathetic human soul. Despite Chaney's pioneering work, this version ranks third.

Today, the anti-fascist propaganda aspects of the 1939 masterpiece are obvious—and what's wrong with that? Even though Charles Laughton's make up doesn't equal Lon Chaney's, he's such a marvelous actor that he's a more sympathetic and moving Quasimodo. Teaming him with Maureen O'Hara's Esmeralda is the magical chemistry that Hollywood creates every decade or so. (If you don't mist up when she gives him water and then when he stumbles back into the cathedral, something's wrong.) Hardwick's Claude Frollo is a complex and sinister villain. The gigantic cathedral facade, the bell tower sets, and the proverbial cast of thousands are just terrific. Also, since the black-and-white film was made for a conventional sized screen, it looks grand on video. The big finish, complete with molten lead spewing from the mouths of gargoyles, is about as good as it gets.

The 1923 version of *The Hunchback of Notre Dame* has Lon Chaney Sr. in some of his best make up ever.

Like the other costume dramas of its time, the 1957 version is slow, showy, long, and overacted. In terms of plot, it is fairly faithful to Hugo's novel. Gina Lollobrigida is a spirited Esmeralda, the sultry gypsy who catches the eye of bell-ringer Quasimodo (Anthony Quinn) and his boss at the cathedral, Claude Frollo (Alain Cuny). The main attraction is La Lollo at the height of the mid-'50s cheesecake phase of her career, and there's a lot to be said for that. To show off his star, director Jean Delannoy often stops the action cold—her dance in a very red, very tight dress, for example. Alas, the rest can't match that moment. Quinn is trapped under heavy, stiff prosthetic make up and Cuny is a mopey villain. This version runs a distant fourth.

The 1982 made-for-TV production isn't as lavish as the 1939 film, but it's still one of the most enjoyable screen adaptations. The key is the casting. Lesley-Ann Down is at her loveliest as the gypsy Esmeralda. Derek Jacobi's Dom Claude Frollo has the right combination of villainy and love. Anthony Hopkins, nearly unrecognizable under the makeup, deserves comparison to Charles Laughton and Lon Chaney Sr. Quasimodo is one of horror's great characters—the monster we fear but come to love—and Hopkins wrings every drop of emotion out of him. (For comparative purposes, notice how differently he handles Dr. Hannibal Lecter in *Silence of the Lambs.*) The story of love and adventure in an exotic medieval setting is probably too complicated for very young viewers, but horror fans of any age who enjoy spectacle and can understand the emotions involved will be fascinated.

Hunger, The (1983)

Miriam (Catherine Deneuve), a beautiful two-thousand-year-old vampire, needs help when she realizes that John (David Bowie), her current lover, is aging fast. Enter Sarah Roberts (Susan Sarandon), a blood specialist whose research involves geriatrics. Tony Scott's visually sumptuous tale is spun out at an appropriately languid pace, complete with relatively tame soft-focus lesbian love scenes between Deneuve and Sarandon, and an understated mix of violence and sly humor. Bowie adds the right element of sexual mystery to the proceedings. This one paves the way for a generation of MTV-influenced escapist films emphasizing glossy style over story. It's also the titular source for a cable-TV horror series.

Hungry Wives

See Season of the Witch

Hush, Hush, Sweet Charlotte (1964)

Let's get past the flaws first: It's long, slow by today's standards, and most of the Southern accents and idioms are as phony as they come. Forgot those. This is a terrific faux-Faulkner Gothic with Grand Guignol flourishes. Did the young Charlotte really kill her lover (Bruce Dern) back in 1927? Thirty-seven years later, is she (Bette Davis) insane, or, as the sheriff says, "She's not really crazy. She just acts that way because other people seem to expect it of her." That's the center of the film. The performances by Davis and her co-stars Olivia de Havilland, Joseph Cotten, and Agnes Moorehead are some of their most delightful (and nasty). The last reels show how much can be done with black-and-white cinematography. Director of photography Joseph Biroc was nominated for an Academy Award. (So was Agnes Moorehead.)

I

I Am Legend (2007)
Last Man on Earth, The (1963)
Omega Man, The (1971)

Richard Matheson's brilliant post-apocalypse vampire novel has been filmed three times. The first version, *The Last Man on Earth* (written by Matheson) is the most faithful in its bleak tone and plot. A restrained Vincent Price is Dr. Robert Morgan who's still searching for a cure to the vampire plague after society has disintegrated and his city has become a haunted empty place. In many ways, the film is a prototype for George Romero's zombie films. The hero has locked himself into a fortress-like house, and these vampires are slow, clumsy, and pasty.

In the 1970 version, *The Omega Man,* Matheson's story becomes an allegory for the societal conflicts of the late 1960s. After Sino-Russian germ warfare starts a plague, Neville (Charlton Heston) is the only "normal" human in a Los Angeles overrun by an insane cult of albino, neo-Luddite barbarians. He happily slaughters them until he finds more survivors. From the opening scene—where he pops in an 8-track tape and plays the theme to "A Summer Place," to the trenchant comments on consumerism and responsibility, the film is a series of surprises with a remarkable sense of desolation and dour, deadpan humor. In many ways, it can be seen as a companion piece to *Night of the Living Dead,* made two years before. Both are about things falling apart. The main difference is an excellent, though undervalued performance by a major star in an unorthodox role.

I Am Legend (2007) is a big-budget Will Smith action film. His Robert Neville is an army scientist who's the last uninfected human in Manhattan. He's looking for a vaccine against the KV virus, which was developed as a cancer cure but turned out to have the unfortunate side effect of turning people into vampire-like monsters. The first half is fairly effective and the star has some fine moments, but after the original version suffered poor ratings in preview screenings, a new conclusion was tacked on.

I Dismember Mama (1972)

Albert (Zooey Hall) is convincingly unbalanced, an individual so out of touch with reality that he needs to be institutionalized. Anyone forced to wear his hideous wig would need professional help. And that hairpiece sets the standard for a slice of low-budget misogyny. The film's tension is derived from this murderous lunatic being on the loose with a little girl, and that is not entertainment.

I Know What You Did Last Summer (1997)
I Still Know What You Did Last Summer (1998)

Writer Kevin Williamson's follow-up to *Scream* is loosely based on Lois Duncan's young adult novel. The small town quarterback (Ryan Phillippe), the beauty queen (Sarah Michelle Gellar), the brainy girl (Jennifer Love Hewitt), and the ambitious poor boy (Freddie Prinze Jr.) are the protagonists of the self-aware horror. In the middle of their last summer of irresponsibility after they've graduated from high school, they're involved in an accident, perhaps a murder. They cover it up, but a year later, it's not over. Yes, there's more than a little Hitchcock in the premise, and, for a time, Williamson and Scottish director Jim Gillespie follow the master's lead with a tricky, unpredictable tale. The second half becomes more conventional stalker stuff. The young characters are attractive, though the girls are in constant danger of falling out of their Wonderbras. What the film really lacks is a convincing sense of place. In North Carolina, the mountains and the beach are at opposite ends of the state.

The sequel begins with an unsuspenseful and surprise-free dream sequence, and essentially rehashes the story in the Caribbean. Ms. Hewitt is extremely attractive, and the lighting and photography carefully flatter her. Fans will appreciate Jeffrey Combs' presence. Jack Black has an uncredited cameo as a stoner.

I Sell the Dead (2008)

On the day that he is to be hanged, body snatcher Blake (Dominic Monaghan) tells the story of his distasteful criminal career to the curious Father Duffy (Ron Perlman). In their years together, Blake and his partner Grimes (Larry Fessenden) unearthed many a strange person and creature. The somewhat episodic comedy is divided by comic book-like still frames. The low-budget production is often extremely dark, diverting attention from the minimal sets. The limited but graphic makeup effects aren't bad. The cast handles the talky action well, but the pace is still on the slow side.

I Spit on Your Grave (1978, 2010)

The infamous title is accurate enough for this feminist revenge fantasy. Jennifer (Camille Keaton) is brutally raped in her upstate New York vacation home, and gets even with the four attackers. The crimes, quoting John Boorman's *Deliverance,* are shown with unflinching horror. At first, the male characters are one-dimensional monsters. Later they're revealed to be two-dimensional monsters. Throughout, the viewer is squarely on Jenny's side, though some critics have attacked the film as misogynistic. Anyone who makes it through the first half will get that visceral, atavistic jolt that a good revenge flick—even one as crude and single-minded as this—can deliver. Similar material was handled in Abel Ferrara's *Ms. 45.*

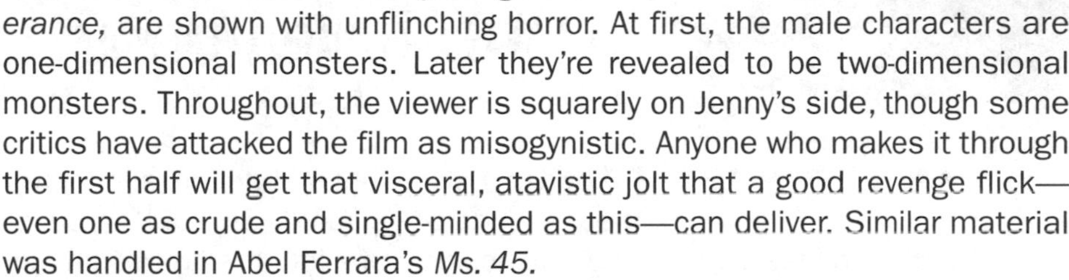

The 2010 version tells the same story with a Southern setting. It presents the sexual violence in more detail and with a crisper image but it still has the studied, soulless quality of twenty-first-century remakes.

I Walked with a Zombie (1943)

Curious variation on *Jane Eyre* (with a hint of *Rebecca*) is widely considered to be Val Lewton and Jacques Tourneur's masterpiece. Like their other collaborations, it's more well-mannered talk than action, beautifully staged and photographed in evocative black and white. Nurse Connell (Frances Dee) goes to the island of St. Sebastian, West Indies, to look after a plantation owner's (Tom Conway) catatonic wife. Though the film's racial attitudes can be seen as paternalistic, at least it presents black characters, and at that time, most Hollywood releases were all-white. Black people simply did not exist. Conway's caddish performance is similar to his work in *The Cat People.* Frances Dee has a simpler role; the camera gives her an elegant glamour. The big voodoo ceremony is an impressive set piece.

Actress Theresa Harris plays a maid, as she often did in her many Hollywood roles, in *I Walked with a Zombie*.

I Was a Teenage Frankenstein (1957)

Made to cash in on the popularity of *I Was a Teenage Werewolf,* this even sillier sequel is most famous for Professor Frankenstein's (Whit Bissell) one-liner about "a civil tongue in your head." Let's not spoil it for anyone who might have missed this oft-broadcast cult favorite. Gary Conway is the bad doctor's creation. In the end, the film delivers the nostalgic thrills the title promises, with considerable humor and a few genuine scares.

I Was a Teenage Werewolf (1957)

"That's a million dollar title on a hundred thousand dollar picture." So said producer Sam Arkoff when his partner James Nicholson came into the office with this one, and he's right. Though the film is a typical piece of American-International, mid-'50s youth exploitation, it's also the debut of Michael Landon. He's Tony, a violent, troubled teen. Dr. Brandon (Whit Bissell) is the semi-mad psychiatrist who leads Tony on a drug-induced journey to his past lives, conjuring up a hairy-faced, slobbering monster. The parallel bars scene has a place in the Alternative Hall of Fame. Bissell would reprise his role in the even more tongue-in-cheek *I Was a Teenage Frankenstein.*

Identity (2003)

Bizarre collection of horror clichés ought to be a derivative mess, but director James Mangold (*3:10 to Yuma, Walk the Line*) inexplicably spins genre straw into gold. At a rundown motel on the far side of nowhere, a group of strangers find themselves stranded: the larcenous hooker, young newlyweds, parents and their young son, a chauffeur driving a spoiled actress. At least, that's what we initially believe them to be. It doesn't take long for the viewer to understand that these people aren't who and what they seem. The resolution may make you want to throw something at your TV, but resist the urge. This is one to like in spite of itself.

Poster for *I Was a Teenage Frankenstein.*

Idle Hands (1999)

Stoner humor and graphic horror make for an uneasy and not particularly funny combination. Slacker Anton (Devon Sawa) doesn't know what to do when his right hand takes on an evil life of its own. Neither his parents (Connie Ray and Fred Willard) nor his pals (Seth Green and Elden Henson) are safe, but the rude appendage actually attracts the interest of Anton's comely young neighbor (Jessica Alba in an early jailbait role). Somehow, I was reminded of the original animated Scooby-Doo on bad acid.

I'm Dangerous Tonight (1990)

Entertaining supernatural hokum is loosely based on a Cornell Woolrich story. A magical Aztec ceremonial cloak releases the darker side of anyone who wears it, initially causing a few offscreen murders and such. But then the cloak falls into the hands of a mousy college student (Madchen Amick). She tailors it into a slinky red party dress, and, PRESTO!, the innocent undergrad becomes a femme fatale reincarnation of Rita Hayworth in *Gilda.* That's the finest moment, though the rest of the movie benefits considerably from fine supporting work. This one was made for the USA cable network and so Tobe Hooper's approach to violence and gore is relatively tame.

In the Mouth of Madness (1994)

Like *Wes Craven's New Nightmare* this is a horror film about imagination, the source of all horror. But writer Michael De Luca and director John Carpenter are telling a more traditional story that's firmly rooted in the H.P. Lovecraft mythos. As no-nonsense investigator John Trent (Sam Neill) searches for missing horror author Sutter Cane (Jurgen Prochnow), he finds that the novels have an odd effect on him. Be patient with the complex structure. This

The Top Eleven Classic Ghost Stories

The Others
The Changeling
Ghost Story
Sixth Sense
A Christmas Carol
Devil's Backbone
Haunted
Poltergeist
What Lies Beneath
The Forgotten One
A Stir of Echoes

is a well-made film with some genuinely creepy moments. Sam Neill is a fine hero. The subtle special effects created by Industrial Light and Magic and KNB EFX Group are excellent.

Incredible Shrinking Man, The (1957)

By today's standards, the special effects would hardly rate a raised eyebrow, though the fight with the spider still scares me. And the idea of shrinking humans, or enlarging their surroundings, has been used often enough in movies before and since. The real difference here is Richard Matheson's intelligent, serious script, based on his novel. It takes the stuff of pulp horror and refines it into something that approaches poetry at the conclusion, and raises the archetypal material far above the B-level. Add to that, veteran Jack Arnold's sure handed direction and a surprisingly effective performance by Grant Williams in the lead.

Indestructible Man (1956)

Curious low-budget horror places veteran Lon Chaney Jr., near the end of his career, in a *Dragnet* style crime tale complete with voice-over narration, unemotional dialogue, and immobile camera work. A not-particularly-mad scientist accidentally revives "Butcher" Benton (Chaney) after he's been executed. Now invulnerable and superhumanly strong, the gangster lumbers off for revenge upon his cronies and his traitorous lawyer. Looking old and tired, Chaney is far past his prime. The best moments are L.A. street scenes with trolley cars, and welcome stock footage of squad cars and motorcycles screaming out of the basement of the police station. Enjoyable mostly as period nostalgia or as an early prototype for *The Terminator.*

Infestation (2009)

Giant carnivorous bugs attack a city and cocoon humans for future dining. Five survivors have no idea what's going on or what they should do. The office misfit Cooper (Chris Marquette) suggests they walk to his father's (Ray Wise) house because it has a bomb shelter. From that standard-issue premise, writer/director Kyle Rankin comes up with some surprises. Early on, the violent action has a slapstick quality. Later, it becomes more serious. Throughout, the nasty computer effects are crystal clear.

Innkeepers, The (2011)

Ti West's second feature is a spare comic tale of a couple of amateur ghostbusters. Claire (Sara Paxton) and Luke (Pat Healy) are in charge of the economically challenged Yankee Pedlar Inn during its final days of operation. They hope to find evidence of the spirit of jilted bride Madeline O'Malley who's said to haunt the place. In practice, they're more interested in sucking down a couple of six packs of Schlitz beer. (Paging Dr. Venkman.) The meanderingly paced action is divided by black-and-white intertitle cards, giving the film an old-fashioned formality. West deserves credit for restraint in a time of overdependence on graphic effects. Still, some viewers will question the payoff after such an extended build-up.

Innocent Blood (1992)

John Landis' guilty-pleasure companion piece to *An American Werewolf in London* might have been called *A French Vampire in Pittsburgh.* Marie (Anne Parillaud) finds herself in the middle of a Mafia gang war and decides to indulge in a little Italian food. Joe Gennaro (Anthony LaPaglia) is a cop who has infiltrated Sal Macelli's (Robert Loggia) family. Don Rickles has a nice cameo as a mob lawyer. Fans will also spot genre luminaries Forest J. Ackerman, Dario Argento, and Sam Raimi in bit parts. Landis is trying to be as irreverent and provocative as possible, and he's generally successful.

John Landis, who directed *An American Werewolf in London,* also had his hand in the companion film *Innocent Blood.*

Inside (2007)

Exceptionally austere, bloody, and bizarre French import has a deliberate pace at the outset. The main characters are Sarah (Allyson Paradis), a pregnant woman who survived a car crash, and an unnamed woman (Béatrice Dalle) who threatens her and her unborn baby. Much of the action takes place at night in a dark house. Directors Alexandre Bustillo and Julien Maury's use of seemingly natural lighting leaves large areas of the screen in murky darkness, lightly muting the brutally graphic violence. Given the structure, the film can be read in at least two ways. Very much not to all tastes.

Interview with the Vampire: The Vampire Chronicles (1994)

The Anne Rice-Neil Jordan adaptation of her famous novel is the *Gone With the Wind* of vampire movies. Like *GWtW* it's long, romantic, and wildly overstated. Unlike *GWtW* it's gruesomely bloody, disgusting and, at the right times, very funny. Louis (Brad Pitt), a centuries-old undead, recounts his story to a reporter (Christian Slater), telling how he was transformed in eighteenth-century New Orleans by Lestat (Tom Cruise), and came to transform young Claudia (Kirsten Dunst). Director Jordan lets the tone tack between opulence and outright horror without ever losing control of the story. He also generates the intensity that any real horror film needs. The gay subtext, so important to Rice's work, is remarkably strong for a mainstream film. Her script is talky and often poetic, and the cast is up to it, though Cruise's fey performance is initially off-putting. Stan Winston's effects are among his best.

Invasion of the Body Snatchers (1956, 1978)
Body Snatchers (1993)
Invasion, The (2007)

"In my practice I've seen how people have allowed their humanity to drain away—only it happens slowly, instead of all at once. They didn't seem to mind." That's how Dr. Miles Bennell (Kevin McCarthy) eventually describes the strange things that are going on in the little town of Santa Mira. How he comes to that understanding is one of the most suspenseful and frightening movies ever made. By now, the story of the pod people is familiar, and the film's dead-on assessment of the 50s' political and social paranoia has

Dana Wynter & Kevin McCarthy starred in the 1956 version of *Invasion of the Body Snatchers.*

been thoroughly discussed. (But consider, for a moment, the religious implications of altogether ordinary-looking monsters who claim to be "reborn into an untroubled world.") The Daniel Mainwaring-Don Siegel film works so well on so many levels that its power as a pure thriller is often overlooked. It's beautifully constructed—steadily, inexorably ratcheting up the pressure. Notice how Siegel changes the lighting from bright sun to tightening shadows that reflect the characters' growing awareness. McCarthy's performance builds from blasé self-satisfaction to raving dementia without a false move. (By the way, that is director Sam Peckinpah—who helped with the script—as Charlie, the gas man.) A shorter alternative version of the film eliminates the framing device.

Philip Kaufman's 1978 remake is livelier, more graphic and violent, but it doesn't replace the original. Kaufman moves the setting from a small town to San Francisco where public health inspector Donald Sutherland slowly comes to discover the pod people. The film is too long with unresolved plotlines, and Kaufman's tendency to show off behind the camera with weird angles becomes obtrusive. Still, it's a good suspenseful story, well-acted by an excellent cast.

For sheer paranoia, Abel Ferrara's 1993 *Body Snatchers* may not be as suspenseful as Don Siegel's original, but it's better than Kaufman's. The inventive special effects are about as skincrawly as any you'll see. They involve soft, gently probing little tendrils that do absolutely revolting things. Sullen, teenaged Marti Malone (Gabrielle Anwar) hates everything about the new military base where her family has moved. She doesn't much care for her dad (Terry Kinney), stepmom (Meg Tilly), or little brother (Reilly Murphy) either. The only thing she likes is a handsome chopper pilot (Billy Wirth). Of course, they're all potential pod fodder. Initially, Ferrara uses a funereal pace to turn the ordinary into the ominous, effectively building tension until the icky effects kick in. On the minus side, he overuses the shortcut of panning his camera through walls between rooms. It's a technique that rudely reminds viewers they're watching a movie when they should be suspending their disbelief. Judged against the rest of the film, it's a minor flaw. This one really works well.

The Invasion (2007) is a leaden star vehicle for Nicole Kidman and Daniel Craig. A troubled production that went through several scripts adds a more overt political element with the aliens taking over governments. Throughout, the action is less than compelling and the resolution is convenient.

Invisible Man, The (1933)
Invisible Man Returns, The (1940)
Invisible Agent (1942)
Invisible Man's Revenge, The (1944)

"Power! Power to walk into the gold vaults of the nations, into the secrets of kings, into the holy of holies! Power to make the multitudes run squealing in terror at the touch of my little invisible finger!" That's how mad scientist Jack Griffin (Claude Rains) proclaims his newly acquired transparency. Director James Whale takes H.G. Well's "scientific romance" on a universal fantasy and turns it into a study of megalomania. (Remember that the film was made at a time when real megalomaniacs were on the rise in Germany and Italy.) Though the effects are dated now, the film zips right along with real energy and the sets are terrific. James Whale's talents as a film director had increased considerably since his horror debut with *Frankenstein.* Deprived of most of an actor's tools, Rains gives his voice a harsh, raspy quality that suits a character who's maddened by the side effects of the drug—monocaine—that renders him pigmentationally challenged. The only flaw is a relatively weak, undramatic conclusion.

The Invisible Man Returns doesn't come close to the original, but it's not bad with important comic elements. Ratcliffe (Vincent Price) is an innocent man who's given a dose of super-Clearasil by the brother of the original "Invisible Man" to spring him from the slammer where he's about to hang for murder. A youthful Price is uncharacteristically restrained while almost everyone else in the cast is shamelessly broad. The effects are the point anyway. Don't miss the invisible hamsters in their little leather harnesses.

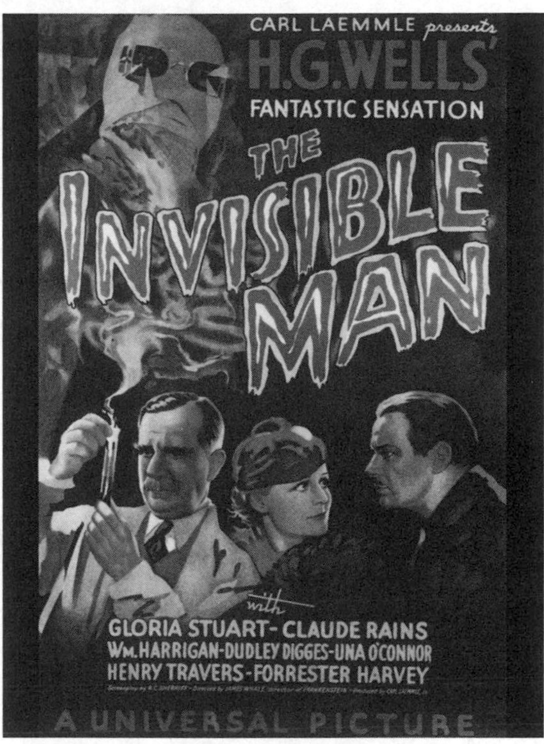

Poster for 1933's *The Invisible Man.*

The Invisible Woman has nothing to do with horror. *The Invisible Agent* (1942) is not so much horror as wartime propaganda, and it's enjoyable as such. Griffin's grandson (Jon Hall) escapes enemy agents led by Peter Lorre, and then takes the invisibility formula behind enemy lines. The black-and-white photography is sharp; top-billed Ilona Massey is glamorous and the invisibility effects are kind of charming.

By the fifth installment, *The Invisible Man's Revenge,* Universal has strayed so far from the source that the credits claim only "suggested by H.G. Wells." That's appropriate for a bizarre, socio-political tale of evil gentry exploiting the common man, sort of. Robert Griffin (Jon Hall) is a semi-psychotic recovered amnesiac who goes from South Africa to England to track down the aristocrats (Lester Matthews and an underused Gale Sondergaard) who bilked him out of his diamond mine. (I am not making this up; writer Bertram Millhauser gets the credit.) After the rich folks slip him a mickey and sic their lawyer on him, Griffin comes across mad doctor John Carradine who's been experimenting with an invisibility drug. The film is slow and so clunky that it's almost a comedy, but it was made on the studio's backlot with the customary attention to detail and some fine black-and-white effects that predate James Cameron's *The Abyss.*

The Twenty-Five (+) Funniest Horror-Comedies

Abbott & Costello Meet Frankenstein
Abominable Dr. Phibes
American Psycho
An American Werewolf in London
Motel Hell
Ravenous
Re-Animator
Return of the Living Dead series
Scary Movie
Scream
Shaun of the Dead
Slither
The Stepfather
Storm Warning
The Surgeon
Theatre of Blood
Tim Burton's Corpse Bride
Tucker and Dale versus Evil
Young Frankenstein
Zombieland
Arnold
Beetlejuice
Not Like Us
Severance
Snakes on a Plane

Island of Lost Souls, The (1932) Island of Dr. Moreau, The (1977, 1996)

Like Robert Louis Stevenson's *Dr. Jekyll and Mr. Hyde,* H.G. Wells' *The Island of Dr. Moreau* finds its horror in the most basic elements of humanity—the nature of good and evil, society, sex, religious belief. The 1932 adaptation, *The Island of Lost Souls,* is by far the most successful and frightening, though Wells himself is said to have disliked it. The main reasons are Charles Laughton's silky performance as the doctor whose experiments attempt to turn animals into men and women; inventive work by director Erle S. Kenton and cinematographer Karl Struss; and simple yet effective makeup. In appearance and attitude, the film resembles *King Kong.* The "are we not men" ritual is terrific, and several of the nocturnal jungle scenes have nightmarish intensity. For a perplexing double feature, watch this one with Tod Browning's *Freaks,* made the same year.

The 1977 *Island of Dr. Moreau* lacks the frightening intensity of Kenton's film, but it's not without winning moments. Those are provided mostly by Burt Lancaster who's conducting bizarre experiments on a remote island. Michael York is the young hero who's stranded there. When the doc goes to work on him, it's a horrifying scene. The human-animal makeup isn't as successful. When the creations are shown in full color sunlight, as they often are, it's pretty obvious that these are people in rubber masks. Some of the dialogue is equally unpersuasive.

Seen strictly as a horror/comedy, the 1996 version is hard to top. Marlon Brando's mountainous Moreau is the *Mad* magazine version of his Col. Kurtz from *Apocalypse Now.* He makes his first entrance in white makeup, an umbrella hat, and a Popemobile. He also adopts a lisping Boris Karloff British accent. Val Kilmer, as his assistant Montgomery, and David Thewlis, as the castaway Douglas, give their characters a curious gay spin. (The fact that top-billed Kilmer plays a supporting role and character actor Thewlis is the protagonist says a lot about the unbalanced dramatic weight.) The story doesn't differ significantly from the original. Director William Friedkin (who took over from writer Richard Stanley after the traditional "creative differences") and director of photography William Fraker keep the action quick and bright. Some of Stan Winston's makeup effects are excellent, but the overall tone is wrong for horror. Still, the entire production is so bizarre that it deserves a look for curiosity value, if nothing else.

Isle of the Dead (1945)

This dark, graceful film is virtually motionless. During the Balkan war, a Greek general (Boris Karloff at his best) is trapped on an island cemetery with seven other people. One old woman believes that a vampiric spirit is loose. The others calmly debate faith versus reason until the end when one of the spookiest shocks you'll ever experience takes place. It's really no more overt than the rest, but it's been so carefully set up that it's a hard jolt. Particularly recommended for older fans. Kids probably won't have the patience for it.

It! (1966)

Arthur Pimm (Roddy McDowall) is a British Norman Bates sort of mamma's boy who's already up to no-good when he comes into possession of the legendary Golem, a massive Hebrew statue that can come to life and do its master's bidding. Will it help him get a promotion at the museum or perhaps to win the lovely Ellen (Jill Haworth)? Filmmaker Herbert Leder gives the material semi-serious treatment. The action gets off to a slow, stiff, talky start and never moves very quickly. With his trademarked light touch, McDowall is fine. The creature looks suspiciously like a stone Conehead.

It's Alive (1974)
It's Alive 2: It Lives Again (1978)
It's Alive III: Island of the Alive (1987)
It's Alive (2008)

Versatile and inventive director Larry Cohen uses horror's most famous line of dialogue as a descriptive title for a monstrous mutant baby. Said infant comes equipped with vampire-like fangs and the leg muscles and jumping power of a mature kangaroo. The little fiend attacks the milkman and, in true B-movie fashion, hides out in the Los Angeles sewers. Bernard Herrmann's score—one of his last—helps to raise this one to genuine cult status.

Although the sequel begins with a paranoid premise of government surveillance of pregnant women, the atmosphere and acting are too laid back to sustain it. Like the first, it's about giant mutant killer babies. The central question here is: Are they good giant mutant killer babies or bad giant mutant killer babies. Do you really care?

The third feature boasts the best cast and highest production values of the trilogy. It also maintains the series' most significant contribution to the genre—the combination of revulsion, fear, and parental love that the mutant infants inspire. Michael Moriarty, Cohen's frequent star and collaborator, is the father who, after many misgivings, stands up for his kid. Some of the creatures are handled with stop-motion animation. The free-flowing story wanders into some odd political and narrative areas as the children grow. For a film with a "III" in the title, this one's interesting, but it's far from Cohen's best.

The 2008 remake retains the premise but moves most of the action to a desert house. Like virtually all of the twenty-first-century remakes, it's much more polished, but despite a few nasty computer effects, it never comes close to the overall weirdness of the original. The cast, particularly Bijou Phillips as the concerned mother, is game.

J–K

Jack Be Nimble (1993)

New Zealand Gothic horror has been properly compared to Stephen King's work and to Peter Jackson's *Heavenly Creatures,* though it's much darker and more frightening. Jack (Alexis Arquette) and his sister Dora (Sarah Smuts-Kennedy) are taken from their parents as children and raised in separate homes. She goes to middle-class suburbia; he winds up in a rural hellhole. His tortured upbringing there turns him into a rebellious, unstable young man who's driven to find his lost sister. By then she has begun an affair with Teddy (Bruno Lawrence) who understands her on an unusually sympathetic level. And that is all anyone should know about the plot. Writer-director Garth Maxwell is an imaginative filmmaker who really knows what he's doing with grim, grainy images. Despite its obviously limited budget, the film is strong stuff, building to an unpredictable finish that's not for everyone.

Jack-O (1995)

The equivalent of a suburban Halloween spook house is a low-budget horror/comedy emphasizing laughs over scares. Like any good spook house, it's also a loving evocation of the season. The opening nursery rhyme, "Mr. Jack will break your back and cut off your head with a whack, whack, whack" sets the tone. The bloody effects that follow are about the least realistic you'll ever see, and the hoary plot revolves around a warlock who's resurrected as a pumpkin-headed slasher. Young Ryan Latshaw is fine as the trick-or-treating hero who shares the screen with a host of horror veterans led by John Carradine, Cameron Mitchell, Dawn Wildsmith, Linnea Quigley, and Brinke Stevens who ham it up happily. If it weren't for one shower scene, this one would be recommended for kids. Instead, it's aimed more at nostalgic drive-in fans.

Jack's Back (1988)

Rowdy Herrington's underpublicized sleeper is a rare treat. The premise—one hundred years later, to the day, someone is recreating Jack the Ripper's crimes in Los Angeles—sounds like the derivative flapdoodle of a bad made-for-cable feature. But writer/director Herrington fills the screen with evocatively lit compositions and surprising plot twists. The first act conclusion is a corker and so's the tricky ending. Star James Spader's sleepy-eyed diffidence cuts against the grain of his character—a dedicated young doctor—but it still works. Ignore the formulaic sound of the synopsis and take a look.

Jacob's Ladder (1990)

The opening scene in Vietnam—featuring a strong early appearance by Ving Rhames—is as shocking a slice of wartime horror as you're likely to see. Flash forward to New York where Jacob (Tim Robbins) is a possibly delusional postman living with Jezebel (Elizabeth Peña). The rest of the plot is virtually review-proof. To reveal any of it would spoil all of it. Director Adrian Lyne's polished visual style mixes the mundane and the nightmarish with frightening originality. Jake may be mad or he may have been driven mad or something else may be going on. The performances couldn't be better. The second half is more problematic.

Jaws (1975)
Jaws 2 (1978)
Jaws 3 (1983)
Jaws: The Revenge (1987)

Technical problems turned what might have been nothing more than another monster movie into one of horror's best. The tales about the difficulties with "Bruce," the mechanical shark, are the stuff of Hollywood legend. (According to one version, the producers initially thought that real sharks could be trained to perform.) When Bruce didn't work, young director Steven Spielberg was forced to shoot around it and to suggest what he couldn't show. In the process, every scene set on or near the ocean became doubly suspenseful. Even in bright daylight, the surface of the water is hiding a creature that comes straight from our collective nightmares. The two main settings—the island village of Amity and the fishing boat—are well realized. The script wisely jettisons the needless subplots from Peter Benchley's novel and focuses on the three protagonists—the sheriff (Roy Scheider), the scientist (Richard Dreyfuss), and the salt (Robert Shaw)—as they hunt for the shark. If the telling of the story is a bit stilted and formal, it was good enough to keep thousands of people out of the ocean during the summer of 1975. John Williams' ominous here-comes-the-shark theme and soaring score add immeasurably. Take another look.

Based on the Peter Benchley bestseller, the original *Jaws* was brilliantly directed by a young Steven Spielberg.

Jaws 2 is a pale shadow that has almost all of the gimmicks of the original but none of the punch. No surprise there; it was a troubled production with original director John Hancock replaced by Jeannot Szwarc three weeks into shooting and the script by Hancock's wife Dorothy Tristan rewritten by Carl Gottlieb. Star Roy Schieder was contractually obligated to make the movie, and the lack of originality and enthusiasm is obvious everywhere. If there were truth-in-titling laws, this, like most sequels, would have been called *Jaws $*.

It's a shame that the long-rumored National Lampoon's *Jaws 3—People 0* project never found its way to the screen. Instead, we've got this waterlogged mess, originally made for 3-D. That 3-D process makes it look cheap and rough on video, with really poor effects. The lame action is set in an aquatic amusement park owned by Calvin Buchard (Lou Gossett Jr.). It's certainly the most embarrassing entry on writer Richard Matheson's resume.

The plot of the unfortunate *Jaws: The Revenge* revolves around the shark essentially stalking the Brody family from Amity to the Bahamas. The overall ridiculousness of the story is matched by the inept mechanical shark. The film is an unintentional comedy and a completely legitimate contender for Worst Sequel Ever. It brought the series to a long overdue end.

Jeepers Creepers (2001)

Bickering brother and sister (Justin Long and Gina Phillips) are in an old Chevy on a lonely stretch of blacktop when they come across a menacing guy in a rusty truck. From that standard set-up, Victor Salva's film shifts gears at regular intervals, generating real surprises, and becoming more and more outlandish as it goes. In fact, it wanders so far afield that some fans hate it. For my money, it's entertaining but not particularly involving because the characters do such unbelievable things to advance said plot. Followed by two sequels.

Jekyll and Hyde (1990)

Tepid retelling never really gets to the heart of the matter. Michael Caine plays the good doctor and his brutal alter ego. The first part follows the familiar plot until Jekyll falls in love with his sister-in-law (Cheryl Ladd). Then for a time, the focus is on Victorian values and mores, complete with egregious overacting from all concerned. When it returns to Mr. Hyde, the film becomes a standard mid-budget monster flick with a surprise ending that's no surprise. The transformation effects are nothing special, and the Hyde makeup looks like a lumpy onion with a bad attitude. In her own way, Cheryl Ladd doesn't fare much better. She has to wear a bustle that is truly remarkable. Hit the pause button when that astonishing appendage appears.

Jennifer's Body (2009)

After her Oscar-winning script for *Juno,* writer Diablo Cody came up with a misfired horror comedy that aspires to be a new *Heathers.* That's a very high bar and the film never comes close. Megan Fox is the titular alpha girl at the high school in Devil's Kettle. After she's transformed into a man-eating demon (literally), her best friend Needy (Amanda Seyfried) is at a loss. The main problem is that Cody and director Karyn Kusama transform Jennifer into a grotesque young harridan. The dialogue is self-consciously arch; the pace is slow and J.K. Simmons wears one of the worst wigs ever to appear on screen. A waste of considerable talent on both sides of the camera.

John Carpenter's Vampires (1998)

The Vatican pays the bills for a team of vampire hunters led by Jack Crow (James Woods). They destroy a nest of bloodsuckers in New Mexico, but the

Big Cheese (Thomas Ian Griffith) eludes them and counterattacks. The action is graphic and bloody, but the film falls short for two reasons. First, the macho posturing on the part of the good guys is ridiculous. Second, Woods turns in the kind of full-throated angry performance that Nic Cage would recreate in similar films a decade or so later.

Jugular Wine: A Vampire Odyssey (1994)

In Alaska, footloose college professor James Grace (Shaun Irons) is bitten by a vampire. Maybe. He might also discover inklings of a larger conspiracy involving a monstrous figure named Legion. Back home in Philadelphia, Grace feels that he's changing or perhaps dying. Whatever, he sets off on a journey to learn what has happened. Young filmmaker Blair Murphy attempts to do more than his meager budget (and probably his experience) will allow. The result is wildly uneven but consistently entertaining and intelligent, combining exploitation with serious literary and philosophical ideas in a tenuous balance. The bloody effects are much more believable than you often see in more sophisticated productions. The rough, picaresque road-movie quality makes virtues of most flaws though it all could make more sense than it does. It's still more enjoyable than *Nadja* or *The Addiction.* That's Murphy as the blond Nickadeamous.

The Top Five Legitimate Contenders for Worst Movie Ever

Plan 9 from Outer Space
Bride of the Monster
Jaws 4
Troll 2
Pet Sematary 2

Jurassic Park (1993)
Lost World: Jurassic Park, The (1997)
Jurassic Park III (2001)

In making an absolutely spectacular dinosaur film, that elusive Hollywood "chemistry" works to perfection ... well, near perfection. First, the monsters created by Dennis Muren, Stan Winston, and Michael Lantieri with live action, stop-motion animation, and computer-generated digital images are magnificent. Even on the small screen, T-rex and Velociraptor are completely frightening. Second, the script by novelist Michael Crichton and David Koepp puts a cast of interesting stock figures through a series of adrenaline-pumping adventures. Finally, director Steven Spielberg mixes image and sound deftly, and keeps the whole thing zipping right along at a potboiler pace. At the same time, his tendency toward oversweetness bubbles close to the surface a time or two. Even so, for some younger horror fans, this movie will generate nightmares that might last for years.

Highly intelligent velociraptors pursue hapless humans in 1993's *Jurassic Park.*

The clumsily plotted sequel, *The Lost World: Jurassic Park,* has more dinosaurs, tinier dinosaurs, faster dinosaurs, cuter dinosaurs, and hungrier dinosaurs than the first film. It also has a ridiculous ending that falls apart completely. Two competing groups—noble scientists and nasty hunters—go to another island where dinosaurs flourish. The first bunch is led by a reluctant Ian Malcolm (Jeff Goldblum) and Kelly, his twelve-year-old black daughter (Vanessa Lee Chester). With them are Sarah (Julianne Moore), his socio-paleontologist girlfriend; brave Greenpeace video documentarian Nick (Vince Vaughn); and "equipment systems specialist" Eddie (Richard Schiff). (That cockamamie collection of cinematic diversity says a lot about the film's lapses.) The human characters aren't as interesting as the dinosaurs which are even more lifelike, complex, and believable. Regarding the film's violence, younger children who could handle the original will be fine with this one. Will they be scared? Sure they will. It's a monster movie; they're supposed to be scared. They'll see one guy turned into T-rex toejam, and several others are eaten. But Spielberg never dwells on the harsher moments or stages them too vividly.

For my money, *Jurassic Park III* is more successful. It's quickly paced and more openly comedic. Dr. Grant (Sam Neill) from the first film is persuaded by Paul Kirby (William H. Macy) to accompany him and his wife on a fly-over of a jungle island where more reconstituted dinosaurs roam. He has ulterior motives. If the T-rexs, raptors, and other saurians aren't as frightening as they were before, the special effects are almost as good.

Keep, The (1983)

Like all of Michael Mann's work, this variation on the Golem legend is so sophisticated in visual terms that it borders on genius. Mann can replace conventional dialogue with image, sound, and music as well as anyone ever has. That also makes for an emotional coolness in the attempt to equate Nazism with a sort of Lovecraftian supernatural evil. In 1941, Germans led by Jurgen Prochnow and Gabriel Byrne let some huge, powerful force loose in a Romanian castle. Ian MacKellan, as a Jewish scholar, and Scott Glenn, as a mysterious partisan who's been transformed, are fine, but Mann is more interested in smoky light, an elegantly composed screen, and bizarre effects. The elaborate style justifies a deliberate pace.

Kill List (2011)

What appears to begin as a domestic drama set in a grim, dry British suburb turns into a crime story about two assassins (Neil Maskell and Michael Smiley). But early on, it's made clear that something else is at play. The naturalistic tone is punctuated by abrupt moments of fairly realistic violence. Action remains unpredictable throughout because director and writer (with Amy Jump) Ben Wheatley refuses to follow any genre conventions. The conclusion is slightly reminiscent of *The Wicker Man,* but that's not really a useful comparison, beyond both films' originality.

King Kong (1933, 1976, 2005)
King Kong Lives (1986)

The original is one of Hollywood's true masterpieces, so richly layered and enjoyable that its simple core is often overlooked. This is the story of an innocent guy from the sticks who's on his own in New York and looking for a girl. Everything about the film fits together perfectly. It begins when Robert Armstrong's gruff Carl Denham says, "All right, the public wants a girl and this time I'm going to give 'em what they want!" and then finds Ann Darrell (Fay Wray, one of the sweetest, sexiest heroines ever and the original Scream Queen). She steals the heart of the King himself, and I don't mean

Stop-motion animation brings a giant gorilla to life to menace poor Fay Wray in the 1933 version of *King Kong*. It still holds up well compared to newer versions with costlier special effects.

Elvis. The combination of Willis O'Brien's effects, Max Steiner's thunderous score, and the terrific sets create the black-and-white reality of a remembered dream. For an unapologetic piece of popular entertainment, the film has been subjected to academic and political analyses of every stripe. It remains, however, stubbornly critic-proof. Most editions are of the original 101-minute 1933 version, not the bowdlerized 1938 re-release that eliminated most of the film's still shocking violence.

Producer Dino De Laurentiis' 1976 remake adds absolutely nothing to the original. All right, it does mark the debut of Jessica Lange, but she has long since lived it down. The special effects, though more advanced in some respects, are not as believable as O'Brien's stop-motion work. Not one moment in this film even comes close to the Kong v. T-Rex fight. Other elements of the original—the protagonist's innocence, the implied sexuality—have been heightened to the point that they smack of parody.

About the best that can be said is that this one's better than the lamentable 1986 sequel *King Kong Lives.* It is worse than I can describe, worse than you can imagine. For starters, Kong has been in a coma since his fall from the World Trade Center ten years before. Dr. Franklin (Linda Hamilton) is about to implant a jumbo-sized artificial heart, but she needs blood, lots of it. That's when Hank (Brian Kerwin) shows up with Lady Kong. The rest is even more insulting to your intelligence with gobs of gooey sentimentality at the end, and not the first trace of intentional humor. Too simple-minded for adults, too graphically violent for kids, and all the way through, it has a leering sexual subtext.

Peter Jackson's loving, self-indulgent 2005 version is almost twice as long as the original. As much as I like and admire it, I've got to admit that it could use some judicious trimming. It's got just a few too many stampeding dinosaurs and giant bugs and spiders. That said, Jackson's evocation of America in the depths of the Depression is vivid. Naomi Watts is the equal of Fay Wray (those are words I never thought I'd write), and Andy Serkis' motion capture performance as the Big Guy is a marvel. Fans of Jackson's early work will catch his little tip of the hat to *Dead Alive* with a poster for the Sumatran rat-monkey.

Kingdom of the Spiders (1977)

Overachieving B-movie is solidly in the tradition of the underrated Jack Arnold films of the 1950s. In rural Arizona, farm animals are dying. Vet William Shatner is baffled; Tiffany Bolling is the obligatory science-babe who deduces that the animals were killed by spider venom. In one neat sequence, the sexual conventions of the genre are turned upside down, and the ending is a nice turn on *Night of the Living Dead.* Writers Alan Caillou and Richard Robinson and director Bud Cardos don't make any apologies for what they're doing and handle things with the right combination of seriousness and humor.

Kiss Me Kill Me (1973)

Valentina (Isabella de Funès) is a swinging photographer who's set upon by Baba Yaga (Carroll Baker), a sort of vampiric witch. She's aided by an evil, sexy S&M doll that comes to life. In many ways, this oddity is an archetypal '60s movie with funky jazzy music, coy sex, radical politics, and hallucinatory dream sequences. Though director Corrado Farina's film is based on a comic book character created by Crepax, the influences of Fellini and Antonioni are just as obvious. Exploitation with several odd twists is recommended mostly to fans of the era. Alternate titles: *Devil's Witch; Baba Yaga; So Sweet, So Perverse; Cosi dolce ... cosi perversa; Baba Yaga—Devil's Witch*.

Kiss of the Vampire (1963)

Hammer's third vampire film (after *Horror of Dracula* and *Brides of Dracula*) is one of its best, despite the absence of Peter Cushing and Christopher Lee. They're replaced by Clifford Evans as the drunken, remorseful vampire hunter Zimmer, and Noel Willman as the aristocratic Ravna. Writer Anthony Hind's script is a simple variation on Bram Stoker's story that the studio would rework time and again over the next decade. Young couple (Edward De Souza and Jennifer Daniel) comes across vampire's castle and is entrapped. Though there's barely a plunging neckline, the sexual aspects are strong, with a faint hint of lesbianism. The introductory burial scene is a tremendous shocker; the effects at the end are comparatively weak. Clearly, the film is a strong influence on Roman Polanksy's *The Fearless Vampire Killers.*

L

Labyrinth (1986)

When self-centered Sarah (Jennifer Connelly) foolishly invites the King of the Goblins (David Bowie) to take the little brother she has to babysit, he accepts. Her suburban neighborhood is transformed into a labyrinth filled with magical creatures; she has thirteen hours to find a castle at the center and rescue the tot. Director Jim Henson quotes Salvadore Dali, Walt Disney, Maurice Sendak, and M.C. Escher in the creation of his frightening, gritty wonderland. In this world of fairy tales, beauty and wonder are never far from ugliness, and they are often all part of the same thing. In the end, the story is about growing up, maturing, accepting responsibility—in short, all of the things that most movies, even those aimed at kids, are not about.

Lady Frankenstein (1971)

Italian import begins as a fairly straightforward variation on the standard themes with the venerable Joseph Cotten playing our man Frank not so much as a mad scientist but more as an aggressive humanist. "Here on earth, Man is God," he says, and "Let man's will be done." Cotten has the presence to bring off such hokum. But he exits at the end of the first act, turning things over to his daughter (Sarah Bay) who follows in daddy's experimental footsteps. Meanwhile, his creation ravages the countryside. With the addition of familiar voice dubbing, the whole thing sounds and looks a little like a gladiator flick. It ends up being fair to middling exploitation.

Lair of the White Worm (1988)

Ken Russell pits paganism (in the form of snake worship) against Christianity in a wonderfully screwy adaptation of Bram Stoker's last novel, a.k.a. *The Garden of Evil.* When Lady Sylvia (Amanda Donohoe), "the fanged princess of darkness," arrives in contemporary England, no boy scout is safe. Our four heroes are the Trent sisters (Catherine Oxenberg and Sammi Davis) whose parents disappeared a year before, archeologist Angus Flint (Peter Capaldi) who finds a huge skull in their backyard, and Lord James (Hugh Grant) the local Pooh-Bah who's still investigating the disappearances. The plot quickly succumbs to Russell's trademark flamboyance.

Lake Placid (1999)

Just about every aspect of this comedy is as ridiculous as the premise—a giant crocodile taking up residence in a lake in Maine. Throughout, the humor is snarky and fresh, and the characters are cheeky. We've got the New York museum paleontologist babe (Bridget Fonda) who's sent up to investigate after the first human is chomped in half, and the globe-trotting mythology professor (Oliver Platt) who's got a thing for crocs. And let's not forget the kindly old lady (Betty White) who makes sure that the visitor gets enough protein in its diet. Stan Winston's effects are up to the frivolous task. Followed by two non-theatrical sequels.

Land of the Dead

See Night of the Living Dead

Last Broadcast, The (1998)

Steven Avkast (Stefan Avalos) and Locus Wheeler (Lance Weiler), hosts of the cable *Fact or Fiction* show, go into the New Jersey Pine Barrens for a live broadcast of their search for the legendary Jersey Devil. They're accompanied by sound technician Rein Clackin (Rein Clabbers) and psychic Jim Suerd (Jim Seward). Only Suerd comes out of the woods alive. A year later, he has been convicted of the murders and documentary filmmaker David Leigh (David Beard) begins to investigate the case. Directors Avalos and Weiler tell much of the story through "found" and "restored" videotape, thereby turning many of the liabilities of low-budget work into assets. Much more importantly to viewers, they have constructed a tricky plot that's held together with excellent writing and a sterling performance from Beard. His dead-pan

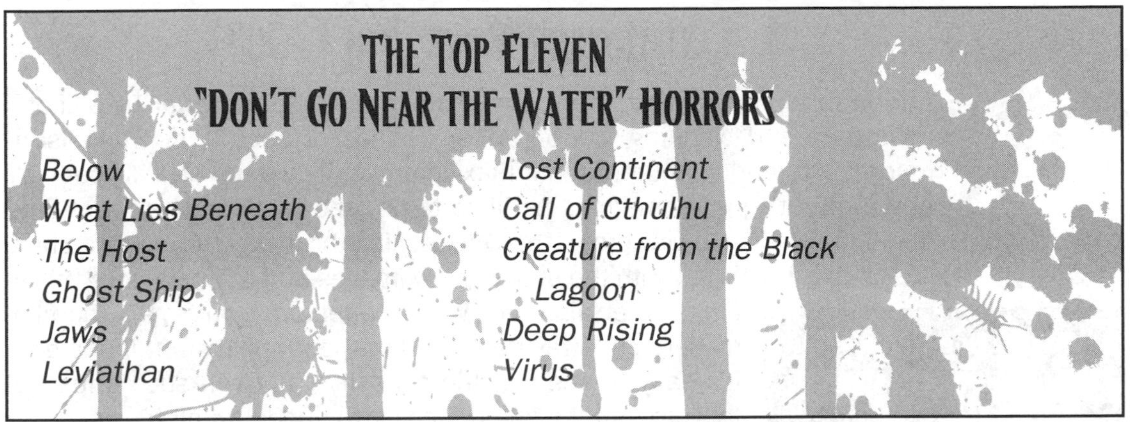

The Top Eleven "Don't Go Near the Water" Horrors

Below
What Lies Beneath
The Host
Ghost Ship
Jaws
Leviathan
Lost Continent
Call of Cthulhu
Creature from the Black Lagoon
Deep Rising
Virus

mock documentary voice-over narration is right on the mark. It's also the glue that holds everything else together. The parallels to *The Blair Witch Project* are hard to ignore, but *The Last Broadcast* was made first.

Last Days of Planet Earth (1974)

Japanese interpretation of the predictions of Nostradamus with a soundtrack that might have come from an Italian spy flick is every bit as gonzo as you might imagine. The film uses so much stock footage that it often looks like a documentary. But then there are the giant sea slugs and the weed-choked subway tunnels and the groovy drug-crazed hippie love-in and the incredible exploding traffic jam. Excessive voice-over narration vainly attempts to impose logic and continuity on the plotless, cataclysmic action. Virtually every line of dialogue is preachy and pedantic, finally endorsing an environmentally-based totalitarianism. With so much hysterical energy in play, this craziness is seldom dull. Personally, I think the whole problem can be traced back to the heroine's thigh-high, white vinyl zipper platform boots.

Last Exorcism, The (2010)

One of the better "found footage" horrors pays as little attention to that dubious premise as possible. Evangelist Cotton Marcus (Patrick Fabian) questions his faith but agrees to participate in a rural exorcism. Why? He wants to prove it false to the camera crew that's following him around. An incredible performance by Ashley Bell as the subject of the possession is the film's main strength. According to the filmmakers, it was accomplished without special effects. Some have criticized the conclusion, but given the structure, it's appropriate. A sequel is in the works.

Last Horror Movie, The (2003)

After a false introduction, the scene shifts to Max (Kevin Howarth), a chatty sociopath and wedding videographer. His assistant (Mark Stevenson) records the random murders that Max commits. Why does Max kill people? Apparently it's just something he likes to do, and he spends a lot of time speaking directly to viewers of the DVD, asking them why they are watching it. The story plays out with the shaky grainy images and stiff posturing of "reality" entertainment. Violent effects are minimal. The filmmakers cut away from most of the graphic stuff. In the end, it's easy to see why the curiosity has been such a festival favorite, but it's still not going to appeal to all fans.

"We're trying to make an intelligent movie about murder while actually doing the murders."
The Last Horror Movie

Last House on the Left (1972, 2009)

Judged by the standards of violence that it helped to establish, this early '70s psycho/revenge cheapie looks fairly tame today. Two not-so-innocent teenage girls (Sandra Cassell and Lucy Grantheim) are brutalized by a semi-comic gang of dimwits who then take refuge in the wrong place. The combination of sadistic horror, generational conflict, and "dumb" comedy is still strong stuff, however crudely made. Filmmakers Wes Craven and Sean Cunningham mean to be provocative. Their work would be more effective with less comic relief—note the goofy deputy played by video stalwart Martin Kove—but the film's influence on the low-budget horrors that would follow is undeniable.

The 2009 remake jettisons the comic elements and keeps the focus squarely on some of the most graphic and horrible sexual violence ever put on screen. The villains, led by Krug (Garrett Dillahunt) are more serious figures, but the second half settles into predictable lines of action. More importantly, the filmmakers water down one key element, considerably lessening the emotional power of the original.

Last Man on Earth

See I Am Legend

Lawnmower Man (1992)

In a loose retelling of *Frankenstein,* Jobe Smith (Jeff Fahey) is a slow-witted handyman whose brain power is boosted by exposure to Dr. Angelo's (Pierce

Brosnan) experiments in virtual reality. The plot has almost nothing to do with Stephen King's short story—he had his name removed from the title—but the tone is faithful to his fictional territory of small towns, bullies, kids, cruelty, abuse, ominous government agencies and, of course, a big pyrotechnic finale. The home video version is thirty minutes longer than the theatrical release with more special effects and a fully developed, coherent story. Its well-deserved popularity on tape and DVD has elevated the film above cult status and into the realm of a solid mainstream hit. Followed by a sequel that's more sci-fi than horror, and has even less to do with King's ideas.

Legend of Hell House (1973)

A dying rich man hires a team of investigators to prove the existence of the afterlife in "the Mt. Everest of haunted houses." A credulous physicist (Clive Revill), his wife (Gayle Hunnicutt), a medium (Pamela Franklin), and a survivor (Roddy McDowall) of a previous examination of the house go there for a week. Richard Matheson's script is a model of efficiency, setting up characters and conflict in the first few minutes without a wasted motion. Once the group's inside the house—a marvelously well-realized place—director Hough creates a dark, threatening atmosphere. By standards of the time set by *The Exorcist,* the action is comparatively inoffensive, but this is top-drawer, well-acted stuff. The electronic score by Brian Hodgson and Delia Derbyshire adds a lot.

Legend of the Werewolf (1975)

Despite transformation and monster effects that aren't all they could be, this interpretation of the wolfman story is worth a look. As he did in *Curse of the Werewolf,* writer Anthony Hinds approaches the story realistically. Young Etoile's (David Rintoul) doomed parents are poor European political refugees. He's raised by wolves and as a boy, is taken in by a carnival barker (Hugh Griffith). The emotional upheavals of puberty spark his murderous changes. Those, of course, bring a curious pathologist (Peter Cushing) into the picture. With that strong cast, including Ron Moody, the acting is excellent and the story is strong. The nineteenth-century French settings and characters recall Lautrec.

Lemora: A Child's Tale of the Supernatural (1973)

Obscure drive-in horror is obviously made by people with more enthusiasm than experience or resources. (In an interview accompanying the film on the videotape release, director Richard Blackburn admits as much when he de-

The Top Twelve Fiendish Family Movies

Parents
Texas Chainsaw Massacre
House of 1,000 Corpses
Cronos
Frailty
Spider Baby
The Stepfather
Poltergeist
The Uninvited
Insidious
Haunting in Connecticut
Hills Have Eyes

scribes the making of the film and its distribution in the early 1970s.) The 1930s story of devout young Christian Lila Lee's (Rainbeaux Smith) search for her gangster father is essentially a classic voyage to the underworld with a seedy bus driver serving as the Charon figure who takes her on the first steps to the title character (a memorable Leslie Gilb). Despite crude production values, the film creates a frightening, hallucinatory mood. It also skirts the exploitation elements so common in the genre (note the subtitle) and deserves its strong cult following.

Leopard Man (1943)

Though many consider this Val Lewton–Jacques Tourneur collaboration to be less successful than either *The Cat People* or *I Walked With a Zombie,* it's cut from the same highly stylized cloth and it isn't derivative of the other two. The story—based on Cornell Woolrich's novel *Black Alibi* and more mystery than true horror—concerns murders in a New Mexico town that are blamed on an escaped leopard. A threatening aura of the unknown is strong, particularly in the famous street scenes. But the film's attempts at social criticism—"The poor don't cheat one another," a character ponderously states, "they're all poor together"—are forced, naïve, and out of place. Today, the lack of location exteriors doesn't help either.

Let the Right One In (2008)
Let Me In (2010)

Oskar (Kåre Hedebrant) is a lonely Stockholm kid who suffers at the hands of school bullies. One night he meets Eli (Lina Leandersson) who's just moved into the apartment next door. She's lonely, too, for her own reasons. So begins the second-best vampire movie of the century (right after *30 Days of Night*). It's spare, moody, quiet, confidently paced, and bloody at the right moments. The two young leads could hardly be better and their evolving relationship is the center of the story. Dialogue has been pared to a minimum and so the subtitles are barely noticeable.

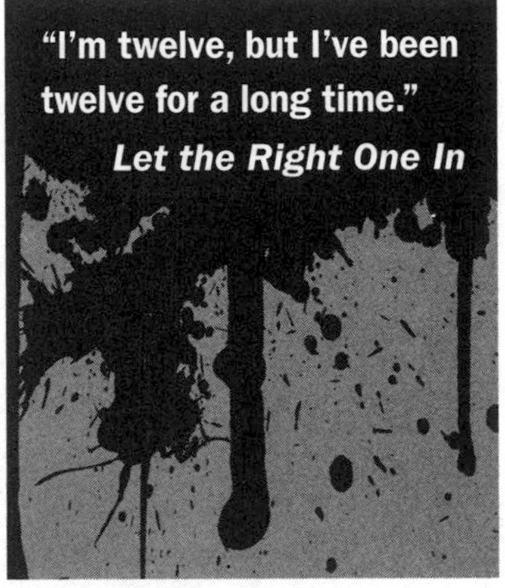

It was remade in 2010 as *Let Me In.* The plot is rearranged to frontload one big scene, and it's been changed in some important ways. Again, the young stars, Kodi Smit-McPhee and Chloë Grace Moretz, are fine. Still, I much prefer the original, particularly at the end, where the bright, climactic scene is reduced to muddy obfuscation in the American version. By the way, it is an appropriate choice to relaunch the Hammer brand, since the studio flourished in the 1960s with remakes of the great Universal horrors.

Leviathan (1989)

Influenced by James Cameron's *The Abyss,* a spate of underwater horror movies were released in the late 1980s. This is one of the better attempts, despite a familiar story—huge monster attacks undersea mining camp, killing the crew. Director George Cosmatos builds suspense through misdirection and downplays graphic special effects. He got good performances from a troupe of fine character actors in stock roles: competent captain (Peter Weller), joker (Daniel Stern), grumbler (Ernie Hudson), his sidekick (Michael Carmine), fitness freak (Amanda Pays), Doc (Richard Crenna), worrier (Hector Elizondo), bright babe (Lisa Eilbacher), and, of course, the critter who owes a debt to *Alien.*

Lifeforce (1985)

Using only the bare bones of Colin Wilson's fine novel, *The Space Vampires,* screenwriters Dan O'Bannon and Don Jakoby add lots of fancy effects and a bizarre, senseless ending. Capt. Carlsen (a manic Steve Railsback) of the space shuttle *Churchill,* discovers a huge ship with dead bat-like creatures and three humans preserved in plastic. Back on Earth, the humans reawaken and zap people. The sequence where a buck naked Matilda May stalks several security guards must be seen to be believed. For an hour and forty minutes of cheap thrills, you could do worse.

Lifespan (1975)

Cerebral sci-fi/horror is too slow and talky, particularly at first, but stick with it. The story of a conspiracy and a search for an immortality drug—or "death control pill," as one character puts it—is rewarding and different. Young Dr. Benjamin Lamb (Hiram Keller) is an American in Amsterdam who tries to find the results of a dead colleague's missing research. In the process, he becomes kinkily involved with the man's mistress, Anna (Tina Aumont), and a suave menacing stranger (Klaus Kinski) from Switzerland. With his images of death, aging, Nazi atrocities, and grave robbing, director Alexander Whitelaw creates a growing atmosphere of menace. It builds a bit too deliberately to a properly unconventional ending. Whitelaw is also responsible for the unusual *Vicious Circles.*

Link (1986)

In the opening scene of this made-for-cable English horror, producer-director Richard Franklin shows off with some flashy camera moves. Dr. Phillip (Terrence Stamp) hires Jane Chase (Elisabeth Shue) to be his assistant. The trouble starts when their primate experiments at a remote seaside mansion result in carnivorous chimps. Even the excellent casting combined with a few good effects aren't enough to overcome the limits of the script which calls for the human characters to aim most of their dialogue at chimps and orangutans. Stamp seems vaguely contemptuous of the material, and not without reason. For a much deeper and frightening examination of similar ideas, see George Romero's *Monkey Shines.*

Lisa and the Devil (1974)

Lisa Reiner (Elke Sommer), a tourist, sees a medieval fresco of a bald devil. Moments later in an antique store, she meets Telly Savalas. They're the same guy! A long dark night of discovery at an ornate mansion ensues, and the action takes on a finely tuned surrealistic edge. According to various reports, soon after it was finished, the film was re-edited (and retitled *House of Exorcism*) to cash in on the popularity of *The Exorcist* and has been seen only rarely in its intended form. That's a real shame because this is one of Mario Bava's most controlled, beautifully photographed, and sumptuous works. Savalas is sardonically superb. Though the film was fairly daring in its day, now the coy nudity is almost charming. At the end of the Anchor Bay VHS edition, three key scenes of sex and violence have been salvaged. They

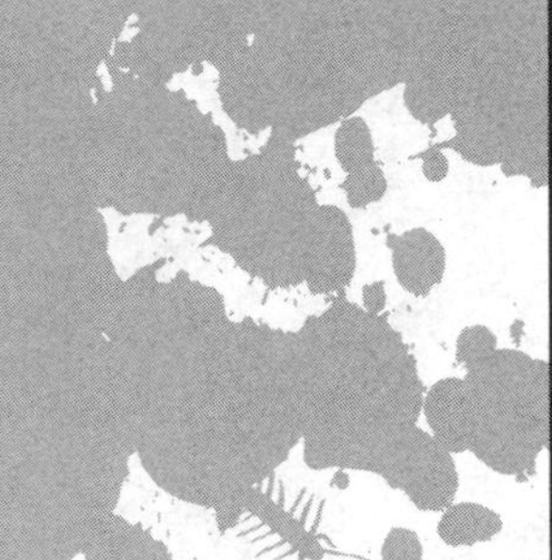

The Top Eight Frighteningly Fearsome Faces

Basketcase
Funhouse
Hills Have Eyes
Phantom of the Opera
Frankenstein
The Dark
Nosferatu
Shadow of the Vampire

provide an interesting look at the filmmaking process, but the end result is actually better without them. A hard-to-find Image DVD contains both titles.

Listen (1996)

Sarah's (Brooke Langton) best pal, the slinky Krista (Sarah G. Buxton), expects more from their relationship, even though Sarah has just moved into her boyfriend Jake's (Gordon Currie from *Blood and Donuts*) San Francisco apartment building. At the same time, another of those pesky psycho serial killers is preying on prostitutes. Canadian director Gavin Wilding and writers Jonas Quastel and Michael Bafaro understand that the serial killer has become such a stock character that the details of that side are merely sketched in. The ending is particularly good with a "it's him - no, it's him - no, it's her - no, it's the first guy!" series of twists. *Scream* fans have seen worse.

Little Shop of Horrors (1960, 1986)

Producer-director Roger Corman brags that he made his most famous cult hit in only two days on a leftover sound stage for a budget somewhere between $22,000 and $100,000. Today it's still enjoyable with some genuinely funny gems surrounded by wall-to-wall, hambone overacting. The carnivorous flower Audrey Jr. is a fair special effect that's easily upstaged by Dick Miller as a florivorous man. Beyond that—and a kinetic last reel—the action is all talk, including a fine Dragnet parody. The story is the basis for a hugely popular stage musical that was filmed in 1986.

It is a lively, funny, snappy, scary, bizarre, and surprising musical horror that strikes a strange edgy tone in the first scene and maintains it all the way through. Somehow, Frank Oz is able to remain true to the double roots of his story—Roger Corman's famous cult hit and the off-Broadway play based on it—without letting a large budget and high-powered cast ruin

Stage production versions of *Little Shop of Horrors* have created elaborate puppet versions of Audrey II, such as this one from the Menier Chocolate Factory in London, England.

things. As the star-crossed lovers Seymour and Audrey, Rick Moranis and Ellen Greene are very good, though they're upstaged by Steve Martin as a sadistic Elvisian dentist and, of course, Audrey II, the carnivorous houseplant that begins looking like a Brussels sprout with lips and ends as a huge, tentacled monster. Great songs.

Living Death (2006)

If director Erin Berry had had a budget that matched his script and his cast, this would be a cult favorite. Victor Harris (Greg Byrk) is a wealthy sadist who loves to torture the women he picks and then to buy them off. His wife (Kristy Swanson) and lawyer (Joshua Peace) put up with that and his personal abuse. Early on, you'll see exactly where the story is headed. But you'll be surprised at how far it goes. Unfortunately, sets, costumes, and sound are threadbare. The gory elements and the humor are fine.

Lodger, The: A Story of the London Fog (1926, 1944)

Like so much of Hitchcock's work, this early silent thriller blurs the lines between horror and mystery. Loosely based on Jack the Ripper, it's a serial killer tale. The title character (Ivor Novello) may be "The Avenger" who murders blonde women. He has a strongly vampiric appearance, both ominous and seductive. The familiar Hitchcock themes emerge—fear of police, the blonde heroine, the man who wants to control her, the innocent on the run from the law—and his simple effective methods of building suspense are already in place. Note the what's-in-the-box scene. Interestingly, at one point, the Lodger wears what appears to be a Freddy Kreuger sweater. Hitch shows up in a newsroom and in a crowd scene on a bridge.

The 1944 sound version holds up quite well. Laird Cregar is superb as the brooding title character and so is George Sanders as the inspector. It's a sleeper worth seeking out by fans who might have missed it.

Lost Boys, The (1987)

Joel Schumacher says, "My fear was that I'd wake up in the middle of the night and thinking, 'My God, you wanted to make *Lawrence of Arabia* and *Grand Illusion* and you're making a teenage vampire movie.' Now, can we make the greatest teen-age vampire in the history of the world?" He may not have accomplished that goal—*Near Dark* comes to mind—but this one's o.k. Michael (Jason Patric) and Sam (Corey Haim) move with their divorced mom (Dianne Wiest) to Santa Carla, CA, "the murder capital of the world" and discover a gang of undead adolescents led by David (Kiefer Sutherland). Schumacher and director of photography Michael Chapman make the flimsy material look much better than it actually is with some dandy visual tricks, and the young cast isn't bad, either. Still, the story relies so much on Hollywood conventions that it's easy to predict what's going to happen, and the big finish is equally stereotyped stuff.

Lost Continent (1968)

Hammer's most bizarre production is impossible to describe. It begins with a wildly inappropriate theme song and electric organ score that could have come from happy hour at a motel cocktail lounge. That introduces a group of characters from a Graham Greene novel inexplicably transplanted into a seagoing Edgar Rice Burroughs plot. A leaky freighter is en route to Caracas with a dangerous explosive cargo, five desperate passengers with secrets of their own, a troubled cynical captain (Eric Porter), and a mutinous crew. On the horizon lie a hurricane, carnivorous seaweed, religious persecution, and giant man-eating mollusks. The whole thing is every bit as strange, screwy, and wonderful as it sounds. No, it's not completely successful but it's never dull. The Anchor Bay DVD contains eight minutes that were too "adult" for American audiences in 1968.

Lost Highway (1997)

David Lynch's surreal horror is a noirish horror-mystery without answers told through the "logic" of a nightmare. To enjoy the film, if that's possible, viewers must forget about narrative conventions and accept Lynch's dreamy evocation of 3:00 A.M. nightworld delirium where nothing is certain. In the opening scene, a voice over an intercom tells saxophonist Fred Madison (Bill Pullman) "Dick Laurent is dead." Fred suspects that his sultry, brunette wife Renee (Patricia Arquette) is unfaithful. A spooky, pop-eyed pasty-faced Mystery Man (Robert Blake) further muddies the waters before Fred is inexplicably transformed into young mechanic Pete Dayton (Balthazar Getty) who falls for Alice (Patricia Arquette again), platinum blonde moll of the vicious mobster Mr. Eddy (Robert Loggia who, according to the credits, is also the aforementioned Dick Laurent). Throughout, the sex is hot and graphic, and so is the violence. Those, of course, are Lynch's stock and trade. This one may please his most rabid fans, but it's unlikely to win many converts to the cause.

Lost Skeleton of Cadavra, The (2001)

Gentle spoof of '50s sci-fi/horror stays true to its source material with black-and-white photography, stilted dialogue, Bronson Canyon locations, and intentionally cheap effects and costumes. The mutant monster is one of the silliest man-in-a-bad-rubber-suit creations you'll ever see. The alien couple who allow him to escape aren't as funny as the Coneheads. Overall, the film lacks the quick pace and energy of the best originals.

Lost Souls (2000)

Once again, Satan is trying to take things over here on Earth, in a variation on *Rosemary's Baby.* His target is writer Peter Kelson (Ben Chaplin). Devout young Maya Larkin (Winona Ryder) and Father Lareux (John Hurt) have stumbled

The Top Nine (+) Horrors Made from "Found" Footage

The Last Broadcast
The Last Exorcism
The Blair Witch Project
Diary of the Dead
Paranormal Activity series
[REC]
Quarantine

onto his wily scheme and stand in the way. Noted cinematographer-turned-director Janusz Kaminski gives the proceedings a more sophisticated look than they really deserve, but he lets the pace mope along. Overall, it's a cut above most of the similarly themed films that were made in those years, with fine support from Philip Baker Hall, but it doesn't come close to *Rosemary.*

Lost World: Jurassic Park, The

See Jurassic Park

Lucinda's Spell (1998)

If Anne Rice and Mel Brooks teamed up to make a sexy horror, they might come up with something like this silly romp. Jason (writer/director Jon Jacobs) is a direct descendant of Merlin the Magician. He's on schedule to conceive a supernatural offspring on the Eve of Beltane. All the witches in New Orleans want to be the lucky bachelorette he chooses. Lucinda (Christina Fulton) is a hooker with a heart of gold and a history with His Wizardness. It plays out as an energetic B-movie with a '60s drive-in feel and an uncertain tone that veers from comic to serious to bawdy.

Lust for a Vampire (1971)

Hammer's follow up to *The Vampire Lovers* is a weak vehicle made without the studio's usually solid plotting. The initial reconstitution of a dead vampire has been done before and much more elaborately. Most of the action is set in a girl's school, giving the producers license to have the young ladies indulge in assorted toplessness, back rubs, and one wrongheaded bit of interpretive dance. Seductress Carmilla (Yutte Stensgaard) is blandly, blondly pretty, and she tends to cross her eyes when feigning ecstasy which is kind of cute. It's obvious throughout that the filmmakers are going through familiar motions. Not the studio's finest hour, but one of its sexier.

Luther, the Geek (1990)

Bizarre little 1990 production has earned itself a strong underground reputation. Here, the word "geek" is used in its original meaning. Forget nerds; it actually refers to carnival performers who bite the heads off of live animals, usually chickens in the United States. That's what the title character does. He's also a homicidal maniac who sets his sights on a rural Midwestern farm house. The result might have been titled *The Chainsaw Massacres of Madison County.* Director Carlton Albright aims for that same Grand Guignol combination of sex and violence. The presence of Stacy Haiduk doesn't hurt a bit.

M (1931)

With a fact-based story, Fritz Lang set the formula for the serial killer/crime/horror film in 1931. Franz Beckert (Peter Lorre) is a compulsive child murderer whose crimes paralyze a city. When the cops clamp down on the local underworld, the crooks decide to catch the killer themselves. Lang tells the story by intercutting among the various forces involved, but at the horrific heart of the story is Lorre's brilliant performance as a human monster. Though the film was released in the same year as Lugosi's *Dracula,* it's by far the more frightening of the two today. Lorre embodies many of the evils that Lugosi symbolizes. At the beginning, Lang uses starkly simple images—a ball, a balloon, an empty dinner plate—to convey the enormity of the crimes. Then Lang turns things around with Lorre's haunted confession. At the end, when various parties comment on the terrible crimes they frame a debate that's still going on today. *M* is simply one of the world's great films.

Mad Doctor of Blood Island (1968)

"Now the Mad Doctor of Blood Island invites YOU to join him in taking the OATH of GREEN BLOOD.... I, a living breathing creature of the cosmic entity, am now ready to enter the realm of those chosen to be allowed to drink of the Mystic Emerald fluids herein offered. I join the Order of Green Blood with an open mind and through this liquid's powers am now prepared to safely view the unnatural green-blooded ones without fear of contamination." Unfortunately, that on-screen introduction is the best part of this campy, politically incorrect Philippine import. It's a standard mad scientist story with a guy in a cheap monster mask and gloves. The directors are fond of an unwatchable pulsing in and out zoom to introduce the critter. The film is also an early appearance of cult favorite Angelique Pettyjohn who died in 1992.

Mad Love (1935)

Yvonne Orlac (Frances Drake) is the reigning "scream queen" of the Parisian Grand Guignol stage. The ominous Dr. Gogol (Peter Lorre in perhaps his most impressive and commanding role after *M*) is her biggest fan and his devotion is indeed, mad love. Though the oft-filmed plot involves Gogol's transplanting hands onto her pianist husband Stephen (Colin Clive), the film belongs to Lorre. The main flaw is the comic relief of the period. The black-and-white photography is superb, and some of the sets are impressive, but nothing on screen tops Lorre's eggshell-smooth bald dome, and the makeup he wears toward the end.

Magic (1978)

The strengths of this psychological horror are writer William Goldman's solid knowledge of the working side of show business and his typically well-constructed plot. On the other side of the camera are three terrific performances by Anthony Hopkins as Corky Withers, the magician with deep problems; Ann-Margret as Peg Snow, the girl from his past; and Burgess Meredith as Ben Green, his caring agent. If Richard Attenborough's direction is a bit too studied, the story is compelling and the whole film has that rough, unpolished quality that makes good '70s movies so rewatchable. The upstate New York locations are fine, and the emotional underpinnings of the story are unusual but accurate.

Manhunter (1986)

Michael Mann's slick psycho-killer film wasn't the huge popular hit that Jonathan Demme's *Silence of the Lambs* became, but it's still a well-made crime/horror tale. Both films tell the same story—FBI agent (William Petersen) enlists the help of jailed psychotic genius Hannibal Lecktor (sic) (deftly underplayed by Brian Cox) in nabbing another psycho. Both films also attempt to get inside the mind of today's most popular stock villain, the serial killer. And, of course, both are based on Thomas Harris's fine novels. (*Silence* is the sequel to *Red Dragon* [see review] the source for *Manhunter.*) Mann is an inventive stylist who can pump up ordinary scenes with pastel light, odd camera angles, and the like. But those same tricks keep him from getting to the

The Top Thirty Golden Oldies That Every Fan Should See

The Raven
The Body Snatcher
Devil Doll (1936)
Devil Doll (1964)
Last Man on Earth (1963)
King Kong
Isle of the Dead
Mad Love
Mark of the Vampire
Nosferatu
The Old Dark House
Premature Burial
Red House
Strange Door
The Tingler
The Uninvited (1944)
Vampire Bat
Vampyr
Wait Until Dark
Walking Dead
What Ever Happened to Baby Jane?
Witchcraft Through the Ages
Cabinet of Dr. Caligari
Horror Chamber of Dr. Faustus
Island of Lost Souls
Peeping Tom
The Changeling
A Christmas Carol
Carnival of Souls
Dr. Jekyll and Mr. Hyde (1941)
Freaks

emotional core that Jodie Foster, Anthony Hopkins, and Demme found in *Silence.* The supporting characters—including Cox, Tom Noonan as the killer, and Joan Allen as the woman who might save him from his madness—are as interesting as the leads. The offbeat rock score has aged poorly.

Maniac (1980)

Director William Lustig collaborated with writer-star Joe Spinnell and effects wizard Tom Savini in the production of this above-average psycho-killer tale. The plot is loosely based, in part, on the New York Son of Sam murders. Frank Zito (Spinnell) is a fat, pathetic loner who murders and scalps women. Some of the physical details of his life and crimes ring true, but the psychological side is a collection of pop clichés, all based on another bad mommy. In the end, it's one of the best examples of a limited and distasteful genre. Spinnell and co-star Caroline Munro would play similar characters in *The Last Horror Movie.*

Maniac Cop (1988)
Maniac Cop 2 (1990)
Maniac Cop 3: Badge of Silence (1993)

First-rate action/horror benefits enormously from an all-star B-movie cast turning in unusually energetic performances. Between them, producer-writer Larry Cohen and director William Lustig have been responsible for some of the best low-budget entertainment (and a few clunkers). This slightly overplotted variation on the slasher stereotype makes good use of New York locations, and it's got a nice sense of humor. The main flaw is supposedly tough vice cop Lauren Landon who shrieks like a schoolgirl at any hint of violence. Yes, that's director Sam Raimi as the TV reporter at the St. Patrick's Day parade.

For those who missed the first film or have forgotten it, *MC2* begins with the big finish wherein the title character (Robert Z'Dar) is impaled through the chest by a large wooden beam. Is that enough to keep a potentially profitable psycho-monster down? You know it's not. Cohen and Lustig create realistically nasty urban squalor. The Hollywood gunplay is standard issue with shotgunned bodies flying through plate glass windows; so are the other cop clichés. Outlandish chases with superb stuntwork are better. Only the last third approaches the filmmakers' better work.

Though begun by Larry Cohen and William Lustig, *MC3: Badge of Silence* has since been disowned by them, acording to Lustig. It opens with a voodoo ritual reviving the oft-deceased psycho-patrolman (Robert Z'Dar). According to co-director Lustig, the people who financed the film were trying, inexplicably, to make a *Maniac Cop* movie for people who don't like *Maniac Cop* movies. The relatively "realistic" urban environment becomes a caricature, and the tone of moral superiority that the film takes to tabloid journalism is thoroughly hypocritical. Like Jason and Freddy, MC gets weaker and more heavily padded with recycled material from the earlier films with each outing.

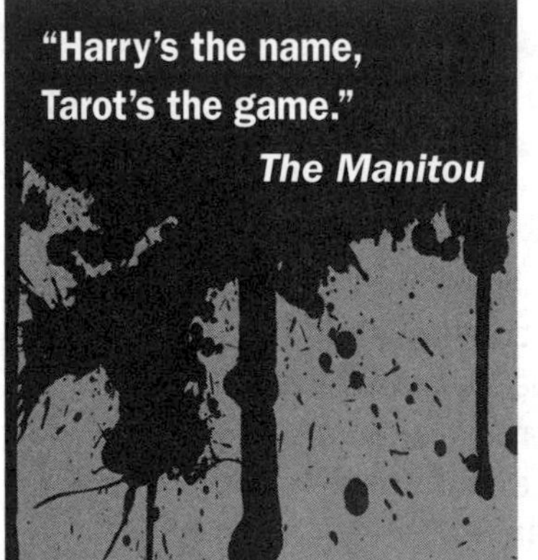

Manitou, The (1978)

Pure hokum at least has the courage of its hokey convictions. It's working in a narrow range between supernatural horror and light comedy, and manages to carry it off entertainingly because the production values are unusually high—the film looks much more polished than many of the period—and because Tony Curtis turns in a canny performance in a role perfectly suited to his skills. He's Erskin, a bogus medium whose ex-girlfriend Karen (Susan Strasberg) has developed a tumor on her neck. The growth eventually becomes a monster that takes over a hospital. Stella Stevens, Ann Southern, Burgess Meredith, and Michael Ansara provide better support than their stereotyped characters deserve. Director William Girdler also made *Grizzly* and *Abby* before he was killed in a helicopter crash.

Manmade Monster (1941)

"Dynamo Dan" McCormick (Lon Chaney Jr.) is already a carnival star when he survives a bus crash into a high tension power pole. The evil "electrobiologist" Dr. Rigas (Lionel Atwill) subjects him to experiments that make Dan a voltage junkie of enormous strength. The result is a crazed variation on *Frankenstein* with indescribable effects. The whole idea of a character invulnerable to electrocution was popular in the early days of cinematic horror. This is neither the best nor the worst example, made with the studio's usual high standards and tight-fisted budget.

Man-Thing (2005)

Silly formula tale never strays far from its shallow comic book roots in terms of plot, acting, and production values. New sheriff Williams (Matthew Le Nevez) finds that the locals are protesting against the Schist Petroleum drilling operation. They're assisted by a creature born out of the fecund, primordial ooze of the Bywater swamp. When the title creature shows up, he seems to share some cinematic DNA with those angry trees that threw their apples at Dorothy and the Scarecrow.

Mark of the Vampire (1935)

Even though the supernatural elements are discounted in the end, and despite egregious comic relief, the strong images, fine acting, and graveyard atmospherics make this one of the 1930s' finest moments. Lionel Barrymore, as the investigating Professor, is almost as impressive as Bela Lugosi's virtually mute Count Mora and his daughter Luna (Carol Borland), who makes one grand airborne entrance. Until the unfortunate denouement, director Tod Browning and cinematographer James Wong Howe create beautiful and spooky black-and-white images that rival *Frankenstein* and *Dracula.* Recommended.

Martin (1976)

Is Martin (John Amplas) a very disturbed young man, or is he an eighty-four-year-old vampire? His older cousin (Lincoln Maazel) from the old country believes the latter and wants to save Martin's soul and then to destroy him. Whatever the truth, Martin is killing people. So what if he uses drugs and razorblades instead of hypnotic gazes and fangs—the results are the same. In the end, George Romero's story is about being human. With its grainy color and closely observed Pittsburgh locations, the film is reminiscent of another often overlooked Romero gem, *Monkey Shines*. The characters have been so thoroughly stripped of conventional movie glamour that the picture is much more realistic than 99 percent of the movies that come out of Hollywood. (That's Romero as Father Howard.) *Martin* is one of horror's most accomplished sleepers.

Mary Reilly (1996)

Director Stephen Frears makes a mistake in his first shot by opening with Julia Roberts on her knees scrubbing a stoop, and the camera focused squarely on her butt. Nobody looks good from that angle. After it, though, Frears settles down to tell the story (based on Valerie Martin's novel) of Dr. Jekyll (John Malkovich) from the point of view of one of his servants, Mary Reilly (Roberts). It's a dark tale made more so by Mary's memories of childhood abuse. The flaws are obvious—slow pace, Roberts' on-and-off Irish accent—and so are the positives—Malkovich's performance, great sets, strong Gothic atmosphere. Each generation reinterprets the Jekyll and Hyde story, and this version makes legitimate and thoughtful contributions, albeit somewhat laboriously and obviously. Recommended to students of Stevenson's original and to those who are curious about the proper method of skinning a live eel.

Mary Shelley's Frankenstein

See Frankenstein

Masque of the Red Death, The (1964, 1989)

In terms of budget, the 1964 production is Roger Corman's most lavish and expensive Poe adaptation. Vincent Price attacks his role as the evil Prince Prospero with obvious delight, but he's still almost upstaged by Hazel Court at her loveliest. Charles Beaumont's script borrows from other Poe stories,

The Top Twenty (+) Gore Intensive Horrors

Borderland
Wrong Turn
High Tension
House of 1,000 Corpses
Dead Alive
Emerald Jungle
Midnight Meat Train
Passion of the Christ
Return of the Living Dead series
Saw series
Storm Warning
Texas Chainsaw Massacre
2000 Maniacs
2001 Maniacs
Undead
Wax Mask
Wizard of Gore
Severance
Wizard of Gore (2007)
Frontier(s)

most obviously "Hop-Frog," and the film is fleshed out with moderate doses of '60s sin, sex, and psychedelia. The result, photographed by Nicholas Roeg, has aged well.

The 1989 Corman-produced remake is curiously slow and dispirited though fairly faithful to Poe's story. Prince Prospero (Adrian Paul) tries to defeat the plague of the Red Death by bringing all of his noble pals inside and sealing the gates of the city. He imports a few comely peasant wenches for entertainment and also invites his old teacher, Machiavel (Patrick MacNee). Prospero is a dark, brooding sort who's prone to sophomoric philosophical reflection when he's not paying more attention than he should to his sister Lucretia (Tracy Reimer). He worries about life and death and the duty of the prince and stuff like that. Despite atmospheric sets; silly costumes, wigs, and dialogue; swordfights; and boiling oil to pour on the peasants, the film lacks the two key ingredients that make the best Corman movies so enjoyable: speed and lack of self-consciousness.

Mausoleum (1983)

Traumatized as a young girl by the death of her mother, Susan (Bobbie Bresee) sees visions in a haunted cemetery. Ten years later, the Nomed family curse strikes. Her eyeballs are tinted green, fog floats down the hallway of her palatial home, and she turns into a monstrous hairy demon with carnivorous breasts. The mix of too-familiar lighting and sound effects generates no real scares, though some of John Buechler's makeup has shock value. The plot is a silly mish-mash of *Carrie* and *The Exorcist* with more exploitation elements, though Bresee and Marjoe Gortner, as her worried husband, handle the material fairly seriously. Fans of cheap thrills have seen worse and much better.

May (2002)

Independently produced psychological horror begins with an act of shocking violence and then backtracks to reveal how and why May Canady (Angela Bettis) came to that point. She's a painfully shy young woman who works for a dubious veterinarian and lives in a cluttered apartment with a weird doll. On her lunch breaks, she watches Adam (Jeremy Sisto at his creepiest) but doesn't know how to approach him. Over time, the line between May's fantasies and reality becomes increasingly blurred. Though the film isn't as polished, Angela Bettis' performance is right up there with Catherine Deneuve in *Repulsion* and Natalie Portman in *Black Swan.* Don't miss the story about Seymour the dog.

Mega-Python versus Gatoroid (2011)

Every aspect of this made-for-TV alternative classic is done on the cheap—casting, writing, locations, sets, effects, even the well-worn premise. Reptile-rights activist (Deborah Gibson) releases laboratory snakes into the swamp. Ranger (Tiffany) has to deal with their gigantic offspring. About the best that can be said of the result is that nobody involved had any illusions about what they were doing. They're looking for laughs, not scares.

Messengers, The (2007)

Handsomely produced but flawed ghost story begins with a family moving into a grim North Dakota farmhouse that might have been moved from that hill behind the Bates Motel. Terrible things have happened there in the recent past and they are soon visited on daughter Jessie (Kristen Stewart, getting warmed up for the *Twilight* movies) and her mute baby brother. At first, the chittering creatures are effective and so is the attention to detail in extreme close-ups. Soon, though, the scares become programmed, particularly the bits lifted from *The Birds,* and a major continuity error pops up. Finally, the goofy conclusion feels like a cheat, leaving lots of loose ends. Followed by a prequel.

The Top Eight Most Memorable Women of Horror

- *Misery*
- *Repulsion*
- *May*
- *Daughters of Darkness*
- *Vampyres*
- *Audition*
- *Black Swan*
- *Ginger Snaps*

Midnight Meat Train, The (2008)

Borrowing bits from *Seven* and *The Vanishing,* this gore-fest certainly lives up to its title. Leon (Bradley Cooper) is a New York photographer who gets a shot of a young woman minutes before she disappears one night on a subway train. He thinks he might also have caught a picture of a spooky butcher (Vinnie Jones) who had something to do with it all. The first act of violence is sudden, brutal, and shocking. The excesses that follow include but are not limited to decapitations, eviscerations, impalements, and stuff that they don't have names for, all shown in the "photo-realism" afforded by computer effects. The action is presented in cold blue tints to distort and darken the most graphic moments. By the end, the plot has taken so many ridiculous turns that even the ultraviolence has lost much of its punch. That said, Ryûhei Kitamura's film is aimed squarely at fans who aren't looking for subtlety.

Mighty Peking Man (1977)

The title character in this bizarre riff on King Kong is a guy in a moth-eaten gorilla/caveman suit who destroys sets of miniature villages and cities. Why? It all has to do with the love of his life, a fetching blonde (Evelyne Kraft) who runs around in a skimpy leather bikini. Frantic energy, delirious pace, and high-camp humor are the main attractions.

Milo (1998)

To my mind, any horror film that involves threats to children has a high bar to cross, and this low-budget effort never comes close. A slow, confusing dreamlike introduction with a group of little girls and an ominous boy sets a distasteful tone. The rest concerns teacher Claire Mullins (Jennifer Jostyn, who's better than the material) who returns to her hometown to face those terrifying childhood memories. The repetitive piano theme is irritating, the acting poor, and the writing is worse.

Mimic (1997)

Guillermo del Toro's *Cronos* is the most innovative and original take on the traditional vampire that anyone's made in decades. With the help of writers John Sayles, Steven Soderbergh, and Matthew Robbins, he does the same with big-bug-sci-fi/horror here, combining humanism with bizarre effects. A snowy New York City introduction establishes Dr. Susan Tyler (Mira Sorvino) as the science babe who inadvertently creates the creatures in question when she cures a devastating cockroach-borne children's plague. Three years later, giant mutant bugs decide it's payback time. Compared to *Cronos,* these scares and jolts are more conventionally telegraphed—not surprising in a big-budget studio release—and the influence of TV's *X-Files* is all too evident. Otherwise, the film boasts great sets, a high-octane third act, and nasty bug effects (and bug guts effects) from Rob Bottin and Tyruben Ellingson. Followed by a direct-to-DVD sequel.

Mirror, Mirror (1990)
Mirror, Mirror 2: Raven Dance (1994)
Mirror, Mirror 3: The Voyeur (1995)

Curious feminist horror is based on a huge old supernatural mirror that bridges generations and dimensions. (Or something to that effect; the details aren't spelled out.) The setting is a small town where oddball newcomer Megan (Rainbow Harvest) has a hard time adjusting to high school. She finds herself captivated by the antique mirror left in the bedroom of her new house. As she spends more time with it, terrible things happen to those who torment her at school. The script—written by four women, one of them director Marina Sargenti—borrows liberally from *Beetlejuice, The Amityville Horror, Carrie,* and several other Stephen King works. Throughout, the male characters are either well-meaning oafs or pawns to be manipulated by their evil girlfriends. At its best, the film avoids blatant violence and instead uses blood as a metaphor.

Mirror, Mirror 2: Raven Dance opens with a tattooed, skinhead band playing at a Catholic orphanage for no audience, so you know that plot doesn't count for much. The effects are all that this one has going for itself. They range from a guy in a silly rubber suit to some really good, inventive work done with lights and computers. The violence is too outlandish to be offensive. A cast of horror vets including Roddy McDowall, Sally Kellerman, William Sanderson, Veronica Cartwright and several continuity errors are part of the fun, too.

Mirror, Mirror 3: The Voyeur begins with some computer-enhanced stuff that's pretty fancy for a low-budget effort and continues to attempt more than it can deliver. The semi-hysterical plot launches into ritual suicide (sort of) by Cassandra (Monique Parent) because she can't be with her lover Anthony (Billy Drago) while her drug-dealing husband has stashed a briefcase full of cash in the living room of the empty mansion where they live. Really poor sound is the most obvious corner that the filmmakers cut. Cheapjack action sequences don't add anything. The recurring image of two rotisserie chickens—apparently meant to represent the lovers—is an appropriately daft touch. The two directors may well have made two separate but tangential movies—one about the drug business involving David Naughton as a cop, the other an erotic reincarnation tale with a fair special effects finish—and chopped them together.

Mirrors (2008)

Remake of the Korean film *Into the Mirror* is roughly as successful as *The Ring* and *The Grudge.* Troubled New York cop Ben Carson (Kiefer Sutherland) takes a job as a night watchman at a burned out department store where he finds troubling images flickering inside the mirrors. They materialize, if that's the right term, to threaten him and his family. Writer/director Alexandre Aja understands the material and works with it well, without letting the inventive optical effects overpower the rest. The violence in the unrated version is properly bloody. I like the ending, too.

Misery (1990)

Annie Wilkes (Kathy Bates) is perhaps Steven King's most impressive and memorable human monster. She's a madwoman whose obsession with the fictional Misery Chastain is transformed into a fantasy-come-true when she rescues Misery's creator (James Caan) from a car accident and imprisons him in her cluttered, claustrophobic Rocky Mountain cabin. William Goldman's script is airtight. The best scares are intense and shocking. Some of King's ideas about the relationship between popular artist and fan are lost in translation to the screen. Bates' Oscar-winning performance is unforgettable and overshadows Caan's more controlled work.

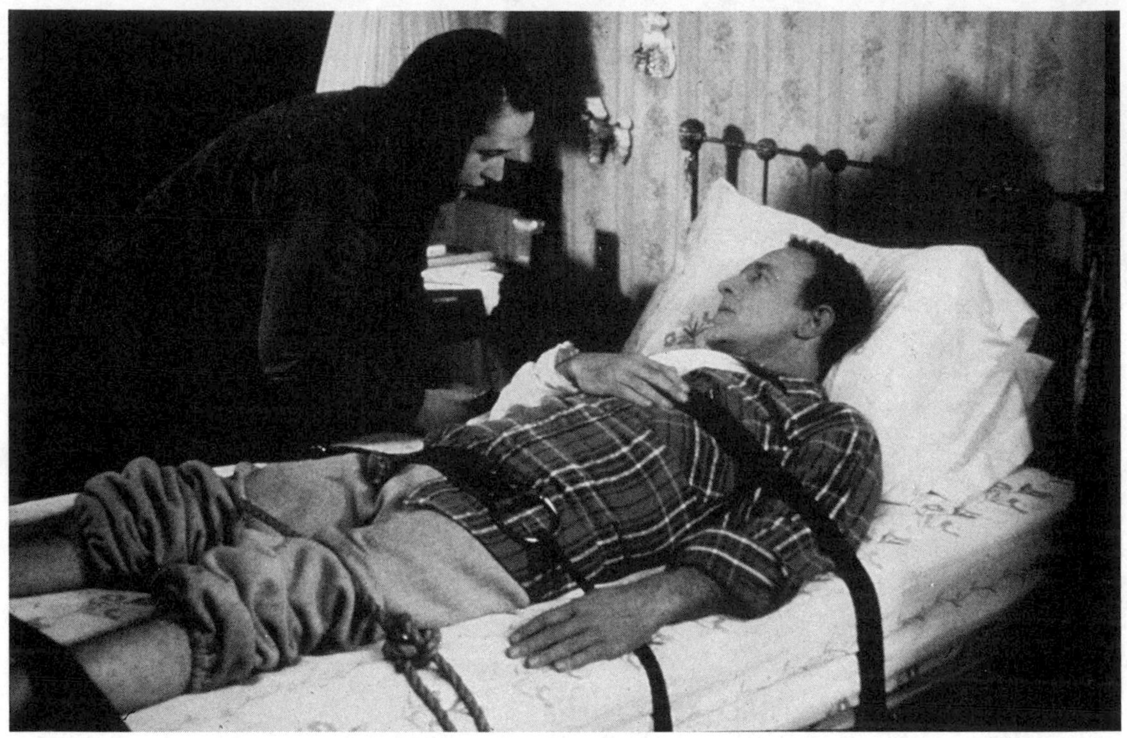

Kathy Bates plays a psychotic nurse who imprisons her favorite author (James Caan) in Stephen King's *Misery.*

Mist, The (2007)

Adaptation of a Stephen King novella is very similar in theme, plot, and characters to *Dreamcatcher.* After a violent electric storm, the residents of a small town awake to find a curious mist approaching them across a lake. David Drayton (Thomas Jane) and his young son are in a grocery store when it closes in over them, and nasty creatures, mostly giant bugs and spiders and toothy tentacles, attack. That part is a good solid B-movie with overachieving special effects and a cast of excellent character actors. But the downbeat ending is still much too heavy for this kind of escapism. A black-and-white version is available on the special-edition DVD.

Mr. Stitch (1995)

Troubled, stylized update of *Frankenstein* starts slow and never generates any real energy. Much of it takes place on a nearly empty white set where the proverbial mad scientist (Rutger Hauer) has created a sexless patchwork man (Wil Wheaton) who combines all races and genders. Following lengthy discussions of innocence and religion, the plot finally makes an entrance. That has to do with sinister government plots, half-hearted chases, and a sympathetic psychologist (Nia Peeples). Producer/director/writer Roger Avary also co-wrote *Pulp Fiction* but you'd hardly guess it on the basis of this Frano-American effort. It's really more akin to George Lucas' student film-turned-feaure *THX-1138.*

Modern Vampires (1998)

Frantic but lame ultra-low budget comedy is often so dark that you can't tell what's going on. The plot revolves around conflicts within the community of hip, young Hollywood vampires. Casper Van Dien and Natasha Gregson Wagner are attractive but little else in the leads. Beyond a few acceptable effects, it's all dime-store fangs and Rod Steiger, as Van Helsing, cutting loose as only he could.

Monkey Shines: An Experiment in Fear (1988)

George Romero uses Pittsburgh as the setting for a story firmly based in reality. When an accident leaves law student Allan Mann (Jason Beghe) a quadriplegic, his friend Geoffrey (John Pankow) arranges for a special monkey, Ella (Boo), to be trained to help him with the tasks most people take for granted. Also on hand when Allan and Boo become psychically linked are an overprotective mother (Joyce Van Patten) and an ill-tempered nurse (Christine Forrest). The real strength of the film is the way it depicts everyday horror, claustrophobia, and helpless anger. At its worst, an enraged supermonkey is much less frightening than well-intentioned, manipulative friends and relatives.

Monolith Monsters, The (1957)

Admittedly, these are not the most frightening monsters ever to hit the silver screen. They're rocks from outer space that grow tall when they're exposed to water and fall over. Yes, they can turn people to stone but we're out in the middle of the desert. Even so, the movie is kind of cool, not silly. From Paul Frees' stentorian opening voice-over to the big finish, director John Sherwood tells the story economically with a fine score and effects that are interesting even if they aren't particularly frightening.

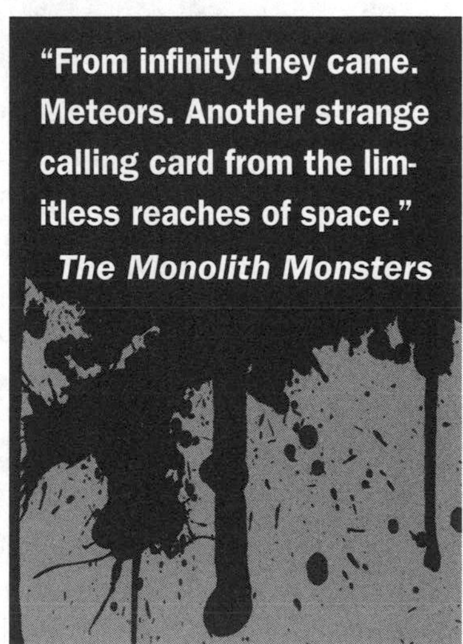

"From infinity they came. Meteors. Another strange calling card from the limitless reaches of space."
The Monolith Monsters

Monster on the Campus (1958)

A defrosted, radioactive coelacanth causes professor Donald Blake (Arthur Franz) to revert to his murderous, lustful caveman roots. Director Jack Arnold handles the slight material with his usual sure touch, but, with its windy speechifying, this is far from his best work. The transformation effects and the rubber-mask creature that results from it are no better or worse than the other Universal releases of the era.

Motel Hell (1980)

"There's all kinds of critters in Farmer Vincent's fritters!" So says the proprietor (Rory Calhoun), famous for his preservative-free, 100-percent natural smoked sausages. But what does he have to do with the automobile accidents that happen nightly near his motel? And what's going on in that walled garden out back? The answers are graphically (but not too graphically) provided in this blackly comic version of *The Texas Chainsaw Massacre.* Before it's over, virtually every melodramatic cliché imaginable—including heroine Nina Axelrod on the buzz saw—has been brought into play. British director Kevin Connor makes good use of stark lighting and gurgling sound effects to create creepy atmosphere. In many ways, this laid the groundwork for *Re-Animator* and the works of Sam Raimi and Peter Jackson.

Mothman Prophecies, The (2002)

Mark Pellington's adaption is completely faithful to the spirit of John Keel's excellent book, if not to the letter. Both are about our deep-seated desire to believe in something. Unable to get over the death of his wife, *Washington Post* reporter John Klein (Richard Gere) inexplicably finds himself in Point Pleasant, West Virginia, where people are scared because very strange things are happening. The unconventional story defies any easy synopsis, and the less you know, the better. The characters all ring true, the performances are moving, and the sense of place is strong. One of the very best.

Mulholland Dr. (2001)

It's pointless to apply a conventional reading of narrative logic to David Lynch's murky work. This film began as a pilot for a TV series. When it did not match studio executives' expectations, Lynch added more material to the story of Betty Elms (Naomi Watts), an ambitious young Canadian actress

The Top Thirteen (+) Guilty Pleasures

Drive Angry
Priest
House That Vanished
House on Straw Hill
Re-Animator
Underworld series
The Wraith
The Banker
Rise: Blood Hunter
Blade Trinity
Dracula 2000
Final Destination series
From Dusk til Dawn

newly arrived in Los Angeles, and the amnesiac Rita (Laura Harring). Tangential subplots involving relatives who shrink, a terrifying meeting at a diner, and a long musical number are all open to several interpretations. Throughout, Lynch maintains the fever dream quality that makes his best work so memorable, not to mention frustrating.

Mummy, The (1932 & 1959)
Mummy's Hand, The (1940)
Mummy's Tomb, The (1942)
Mummy's Ghost, The (1944)
Mummy's Curse, The (1944)

Karloff appears in the famous Mummy makeup only briefly in the memorable first few minutes of this seminal work, made between his initial appearances as the Frankenstein monster. The bandaged image is so memorable, though, that it provides the inspiration for the sequels and remakes that have followed. For most of the film, Karloff is Ardeth Bey, the cold-eyed, glacially slow resurrected Egyptian. In that role, he's really more of a Dracula figure. Helen Grovner (Zita Johnson) is his long-lost love. Karl Freund's stylized direction and the whole art-deco look of the production have aged beautifully. (Some stilted dialogue has not.) Those who know the film only from old creature-feature late shows owe themselves another look. The crisp black and white has been carefully restored to its original clarity, and Boris Karloff's per-

Poster from the original Boris Karloff flick, *The Mummy.*

formance may be the best kept secret of his long career. For those planning a Mummy-thon, the chronological order of the Universal series is as follows.

Things get off to a lighthearted start with *The Mummy's Hand* the second entry which really establishes the ground rules—Tana leaves, high priests of Carnac, princess, etc. Never has Southern California looked less like Egypt than it does here, and when the old priest says "Kharis rests on de udder side ub dis mountain," you know you're not dealing with completely serious material. George Zucco is properly malevolent with Wallace Ford and Cecil Kellaway providing comic relief. Elements of *Dracula* and *The Wolfman* creep in, too.

Lon Chaney Jr. dons the Ace bandages for Mr. M's third outing, *The Mummy's Tomb* and Turhan Bey takes over the priestly skulking duties. A condensed ten-minute version of *Mummy's Hand* sets the scene. After that, the high priest moves to Mapleton, Mass., where he's arranged a job as cemetery caretaker. The dishwater-thin revenge plot depends on the back-lot atmospherics that the studio used so effectively in those days. Chaney's makeup and hum-drum acting are both second rate.

In *The Mummy's Ghost* an uncharacteristically low-keyed John Carradine is the new priest who's called upon to feed Tana-leaf tea to the loosely wrapped Chaney. Even though this entry is marginally less formulaic than the previous entry, it's just as silly and even more unevenly acted by a cast of the studio's stock troupe. The day-for-night effects are noticeably weak. Ramsay Ames does continue the tradition of striking *Mummy* heroines.

Attentive videophiles will remember that at the end of *Ghost,* Kharis (Lon Chaney) shuffled under the surface of the water in a swamp in Mapleton, with his princess sweetie in his arms. At the beginning of *The Mummy's Curse* he emerges from a Louisiana swamp that the government is draining. With equally blithe inexplicability, he has become a part of Cajun lore. A few minutes later, up pops Mrs. Mummy (Virginia Christine) from the muddy tracks of a bulldozer. About the best that can be said of this unapologetically screwloose material is that it's fast, short, and really no worse than you ought to expect for the fifth entry in a series that was always made on parsimonious budgets. The use of the lone black character for comic relief reflects the socially acceptable racism of the 1940s.

Following the success of its versions of *Frankenstein* and *Dracula,* the Hammer studio's third foray into horror, *The Mummy* is one of the studio's most lavish productions. The screen is filled with extravagant sets, costumes, and makeup. (The ancient Egyptians wear enough mascara to supply a dozen New York hookers.) Despite an outfit that virtually immobilizes his face, Christopher Lee makes the title character a creature of impressive strength and size—a four-thousand-year-old fool for love. Even though most of his dialogue is wonderful Egyptological hokum, he maintains a straight face. (It couldn't have been easy.) As always, Peter Cushing is excellent as the doughty hero who does the right thing. Recommended.

In 1999, Universal rebooted the series as big-budget special-effects adventures that have nothing to do with horror.

Murder Weapon (1989)

Legendary low-budget horror reverses all of the conventions of the slasher flick. In this one, the heavy-breathing killer is stalking young guys. Recently released from a psychiatric institution, our heroines Dawn (Linnea Quigley) and Amy (Karen Russell) have, perhaps unadvisedly, gone off their medications. They invite several guys over to their house for an afternoon of beer and whatever. In flashback scenes, their psychiatrist (*Carol Burnett Show* vet-

The Top Seven Heartland Horrors

Children of the Corn
Dario Argento's Trauma
Strange Behavior
Take Shelter
Town That Dreaded Sundown
Tremors
Trick 'R Treat

eran Lyle Waggoner) tries to explain the root of their problems, while, one by one, the guys disappear. There's no real suspense, and the imaginative killings are so illogical and unrealistic that the graphic, prosthetic special effects don't even have much immediate shock value. They're just bloody and silly. The film never tries to be anything more than low-budget escapism and it succeeds at that quite admirably. It's an early effort from the prolific Dave DeCoteau made under his nom de video Ellen Cabot.

My Bloody Valentine (1981, 2009)

In one daring burst of originality, the slasher-killer in this holiday-themed horror uses a pickax instead of a knife. Wow! Beyond that, the rest is a dull repetition of the formula that John Carpenter created in *Halloween,* with a no-name cast of young characters being killed off by a faceless psycho. This is one of the least impressive of the undistinguished imitators that appeared throughout the 1980s.

The 2009 remake is a solid improvement on the original though, admittedly, that's not saying much. It has a cheesy sense of fun and does not take itself seriously for a single frame. The casting of veterans Kevin Tighe and Tom Atkins is a good move and not just for nostalgic reasons. They're absolutely right for the parts. The Grand Guignol gross out stuff is handled well—neither too much nor too little. On DVD, the two-dimensional version is easier on the eyes than the 3-D.

My Soul to Take (2010)

For a comedy, this misfire is filled with long, slow stretches. For a true horror movie, it has too many funny scenes, some of them—notably the riff on the famous Marx brothers mirror routine—intentional. The plot revolves around a killer with a split personality who appears to return sixteen years after his first crimes to prey on seven teenagers. Writer/producer/director Wes Craven is going over much of the same slickly produced ground he has plowed in the *Elm Street* and *Scream* series, with little new to offer.

Mystery of the Wax Museum (1933)

Early two-color Technicolor horror is a companion piece to director Michael Curtiz's *Doctor X* (1932). Lionel Atwill is the wax sculptor who's driven mad by an unscrupulous partner; Glenda Farrell is the sassy reporter on the trail of a story about missing bodies; Fay Wray is her innocent roommate. The story, remade in 3-D as *House of Wax* (see review) with Vincent Price, is never very frightening, but the cast and the impressive sets are excellent.

N

Naked Lunch (1991)

Bizarre drug comedy is more polished than *Trainspotting,* but, in its way, just as demented, funny, and disgusting. William Lee (Peter Weller) is a brown-suited exterminator and sometimes writer whose various addictions and compulsions coalesce into a phantasmagoric hallucination. The material is so strong that even some of David Cronenberg's fans may have trouble getting with it. Weller's dazed, not-quite-earthbound performance is pretty extreme, even for him. It matches the rest of the story. Inanimate objects sprout sexual organs and indescribable perversions are tossed out like jokes when Bill ingests "black meat," a drug made from "the flesh of the giant aquatic Brazilian centipede." As the introductory quote states, "Nothing is true; everything is permitted." Not surprisingly, the material loses its edge before the film is over.

Nature of the Beast (1995)

Jack (Lance Henriksen) is a paunchy traveling salesman. Adrian (Eric Roberts) is a spooky hitchhiker. They meet on the road in a remote California desert, miles away from the interstate. We also know that a serial killer is chopping up people, and a million bucks-plus is missing from a Las Vegas casino. What does Adrian have in his daypack? Why is Jack so protective of his locked briefcase? Writer-director Victor Salva uses a deliberately slow pace and edgy characterizations to maintain suspense. Henriksen and Roberts have built their careers on quirky, colorful roles and these are two of their best. Henriksen is particularly strong—he also gets credit as "creative consultant"—and his performance carries the spooky story over several rough spots.

Near Dark (1987)

Kathryn Bigelow's directorial debut is just your basic, contemporary Western/vampire/Peckinpah-homage. It's a frightening, violent, erotic story told with a sly touch of black humor. Young Caleb (Adrian Pasdar) is seduced by Mae (Jenny Wright) and kidnapped by a gang of vampires (though that word is never used) who travel around the Southwest in stolen cars at night. Then unknown Lance Henriksen, Bill Paxton, and Tim Thomerson do fine work. The best parts are a grotesque, bloody set-piece in a roadhouse and a shootout with the cops at a seedy motel. The only flaw is a weak ending. Bigelow's flair for action gives the film a gritty texture that helps it past the lapses.

Needful Things (1993)

In style and appearance, this Stephen King adaptation is similar to Stanley Kubrick's *The Shining.* Both are visually impressive, slow moving, and brightened by mordant, dry wit. Neither is particularly frightening. The Devil (Max von Sydow) opens an antique store in Castle Rock, Maine, and touches the townspeople's deepest desires. Writer W.D. Richter does a good job of compressing the long novel, but some of the subplots may not make sense to those who haven't read it. Director Fraser Heston gets journeyman work from a cast of first-rate character actors (Ed Harris, Bonnie Bedelia, Amanda Plummer, J.T. Walsh) but the film belongs to Von Sydow's affable, persuasive Satan.

Max von Sydow played the Devil in *Needful Things.*

Nest, The (1988)

Killer mutant cockroaches take over a small resort island, resulting in deliciously nasty special effects and lots of creepy, crawly critters. The cast is better than you'd expect, too, especially Terri Treas, as the scientist who turns out to be a little kinky for her insects.

The story gets funnier and grosser as it goes along, giving bug-monster fans everything they could ask for.

Netherworld (1992)

Curiously, this slick Full Moon production has never caught on with fans the way that some of its lesser efforts have. The story has to do with reincarnation, magic, and such on a plantation in the Louisiana backwater. Director David Schmoeller creates an odd waking-nightmare quality that's really chilling in its best moments. Some of the effects are ingenious, but the show is stolen by character actor Robert Burr as a deliciously decadent, Edsel-driving lawyer. Also, the Edgar Winter blues score is terrific. Watch all the way through the end of the credits for a nice final joke.

New Moon

See Twilight

Night Angel (1990)

The setting is a fashion magazine. Lilith (Isa Andersen) is a female demon who returns to seduce and destroy. Most of the time she looks like any other skinny fashion model, but when she turns up the heat, she changes. Her mascara looks like it was applied with a pallet knife and she grows shiny black fingernails about three inches long. When she goes after her victims, she's so trashy she makes Madonna look like Martha Stewart. Director Dominique Othenin-Girard keeps it all campy, flashy, and slick. The action peaks in the long, phantasmagorical dream sequence.

Night Junkies (2007)

Unsubtle, unpleasant, low-budget British horror equates vampirism with intravenous drug use and sexual degradation. From the impossible-to-read opening credits to the subtitle-free accents, the story of lap dancer Ruby (Katia Winter) and vampire Vincent (Giles Alderson) is difficult to follow. Colored lights make the cheap sets look even more scabrous, and they do the cast no favors.

Night of the Comet (1984)

After a comet zaps the world, wiping out most of the people but leaving the material goods intact, tough-minded Valley Girls Reggie (Catherine Mary

The Top Eleven High School Horrors

Christine
Buffy the Vampire Slayer
Carrie
Cry Wolf
The Faculty
Haunting of Molly Hartley
Jennifer's Body
The Lost Boys
Idle Hands
Disturbing Behavior
The Hole

Stewart) and Samantha (Kelli Maroney) Belmont don't even need credit cards to clean out the mall. If only there weren't all these darn zombies wandering around, not to mention the mad scientists (Geoffrey Lewis and Mary Woronov). Writer/director Thom Eberhardt makes his heroines appealing young women, but toward the end, the story takes on a tired, almost nihilistic cast which, like the zombies, seems to have been borrowed from a *Living Dead* film. By the way, the premise is lifted from one of Sir Arthur Conan Doyle's Prof. Challenger stories.

Night of the Creeps (1986)

Schlocky little B-horror revels in its own schlock. The plot is standard stuff involving parasitic slugs from outer space that infect a college town and turn the kids into living-dead zombies. Writer-director Fred Dekker keeps the pace zipping right along and he collected a troupe of seasoned professionals, including Tom Atkins, Dick Miller, and Kenneth Tobey. For once, the humor and the scares complement each other well.

Night of the Demon

See Curse of the Demon

Night of the Lepus (1972)

"They're as big as wolves—and just as vicious!" says Dr. Clark (DeForest Kelley). They're … They're giant mutant carnivorous bunny rabbits! The earth trembles beneath the thunder of their mighty paws! Grown men weep at the sight of their twitching noses! Well, actually, they don't weep and the earth doesn't tremble, but you will giggle when you see these little critters hopping around HO-scale sets in slow motion to make them appear large and powerful. If the filmmakers had only embraced the humor of their subject and coaxed their cast into the same spirit, this might have been a cult classic. Instead, they brought together a group of so-so character actors—and one genuine star, Janet Leigh—who turn in wooden performances that match the lame script. It's interesting to compare this laugher with *Ben* and *Willard,* all three about small, furry mammals and all produced at about the same time. Rats are scary; rabbits are not. Even a bad movie about rats will have a few frightening moments, but not even Steven Spielberg could invest bunnies with credible ferocity.

Night of the Living Dead (1968 and 1990)
Dawn of the Dead (1978 and 2004)
Day of the Dead (1985 and 2008)
Land of the Dead (2005)
George Romero's Diary of the Dead (2007)
Survival of the Dead (2009)

Raymond Chandler said that hard-boiled mystery writer Dashiell Hammett gave murder back to the people who were good at it by setting his stories in a real world populated by believable characters. In 1968, George Romero did the same thing for horror. At that time, Roger Corman's low-budget Poe adaptations were pretty well played out, and on the other end of the spectrum, Roman Polanski's baroque *Rosemary's Baby* was the kind of movie that could come only from a big studio. Romero and a group of his friends who were also investors decided to make a "little" black-and-white movie where they lived, in Pittsburgh. After considerable squabbling (which is reflected in the film itself), they settled upon a simple story about the recently deceased rising up to eat the flesh of the non-deceased.

Several people—with nary a stereotype in the bunch—are trapped in a farmhouse by these stumbling zombies. Over the course of a day and a night, they try to survive, making one wrong decision after another as the horror and suspense steadily increase. Romero found uniformly good and natural performances from an unknown cast. As the sheriff, George Kosana is outstanding, and his most famous line—"They're dead; they're all messed

Poster from the 1968 horror classic *Night of the Living Dead.*

up."—was an improvisation. Though the film has been copied, imitated, remade, and parodied countless times, it remains an intense experience.

The offbeat 1990 remake may not be completely necessary but it's not altogether bad, either. The main strengths are commanding performances by Tony Todd and Patricia Tallman in the leads. (Her Barbara is a much more active and assertive character than she was before.) The main weakness is lack of originality. The story doesn't vary significantly from the first version, and how many "living dead" zombies have stumbled across the screen in the past decades? The technical advances in effects and a more generous budget actually work against the claustrophobic intensity that made the first film a cult hit.

The ambitious 1978 sequel, *Dawn of the Dead,* actually builds on the premise of the first film and expands into more overtly political realms. After the "living dead" plague spreads into cities, four survivors (Gaylen Ross, David Emge, Ken Foree, and Scott H. Reiniger) take refuge in a huge shopping mall and try to seal it off from the flesh-eating zombies. George Romero says that the Monroeville Shopping Center where the film was made is "a temple to consumer society." Does he then mean to drive the money-changers from that temple? Zach Snyder's 2004 remake of *Dawn* was one of the first to posit fast zombies who can run. It also speeds things up by having the bitten become zombified within seconds of their initial infection. While Romero's political dimension is largely ignored, the film is exceptionally well cast and it maintains a good sense of humor. The CGI effects are technically accomplished.

Day, the third installment, opens inside a bare cinderblock room where Sara (Lori Cardille) stares at a calendar on the wall. Clearly, the original situation where bodies rise up to devour the living has deteriorated. A small group of scientists and soldiers is trapped inside an underground Florida missile installation. Do they study the living dead and possibly learn how to domesticate them? Or will the military types, under the command of a martinet, screw things up even more? Romero's social criticism is even stronger than it was in *Dawn,* making for a slow first hour. The conclusion contains some of Tom Savini's most grotesque, detailed, and sophisticated gore effects.

(Despite the title, the 2008 *Day of the Dead* is not really a remake of Romero's film though they share some plot similarities and names. A virus causes an outbreak of a disease that turns the infected into fast predatory zombies in a small Colorado mountain town. Neither dialogue nor characters' actions ring true. Acting and makeup effects are so-so.)

Twenty years after *Day,* Romero returned to his creations with *Land of the Dead,* his most complicated, polished, and overtly political zombie effort. The focus is on Fiddler's Green, a high rise "gated community" for the wealthy, surrounded by a fortified town where the less-fortunate survivors live. It, in turn, is surrounded by the "stenches" or "walkers" who have begun to evolve and organize under the leadership of Big Daddy (Eugene Clark). Mr. Kauffman (Dennis Hopper) is the corrupt boss of the tower who sends out parties of scavengers led by Riley (Simon West), his scarred pal Charlie (Robert Joy), and Cholo (John Leguizamo). If the film's politics are more sharply pointed, so is the violence with the focus on cannibalism, entrails, and gore. For my money, this is the best of its kind. Check the credits for cameos.

"Everyone who dies will become one of them. If you are bitten, you will just become one of them that much sooner."

Land of the Dead

Romero's fifth "dead" film, *Diary,* is much more entertaining and thoughtful than most "found footage" horrors. A group of college students and their dyspeptic professor are making a mummy movie when they learn of the first zombie awakenings and societal order collapses. They set off in a Winnebago as Jason (Josh Close), the would-be director, keeps his video cameras running. The violent effects are graphic and the dialogue is sharp with properly mordant humor. It's a road movie with the bleakest of endings.

Survival of the Dead, the semi-comic sequel to *Diary,* begins with Romero delivering a light director's introduction and then descends into self-parody. Some of the characters introduced in the previous film return and are lured to a Delaware island where two feuding family patriarchs (Kenneth Welsh and Richard Fitzpatrick) cannot agree on the proper way to handle the living dead apocalypse. The acting is overly broad and the zombie makeup is slipshod.

Night of the Seagulls

See Tombs of the Blind Dead

Night Stalker, The (1972)
Night Strangler, The (1973)

When it aired in 1972, *The Night Stalker* was generally regarded as the best movie ever made for television, and it's aged more gracefully than many of its theatrical contemporaries. It was one of the first horror films to combine realistic police procedural details and a contemporary setting with vampire lore. Add in solid characters based on familiar stereotypes—wisecracking reporter, tough editor, weasely politico—and a winning off-the-cuff comic performance by Darren McGavin in the lead and Simon Oakley as his long-suffering editor Vincenzo. Both Richard Matheson's script and the photography are rock solid. Journeyman director John Moxey never lets the pace flag.

The sequel, *The Night Strangler,* shifts the scene to Seattle where more mysterious murders are occurring. An alchemist (Richard Anderson) and his search for the "elixir of life" are involved. McGavin and Oakland are at their hammiest. The comedy is played more broadly and the supporting cast is filled with familiar faces, the most welcome being Margaret Hamilton.

Night Watch (2004)
Day Watch (2006)

A lengthy pseudo-medieval introduction establishes the ground rules for a Russian take on the eternal battle between Good and Evil. After it, the scene shifts to the present where regular guy Anton (Konstantin Khabenskyi) becomes a key figure. The tone swings quickly and often between extremes of slapstick and seriousness, though I have to admit that for long stretches, I had only a tenuous grasp on what was happening and why the characters were doing what they were doing. Even so, the pace is energetic and the film looks terrific.

The sequel, *Day Watch,* makes even less sense. It begins with more historical business about Tamerlane and the "chalk of fate," literally a piece of chalk with which you can rewrite history. It's really more about CGI effects than true horror. Again, a firm grasp on the details of the plot eludes me.

Nightcomers, The (1971)

Michael Winner's "prequel" to Henry James' *Turn of the Screw* is much trashier and more enjoyable than the source material. Screenwriter Michael Hastings' (*Tom & Viv*) interpretation of the characters and their story is just

The Top Ten
Horrible Hospitals and Medical Horrors

Anatomy
Anatomy 2
Boxing Helena
Contagion
Coma
Human Centipede [first sequence]
Manitou
Halloween 2
Gothika
Session 9

as transparent as James' is opaque. Quint (Marlon Brando) is carrying on an overheated, kinky S&M affair with Miss Jessel (Stephanie Beacham) under the curious eyes of two watchful children. Brando's animated performance as a cheerful, conniving manchild is a delight and can be seen in some ways as a dry run for *Last Tango in Paris.* The film benefits from Robert Paynter's handsome photography, excellent locations, and a fine Jerry Fielding score. The conclusion's a shock.

Nightmare (1984)

Virtually everything that is made fun of in the *Scream* films is trotted out with complete seriousness in a weirdly complicated plot that doesn't stand up to any logic tests. It all begins in New York where George (Baird Stafford) suffers terrifying dreams, but much of the action takes place in Florida where flighty mother Susan (Sharon Smith) lets her young kids take care of themselves while she carries on an affair. The Times Square material is sweaty and seedy, and one toxic green shag carpet isn't much more enticing. Add in some amateurish acting in supporting roles and often inaudible dialog, and you've got a prime piece of '80s exploitation.

Nightmare before Christmas, The (1993)

Producer Tim Burton and director Henry Selick sustain a dark, charmed mood in this stop-motion animation feature. When Jack Skellington, the King of Halloween, discovers Christmastown, he decides that the two holidays should be combined. The filmmakers are trying to create another variation on the whimsical atmosphere that was so important to *Edward Scissorhands* and *Beetlejuice,* a mixture of childlike wonder and horror that isn't truly frightening. Danny Elfman's songs carry much of the action. Only "What Is This?" really cuts loose, but Elfman's instrumental score is terrific. In the end, the film is so unusual that animation fans are the real audience.

Nightmare on Elm Street, A (1984 and 2010)
Nightmare on Elm Street Part 2, A: Freddy's Nightmare (1985)
Nightmare on Elm Street 3, A: Dream Warriors (1987)
Nightmare on Elm Street 4, A: The Dream Master (1988)
Nightmare on Elm Street, A: The Dream Child (1989)
Freddy's Dead: The Final Nightmare (1991)
Wes Craven's New Nightmare (1994)

Consider for a moment the marketing genius behind Freddy Krueger and the "Elm Street" series. Freddy (Robert Englund) is a ghost, in the loosest sense of the term—the spirit of a child molester who was burned to death by the parents of his victims. Now he comes back with his razor-fingered glove-thingy. He can appear and disappear at will. He can pop from here to there instantaneously. He can do terrible things in either the visible or invisible mode, in either the dream world or the real world. And he has no real motivation; he's just mean, hating everything and everybody. Because his powers are so elastic, this little moneymaker can be killed and resurrected as long as he stays in the black.

Fans of this popular but overrated series have long held that the even-numbered entries are the worst, and *Part 2: Freddy's Revenge* certainly bears them out. Some of the sillier effects involve flying tennis balls, exploding hot-dogs, and a possessed parakeet, not to mention the boy who talks with his mouth full. Everything about this one from the opening dream sequence to the slaughtered teens to the clichéd ending strictly follows the formula. The unintentional humor is a relief from the numbing routine.

Sheer inventiveness alone does not a good horror movie make. Neither do special effects involving tongues and the third installment, *Dream Warriors,* is the virtual *Gone With the Wind* of tongue-effect movies. Other than those, it's more of the same as the ubiquitous Freddy (Englund) shows up everywhere, even on *The Dick Cavett Show,* and preys on institutionalized kids

The ghost of an evil child molester returns over and over to kill again in the "Elm Street" series starring actor Robert Englund as Freddy Krueger.

including the then almost-famous Patricia Arquette and Laurence (then Larry) Fishburne, whose resume already included *Apocalypse Now* and the TV soap *One Life To Live.* Original heroine Heather Langenkamp returns. (She also plays herself in the final installment, *Wes Craven's New Nightmare.*) Throughout, the pace is quick and director Charles Russell (*The Mask*) never seems to take this dumb stuff seriously. Though fans praise this one highly, it's still got a "3" in the title.

Since, as the *Dream Master* subtitle indicates, part four is essentially a dream from the first shot, it contains no real scares—just shocks and surprises on some remarkable sets. As you ought to expect from any sequel with a "4" in the title, the plot is familiar. The main characters are blandly, generically attractive. Director Renny Harlin shows off with flashy overdirection whenever he can. He gives the production such a high gloss that it's the most glittering piece of eye-candy in the series.

In *The Dream Child,* Freddy (Robert Englund) attacks Alice's (Lisa Wilcox) unborn fetus. (No, the film has nothing to add to the abortion de-

Robert Englund, sans make-up, looking much better than his alter ego, Freddy Krueger.

bate.) Again, the dream structure eliminates real scares, so the filmmakers concentrate on imaginative effects. Also, since so much of the horror is based on pregnancy, childbirth, and monster infants, women may react to the story on a more fundamental level. Credit writer Leslie Bohem.

If nothing else, *Freddy's Dead: The Final Nightmare,* an unnumbered 6, proves that women can make horror sequels just as poorly as men. Director Rachel Talalay quotes the *Twilight Zone*'s *Nightmare at 10,000 Feet* and *The Wizard of Oz* early on, and her substantial budget allows for a barrelful of crackerjack visual effects. So what? The rest is more of the same bad acting from another bland young cast. In Ms. Talalay's favor, it should be noted that the violence is handled with cartoonish exaggeration and so it's not particularly sadistic.

With *Wes Craven's New Nightmare* the series takes an unexpected intellectual turn and becomes an entertaining exercise in horror. Most of the characters play themselves. They are the actors, filmmakers, and studio executives who are involved in a work in progress, *Wes Craven's New Nightmare.* Craven has not finished the script yet but Robert Englund is definitely interested in the project. So are producers Marianne Maddalena and Sara Risher and New Line Cinema chairman Robert Shaye. Star Heather Langenkamp, needs to be persuaded. When she learns that her husband (David Newsom) is secretly working on new special effects for Craven's project, she's really scared. Upon that premise, Craven builds an intricate construction about the act of storytelling and the power that some stories have. References to Hansel and Gretel are well taken. They bring up the responsibility of storytellers to their audience, particularly when children are involved. In the last reels, Craven returns to the simple, effective thrills of a good horror movie, from a harrowing freeway scene to the wild finale.

As for the 2010 remake of the original, fans really need to know only two things: Wes Craven had nothing to do with it; Michael Bay did. Jackie Earle Haley certainly has the right looks and intensity to portray Freddy. Beyond that, it's the same old same old. The dream structure is played out with CGI effects which proves, once again, that in horror, more can be less.

The Top Thirteen Literary Adaptations

- *Something Wicked This Way Comes*
- *Ghost Story*
- *Dr. Jekyll and Mr. Hyde*
- *Dorian Gray*
- *Portrait of Dorian Gray*
- *The Stepford Wives*
- *Rosemary's Baby*
- *A Stir of Echoes*
- *I Am Legend*
- *Summer of Fear*
- *Witches*
- *Witches of Eastwick*
- *Curse of the Demon*

Nightscare (1994)

Rare horror/comedy actually manages to be frightening, funny, and original. It's obvious from the first shot—an extreme close up of a hypodermic needle entering flesh—that director Vadim Jean is trying to work on a primal level. Gilmore (Keith Allen) is an insane murderer. Dr. Lyell (Elizabeth Hurley) is the neurologist who's treating him with an experimental drug which she's also testing herself. Detective Hamilton (Craig Fairbrass) is the cop who arrested Gilmore and still has reason to hate him. The drug brings the three of them together. Jean does a fine job of depicting different states of perception—dream, drugged, memory, sobriety—and making them equally "real" on screen. Whenever the film threatens to take itself too seriously, a dry, mordant humor shows up. Don't miss the last little visual joke that's tossed in at the end of the closing credits.

Nightwing (1979)

Well-intentioned adaptation really doesn't do justice to Martin Cruz Smith's fine novel, despite its faithfulness to the plot. Duran (Nick Mancuso) is an Indian deputy who discovers a flock of vampire bats carrying plague. The main problem is the bats—they're never remotely believable or frightening. The script isn't much better. The flaky characters from Smith's novel have been replaced by a series of clichés. The rest of the cast, including Kathryn Harrold, Stephen Macht, and David Warner, are capable but they have nothing to work with. Coulda been a contender.

Ninth Gate, The (1999)

Roman Polanski's horror conspiracy tale can be seen as an embarrassing companion piece to *Rosemary's Baby.* Almost nothing about the film works as it should. Crooked book dealer Dean Corso (Johnny Depp) is hired by billionaire Boris Balkan (Frank Langella) to authenticate a copy of *The Nine Gates of the Kingdom of Shadows.* The medieval text is rumored to have been co-written by Satan himself. Corso heads off to Europe where the other two copies are located, but even before he leaves, almost everyone he meets comes to an untimely violent demise. Throughout, the pace is slow, and despite the subject matter, there's not a hint of suspense or dread. The acting is mannered and so is the writing. Depp's character is an unusually ineffectual protagonist. The fiery finish is, I think, not meant to be funny.

Nosferatu (1922, 1979)

The first feature-length adaptation of Bram Stoker's *Dracula* is still one of the best horror films ever made—complex, serious, and frightening. The famous makeup has lost none of its power. Note how Renfield's (Alexander Granarch) appearance foreshadows Dracula's (Max Schreck). That creature with the elongated fingers, ratlike fangs and face is an indelible part of horror cinema, as much as Lon Chaney Sr.'s Phantom and Boris Karloff's Monster. Famous copyright infringement legal questions caused English language versions of the film to change the name "Dracula" to "Orlok," but it's been restored in some video and DVD editions. If some devices don't work now—using fast motion to indicate power; having Dracula rise rigidly from his coffin as if on hinged feet—director Murnau's miasmic, dreamlike atmosphere is a remarkable creation. Also, the relationship between Dracula and Nina (Greta Schroeder) is much more complicated. Required viewing, particularly for younger fans. (The making of the film is the subject of *Shadow of the Vampire.*)

Warner Herzog's 1979 remake is faithful to the original, most importantly in the makeup for Klaus Kinski which reproduces Schreck's terrifying devil-rat face. Isabelle Adjani, an actress who's seen far too seldom in American film, is very good, too, but the whole production somehow lacks energy and passion.

Not Like Us (1995)

This offbeat comedy is a neat sleeper. The opening scene combines ominous music with idealized pictures of a bucolic small town named Tranquility. That juxtaposition of sound and image continues as mysterious deaths accu-

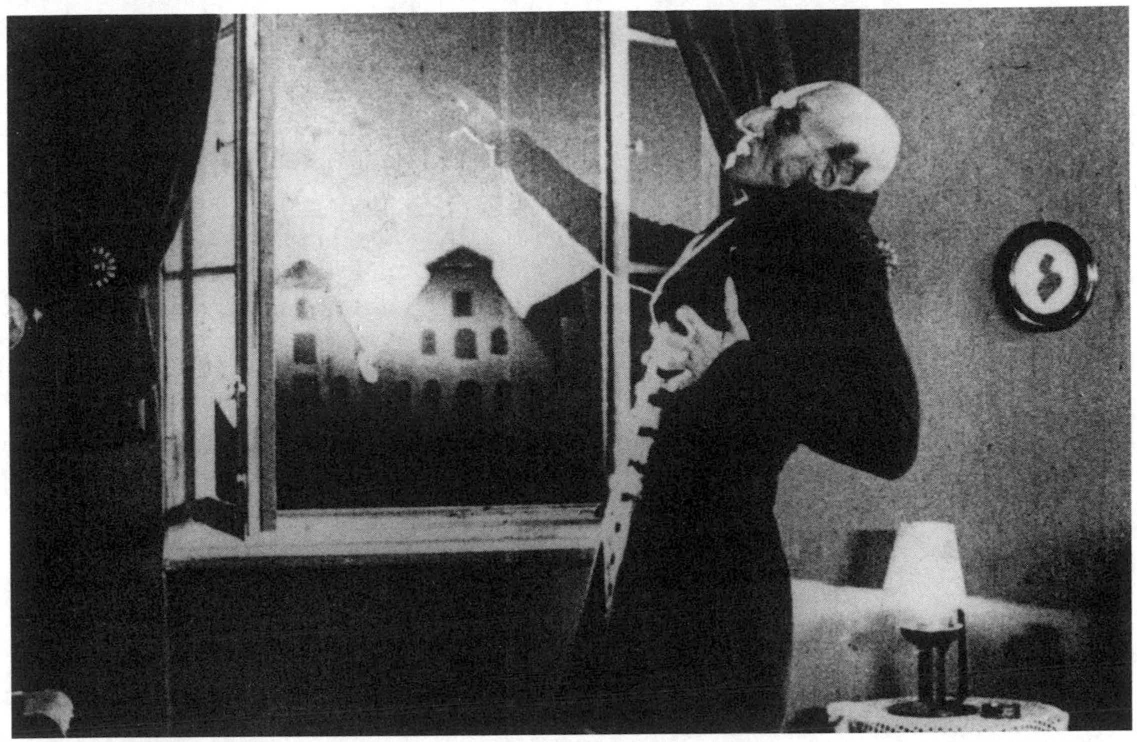

The original vampire movie, *Nosferatu* still holds up as creepy, frightening horror fare almost a century later.

mulate. The local coroner attributes them to "multiple purple rash wounds of the epidermis." Another "expert" suspects insufficient fiber in the victims' diet. Could the newcomers John (Morgan Englund) and Janet Jones (Rainer Grant) have anything to do with it? Anita (Joanna Pacula) says no. She likes Janet but her suspicious, insular neighbors disagree. If that weren't enough, homewrecker Vicki (Annabelle Gurwitch) is trying to steal Anita's hubby (Peter Onorati). Writer Daniella Purcelli and director Dave Payne have drawn inspiration from a host of sources—*Motel Hell, Parents, Meet the Hollowheads, Not of This Earth.* The humor is cheeky, gory, and light. Joanna Pacula is a little too serious as the heroine who tends to overlook important information. Rainer Grant steals the show as the ballbreaker from another world. It all ends with wicked red-meat special effects.

Not of This Earth (1988, 1996)

The first remake of Roger Corman's hard-to-find 1957 original has virtually everything that a B-movie fan could ask for: total lack of seriousness, zippy plot, cheesy special effects, and oodles of gratuitous nudity. Arthur Roberts is a vampire from the planet Davonna who collects human blood and sends it to the folks back home. Traci Lords is the nurse who unwittingly helps him by providing transfusions. But why is smoke coming from the furnace when the temperature is close to 100 outside? Is someone getting rid of the remains of an unlucky door-to-door vacuum cleaner salesman?

In the 1996 version, the effects range from amateurish to innovative. Michael York is a fine alien. As Nurse Amanda, Elizabeth Barondes is easily the equal of Beverly Garland and Traci Lords, and director Terry Winkless might follow in the footsteps of Corman himself and schlockmeister Jim Wynorski who handled the first remake.

O

Oblong Box, The (1969)

In nineteenth-century England, Julian Markham (Vincent Price) keeps his brother Edward (Alistair Williamson) chained and locked up in the family mansion. The reasons why go back to a gruesome crucifixion ritual that took place sometime before in Africa. Christopher Lee is a grave-robbing doctor who becomes embroiled in the Markhams' problems. The source of the horror is upper class hypocrisy and arrogance. In both the expensive look and neatly written script, the film is comparable to the Hammer productions of the late 1960s.

Of Unknown Origin (1983)

Slickly made Canadian production is actually one of the better rat-themed horrors. With his wife (Shannon Tweed) and young son gone on vacation, hardworking businessman Bart Hughs (Peter Weller) finds his brownstone under attack by an oversized mama rat. Gradually, his obsession with work is transferred to the vermin. His tactics steadily escalate. The rat's tactics escalate right back. Weller brings his usual intensity to the role, and the various interiors become an integral part of the story. The rat's first big appearance is a real flesh-crawling shocker. Toward the end, it goes too far and the physical action meant to be tragic becomes comic, but this one's still worth a look.

Old Dark House, The (1932)

Three travelers (Raymond Massey, Gloria Stuart, Melvyn Douglas) are trapped by a storm at a nasty country manse inhabited by Femm (Ernest Thesiger), his deaf sister (Eva Moore), and his hideously scarred butler (Boris Karloff), "an uncivilized brute." Soon Porterhouse (Charles Laughton) and Gladys (Lillian Bond) join the bedraggled band. The film is remarkably sexy and frank for the 1930s, and the sardonic humor is still fresh. The acting is theatrically broad. In the expansive troupe, Laughton is the most flamboyant. All in all, a treat.

Omega Man, The

See I Am Legend

Omen, The (1976, 2006)
Damien: Omen II (1978)
Omen III: The Final Conflict (1981)
Omen IV: The Awakening (1991)

The first part of what must be Hollywood's most successful supernatural series has aged gracefully. Director Richard Donner, known best for the *Lethal Weapon* series, turns David Seltzer's preview-to-Armageddon story into a first rate potboiler. Evil is incarnated in a rosy-cheeked little cherub. His spooky nanny—effectively underplayed by Billie Whitelaw—is a lethal Mary Poppins who's given in to the dark side of the force. The plot is filled with inventive twists and shocks and a welcome restraint in the effects department.

The sequel, *Damien: Omen II,* is easily the weakest of the three. It plods along, killing off supporting characters at a predictable rate in increasingly grotesque ways. Now grown to a teenager, the son of Satan (Jonathan Scott-Taylor) goes off to military school where Lance Henriksen is the Staff Sergeant of Satan. The relative subtlety of the first film is nowhere to be found. In its place is cliched Hollywood nonsense involving a crow that apparently scares people to death. The best supernatural stories of this school use the religious element much more sparingly. The basic problem here is poor writing—in both plot and character development—so the presence of star William Holden is mostly wasted. An over-reliance on Jerry Goldsmith's hyperventilating music doesn't help either.

The series returns to something like its former level of quality for *The Final Conflict.* Perhaps the presence of Richard Donner, director of the original, as executive producer has something to do with it. Star Sam Neill, one of the best character actors in the business, makes the most of a well-written role. He carries off potentially hilarious dialogue with absolute conviction and believability, giving the adult Damien a strong streak of Nixonian bravado. The gruesome effects and stunts are better, too, particularly a long fox hunt scene. The plot is strong and the trilogy ends on a note of religio-cinematic excess worthy of Cecil B. DeMille. It was followed by a made-for-TV fourth installment.

The 2006 version of the original is actually one of the more enjoyable remakes. It's every bit as much fun as the original for the same cheesy reasons, and the expensive studio production has a glossy Hollywood patina. Liev Schreiber and Julia Stiles are well cast in the leads. Having the original Rosemary (Mia Farrow) take over for Billie Whitelaw is a fine touch, and young Seamus Davey-Fitzpatrick has all the prepubescent creepiness that the role requires.

One Missed Call (2003, 2008)

Horror based on ringtones and voice mail just doesn't resonate with some (i.e. older) audiences. Even so, Takashi Miike's tale of fatal cell phone messages from the future is visually and aurally inventive. It has a dark, shadowy look, and the interaction among the young characters has a loose realism. For me, the busy, febrile plot is less successful than *The Ring.*

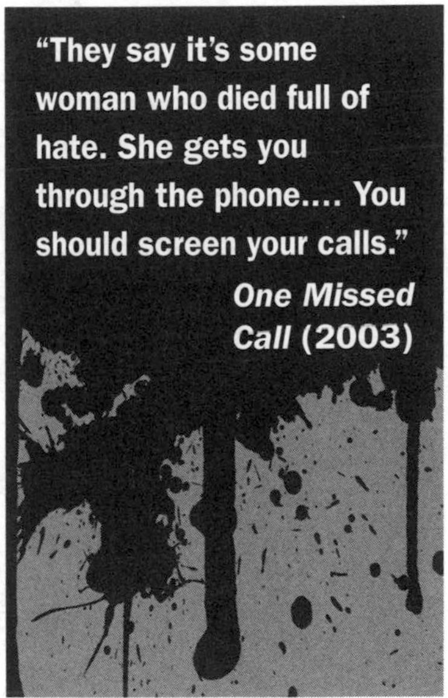

The 2008 American version follows all the rules for Asian horror. We've got the vengeful ghost using new technology to do terrible things, a series of murders, and a plucky heroine (Shannyn Shossamon). One problem: technology advances so quickly that the cell phones themselves already look clunky and dated. Director Eric Valette has a jazzy sense of style with lots of flashy camerawork. Most of the startling images come from the original.

Opera (1987)

Dario Argento translates the familiar *Phantom of the Opera* plot into a baroque slasher tale. The sumptuous production is visually fascinating eye-candy with a strange humor which often appears to be intentional, though where both opera and horror are concerned, the line between intentional and not is often hard to distinguish. Argento begins with crisp editing and flowing camerawork, but as the story goes on, it loses focus and the director indulges his love for visual flourishes. Happily, even eagerly, he sacrifices logic and coherence to flashy images, no matter how pointless. (In a typical moment, Argento flips the camera over for no reason.) That said, he also gives fans what they want to see in the bloody scenes. In his best bits, sharp metal meets soft tissue in graphic close-up. It all arrives at a grand nutball conclusion with a "ravencam" point of view and finally—so help me—a quote from *The Sound of Music.* This version is much more successful than his version of the LeRoux's story (see review). (Alternate title: *Terror at the Opera.*)

The Top Seven H.P. Lovecraft Adaptations

Call of Cthulhu
Re-Animator
Dagon
The Unnamable
Dunwich Horror
Bride of Re-Animator
Beyond Re-Animator

Orphan, The (2009)

The nightmarish introduction may be the most unsettling and frightening part of this evil-kid horror. Kate (Vera Farmiga) and John (Peter Sarsgaard) have two children but want to adopt. They choose Esther (Isabelle Fuhrman) and things start to go bad from the moment she enters their already ominous and intimidating contemporary home. For those familiar with the genre, the story is on the predictable side but the film still deserves a solid recommendation for the superb casting, both in the leads and the supporting cast, the bleak winter landscape, and a satisfying conclusion.

Other, The (1972)

Writer-producer Tom Tryon's adaptation of his best-selling novel is one of the most gripping evil child tales ever put on screen. Most viewers will probably figure out one part of the story a little early, but that's not a real problem. Holland and Niles Perry (Martin and Chris Udvarnoky) are good and evil young twins. The "accidents" that happen around them are suspenseful and shocking, and built on real insights into the world of children. The combination of rural setting and '30s nostalgia creates a strong sense of place. Director Robert Mulligan is restrained in the violence he chooses to show and the film is all the creepier and more frightening for that restraint.

Others, The (2001)

Nicole Kidman's steely beauty has seldom been used so effectively. She plays a demanding war widow who lives with her two young children in a fog-shrouded mansion on the Channel Islands, 1945. The kids are allergic to sunlight and so the heavy curtains must be kept drawn at all times. Or so she tells the new maid (Fionnula Flanagan) who seems to know more than she should. On one level, the story is a variation on *The Turn of the Screw.* Writer/director Alejandro Almenabar gets many of the scares from simple sound effects and editing choices, and they're just as effective as more graphic nastiness. The film works as a classic ghost story through a believably eerie setting, unusual characters, a solid plot structure, and the right ending.

P–Q

Pale Blood (1990)

The idea of a European vampire in a modern American city is nothing new but director V.V. Dachin Hsu gives it a fresh spin. A serial murderer is draining young women's blood in Los Angeles. Romanian Michael Fury (George Chakiris from *West Side Story*) is so interested that he's hired a detective (Pamela Ludwig) to keep him informed. Van (Wings Hauser), a video artist with several loose screws, is obsessed with the killings. Hsu seems more comfortable with stylistic touches and a strong dreamy atmosphere than with plot and so the pace is slow. Genre veteran Hauser has a grand time with the material and injects some real energy, especially at the end. Good location work, too.

Pan's Labyrinth (2006)

Guillermo del Toro's Oscar-winner is simply one of the great horror films. In the last days of World War II in Spain, Captain Vidal (Sergi López) commands a garrison and casually executes anyone he cares to. His pregnant wife, Carmen (Ariadna Gil), is traveling to the outpost with her daughter (his stepdaughter) Ofelia (a brilliant young Ivana Baquero). Even before they arrive, the girl discovers a magical place within the horror of a war she barely comprehends. Del Toro then follows two storylines, one magical, the other "real." His monsters are all too human. The similarities to *The Devil's Backbone* are intentional. Del Toro sees the films as companion pieces.

Paranoiac (1963)

Eleanor (Janette Scott) thinks that she sees her dead brother Anthony (Alexander Davion) at church, but it's obvious from the first scene that her other brother, the no-good rotten Simon (Oliver Reed), is up to something. Like Hammer's other black-and-white horror/thrillers of the early 1960s, this one is built on such a shaky psychological foundation that it's never particularly frightening. It's still sharply photographed and well-acted by all concerned, particularly Reed.

Paranormal Activity (2007)
Paranormal Activity 2 (2010)
Paranormal Activity 3 (2011)

By some measures, this is the most successful series in the history of movies. The films cost pennies to produce in Hollywood terms, and they have earned hundreds of millions of dollars. The stories of demonic possession are told with home video and surveillance equipment, and the settings are suburban houses. Unknown actors are used for a cast limited to a dozen or so characters. In carefully crafted promotional campaigns, the studio has done nothing to dissuade credulous viewers from believing that they are seeing "reality," whatever that means these days. The films begin without conventional titles and opening credits.

In the first, Katie (Katie Featherston) and Micah (Micah Sloat) are troubled by things that are happening in their San Diego home at night. He buys a fancy video rig to record what goes on in their bedroom while they're asleep. Initially, it's easy to believe these are two real people, not actors. The performances have a relaxed, unforced quality. The characters live in an ordinary, cluttered suburban house. She's sexy but in a regular way. You understand their fear when the stranger things happen.

Taking its cue from *Godfather, Part II, Paranormal Activity 2* is both a prequel and a continuation of the first film. The focus is on Katie's sister Kristi (Sprague Grayden) and her new baby. The house is larger, some of the scares are pretty good, and bloody stuff is kept to a minimum.

The third entry uses the same limited sets and tosses in variations on the security camera point of view with old VHS tapes from the 1980s and some oscillating mobility in a few scenes. Like the others, it relies more on shocks than traditional scares and is relatively restrained. Finally, it's not much better or worse than most titles that end with the number "3." Another is in production.

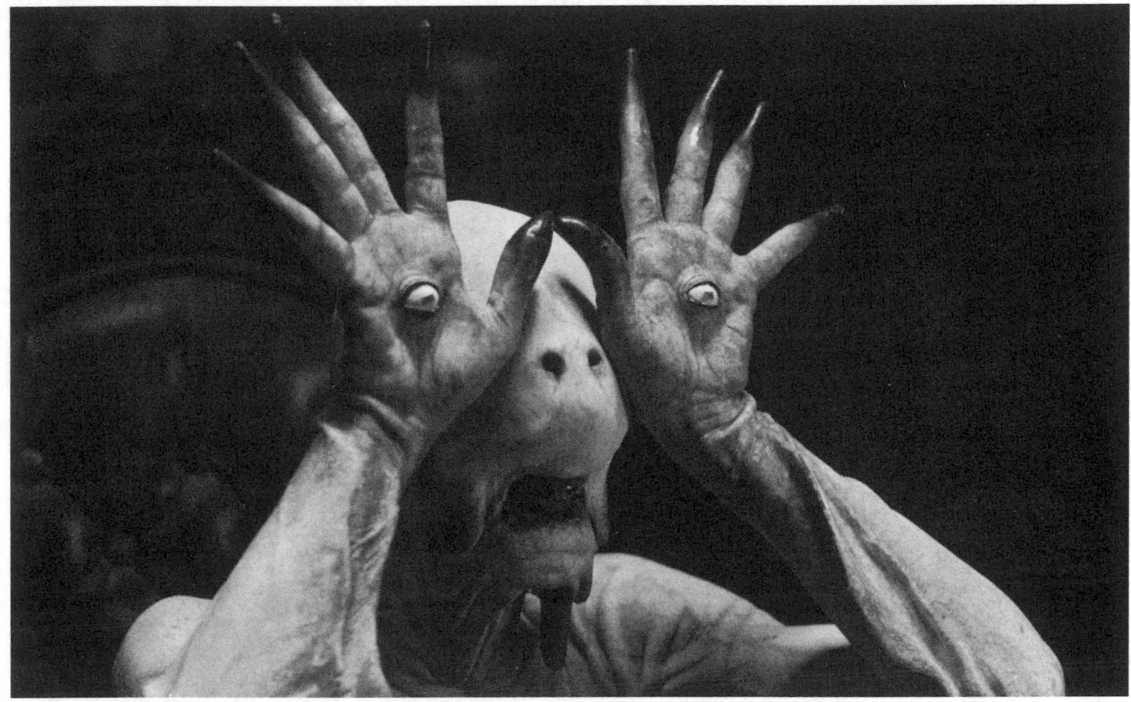

The Oscar-winning *Pan's Labyrinth* is about a young girl escaping the horrors of war by entering a fantasy realm that also contains its own nightmares.

Parasomnia (2008)

Despite a modest budget, writer/director William Malone creates a dark, fairy tale-like horror. Sleeping beauty Laura (Cherilyn Wilson) suffers from a condition that keeps her in coma-like unconsciousness for hours with only brief periods of wakefulness. Even worse, her hospital room is right next door to psychic serial killer Byron Volpe (an impressive Patrick Kilpatrick). Young Danny (Dylan Purcell) thinks he can save her, even though a little kidnapping might be necessary. From that curious beginning, the story takes even more wonderfully unpredictable turns. Though the image is often frustratingly dark, Malone pulls off some impressive visuals—note the long opening shot—and cool optical distortions that morph between color and black and white. Yes, that's John Landis in the department store.

Parents (1989)

In a deeply distorted vision of the 1950s, young Michael (Bryan Madorsky), Mom (Mary Beth Hurt), and Dad (Randy Quaid) move to a new town and a

The Top Eight Meteorites Bearing Unwelcome Visitors Movies

The Blob
Giant Spider Invasion
Alien Trespass
Slither
Color Out of Space
Monolith Monsters
Undead
Night of the Creeps

split-level filled with coral and turquoise furniture and appliances. The shy, silent, and basically unlikable boy is troubled by visions of his parents with bloodstained mouths. When they give evasive answers about the main course at dinner, he comes to believe that they are cannibals. Is that the truth, or is he a very disturbed child? The script presents no easy answers or escapes. For the most part, actor-turned-director Bob Balaban succeeds in making this a disturbing, unnerving piece of work. All of the colors are slightly off, too intense. Food has seldom been so revoltingly photographed. The characters are just a notch or two off dead center and a soundtrack of syrupy big band hits has been poured over these disquieting visual images. Though there is a grimly humorous angle to the story, this is not a comedy. It's the stuff of nightmares.

Passion of the Christ (2004)

Though Mel Gibson's blockbuster is not often thought of as horror, it is possibly the most sadistic mainstream film ever released, one that rivals torture porn in the sheer intensity of its violence. Virtually the entire film is a heavy-handed variation on one scene: a bloody unresisting Jesus (Jim Caviezel) being beaten, flayed and/or whipped with bits of flesh flying off the body, while a crowd looks on, most of them excited, a few appalled. Lurking in the background is an hermaphroditic Satan (Rosalinda Celentano) with worms crawling out of her nostrils and a monstrous baby in her arms. Whatever Gibson's intentions, the images are terrifying.

Peeping Tom (1960)

It's impossible to overestimate the influence of Michael Powell's brilliant but rarely screened 1960 masterpiece. It can be seen as the missing link between

Fritz Lang's *M* and *Psycho* in the realistic school of horror. Essentially, it's the story of Mark (Carl Boehm), a twisted, young film technician driven to murder women as he photographs them. He falls in love with Helen (Anna Massey), but her blind mother (Maxine Audley) seems to know everything about him. Voyeurism is a prime subject but Powell is also concerned with the nature of film itself, from the perspective of both the creator and the viewer. Viewed simply as a thriller, it's Hitchcockian in the very best sense of the term—complex, witty, suspenseful, unpredictable. Even though the violence is not explicit by today's standards, it's still a deeply disturbing piece of work. The Criterion edition recreates Powell's vivid use of color, and also the sound that's remarkably clear and important to the film. Required viewing for any serious student of horror.

Carl Boehm is a murderous photographer in *Peeping Tom.*

People under the Stairs (1991)

Wes Craven addresses capitalism and the nuclear family in a subversive Grand Guignol horror. Evil is represented by seemingly "normal" white adults. Poor black kids, burglars, and horribly deformed "freaks" are the heroes. Using Tarot cards as a structure, the film follows young Fool (Brandon Adams) on his journey of discovery in the world of two slumlords (Everett McGill and Wendy Robie). The core of the story is the eternal rebellion of children against parents, and a teenaged audience will probably appreciate it more than parents think they should.

Pet Sematary (1989)
Pet Sematary II (1992)

Stephen King's version of *The Monkey's Paw* is one of his most frightening novels, and Mary Lambert's film, made from his script, is one of the best adaptations of his work. Lewis and Rachel Creed (Dale Midkiff and Denise Crosby) and their two kids move into a Maine country house on a busy road. Jud (Fred Gwynne) warns them that it won't be safe for the family cat. The road has claimed so many animals that there's a "Pet Sematary" in the forest. Deeper in the forest, there's another pet cemetery with a darker purpose. Toward the end, some comic relief is dubious, and the film lasts thirty seconds too long, but it's still a potent chiller about the destructive, possessive side of love.

The lamentable, nasty little sequel is notable only for the sadistic quality of its graphic violence. It's one thing for a film to depict children and animals in life-threatening situations. It's another to show the perpetrators of the violence taking such glee in the torture they inflict. But the film is so ineptly made that it will never attract a large audience. Richard Outten's script blunders from one contrived confrontation to the next and director Lambert does a poor job of it, as well. Where the original film is about familial love gone bad, *II* is about special effects.

Phantasm (1979)
Phantasm II (1988)
Phantasm III: Lord of the Dead (1994)

The ads call this one "a truly bizarre science-fiction horror fantasy" and for once they aren't exaggerating. The senseless plot concerns two parentless brothers who discover weird goings-on at the local funeral parlor, including the infamous airborne, brain-drilling chrome ball; malevolent hooded midgets in monk's robes; and the Tall Man (Angus Scrimm), a mortician with yellow goop for blood. Creepy, unpredictable nightmare fashioned on a shoestring by young, independent producer-writer-director Don Coscarelli contains enough wildly imaginative twists and inventions for a dozen horror movies, but not enough logic for one. The plot and sensibility could have come straight from a Road Runner cartoon, with about as much attention paid to the laws of physics. Scenes were cut out of the original film to avoid an X rating.

The 1988 sequel is almost as screwy and weird as the original with lots of gruesome special effects. Do not expect the plot to make sense. Coscarelli's not interested. His story just rolls along from one bizarre event to the next, finally arriving at a predictable ending.

The horror-comedies don't follow any internal logic. A character who's killed in one scene, reappears in the next without explanation; dream and reality are constantly confused; etc.—you know the drill. In *Phantasm III,* the events on screen are nothing more than an excuse to trot out special effects of amputations, decapitations, lobotomies, and the like involving the now-familiar Tall Man and flying chrome softballs. For better or worse, the gory stuff is played strictly for laughs. Even though the effects have become much more polished, that's not necessarily an improvement.

Another sequel has followed.

Phantom of the Opera (1925, 1943, 1962, 1989, 1998)

Gaston LeRoux's tale is one of the most popular potboilers of all time—on stage, page, or screen. Lon Chaney Sr.'s 1925 version is the most famous and rightly so. The big scenes—the falling chandelier, the underground lake, the masked ball, the final chase, and, of course, the unmasking—are still terrific. Despite changes in dramatic style, this is one of Chaney's most impressive acting jobs. If you can take your eyes off his makeup, notice how expressively he uses his hands. Since the title is in public domain, the film is available from several labels. The versions vary widely in quality. Look for one that has a musical soundtrack, the tinted scenes, and, more importantly, be sure that the transfer has been made from a print projected at silent speed (16 frames per second), not sound speed (24 frames per second) which gives normal motion the fast, jerky quality mistakenly associated with early films.

Master of make-up Lon Chaney Sr. transforms into the horrific Phantom of the Opera in the 1925| film version.

Claude Rains, one of the most versatile and effortless actors ever to grace the screen, is a thoroughly sympathetic Phantom, but the expensive 1943 production is a failure as a horror film. Far too much time is spent on the trivial romantic triangle and light opera performances. Tellingly, in the credits, Rains gets third billing after Nelson Eddy and Susanna Foster. The allegedly frightening elements are largely reduced to silliness involving a cape and a broad-brimmed hat. Even the chandelier, unmasking, and sewer scenes are disappointing.

The 1962 Hammer version takes more care with backstage details than most. It also pays too much attention to the caterwauling on stage. Herbert Lom doesn't have much to do as the Phantom. Michael Gough is at his sly, villainous best. The violence is surprisingly explicit for the time, though the film lacks the energy, sexiness, and suspense of the studio's best work.

The Top Seven Mini-Monsters Movies

Trilogy of Terror
The Brood
Don't Be Afraid of the Dark
Ben
Island of Dr. Moreau
Willard
Slither

Robert Englund won't make anyone forget Lon Chaney, but his full-bore Phantom is nothing to be ashamed of. In fact, director Dwight Little and writer Duke Sandefur's 1989 interpretation of the story is underrated and surprisingly well-crafted. In this gory version, made in Hungary, Erik is equal parts Faust and Jack the Ripper. As the aspiring opera star Christine, Jill Schoelen's studied girlishness is irritating but in character. The whole film might have been better with a little less gore and a good falling chandelier scene. Curiously, it begins with shots of two now vanished New York landmarks, the World Trade Center and Tower Records.

In Dario Argento's 1998 version, the Phantom (Julian Sands) is not disfigured. As a boy, he was set afloat in a basket and saved by rats who raised him as one of their own in the caverns beneath the Paris Opera House. Asia Argento is one of the sexier Christines, but the dubbing of the English version is so slipshod that her singing voice seldom has much to do with the movements of her mouth. The same goes for the other, singers, too. Several scenes have a Felliniesque comic touch. This one's not nearly as much fun as Argento's 1987 *Opera* (see review).

By the way, the 2004 adaptation of Andrew Lloyd Webber's successful musical has virtually nothing to do with horror.

Phantoms (1998)

Dean Koontz's town-that-vanished tale boasts a top-drawer cast and so-so effects. Feuding sisters Lisa (Rose McGowan) and Jennifer (Joanna Going) arrive in Snowfield, Colorado, to find themselves alone. Most residents have vanished; some bodies that remain have been exsanguinated; cars and telephones suddenly stop working. Most of the scares are standard stuff—shadows zipping across the frame, quick cuts, sudden loud noises. The atmospherics are o.k. but the pace lags and it's all pretty silly by the end. (As is almost always the case with this kind of story, the set-up is stronger than the revelation.) Peter O'Toole's disgraced academic turned tabloid hack livens things up and Patsy Cline songs are always welcome, whatever the setting.

Phenomena (1985)

Young Jennifer Corvino (Jennifer Connelly) is telepathically connected to the insect world. She finds that bizarre murders are being committed around the spooky Swiss private school where she's just enrolled. Perhaps if she teams up with the eminent entomologist Dr. McGregor (Donald Pleasence) and his sidekick, a genius chimpanzee, they can solve the crimes. No, this is not a comedy, but in most of Dario Argento's films, the plots are not meant to be taken realistically. They're vehicles for his ideas and striking set pieces. He exaggerates the conventions of horror in the same ways that the Italian westerns of the 1960s and 1970s built on their American predecessors. The Grand Guignol conclusion is a maggot-infested doozie. A shortened, pan-and-scan version of the film has been distributed on tape under the title *Creepers.*

Picture of Dorian Gray, The (1945)

Pandro Berman, the producer who was responsible for so many of the best RKO and MGM films, is also behind the most opulent version of Oscar Wilde's famous story of youth and corruption. Though expressionless, Hurd Hatfield is fine as the far-too-handsome Victorian aristocrat, and though Angela Lansbury received an Oscar nomination for her performance as his first victim, the film belongs to George Sanders. His Lord Henry Wootten is the epigrammatic voice of the author. The portrait itself—"the emblem of his own conscience ... that would teach him to loathe his own soul"—is shown in Technicolor, but Harry Stradling's Oscar-winning black-and-white cinematography is lush.

Pillow of Death

See Dead Man's Eyes

Pin (1988)

Disturbed young Leon (played successively by Jacob Tierney, Steven Bednarski, and David Hewlett) is an apple who hasn't fallen from the tree. His father, Dr.

Linden (Terry O'Quinn) is a strange disciplinarian while his mother (Bronwen Mantel) keeps clear plastic slipcovers on all the furniture and thinks that Leon's friends are germ-ridden disease carriers. His younger sister Ursula (Michelle Anderson, Katie Shingler, and Cyndy Preston) has survived relatively unscathed. Pin is the transparent dummy in dad's office with which Leon develops an obsessive attachment. Few mainstream films deal with the changes in childhood and adolescence as well as this one. Writer-director Sandor Stern also delivers the goods with surprising scares that are developed through the characters. One of the best and least-recognized recent sleepers.

Piranha (1978, 1995, 2010)
Piranha II: The Spawning (1981)

A rural Texas resort area is plagued by attacks from ferocious, man-eating fishies created by a scientist to be used as a secret weapon in the Vietnam War. Spoofy horror film—the title monsters are little more than bubbles and red dye in the water—follows the familiar quick-and-dirty Roger Corman formula, and features director Joe Dante's signature in-jokes in the background. One tiny stop-motion critter appears in an all-too-brief cameo. This was the first script by novelist/filmmaker John Sayles to be produced. He also appears as the Army sentry.

Piranha II: The Spawning, James Cameron's directorial debut, stinks. The whole idea of carnivorous flying fish zipping up out of the ocean and going for people's jugulars is just so damn silly that there's nothing anyone could have done with it. Because of that, the fact that nothing much happens in the first half isn't that serious. Give Cameron and writer H.A. Milton credit for trying to take their main characters beyond stereotypes. In the leads, Tricia O'Neil and the ever-reliable Lance Henriksen are fine, but in 1981, conventional special effects simply could not create believable flying creatures—not bats and certainly not fish. The filmmaker has made considerable strides in recent years.

The 1995 remake of the original adds nothing. In fact, it lacks that nice flourish of stop-motion animation and it may even reuse some of the silly little two-dimensional fish "monsters" from the original. The rest of the effects are accomplished, as they were before, with red dye and a submerged bubble machine. Alexandra Paul and William Katt are the less-than-dynamic duo who must save the summer camp and the new lakefront development from the titular carnivorous fish, created by the government as a secret weapon. If you have the choice, give this one a pass and find the real thing.

The 2010 remake adds 3D, hundreds of digital critters, and a massive dollop of bad taste. Actually, director Alexandre Aja never misses an opportunity to be outrageous. From parasailing porn stars to severed organs, he tries so hard to break boundaries that the humor becomes a bit tiresome.

The Top Six Modern Witches and Warlocks Movies

The Craft
Rosemary's Baby
Burn Witch Burn
Curse of the Demon
Drag Me to Hell
Simon King of the Witches

Pit and the Pendulum, The (1961, 1991)

Roger Corman's second foray into Poe territory takes a more active approach. The relative restraint of *Fall of the House of Usher* is replaced by some hammy overacting and a Richard Matheson script that's unusually stilted at first. "The point seems of vital import to you," one character orates without an ounce of believability. Vincent Price is Nicholas, the son of an inquisitor who isn't over the death of his wife Elizabeth (Barbara Steele). If you can put up with the talky first half, the second pays off with a grand conclusion. The torture sequence may be Roger Corman's finest combination of sets, sound, action, and editing.

Told in the spirit of Corman, the 1991 version is a tongue-in-cheek version of several of Poe's stories, with a small tip of the hat to Mel Brooks' *History of the World—Part 1.* The mad inquisitor Torquemada (Lance Henriksen) is attracted to a baker's wife (Rona De Ricci) who's mistakenly imprisoned for witchcraft. An Italian Cardinal (Oliver Reed) has come to town to restrain the excesses of the Spanish Inquisition, but Torquemada, a slave to his obsession, tries to torture a confession, and perhaps more, from the woman. The Grand Guignol torture scenes are inventive and repulsive, though, doubtless, not as inventive and repulsive as the real thing. A shocking streak of sardonic humor keeps the action from becoming too sadistic. Director Stuart Gordon (*Re-Animator*) does fine work, even if he can't match the conclusion of Corman's original.

Plague of the Zombies (1966)

Sure the title is silly and the plot does revolve around zombies in nineteenth-century Cornwall, England—not the usual setting—but that's not a problem. This is essentially a vampire story with a twist. Relative unknowns Andre Morell, as the Van Helsing character, and John Carson as the villainous Squire, are every bit as good as Peter Cushing and Christopher Lee. Jacqueline Pearce and Diane Clare are demurely sexy Hammer heroines. The presence of familiar character actor Michael Ripper doesn't hurt either. The

One of the worst films ever made, *Plan 9 from Outer Space* is so poorly done it has become a laughable cult hit.

makeup is easily the equal of more recent living dead movies. And let's not overlook the political aspects of a story about the relationship between the upper class and workers. Zombies of the world, unite! You have nothing to lose but your shrouds!

Plan 9 from Outer Space (1959)

In his famous and sad final role, Bela Lugosi's screen time is less than two minutes. (See Tim Burton's *Ed Wood* for the full version of the relationship between Lugosi and the young director.) Wood's wife's chiropractor replaced the star and kept himself hidden behind cape and hat. The rest of Wood's alternative masterpiece—almost universally acknowledged to be the "worst" film ever made—is the stuff of Hollywood legend. Aliens in silk pajamas conspire to resurrect several slow-moving zombies from a cardboard graveyard and to conquer Earth before we warlike humans destroy the rest of the universe with "solarite bombs." Spaceships that look suspiciously like paper plates blaze across the sky, and Wood's famous penchant for rambling philosophical dialogue is given free rein.

JoBeth Williams is blocked from entering her child's bedroom by a really cool special effect in *Poltergeist.*

Poltergeist (1982)
Poltergeist II: The Other Side (1986)
Poltergeist III (1988)

Though Tobe Hooper directed this hugely popular horror hit, it was produced and co-written by Steven Spielberg. In some ways, then, it can be seen as the dark side of *E.T.,* also released in the summer of 1982. The Freelings (JoBeth Williams and Craig T. Nelson) learn why they got such a good deal on their suburban tract house when it attacks them and their kids. Most of the scares are original and frightening. Structurally, the film is sound with careful preparation establishing place and mood. The main flaw is the conclusion which ought to be more solidly connected to the earlier action. At the end, the characters simply need a better reason to spend more time in the place. Critics have floated many theories about the film's success—it's about the destruction of suburbia, Reagan-era politics, etc.—but it's simply a good, well-acted spooky movie.

The humor and homey sense of the first film seems forced in *Poltergeist II: The Other Side.* That suburban "realism" has been replaced by dopey special effects. Geraldine Fitzgerald's kindly old grandma and Heather O'Rourke's psychic cherub are cloyingly sweet. A few of the scares work well—notably the cadaverous Julian Beck's first appearance and a worm monster created by H.R. Geiger—but most of the action is a rerun of the first film and lightning does not strike twice.

III finds young Carol Anne (Heather O'Rourke, who died before the film's release) staying with her aunt and uncle (Nancy Allen and Tom Skerritt) in a ritzy Chicago high-rise. Watered down versions of those silly spooks from the first two show up again. Slick production values can't cover up a lack of originality. Many of the effects involve mirrors and ice. Overall, it's a solid step down from the disappointing *II.* Followed by a cable TV series.

Pontypool (2008)

Defiantly offbeat and original, this slow-starter posits the outbreak of a zombie plague as a result of language. Unhappy, egotistical Grant Mazzie (Stephen McHattie) is hosting a morning radio show in a small Canadian town. While he's on the air, a mob inexplicably surrounds a doctor's house. Mazzy, his producer Sydney (Lisa Houle), and his engineer Laurel Ann (Georgina Reilly) don't know what to make of it or what to do. Most of the action is focused on those three inside the basement radio station. It's light on the violence usually associated with the genre, but it certainly has its gross, surprising moments. Still, this one is best appreciated for the smart witty script, a sure understanding of radio, and letter-perfect performances.

Premature Burial (1962)

Guy Carrell (Ray Milland) is certain he'll be interred before he's completely inert. His fiancé Emily (Hazel Court) tut-tuts his obsession. Justifiably famous for his budgetary tight-fistedness, producer-director Roger Corman makes the fullest possible use of a few richly decorated and fog-shrouded Gothic sets, including a crypt with an escape route. Veteran writers Charles Beaumont and Ray Russell use Poe's morbid fear as the premise for a cracking good yarn. Like Shakespeare, they leave the stage littered with bodies.

Priest (2011)

In a desolate post-apocalyptic world, humans have defeated vampires and the few remaining undead survivors are kept on reservations. The title character (Paul Bettany) is a vampire-hunting samurai without a master. He returns to the fight after his niece (Lily Collins) is taken by the bloodsuckers. Yes, the first reference point is *The Searchers.* After that, you'll see stolen bits from *Blade Runner, The Road Warrior,* and any number of Sergio Leone westerns and Asian martial arts films. Throughout, the action pays as much attention to the laws of physics as a Road Runner cartoon. That said, this adaptation of a series of graphic novels is a prime guilty pleasure. The big finish on a speeding locomotive is wonderful.

Primeval (2007)

"Inspired by true events" giant crocodile adventure comes in third to *Rogue* and *Lake Placid.* A TV crew (Dominic Purcell, Brooke Langton, and an underused Orlando Jones) is sent to Burundi in the middle of a civil war to get footage of a huge reptile named Gustav that's dining on the locals. Said beast is wisely kept off camera most of the time or shown in silhouette. Though the story is told with some humor and attention to the political situation, it's not on a level with the best of its kind.

Prince of Darkness (1987)

One of John Carpenter's best and most underrated films works through intelligent dialogue, carefully measured special effects, and excellent performances from an ensemble cast. When a priest (Donald Pleasence) learns that the last member of an odd order, the Brotherhood of Sleep, has died, he inspects the church that the brothers guarded. Why are street people so attracted to it, and what is that big jar of goop that looks like molten lime Jell-O in the basement? Theoretical physics and ultimate evil are involved. Fans will catch echoes of *Poltergeist* and Carpenter's own *Assault on Precinct 13.*

Prisoner (2007)

Derek Plato (Julian McMahon), obnoxious auteur of controversial violent movies, is scouting locations at a prison when he finds himself locked up in a cell. It's unclear exactly what his captor (Elias Koteas) is up to. The independent production has a sophisticated look and the penitentiary where it was filmed seems grimly authentic. Even though punch sound effects are overused, the film earns a qualified recommendation to fans looking for something on the arty side. As for the big revelation at the end, I laughed when I wasn't supposed to.

The Top Thirteen Must-Be-Seen-to-Be-Believed Movies*

Blood Feast
Blood of Dracula
Brain That Wouldn't Die
Gamera: Guardian of the Universe
Island of Dr. Moreau (1996)
Kiss Me Kill Me
Lair of the White Worm
Lifeforce
Lost Continent
Lost Highway
Night of the Lepus
Blood Freak
Opera

**Group viewing recommended*

Prom Night (1980, 2010)
Hello, Mary Lou: Prom Night II (1987)
Prom Night III (1990)
Prom Night IV: Deliver Us from Evil (1992)

Good acting and above average production values are put in service of a plot that doesn't deviate a millimeter from the standard dead teenager slasher/stalker formula. It borrows most blatantly from *Halloween* with the "six years before" prologue, and from *Carrie* in the second half. Jamie Lee Curtis and four of her high school friends are the prey of a killer out to avenge an earlier murder. But much more terrifying than that plot is the "Disco Madness" theme of the titular dance. Flashing lights, raised arms, pointing fingers, polyester—the horror, the horror.

Despite the *Prom Night II* subtitle, *Hello, Mary Lou* isn't a sequel. It really owes more to *Nightmare on Elm Street.* Thirty years after she was burned to death on the bandstand as she accepted her crown, Mary Lou's (Lisa Schrage) spirit rises from the grave and tries to inhabit Vicki's body. The thing is, Vicki is a good girl, while Mary Lou, alive or dead, is an unrepentant temptress, who wants vengeance on the people (including Michael Ironside) responsible for her death. Think Freddy Kreuger with PMS. Some of the hallucinatory scares are unexpected. So is the serious religious element.

Prom Night III is a sequel to *Mary Lou,* and has nothing to do with the first film. As it opens, Mary Lou Maloney (Courtney Taylor), the unrepentant party girl and murderess, breaks out of her shackles in hell with a nail file and returns to high school. She sets her sights on struggling student Alex (Tim Conlon) and does everything in her devilish powers to further his academic career. This time out, the recycled plot is treated as comedy. Despite fair effects and production values, it remains pretty wrapping around an empty box.

In *Prom Night IV: Deliver Us From Evil,* Father Jonas (James Carver) prays to "save sluts and whores" as the stigmata bleed on his palms. Moments later, the psycho-priest is killing kids at the prom and indulging in self-flagellation. About the best that can be said of this tedious Canadian production is that it ended the series until the forgettable 2008 in-title-only remake. It has to do with an escaped murderer coming after a high school girl.

Prometheus (2012)

Ridley Scott's "prequel" to *Alien* is as much science-fiction as pure horror. After a visually stunning introduction presenting the introduction of life on Earth, the scene shifts to the future where a team of scientists head off in the titular spaceship to the planet that would later be visited by the *Nostromo.* The two most interesting characters are Dr. Shaw (Noomi Rapace), a scientist who turns out to be as tough as Ripley, and the obligatory robot, David (Michael Fassbender), who models himself on Peter O'Toole's T.E. Lawrence. Given the advances in special effects, the horrors that they encounter are much more graphic and intricate, and, in one case, almost as shocking. Even if the film isn't another masterpiece, it's a fascinating work.

Prophecy, The (1995)
Prophecy II, The (1998)

Enjoyable and surprisingly witty religious horror goes beyond the traditional structure of Good versus Evil as represented by God and Satan. The key combatants are angels involved in an eons-long war with each other. These angels are not halo-topped sweetie pies who float around performing the odd miracle here and there. To these creatures, humans are "talking monkeys" who have usurped their favored place in the presence of God. It's hard for Harry (Elias Koteas), a priest-turned-cop, to know which side to take in the conflict. On one hand, Gabriel (Christopher Walken, at his deadpan creepiest) is willing to kill anyone who gets in his way. But since he can't drive, his mobility is limited. His opposite number Timothy (Eric Stoltz) seems to be looking for a soul to steal. They're after a young Arizona Indian girl whose only protection is her elementary school teacher (Virginia Madsen). First-time writer-director Gregory Widen gets excellent performances from a seasoned cast, and he gives the whole film a gritty, intense look that fits the subject. He also avoids most of the genre's clichés, and the film's intelligent black humor keeps it from being too heavy.

The rare sequel is just as good, just as off beat as the original, and even funnier. The heavenly Terminators are back, and Gabriel (Christopher Walken) is the baddest of the bunch. He's after Valerie Rosales (Jennifer Beals), a nurse who's been impregnated by Daniel. Director Greg Spence, also responsible for the surprise sleeper *Children of the Corn IV,* brings real wit and innovation to the story. Gabriel's entrance is a terrific set piece and the ending is even better. Some of the plotting is a tad too elaborate but that's not a real problem. Inexplicably, this gem made its debut on video.

Psycho (1960, 1998)
Psycho II (1983)
Psycho III (1986)
Psycho IV: The Beginning (1990)

In 1960, Alfred Hitchcock invented the modern horror film with a modest masterpiece that has influenced virtually everything in the field that's been made since. Loosely inspired by infamous killer Ed Gein, the movie deliberately and constantly misleads audiences. Today, everybody knows the story, and the big scenes are built on images that have become cinematic archetypes. But that's hindsight. In 1960, no one expected the leading lady (Janet Leigh) to make such an early and shocking exit, and no one expected a murderer to look like the boy next door. Co-star Tony Perkins had been known for serious, generally "nice" roles. More to the point, the whole idea of an opportunistic serial killer was unheard of. Today, the only part of the film that's at all dated is Simon Oakland's lengthy concluding explanation. The film itself is so craftily constructed that even Hitchcock's fans will find something new when they see it again. In his interviews with François Truffaut, Hitchcock said that he didn't consciously recreate "an old-fashioned Universal horror-picture" but that's precisely what the Bates Motel is. He also said that he was consciously working within the economic limits of a television production (except for the shower scene), and so now the film plays beautifully on home video.

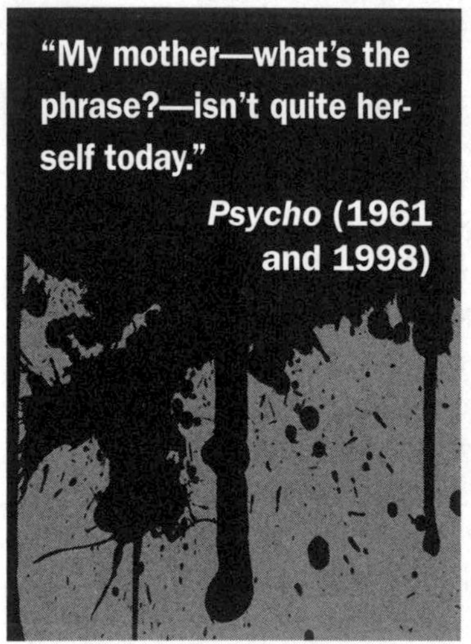

"My mother—what's the phrase?—isn't quite herself today."

***Psycho* (1961 and 1998)**

The house used in *Psycho* can still be seen on the Universal Studios lot in California.

Psycho II doesn't come close to the original, but it's not a bad horror movie, either. And it is a true sequel, a logical continuation of the characters and story of Hitchcock's low-budget masterpiece with several genuinely suspenseful moments. More importantly, Tom Holland's script has a wickedly funny sense of black humor. After being institutionalized for twenty-two years, Norman Bates (Anthony Perkins) is declared sane, over the loud objections of Lila Loomis (Vera Miles, continuing her role from the first film). Back at the old motel, the first thing Norman sees is a shape in the upper left window of the house on the hill. Then his mother calls. Is someone trying to drive him mad again, or is Norman just doing what comes naturally?

Beyond a few references to other Hitchcock films, *Psycho III* is just another slasher flick. After a reprise of the ending to *II,* a young nun, Maureen (Diana Scarwid), leaves her convent under horrible (and funny) circumstances borrowed from *Vertigo.* Eventually, she and Duane (Jeff Fahey) find themselves as the only guests at the Bates Motel where Norman (director Perkins) is still having conversations with Mom up in the house on the hill. Though the violence is handled with some restraint, the action is poorly written and poorly paced.

The Top Five Nazi Horrors

Zombie Lake
Dead Snow
Bloodsucking Nazi Zombies
Shock Waves
Frontier(s)

In *Psycho IV: The Beginning,* Fran Ambrose's (C.C.H. Pounder) radio talk show is focused on "boys who kill their mothers." Naturally, Norman (Anthony Perkins) calls in to share. In flashback, young Norman (Henry Thomas, from *E.T.*) remembers dear old mom (Olivia Hussey). Like the other entries in the series, it's partially tongue-in-cheek and enjoyable enough if you don't compare it to the original. Thomas is eerily reminiscent of Perkins as he was in 1960. Graeme Revell's score is built around Bernard Herrmann's original music. Director Mick Garris is also responsible for *Stephen King's The Stand.* This one was made for cable with exceptionally high production values.

In 1998, Gus Van Sant remade the original film in color. Though it was said to be a shot-for-shot duplicate, there are not-so-subtle differences in dialogue and action. In the leads, Vince Vaughn and Anne Heche are certainly adequate, though her short spiky hair and bizarrely colored wardrobe stand in stark contrast to Janet Leigh's understated beauty. To me, it's an intriguing experiment in filmmaking, of more interest to students than to general viewers.

Psycho Beach Party (2000)

Impoverished parody looks just as inexpensive as the '60s drive-in flicks that it's imitating, and is almost as much fun. Almost. A serial killer is preying on the teenagers in a Southern California beach town. That puts a bit of a crimp in young Chicklet's (Lauren Ambrose) attempts to become the first girl to join the Big Kanaka's (Thomas Gibson) band of surfers. It doesn't help that she goes a little bit nuts from time to time when she sees certain patterns. The cast is certainly game and in tune with the cheesy, sexy action, but there's really nothing here that John Waters hasn't done with more wit and energy.

Pumpkinhead (1988)
Pumpkinhead II: Blood Wings (1994)

TV host and drive-in movie critic emeritus Joe Bob Briggs has said that this is the most requested title among his incarcerated fans. It's easy to see why. At the beginning, special effects master Stan Winston's directorial debut hammers on emotional buttons without wasting a single motion. Grotesque monster (Tom Woodruff Jr. in terrific makeup), loving widowed father (Lance Henriksen), his young son, thoughtless rich city kids ripping up the rural setting on their dirt bikes—that's the set-up. But once the conflicts are being engaged, Winston gives the story a serious twist, refusing to take the easy, expected path. Throughout, his direction is sure-handed; just notice the way he uses light and smoke. In Henriksen's long career, this is one of his most complex roles and the whole film is one of the unrecognized greats.

The elements that were combined so gracefully in the original—the memorable atmosphere, strong characters, intelligent twists on the revenge formula—come back as hollow clichés in *Pumpkinhead II: Blood Wings,* a story that's really a remake, not a sequel. Obnoxious teens in an Arkansas backlot resurrect the son of the first title character. Some of the effects are excellent, and it's good to see Andy Robinson, the psycho killer in *Dirty Harry,* who almost always plays villains, cast as the hero. He's a New York cop who becomes a rural sheriff. Beyond that, the film is a competently made, polished slasher flick with Bill Clinton's brother Roger as the mayor.

Followed by two more direct-to-DVD sequels.

Director Alfred Hitchcock was behind some of the best horror and thriller films ever made.

Quarantine

See [REC]

Queen of the Damned (2002)

Lestat, played by Tom Cruise in *Interview With the Vampire,* returns in a much more modest production. Played by Stuart Townsend, he wakes up in New Orleans, joins a band, and becomes an international rock star. The largest part of the wide-ranging plot involves Jesse (Marguerite Moreau), a young woman who's infatuated with him, and Marius (Vincent Perez), the vampire who "made" Lestat. Though Aaliyah, who was killed in an airplane accident before the film was released, gets star billing, she's a supporting character. For all the heavy breathing and bodice-ripping, it's relatively tame stuff. *Queen of the Darned* would have been more appropriate.

Rabid (1977)

Though it's not David Cronenberg's best, by any means, this combination of medical, sexual, and mechanical horrors provides an early look at some of the themes he would explore more fully in other films. In a triumph of casting, porn star Marilyn Chambers is Rose, a motorcycle accident victim whose skin grafts mutate, turning her into a vampiric carrier of a new strain of rabies. In the first half, the horror is based on intimate surgical fears which turn into larger and less frightening *Living Dead* excesses later. Cronenberg's fans will spot the thematic and symbolic links to the later, more serious work.

Raisins de Mort, Les (1978)

Attacked by a man whose face rots before her eyes, Elizabeth (Marie-Georges Pascal) flees across a barren French countryside where she encounters more predatory zombies. Actually, this is one of the prolific Jean Rollin's better efforts, though it is squarely in the Euro-gore tradition of the 1970s. The opening scenes on an almost empty train are particularly good, and the plot recalls *Night of the Living Dead* without being imitative. In an on-screen introduction, Rollin remembers how bitterly cold it was when the film was made and that fits the bleak tone. The title refers to the wine grapes that cause the zombie plague.

Rapture, The (1991)

Too original, daring, and unsettling for a timid theatrical market, this controversial religious horror has become a cult favorite on video. Though it's

The Top Nine Encounters with Old Scratch Movies

Devil's Advocate
Angel Heart
End of Days
Needful Things
Prince of Darkness
Witches of Eastwick
Devil
The Evil
House of the Devil

far from a perfect film, Michael Tolkin's story of conversion treats charismatic Christianity with a seriousness that's almost never seen in popular entertainment. Mimi Rogers plays a woman who renounces an empty life of sexual experimentation and becomes devoutly religious, only to be betrayed by God. Perhaps. Whatever beliefs viewers bring to the film, it's a disturbing, thought-provoking experience. Recommended.

Rasputin, the Mad Monk (1966)

Hammer recycles both the principal sets and cast members from *Dracula Prince of Darkness* for this grand melodrama. Naturally, the key is Christopher Lee's energetic portrayal of the famous character—though for American audiences there is some unintentional humor in the pronunciation of his name as Ras-POOTIN. Barbara Shelley is excellent as the royal lady-in-waiting he seduces. Lee interprets the monk as a charismatic combination of Jesus, Dracula, and Walt Whitman. Ignore the beard and wig. Listen to his rough, loud voice, and notice the way he uses his hands. Though the film lacks a persuasive Russian setting, it's still a lot of fun for Hammer fans. Liner notes claim that a nine-year-old Lee actually met Prince Yusupoff, one of the assassins.

Raven, The (1935)

Lugosi and Karloff's second teaming is a real disappointment following the brilliant *Black Cat,* though it is closer to Edgar Allan Poe's themes. Bela Lugosi is a half-mad surgeon who thinks that he's a god "with the taint of human emotion." He enlists a criminal (Boris Karloff) to help him get rid of an inconvenient judge. The main problem is unintentional humor, nowhere more evident than in the modern dance interpretation of Poe's poem, "The Raven." Karloff's makeup and one strong mirror scene are the best moments.

The real Grigori Rasputin was a controversial figure who gained influence over Russia's Romanov dynasty and was later assassinated.

Raven, The (1963)

Egged on by the pixilated Dr. Bedlo (Peter Lorre), Dr. Erasmus Craven (Vincent Price) confronts the powerful sorcerer Scarabus (Boris Karloff) to find his lost Lenore (Hazel Court). Along for the ride are Bedlo's son (Jack Nicholson) and Craven's daughter (Olive Sturges). The picture was filmed in three weeks with considerable comic improvisation by Lorre and Nicholson which, according to producer/director Roger Corman, Karloff disliked. The three veterans have a wonderful time with the material, particularly Lorre. He's really funny with some of his best light physical comedy. The duelling sorcerers finale is fine, too. Despite a typically penurious Corman budget, the film looks good.

Ravenous (1999)

The humor in this dark black comedy begins with the opening on-screen foreword. The Western that follows looks like *Dances with Wolves,* if they'd called it *Dines with Cannibals.* After a bloody encounter in the Mexican-American War, John Boyd (Guy Pearce) is sent off to Fort Spencer, high in the wintry California mountains. He has hardly arrived when Colqhoun (Robert Carlyle) shows up with a horrible story. The party he was traveling with was trapped by the snow in a cave. Facing starvation, they resorted to the unspeakable.

A rescue party sets out, and the rest is one bloody surprise after another. The ensemble cast handles the material with just the right touch. In the end, this sleeper is a rare and tasty treat.

In the horror genre, Jack Nicholson is probably best remembered for his role in *The Shining,* but he has starred in many other creepy films in his long career, including *Wolf* and *the Raven.*

Re-Animator (1985)
Bride of Re-Animator (1990)
Beyond Re-Animator (2003)

Few if any horror films mix strong sexual humor and equally strong effects as well as this cult favorite. H.P. Lovecraft's serial novella, "Herbert West, Reanimator," about a serum that revives the dead (sort of) is brought to the screen with all the grotesque inventiveness that the special effects folks can provide. Richard Band's music shamelessly "borrows" from Bernard Herrmann's scores for *The Trouble With Harry* and *North by Northwest.* The famous "head" scene has never been duplicated. On home video, the film exists in three editions. The R-rated theatrical release is the tamest of the three. Most DVDs are unrated.

The sequel, *Bride of Re-Animator,* is a thorough disappointment, going too far in all the wrong directions. Of course, the prosthetic special effects are graphic, but severed body parts have been so overused that they don't even have the power to shock any more. The strong, flippant humor of the first film has become studied, though star Jeffrey Combs gives it his best. Worst of all, the filmmakers don't even pay attention to plot details from the original. Characters who were clearly dead and/or squashed are brought back without explanation. No, logic is not a prime consideration in cheap horror movies, but that kind of unimaginative sloppiness is an insult to fans.

Beyond Re-Animator marks something of a return to form. Dr. Howard Phillips (Jason Barry) arranges to take a position at the Arkham State Penitentiary so that he can meet and work with Dr. West (Combs) who's incarcerated there. What follows goes over some of the same fertile ground as the original but within the prison setting and with the use of twenty-first-century computer effects.

Reaping, The (2007)

LSU professor Katherine Winter (Hilary Swank) has debunked forty-eight miracles when she learns that people in the little bayou town of Haven believe that they're experiencing biblical plagues and that young Loren McConnell (AnnaSophia Robb) has something to do with it. Off Winter and her assistant Ben (Idris Elba) go. They find friendly fundamentalist locals and rivers of blood, flies, boils, dead livestock, locusts and the like. The effects are inventive and disgusting but when the film delves into its ridiculously convoluted mythology, gasps of fright become giggles of derision.

"I must say, Dr. Hill, I'm very disappointed in you. You steal the secret of life and death, and here you are trysting with a bubble-headed coed."

Re-Animator

[REC] (2007)

Perhaps the best of the "reality" based horrors combines the immediacy of *Blair Witch* with raving, ravenous zombies. Ambitious young feature reporter Angela Vidal (Manuela Velasco) and her unseen photographer Pablo (Pablo Rosso) are following a crew of firefighters one night when an emergency call comes in. A woman is in distress in an apartment building. No sooner have they arrived than they find themselves locked in. The filmmakers make good use of natural sounds in place of a musical soundtrack. The pace is so quick that logical lapses and convenient plotting aren't a problem, either, and the whole thing clocks in at a sleek seventy-eight minutes. The American remake, *Quarantine,* follows the original faithfully in plot, setting, characters, and tone. Jennifer Carpenter brings the same kind of energy and curiosity to the lead. Both have been followed by sequels.

Red Dragon (2002)

Writer Ted Tally and director Brett Ratner stick closer to Thomas Harris's novel than Michael Mann did when he made *Manhunter* from the same material. The difference is Anthony Hopkins returning to the character of Hannibal Lecter from *Silence of the Lambs.* Where Brian Cox turned in a carefully shaded, small performance in Mann's film, the role is enlarged with a long introduction involving Hopkins and Edward Norton as FBI agent Will Graham, and extended scenes between them in the psychiatric facility. The rest follows Harris's plot with a top drawer cast. Harvey Keitel, Philip Seymour Hoffman, Ralph Fiennes, and Emily Watson are certainly the equals of their counterparts in the first film. What's missing is the fevered intensity Mann brought to the story, and his striking but dated '80s visuals and score.

THE TOP NINE
HORRIBLE HIGHWAYS AND BYWAYS MOVIES

Identity
The Forsaken
Twentynine Palms
Vacancy
Duel
Jeepers Creepers
Prophecy
Splinter
Wind Chill

RED HOUSE, THE (1947)

Avoid the cut-rate DVDs of this sharp sleeper. The 2011 restoration is a revelation. Edward G. Robinson is Pete Morgan, an uncle who is far too interested in his teenaged niece Meg (Allene Roberts, whose unblinking close-ups are really strange). Their questionable relationship is mirrored in all of the other characters. An undercurrent of guilty sexuality runs throughout, most obviously in Meg's flirty friend Tibby (Julie London), but also in their pal Nath (Lon McCallister) and his widowed mother (Ona Munson). It's the kind of thing that David Lynch has used so effectively. Comparisons to *Night of the Hunter* are not out of order.

RED RIDING HOOD (2011)

Director Catherine Hardwicke brings a bit of the *Twilight* sensibility to this werewolf fantasy. Fans will see some similarities to *The Company of Wolves,* too. When a vaguely medieval village is attacked by the beast, young Valerie (Amanda Seyfried) finds that she can talk to it. Could it be one of her suitors (Max Irons and Shiloh Fernandez) who is being transformed? A visiting Inquisitor, Father Solomon (Gary Oldman), will do whatever it takes to find the monster. Detailed CGI backgrounds give the film a painterly look. The creature effects are dark, and violence and blood are kept well within the limits of a PG–13 rating.

RELIC, THE (1997)

A slickly produced by-the-numbers variation on the *Alien* formula became something of a surprise hit in theatrical release, and has been even more popular

Edward G. Robinson (second from right) is a creepy uncle in *The Red House.*

with audiences on home video. Following an exposition-packed introduction, the scene shifts to a Chicago natural history museum and the labyrinth of sewers and tunnels beneath it where a South American mutant monster decapitates supporting characters and eats their hypothalamuses (hypothalami?). Tough cop Tom Sizemore and tough evolutionary biologist Penelope Ann Miller set things right. Clayton Rohmer, Linda Hunt, and James Whitmore make the most of their tissue-thin backup roles. Journeyman filmmaker Peter Hyams is an excellent director of photography and a so-so director. He creates an effective sense of place and wisely keeps his monster under wraps until the third act when he reveals just enough of Stan Winston's beastie. Somehow, the whole thing is much more entertaining than it ought to be.

Repulsion (1965)

Carol (Catherine Deneuve) is a young beautician who descends into madness when her sister (Yvonne Furneaux) leaves her in their London apartment. "She's a bit strung up, isn't she?" sis's beau (Ian Hendry) observes. Deneuve's virtually mute and expressionless performance is somehow right for a character whose emotional collapse goes back to her childhood, though sexual explanations are strongly suggested, too. Younger viewers should understand the sexual relationship in the film was fairly scandalous in its time. Polanski finds horror in the most mundane details of everyday life—a wall, a crack in the sidewalk, and of course that famous rabbit. The apartment itself becomes a reflection of deliberately paced and deeply personal terrors. On the Criterion Collection disc, Polanski explains the purely commercial roots of the film's production. For whatever reason it was made, this remains one of the most excruciating films of the 1960s.

Resident Evil (2002)
Resident Evil: Apocalypse (2004)
Resident Evil: Extinction (2007)
Resident Evil: Afterlife (2010)
Resident Evil: Retribution (2012)

The most popular films based on a video game are built around hordes of zombies, mutant attack Dobermans, and assorted monsters with tentacles and other repulsive body parts. The series begins with the nasty T-virus that gets loose in the Hive, a research lab beneath Raccoon City. The evil Umbrella Corporation is behind it all. Our heroine Alice (Mila Jovovich) is an amnesiac (as are several of the supporting characters from time to time) who fights back and gains powers. Violent effects focus on slice-and-dice lasers and the like. Writer/director Paul W.S. Anderson, the star, and her stunt doubles handle the action competently and so the films are not limited to audiences who play the games.

"THE DEAD WALK!" **headline in** ***The Raccoon City Times.***

Resident Evil

The second entry, *Resident Evil: Apocalypse,* revolves around the outbreak of the zombie infestation in Raccoon City. The origins of the T-virus are explained, and the action scenes are even more elaborately choreographed with bigger, badder monsters and lots of guns. Special effects are more complex, too.

Resident Evil: Extinction finds the zombie apocalypse in full flower. Much of the action is set in the desert, giving the film a *Road Warrior* feel. The mutant crow attack recalls Hitchcock's *The Birds.* More continuing supporting characters are introduced.

As *Resident Evil: Afterlife* begins, Alice has become a psychic, gravity-defying, multiple-self samurai superhero. The elaborate action scenes are as important as traditional

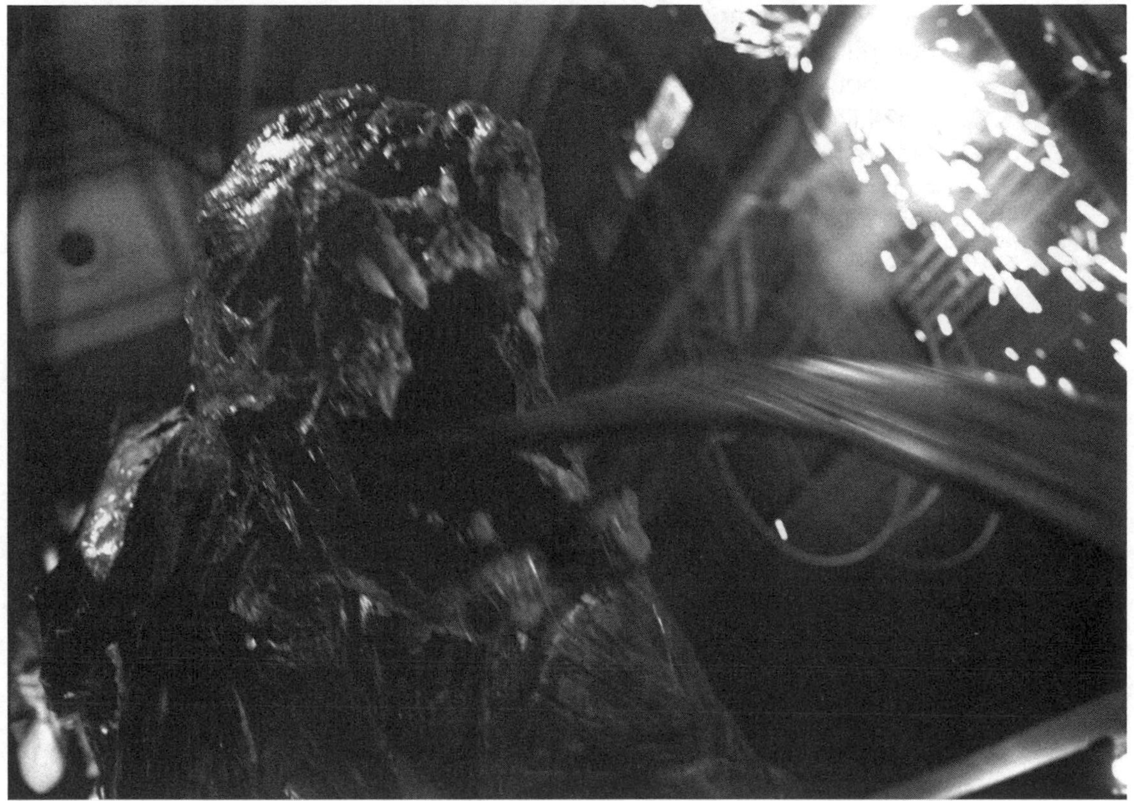

Genetic research orchestrated by an evil corporation goes horribly awry in the "Resident Evil" series.

horror, but there are still plenty of monsters and zombies. Throughout all four films, production values are first rate, and the continuing narrative unfolds like an old Saturday morning serial.

Things start to slip in the fifth film as so-so 3-D and CGI effects take precedence over any narrative coherence. The action scenes are a bit tired, too, and even judged by the standards set by the earlier installments, the costumes are very strange. Alice's get-ups range from a bondage-inspired leather and buckles outfit to two small towels, fore and aft, held in place by transparent tape.

Resurrected, The (1992)

A good eerie plot—slightly similar to director Dan O'Bannon's script for *Dead and Buried* and based on a Lovecraft story—loses focus through some little mistakes. Clair Ward (Jane Sibbett) hires detective John March (John

Terry) to discover the reason behind her husband Charles Dexter's (Chris Sarandon) obsession. He claims to be involved in "the interrogation of matter," but why have the cops found body parts in his riverfront Rhode Island lab? Like a supernatural *Double Indemnity,* the film is built around March's tape-recorded narration. Small scenes—getting a phone number, changing a shirt—needlessly call attention to themselves, and the impressive ending isn't all it could be. On the other hand, a long subterranean finale is excellent and Todd Master's monster effects are unsettling.

Return of Count Yorga

See Count Yorga, Vampire

Return of Dr. X, The (1932)

Despite the title, this one has virtually nothing to do with Michael Curtiz's *Doctor X,* made seven years before. It's a campy B horror/comedy that gets off to a rocky start when wise-cracking reporter Walt Barnett (Wayne Morris) discovers a disappearing body. It doesn't really kick into gear until Humphrey Bogart (in his only horror role) shows up as Dr. Quesne, a twitchy, lispy, vampiric medico who's up to no good. Not one frame is meant to be taken seriously, and so it's a lot of fun.

Return of the Blind Dead

See Tombs of the Blind Dead

Return of the Living Dead (1985)
Return of the Living Dead Part II (1988)
Return of the Living Dead Part III (1993)

Comic sequel, of sorts, to *Night of the Living Dead* begins with the idea that George Romero's cult hit is based on a real incident, and the truth behind it is that a combination of hazardous-waste spill and military cover-up created the carnivorous corpses. A series of Three-Stoogian blunders reignites the plague, setting a graveyard full of fresh bodies loose on a bunch of teens. Director Dan O'Bannon keeps things popping right along, and the yuck-factor goes right off the scale with some impressively staged bloody effects. It's all so far-fetched and outrageous that this one's recommended to gore fans only.

The Top Thirteen Period Horrors

The Wolf Man
Horror Express
Dorian Gray
Kiss of the Vampire
Legend of the Werewolf
The Terror
American Haunting
Brotherhood of the Wolf
Conqueror Worm
From Hell
Gothic
Haunted Summer
Ravenous

As sequels to horror-comedies go, *RotLD Part II* is o.k., but it's no *Evil Dead II.* It simply takes the based-on-a-true-story premise of the first and treats it even more frivolously. The Army spills a can of gas that recharges corpses who then set upon teenagers. Heads are lopped; limbs are hacked; blood cascades. Ho-humm. Seen it a hundred times.

In *Part III,* love-smitten teen Curt (J. Trevor Edmond) uses the government's secret Trioxin gas to reanimate his girlfriend Julie (Mindy Clarke) after she's a little bit killed in a motorcycle accident. The result is another gore comedy with gross effects and a predilection for self-mutilation. The third time around, this one-joke wonder is wearing paper thin. As the colonel in charge, Kent McCord ("One Adam-12, see the zombie") is his usual ramrod stolid self. The imaginative corpse effects are the point. Two more sequels were made for television in 2005.

Return of the Vampire (1944)

The Columbia studio attempts to recreate the successful Universal formula, whipping together several elements in a lumpy half-baked loaf. The story begins in 1918 with the vampire Armand Tesla (Bela Lugosi) being guarded by a werewolf (Matt Willis). Flash forward to the London Blitz of World War II where Tesla is resurrected and goes after the family who staked him years before. The wolf transformation effects aren't much, and Lugosi's first return to the role of a vampire after *Dracula* is a bit of a letdown, too. He has some very smooth scenes and energetic flashes, but the wartime setting is a distraction. So is the werewolf angle, and why is the hairy-faced fellow always wandering around with brown paper packages? The basic problem is a silly script. Sample dialogue: "Poor Andreas ... what a tragedy to lose his soul again."

Return to Salem's Lot, A

See Salem's Lot

Revamped (2007)

Ultra-low-budget comedy has a few moments of wit, but most of its humor is based on dime store plastic fangs and the like. Distraught over his wife's infidelity, Richard (producer/writer/director Jeff Rector) happens upon cable channel 666 and an infomercial for Kiss of Death, Inc, which promises vampires who will solve all his problems. He calls the toll-free number and signs up. When he awakens five years later, he finds that things have changed. Abominable lighting does no favors to an ensemble cast who have specialized in video premieres.

Revenge of the Creature

See Creature from the Black Lagoon

Riding the Bullet (2004)

It's Halloween night, 1969, at the University of Maine when unhappy student Alan Parker (Jonathan Jackson) is called home. His mother (Barbara Hershey) is seriously ill. His hitchhiking road trip becomes a long dark night of the soul even before George Staub (David Arquette), an emissary of hell, shows up. The source material, a Stephen King novella, contains autobiographical elements and nods to other works. Though some scenes misfire, overall, it's a solid combination of scares, bizarre laughs, honest emotion, and great oldies.

Ring, The (2002)
Ring Two, The (2005)

The first big-budget remake of an Asian hit created a new school of American horror with technology-based possession, or something to that effect, at the heart of the story. Conventional monsters are replaced by creepy kids, catatonic teenage girls, water images, and off-putting sound design. (The subtitle track on the DVD describes the background noises as "eerie rumbling" and "unearthly whistling.") The premise—watch a particular videotape and you die within seven days—has an urban legend vibe, and an A-list cast pulls it off flawlessly. The big scare at the end is a terrific moment.

The sequel was directed by Hideo Nakata, who also made the first two Japanese *Ring films.* Naomi Watts and young David Dorfman reprise their roles, and the film has an exceptionally sharp look. Even though Nakata attempts some interesting, even striking variations on the most memorable moments of the original film, the element of surprise is diluted. Some sketchy narrative choices don't help.

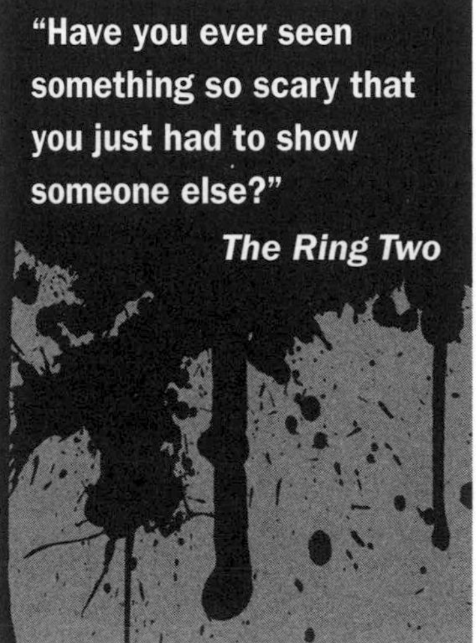

Rise: Blood Hunter (2007)

Newspaper reporter Sadie Blake's (Lucy Liu) story about a subculture of young wannabe vampires attracts the attention of the real thing, leading to a complicated, violent, sexy story with a strong element of Quentin Tarantino and a properly dark sense of humor. Writer/director Sebastian Gutierrez's plot moves back and forth in time but remains easy to follow. Performances from excellent supporting actors are very good. So is the contemporary Gothic atmosphere, and the bad vampires are ominously weird. Some may find the pace of the unrated two hour-plus version too slow. I think it's properly deliberate, adding emotional weight to the proceedings. Recommended.

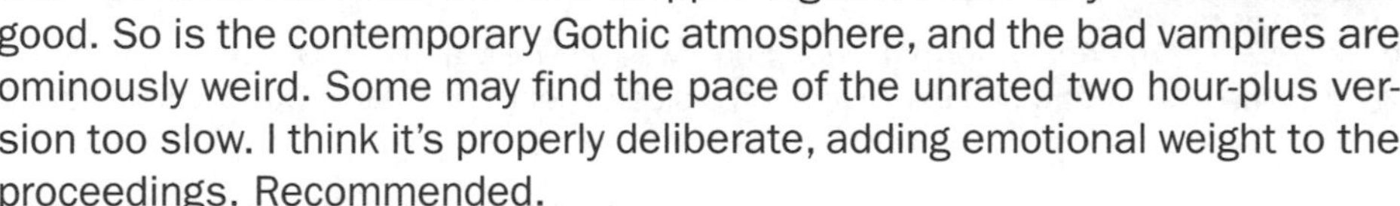

Rite, The (2011)

As played by Anthony Hopkins, Father Lucas isn't going to make anyone forget Hannibal Lecter, but he is a good character and the film is a cut above the norm for exorcism horror. Doubting seminarian Michael Kovak (Colin O'Donoghue) is ready to resign the priesthood before he takes his vows, but is persuaded to put off his decision until he takes a special course in the finer details of performing exorcisms at the Vatican. For the young man, it's more a matter of two months in Rome than spiritual fulfillment. He meets Father Lucas who is the church's go-to guy for driving out demons. He has performed thousands of the rites. As long as the focus is on their faith versus reason argument, things stay interesting. Throughout, director Mikael Håfström maintains the highest production values in terms of sets, photography, acting, and writing, just as he did in *1408.* But by the end, we're into contortions and spitting up nasty objects and the devil's red-eyed mule

A kinky cult classic for decades, *The Rocky Horror Picture Show* was originally a theatrical bomb, until audiences started bringing props to the show and dancing in the aisles to songs like "Let's Do the Time Warp."

(really). Not surprisingly, the film unquestioningly sides with church doctrine and that, I suppose, is what fans want to see.

Rocky Horror Picture Show, The (1975)

On DVD, the audience-participation element of the Mother of All Midnight Screenings is lost, though what you and your friends want to do and wear in the privacy of your own place is nobody's business. So, what about the movie itself? As a kinky musical sendup of old horror movies, it's campy, vampy, and not bad at all. The rock score is loud and energetic; the lyrics surprisingly witty. Susan Sarandon and Barry Bostwick are fine as the innocent heroine and hero, but the film belongs to Tim Curry's Dr. FrankNFurter. He redefines outrageous excess as the mad scientist who favors mascara, high heels and fishnet hose. Curry wrings every drop of humor from the role—and there's a lot to wring. In the process, he shows how a talented stage actor can overpower a screen production, either on film or DVD.

Rodan (1956)

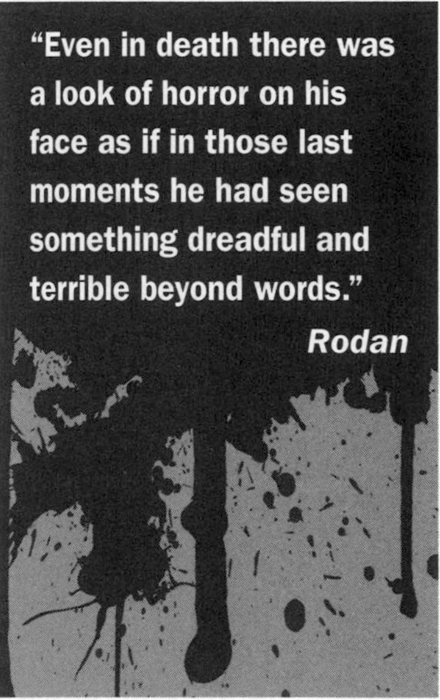

Five minutes of stock footage of hydrogen bomb tests establish the fact that Japanese underground monsters are more than a little miffed at being disturbed. Mysterious attacks first occur in a mine, and when one of the critters makes his big entrance, it's a grand moment of surprise and laughter. The freewheeling plot has several flying monsters, including the titular guy and his squeeze Rodina, earthquakes, volcanoes, amnesia, and some impressive sets for the caverns. Director Ishirô Honda may have used some of the same exteriors for the big crowd scenes that were seen in *Godzilla*. It ends with a decisively positive or at least sympathetic view of Rodan and Rodina.

Rogue (2007)

In the Northern Territories of Australia, the tour boat *Suzanne* sets off for a three-hour cruise. It does not end at Gilligan's Island. At heart, this is a superb big lizard (all right, big reptile) movie. The monster is a huge salt water crocodile that's realized on screen by visual effects supervisors Dave Morley and Andrew Hellen. They studied real crocs and their creation is one of the most realistic you'll ever see. It just looks and moves and sounds right. Their efforts would mean little if the characters didn't engage us and these, like the critter, are much more believable than the usual collection of stereotypes. Things do start slowly because writer/director Greg Mclean takes time to establish the environment with stunning nature photography.

Rosemary's Baby (1968)

Few works of fiction or film can succeed both as horror and as mainstream entertainment. This one does, and it's as suspenseful and enjoyable today as it was when it was made. The solidly plotted story revolves around an innocent Midwestern girl (Mia Farrow) married to an ambitious young New York actor (John Cassavetes) who'll do almost anything to advance his career. Ruth Gordon won an Oscar for her scene-stealing performance as a nosy neighbor in a spooky apartment building. Not to take anything away from writer/director Roman Polanski—countless good novels have been screwed up on their way to the screen—but both the dramatic structure and the characters come straight from Ira Levin's novel. Polanski did bring a sexual frankness to the story that was unknown in popular film of the time.

The Top Seven (+) Tales of Possession

The Exorcist
Temptress
Paranormal Activity series
Exorcism of Emily Rose
The Rite
The Last Exorcism
Insidious

A rarely-seen sequel, *Look What's Happened to Rosemary's Baby,* was made for television in 1976, and Ira Levin wrote an abominable, slapdash novel, *Son of Rosemary,* in 1998.

Ruins, The (2008)

Two young American couples (Jena Malone and Jonathan Tucker, and Laura Ramsey and Shawn Ashmore) are drinking beer and margaritas on a Mexican beach when they learn of a Mayan temple that's "off the beaten path" in the nearby jungle. They find a squat, vine-choked pyramid and things immediately go south. Writer Scott Smith and director Carter Smith wisely keep their cards close and give things away gradually, as the characters, who do have some depth, come to realize the real nature of what's happening. Later, the action is properly bloody, skin-crawly, and surprising without overindulgence in graphic effects.

S

Salem's Lot (1979)
Return to Salem's Lot, A (1987)
'Salem's Lot (2004)

The 1979 mini-series cut to feature length as *Salem's Lot: The Movie* is rather abruptly edited at the beginning. Introductory material involving key characters has been left on the cutting room floor, and the obvious commercial breaks are intrusive. The made-for-TV production values haven't improved with age, either, but James Mason's dapper, effortless performance as the villainous Straker is still superb. Nobody else in the cast comes close to him. The scares work fairly well, too, though the vampire effects have been eclipsed in several theatrical films that have been made since. The Barlow vampire makeup is based on the original *Nosferatu.* The full 183-minute version is available on DVD.

A Return to Salem's Lot, Larry Cohen's 1987 semi-comic vampire tale is not really a sequel to Tobe Hooper's mini-series. Instead, he uses Stephen King's premise of a small town overrun by bloodsuckers as a platform from which he can satirize conservative American smugness. Under the leadership of Judge Axel (Andrew Duggan), the undead inhabitants of Salem's Lot are afraid of change, drugs, and AIDS. They have their own version of history that casts them as outsiders who came to this country seeking freedom from unjust persecution. It wouldn't be fair to reveal what they want of anthropologist Joe Weber (Michael Moriarty) and the cigar-chomping Van Meer (actor-director Sam Fuller). At best, Cohen is half successful; the snappy, sexy moments aren't consistent. The whole film has an unfinished, hurried

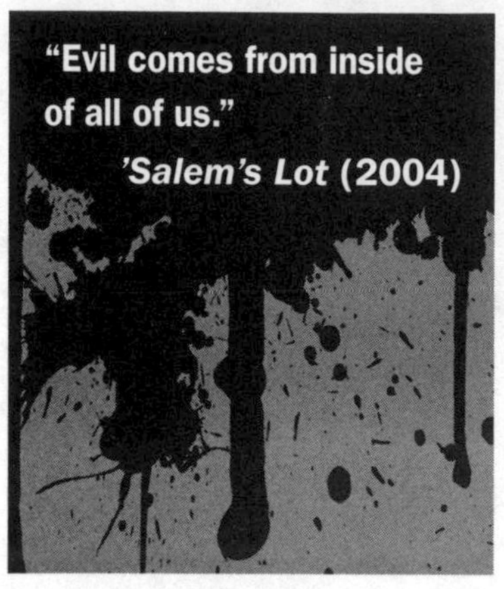

feeling and not very impressive effects. Recommended more to Cohen's fans than to King's.

'Salem's Lot (with the first apostrophe), the 2004 remake of the original is a solid step up in terms of production values and casting, particularly in the supporting roles. The plot has been updated in a few details but not significantly changed. Rob Lowe is understated in the lead. Donald Sutherland may not be James Mason, but he's every bit as smooth and charming. More important, the special effects are infinitely superior and with the relative freedom accorded to made-for-cable works, the graphic fantasy violence is appropriate to King's fiction.

Santa Sangre (1989)

Felliniesque fantasy opens with a naked man (Axel Jadorowsky) on a perch in a cell, and immediately flashes back to a Mexico City circus filled with grotesques. Director Alejandro Jadorowsky (father of Axel) tackles organized religion, greed, castration, sex, and various Oedipal relationships with bucketsful of symbolism. It's difficult to tell how much of this is meant to be taken seriously in any respect—very little, I suspect—because the violence and sex are cartoonishly broad, and chickens figure prominently. Some of the graveyard images, however, are hauntingly lovely and at the end, the story somehow becomes touching. Wonderful soundtrack.

Saw (2004)
Saw II (2005)
Saw III (2006)
Saw IV (2007)
Saw V (2008)
Saw VI (2009)
Saw: The Final Chapter (2010)

James Wan's theatrical debut introduced the term "torture porn" into the filmic lexicon. It describes a new iteration of Grand Guignol horror focusing on graphic depictions of prolonged pain inflicted by elaborate mechanical de-

In the "Saw" series can best be described as "torture porn," as prisoners of a weird doll are forced to mutilate themselves.

vices that can be defeated only by acts of extreme self-mutilation. The perpetrator is John Kramer, aka Jigsaw (Tobin Bell). The setting is usually a noxious, dank industrial bathroom or its equivalent. The first film and the ones that have followed borrow visual elements, themes, and characters from *Se7en.* They are completely original in the infernal machines which have unusual realism in both their design and the sounds that accompany them. Also, it's impossible to overstate Tobin Bell's contribution. His dry, whispery voice and quiet intensity carry the films over numerous narrative rough patches.

Saw is built around two guys (Cary Elwes and Leigh Whannell) who must cut off their feet. Another bit involves a reverse bear trap that rips open jaws. Why is all this going on? The victim is guilty of something evil—jaywalking, adultery. Jigsaw's schemes flummox the police (Danny Glover and Ken Leung). Wan left the director's chair after this one, but has remained involved with the films as writer and producer.

Saw II begins with Jigsaw giving himself up (much as Kevin Spacey's John Doe did in *Se7en*). That doesn't slow him down for a moment and more

The Top Eleven (+) Post-Apocalyptic Horrors

Priest
Resident Evil series
Dawn of the Dead
Land of the Dead
Zombieland
Day of the Dead
Carriers
Omega Man
Last Man on Earth
Night of the Comet
The Stand

intricate torture devices are brought out, involving a larger pool of victims and more graphic effects. The pit filled with dirty hypodermic needles is undeniably upsetting.

In *Saw III* Jigsaw is loose and much of the focus is on exceptionally strong medical horror, including graphic brain surgery. The already byzantine back story involving Jigsaw and the police is twisted into even more bizarre permutations that really don't deserve comment. Characters thought to be dead turn out to be alive. Bad guys become good guys become ... whatever.

Saw IV starts with Jigsaw's autopsy. Flashbacks repeat and amplify key nasty bits from the earlier entries. Even so, the filmmakers maintain the grim, grainy look of the first three.

By *Saw V* some slippage shows up in the production values of the non-torture scenes. The big moments are a rehash of Edgar Allan Poe's famous razor sharp pendulum (but it's not tempered steel, tsk, tsk) and a self-tracheotomy.

Saw VI tries to wrap everything up in a neat, albeit bloody package with an explanation of how it all came to pass. The main bad guys are health insurance company executives, but it's easy to see that much of the air has leaked out of the balloon.

Tellingly, *Saw: The Final Chapter* moves the first big scene out of the torture chamber and into a brightly lit city square where it immediately turns into bad comedy. The theatrical release was 3D. With any number of Ds, the mojo is gone.

Scalpel (1977)

Often surprising Southern Gothic sleeper involves a plastic surgeon (Robert Lansing) who's been cut out of his father-in-law's will because the granddaughter (the surgeon's daughter) has disappeared. Why? Because she saw her father drown her boyfriend. Soon after grandad's demise, the surgeon finds a girl (Judith Chapman) with a disfigured face which he can transform into the image of his missing daughter. Yes, it's contrived and convoluted, but writer-director John Grissmer twists his tale in unexpected directions. Unavailable on DVD.

Scanners (1981)

Exploding head effects burst onto the screen with David Cronenberg's story of dueling telepaths and government agents. (Yes, it's a lot like *Firestarter* and *The Fury.*) At its best, the film makes the experience of telepathy seem real as an uncontrollable babble of interior voices, and, as Cronenberg carefully points out, isn't that what madness is? At its worst, the special effects take over, and they're still pretty good. Michael Ironside's insane Revok steals the show. The wild plot is pretty tame compared to some of Cronenberg's more recent work.

Scary Movie (2000)

The Wayans brothers' parody of popular horror movies is aimed mainly at the *Scream* series and other slasher films. Since those pictures virtually mock themselves these days, the focus of the humor is more on sex than scares, and the more outrageous bits take an R rating to its limits. Gay viewers may not be amused, but when it comes to orientation, the film is an even-handed offender. It has been followed by four sequels of varying quality to date.

Scream (1996)
Scream 2 (1997)
Scream 3 (2000)
Scre4m (2011)

Wes Craven understands his audience as well as any filmmaker in the business. He aims the first film at kids who have seen every movie in the horror section of their local video store, and assumes that they understand the rules and conventions of teen slasher flicks. Then he and writer Kevin Williamson base their scares and twists on those assumptions, making references to virtually every major American horror film from *Frankenstein* to *Elm Street.* At the end, after they've laughingly described and demonstrated all of the genre's

Yet another series of slasher films, the makers of the "Scream" movies have fun making references to other American horror movies.

clichés, they twist them around to a satisfying and unusual conclusion. Clearly, it's the kind of movie that could be too self-aware and self-referential for its own good, but it strikes the right note with young viewers who have made it a huge sleeper hit in theatrical release and on video. The sequels that followed in the 1990s built on the premise without really adding much.

Scream 2 cranks the "meta" aspects up to eleven. The first murders are committed at a preview screening of *Stab,* an adaptation of a book about the killings in the first film. The top drawer cast is called upon to handle an awful lot of dialogue.

Scream 3 finds Dewey (David Arquette) working as a technical advisor on *Stab 3.* For those who may have come in late, the rules for a third entry in a trilogy are laid out early on. The screen is filled with cameos.

In 2011, Craven and Williamson returned with *Scre4m,* a "re-boot" that essentially recreates the original as an out-and-out comedy. In tone, it's only a short step from the *Scary Movie* franchise. It does, however, contain an impassioned argument against talking in theaters.

Scream and Scream Again (1970)

Horror, sci-fi, spies, and archetypal '60s music are whipped into a semi-coherent froth. Dr. Browning's (Vincent Price) nurse is murdered in a vampire-like sexual attack, and a hard-case cop (Alfred Marks) investigates. At the same time, a totalitarian spy is up to something, and a guy in the hospital finds that he's missing a new extremity every time he wakes up. (His reaction is apparently the source of the title.) Peter Cushing's appearance is a cameo; Christopher Lee is an intelligence officer who's only tangentially involved. A long chase scene filled with surprising twists is the highpoint.

Screaming Mimi (1958)

Overwrought serial killer tale had an immediate influence on giallo horrors that would follow a decade or so later. (It's based on a novel that's an uncredited source for Argento's *Bird with Crystal Plumage.*) Virginia (Anita Ekberg) is enjoying an outdoor shower when she's attacked by a knife-wielding lunatic who's escaped from the nearby Highland Sanitarium. Even though the maniac is dispatched by her half-brother, Virginia is so traumatized that she finds herself in Highlands under the tender care of Dr. Greenwood (Harry Townes) who becomes obsessed with the statuesque Scandinavian stunner. Before long, Virginia is reborn as the exotic dancer Yolanda who works at Gypsy Rose Lee's San Francisco nightclub. More murders follow and a sexy little statue of Virginia/Yolanda is somehow involved. The thoroughly enjoyable foolishness would hardly be worth noting if it weren't for the star at the height of her considerable sex appeal and an overall atmosphere of seedy madness.

Season of the Witch (1972)

Originally released in the United States as *Hungry Wives,* when it was produced in 1972, George Romero's self-described "feminist film" may have had more social relevance than it does now. Today its sexual politics are obvious and off-putting. It's more successful as a portrait of a middle-aged woman's emotional disintegration. As Joan Mitchell (Jan White) approaches the big 4-0, she experiences dreams or hallucinations that portray her life as surreal fantasies. The "empty nest syndrome" is taken to new heights when Joan becomes interested in a neighborhood witch and her coven. Like most of Romero's work, it's made mostly on suburban locations and subtly acted by a de-glamorized unknown cast. The too-talky story can be seen as strict realism without any supernatural elements. In that respect, it's a companion piece to Romero's *Martin,* though not nearly as suspenseful or engrossing.

Secret Window (2004)

On one level, this is a gimmick movie, but it's so solidly constructed, enjoyable, and funny that it stands up just fine to a second viewing. Troubled writer Mort Rainey (Johnny Depp) is confronted by a wild-eyed redneck (John Turturro), who claims that Rainey stole one of his short stories. Rainey professes complete innocence, but it's obvious from the beginning that something else is going on. Performances and production values are fine. The effects never detract from the characters. Recommended to fans of *1408,* based on another Stephen King story, and of writer/director Koepp's *A Stir of Echoes.*

Seed of Chucky

See Child's Play

Seizure (1974)

Oliver Stone's debut is a variation on *Dead of the Night.* Horror author Edmund (Jonathan Frid) invites a group of friends and associates to his country house for a weekend visit after recurring dreams of the horrors that will befall them. Cult favorites Mary Woronov, Martine Beswick, Troy Donahue, and Herve Villechaize are among them. Inexpertly made on a low budget—you can see shadows of cameras in some scenes—the film has aged poorly, but like so many of Stone's works, its excesses (like the three escaped lunatics, one a female Harvard professor!) are perversely enjoyable. The cast handles the bizarre material rather well, particularly Frid.

Sentinel, The (1977)

Big-budget horror borrows freely from *Rosemary's Baby* and *The Exorcist*—too freely, really—but it's still entertaining in a mainstream vein with a few solid scares. Supermodel Alison Parker (Christina Raines) is going through serious personal problems which are revealed in ham-fisted flashbacks when she moves into a new Brooklyn brownstone and meets her "very strange" neighbors. For openers, they may be ghosts, but cops Eli Wallach and Christopher Walken suspect that all may not be kosher with Alison and her fiancé Michael (Chris Sarandon). The apartment building's sense of reality helps considerably. The big spooky finish directly quotes Tod Browning's *Freaks.*

The Top Eight Psychological Horrors

Afraid of the Dark
Black Swan
Take Shelter
301/302
Audition
Chasing Sleep
Dead Ringers
Fade to Black

Serpent and the Rainbow, The (1988)

Ambitious Wes Craven effort is far from his best. It's a handsome production—too handsome in ways. Out in the Amazon jungle, a shaman gives credulous Harvard don Dennis Allan (Bill Pullman) some magic mushroom juice. He has visions and seven years later pops down to Haiti to investigate "zombification" drugs. The rest wanders through grotesque horror, gauzy romanticism, political terror, and hallucinations. The acting is mannered, and though some of the shocks are really jolting, the whole unfocused thing takes itself far too seriously. Zakes Mokae steals the film as the Ton Ton Macute villain. The credits claim "based on a true story." That's no excuse.

Session 9 (2001)

Complex, involving, frustrating, and somewhat inconclusive, this psychological horror is built on an unusual premise and takes an equally difficult course in working it out. The setting is the Danvers State Hospital for the insane, built in 1871 and closed since 1985. Five guys are hired to clean out hazardous asbestos. They have their own demons to deal with, or are those the ghosts of past residents? I can't say that I fully understand everything that's going on at the end, and director Brad Anderson's affinity for low-angle close-ups and mumbled dialogue didn't help either, but the film kept me involved all the way through.

Se7en (1995)

Stuck with a collection of clichéd characters and a story that makes absolutely no sense (just try to figure out how the concluding actions are planned and executed), director David Fincher and production designer Arthur Max wrestle the film into submission with sheer style. The plot involving a serial killer working his way through the seven deadly sins means nothing compared to the overall texture of depravity and palpable horror. The story has carefully removed any hint of reality. It takes place in a rainy city without name or location. The keys to the film's popularity are a terrifically understated performance by Morgan Freeman as Somerset, the cop a week from retirement, and very good work from Brad Pitt whose star was on the rise. Though that ending makes no rational sense, it is undeniably suspenseful.

Seventh Sign, The (1988)

Relatively effective apocalyptic thriller based on the Book of Revelation shares the basic credibility problem that plagues any work of the genre. To some viewers, it's dealing with the literal word of God; to others it's the pure baloney of tabloid headlines. I tend toward the luncheon meat school of criticism, but I try to keep an open mind. This one revolves around a troubled pregnant woman (Demi Moore) and a taciturn stranger (Jurgen Prochnow). She gives a good, convincing performance reminiscent of Mia Farrow in *Rosemary's Baby,* and Australian director Carl Schultz keeps the special effects to a minimum.

Severance (2006)

Seven staffers from the marketing department of the Palisade Defense company head off for a team-building weekend. They're supposed to stay in a luxury lodge but their ill-tempered bus driver leaves them stranded in the woods, somewhere in either Hungary or Romania or Serbia. Location turns out to be the least of their problems. Think the graphic violence of *Hostel* with the wit of *Shaun of the Dead.* Most of the humor comes from Andy Nyman and Danny Dyer. The violence is some of the most bizarre you'll ever see. (People walked out of a film festival screening where I first saw it.) The political points are well taken.

Sh! The Octopus (1937)

Fast-paced parody of the old-dark-house formula is impossible to describe. Set in a lighthouse on a dark and stormy night, it's trippily reminiscent of *Peewee's Playhouse* with black-outs, pratfalls, and trap doors, and, of course, tentacles appearing from off stage. Two comic detectives (Hugh Herbert and Allen Jenkins) attempt to solve the murder of a body that's hanging from the rafters while a dozen or so other characters wander in and out virtually at random. The slight film might not be worth mentioning if it weren't for one bizarre transformation effect at the end that's accomplished with makeup and lens filters. Today, the moment would be easy enough to accomplish with computers but in 1937 it was something special.

Shadow of the Vampire (2000)

If you can get through the torpid opening credits without falling asleep, you'll find that the pace doesn't really quicken. It takes a bit of time to get to the conceit of Steven Katz's script. He suggests that director F.W. Murnau (John Malkovich) found a real vampire, Max Schreck (Willem Dafoe), to play the role of Orlok in his seminal 1922 horror film *Nosferatu.* Having a hungry bloodsucker on location with cast and crew creates some problems. The film follows the making of the silent masterpiece, recreating key scenes, and, of course, the iconic rat-like makeup. The transitions between black and white and color are seamless and effective, and the whole thing is surprisingly funny at odd moments. It comes to life in the moments where Murneau is behind the camera guiding his cast.

Shaun of the Dead (2004)

Shaun (co-writer Simon Pegg) faces trouble at every turn. His girlfriend Liz (Kate Ashfield) thinks he neglects her for his slacker friend Ed (Nick Frost). He's forgotten to make reservations for their anniversary dinner at Fulci's restaurant. His mother is put out with him and he's stuck in a crummy job selling appliances. Then the deep space probe Omega 6 breaks up over southeast England and the zombie plague erupts. It's clear from the outset that Pegg and director Edgar Wright know their horror movies and they bring a fan's enthusiasm to this comedy. If Wright shows off a bit with extended tracking shots, he's entitled. Pegg's love of American genres extends to cop movies (*Hot Fuzz*) and sci-fi (*Paul*).

Shining, The (1980, 1997)

Director Stanley Kubrick boasted during production that his adaptation of Stephen King's novel of a haunted hotel would be the most terrifying film ever made. It's not. It is handsome and well-acted, but it's almost more a suspense film in the traditional sense than a horror film. Kubrick makes full use of his intricate, grandiose sets and caresses them with his constantly moving camera. In the big finish, when Jack Nicholson is chasing his son

Writer's block and an isolated, haunted hotel drive Jack Nicholson to murder in *The Shining*.

through snow-covered topiary, the sheer beauty of the scene is more impressive than its menace. And the famous moment with the spectral bartender, where Nicholson is having his first drink in five months, is so evocatively lit and carefully crafted that you can almost taste the bourbon.

King was never happy with Kubrick's interpretation. In 1997, he served as executive producer and writer for a much longer (273 minutes) TV mini-series. The form suits the 504-page source material. Given the extended time for character development, Steven Weber and Rebecca De Mornay are as believable as Nicholson and Shelley Duvall. Director Mick Garris makes his Overlook Hotel as real as Kubrick's, even if he doesn't match such memorable set pieces as the ghostly bar. My only criticism: young Courtland Mead is too cherubic. A sequel to the novel (and certainly the film) is in the works.

Shock Waves (1977)

This is arguably the best example of a curious subgenre of horror—the underwater Nazi zombie movie. Rose (Brooke Adams) tells the flashback story of a Caribbean excursion boat, captained by John Carradine, that lands on an island inhabited by a mad German doctor (Peter Cushing). You do not need three guesses to figure out what he's up to. Some of the locations, notably an old hotel, are spooky and director Ken Weiderhorn is able to give the fascist creatures their moments, too.

Shocker (1989)

On one hand, Wes Craven creates a fierce satire on television and the way the medium distorts our view of reality. On the other, he panders to his young male target audience by presenting the horror—yet another psychotic mass murderer, Horace Pinker (Mitch Pileggi)—as a heroic villain, and violence becomes a thoughtless end in itself. Most of the time, though, the film is just another derivative exercise in obvious special effects, borrowing liberally from Craven's own work, as well as *The Hidden* and *Horror Show.* After he's elec-

The Top Fifteen Reasons-Not-to-Visit-New-York Movies

Midnight Meat Train
Godzilla (1998)
End of Days
King Kong
Ghostbusters
Gremlins II
Jacob's Ladder
The Believers
Black Swan
God Told Me To
Dark Water
Hellboy
Hellboy II
Maniac Cop
The Sentinel

trocuted, Pinker, who has literally worshipped at the feet of the god of TV, becomes a channel-surfing Freddy Kreuger who returns to attack his enemies.

Silence of the Lambs, The (1991)

Three filmmakers—director Jonathan Demme and stars Jodie Foster and Anthony Hopkins—are at the top of their form, creating a rare hit that is both a mainstream, Oscar-winning success and a first-rate horror film. Foster is Clarice Starling, an ambitious young FBI trainee who is sent to interview imprisoned serial killer Hannibal Lecter (Hopkins) to catch another murderer (Ted Levine, whose carefully shaded performance is easy to overlook). Writer Ted Tally deftly compresses Thomas Harris' fiction, and Demme handles the action with a sure touch, mixing character, complex plotting, and locations that have a feeling of absolute authenticity. Repeated viewings reveal what a careful craftsman Demme is, and even the most superficial glance reveals how much TV's *The X-Files* has lifted from the film. Yes, that is producer Roger Corman, who gave Demme his start, as the FBI director. Followed by the sequel *Hannibal*.

Silent Hill (2006)

Feature-length adaptation of a video game gets full marks for atmospherics, not so much for narrative coherence. Sexy mom (Radha Mitchell) runs out into the night looking for her daughter who has sleep-walked to the unprotected edge of a vast pit right next door to their expensive house, thereby establishing a dream-like logic. The action eventually shifts to the little town of Silent Hill, West Virginia, where ash falls like gray snow, and assorted nasty and often-faceless critters threaten the uninteresting, tissue-thin characters. Maybe it makes more sense to those who have played the game.

Silent Scream, The (1980)

Scotty Parker (Rebecca Balding) arrives late at a Southern California college and has to scrounge up off-campus living arrangements. The clifftop place she finds bears a certain resemblance to the Bates residence, but she's desperate. Though at first, the film appears to be just another stalker tale, it's carefully constructed with believable, sympathetic characters who avoid clichés. The younger cast members are fine and their elders—particularly Yvonne DeCarlo, Barbara Steele, Cameron Mitchell, and comedian Avery Schreiber in a serious role—are even better. Director Denny Harris makes inventive use of the house's interior spaces to create suspense. For horror fans, the levels of graphic violence and titillation may be too low, but the Hitchcockian story is tightly written with a strong ending.

Silver Bullet (1985)

The first half of Stephen King's no-frills werewolf story focuses on the daylight side of the creature and its nighttime activities. Then in the second, the action focuses on Marty (Corey Haim), a wheelchair-bound boy who has discovered that identity. He persuades his sister (Megan Follows) and uncle (Gary Busey) to believe him, and they have to face the beast. King's script doesn't fool around much and novice director Daniel Attias handles his job the same way. The only real flaw is a lack of sense of place.

Simon, King of the Witches (1971)

"My name is Simon and I live in the storm drain," our hero (Andrew Prine) states, leading even the slowest viewer to wonder just how powerful this would-be regent really is. Actually, Prine isn't bad at all and the late-'60s hippy-dippy milieu is a trip. Both the humor and the loose plot involving Simon's episodic encounters with corrupt officials, bogus witches, and drug dealers are reminiscent of Russ Meyers' *Beyond the Valley of the Dolls,* but without the crazier excesses. Magic itself is treated in a mostly matter-of-fact manner with low-tech effects.

A therapist (Bruce Willis; left) has a surprise in store for him when he decides to treat a troubled boy (Haley Joel Osment) who sees ghosts in M. Night Shymalan's *The Sixth Sense.*

Sixth Sense, The (1999)

Yes, it's a "gimmick" movie, but M. Night Shyamalan's debut is a classically constructed ghost story with good characters, legitimate scares, and all the technical brilliance of a big-budget studio production. The film finally works through excellent performances by Bruce Willis as a child psychiatrist, Haley Joel Osment as his patient, and Toni Collette as the boy's overworked mother. Take a second look. This one stands up well to repeated viewings.

Skeleton Key, The (2005)

Geriatric nurse Caroline (Kate Hudson) is burning out professionally when she takes a job deep in the Louisiana bayou country. It's clear from the outset that something untoward is going on with her charge, Ben Devereaux (John Hurt) and his wife Violet (Gena Rowlands). But what is it? Writer Ehren Kruger and director Iain Softley play their cards carefully, and the film is more enjoyable if you don't anticipate the twists. The ensemble cast does fine work, even though Peter Sarsgaard's Southern accent is iffy. The house where much of the action takes place is effectively realized, and the occasional directorial flourishes are easily ignored.

Sleepless (2001)

Giallos seldom make much sense but this one is particularly loosey-goosey. It has to do with two sets of murders, one contemporary and the other seventeen years earlier believed to have been committed by the "killer dwarf," now deceased. Police detective Moretti (Max von Sydow) comes out of retirement to work on the new killings. Dario Argento's plot quickly boils down to a series of elaborately staged acts of lethal violence, usually against women. The star brings more gravitas to the film than it needs or deserves.

Sleepy Hollow (1999)

In most Tim Burton films, production design is as important as the story. That's true here with his creation of an eighteenth-century upstate New York hamlet and the dense forest that surrounds it. In this version, Icabod Crane (Johnny Depp) is a police constable who's sent from New York City to investigate a series of beheadings. Those murders are sufficiently graphic but not dwelt upon to the point that they're excessive. Depp is a somewhat goofy protagonist, adding a note of humor, and Christopher Walken is effectively grotesque and horrifying as the Horseman. Note Burton's tip of the hat to the original *Frankenstein* in part of the big finish.

Slither (2006)

Another of those pesky meteorites encasing parasitic, carnivorous aliens lands in the woods near the little town of Wheelsy. Grant Grant (Michael Rooker) is the first victim. His wife Starla (Elizabeth Banks) tries to stand by her man, but it's hard when he swells up and grows tentacles. The humor is as important as the effects; the pace zips right along; star Nathan Fillion brings his easy-going charm to the role of the beleaguered sheriff. Great stuff for fans.

Slumber Party Massacre (1982)

Noted feminist author Rita Mae Brown has said that she meant for this script to be a parody of dead teen slasher flicks. That's easy to believe, but the movie sure didn't turn out that way, despite some intentional humor and an understanding of adolescent girls' behavior. A killer (Michael Villella) with an electric drill and a long bit is loose on the weekend that Trish's (Michelle Michaels) parents leave her home alone and she invites some girlfriends over. A surfeit of T&A, including a Brinke Stevens cameo, is really all this pedestrian entry has going for it. And, at seventy-eight minutes, it is short. Two sequels have followed.

Snakes on a Plane (2006)

The title really does say it all, and the film delivers. Much of the structure is borrowed from *The High and the Mighty.* We've got a flight from Hawaii to Los Angeles with a diverse passenger and crew list, including the rap artist with entourage, the celebutante with Chihuahua, the flight attendant on her last flight. And, of course, the snakes—a bushel of brightly colored, shiny CGI serpents that pop up everywhere. In the leads, Samuel L. Jackson and Julianna Margulies handle the material with a light touch, but not too light, embracing its essential cheesiness. And the ending is terrific.

Snow White: A Tale of Terror (1997)

Michael Cohn's made-for-cable interpretation of the Grimm fairy tale is more imaginative, thoughtful, and insightful than 99 percent of the horror movies that go to theaters. The visual influences range from Vermeer to Cocteau's *Beauty and the Beast* and *Night of the Living Dead.* The changes in story and character are unsettlingly perceptive. In this version, the conflict between Snow White (played by Taryn Davis as a child and Monica Keena as a teen) and the Queen (Sigourney Weaver) is much more complicated and competitive. The girl isn't completely innocent and the older woman has reason to feel threatened. Sam Neill is the father and husband who's caught in the middle. A bleak wintry-autumnal medieval atmosphere bolsters some excellent acting from all concerned. Give writers Thomas Szollosi and Deborah Serra considerable credit for going back to the Grimm Brothers' archetypal roots and weaving them into new patterns. Fans should make an extra effort to find this one.

Sole Survivor (1983)

At first the plot and the eerie alienated atmosphere are straight from *Carnival of Souls.* Denise Watson (Anita Skinner) is the sole survivor of an airplane crash that unstable, psychic actress Karla Davis (Caren Larkey) somehow predicts. After it, strange visions plague Denise, or is she seeing real dead people? Some of the acting isn't all it could be, but Thom Eberhardt's

The Top Thirteen Most Remarkable Remakes

House on Haunted Hill
The Omen
Tale of Two Sisters
Thirteen Ghosts
The Uninvited (2009)
The Wolf Man (2010)
Willard
The Crazies
The Shining
'Salem's Lot
The Fly
2001 Maniacs
Wizard of Gore (2007)

dialogue is offhandedly realistic. Given the nature of the supernatural material, it's realistic, too, and the plot manages to maintain its trickiness all the way through. This is one of the best hidden treasures tucked away in the back of your favorite video store. Look for Brinke Stevens in a small role and Leon (credited as Leon Robinson) in a cameo.

Something Wicked This Way Comes (1983)

"First of all, it was October...." That's the way both Ray Bradbury's famous novel and his adaptation begin. It's a lyrical, unashamedly nostalgic horror film that remains strictly faithful to the magical tone of the fiction. Will Halloway (Vidal Peterson) and Jim Nightshade (Shawn Carson) are twelve years old and about to learn "the fearful needs of the human heart" when Dark's Pandemonium Carnival arrives in their small town. It's evil, seductive entertainment where wishes are granted at a terrible price. Dark (Jonathan Pryce) and the mute Dust Witch (Pam Grier) know those wishes and are ready to accommodate them. Will's father (Jason Robards Jr.), the town librarian, is the boys' guide. Director Jack Clayton creates some truly frightening moments—particularly for those bothered by spiders—but he's more successful in evoking Bradbury's unique vision of youth and magic and things that cannot be explained.

Sometimes They Come Back (1991) Sometimes They Come Back ... Again (1996)

Jim Norman (Tim Matheson) and his wife Sally (Brooke Adams) move back to the small town his parents left twenty-seven years before. Jim finds that the horrors of his past haven't diminished and the ghosts are still there. Writers Lawrence Konner and Mark Rosenthal and director Tom McLoughlin effectively flesh out King's short story while retaining his weathered small town atmosphere and his understanding of the enduring power of childhood bullies. Matheson's very good in a straight dramatic role. On video, the made-for-TV feature contains extra footage of violence and grotesque special effects.

The plot to the sequel-remake *Sometimes They Come Back ... Again* is nothing special. It cannibalizes several other Stephen King works and tosses in a ton of witchcraft hokum. That said, the story of resurrected Satanic teen bullies who terrorize John Porter (Michael Gross) and his daughter Michelle (Hilary Swank) is not without style and polish. A few of the effects are really striking. Alexis Arquette is very good as the lead bad guy, and so are Gross and Swank.

Son of Dracula (1943)

The first use of Alucard for Dracula is underlined for slow learners as the Count (Lon Chaney Jr.) makes a less than spectacular debut in America. He arrives by train at Dark Oaks plantation at the invitation of Kay (Louise Albritton), a credulous Southern belle who believes in the occult. Chaney isn't completely comfortable with the role. Perhaps that's why he's largely absent in the opening reels. The film really owes more to the carefully crafted, mid-budget horrors that Universal was cranking out at a steady pace during those years than it does to the original *Dracula* or to the sequel *Dracula's Daughter.* It does contain some neat scenes, like the coffin rising up out of the swamp, and the second half is stronger with inventive plot twists and a spookier atmosphere.

Son of Frankenstein (1939)

Though it's generally considered to be the weakest of the three films in which Boris Karloff played the Creature, in many ways, this one is more enjoyable today. Under the direction of veteran Rowland V. Lee, it's certainly less fantastic and overwrought than James Whale's work. Wolf Frankenstein (Basil Rathbone) returns to the ancestral castle, only to find that the villagers still haven't forgiven him for what his daddy did. He's trying to make amends when old Ygor (Bela Lugosi) tells him that the monster still lives. But it seems that Ygor left the headlights on and now the big guy needs a recharge. The sets and the sharp black-and-white cinematography are first-rate, but the act-

ing carries the film. Lugosi was never more restrained and seldom better than he is here. Karloff, as always, is excellent. (This was the last time he played the role.) Even facing that kind of competition, Rathbone and Lionel Atwill (as Krogh, the sympathetic local cop) are never upstaged.

Sorority Row (2009)

Highly polished exploitation begins with some flashy visuals, and it looks terrific all the way through. The premise is your basic prank-gone-wrong that results in a murder and cover-up. Eight months later, someone starts knocking off the sorority sisters involved. The murders are preposterous, inventive impalements. The script is bitchy. The young actresses are brittle and attractive. Nothing about the film pretends to be the least bit serious. It's a loose remake of the 1983 *House on Sorority Row.*

Soul Survivors (2001)

Four friends with complicated romantic entanglements head off for college. On their first night, Sean (Casey Affleck) is killed in a car accident. Cassandra (Melissa Sagemiller) was driving. After she's released from the hospital, she's plagued by frightening visions of a killer in a bizarre, translucent plastic mask, and Sean's ghost. Like the *Elm Street* films, many of the scares are built on the dream-reality business. As long as we're unsure about Cassie's state of mind, the action has a nicely unbalanced feeling. By the end, though, the plot has been reduced to one long, tiresome chase scene.

Species (1995)

At heart, this is an *X-Files*-inspired B-horror that's been pumped up with a classy cast and expensive effects, and is trying to pass itself off as serious escapism. Sil (Natasha Henstridge), created from outer space DNA, can be an icy blonde babe one moment and a disgusting alien creature (created by H.R. Geiger) the next. She's loose in Los Angeles and her biological clock is ticking. A government team (Marg Helgenberger, Alfred Molina, Forest Whitaker, Michael Madsen) is on her trail. The plot tends to ramble pointlessly for long stretches of time, and in key scenes the dialogue states the obvious with unintentionally hilarious results. Some of the bits of business there are funny and surprising. Others—including a weak conclusion—are strictly formula. Throughout, the thrills are slick and cheap. Followed by three sequels.

Specters (1987)

Subway work uncovers the entrance to Demetiano's Tomb off the Roman catacombs. Prof. Lasky (Donald Pleasence), an archeologist, thinks that an ancient evil lies beneath the Christian crypt. Yes, the influence of *Five Million Years To Earth* is obvious in plot details, but this one stands on its own. The subterranean atmosphere is well-realized, and, despite contributions by four writers, the story is strong. So are the acting, dubbing, and pace. Though the film isn't as graphically violent as many recent Italian horrors, it compares favorably to the best of Amando de Ossorio and Dario Argento, making clearly defined parallels between supernatural evil and more recognizable human evil—greed, lust, covetousness. The ending's weak.

Spider Baby (1968)

The mad Merrye family lives in a remote, decaying mansion somewhere between the Little Shop of Horrors and the Bates Motel. Chauffeur Lon Chaney Jr. protects the kids—Virginia (Jill Banner), a Leatherface Lolita, Elizabeth (Beverly Washburn), and Ralph (Sid Haig), their doglike brother—from lawyers, greedy relatives, and other predators. Veteran exploitation director Jack Hill cranked this comic quickie out in record time. It's cut from the same cloth as *Little Shop* and *Bucket of Blood,* but it's more twisted than either of them. Enjoyed a theatrical re-release thirty years after its 1968 run, and has earned an understandably strong cult following.

Splice (2009)

Clive (Adrian Brody) and Elsa (Sarah Polley) are modern day Frankensteins busily creating new life forms with genetic tinkering in their lab. These critters are used for medical research, and the hot, young scientists are ready to move on to work with human DNA until their corporate backers say no. Of course, they proceed anyway, and Dren is born. She's a weirdly strange, dangerous, and finally sexy creature who's realized on screen through a combination of CGI effects, prosthetics, and performances by Abigail Chu (as the child) and Delphine Chanéac (as the more mature character). One demonstration scene doesn't work as well as it might, but the third act approaches early David Cronenberg levels of imagination and bizarre, sexual violence. Not to all tastes, certainly.

The Top Nine Horrors from Richard Matheson

- *Trilogy of Terror*
- *Duel*
- *Incredible Shrinking Man*
- *A Stir of Echoes*
- *Bram Stoker's Dracula*
- *Burn Witch Burn*
- *Pit and the Pendulum*
- *The Night Stalker*
- *The Night Strangler*

Splinter (2008)

When you're kidnapped by an escaped convict (Shea Whigham) and his girlfriend (Rachel Kerbs) and that's not the worst thing that happens to you, you're having a really bad day. That's the case for Polly (Jill Wagner) and Seth (Paulo Costanzo) when they and their captors are trapped in a rural gas station by a bizarre, spiky creature that does extremely nasty things to its victims. Director (Toby Wilkins) avoids the redneck horror stereotypes and keeps things interesting despite budgetary limitations. The monster effects are inventive without wallowing in excess.

Spontaneous Combustion (1990)

The title refers to spontaneous "human" combustion, an occurrence fairly widely reported by eighteenth-century paranormal investigators, but somewhat déclassé among today's believers. David (Brad Dourif) is the child of parents who took part in a strange 1955 nuclear experiment. The opening contrast of feel-good newsreel images of the 1950s with the realities is handled nicely, if a little too slowly. Dourif does some of his best and most sympathetic work as the grown child who's become an anti-nuclear activist with a great vintage Studebaker. The rest is a companion piece to *Firestarter* and thoroughly enjoyable in its own crazed way. Yes, that is Dick Butkus and director John Landis.

Stendahl Syndrome, The (1996)

Dario Argento takes his hallucinatory explorations of the relationship between art and sexual violence to a rarified level. Anna Manni (Asia Argento), an Italian plainclothes cop, is both the victim and pursuer of a serial rapist. The film opens with a long sequence in the Ufizzi Museum where Argento loosely quotes Brian DePalma's *Dressed To Kill* with his restlessly roving camera. Before it's over, you'll also catch references to *Silence of the Lambs* and *The Twilight Zone,* though Argento isn't imitating anyone. The title refers to a condition in which a person is so overpowered by a work of art that he or she becomes delirious. At one point, Argento takes the concept to a new extreme when Anna walks through a painting and into her immediate past. Fans will recognize his recurring visual themes—razor blades, running water, sexual role reversal, blood. For me, this is one of the director's best.

Stepfather, The (1987, 2009) Stepfather II (1989)

In the opening scene, we learn that a man (Terry O'Quinn, in a career-defining role) has savagely murdered his suburban family. He alters his identity and escapes. Then we meet the new family he has gathered around himself a year later. The teen daughter (Jill Schoelen) thinks he's creepy, but she's can't make her mother (Shelley Hack) or anyone else believe her. The rest is a combination of brutal surprises, the blackest of black humor, and terrific suspense. Writer Donald Westlake makes this guy a combination of Ward Cleaver and Norman Bates. (He's loosely based on the real John List.) For any horror fan who's missed this brilliant independent production, it's required viewing.

Stepfather II, from 1989, is not so much a true sequel as a recycling of the first plot. Terry O'Quinn returns as the homicidal maniac who survived the shooting, stabbing, and whatall that ended the first film and is locked up in a psychiatric hospital. John Auerbach's script is faithful to the character and it has a few good one-liners, but it's still predictable. So is Jeff Burr's direction. Altogether unnecessary.

The 2009 remake lacks the surprise, the charismatic star, and the subversive politics of the original. It also strains credibility in several key scenes. But any film that puts Amber Heard in a bikini as often as this one does can't be all bad.

Stepford Wives, The (1975)

Few films—and even fewer horror films—become part of the language, but "Stepford" is an all-purpose adjective for robotic mindlessness. It should be. Ira Levin's tale is one of the defining works of late twentieth-century American horror. His novel and William Goldman's screen adaptation are companion pieces to *Rosemary's Baby,* sharing the same respectable, affluent villains and, more importantly, perfectly tuned paranoia. Director Bryan Forbes effectively creates menace out of the commonplace and ordinary. In the lead, Katharine Ross may be too restrained, but that's all right; the supporting cast (Paula Prentiss, Nanette Newman, Tina Louise) picks up the slack. Beyond the obvious feminist message, the film is really about the horror of bland, comfortable suburban conformity. And in a way, the passage of time has proved the truth of Levin's central idea. Today, successful middle-aged corporate executives don't have "Stepford Wives"; they have "trophy wives." Some might say that's a distinction without a difference. The pallid 2004 Nicole Kidman remake has virtually nothing to do with horror.

Stephen King's It (1990)

Stephen King's huge novel fared better than many of his works when it was transformed into a miniseries. The lengthy plot is still simplified, but even at three hours plus, the pace zips right along. The story concerns a group of childhood friends who, in their youth, overcame a hazily defined, protean critter. It often appears as Pennywise (Tim Curry), the evil clown, but it can assume other incarnations, many involving inventive special effects. Years later, when the kids have grown up, the boogie man comes back. An ensemble cast of TV veterans including Harry Anderson, Dennis Christopher, Richard Masur, Annette O'Toole, Tim Reid, John Ritter, and Richard Thomas does commendable work. Director Tommy Lee Wallace doesn't let the effects overpower the story.

Stephen King's Night Flier (1997)

You'd think that a vampire (Michael H. Moss) who learns to fly a Cessna would update his wardrobe, but this one wears the full-length satin-lined cape. Though this made-for-cable feature is based on a King short story, it owes almost as much to *Kolchak, The Night Stalker*. Richard Dees (Miguel Ferrer) is a supermarket tabloid reporter who, after baring his burnt-out soul at length, goes on the trail of a bloodsucker who finds his victims at small airports. Dees' more enthusiastic competition is Katherine Blair (Julie Entwisle, who looks like a perky young Phoebe Cates). The effects are graphic enough to satisfy gore fans, but some of the early physical action is stiffly choreographed. The film has a bright polish, clever structure, acting that's well above average, and a bang-up finish. It did so well on cable that it earned a theatrical release.

Stephen King's Sleepwalkers (1992)

Arguably King's worst film work is about shape-shifting monsters who feed on the life force of virgins and are vulnerable only to cat scratches. Incestuous mother Mary (Alice Krige) and son Charles (Brian Krause) set their sights on young Tanya (Madchen Amick). King's script meanders through pointless chitchat scenes. Unless something is blowing up or bleeding right in front of director Mick Garris' camera, he doesn't know how to photograph it. At one point, he tosses in close-ups of knees. The only cast member who doesn't shame him- or herself is Sparks who plays Clovis, the brave cat.

Stephen King's The Stand (1994)

Since King's huge novel has been a bestseller twice, everyone must be familiar with the story of an America decimated by "superflu" and turned into a battleground between Good and Evil. This adaptation, written by King and directed by Mick Garris, is faithful in tone and form to the fiction. Even at six hours, though, it still leaves out some material. Fans of the novel will also see where it cuts some corners in the big scenes, most notably those in the corn fields. The film is well cast with Gary Sinise, Jamey Sheridan, Molly Ringwald, Laura San Giacomo, Ruby Dee, Ossie Davis, Rob Lowe, and Ray Walston handling most of the dramatic action. And yes, that's John Bloom (a.k.a. drive-in critic Joe Bob Briggs) as the Texas highway patrolman and director Sam Raimi as a road guard. All in all, this is one of the more successful adaptations of King's longer fiction which tends to suffer when forced into the length of a conventional theatrical feature.

Stephen King's The Tommyknockers (1993)

One of King's better evil-underground-monster tales translates well to video, A writer (Marg Helgenberger) uncovers something on her farm that gives various inhabitants of Haven, Maine, strange new creativity and intelligence among other powers. The story flows smoothly with some good non-spectacular effects and the usual assortment of familiar types portrayed by a troupe of first-rate character actors. Unfortunately, the best inventions of King's fiction don't make it to the screen. Structurally, this one's similar to *Needful Things* and *It* with a strong touch of *Invasion of the Body Snatchers.* For those unfamiliar with the story, the ending's a terrific payoff. The VHS tape is a 120-minute condensation. DVD contains the original 181-minute version.

Stigmata (1999)

One of Hollywood's better possession efforts begins with a bleeding statue of the Virgin in a Brazilian backwater. Father Andrew (Gabriel Byrne), sent by the Vatican to investigate, thinks it may be a genuine miracle. His superior (Jonathan Pryce) disagrees and dispatches him to Pittsburgh to find out why beautician and atheist Frankie Page (Patricia Arquette) is displaying the wounds of Christ on her wrists. Are they psychological or supernatural? The conspiratorial and theological aspects of the story may be a bit muddled but writer Tom Lazarus and director Rupert Wainwright treat religious belief seriously. The leads are very good, even in the rough spots, making the characters believable and sympathetic. The grey, dripping locations are effective, and the special effects don't overpower the action. Devout Catholics may object to the treatment of the church.

Stir of Echoes (1999)

Excellent adaptation of an undervalued novel moves the setting from Los Angeles to a Chicago neighborhood, but the heart of Richard Matheson's story is intact. After his sister-in-law hypnotizes him, Tom Witzky (Kevin Bacon) sees ghosts and disturbing visions that seem to be connected to the house where he and his family are living. Overall, the use of effects and sound are properly understated, and one of the first big scares is a genuine jump-in-your-seat moment. Writer/director Dave Koepp adds some sly humor to the story, too. The resolution and the conclusion are both strong.

Storm Warning (2007)

Like so many Australian productions, this one boasts spectacular locations and striking photography in the opening scenes. Then it pivots to a conventional story of a city couple (Nadia Farès and Robert Taylor) trapped in the country by three degenerates. These cretins are so bizarrely exaggerated that they aren't believable enough to be properly frightening. In the same vein, the action becomes more and more outrageous as it goes along. By the end, it's so crazed that the film becomes a comedy of ultraviolence. In those scenes, the crisp clarity of the image actually works against the content. This kind of "redneck horror" is best served by a garish, grainy look.

Stormswept (1995)

Soft-core, Southern Gothic horror-comedy begins on a familiar note with six crew members of a film production company trapped by a thunderstorm in

The Top Nine Sexiest Horrors

- *Daughters of Darkness*
- *Don't Look Now*
- *Dressed to Kill*
- *House That Vanished*
- *Embrace of the Vampire*
- *Lust for a Vampire*
- *The Hunger*
- *Screaming Mimi*
- *Vampyres*

a haunted Louisiana mansion. An unspeakable crime occurred there years before. Now, an evil, sexually charged spirit pervades the place and a mysterious blonde (Kathleen Kinmont) has set up housekeeping in the basement. An early establishing shot of a spider walking through an ornate chandelier sets the mood, and the rest of the film pretty much lives up to it. Some of writer-director David Marsh's scares are conventional dark-and-stormy-night stuff, but there are enough inventive moments to keep your interest. Fans have seen much worse.

Strait-Jacket (1964)

William Castle's attempt to cash in on the success of Robert Aldrich's *Whatever Happened to Baby Jane?* opens with a scream, shattering glass, and lurid headline. Lucy Harbin (Joan Crawford)—"very much a woman and very much aware of the fact," our narrator claims—uses an ax to knock off her two-timing hubby and his girlfriend. Twenty years later, her daughter Carol (Diane Baker), who witnessed the whole thing, is waiting when Mommie Dearest is released from the asylum. To nobody's surprise, more chop-chop murders ensue. The plotting isn't as tight as it is in Aldrich's films. If the black-and-white photography isn't as sparkling, the work is still an effective period piece that's not without its moments. Robert Bloch's script is not another *Psycho.*

Strange Behavior (1981)

Writer Bill Condon and director Michael Laughlin try their hands at a Stephen King tale of a small town where teens are transformed into murderous zombies. Could Dr. Parkinson's (Fiona Lewis) drug-based behavior modification experiments with students have anything to do with it? The filmmakers use a few simple tricks well enough, and they treat the characters seriously, but the pace is pokey and some of the violent effects don't measure up to the level of believability that the story demands. The old needle-in-the-eyeball routine still works, though. Made in New Zealand with a good cast including Michael Murphy, Scott Brady, Louise Fletcher, and Charles Lane.

Strange Door (1951)

Charles Laughton is at his mischievous best as the evil Sire de Maletroit, a seventeenth-century aristocrat who has a nasty plan in mind for his niece Blanche (Sally Forrest). ("I'll feed your liver to the swine," he threatens a cohort.) With its impressive dungeons and secret passages, and Boris Karloff in support as Voltan, the film looks as good as the best Universal horrors of the '30s and '40s. Throughout, the physical action is lively and the ending's a doozy. The main attraction, though, is Laughton's zesty performance.

Strangeland (1998)

Poorly written, woodenly acted, and morally uncertain psycho-thriller is enthusiastic in its affinity for needles, piercings, and torture. The thin story revolves around Capt. Howdy (writer Dee Snider), an Internet predator who lures young women to his suburban Colorado house where he does unspeakable things in his chamber of horrors. One of his victims is Genevieve (Linda Cardellini), daughter of police detective Gage (Kevin Gage). The first half or so involves his perfunctory search for the girl. As things progress, a vigilante (Robert Englund, of Freddy fame) with a taste for teen porn is presented as being more reprehensible than a man who kidnaps, mutilates, and murders. The only energy is generated in those torture scenes. Away from the dark side, the actors are going through the motions. No surprise there, given the ham-fisted plotting.

Strangers, The (2008)

An introduction claims that this home invasion horror is based on fact, and at first, it does have a certain grim realism. James (Scott Speedman) and Kristen (Liv Tyler) are an unhappy couple who could have wandered in from a particularly gloomy Ingmar Bergman film. Director Bryan Bertino favors a shaky handheld camera, mumbled unintelligible dialogue, and dim lighting that leaves much of the screen in darkness. For me, though, this kind of "naturalistic" domestic horror is not entertainment. I feel the same about the even more unsettling German film *Funny Games*.

Subspecies (1991)
Bloodstone: Subspecies II (1993)
Bloodlust: Subspecies III (1994)

With this video premiere, producer Charles Band and director Ted Nicolaou began a partnership that became a virtual mini-studio in Romania. The no-frills vampire story is an updated Hammer film. The terrific opening scene takes place inside a castle where two really hideous guys (one of whom has a serious problem with drooling) are doing absolutely disgusting stuff. Throughout, the Gothic sets and locations are properly atmospheric with creaking doors and heavy organ music. The plot, revolving around good and bad vampire brothers, is acceptable. The evil Radu's (Anders Hove) makeup is based on the original *Nosferatu* and if the whole thing seems more than a little overdone, that's what the material calls for. It isn't meant to be subtle.

In the first sequel, the good vampire's American girlfriend (Denice Duff) steals the Bloodstone, a supernatural lava light, and heads for Bucharest. The rest contains enough imaginative, grotesque effects to keep even the most jaded fan happy and nauseous. *III* is the weakest of the series, though the gooey effects will appeal to hardcore fans. A fourth was made.

Summer of Fear (1978)

When young Julia's (Lee Purcell) parents are killed in a wreck, she moves in with Rachel (Linda Blair) and her family. Rachel comes to believe that the standoffish newcomer is a witch who's out to steal her boyfriend, her father, and her new party dress. The story, based on Lois Duncan's well regarded young adult novel, is similar to Fritz Leiber's *Conjure Wife,* filmed as *Weird Woman* and *Burn, Witch, Burn.* For Linda Blair, the role marks a transition between her prepubescent *Exorcist* character and the flashy sexpots she'd play a few years later. In the same way, for director Wes Craven the film is a large step away from his early exploitation and toward mainstream respectability. Yes, that's Fran Drescher as Rachel's friend.

Supernova (2000)

Troubled production was radically re-edited from the PG-13 theatrical release for an R-rated DVD. At heart, it reworks the *Alien* playbook in plot and smoky look. The quirky crew of an emergency medical rescue vessel received a distress call from a mining outpost. The lone survivor, Karl (Peter Facinelli) is up to no good and has a thing that looks like a warped crystal bowling ball which might destroy the known universe. Nice looking visual effects and arty love scenes involving Robin Tunney are the main attractions.

Surgeon, The (1995)

Think *E.R.* meets *Re-Animator* in a dandy little medical horror/comedy with a first-rate ensemble cast. The title character (Sean Haberle) is the proverbial mad scientist—actually he's a little madder than most—who's out to get everyone who has thwarted his research into "pituitary extract." Those include Malcolm McDowell and Charles Dance. Isabel Glasser and James Remar are the good doctors. Peter Boyle is the cop on the case. Director Carl Schenkel and special effects co-ordinator Steve Johnson have come up with some genuinely creepy moments, most of them infused with strong humor. It's difficult to maintain an effective ratio of laughs and scares, but they manage.

Survival of the Dead

See Night of the Living Dead

Suspiria (1977)

On the darkest and stormiest night of them all, a young American dancer (Jessica Harper) goes to a new school in Germany. Before she can set foot inside the door, her fellow students are being killed. Director Dario Argento introduces some of the same characters, ideas, and motifs he works with in later films, notably *Phenomena.* They share the same flaws, too. Plot coherence is flimsy at best, and realistic motivations for some of the excesses are hard to find. To my taste, Argento is also overly dependent on loud sound effects and music to make the visuals more upsetting. The acting varies from understated realism, despite often ludicrous dialogue, to a crazed Teutonic caricature. That said, Argento can create striking images, and he tosses in Hitchcock quotes from such odd sources as *North by Northwest* and *The Birds.* Like so much of Argento's work, this is easier to admire than to like.

T

Take Shelter (2011)

Curtis (Michael Shannon) works construction in rural Ohio. He's the devoted husband of Samantha (Jessica Chastain) and father of a little girl. When he suffers terrifying nightmares and visions of storms and slightly unnatural phenomena, he suspects that it's madness. He might have inherited it from his mother, but everything seems so real that he's frightened and feels that he has to do something. Special effects are deployed with intelligence and they never overpower the human side of the story. That's where the film works best. Writer/director Jeff Nichols and Shannon are able to make that fear all too believable, and so everything hits much closer to home than it does in conventional horror. The conclusion might have moved more quickly, but it's honest and well-earned.

Tale of Two Sisters, A (2003)

Writer/director Jee-woon Kim sets a methodical pace to tell the story of a broken family. He seems more interested in strictly formal compositions and striking colors than moving things along. Most of the action takes place inside a gloomy house, and it's so stylized that I never fully engaged with the film. Part of the problem may be mine since I had already seen the American version, titled *The Uninvited* (see review). I still prefer it.

Tales from the Crypt: Demon Knight (1995)

First-rate little horror-comedy based on the popular cable TV series—and before that, the lurid EC Comics from the 1950s—boasts excellent production

Inspired by a comic book series, *Tales from the Crypt* is hosted by the devilishly witty Crypt Keeper.

values, a smart script, and a talented cast. In terms of plot, this is your basic Good versus Evil, End of the World as We Know It story. (Pay no attention to the framing device with the Crypt Keeper.) Outside a little New Mexico town on a dark and stormy night, the Collector (Billy Zane) chases a mysterious stranger, Brayker (William Sadler), and traps a doughty group of characters in a hotel. It's not giving anything away to reveal that the Collector is a cheerful demon who conjures up a host of disgusting monsters. Director Ernest Dickerson (*Juice, Surviving the Game*) made his reputation as Spike Lee's cinematographer, and is particularly careful with lighting, using shadows to dampen the more grotesque special effects—beheadings, arms being ripped off, etc. The horror is also leavened with a generous streak of saucy wit.

Tales from the Crypt Presents Bordello of Blood (1996)

In an uninspired follow-up to *Demon Knight,* both the bloody special effects and the humor are based on overly familiar clichés. Despite the expensive polish of the production, the film has a careless, thrown-together quality. A half-hearted prologue introduces supervampire Lilith (Angie Everhart). The scene abruptly shifts to Los Angeles where she runs the titular establishment out of a mortuary. Katherine (Erika Eleniak) hires comic detective Rafe Guttman (Dennis Miller) to find her brother (Corey Feldman) after the wayward sibling visits Lilith. A TV preacher (Chris Sarandon) is involved, too, but exactly what he's doing is never clear. Not that it matters. Writer/director Adler is more interested in exploding bodies and bad one-liners.

Tales from the Darkside: The Movie (1990)

Four-part anthology of three comedies and an odd love story varies in quality, though it is well made. For those whose taste runs to visceral black humor, the film is funny and even enjoyable. In the wraparound story, Deborah Harry is a society matron planning a dinner party. "Lot 249" is a Mummy tale with Christian Slater. The strongest segment is "The Cat from Hell," written by George Romero from a Stephen King story. "Lover's Vow" is a predictable entry about an artist (James Remar) and a mystery woman (Rae Dawn Chong). The "yuck" factor is high with inventively bloody effects, but the sly, gleeful tone keeps these stories from becoming oppressive.

Tarantula (1955)

The effects are nothing special, from the fuzzy black giant spider to the rubber masks and hands, but this Jack Arnold effort boasts his usual tight storytelling and a supporting cast filled with familiar faces from the 1950s. The plot pits the Good Doctor (John Agar) against the Mad Scientist (Leo G. Carroll) with the Gorgeous Grad Student (Mara Corday) in the middle. The best moment has to be when the titular tarantula, who's bigger than a split-level house, sneaks up on the heroine as she's getting ready for bed and peeks through her window. Yes, that's Clint Eastwood in the jet at the end.

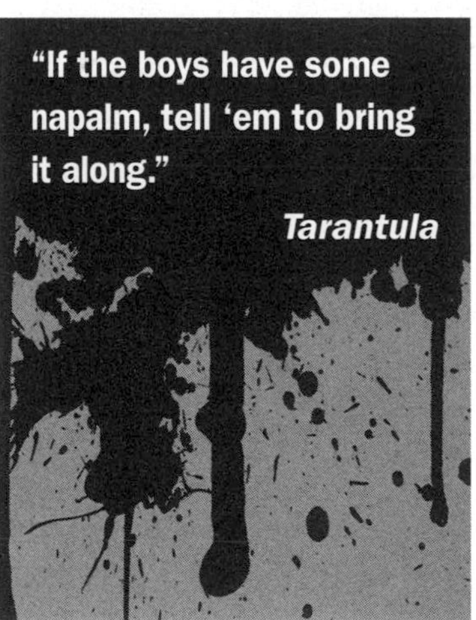

Targets (1968)

Not on the National Rifle Association's top-ten list, Peter Bogdanovich's debut is a fine, economically made horror film that neatly brings the conventions of the past into the violent present of 1968. In those days, America was just getting used to the idea that someone might take a rifle onto a

The Top Twenty-Seven Sleepers

Below
The Dark (1993)
Dead and Buried
Creep
Cronos
Devil
Frailty
Hands of the Ripper
Jack Be Nimble
Jack's Back
Lemora: A Child's Tale of the Supernatural
The Lodger
Martin
May
Mothman Prophecies
Parasomnia
Rise: Blood Hunter
Silent Scream
Snow White: A Tale of Terror
Sole Survivor
The Stepfather
Take Shelter
They Live
Tale of Two Sisters
Urban Ghost Story
Wendigo
Wind Chill

tower and shoot people for no reason. Boris Karloff plays Byron Orlok, an aging horror star; Bogdanovich is Sammy Michaels, a young director trying to persuade Orlok to act in his film. Tim O'Kelly is Bobby Thompson, a conservative young man filled with family values who's about to go over the edge. How those three and a few others converge at a drive-in theater makes for a grim, fascinating tale.

Taste the Blood of Dracula (1970)

A debauched British Lord (Ralph Bates) takes the title literally and puts a curse on his cowardly associates—three outwardly proper gentlemen who have secretly formed a hellfire club. The development turns Dracula (Christopher Lee) into a partially sympathetic figure. Shifting the scene to Victorian England further distances the film from earlier entries in the then-twelve-year-old series. A strong autumnal atmosphere helps considerably, but the film isn't as tightly structured as its predecessors. Key characters tend to pass out and regain consciousness at convenient moments. The generational conflicts that had been subplots are central here.

Temptress (1995)

Photographer Karin Swann (Kim Delaney) returns from India with a suggestive new tattoo to remind her of the "spiritual reawakening" that she found when she tapped into her "goddess energy." Actually, she tapped into a little more than she realized and her goddess is one mean mother. Her live-in boyfriend (Chris Sarandon) is not amused. A mysterious stranger (Ben Cross) says that he understands. The possession story that follows is extremely well told. Writer Melissa Mitchell and director Lawrence Lanoff manage to combine the supernatural with everyday reality and psychological reality remarkably well. They also use the conventions of the genre to show both the creative and destructive aspects of sex. A sleeper.

Tenebre (1982)

As is usually the case with Dario Argento movies, the plot is complicated and pretty much dispensable. It serves merely as a clunky, coincidence-driven device to string together a series of sexual and violent images that often involve beautiful women in some stage of undress. In Rome, American horror novelist Peter Neal (Anthony Franciosa) finds that someone is copying passages from his book *Tenebrae* in real razor murders. The silliness of that side of the film is balanced against Argento's inventive camerawork which alternates between careful attention to extreme close-up detail and long, complex tracking and crane shots. Argento deserves full credit for his stylish visuals, but the material so flamboyantly ignores the conventions of cinematic "realism" that many viewers won't appreciate it.

Terror, The (1963)

Legendary Roger Corman production boasts no less than five directors. Corman has written that he began the film hoping to crank out another Poe-inspired Gothic quickie. As various complications ensued, he had young Francis Ford Coppola shoot some footage in Big Sur; and co-writer Jack Hill also took a crack. So did Monte Hellman, and finally star Jack Nicholson got behind the camera. Why not? He was then married to his pregnant co-star Sandra Knight. This serial collaboration begins as a hallucination with a delirious Napoleonic officer (Nicholson) riding down a beach. Then it becomes a turgid period piece when he reaches Boris Karloff's castle, and finally the oft-revised plot virtually disintegrates. In the end, it's mostly about characters wandering down dark hallways and paths for no discernible reason.

Terror at Red Wolf Inn (1972)

Upside—impoverished college student Regina (Linda Gillen) wins a free vacation at Red Wolf Inn. Downside—the owners (Mary Jackson and Arthur Space) may be cannibals. That's not to say they aren't nice people, and their grandson (John Neilson) is really cute. The humor avoids the excesses typical to this kind of horror/comedy in favor of a kinder, gentler *Arsenic and Old Lace* tone. Mostly. The ending is very much in keeping with the rest.

Terror Train (1980)

A first-rate cast does fair work with imitative material. It's *Halloween on Amtrak* as someone knocks off masked partygoers on a train. Jamie Lee Curtis is our full-throated heroine. Ben Johnson is the conductor. Writer T.Y. Drake and director Roger Spottiswoode let the pace drag, even toward the end, though they are somewhat restrained with the graphic violence. Director of photography John Alcott makes the interior of the train a vivid setting with his inventive use of light and gauze filters. Fans may not be disappointed, but they won't find much they haven't seen before.

Texas Chainsaw Massacre (1974, 2003)
Texas Chainsaw Massacre 2 (1986)
Leatherface: Texas Chainsaw Massacre 3 (1990)
Texas Chainsaw Massacre 4: The Next Generation (1994)
Texas Chainsaw Massacre: The Beginning (2006)

The purity of Tobe Hooper's low-budget psychotic vision has often been copied—by him and by others—but the inescapable, fully realized insanity of the film has never been equaled. It's an essentially plotless story of kids who wander off the main road and into a rural house full of cannibals. The film moves with the free association "logic" of a nightmare. Horror piles upon horror ignoring conventional narrative structure. It's the repetitive nature of the events that has earned the film its undimmed reputation. Decades after its debut, *TCM* is still the ultimate "meat movie." If anyone has surpassed it, I don't want to know.

The 1986 sequel, *Texas Chainsaw Massacre 2,* begins with a breathless voice-over narrator claiming that the Lonestar cannibals of the first film sim-

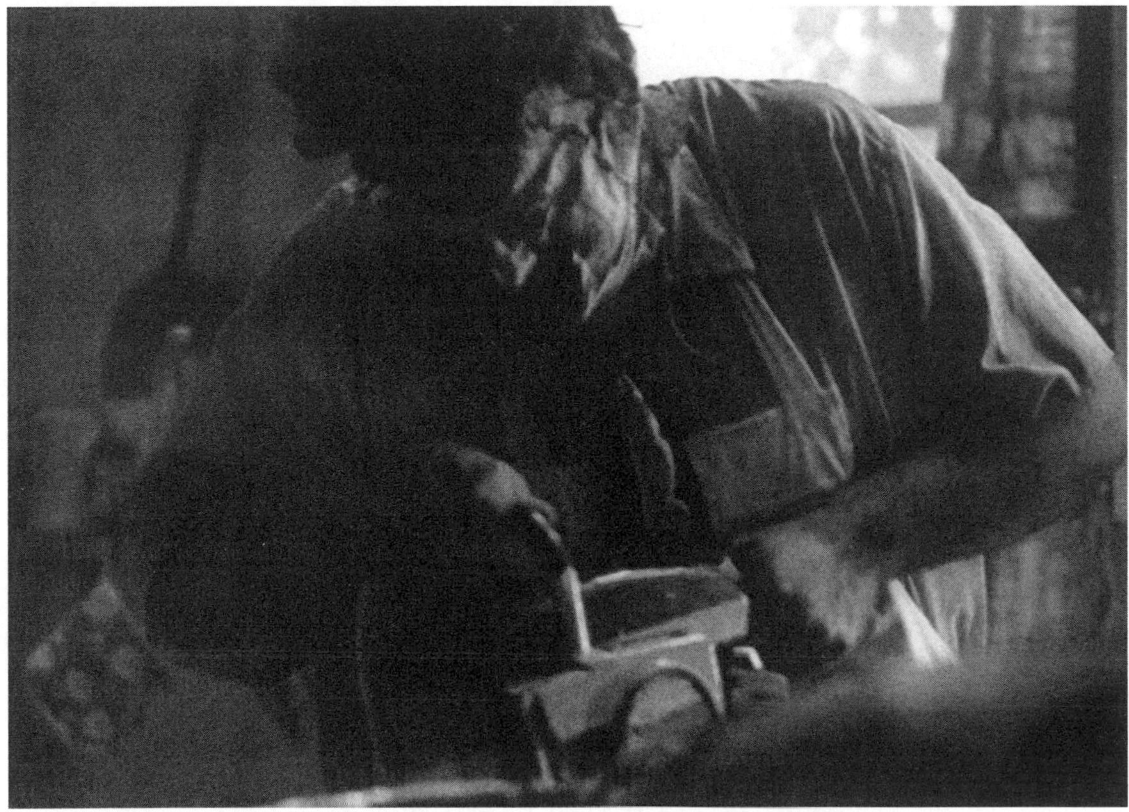

A bad ad for gas-powered tools, *Texas Chainsaw Massacre* is all about a house full of cannibals who like their meat fresh.

ply disappeared despite the best efforts of the cops to find them for thirteen years. It turns out that the Sawyer family has been winning chili cook-offs and living under an amusement park. The intensity of the original has been replaced with outrageous stunts and jokes. Dwarfed beneath a huge cowboy hat, Dennis Hopper is a vengeance-seeking Texas Ranger. Tom Savini's bloody effects are more sophisticated than they were in the original, but more is definitely not better.

It was followed in 1990 by *Leatherface: Texas Chainsaw Massacre 3.* Californians Michelle (Kate Hodge) and Ryan (William Butler) stop at the wrong Texas gas station and wind up in the clutches of the Sawyer family. Though the violence is just as graphic as the original with even more sophisticated production values, it's still a conventional *3.* The intentional humor further diminishes the aura of palpable dread created by the original. Spirited performances from Kate Hodge and Ken Foree are not enough to earn a recommendation.

Four years later, the series resurfaced with *Texas Chainsaw Massacre 4: The Next Generation.* Four prom-goers, including Jennie (Renée Zellweger), who are so obnoxious that they deserve anything that happens to them, wander out into the boonies. They're attacked by the familiar family of maniacs led by Vilmer (Matthew McConaughey) who has a mechanical leg. The plot is essentially a slightly comic parody of the original. The production values are much higher, but so what? Curiosity value from the early presence of the two stars is all the derivative flick has to offer.

In 2003, Michael Bay's production company restarted the series telling the same story with a few narrative tweaks, slick production values, and big stars (Jessica Biel, R. Lee Ermey). Of all the twenty-first-century attempts to recapture the spirit of the spirit of '70s horror, this is probably the least successful. Slick production values and big stars are precisely not the point. The reboot was followed in 2006 by *Texas Chainsaw Massacre: The Beginning.* The prequel to a remake is just what you'd expect it to be. It touches on key points of the original, including the harrowing "dinner" scene, and has a bronzy/coppery color scheme that approximates the harsh, garish look. R. Lee Ermey's believable performance is wasted.

Theater of Blood (1973)

In a companion piece to *The Abominable Dr. Phibes,* Vincent Price is Edward Lionheart, a hammy Shakespearian actor who takes vengeance on anyone who has written an unfavorable review of his work. With the help of a mob of crazies and his daughter Edwina (Diana Rigg), he concocts baroque schemes to get rid of London's drama critics, each murder quoting a bloody moment from the Bard. Like so many films of its time, it's also about the establishment under siege by the rabble. The wit is sharp and the whole film plays to Price's strengths as an actor. (It ends with his literally attacking the scenery.) Douglas Hickox's energetic, swiftly paced direction keeps the theatrical aspects from ruining the film. Note Lionheart's "suicide" scene. One quibble: Diana Rigg spends far too much time in disguise.

Them! (1954)

Mutated giant ants wreak havoc on a New Mexico town in the first of the big-bug horrors. It far surpasses the rest, mostly because the formula hadn't been set in cinematic stone yet. The script contains several human touches, and the whole production benefits from neat WWII hardware—flame throwers, Tommy guns, B-24s. Throughout, the focus is more on the characters' reactions to the situation than on the critters themselves. That's fine because these ants are not particularly convincing and the real point is audiences' fears concerning the then-new "atomic age." See how many names you can spot among the supporting cast.

They (2002)

It was a dark and stormy night when little Billy realized that the monsters hiding in his closet were real. As an adult, he still suffers from night terrors and tries to persuade his childhood friend Julia (Laura Regan) that as children they were "marked" by these creatures who are coming for them. Not what she wants to hear right before she has to defend her psychology doctoral thesis. The handling of this familiar and difficult subject is slow, dark, and unfocused. Alternate title: *Wes Craven Presents: They*.

They Came from Within (1975)

In the spirit of the times, David Cronenberg's debut combines elements of *Night of the Living Dead* and *Deep Throat.* From the bizarre opening shots, Cronenberg's trademark combination of outrageous violence, medicine, and sex is right up front. The setting is a luxurious Montréal high-rise apartment where turdlike parasitic creatures infect human hosts. Though the prosthetic effects aren't as blatant as they are today, they're every bit as revolting. Visually and thematically, the film sets the tone for Cronenberg's later work from *Rabid* to *Crash.* The aphrodisiacal horror isn't sustained all the way through, and toward the end, some of the sexual material comes across as comic. Alternate title: *Shivers*.

They Live (1988)

Nada (Roddy Piper) is a drifter who tumbles onto an alien mind-control conspiracy. Special sunglasses reveal their insidious propaganda and skeletal faces. The sci-fi/horror is an unsubtle criticism of conservative economic and social policies, but director John Carpenter spins things out with his usual sure touch for escapism and wrestler Piper is a fine hero. As for the plot, it's pretty easy to accept, particularly for those who've always had their doubts about Newt Gingrich and his crowd. Though the film is based on a short

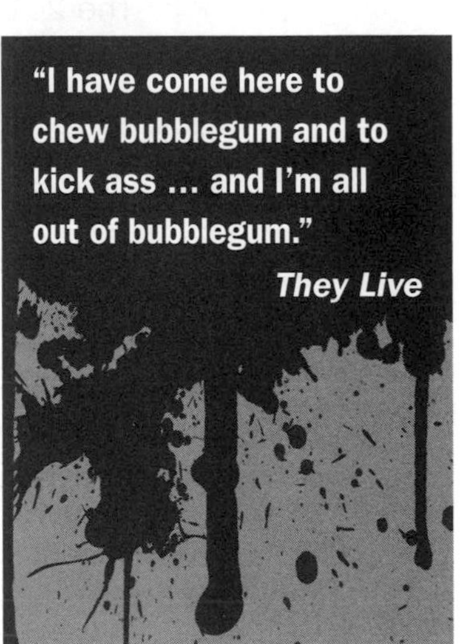

story by Ray Nelson, many of the film's ideas are also used in the great *Illuminatus* cult novels of Robert Shea and Robert Anton Wilson. (The clip in the film is from *The Monolith Monsters.*)

Thing, The (from Another World) (1951, 1982, 2011)

A vampire vegetableman (James Arness) from outer space crashes his saucer into the arctic ice. Soldiers and scientists, led by Kenneth Tobey and Robert Cornthwaite, thaw him out and then do a lot of squabbling among themselves. The Killer Carrot is a giant, hungry, seed-dispersing creature run amok, unaffected by missing body parts, bullets, or cold. Director Christian Nyby—with considerable help from producer Howard Hawks, writers Charles Lederer, and an uncredited Ben Hecht—makes this one of the most tightly constructed stories of the 1950s. Equally important is the film's atmosphere of frozen claustrophobia and isolation. In every respect, save faithfulness to John Campbell's original story "Who Goes There," this one is superior to the remakes that have followed.

Writer Bill Lancaster goes back to John Campbell's story for John Carpenter's version. It's more horrifying than the first (which is really more sci-fi than horror) with the premise of a shape-changing alien whose ship crashes in Antarctica. The British Columbian and Alaskan locations are convincingly cold and bleak, but the characters are generally unsympathetic, led by Kurt Russell's sombrero-topped McCready. The real point of the film is Rob Bottin and Albert Whitlock's baroque monster effects which lose their shock value well before the film's over.

The 2011 version is actually a prequel to Carpenter's. The focus is on the Swedish Antarctic scientists who discover the spaceship buried in the ice and release the shape-changing bug-like critter. Though the icy, snowy landscape is striking, the film is mired in a low-energy pace and tenuous realism in the characters' actions.

Thirst (2009)

Father Sang-hyeon (Kang-ho Song) is a devout Catholic until he's infected by a blood transfusion and becomes a vampire. His transformation opens him to vast new worlds of sin and temptation with housewife Tae-ju (Ok-bin Kim). The first act is mundane and homey. Things get much stranger and surprising in the second half. Throughout, Chan-wook Park's direction is sure-handed. Special effects are handled judiciously and well, and the humor is unexpectedly sharp. Cultural differences make it difficult to judge performances

The 1982 remake of *The Thing* changes the premise of the original, exchanging a Killer Carrot for a shape-shifting alien.

but these are superb. Kang-ho Song (*The Host*) is an energetic star reminiscent of Jack Black.

Thirteen Ghosts (2001)

Remake of William Castle's 1960 film certainly has all the spirit of the original and a budget that the famous schlockmeister could only have dreamed about. Arthur Kriticos (Tony Shaloub) and his two kids inherit a clockwork glass house from his nutty Uncle Cyrus (F. Murray Abraham). The problem is, there are a dozen ghosts imprisoned in the basement. After they find themselves locked inside the place, psychic Dennis Rafkin (a hyper-caffeinated Matthew Lillard) tries to help. The explanatory material is crazily complicated, and it's all handled with the same combination of humor and horrific violence that fans have seen in the remake of Castle's *House on Haunted Hill.* This one is somewhat less successful, though the sets and ghosts, from that time before CGI effects became so ubiquitous, have a solidity you don't see now.

30 Days of Night (2007)

No question, this is the best vampire movie of the twenty-first century. Barrow, Alaska, is completely without sunlight for one month every year. A shipload of the undead arrives as the prolonged darkness begins and they take over the small town. Sheriff Eben (Josh Hartnett) and his wife Stella (Melissa George) and a few others manage to survive the initial attack and try to fight back. Ben Foster is memorable in the skuzzy, foaming-at-the-mouth Renfield role of the monsters' assistant, but the film really belongs to Danny Huston's nameless, screeching vampire leader. He's an incredibly nightmarish figure without the use of the more extreme make up and effects. New Zealand sets and locations make a believable Alaska. Initially, the filmmakers use the simple visual device of large dark splashes of red blood on white snow. Later they amp up the more graphic violence to just the right level—shocking, inventive, and properly excessive. Followed by a sequel.

301/302 (1995)

The woman in apartment 301 (Eun-Jin Bang) is a recently divorced chef. The woman across the hall in 302 (Sin-Hye Hwang) is a shy, self-loathing, bulimic writer. In the opening scenes, we learn that 302 has disappeared. 301's flashbacks slowly reveal their relationship from the day she moved into the building. Writer Sur-Goon Lee and director Chul-Soo Park set much of the story within the apartment building and the other homes that have made the two women who and what they are. The most obvious influence is Roman Polanski's *Repulsion,* but you can also see hints of *Heavenly Creatures, An Untold Story,* and other more recent works. If some of the revelations are trite, others are shocking, and the film's humor is sharply edged and hard to define. The story is beautifully constructed with rare intelligence. An award winner in Korea and at several festivals.

Thrill of the Vampire (1971)

Of all the tacky '70s exploitation horror flicks, this is probably the tackiest and most exploitative. Though the synopsis—honeymooners (Sandra Julien and Jean-Marc Durand) stop by a castle to visit her cousins and are seduced by hippie vampires (Michel Delahaye, Jacques Robiolles, and Dominique who's the spitting image of Olive Oyl), sounds like *Daughters of Darkness,* the films could not be more different. In an introduction, director Jean Rollin admits that he was making a parody, something "between a comedy and a vampire film." His combination of the mundane and the surreal might have served as an example for TV perfume commercials of the 1990s. The soundtrack contains some of the worst garage rock ever recorded.

The Top Seven Nasty Spider Horrors

Arachnophobia
Giant Spider Invasion
Deadly Blessings
Earth versus the Spider
Eight-Legged Freaks
King Kong (2005)
Kingdom of the Spiders

Tim Burton's Corpse Bride (2005)

Stop-motion animated musical can be seen as a companion piece to *Edward Scissorhands* and *The Nightmare Before Christmas.* It's a sweetly romantic story with a dark side that probably makes it inappropriate for some young audiences. In a vaguely Victorian world, Victor (voice of Johnny Depp) and Victoria (Emily Watson) are about to be married when he inadvertently resurrects Emily (Helena Bonham Carter) by putting a ring on her bony finger. Burton's instantly recognizable visuals are evident in every frame with well-defined characters and smart mordant wit. The physical humor is inventive. Danny Elfman's score and songs are fine. The action aboveground is presented in severe, washed out blues and grays. Bright spots of color and music are reserved for the underworld.

Tingler, The (1959)

Producer-director William Castle's on-screen introductory warning about the "tingling sensation" that some viewers may experience refers to the famous gimmick he'd planned for the film's theatrical release. Some theater seats were to be wired to give audience members a mild shock in key scenes. The Tingler is an insect-like creature created in the spine by "the force of fear." It's all as hokey and silly as it sounds. Vincent Price's conversational, understated performance as a curious coroner with a faithless frau (Pamela Lincoln) is one of his best. Beyond the loopy horror aspects, which are a ton of fun, the film's subtext of male-female sexual and economic competition in the 1950s is fascinating.

To Sleep with a Vampire (1993)

Intelligent two-character vampire story is a remake of *Dance of the Damned.* The protagonists are a sensitive, nameless vampire (Scott Valentine) and

This poster for *The Tingler* advertises the famous gimmick of theater chairs wired to mildly shock the audience.

Nina (Charlie Spradling) a suicidal stripper. She desperately wants to see her estranged young son before she ends her life; he wants to know what the sun feels like. In Patricia Harrington's script (based on the original by Katt Shea and Andy Ruben), they come to an understanding. Director Adam Friedman makes the most of limited special effects (including switchblade fingernails) and he gets moving performances from his leads. Though they sound like clichés, these two become sympathetic, fully believable characters before it's over. Recommended.

To the Devil a Daughter (1976)

In the opening scene, Father Michael (Christopher Lee) questions his faith, perhaps even actively renouncing it. Twenty years later, he leads a young nun, Catherine (Nastassja Kinski) out of a nunnery and into some form of vague danger. That uncertainty is the point. The other key player is John Verney (Richard Widmark), an occult writer. Chris Wicking's script—based on a Dennis Wheatley novel—avoids clichés and, at the risk of confusing the viewer, creates real suspense. The presence of a veteran ensemble cast (including Honor Blackman and Denholm Elliott) not normally associated with horror adds to that quality. Comparison's to *The Devil's Bride* and *The Exorcist* are not out of place.

Tombs of the Blind Dead (1972)
Return of the Blind Dead (1973)
Ghost Galleon (1974)
Night of the Seagulls (1975)

Amando de Ossorio's first use of the resurrected Knights Templar is one of the most influential horrors of the early 1970s. Though the film is clumsily plotted, it sets the stage for several sequels and the more general trend, particularly in European films, of mixing sex (exploitative and otherwise) and graphic horror. Ossorio's Templars are thirteenth-century Portuguese knights who torture young women and drink their blood to gain immortality. They're executed and blinded by crows that peck out their eyes, but they rise up out of their graves centuries later whenever young women are nearby. Though they cannot see, they locate their victims by sound and, like American "living dead," eat them. (Later films would correct the illogical nature of the Templars' condition by changing the backstory to have them blinded before they're executed.) Questions of sexual politics aside (and the film does raise many issues in that area), the Templars are memorable, nightmarish figures.

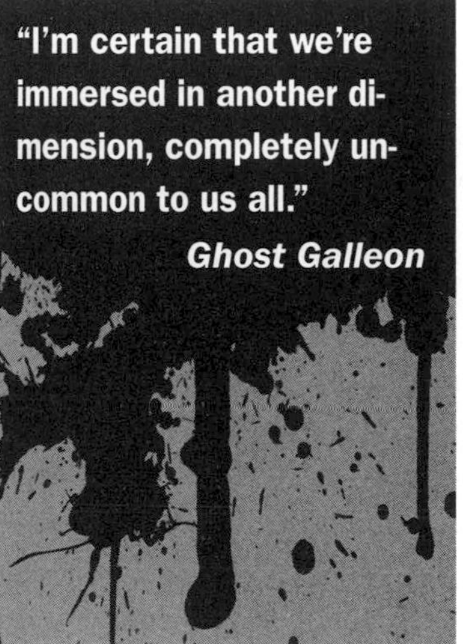

Return of the Blind Dead is a strong sequel, much more tightly plotted than the original. Resurrected, cannibalistic Medieval knights have become something of a cottage industry in European horror. These Templars pop back up for the five-hundredth anniversary of their execution, and trap a diverse group of squabbling people in a building. The Knights themselves look like Klansmen in dirty sheets. But when they're riding their hooded horses in slow motion, they make an impression.

The third film, *Ghost Galleon,* is simply atrocious. A slow, talky introduction sets up two bikini models involved in some kind of publicity stunt adrift on the ocean in a small boat. They bump into the titular vessel. At tedious length, they and four others are trapped there, along with a treasure and the cannibalistic Templars. Without their horses, they mostly shuffle menacingly. The result is unintentional comedy that's a prime candidate for the Mystery Science Theater treatment.

Night of the Seagulls (1975) brings the series to a pallid close. The pace is slow; the story is simple; the effects are nothing new.

Torso (1973)

Many fans and critics claim that Sergio Martino's giallo is the best of the genre, and they may well be right. It's certainly one of the most logical. For once, the stylistic excesses—wonderfully bizarre camera angles and movement, fevered sexual action, carefully detailed Italian settings—are put in service of a story that mostly makes sense. Jane (model Suzy Kendall) is an American graduate student in art history. A killer is stalking her beautiful friends and always seems to catch them in compromising situations. As Eli Roth notes in his DVD introduction, by the end, you'll believe that every man who appears in the film could be the murderer because they're all such unalloyed, sexist cretins. Throughout, the film is a product of its time in terms of fashion, hairstyles, and politics. The influence of *Psycho* is obvious, particularly in the nearly wordless, extended conclusion. The film has been available under various titles and running times. The Blue Underground disc is the full-length version, and it's remarkably sharp and clear.

Torture Chamber of Baron Blood (1972)

Peter Kleist (Antonia Cantafora), a young American, goes to Austria to discover his family roots. He's the ancestor of a particularly vicious Baron and ignorantly resurrects the guy. Most of the action is set in a castle where director Mario Bava makes full use of the towers, dungeons, and secret passageways. The film has a strange and more ominous atmosphere than Bava's previous effort, *Lisa and the Devil.* He also revisits some of the images he first used in *Black Sunday.* The highpoint is a long, strikingly lit night chase scene. In the big torture sequence at the end, the participants are less than completely persuasive.

Tourist Trap (1979)

Solid little B-picture makes the most of its budget and tells a scary yarn solidly in the *Psycho-Halloween-Texas Chainsaw Massacre* tradition. A group of kids searching for their missing friend are stranded at the remote Slausen's Desert Oasis motel. Slausen (Chuck Connors) is an affable sort who helps them with their car trouble, but tells them to stay away from the house down the hill where "Davey" lives. You know what they're going to do, but so what? Director David Schmoeller frightens you when he means to and that's enough. Good ending, too.

Town That Dreaded Sundown, The (1976)

Early serial killer story is supposedly based on truth and is told as a documentary with lots of local (Texas, Arkansas) color and non-professionals as extras. In Texarkana, 1946, a masked man is attacking couples in Lovers' Lane. Top Texas ranger Ben Johnson is brought in to head up the task force. The attacks are presented mostly with grim, grainy naturalism. Set at night, they're hard to make out. Director Charles Pierce depends more on sound and atmosphere than visuals. Considerable cornball, redneck humor doesn't help much. Careful viewers will see a cameraman in the train sequence.

The Top Eight Horrors from Stephen King

'Salem's Lot
The Shining
Stephen King's Night Flyer
The Stand
Dead Zone
Dolores Claiborne
Riding the Bullet
Misery

Transmutations (1985)

Genre-bender begins well with lots of action setting up the conflict virtually without dialogue. Based on a Clive Barker story, the film mixes detection and horror fairly well, but the ending is a letdown. A solid cast of character actors does good work. The special effects are relatively restrained because the aim is a certain thoughtfulness. The result is similar to *Hellraiser* in some ways, though not as impressive.

Trauma (2004)

Not to be confused with the 1993 Dario Argento film, this one is a Hitchcockian portrait of a damaged man. Ben (Colin Firth) has been devastated by the death of his wife and the injuries he suffered in a car accident. But Ben (and the viewer) can't really know what's real. A slow beginning establishes his unstable state of mind. He talks to an unseen psychiatrist, sees a hooded figure, and keeps a creepy ant farm in his apartment. He's also a suspect in another murder when he decides that his wife might not be dead after all. In the quieter moments, Firth's performance can be seen as a warm-up for the similar role he played five years later in *A Single Man.*

Tremors (1990)
Tremors 2: Aftershocks (1996)
Tremors 3: Back to Perfection (2001)

Universal has always been known for its horror films, and this updated version of such grand '50s big-creature features as *Them* and *The Beast from 20,000 Fathoms* is one of the studio's better recent efforts. It's told with ex-

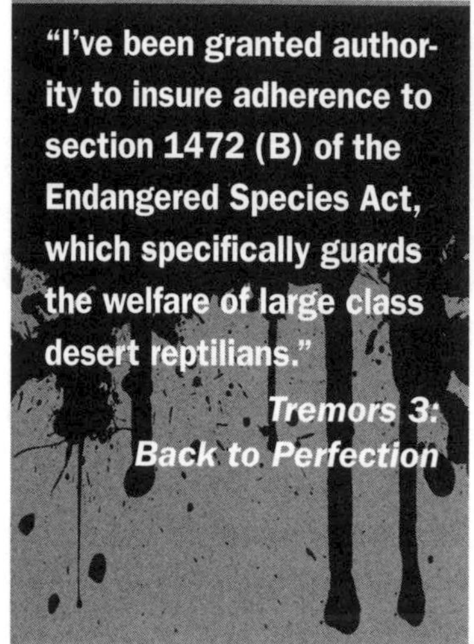

cellent production values—even on the small screen, the picture is remarkably crisp—a solid ensemble cast (Kevin Bacon, Fred Ward, Michael Gross, singer Reba McIntyre), no-nonsense direction, and a script that manages to combine laughs and scares in the right ratio. The plot revolves around a race of carnivorous superworms who live underground and surface in the desert town of Perfection, Nevada, where they decide to have lunch. Given that premise, you might expect the effects to be on the humorous side, but they're actually quite good.

Above average sequel, *Tremors 2: Aftershocks,* recreates the original's sense of humor and builds on the inventive special effects that were so much fun before. Fred Ward and Michael Gross reprise their roles as cowboy and survivalist. Writer-director S.S. Wilson co-wrote the first film, so this one retains its offbeat sensibility. Monster earthworms, called "Graboids," have returned to the oilfields of Chiapis, Mexico. Since Earl Bassett (Ward) has frittered away the wealth and fame that came from his earlier triumph over the monsters, he accepts an offer from the Mexican government to hunt down this infestation. Off he goes with new sidekick Grady (Christopher Gartin). Not surprisingly, this one isn't as lively or as explosive as the first film but it's still enjoyable because the characters are treated seriously, and the violence isn't excessive. Fine fare for younger horror fans.

The third film is a bare-bones affair with a small no-name cast, so-so effects, and a much stronger emphasis on humor. It was followed by a fourth.

Trick or Treat (1986)

In this low-budget *Carrie,* geekish Eddie (Marc Price) finds refuge from the torment of his classmates in head-banger heavy metal, and so he's distraught when his hero Sammi Curr (Tony Fields) is killed in a motel fire and won't be biting off the heads of any more live snakes. When Eddie electronically resurrects Curr, he gets revenge. Rhet Topham's script neither condemns nor blindly accepts the music business, and director Charlie Martin Smith (Terry the Toad in *American Graffiti*) gets fine work from a young cast, and he makes good use of some surprising effects. Definitely a sleeper.

Trick 'R Treat (2007)

In the little town of Warren Valley, Ohio, they celebrate Halloween with almost orgiastic enthusiasm. Overlapping stories follow Emma (Leslie Bibb) who has over-decorated her yard. The school principal (Dylan Baker) seems to be poisoning a bratty, greedy kid, and it's hard to say what his creepy neighbor (Brian Cox) is up to. Then there's the good girl (Anna Paquin) who's looking to go bad, and a group of kids who want to know more about the famous Halloween School Bus Massacre that happened a few years back. Not to mention the serial killer. As an homage to E.C. Comics, it's easily the equal of *Creepshow.* Despite a modest budget, writer/director Michael Dougherty gives the film a beautifully textured, atmospheric look.

Trilogy of Terror (1975)
Trilogy of Terror II (1996)

Anyone who's wondered about the source of the band name "The Voluptuous Horror of Karen Black" hasn't seen this video masterpiece. She stars in three Richard Matheson stories directed by Dan Curtis of *Dark Shadows* fame. "Julie" is a nice reversal on an adolescent male fantasy. "Millicent and Therese" is a transparent sisters story. "Amelia" brings Matheson's famous Zuni Fetish Doll from the story "Prey" to the screen. It's simply one of the scariest mini-monster yarns ever written and this adaptation is terrific. It's perfectly constructed with a final image that comes straight from a nightmare.

The three video campfire tales in *Trilogy of Terror II* are told by old pros who know exactly what they're doing. The title says it all with "Graveyard Rats." "Bobby" is a neat variation on "The Monkey's Paw," and "He Who Kills" is a sequel to "Prey" about a murderous Zuni Fetish Doll. Lysette Anthony is a spirited protagonist in all three. Curtis directs with an appreciation for the material. Forget the self-consciousness of "Scream." These are unashamedly old-fashioned stories meant to frighten. Turn out the lights and enjoy.

Troll (1986)
Troll 2 (1990)

Italian-American production isn't completely successful, but it has its moments. When a troll sets out to take over an apartment building, only young Harry (Noah Hathaway) realizes it. Eunice St. Clair (played at various times by June Lockhart and her daughter Anne) seems to know what's going on. The other key character is a dwarf named Mallory (Phil Fondacaro). When they're at the center of the action, Ed Naha's script is as good as it's trying to be. At other times, though, director John Buechler's elaborate troll creatures and makeup effects are transparent camera tricks. You can almost see the wires. Overall, though, the good outweighs the bad.

Troll 2, a sequel in title only, is mentioned often and rightly in discussions of the worst movie ever. The critters are goblins, not trolls, and the makeup effects are rudimentary. Ditto the acting and writing.

Trollhunter (2010)

The "found footage" element of this surprising import is its weakest part, and toward the end, the filmmakers pretty much abandon it. A crew of college students armed with camera and microphone set out to interview a poacher. They wind up with cranky Hans Kalle (Otto Jespersen) who turns out to be a civil servant tasked with keeping gigantic trolls in the proper place. These CGI creations are pretty impressive, even within the limits of the grainy, low-definition video. The same goes for the rugged Norwegian locations. At times, the action morphs into sly comedy. Comparisons to *Cloverfield* are apt. This one is simpler and, to my taste, just as enjoyable.

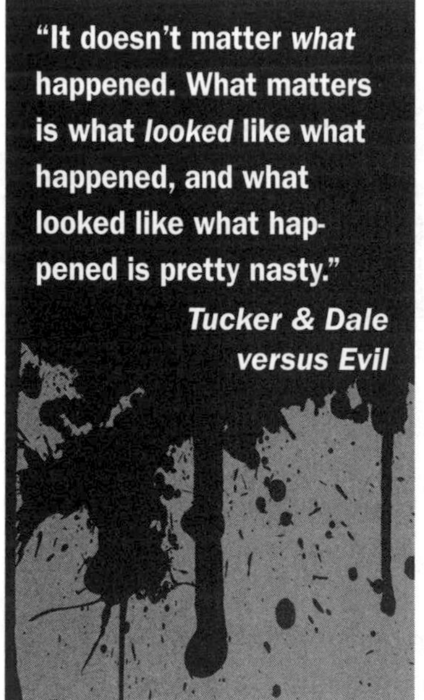

Tucker & Dale versus Evil (2010)

Smart, funny variation on rural horror finds a bunch of city kids on spring break in the West Virginia mountains where they're terrified by two literal good ol' boys, Tucker (Alan Tudyk) and Dale (Dale Dobson). The guys plan to spend the weekend fixing up their new "vacation home," but the visitors won't leave them alone when they think that their friend Ally (Katrina Bowden) has been taken prisoner by the rapacious rednecks. The film then becomes a dark farce with all the blood and gore that the most extreme fan could want. Director/co-writer Elijah Craig knows the rules of the game and toys with viewers' expectations but he's never tongue-in-cheek.

Turistas (2006)

Alex (Josh Duhamel), his sister Bea (Olivia Wilde), and her friend Amy (Beau Garrett) are traveling in a remote part of Brazil when a believably scary bus accident strands them at a beautiful beach straight out of a beer commercial—sparkling white sand, friendly locals, cheap drinks, lots of other attractive kids. What could possibly go wrong? When the action moves into the jungle, it's be-

The Top Seven Creepy Sexy Horrors

The Astronaut's Wife
Galaxy of Terror
Don't Look Now
Demon Seed
Rosemary's Baby
House on Straw Hill
Vampyres

lievably dank and nasty. The horrors that follow are cut from the same cloth as *Hostel,* but somehow, it's never quite as satisfying or engaging.

28 Days Later (2002)
28 Weeks Later (2007)

Technically, these fast zombies aren't really zombies at all. They're victims of the "rage" plague that was set loose upon England and the world by animal rights activists. Four weeks after the outbreak, bicycle messenger Jim (Cillian Murphy) wakes up in an empty hospital and an empty city to find that society has disintegrated. He meets fellow survivors, the hard-headed Selena (Naomie Harris) and the friendlier Frank (Brendan Gleeson), and they try to find a safe place. Director Danny Boyle brings his bravura style to the fast-paced story. His shot-on-video image sacrifices polish and clarity for immediacy. The fully drawn characters react more realistically than they often do in this kind of film. For those who disagree with the upbeat ending, several others are included on the DVD.

The sequel, *28 Weeks Later,* works with a larger and equally talented cast to tell the story of the resurgence of the plague. Strictly in visual terms, the image is clearer and easier on the eyes than the first film. It's also more complex in terms of plot and emotion, but it's also deeply flawed by two lapses in logic at the center of the plot. The first is large; the second is massive, and by the end, much of the action is cartoonishly unrealistic.

Twentynine Palms (2003)

Certainly one of the most fast-forwardable, dogma-tinged films ever made, this one is classified as horror because it involves a couple on a lonely road in the middle of the desert. David (David Wissak) and Katia (Yekaterina Golubeva) run into extremely violent trouble. Mostly, they ride around in their Hummer, have near-X-rated sex, and stay at a cheap motel. Those looking for cheap thrills or sustained scares (other than boredom) will be disappointed.

Twilight (2008)
New Moon (2009)
Twilight Saga: Eclipse (2010)
Twilight Saga: Breaking Dawn—Part 1 (2011)
Twilight Saga: Breaking Dawn—Part 2 (2012)

Arguably the most popular horror series ever made, these films really have little to offer the true horror fan. Like Stephenie Meyer's novels, they're aimed squarely at a young female audience that's more interested in close-ups of Edward (Robert Pattinson), the undead dreamboat, and Bella (Kristen Stewart), his high school honeybunch. (I dare you not to laugh when they share their first smoldering glance.) The first film begins when she moves to Forks, Washington, where it's cloudy and foggy enough for vampires to come out in daylight. Overall, the sense of place and the teen-aged characters' anguished emotions are more important than the traditional tropes of horror—particularly the special effects which simply don't measure up. Edward and his family are good "vegetarian" vampires who feed on animal blood, but still hunger for the hard stuff. Ergo, Edward and Bella can't "do it," and that's only part of the complicated plot.

Heart throb Robert Pattinson plays the vampire Edward in the blockbuster "Twilight Saga" series.

There are also bad vampires and the second film, *New Moon,* introduces werewolves who hate vampires, and the Vulturi, effete powerful Eurovamps who take over as the main villains. Most of the action, though, is teen romance and break-ups, all played out with maximum emotion under Chris Weitz's direction. The effects may be a marginal improvement over the first film but they're still less than stellar.

In the third film, *Twilight Saga: Eclipse,* the larger conflicts among vampires and be-

The Top Thirteen Surprising Sequels

Addams Family Values
Hostel III
Gremlins 2
Children of the Corn IV
Seed of Chucky
Evil Dead II: Dead by Dawn
Army of Darkness
Final Destination 2
Halloween H20
Land of the Dead
Prophecy II
Witchboard: Possession
Fly 2 (1986)

tween vampires and werewolves come into sharper focus. The superfast vampire stuff is still lame and the giant werewolves look like they wandered in from Narnia. Those could not be less important to fans who want to see two hunks—one bare-chested and the other all sparkly—fighting over Bella.

Perhaps because it's only telling the first half of Meyer's final novel in the series, the fourth installment has a sluggish pace. Fans are clearly fascinated by the details of the wedding and honeymoon of the couple. Those more interested in the horror elements will disagree.

Twins of Evil (1971)

Hammer adds two interesting new wrinkles to the vampire story with this late entry. First, having a misogynist, Puritan witch hunter, Gustav Weil (Peter Cushing) in opposition to the Countess Mircalla (Katya Keith) and Count Karnstein (Damien Thomas) places the viewer on uncertain ground. Whose side are you on? Second, casting Madeleine and Mary Collinson, twin Playboy models of limited acting abilities, as the heroines is less than edifying. Writer Tudor Gates and director John Hough create a few memorable scenes, but the exploitation elements are so strong that they unbalance the film, and many of the conventions of the genre are treated with casual, almost comic lightness. In the third act, the generational and political conflicts of the early 1970s take center stage.

Two Evil Eyes (1990)

Two of horror's best—George Romero and Dario Argento—take inventive approaches to Poe stories with the advantage of fine casts and production values.

Adrienne Barbeau and her lover (Raimi Zada) loot her rich dying husband's bank accounts in "The Facts in the Case of Mr. Valdemar." Romero treats the story as an exercise in Hitchcockian suspense with some terrific visual shocks at the end. In "The Black Cat," Dario Argento transforms Poe's tale of retribution into a nightmare. Tequila-swilling photographer Harvey Keitel has a fondness—or is it an obsession?—with gory crime scenes. He also has a poor relationship with his weird lover Annabelle's (Madeleine Potter) cat. It becomes a blood-stained slice of Grand Guignol grotesquery with Keitel giving another full bore performance. The two films share intense claustrophobia and crazed endings.

Two Faces of Dr. Jekyll (1960)

Dr. Jekyll (Paul Massie) divides individual personality into two parts, "an inner man beyond good and evil" and "man as he would be, free of the restrictions society places upon us, subject only to his own will." Director Terence Fisher takes a tack that others have used with equal success, in making Hyde the smoother, more calculating, and sophisticated side of the tweedy, brusque Jekyll. The various parallels at work in Wolf Mankowitz's adaptation of Stevenson have seldom been drawn so blatantly. Here, for example, Jekyll's wife, Kitty (Dawn Addams), has her own conflicting natures. As her lover, Christopher Lee almost steals the film.

2000 Maniacs (1964)
2001 Maniacs (2005)

To contemporary audiences accustomed to hyper-realistic violent effects, Herschell Gordon Lewis' pioneering effort in gore is almost pure comedy. The giggling rednecks of Pleasant Valley, Georgia, trick vacationing Yankees into their small town, planning to make the visitors the guests of honor at the centennial barbecue. The hayseed humor and the soundtrack of folk music and cheap electric organ make it resemble an episode of *Hee-Haw* that's given in to the dark side of the force.

The 2005 version, *2001 Maniacs,* is one of the better of the sorry lot of twenty-first-century remakes. It's every bit as overstated and unashamed as the original. In this iteration, college students on the way to spring break in Florida, are detoured to the little backwater burg and invited by the unreconstructed Mayor Buckman (Robert Englund) to stick around for the Guts 'N Glory Jubilee. Curiously, the more sophisticated CGI techniques used on the violence and gore effects seem every bit as unrealistic as Lewis' did a half century before. Followed by a sequel.

U–V

Un Chien Andalou (1929)

From the opening images of a man sharpening a straight razor, then slicing open a woman's eyeball, this short film from director Luis Bunuel and Salvador Dali has set standards of shock value that few of today's horrors can match. It's sixteen minutes of surrealistic sex, violence, comedy, disembodied hands, dead horses, and hairy armpits. Echoes and quotes can be seen in *Naked Lunch, Silence of the Lambs,* and even TV's *Laugh-In.*

Unborn, The (2009)

Director David S. Goyer lifts bits from Japanese imports like *The Ring* and older mainstream American films like *The Mephisto Waltz* and *Poltergeist* for polished if familiar scares. Teenaged Casey (Odette Yustman, now credited as Odette Annable) has visions of a creepy little kid that lead her to investigate her own past. Really big, ugly-looking potato bugs and upside down heads have their moments, and, overall, CGI effects are not overused. Cold Chicago locations are a fine setting. The ending is weak.

Undead (2003)

Aussie zombie comedy is marked by over-the-top ultraviolence and a quirky visual style that tints many scenes with off-putting colors. The oddball residents of Berkeley become brain-eaters after meteorite-like thingies fall from the sky. Six survivors lock themselves up underground where they bicker and attempt to escape. As inventive as the plot and the effects are, virtually nothing about this low-budget debut suggests the proficiency and polish that the Spierig brothers would demonstrate with their next feature, *Daybreakers.*

Underworld (2003)
Underworld: Evolution (2006)
Underworld: Rise of the Lycans (2009)
Underworld: Awakening (2012)

Predating Stephenie Meyer's *Twilight* novels, these wild action horrors pit vampires against werewolves, or rather, Lycans. A crazily complicated backstory, revealed and revised over the course of the films, establishes how these two creatures can trace their lineage back to the same ancestors, when one brother was bitten by a bat and one by a wolf, and they've been pissed at each other ever since. Once they fought with swords and crossbows. In the present, they use ultraviolet ammunition and silver bullets. Selene (Kate Beckinsale) is a Death Dealer vampire in fetchingly snug black leather outfits who kills Lycans. Michael Corvin (Scott Speedman) is a regular human who is somehow different. The various transformations work well enough. Like the graphically violent action scenes, they benefit from dark, desaturated, blue-tinted night scenes.

The first film establishes the conflicts in the present. The second goes into more detail about the root causes and provides a conclusion to the contemporary story. Throughout, director Len Wiseman's background in commercials and music videos is apparent, but he is also comfortable with the maddeningly complex soap opera elements. The third installment goes back to medieval times for a more detailed origin story about the beginnings of the conflict when Lycans were created by vampires from werewolf stock for use as slaves and guards. Computer effects and action scenes are not as grandly staged as they are in the first two, due in part to the lack of firearms. In all three, Bill Nighy attacks his role as the bull-goose vampire with particular relish, and these movies are much more entertaining and engaging than they ought to be.

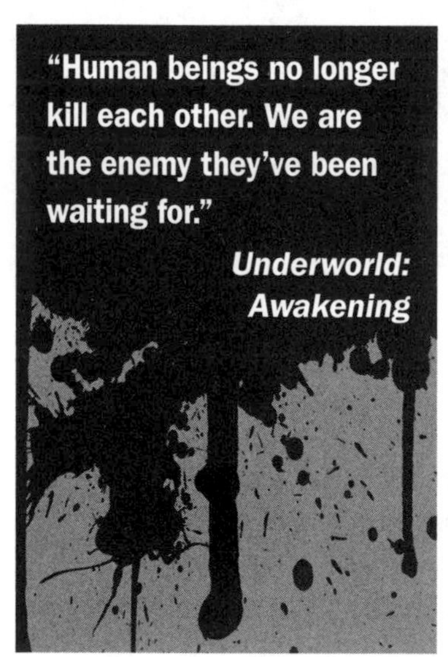

Underworld: Awakening returns to the present where humans have finally tumbled onto the existence of vampires and werewolves and set out to get rid of them. Selene winds up flash-frozen for twelve years. Defrosted, she finds a new world. Despite being the fourth entry, the film maintains the series' level of quality in terms of effects, fight cho-

Werewolves (lycans) battle vampires in the "Underworld" series.

reography and the casting of good character actors in key roles. Like the others, this one is as much about stylized visuals and action as it is about plot.

Unearthed (2007)

Low-budget genre piece is something of a throwback to those '50s films where something horrible and hungry shows up in a little desert town, and the sheriff and the scientist have to figure out how to kill it. Now, instead of a guy in a bad rubber suit, we've got some limited reptilian CGI effects. As the tortured sheriff, hot babe Emmanuelle Vaugier is not remotely convincing. Equally hot babe Tonantzin Carmelo is somewhat better. At least, she's got better lines. More problematic, the daylight exteriors and interiors have a muddy, ugly look, and the night scenes are far too dark. The action sequences are generally well choreographed.

Uninvited, The (1944)

One of Hollywood's best love/ghost stories is old-fashioned in the best sense of the term. It's deftly plotted and atmospheric with well-developed charac-

The Top Seven Towns with a Secret

Brotherhood of Satan
House of Wax (2005)
Phantoms
Children of the Corn
Dark Secret of Harvest Home
Beast Within
Wicker Man

ters. In 1937, London music critic Rick Fitzgerald (Ray Milland) and his sister Pamela (Ruth Hussey) impulsively buy an old house in Cornwall on a cliff overlooking the Atlantic. The initially cozy tone turns chilly as Rick falls for the daughter (Gail Russell) of the deceased owner. Crisp black-and-white photography was nominated for an Oscar. Victor Young's music's not bad either. The weak link is the visible "ghosts" which reportedly do not exist in British prints of the film.

Uninvited, The (2009)

Nicely done remake of the Korean *A Tale of Two Sisters* (see review) features solid performances and production values, and a plot that will trick some viewers while others figure it out early on. Teenaged Anna (Emily Browning) can't get over the death of her mother in a fire. She and her sister Alex (Arielle Kebbel) come to suspect that Rachel (Elizabeth Banks), a nurse, had something to do with it. Or are they simply jealous of the woman's romantic relationship with their father (David Strathairn)? All in all, this one's a cut above the norm for American adaptations of Asian horrors.

Unnamable, The (1988)
Unnamable II: The Statement of Randolph Carter (1992)

Though the film has little to do with H.P. Lovecraft's lightly plotted short story, writer-director Jean-Paul Ouellette is mostly faithful to the master's heightened sense of horror. At least he is at first when Randolph Carter (Mark Kinsey Stephenson) challenges his fellow Miskatonic University students to spend a night in a house where a wizard was killed. The middle is uninspired and repetitious things-that-go-bump-in-the-night stuff when two couples go to the house. Curiously, the creature is portrayed by a woman, Katrin Alexandre, inside a fairly impressive monster suit.

Stephenson returns as Carter in the sequel. A poised, intelligent Lovecraftian figure, he pores over the copy of the *Necronomicon* he found in the first film. The monster—B-diva Julie Strain in an even better suit—is ready to cut loose in the little college town of Arkham. Prof. Warren (John Rhys-Davies) helps Carter figure out what's in the caverns beneath the graveyard. The hokum is no closer to the source material than the first film. Alyda (Maria Ford) wandering around naked beneath a long Lady Godiva wig sets the semi-comic tone.

Untold Story, The (1992)

Gamy Hong Kong horror/crime/gross-out comedy is guaranteed to offend just about everyone. The plot, based on a true story, revolves around a mass murderer. The mildest elements are cannibalism and rape. The rest is so graphic, revolting, and grotesque that it's almost impossible to watch without the fast-forward button. That said, star Anthony Wong's offhand portrayal of a murderous sociopath is every bit as authentic as Michael Rooker in *Henry: Portrait of a Serial Killer* and Anthony Perkins in *Psycho. An Untold Story* goes much farther than either of them, mixing horrific violence with broad humor in a manner that most Western viewers have never seen. Jaded horror fans who yawn through the silly special effects of Jason, Freddy, et al, will get a real jolt out of this one.

Urban Ghost Story (1998)

Believably flawed, sympathetic characters and a grim inner-city Glasgow setting are the strongest parts of a solid little sleeper. After an auto accident in which she "dies," sees the white light, and comes back to life, young Lizzie (Heather Ann Foster) experiences poltergeist phenomena. Her mother (Stephanie Buttle) contacts a tabloid reporter (Jason Connery) who doesn't believe her but sees a story that will sell newspapers. Before long, bogus psychics, paranormal investigators, and even her own friends are trying to exploit the situation. One subplot takes a strange turn and the ending may not satisfy all fans. Still, for my money, it works just fine.

Urban Legend (1998)

College students Natalie (Alicia Witt) and Brenda (Rebecca Gayheart) are shocked when their friends are bumped off in recreations of the titular tales. It's standard stuff with an attractive young cast, lots of smutty talk, and relatively graphic and inventive violence. Overall, the film is slightly more serious than the *Scream* series, and cut from the same polished cloth. Two direct-to-DVD *Urban Legends* films are not sequels; they simply use a variation on the title and work with similar plots.

Vacancy (2007)

The bickering couple is lost on a lonely two-lane blacktop late at night. They have car trouble, but there's a gas station and motel just ahead. Ever since *Psycho,* and probably before, this is a standard-issue recipe for trouble. This time out, Kate Beckinsale and Luke Wilson handle the leads well enough and Frank Whaley is fine as the overly friendly clerk. As for the surprises, they're properly brutal, but about as familiar as everything else. Followed by a sequel.

Vamp (1986)

Three college boys (Chris Makepeace, Robert Rusler, and Gedde Watanabe) go to the city to find an ecdysiast for a frat party and wind up in the strip joint of the undead. Grace Jones is the lead dancer. Her "chair" routine in white face and adhesive tape is too bizarre for words, and, in one incarnation, her makeup is based on the original *Nosferatu.* The story takes place over one long night, and the joke wears thin early. In the narrow subgenre of teen/vampire/comedy, this ranks third behind *Fright Night* and *The Lost Boys.* Body builder Lisa Lyons appears briefly as a dominatrix vampire.

Vampire Bat (1933)

Bats infest a small town and a series of vampiric murders ensue. The cast is the main reason to see this otherwise stodgy tale. Melvyn Douglas is at his suave best as the skeptical hero. Lionel Atwill is fine as the villainous mad scientist. Dwight Frye's character is a caricature of Renfield. Fay Wray isn't given nearly enough to do. Too much comic chit-chat doesn't help the short film, though it does have a few eerie moments.

Vampire Circus (1972)

Relatively obscure Hammer entry lacks the tight plotting of the studio's early work. Director Robert Young replaces it with some above-average transformation effects and soft-core sex scenes. It's about a troupe of vampires who perform as a circus and return to a remote village for revenge a century after they were killed there. Though the cast lacks star power, they do acceptable work with the material.

Vampire in Brooklyn (1995)

Yucky laughs, fairly inventive special effects, and Eddie Murphy doing another star-turn are the main attractions. Not so evident is the offbeat innovation that director Wes Craven brings to his better work—*Nightmare on Elm Street, People under the Stairs, Shocker.* As the title suggests, the story bears a strong resemblance to *An American Werewolf in London.* The humor

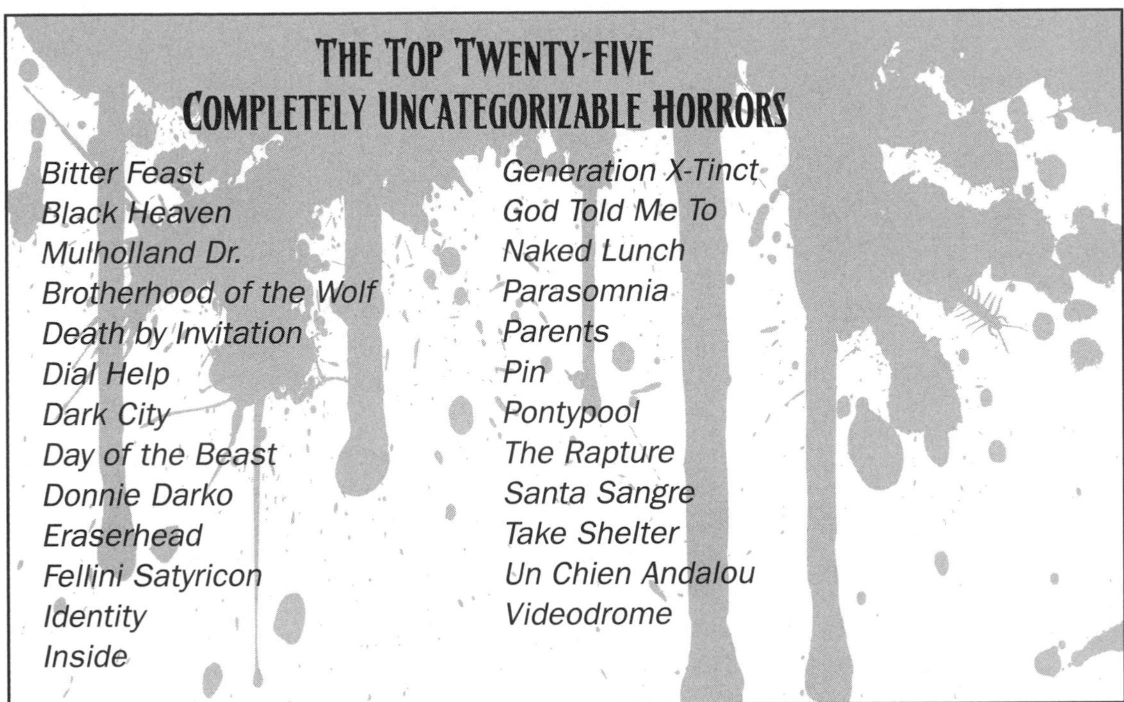

The Top Twenty-Five Completely Uncategorizable Horrors

Bitter Feast
Black Heaven
Mulholland Dr.
Brotherhood of the Wolf
Death by Invitation
Dial Help
Dark City
Day of the Beast
Donnie Darko
Eraserhead
Fellini Satyricon
Identity
Inside
Generation X-Tinct
God Told Me To
Naked Lunch
Parasomnia
Parents
Pin
Pontypool
The Rapture
Santa Sangre
Take Shelter
Un Chien Andalou
Videodrome

is virtually identical, and so is the serious/spoofy approach to horror. Maximillian (Murphy) arrives in Brooklyn looking for the only other surviving member of his race, policewoman Rita Veder (Angela Bassett). He enlists the assistance of a new "ghoul," Julius (scene-stealing Kadeem Hardison) who gives new meaning to the old druggie phrase "eat the roach." Craven keeps the pace moving right along and he gives the production an appropriately rough, gritty look.

Vampire Lovers (1970)

Beyond the nudity which was the film's drawing card when it was first released, this one's a mixed bag. The production values are top-notch and the key images are memorable. But the script is weak with several scenes needlessly repeated to pad it out to feature length, and though it dispenses with some of the vampiric conventions—sunlight, mirrors, coffins—it doesn't replace or explain them. As Carmilla, the predatory lesbian vampire, Ingrid Pitt radiates eroticism. As her antagonist, the General, Peter Cushing is curiously removed from most of the action. In fact, he's absent for most of the picture. The film never really goes into the various male-female conflicts inherent to the subject matter, so it's not as compelling as it could be.

Vampire's Kiss (1980)

Nicolas Cage is a talented, versatile actor, but his fey performance here is so snotty and off-putting that only his most ardent admirers will stick with the story. And, for horror fans, the film is curiously embarrassed by its subject. Literary agent Peter Loew (Cage) has already confessed to his therapist (Elizabeth Ashley) that he has "issues" concerning bats when he picks up Rachel (Jennifer Beals) who bites his neck. Is she real or is she a product of his loneliness? Cage's bug-eyed (and bug-eating!) excesses render the point moot.

Vampyr (1932)

Carl Dreyer's seminal horror film admits that it's a dream in the opening scenes and never pretends to have a formal "realistic" plot structure or a reliable protagonist. David Grey (Julian West) may well have hallucinated the whole slow-moving tale for all the logical sense it makes. Barely connected images of death, sickness, and burial hint at a vampire story, and all of the key moments have been copied countless times since. By today's standards of sound and image, the film is very rough but any serious fan has to see it.

Vampyres (1975)

Considered by many to be José Larraz's best film, this one has gained a reputation for its erotic, exploitative angle, but also works well as a grim Gothic horror. In plot and appearance, it's a companion piece to Larraz's other low-budget work of the period, *The House That Vanished* (see review). Ted (Murray Brown) picks up Fran (Marianne Morris), an attractive hitchhiker. At her moldering country estate, he allows himself to be seduced by her and her lover Miriam (Anulka). The look is grainy, and the sex is athletic and bawdy with a fevered edge that creates a specific equation between vampirism and desire. Larraz uses a constant moaning wind and other heightened natural sound effects to accentuate the cold, autumnal feeling. The main flaw is some ungainly physical action, notably in the outdoor scenes.

Videodrome (1983)

"The battle for the mind of North America will be fought in the video arena—the videodrome." That's one aspect of David Cronenberg's perverse, challenging, unnerving exploration of violence, both real and vicarious. Max Wren (James Woods) is a cable programmer who wants to challenge the limits of his medium—a fledgling operation in the early 1980s. On a pirated satel-

Ultraviolent television is used to battle for the minds of Americans in *Videodrome.*

lite signal, he discovers "Videodrome," ultraviolent stuff masking an even darker purpose. In some ways, the film can be seen as a transition between Cronenberg's early, relatively conventional works (*Scanners, Rabid*) and his more ambitious (*Dead Ringers, Naked Lunch*). It's also a companion piece to *Crash* with its explicit, hypnotic connections between sexual arousal and pain. Though it's certainly not to all tastes, this is one of the most fiercely original horror movies ever made. Is it completely successful? No, it doesn't really make sense and it goes too far. Appropriately, the video version is slightly longer and more grotesque than the theatrical release.

Virus (1999)

In the calm eye of a massive typhoon, a damaged salvage ship comes across a Russian research vessel. It's empty and all the power has been shut off. As soon as they get the lights on, strange things happen. Some of the mechanical and biomechanical monsters are pretty cool, and the special effects are the only interesting part, beyond really bad over-acting by the entire ensemble. Very similar to *Deep Rising,* made a year earlier.

W-Z

Wait until Dark (1967)

Few plays make the transition to the screen as smoothly as this one because the limitations of the stage play to the film's strengths: claustrophobic basement set, flamboyant characters, brick solid storyline. Combine those with ideal casting and you've got one of Hollywood's best. The basic conflict—placing a blind woman, Suzy (Audrey Hepburn), and a girl against three murderous thugs—is still as compelling as ever with deftly timed shocks and revelations. Yes, it's dated for good and for ill. The opening is a fine snapshot of mid-'60s New York, but Suzy's attitude toward her husband will set feminist teeth on edge. It's supposed to. That's part of the film's subtle take on the balance of power between women and men. Audrey Hepburn was nominated for an Oscar, and Alan Arkin as Harry Roat Jr., from Scarsdale, who "wants to do evil things" is an unforgettable villain. The last reel is about as good as horror gets.

Walking Dead, The (1936)

Boris Karloff stars as an ex-con framed for murder, executed, and resurrected in a neatly done lab scene that deliberately recalls his creation as The Monster in *Frankenstein.* Photography, music, and even dialogue are an affectionate tip of the cinematic hat to James Whale's film, made five years before. Director Michael Curtiz's only foray into horror is an impressive and compact piece of work with a touching performance by the star and a fine turn by Ricardo Cortez as the sleek villain. Pay no attention to the details of the almost tongue-in-cheek plot. This fine, largely unknown entertainment ought to be a prime candidate for a remake.

Warlock (1989)
Warlock: Armageddon (1993)

Passable little supernatural thriller mixes a comic book plot with unpersuasive special effects, above average acting, and a strong sense of humor. Back in 1691, a warlock (Julian Sands) escapes execution by conjuring up some kind of timestorm. He and witchhunter Redfern (Richard E. Grant) whisk forward three hundred years to the living room of Kassandra (Lori Singer) a plucky Los Angeles airhead. Before long, they're all hunting for the three parts of the Grand Grimoire, a book that will bring about the "uncreation" of the universe. The pace is quick, the laughs intentional and the plot avoids clichés.

The sequel, *Warlock: Armageddon,* boasts better effects than the original and a plot that's just as nonsensical. The titular supernatural creature (Sands) tries to collect special runestones to bring his daddy Satan into the world, etc. etc. Small town teens Kenny (Chris Young) and Samantha (Paula Marshall) must stop him. The inventive, graphic violence is leavened with equally bloody humor. Similar stuff is found in the 1995 *Prophecy* and *Buffy, the Vampire Slayer.*

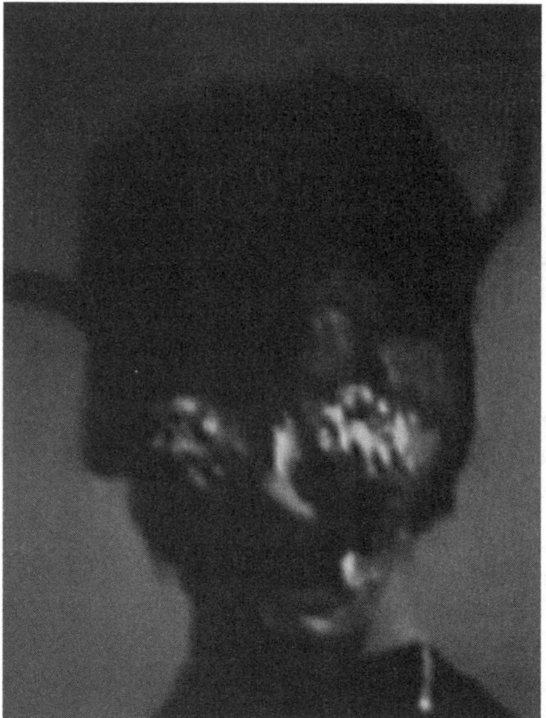

Susan Cabot is the original Wasp Woman in the 1959 film.

Wasp Woman, The (1959, 1996)

Today, the most interesting aspect of this early Roger Corman effort from 1959 is the fact that its protagonist, Janice Starlin (Susan Cabot), is the boss of her own company. Much of the conflict has to do with corporate infighting. In fact, it takes almost an hour for the first monster to appear and when it does, it leaves something to be desired. As the model and spokeswoman for her company, Janice relies on her looks. Age is taking its toll, until a scientist cooks up some supercharged royal wasp jelly for her. The side effects—psychopathic rage, murder—are unpleasant, but ... for a worldclass semi-permanent makeover, they may be worth it. For an offbeat feminist triple bill, run it with *The Blood Spattered Bride* and *Invasion of the Bee Girls.*

The 1996 made-for-cable version stars Jennifer Rubin as model and cosmetics executive Janice Starlin. When she sees the first sign of aging in the mirror, she refuses to go gentle into that good night. Instead, she takes an experimental wasp hormone—"It's going to be bigger than silicone implants!" claims its maker—and looks like she's twenty-five again. A side effect occasionally turns her into a six-legged insect monster with a huge butt. Bummer. Director Jim Wynorski makes movies fast and cheap and this one's no exception. The more you see of the silly makeup, the less effective it is.

Wax Mask (1997)

Dario Argento production is essentially a reworking of the Vincent Price *House of Wax,* with nods to *Dr. Phibes* and *Re-Animator.* Director Sergio Stivaletti's first area of expertise is mechanical effects. He took over the production after Lucio Fulci died. After witnessing the horrible murder of her parents in 1900, Sonia (Romina Mondello) grows up and goes to work at Count Volkoff's (Robert Hossein) wax museum where very strange things are going on in the basement. The Grand Guignol effects may not be as emotionally wrenching as some, but they're certainly graphic enough.

Wendigo (2001)

This independent production lacks polish and dazzling creature effects. In their place, it boasts a perceptive script, complex characters, and a first-rate cast. Kim (Patricia Clarkson), George (Jake Weber), and their young son Miles (Erik Per Sullivan) are on their way to a vacation in snowy, rural Connecticut when they run up against Otis (John Speredakos), a belligerent backcountry cracker. What follows is a slowly paced mixture of conflicts both realistic and supernatural. The use of natural light in interiors makes night scenes too dark at times, though you can see everything you need to see. The four characters are the point, anyway. An excellent sleeper.

Werewolf of London (1935)

Wild and wooly, semi-sci-fi, shapeshifting tale begins in Tibet where botanist Dr. Glendon (Henry Hull) is bitten by a man-beast as he finds the rare *Marifasa lumina lupina* which blooms only under the full moon. Back in England, the ominous Dr. Yogami (Warner Oland) appears to warn of "werewolfery; lycanthraphobia is the medical term." Neither Jack Pierce's makeup nor the unfocused script filled with comic relief equal the Lon Chaney *Wolf Man* though the big fight scene isn't bad and Valerie Hobson is one of the most glamorous

Universal heroines. The main problem is that Glendon is such a cold protagonist that it's difficult to muster up much sympathy for his predicament.

Werewolf of Washington (1973)

Tongue-in-cheek horror was made at the height of the Watergate scandal. Jack Whittier (Dean Stockwell) is the reporter turned White House assistant press secretary who's bitten by a wolf in Budapest. Jack is such a political animal that when he's told about the sign of the Pentagram, he thinks it has something to do with the military. Unfortunately, the dark interiors and grainy night scenes fare poorly on the small screen, and the broad humor lacks the sharp edge that political comedy needs, though as the President, Biff McGuire is presciently Reaganesque. Both the transformation scenes and the makeup effects are on a par with the Lon Chaney *Wolf Man.*

What Ever Happened to Baby Jane? (1962)

Bette Davis's fearless, Oscar-nominated performance is the spark that drives this remarkable *noir* horror. For those who have missed it, think *Sunset Boulevard* with an even more twisted pathology. Baby Jane (Davis) and her sister Blanche (Joan Crawford) are aging, mostly forgotten stars. Blanche is crippled and Jane is insane, though that's putting it much too lightly. Compared to Glenn Close's bunny boiler in *Fatal Attraction,* Jane is the Queen Mother psycho. Her first appearance as a raddled harridan is a real jaw-dropper, and the rest of the film lives up to it. Though the pace is slow by current standards, it generates considerable suspense. Note the way director Robert Aldrich and writer Lukas Heller use parallel images to tighten the various elements of the story. The brightly-lit conclusion is still chilling.

Bette Davis delivers a remarkably chilling performance in *What Ever Happened to Baby Jane?*

What Lies Beneath (2000)

Classy ghost story boasts a first-rate cast, tricky script, and a crackerjack ending. A measured introduction establishes the

Spencers (Michelle Pfeiffer and Harrison Ford), successful empty-nesters with a palatial lake house and irritating new neighbors. The rest is Hitchcockian in the best sense of the term, right down to the score that's reminiscent of Bernard Herrmann. The simple, careful accumulation of details and information in the first half becomes much quicker and livelier and nastier in the second. Well worth a second look.

When a Stranger Calls (1979, 2006) When a Stranger Calls Back (1993)

As proven by the homage paid to it in *Scream,* this film's influence has spread far beyond its theatrical release. The amplification of an urban legend about the threatened babysitter—"the phone calls are coming from inside the house!"—has been one of the most enduring cult favorites on home video. Part of the popularity comes from the casting. As the babysitter, Carol Kane is excellent, and so is Charles Durning as the cop obsessed by an insane killer (Tony Beckley) who turns out to be an unusually complex figure. Add in unconventional plotting that hits all the right emotional buttons and a solid feel for the suburbs and mean streets of Los Angeles. Favorable comparisons to the original *Halloween* are not out of place.

It took the producers more than a decade to come up with the above-average sequel, *When a Stranger Calls Back,* and it's easy to see why. The first film is so curiously but well constructed that it rules out standard follow-up stuff. The original villain is a fully realized individual, not a clichéd movie psycho. The main characters grow during the film and the bad guy is definitely dead at the end. Still, the stalker-v.-babysitter plot is repeated so often because it works, and writer-director Fred Walton handles it with real care. He treats the whole subject of violence against women seriously, and he comes up with an inventive (if not too believable) twist on the formula. It's also well acted with Jill Schoelen taking over as protagonist and Carol Kane and Charles Durning repeating their famous roles.

The 2006 remake of the original begins with a confusing introduction involving the usual threatening call, a suburb, a carnival, an oil well, kids, murders, and another town 125 miles away from all that stuff. Despite expensive production values, it doesn't even come close to the original.

White Zombie (1932)

Though it's terribly dated, Bela Lugosi's follow-up to *Dracula* is still important as the first of its kind and the progenitor of today's *Living Dead* horrors. In

Poster for the 1932 horror flick *White Zombie.*

a backlot in Haiti, a rich lecher engages Lugosi to zombify a young bride he lusts for. The main flaws now are a florid acting style and Lugosi's silly makeup with its exaggerated widow's peak, caterpillar eyebrows, and bald-chinned beard. Some older bargain basement tapes and discs have a scratchy soundtrack and a muddy black-and-white image that lessens the power of impressive sets. A restored version is available on DVD.

Wicker Man, The (1973, 2006)

Playwright Anthony Shaffer's deftly plotted, town-with-a-secret story is genuinely intelligent and suspenseful. It's built on solid philosophical conflicts—Christianity versus paganism, piety versus lust, reason versus revelry. Scottish policeman Sgt. Howie (Edward Woodward) flies to remote Summerisle to investigate the reported disappearance of a young girl. Modishly coiffed Christopher Lee is the laird of the island. Everything Howie finds challenges his strong religious beliefs in ways that neither he (nor the viewer) could have anticipated. Director Robin Hardy combines plain everyday realism with dreamlike hallucinatory images. Woodward's stiff-backed performance gives his role the gravity and authority that the film needs to work. And it does work. Wonderfully.

The 2006 remake is one of the clumsiest ever produced. Relocated to America, the plot makes no sense when it calls for California motorcycle cop (Nic Cage) to go to an island in Washington state, where he has absolutely no jurisdiction, to "investigate" an alleged disappearance. That's really the least of the film's problems. Wherever the original is subtle and suggestive, this one is blatant and blunt.

Wicker Tree, The (2010)

Robin Hardy's comic semi-sequel to *The Wicker Man* is a real disappointment. It reworks key plot points without surprises, and the premise is thoroughly unrealistic. Christian pop star Beth Boothby (Brittania Nicol) goes on a mission to bring the Word of God to Scotland. She travels with her fiancé

Steve (Henry Garrett) though they proudly display their silver chastity rings. Like the rest, they are more caricatures than characters. Neither the scares nor the jokes work very well, but Garrett bears such a strong resemblance to Monty Python's Michael Palin that I expected him to break into "The Lumberjack Song" at any moment.

Willard (1971, 2003)

Though this tepid horror became an unlikely commercial hit for its vengeful rats, its real subject is more Oedipal. Willard (Bruce Davison) still lives with his daft mother (Elsa Lancaster) while working for Martin (Ernest Borgnine), who stole the company from his dead father. Though the pace is slow, journeyman director Daniel Mann gets effective performances from his leads, particularly Borgnine and Davison, and the rats are inherently creepy.

In the 2003 remake, star Crispin Glover and director Glen Morgan give the story an exceptionally weird brand of humor. Glover is made to look like a rat in one shot where the light behind him is shining through his pink ears. But their real parallel is Norman Bates. The two mamma's boys really are a lot alike. The rodents, both real and computer-generated, are still skin-crawly. Jackie Burroughs has some excellent material to work with but she can't really replace Elsa Lancaster (no one could). R. Lee Ermey fills Borgnine's shoes just fine.

Wind Chill (2007)

Nice variation on the "couple lost on a lonely highway" premise has two testy strangers (Emily Blunt and Ashton Holmes) heading off from college for Winter Break. Before they get stuck in the snow, she realizes that something's not right with him. Both the car's messy interior and the rural snowscapes seem completely real. The characters are believable and interesting, and the filmmakers avoid the many clichés associated with this kind of road horror. A solid sleeper.

Witchboard (1986)
Witchboard II (1993)
Witchboard: The Possession (1995)

For the first third or so, this low-budget effort overachieves. Jim (Todd Allen) and Brandon (Stephen Nichols) are both interested in Linda (Tawny Kitaen), but she's just met a ghost through her Ouija board. When the gum-snapping psychic Sarah (Kathleen Wilhoite) shows up, things get really interesting, but her appearance is all too brief and after it, the action settles into standard bump-in-the-night tricks. Even so, this one has enough going for it to earn a qualified recommendation for fans.

In *Witchboard II,* young accountant Paige (Ami Dolenz) moves into a loft to discover her artistic side. A Ouija board left in a closet introduces her to a spirit named Susan who seems to have an agenda. Supporting characters soon drop like flies. Director Kevin Tenney shows off with some interesting but often pointless Argento-inspired camera swoopery, at one point even seeming to go through a moving car. Ami Dolenz isn't accomplished or experienced enough to be much more than a cute, clueless heroine.

The third film, *Witchboard: The Possession,* is what low-budget horror is supposed to be: inventive, spooky, well-made, and with a nasty little sense of humor. The story begins with a tip of the hat to *Rosemary's Baby* and then goes on to tell a story of demonic possession via Ouija board (the only slender connection with the other entries in the series). It lures newlywed stockbroker Brian Fields (David Newman) into all sorts of nastiness. His wife Julie (Locky Lambert) doesn't know what Brian and their creepy landlord (Cedric Smith) are up to, but when Brian brings home a new Miata, she doesn't ask too many questions. The script by Kevin S. Tenney and Jon Ezrine has little to do with the first two films, and director Peter Svatek moves things along at a nice clip. Though he's not above a few moments of Grand Guignol yuckiness, he doesn't over-rely on effects. Great stuff.

Witchcraft (1988-2008)

The first entry in an astonishingly popular series of video premieres borrows from *Rosemary's Baby, The Exorcist,* and *The Amityville Horror.* It lacks the grotesque special effects and overall meanness so prevalent in many theatrical horrors. The plot concerns a young woman's worries about her husband and creepy mother-in-law after the birth of her first child. A weird opening juxtaposes the Lamaze method with burning at the stake. Horror fans have seen better and much, much worse. The series has continued with thirteen inexpensive entries focused on the character of Will Spanner, son of Satan, who's a lawyer by day and a warlock by night. Throughout, the emphasis has been on exploitation and the films have stayed true to their low-budget roots.

Witchcraft through the Ages (1922)

One video version of the famous 1922 silent film is a 1969 condensation with narration by William Burroughs and a Jean-Luc Ponty soundtrack. It's a mix of

Witchcraft through the Ages is a quirky mix of pseudo-documentary and illustrative vignettes.

medieval book illustrations and vignettes that dramatize the black arts—witches nibbling on corpse fingers, putting frogs and snakes into the stewpot, that sort of thing. Spooky scenes, including director Benjamin Christensen as a long-fingered Devil, are mixed with comedy in a pseudo-documentary format that often looks and sounds like an instructional film. The Criterion Collection DVD also contains a restored version of the full-length (104 minutes) release. Despite the inescapably dated quality of the material, it's so unusual that it's recommended, particularly for group viewing by horror fans.

Witches, The (1990)

"Mysterious things go on in the world of witches." So says Luke's (Jasen Fisher) cigar-smoking grandmother Helga (Mai Zetterling), and she knows of what she speaks. She and the boy are at a seaside resort when they come across the Grand High Witch (Anjelica Huston) who's there for a witches' con-

vention. Despite some comic elements, including Rowan Atkinson as the hotel manager, these witches, who hate children, are frightening characters, particularly when they're done up in Jim Henson's creature makeup. Admittedly, those effects may seem dated and old-fashioned for younger viewers weaned on CGI. The sardonic Roald Dahl touch is evident throughout, particularly in the sharp dialogue. Sample: "Real witches have no toes. Their feet have square ends, revolting stumps where their toes should be, so they never wear pointed or pretty shoes, just plain sensible shoes."

Witches of Eastwick, The (1987)

Think a literate, raunchy feminist *Ghostbusters* with Jack Nicholson at his absolute wildest. One night after a few too many martinis, Jane (Susan Sarandon who's excellent), Sukie (Michelle Pfeiffer who's very good) and Alexandra (Cher who's blah) concentrate on the perfect man. He appears as Daryl Van Horne (Nicholson), the devil himself. He writhes, he wriggles, he slithers, he lolls, he seduces each of them. After that ... director George Miller surrenders to every excess imaginable. You may be delighted or you may be offended. You will not be bored.

Witching, The (1972)

In his long and checkered career, Orson Welles was forced to take work in many less than sterling pictures, but this is probably the first one he'd have wanted to be lost and forgotten. It's a half-baked, exploitative rip-off of *Rosemary's Baby* with Welles, affecting an Anglo-Irish accent, as Mr. Cato, boss of a coven in the small town of Lilith, California. Lori (Pamela Franklin) is the object of their transparent ambitions. Welles' performance is limited to a few short, unembarrassing scenes.

Wizard of Gore, The (1970, 2007)

Both the hammy overacting and the gore effects are slightly more sophisticated here than they were in Herschell Gordon Lewis' early work. The disposable story concerns Montag the Magnificent (Ray Sagar), whose bloody stage illusions are so real that TV host Sherry Carson (Judy Cler) looks for the truth behind them. With Lewis' work, though, sophistication isn't really a virtue. This one's too slow, too talky, and lacking the hokey shock value of his first films.

Michelle Pfeiffer, Susan Sarandon, and Cher are modern-day witches in *The Witches of Eastwick.*

The 2007 remake is everything that the original is not—sophisticated, complex, and challenging. Crispin Glover is an inspired choice for Montag. Ed (Kip Pardue) is a dilettante journalist-boulevardier who can't decide if the magician is a charlatan. The unpleasantness begins with leeches and maggots and get much worse. In part, the reality-bending tale is the grandest of Grand Guignols. Seldom has gore been handled so artfully.

Wolf (1994)

Judged strictly as an old-fashioned horror movie, this one is better than some of star Jack Nicholson's other work in the genre, particularly *The Shining.* With a solid script by novelist Jim Harrison and Wesley Strick and equally capable direction from Mike Nichols, it's scary, smart, and funny. Nicholson is fine as a book editor who's bitten by a wolf on a snowy road. Costar Michelle Pfeiffer plays a curiously unsympathetic heroine. She and Nicholson never develop any screen chemistry, but the last reel is terrific. The wolf makeup owes more to Lon Chaney Jr.'s *The Wolf Man* than to recent work like *The Howling.*

The Top Six Urban Legend Movies

Candyman
The Harvest
Chain Letter
Urban Legend
One Missed Call
The Ring
Cropsey

Wolf Creek (2005)

In terms of plot, this road horror is fairly standard stuff. A slowly paced beginning introduces three realistic characters (Cassandra Magrath, Kestie Morassi, Nathan Phillips) who set out on a long drive across a wild stretch of Australia where they run across a cheerful psychopath (John Jarratt). Two things set the film apart: First, the camerawork by cinematographer Will Gibson is astonishing. The lonely desolate landscape has seldom been captured so beautifully. Second, Jarratt's combination of Crocodile Dundee and Norman Bates is a memorable monster. A sequel is in the works.

Wolf Man, The (1941, 2010)

Though he's usually ranked below the Frankenstein Monster and Dracula in Universal's roster of horror stars, the Wolf Man is one of the studio's most sympathetic creations, and he's always been popular with audiences. The key is the way the role of Lawrence Talbot plays to Lon Chaney's strengths as an actor. He combines physical power with vulnerability in both Talbot's guilt-ridden human side and his nocturnal, lunatic, bestial self. He shares that mixture of pathos and horror with Boris Karloff's Monster. In one of his rare appearances in the genre, Claude Rains is excellent as the elder Talbot. To my mind, the poetic script and the lavish sets make the film much more successful and less dated than others of its time. It's a masterpiece that's been more often overlooked by critics than by fans.

The 2010 version is a much larger and more opulent production set in the Victorian England of 1891. This Lawrence Talbot (Benicio del Toro) is an actor who returns home reluctantly after his brother has been killed by a beast. Talbot has a difficult relationship with his father (Anthony Hopkins). Working with a wider canvas, writers Andrew Kevin Walker and David Self and director Joe Johnston go more deeply into the background of the story and expand the action in the present. As much as I like and admire this version, I have to admit that the third act goes on too long. But that's a minor flaw compared to the wrenching transformation scenes, and del Toro's performance which is as heartfelt as Chaney's.

Wolfen (1981)

Some good ideas are mixed with murky intentions for a very mixed bag. Albert Finney and Gregory Hines are the cop and the coroner trying to find the

Maria Ouspenskaya as the gypsy who explains the curse to the ill-fated Lon Chaney in 1941's *The Wolf Man.*

connection between the murders of a New York socialite and South Bronx derelicts. The titular creatures are responsible and given the film's screwball enviro-political sensibility, they're good guys, sort of. Still, the gory effects and deadpan humor deliver what fans expect. When you consider that director Michael Wadleigh's previous experience was the documentary *Woodstock,* and novelist Whitley Strieber would go on to popularize the alien-abduction foolishness with *Communion,* maybe this one's not so strange after all.

Woman in Black, The (2012)

Arthur Kipps (Daniel Radcliffe) is a widower who's still mourning his wife four years after her death. He leaves his young son in London for a job sorting out an estate in a dark, decaying mansion. The residents of the remote seaside town where he stays are unwelcoming. The performances are fine. The house is an impressive piece of set design. Actually, the entire film is properly foreboding and bleak. The deliberate pace and restrained effects may test some viewers' patience.

Woods, The (2006)

In 1965, young Heather (Agnes Bruckner) has indulged in a bit of pyromania and so her folks (Emma Campbell and Bruce Campbell) ship her off to Falburn Academy and the tender tutelage of Miss Traverse (Patricia Clarkson). Turns out that the mean girls and the very strange teachers are the least of Heather's problems. The school is deep in a New England forest that actually seems to be encroaching into the buildings. The first half establishes a sense of mystery that weakens considerably toward the end. Still, the performances are excellent and so is the world of the school.

Wraith, The (1986)

Amazingly, this ambitious teen-horror-car flick manages to hit on all cylinders. Can Jake (Charlie Sheen), the new kid in town, rescue sexy Keri (Sherilyn Fenn) from the unwanted advances of the thuggish Packard (Nick Cassavetes), leader of a gang of young car thieves? With names like Skank, Rughead, and Gutterboy, they are wonderfully mean and funny villains. Writer-director Mike Marvin doesn't waste much time on explanations for this brainless nonsense; he just lets it rip. If it becomes a little predictable by the last reel, the trip is still fun.

Wrong Turn (2003)

Inbred, redneck cannibals don't come any nastier than these monsters. After an effectively brutal introduction, five city slickers—two very sexy girls, two overbearing guys, and our hero (Desmond Harrington)—find themselves stranded on the wrong dirt road in West Virginia. What follows is straight from the *Hills Have Eyes/Texas Chainsaw* playbook, but the action is so swiftly paced and tightly constructed that it is in no way imitative. And with a running time of less than ninety minutes, it doesn't wear out its welcome. To date, four sequels have followed.

Young Frankenstein (1974)

Unlike virtually all horror-comedies, Mel Brooks' affectionate tribute works as both a parody and a horror film. Note the wonderful opening shot and the

Mel Brooks's hilarious spoof of the Frankenstein movies has Gene Wilder—as the son of the original doctor—taking his creation to perform in the theater. Marty Feldman (left) is also hysterical as Igor.

superb lab scenes. (The credits thank Kenneth Strickfaden for the "original Frankenstein laboratory equipment.") Brooks is also true to the original "Golden Age" films to a remarkable degree with lavish sets, costumes, Gerald Hirschfeld's superb black-and-white photography, and a first-rate comic cast doing inspired work. As the Monster, Peter Boyle is worthy of Boris Karloff. Madeline Kahn, Teri Garr, and Cloris Leachman are never upstaged by their co-stars—except maybe Marty Feldman who steals the film as Igor; but the film belongs to Gene Wilder. No surprise there; he wrote the script with Brooks. Most of their fans would agree that this is their finest work, still as fresh, funny, and as worthy of another look as it's always been. One of horror's finest moments, and certainly the funniest.

Zeder (Voices from the Beyond) (1983)

Fevered, semi-coherent, supernatural conspiracy horror that doesn't get properly cranked up until the midpoint. Young writer Stefano (Gabriele Lavia) is driven to investigate a cryptic letter he discovers from a dead priest, and becomes involved in some complicated paranormal rigmarole. His wife (Anne Canovas) reluctantly agrees to help. The overall look, score, sound effects

The Top Seventeen (+) Zombie Movies*

Cemetery Man	*28 Days Later*
Night of the Comet	*Zombieland*
Night of the Living Dead	*Dead Snow*
Pontypool	*Return of the Living Dead*
Plague of the Zombies	*Carriers*
Les Raisins de Mort	*Rabid*
[REC]	*Undead*
Resident Evil series	*White Zombie*
Dawn of the Dead	**and zombiesque creatures*

and voice dubbing recall the giallos of roughly the same period. Exploitation elements, though, are comparatively restrained.

Zombie (1979)

Italian gore-epic—perhaps the best of its kind—opens with a sailboat adrift in New York harbor and a zombie attack. After it, reporter Peter West (Ian McCullough) and Ann Bowles (Tisa Farrow), daughter of the missing boat owner, head for the Caribbean where they find dozens of the living dead. Lucio Fulci's film was promoted as a sequel to George Romero's *Dawn of the Dead,* and thematically and structurally, it is. Gianetto De Rossi's makeup effects are certainly the equal of Tom Savini's and such key moments as the infamous splinter through the eyeball are as visceral as any in the genre. A few little continuity glitches don't detract from the bloody excesses and, to a lesser degree, the sexual exploitation.

Zombie Lake (1981)

A skinny-dipping babe jump-starts underwater Nazi vampire zombies. After extended exposition explaining how the Nazis were killed, a girl's basketball team stops at the lake and one of the zombies pays a visit to his daughter. (I swear I am not making this up.) Under the name J.A. Lazer, Jean Rollin replaced Jesús Franco on this low-budget exploitation quickie. Amazingly, it is not the worst Nazi zombie movie. (See review of *Bloodsucking Nazi Zombies.*)

Zombieland offers a humorous twist to the zombie genre when bad fast food tainted with mad cow disease turns the masses into the walking dead.

Zombie Strippers (2008)

Like *Snakes on a Plane,* the title of this ultra-low-budget effort tells you all you need to know. It opens with cheap jokes about George W. Bush but does get funnier later. Throughout, it's obvious that a large part of the budget was spent on oozing zombie makeup and graphic gore effects. This plague of the living dead is created by a "chemo-virus designed to reanimate dead tissue." Almost all of the action takes place in a dark, threadbare strip club. The focus is on exploding heads and the like, not sex.

Zombieland (2009)

Horror/comedy has all the nasty bloody effects and scares that fans expect, and those are matched by sharp visual and verbal humor. In a post-apocalyptic America, young Columbus (Jesse Eisenberg at his twitchiest) sets off from Texas to Ohio in hopes that his parents might still be alive. Things change first when he meets Tallahassee (Woody Harrelson) and hitches a ride in his SUV. Things change again when the guys cross paths with sisters Wichita (Emma Stone) and Little Rock (Abigail Breslin). Eventually the four set off to find a rumored zombie-free zone in the West. The intelligent script is handled beautifully by actors who understand it and don't work too hard for laughs. In short, one of the best of recent years.

APPENDIX: MOVIE CREDITS

(**A** = actors; **D** = directors; **W** = screenwriters)

Abbott and Costello Meet Dr. Jekyll and Mr. Hyde
A: Bud Abbott, Lou Costello, Boris Karloff, Craig Stevens, Helen Westcott
D: Charles Lamont
W: John Grant, Leo Loeb

Abbott and Costello Meet Frankenstein
A: Bud Abbott, Lou Costello, Lon Chaney, Jr., Bela Lugosi, Glenn Strange, Lenore Aubert
D: Charles T. Barton
W: John Grant, Robert Lees, Frederick Rinaldo

Abbott and Costello Meet the Invisible Man
A: Bud Abbott, Lou Costello, Nancy Guild, Adele Jergens
D: Charles Lamont
W: Frederick Rinaldo, John Grant, Robert Lees

Abbott and Costello Meet the Killer, Boris Karloff
A: Bud Abbott, Lou Costello, Boris Karloff, Lenore Aubert.
D: Charles T. Barton
W: John Grant, Hugh Wedlock Jr., Howard Snyder

Abbott and Costello Meet the Mummy
A: Bud Abbott, Lou Costello, Marie Windsor, Michael Ansara, Dan Seymour
D: Charles Lamont
W: John Grant

Abominable Dr. Phibes
A: Vincent Price, Joseph Cotten, Hugh Griffith, Terry-Thomas, Virginia North, Caroline Munro
D: Robert Fuest
W: William Goldstein, James Whiton

Abraham Lincoln: Vampire Hunter
A: Benjamin Walker, Rufus Sewell, Dominic Cooper, Mary Elizabeth Winstead, Anthony Mackie, Marton Csokas, Jimmi Simpson,
D: Timur Bekmambetov
W: Seth Grahame-Smith

Addams Family
A: Anjelica Huston, Raul Julia, Christopher Lloyd, Dan Hedaya, Elizabeth Wilson, Christina Ricci
D: Barry Sonenfeld
W: Caroline Thomposn, Larry Thompson

Addams Family Values
A: Anjelica Huston, Raul Julia, Christopher Lloyd, joan Cusack, Carol Kane, Christina Ricci
D: Barry Sonnenfeld
W: Paul Rudnick

Addiction, The
A: Lili Taylor, Christopher Walken, Annabella Sciorra, Edie Falco, Katheryn Erbe, Michael Imperioli
D: Abel Ferrara
W: Nicholas St. John

Afraid of the Dark
A: Ben Keyworth, James Fox, Fanny Ardant, Paul McGann, Clare Holman, Robert Stephen
D: Mark Peploe
W: Mark Peploe

After.life
A: Christina Ricci, Liam Neeson, Justin Long, Chandler Canterbury
D: Agnieszka Wojtowicz-Vosloo
W: Agnieszka Wojtowicz-Vosloo, Paul Vosloo, Jakub Korolczuk

After Midnight
A: Marg Helgenberger, Marc McClure, Alan Rosenberg, Pamela Segall, Nadine Van Der Velde
D: Jim Wheat, Ken Wheat
W: Jim Wheat, Ken Wheat

Alice Sweet Alice
A: Linda Miller, Paula Sheppard, Mildred Clinton, Niles McMaster, Brooke Shields
D: Alfred Sole
W: Alfred Sole, Rosemary Ritvo

Alien
A: Tom Skerritt, Sigourney Weaver, Veronica Cartwright, Yaphet Kotto, Harry Dean Stanton, Ian Holm, John Hurt
D: Ridley Scott
W: Dan O'Bannon

Aliens
A: Sigourney Weaver, Michael Biehn, Lance Henriksen, Bill Paxton, Paul Reiser, Carrie Henn, Jenette Goldstein
D: James Cameron
W: James Cameron, Walter Hill

Alien 3
A: Sigourney Weaver, Charles S. Dutton, Charles Dance, Paul McGann, Brian Glover, Ralph Brown, Lance Henriksen, Danny Webb, Christopher John Fields, Holt McCallany
D: David Fincher
W: Dan O'Bannon

Alien Trespass
A: Eric McCormack, Jenni Baird, Dan Lauria, Robert Patrick, Jody Thompson, Aaron Brooks, Sarah Smyth
D: R.W. Goodwin
W: Steven P. Fisher

Alligator
A: Robert Forster, Jack Carter, Henry Silva, Robin Riker, Dean Jagger, Michael V. Gazzo, Perry Lang, Bart Braverman, Angel Tompkins, Sue Lyon
D: Lewis Teague
W: John Sayles, Frank Ray Perilli

Alligator 2: The Mutation
A: Steve Railsback, Dee Wallace Stone, Joseph Bologna, Woody Brown, Bill Daily, Brock Peters, Richard Lynch, Holly Gagnier
D: John Hess
W: Curt Allen

Alone in the Dark
A: Christian Slater, Tara Reid, Stephen Dorff, Frank C. Turner, Matthew Walker, Will Sanderson, Mark Acheson, Darren Shahlavi, Karin Konoval
D: Uwe Boll
W: Elan Mastai, Michael Roesch, Peter Scheerer

American Haunting, An
A: Donald Sutherland, Sissy Spacek, James D'Arcy, Matthew Marsh, John Bell Jr., Rachel Hurd-Wood
D: Courtney Solomon
W: Courtney Solomon

American Horror Story
A: Jessica Lange, Evan Peters, Lily Rabe, Zachary Quinto, Sarah Paulson, Dylan McDermott, Joseph Fiennes, Lizzie Brochere, James Cromwell, Frances Conroy, Connie Britton, Taissa Farmiga
D: Various
W: Various

American Nightmare
A: Debbie Rochon, Brandy Little, Robert McCollum, Kristin McCollum, Heather Haase, Kenyon Holmes, Rebecca Stacey, Kimberly Grant
D: Jon Keeyes
W: Jon Keeyes

American Psycho
A: Christian Bale, Justin Theroux, Josh Lucas, Bill Sage, Chloe Sevigny, Reese Witherspoon, Samantha Mathis, Matt Ross, Jared Leto, Willem Dafoe, Cara Seymour, Guinevere Turner
D: Mary Harron
W: Mary Harron, Guinevere Turner

American Werewolf in London
A: David Naughton, Griffin Dunne, Jenny Agutter, Frank Oz, Brian Glover, Lila Kaye, David Schofield, John Woodvine, Don McKillop, Paul Kember, Colin Ferandes
D: John Landis
W: John Landis

American Werewolf in Paris
A: Julie Delphy, Tom Everett Scott, Julie Bowen, Pierre Cosso, Thierry Lhermitte, Vince Vieluf, Phil Buckman, Tom Novembre, Isabelle Constantini, Anthony Waller
D: Anthony Waller
W: Anthony Waller, Tim Burns, Tom Stern

Amityville Horror
A: James Brolin, Margot Kidder, Rod Steiger, Don Stroud, Murray Hamilton, Helen Shaver, Amy Wright, Val Avery
D: Stuart Rosenberg
W: Sandor Stern

Amityville 2: The Possession
A: James Olson, Burt Young, Andrew Prine, Moses Gunn, Rutanya Alda
D: Damiano Damiani
W: Tommy Lee Wallace

Amityville 3: The Demon
A: Tony Roberts, Tess Harper, Robert Joy, Candy Clark, Jonn Beal, Leora Danna, John Harkins, Lori Laughlin, Meg Ryan
D: Richard Fleischer
W: William Wales

Amityville 4
A: Parry Duke, Jane Wyatt, Norman Lloyd, Frederic Lehne, Barndy Gold
D: Sandor Stern
W: Sandor Stern

Amityville: A New Generation
A: Ross Partridge, Julia Nickson-Soul, David Naughton, Richard Roundtree, Terry O'Quinn
D: John Murlowski
W: Christopher DeFaria, Antonio Toro

Amityville Curse
A: Kim Coates, Dawna Wightman, Helen Hughes, David Stein, Cassandra Gava, Jan Rubes
D: Tom Berry
W: Michael Krueger, Norvell Rose

Amityville Dollhouse
A: Robin Thomas, Starr Andreeff, Allen Cutler, Rachel Duncan, Jarrett Lennon, Clayton Murray, Frank Ross, Leonora Kardorf, Lisa Robin Kelly
D: Steve White
W: Joshua Michael Stern

Amityville 1992: It's About Time
A: Stephen Macht, Shawn Weatherly, Megan Ward, Damon Martin, Nita Talbot, Dick Miller
D: Tony Randel
W: Christopher DeFaria, Antonio Toro

Anaconda
A: Jon Voight, Jennifer Lopez, Ice Cube, Eric Stoltz, Owen C. Wilson, Kari Wuhrer, Jonathan Hyde, Vincent Castellanos
D: Luis Llosa
W: Jim Cash, Jack Epps Jr., Hans Bauer

Anatomy
A: Franka Potente, Benno Fuermann, Anna Loos, Sebastian Blomberg, Holger speckhahn, Traugott Buhre, Oliver Wnuk
D: Stefan Ruzowitzky
W: Stefan Ruzowitzky

Anatomy 2
A: Ariane Schnug, August Diehl, Herbert Knaup, Birgit von roenn, Klaus Schindler, Barnaby Metschurat, Hanno Koffler
D: Stefan Ruzowitzky
W: Stefan Ruzowitzky

And Now the Screaming Starts
A: Peter Cushing, Herbert Lom, Patrick Magee, Ian Ogilvy, Stephanie Beacham, Geoffrey Whitehead, Guy Rolfe, Rosalie Crutchley, Gillian Lind, Janet Key
D: Roy Ward Baker
W: Roger Marshall

Andy Warhohl's Dracula
A: Udo Kier, Arno Juerging, Maxine McKendry, Joe Dallesandro, Vittorio De Sica, Milena Vukotic, Dominique Darel, Stefania Casini, Silvia Dionisio. Cameo: Roman Polanksy
D: Paul Morrisey, Anthony (Antonio Margheriti) Dawson
W: Paul Morrisey

Andy Warhohl's Frankenstein
A: Udo Kier, Monique Van Vooren, Joe Dellasandro, Dalia di Lazzaro, Arno Juerging, Nicoletta Elmi, Srdjan Zelenovic, Marco Liofredi, Cristina Gaioni
D: Paul Morrissey
W: Paul Morrissey

Angel Heart
A: Mickey Rourke, Robert De Niro, Lisa Bonet, Charlotte Rampling, Michael Higgins, Charles Gordone, Kathleen Wilhoite, Stocker Fountelieu, Brownie McGhee
D: Alan Parker
W: Alan Parker

Apprentice to Murder
A: Donald Sutherland, Mia Sara, Chad Lowe, Eddie Jones
D: Ralph L. Thomas
W: Allan Scott, Wesley Moore

April Fool's Day (1986)
A: Deborah Foreman, Jay Baker, Pat Barlow, Lloyd Berry, Deborah Goodrich, Ken Olandt
D: Fred Walton
W: Danilo Bach

April Fool's Day (2008)
A: Taylor Cole, Josh Henderson, Scout taylor-Compton, Joe Egender, Jennifer Siebel Newsom, Samuel Child, Joseph McKelheer
D: Mitchell Altieri, Phil Flores
W: Mikey Wigart

Arachnid
A: Chris Potter, Alex Reid, Jose Sancho, Neus Asensi, Ravil Isyanov, Luis Lorenzo Crespo
D: Jack Sholder
W: Mark Sevi

Arachnophobia
A: Jeff Daniels, John Goodman, Harley Jane Kozak, Julian Sands, Roy Brocksmith, Stuart Pankin
D: Frank Marshall
W: Wesley Strick, Don Jakoby

Army of Darkness
A: Bruce Campbell, Embeth Davidtz, Marcus Gilbert, Ian Abercrombie, richard Grove, Bridget Fonda, Ted Raimi
D: Sam Raimi
W: Sam Raimi, Ivan Raimi

Arnold
A: Stella Stevens, Roddy McDowall, Elsa Lanchester, Victor Buono, Bernard Fox, Farley Granger, Shani Wallis, Jamie Farr, Patric Knowles, John McGiver, Norman Stuart
D: Georg Fenady
W: Jameson Brewer, John Fenton Murray

The Arrival
A: Charlie Sheen, Ron Silver, Lindsay Crouse, Teri Polo
D: David Twohy
W: David Twohy

Art of Dying
A: Wings Hauser, Michael J. Pollard, Sarah Douglas, Kathleen Kinmont, Sydney Lassick, Mitch Hara, Gary Werntz
D: Wings Hauser
W: Joseph Mehri

Ashes and Flames
A: Aisha Prigann, Sasha DeMarino, Mark Schultz
D: Anthony Kane
W: Anthony Kane

Astronaut's Wife, The
A: Johnny Depp, Charlize Theron, Joe Morton, Clea DuVall, Donna Murphy, Nick Cassavetes, Samantha Eggar, Blair Brown, Tom Noonan
D: Rand Ravich
W: Rand Ravich

Asylum
A: Peter Cushing, Herbert Lom, Britt Ekland, Barbara Parkins, Patrick Magee, Barry Morse, Robert Powell, Richard Todd, Charlotte Rampling, Ann Firbank, Sylvia Syms; James Villiers, Geoffrey Bayldon, Megs Jenkins
D: Roy Ward Baker
W: Robert Bloch

Attack of the Giant Leeches
A: Ken Clark, Yvette Vickers, Gene Roth, Bruno Ve Sota, Michael Emmet
D: Bernard Kowalski
W: Leo Gordon

Attack of the Killer Tomatoes
A: George Wilson, Jack Riley, Rock Peace, Eric Christmas
D: John DeBello
W: Jonn DeBello

Attack the Block
A: Jodie Whittaker, John Boyega, Alex Esmail, Leeon Jones, Franz Drameh, Simon Howard
D: Joe Cornish
W: Joe Cornish

Audition
A: Ryo Ishibashi, Eihi Shiina, Tetsu Sawaki, Jun Kunimura, Renji Ishibashi, Miyuki Matsuda
D: Takashi Miike
W: Daisuke Tengan

Audrey Rose
A: Marsha Mason, Anthony Hopkins, John Beck, John Hillerman, Susan Swift, Norman Lloyd
D: Robert Wise
W: Frank de Felitta

Awakening
A: Charlton Heston, Susannah York, Stephanie Zimbalist, Patrick Drury, Ian McDiarmid, Bruce Myers, Nadim Sawalha, Jill Townsend
D: Mike Newell
W: Allan Scott, Chris Bryant, Clive Exton

Awful Dr. Orloff
A: Howard Vernon, Diana Lorys, Frank Wolff, Riccardo Valle, Conrado San Martin, Perla Cristal, Maria Silva, Mara Laso
D: Jess (Jesus) Franco
W: Jess (Jesus) Franco

Bad Moon
A: Mariel Hemingway, Michael Pare, Mason Gamble, Ken Pogue
D: Eric Red
W: Eric Red

Bad Seed
A: Patty McCormack, Nancy Kelly, Eileen Heckart, Henry Jones, Evelyn Varden, Paul Fix
D: Mervyn LeRoy
W: Alex North

Bad Taste
A: Peter Jackson, Pete O'Herne, Mike Minett, Terry Potters, Craig Smith, Doug Wren, Dean Lawrie
D: Peter Jackson
W: Peter Jackson

Banker, The
A: Robert Forster, Jeff Conaway, Leif Garrett, Duncan Regehre, Shanna Reed, Deborah Richter, Richard Roundtree, Teri Weigel, E.J. Peaker
D: William Webb
W: Dana Augustine

Basket Case
A: Kevin Van Hentenryck, Terri Susan Smith, Beverly Bonner, Robert Vogel, Diana Browne, Lloyd Pace, Bill Freeman, Joe Clarke, Ruth Newman, Richard Pierce
D: Frank Henenlotter
W: Frank Henenlotter

Basket Case 2
A: Kevin Van Hentenryck, Annie Ross, Kathyrn Meisle, Heather Rattray, Jason Evers, Ted Sorel, Matt Mitler
D: Frank Henenlotter
W: Frank Henenlotter

Basket Case 3: The Progeny
A: Annie Ross, Kevin Van Hentenryck, Gil Roper, Tina Louise Hilbert, Dan Biggers, Jim O'Doherty, Jackson Faw, Jim Grimshaw
D: Frank Henenlotter
W: Frank Henenlotter

Beast Must Die
A: Peter Cushing, Calvin Lockhart, Charles Gray, Anton Diffring, Marlene Clark, Ciaran Madden, Tom Chadbon, Michael Gambon
D: Paul Annett
W: Michael Winder

Beast of the Yellow Night
A: John Ashley, Mary Wilcox, Eddie Garcia, Vic Diaz
D: Eddie Romero
W: Eddie Romero

Beast With Five Fingers
A: Robert Alda, Andrea King, Peter Lorre, Victor Francen, J. Carrol Naish, Charles Dingle
D: Robert Florey
W: Curt Siodmak

Beast Within
A: Ronny Cox, Bibi Besch, L.Q. Jones, Paul Clemens, Don Gordon, Katherine Moffat, Ron Soble, John Dennis Johnston
D: Philip Mora
W: Tom Holland

Beetlejuice
A: Michael Keaton, Geena Davis, Alec Baldwin, Sylvia Sidney, Catharine O'Hara, Winona Ryder, Jeffrey Jones, Dick Cavett, Glenn Shadix, Susan Kellerman, Robert Goulet
D: Tim Burton
W: Michael McDowell, Warren Skaaren

Before I Hang
A: Boris Karloff, Evelyn Keyes, Bruce (Herman Brix) Bennett, Edward Van Sloan, Ben Taggart, Pedro de Cordoba, Wright Kramer, Bertram Marburgh, Don Beddoe, Robert Fiske
D: Nick Grinde
W: Robert D. Andrews

Beginning of the End
A: Peter Graves, Peggy Castle, Morris Ankrum
D: Bert I. Gordon
W: Fred Freiberger, Lester Gorn

Believers, The
A: Martin Sheen, Helen Shaver, Malick Bowen, Harris Yulin, Robert Loggia, Jimmy Smits, Richard Masur, Harley Cross, Elizabeth Wilson, Lee Richardson, Carla Pinza
D: John Schlesinger
W: Mark Frost

Below
A: Matthew Davis, Bruce Greenwood, Holt McCallany, Dexter Fletcher, Nick chinlund, Olivia Williams, Scott Foley, Andrew Howard, Christopher Fairbank
D: David Twohy
W: Lucas Sussman, Darren Aronofsky, David Twohy

Ben
A: Joseph Campanella, Lee Montgomery, Arthur O'Connell, Rosemary Murphy, Meredith Baxter, Norman Alden, Paul Carr, Kaz Garas, Kenneth Tobey, Richard Van Heet
D: Phil Karlson
W: Gilbert Ralston

Beneath Still Waters
A: Michael McKell, Raquel Merono, Charlotte Salt, Patrick Gordon, Manuel Manquina, Pilar Soto
D: Matthew Costello
W: Mike Hostench, Angel Sala

Beyond Re-Animator
A: Jeffrey Combs, Tommy Dean Musset, Jason Barry, Barbara Elorrieta, Elsa Pataky, Angel Plana
D: Brian Yuzna
W: Jose Manuel Gomez

Billy the Kid versus Dracula
A: Chuck Courtney, John Carradine, Melinda Plowman, Walter Janovitz, Harry Carey, Jr., Roy Barcroft, Virginia Christine, Bing Russell, Olive Carey
D: William Beaudine
W: Carl K. Hittleman

Birds, The
A: Rod Taylor, Tippi Hedren, Jessica Tandy, Veronica Cartwright, Suzanne Pleshette, Ethel Griffies, Charles McGraw, Ruth McDevitt
D: Alfred Hitchcock
W: Evan Hunter

Bite Me
A: Misty Mundae, Julian Wells, Rob Monkiewicz, Erika Smith, Michael R. Thomas
D: Brett Piper
W: Brett Piper

Bitter Feast
A: James LeGros, Joshua Leonard, amy Seimetz, Larry Fessenden, Megan Hilty, John Speredakos, Mario Batali, Tobias Campbell
D: Joe Maggio
W: Joe Maggio

Black Cat, The (1934)
A: Boris Karloff, Bela Lugosi, David Manners, Jacqueline Wells, Lucille Lund, Henry Armetta
D: Edgar G. Ulmer
W: Edgar G. Ulmer

Black Cat, The (1981)
A: Patrick Magre, Mimsy Farmer, David Warbeck, Al Cliver, Dagmar Lassander, Geoffrey Copleston, Daniela Dorio
D: Lucio Fulci
W: Lucio Fulci, Biagio Proietti

Black Friday
A: Boris Karloff, Stanley Ridges, Bela Lugosi, Anne Nagel, Anne Gwynne, Paul Fix, Virginia Brissac, James Craig
D: Arthur Lubin
W: Curt Siodmak, Eric Taylor

Black Heaven
A: Gregoire Leprince-ringuet, Louise Bourgoin, Melvil Poupaud, Pauline Etienne, Pierre Niney, Ali Marhyar
D: Gilles Marchand
W: Dominik Moll, Gilles Marchand

Black Room
A: Boris Karloff, Marian Marsh, Robert Allen, Katherine DeMille, John Buckler, Thurston Hall
D: Roy William Neill
W: Henry Myers, Arthur Strawn

Black Sabbath
A: Boris Karloff, Jacqueline Pierreux, Michele Mercier, Lidia Alfonzi, Susy Anderson, Mark Damon, Rika Dialina
D: Mario Bava
W: Alberto Bevilacqua, Marcello Fondato, Mario Bava

Black Sunday
A: Barbara Steele, John Richardson, Ivo Garrani, Andrea Checchi, Arturo Dominici, Antonio Pierfederici, Tino Bianchi, Clara Bindi, Enrico Oliveri, Germana Dominici
D: Mario Bava
W: Mario Bava, Ennio de Concini, Mario Serandrei

Black Swan
A: Natalie Portman, Mila Kunis, Vincent Cassel, Barbara Hershey, Winona Ryder, Benjamin Millepied
D: Darren Aronofsky
W: Mark Heyman, Andres Heinz, John J. McLaughlin

Blade
A: Wesley Snipes, Kris Kristofferson, Stephen Dorff, N'Bushe Wright, Donal Logue, Udo Kier, Arly Jover, Traci Lords, Tim Guinee, Sanaa Lathan, Eric Edwards
D: Stephen Norrington
W: David S. Goyer

Blade II
A: Wesley Snipes, Kris Kristofferson, Ron Perlman, Leonor Vaerla, Norman Reedus, Thomas Kretschmann, Luke Goss
D: Guillermo del Toro
W: David S. Goyer

Blade: Trinity
A: Wesley Snipes, Kris Kristofferson, Dominic Purcell, Jessica Biel, Ryan Reynolds, Parker Posey, Mark Berry
D: David S. Goyer
W: David S. Goyer

Blade of the Ripper
A: George Hilton, Edwige Fenech, Alberto De Mendoza, Ivan Rassimov
D: Sergio Martino
W: Ernesto Gastaldi, Eduardo Brochero

Blair Witch Project, The:
A: Heather Donahue, Joshua Leonard, Patricia DeCou, Michael C. Williams
D: Daniel Myrick, Eduardo Sanchez
W: Daniel Myrick, Eduardo Sanchez

Bless the Child
A: Kim Basinger, Jimmy Smits, Rufus Sewell, Holliston Coleman, Angela Bettis, Christina Ricci
D: Chuck Russell
W: Thomas Rickman, Clifford Green, Ellen Green

Blessed
A: Heather Graham, James Purefoy, Fionnula Flanagan, Michael J. Reynolds, Debora Weston, Alan McKenna, Andy Serkis, David Hemmings
D: Simon Fellows
W: Jayson Rothwell

Blob, The (1958)
A: Steve McQueen, Aneta Corsaut, Olin Howlin, Earl Rowe, Steve Chase, John Benson
D: Irvin S. Yeaworth, Jr.
W: Kate Phillips, Theodore Simonson

Blob, The (1988)
A: Kevin Dillon, Candy Clark, Joe Seneca, Shawnee Smith, Donovan Leitch, Jeffrey DeMunn, Ricky Paull Goldin, Del Close
D: Chuck Russell
W: Chuck Russell, Frank Darabont

Blood and Donuts
A: Gordon Currie, Justin Louis, Helene Clarkson, Fiona Reid, Frank Moore Cameo: David Cronenberg
D: Holly Dale
W: Andrew Rai Berzins

Blood and Roses
A: Mel Ferrer, Elsa Martinelli, Annette Vadim, Marc Allegret, Jacques-Rene Chauffard
D: Roger Vadim
W: Roger Vadim, Claude Martin, Roger Vailand, Claude Brule

Blood Beach
A: David Huffman, Marianna Hill, John Saxon, Burt Young, Otis Young, Pamela McMyler, Bobby Bass, Darrell Fetty, Stefan Gierasch, Harriet Medin
D: Jeffrey Bloom
W: Jeffrey Bloom

Blood Feast
A: Connie Mason, Thomas Wood, Mal Arnold, Scott H. Hall, Lyn Bolton, Toni Calvert, Gene Courtier
D: Herschell Gordon Lewis
W: Allison Louise Downe

Blood Feast 2: All U Can Eat
A: Mark McLachlan, Trey Bosworth, Lavelle Higgins
D: Herschell Gordon Lewis
W: W. Boyd Ford

Blood Freak
A: Steve Hawkes, Dana Cullivan, Randy Grinter Jr., Tina Anderson, Heather Hughes
D: Steve Hawkes, Brad Grinter
W: Steve Hawkes, Brad Grinter

Blood of Dracula
A: Sandra Harrison, Louise Lewis, Gail Ganley, Jerry Blaine, Heather Ames, Malcolm Atterbury, Richard Devon, Thomas B. Henry
D: Herbert L. Strock
W: Ralph Thornton

Blood of Dracula's Castle
A: John Carradine, Alexander D'Arcy, Paula Raymond, Ray Young, Vicki Volante, Robert Dix, John Cardos
D: Al Adamson, Jean Hewitt
W: Rex Carlton

Blood on Satan's Claw
A: Patrick Wymark, Linda Hayden, Barry Andrews, Michele Dotrice, James Hayter, Avice Landon, Simon Williams, Tamara Ustinov
D: Piers Haggard
W: Robert Wynne-Simmons, Piers Haggard

Blood Orgy of the She-Devils
A: Lila Zaborin, Tom Pace, Leslie McRae, Ray Myles, Victor Izay, William Bagdad
D: Ted V. Mikels
W: Ted V. Mikels

Blood Relations
A: Jan Rubes, Ray Walston, Lydie Denier, Kevin Hicks, Lynne Adams, Sam Malkin, Steven Saylor, Carrie Leigh
D: Graeme Campbell
W: Steven Saylor

Blood Salvage
A: Danny Nelson, Lori Birdsong, John Saxon, Ray Walston, Christine Hesler, Ralph Pruitt Vaughn, Laura Whyte, Evander Holyfield
D: Tucker Johnson
W: Tucker Johnson, Ken Sanders

Blood Spattered Bride
A: Simon Andreu, Maribel Martin, Alexandra Bastedo, Dean Selmier, Montserrat Julio, Maria Rose Rorrigues, Angel Lombarte
D: Vincent Aranda
W: Vincent Aranda

Blood Ties
A: Harley Venton, Patrick Bauchau, Kim Johnson-Ulrich, Michelle Johnson, Jason London, Bo Hopkins, Grace Zabriski, Salvator Xuereb
D: Jim McBride
W: Richard Shapiro

Bloodlust: Subspecies 3
A: Anders Hove, Kevin Blair, Denice Duff, Pamela Gordon, Ion Haiduc, Michael DellaFemina
D: Ted Nicolaou
W: Ted Nicolaou

Bloodstone: Subspecies 2
A: Anders Hove, Denice Duff, Kevin Blair, Michael Denish, Pamela Gordon, Ion Haiduc
D: Ted Nicolaou
W: Ted Nicolaou

BloodRayne
A: Kristanna Loken, Ben Kingsley, Michelle Rodriguez
D: Uwe Boll
W: Guinevere Turner

Bloodsuckers
A: Patrick Macnee, Peter Cushing, Patrick Mower, Edward Woodward, Alex Davion, Imogen Hassall, Madeline Hinde, Johnny Sekka
D: Robert Hartford-Davis
W: Julian Moore

Bloodsucking Nazi Zombies
A: Manuel Gelin, France Jordan, Jeff Montgomery, Miriam Landson, Eric Saint-Just, Caroline Audret, Henry Lambert
D: Jess (Jesus) Franco
W: A.L. Mariaux

Boccaccio '70
A: Anita Ekberg, Romy Schneider, Tomas Milian, Sophia Loren, Peppino de Filippo
D: Vittorio De Sica, Luchino Visconti, Federico Fellini, Mario Monicelli
W: Federico Fellini, Mario Monicelli

Body Snatcher, The
A: Edith Atwater, Russell Wade, Rita (Paula) Corday, Boris Karloff, Bela Lugosi, Henry Daniell, Sharyn Moffett, Donna Lee
D: Robert Wise
W: Philip MacDonald, Val Lewton, Carlos Keith

Body Snatchers
A: Gabrielle Anwar, Meg Tilly, Terry Kinney, Forest Whitaker, Billy Wirth, R. Lee Ermey, Reilly Murphy
D: Abel Ferrara
W: Stuart Gordon, Dennis Paoli, Nicholas St. John

Bones
A: Pam Grier, Snoop Dogg, Michael T. Weiss
D: Ernest R. Dickerson
W: Adam Simon, Tim Metcalfe

Boogens
A: John Crawford, Fred McCarren, Rebecca Balding, Ann-Marie Martin, Med Flory, Jeff Harlan
D: James L. Conway
W: David O'Malley, Bob Hunt

Boogeyman, The
A: Lucy Lawless, Barry Watson, Emily Deschanel
D: Stephen Kay
W: Eric Kripke

Book of Shadows: Blair Witch 2
A: Kim Director, Erica Leerhsen, Stephen Barker Turner, Jeffrey Donovan
D: Joe Berlinger
W: Dick Beebe, Joe Berlinger

Borderland
A: Brian Presley, Rider Strong, Jake Muxworthy, Beto Cuevas, Martha Higareda, Sean Astin, Damian Alcazar, Marco Bacuzzi
D: Zev Berman
W: Eric Poppen, Zev Berman

Boxing Helena
A: Julian Sands, Sherilynn Fenn, Bill Paxton, Kurtwood Smith, Betsy Clark, Nicolette Scorsese, Art Garfunkel
D: Jennifer Lynch
W: Jennifer Lynch

Brain Damage
A: Rick Herbst, Gordon MacDonald, Jennifer Lowry, Theo Barnes, Lucille Saint Peter. Cameos: Kevin Van Hentenryck, Beverly Bonner
D: Frank Henenlotter
W: Frank Henenlotter

Brain Dead
A: Bill Pullman, Bill Paxton, Bud Cort, Patricia Charbonneau, Nicholas Pryor, George Kennedy
D: Adam Simon
W: Charles Beaumont

Brain That Wouldn't Die
A: Herb Evers, Virginia Leith, Adele Lamont, Leslie Daniel
D: Joseph Green
W: Joseph Green

Bram Stoker's Burial of the Rats
A: Adrienne Barbeau, Maria Ford, Kevin Alber
D: Kevin Alber
W: Somtow Sucharitkul

Bram Stoker's Dracula
A: Gary Oldman, Winona Ryder, Anthony Hopkins, Keanu Reeves, Richard E. Grant, Cary Elwes, Bill Campbell, Sadie Frost, Tom Waits
D: Francis Ford Coppola
W: Jim V. Hart

Breed, The
A: Michelle Rodriguez, Oliver Hudson, Taryn Manning, Eric Lively, Hill harper, Lisa-marie Schneider, Nick Boraine
D: Nicholas Mastandrea
W: Robert Conte, Peter Worthmann

Bride of Chucky
A: Jennifer Tilly, Brad Dourif, Katherine Heigl, Nick Stabile, Alexis Arquette, Gordon Michael Woolvett
D: Ronny Yu
W: Don Mancini

Bride of Frankenstein
A: Boris Karloff, Elsa Lanchester, Ernest Thesiger, Colin Clive, Una O'Connor, Valerie Hobson, Dwight Frye, John Carradine, E.E. Clive, O.P. Heggie, Gavin Gordon, Douglas Walton
D: James Whale
W: John Balderston, William Hurlburt

Bride of Re-Amimator
A: Bruce Abbott, Claude Earl Jones, Fabiana Udenio, Jeffrey Combs, Kathleen Kinmont, David Gale, Mel Stewart
D: Brian Yuzna
W: Rick Fry, Woody Keith

Bride of the Monster
A: Bela Lugosi, Tor Johnson, Loretta King, Tony McCoy, Harvey B. Dunn, George Becwar, Paul Marco, Billy Benedict, Dolores Fuller
D: Edward D. Wood Jr.
W: Edward D. Wood Jr., Alex Gordon

Bride with White Hair
A: Leslie Cheung, Brigitte Lin
D: Ronny Yu
W: Kee-tu Lam

Bride with White Hair II
A: Brigitte Lin, Leslie Cheung, Christy Chung
D: David Wu
W: David Wu

Brides of Dracula
A: Peter Cushing, Martita Hunt, Yvonne Monlaur, Freda Jackson, David Peel, Mona Washbourne, Miles Malleson, Henry Oscar, Michael Ripper, Andree Melly
D: Terence Fisher
W: Peter Bryan

Brood, The
A: Samantha Egger, Oliver Reed, Art Hindle, Susan Hogan, Nuala Fitzgerald, Cindy Hinds, Robert A. Silverman
D: David Cronenberg
W: David Cronenberg

Brotherhood of Satan
A: Strother Martin, L.Q. Jones, Charles Bateman, Ahna Capri, Charles Robinson, Alvy Moore, Geri Reischl
D: Bernard McEveety
W: William Welch

Brotherhood of the Wolf
A: Samuel Le Bihan, Vincent Cassel, Emilie Dequenne, Monica Bellucci, Jeremie Renier, Mark Dacascos
D: Christophe Gans
W: Stephane Cabel, Christophe Gans

Bucket of Blood
A: Dick Miller, Barboura Morris, Anthony Carbone, Julian Burton, Ed Nelson, Burt Convey, Judy Bamber, John Brinkley
D: Roger Corman
W: Charles B. Griffith

Buffy the Vampire Slayer
A: Kristy Swanson, Donald Sutherland, Luke Perry, Paul (Pee Wee Herman) Reubens, Rutger Hauer, Michele Abrams, Randall Batinkoff, Hilary Swank, Paris Vaughan, David Arquette, Candy Clark, Natasha Gregson Wagner
D: Fran Rubel Kazui
W: Joss Whedon

Bug
A: Bradford Dillman, Joanna Miles, Richard Gilliland, Jamie Smith-Jackson, Alan Fudge, Jesse Vint, William Castle, Patty McCormack
D: Jeannot Szwarc
W: William Castle

Buried Alive
A: Terence Jay, Leah Rachel, Steve Sandvoss
D: Robert Kurtzman
W: Art Monterastelli

Burn, Witch, Burn!
A: Peter Wyngarde,Janet Blair, Margaret Johnston, Anthony Nicholls, Colin Gordon, Kathleen Byron, Reginald Beckwith, Jessica Dunning, Norman Bird, Judith Scott
D: Sidney Hayers
W: Richard Matheson, Charles Beaumont, George L. Baxt

Burning, The
A: Brian Matthews, Leah Ayres, Brian Backer, Larry Joshua, Jason Alexander, Ned Eisenberg, Garrick Glenn, Carolyn Houlihan, Fisher Stevens, Lou David, Holly Hunter
D: Tony Maylam
W: Bob Weinstein, Peter Lawrence

Cabin Fever
A: Jordan Ladd, James DeBello, Rider Strong, Cerina Vincent, Joey Kern
D: Eli Roth
W: Eli Roth, Randy Pearlstein

Cabin in the Woods
A: Kristen Connolly, Anna Hutchison, Chris Hemsworth, Jesse Williams, Fran Kranz, Richard Jenkins, Bradley Whitford
D: Drew Goddard
W: Drew Goddard, Joss Whedon

Cabinet of Dr. Caligari
A: Conrad Veidt, Werner Krauss, Lil Dagover, Friedrich Feher, Hans von Twardowski, Rudolf Klein-Rogge, Rudolf Lettinger
D: Roberte Wiene
W: Carl Mayer, Hans Janowitz

Call of Cthulhu
A: Matt Foyer, John Bolen, Ralph Lucas, Susan Zucker, Chad Fifer
D: Andrew Leman
W: Sean Branney

Candyman
A: Virginia Madsen, Tony Tod, Xander Berkeley, Kasi Lemmons, Vanessa Williams, DeJuan Guy, Michael Culkin, Gilbert Lewis, Stanley DeSantis
D: Bernard Rose
W: Bernard Rose

Candyman 2: Farewell to the Flesh
A: Tony Todd, Kelly Rowan, Veronica Cartwright, Timothy Carhart, William O'Leary, Bill Nunn, Fay Hauser
D: Bill Condon
W: Rand Ravich, Mark Kruger

Cape Fear
A: Robert De Niro, Nick Nolte, Jessica Lange, Juliette Lewis, Joe Don Baker, Illeana Douglas, Fred Dalton Thompson
D: Martin Scorsese
W: Wesley Strick

Captivity
A: Daniel Gillies, Elisha Cuthbert, Pruitt Taylor Vince, Michael Harney, Laz Alonso
D: Roland Joffe
W: Larry Cohen, Joseph Tura

Carnival of Souls (1962)
A: Candace Hillegoss, Signey Berger, Frances Feist, Stan Levitt, Art Ellison, Harold (Herk) Harvey
D: Harold (Herk) Harvey
W: John Clifford

Carnival of Souls (1998)
A: Shawnee Smith, Larry Miller, Bobbie Phillips, Paul Johansson
D: Adam Grossman, Ian Kessner
W: Adam Grossman

Carnosaur
A: Diane Ladd, Raphael Sbarge, Jennifer Runyon, Harrison Page, Clint Howard, Ned Bellacy
D: Adam Simon
W: Adam Simon

Carnosaur 2
A: John Savage, Cliff DeYoung, Arabella Holzbog, Ryan Thomas Johnson
D: Louis Morneau
W: Michael Palmer

Carnosaur 3
A: Primal Species
A: Scott Valentine, Janet Gunn, Rick Dean, Rodger Halstead, Tony Peck
D: Jonathan Winfred
W: Rob Kerchner

Carpenter, The
A: Wings Hauser, Lynne Agams, Pierce Lenoir, Barbara Ann Jones, Beverly Murray
D: David Wellington
W: Doug Taylor

Carrie
A: Sissy Spacek, Piper Laurie, John Travolta, William Katt, Amy Irving, Nancy Allen, Edie McClurg, Betty Buckley, P.J. Soles, Sydney Lassick, Stefan Geirasch
D: Brian DePalma
W: Lawrence D. Cohen

Carriers
A: Chris Pine, Lou Taylor Pucci, Piper Perabo, Christopher Meloni, Kieman Shipka, Emily VanCamp
D: Alex Pastor, David Pastor
W: Alex Pastor, David Pastor

Case 39
A: Renee Zellweger, Ian McShane, Jodelle Ferland,
D: Christian Alvart
W: Ray Wright

Cat and the Canary (1927)
A: Laura La Plante, Creighton Hale, Tully Marshall, Gertrude Astor, Arthur Edmund Carewe, Lucien Littlefield
D: Paul Leni
W: Robert F. "Bob" Hill

Cat and the Canary (1939)
A: Bob Hope, John Beal, Paulette Goddard
D: Elliott Nugent
W: Walter DeLeon, Lynn Starling,

Cat and the Canary (1978)
A: Carol Lynley, Michael Callan, Wendy Hiller, Olivia Hussey, Daniel Massey, Honor Blackman, Edward Fox, Wilfrid Hyde-White, Beatrix Lehmann, Peter McEnery
D: Radley Metzger
W: Radley Metzger

Cat People (1942)
A: Simone Simon, Kent Smith, Jane Randolph, Jack Holt, Elizabeth Russell, Alan Napier, Tom Conway
D: Jacques Tourneur
W: DeWitt Bodeen

Cat People (1982)
A: Nastassia Kinski, Malcolm McDowell, John Heard, Annette O'Toole, Ruby Dee, Ed Begley Jr., John Larrouquette
D: Paul Schrader
W: Alan Ormsby

Cat's Eye
A: Drew Barrymore, James Woods, Alan King, Robert Hays, Candy Clark, Kenneth McMillan, James Naughton, Charles S. Dutton
D: Lewis Teague
W: Stephen King

Cave, The
A: Piper Perabo, Cole Hauser, Morris Chestnut, Eddie Cibrian, Lena Headley, Rick Ravanello, Daniel Dae Kim, Kieran Darcy-Smith
D: Bruce Hunt
W: Michael Steinberg, Tegan West

Cemetery Man
A: Rupert Everett, Anna Falchi, Francois Hadji-Lazaro
D: Michele (Michael) Soavi
W: Gianni Romoli

Chain Letter
A: Nikki Reed, Keith David, Brad Dourif, Matt Cohen
D: Deon Taylor
W: Michael J. Pagan, Deon Taylor, Eiana Erwin

Changeling
A: George C. Scott, Trish Van Devere, John Russell, Melvyn Douglas, Jean Marsh, John Colicos, Barry Morse, Roberta Maxwell, James B. Douglas
D: Peter Medak
W: William Gray, Diana Maddox

Chasing Sleep
A: Jeff Daniels, Molly Price, Ben Shenkman, Gil Bellows, Emily Bergl, Julian McMahon
D: Michael Walker
W: Michael Walker

Children of the Corn
A: Peter Horton, Linda Hamilton, R.G. Armstrong, John Franklin, Courtney Gains, Robbie Kiger
D: Fritz Kiersch
W: George Goldsmith

Children of the Corn 2
A: Terence Knox, Paul Scherrer, Rosalind Allen, Christie Clark, Ned Romero, Ryan Bollman, Red Travelstead
D: David F. Price
W: Gilbert Adler

Children of the Corn 3
A: Daniel Cerney, Ron Melendez, Mari Morrow, Duke Stroud, Jim Metzler
D: James D.R. Hickox
W: Dode Levenson

Children of the Corn: The Gathering
A: Naomi Watts, Brent Jennings, Jaime Renee Smith, William Windom, Karen Black
D: Greg Spence
W: Stephen Gerger, Greg Spence

Child's Play
A: Catherine Hicks, Alex Vincent, Chris Sarandon, Dinah Manoff, Brad Dourif, Tommy Swerdling, Jack Colvin
D: Tom Holland
W: Don Mancini, John Lafia, Tom Holland

Child's Play 2
A: Alex Vincent, Jenny Agutter, Gerrit Graham, Christine Elise, Grace Zabriskie
D: John Lafia
W: Don Mancini

Child's Play 3
A: Justin Whalin, Perrey Reeves, Jeremy Sylvers, Andrew (Andy) Robinson
D: Jack Bender
W: Don Mancini

Chinese Ghost Story
A: Leslie Cheung, Won Tsu Hsien, Wu Ma, Joey Wong
D: Ching Siu Tung
W: Songling Pu

Christine
A: Keith Gordon, John Stockwell, Alexandra Paul, Robert Prosky, Harry Dean Stanton, Kelly Preston, Christine Belford, Roberts Blossom
D: John Carpenter
W: Bill Phillips

Christmas Carol (1984)
A: George C. Scott, Nigel Davenport, Edward Woodward, Frank Finlay, Lucy Gutteridge, Angela Pleasence, Roger Rees, David Warner, Susannah York
D: Clive Donner
W: Roger O. Hirson

CHUD
A: John Heard, Daniel Stern, Christopher Curry, Kim Greist, John Goodman, Jay Thomas
D: Douglas Cheek
W: Parnell Hall

CHUD 2
A: Brian Robbins, Bill Calvert, Gerrit Graham, Tricia Leigh Fisher, Bianca Jagger, Robert Vaughn, Larry Cedar
D: David Irving
W: Ed Naha

Church
A: Tomas Arana, Hugh Quarshie, Feodor Chaliapin Jr., Barbara Cupisti, Asia Argento

D: Dario Argento
W: Dario Argento, Michele (Michael) Soavi

Climax
A: Boris Karloff, Susanna Foster, Turhan Bey, Gale Sondergaard, Thomas Gomez, June Vincent
D: George Waggner
W: Curt Siodmak

Closure
A: Gillian Anderson, Danny Dyer, Adam Rayner, Antony Byrne, Anthony Calf, Ralph Brown
D: Dan Reed
W: Dan Reed

Cloverfield
A: Jessica Lucas, Mike Vogel, Lizzy Caplan, T. J. Miller, Michael Stahl-David, Odette Annable
D: Matt Reeves
W: Drew Goddard

Club Dread
A: Elena Lyons, Tanja Reichert, Michael Weaver, Jay Chandrasekhar, Kevin Heffernan, Dan Montgomery Jr., Nat Faxon, Jordan Ladd, Richard Perello, Brittany Daniel, Steve Lemme, Lindsay Price, Erik Stolhanske, Paul Soter
D: Jay Chandrasekhar
W: Jay Chandrasekhar, Kevin Heffernan, Paul Soter, Steve Lemme, Erik Stolhanske

Cobra Woman
A: Maria Montez, Jon Hall, Sabu, Edgar Barrier, Lon Chaney Jr.
D: Robert Siodmak
W: Gene Lewis, Richard Brooks

Cold Sweat
A: Ben Cross, Shannon Tweed, Adam Baldwin, Dave Thomas
D: Gail Harvey
W: Richard Beattie

Collector, The
A: Josh Stewart, Juan Fernandez, Andrea Roth, William Prael, Diane Ayala Goldner, Michael Reilly Burke, Andrea Roth, Karley Scott Collins, Madeline Zima, Haley Pullos
D: Marcus Dunstan
W: Marcus Dunstan, Patrick Melton

Color Me Blood Red
A: Don Joseph, Candi Conder, Elyn Warner, Scott H. Hall
D: Herschell Gordon Lewis
W: Herschell Gordon Lewis

Colour from the Dark
A: Debbie Rochon, Marysia Kay, Michael Segal, Eleanor James, Gerry Shanahan
D: Ivan Zuccon
W: Ivo Gazzarrini

Coma
A: Genevieve Bujold, Michael Douglas, Elizabeth Ashley, Rip Torn, Richard Widmark, Lois Chiles, Hari Rhodes, Tom Selleck, Ed Harris
D: Michael Crichton
W: Michael Crichton

Comedy of Terrors
A: Vincent Price, Peter Lorre, Boris Karloff, Joe E. Brown, Basil Rathbone, Joyce Jameson
D: Jacques Tourneur
W: Richard Matheson

Company of Wolves
A: Angela Lansbury, David Warner, Stephen Rea, Sarah Patterson
D: Neil Jordan
W: Neil Jordan, Angela Carter

Conqueror Worm
A: Vincent Price, Ian Ogilvy, Hilary Dwyer, Rupert Davies
D: Michael Reeves
W: Michael Reeves, Louis M. Heyward, Tom Baker

Contagion
A: Matt Damon, Kate Winslet, Jude Law, Gwyneth Paltrow, Laurence Fishburne, John Hawkes, Tien You Chui, Josie Ho, Daria Strokous, Elliott Gould, Demetri Martin
D: Steven Soderbergh
W: Scott Z. Burns

Count Dracula
A: Christopher Lee, Herbert Lom, Klaus Kinski, Maria Rohm
D: Jess (Jesus) Franco
W: Jess (Jesus) Franco, Augusto Finochim, Peter Welbeck, Milo G. Cuccia, Carol Fadda

Count Yorga, Vampire
A: Robert Quarry, Mariette Hartley, Roger Perry, Yvonne Wilder, Rudy DeLuca, George Macready, Walter Brooke, Tom Toner, Karen Huston, Paul Hansen, Craig T. Nelson
D: Bob Kelljan
W: Bob Kelljan, Yvone Wilder

Countess Dracula
A: Ingrid Pitt, Nigel Green, Sandor Eles, Maurice Dehnam, Lesley-Anne Down
D: Peter Sasdy
W: Jeremy Paul

Craft, The
A: Robin Tunney, Fairuze Balk, Neve Campbell, Rachel True, Skeet Ulrich, Helen Shaver, Cliff DeYoung, Christine Taylor, Assumpta Serna
D: Andrew Fleming
W: Andrew Fleming, Peter Filardi

Crash
A: James Spader, Holly Hunter, Elias Koteas, Deborah Kara Unger, Rosanna Arquette, Peter MacNeill
D: David Cronenberg
W: David Cronenberg

Craving
A: Paul Naschy, Julie Saly, Silvia Aquilar
D: Jack Molina, Paul Naschy
W: Paul Naschy

Crawling Hand
A: Alan Hale Jr., Rod Lauren, Richard Arlen, Peter Breck, Sirry Steffen
D: Herbert L. Strock
W: Bill Idelson

Crazies (1973)
A: Lane Carroll, W.G. McMillan, Harold W. Jones, Lynn Lowry
D: George Romero
W: George Romero

Crazies (2010)
A: Timothy Olyphant, Danielle Panabaker, Radha Mitchell, Joe Anderson, Christie Lynn Smith, Brett Rickaby, Preston Bailey
D: Breck Eisner
W: Ray Wright, Scott Kosar

Creature from the Black Lagoon
A: Richard Carlson, Julie Adams, Richard Denning, Antonio Moreno, Whit Bissell, Nestor Paiva, Ricou Browning
D: Jack Arnold
W: Arthur Ross

Creature Walks Among Us
A: Jeff Morrow, Rex Reason, Leigh Snowden, Gregg Palmer, Ricou Browning, Don Megowan
D: Don Sherwood
W: Arthur Ross

Creep
A: Franka Potente, Vas Blackwood, Sean Harris, Ken Campbell, Grant Ibbs, Jeremy Sheffield
D: Christopher Smith
W: Christopher Smith

Creeping Flesh
A: Peter Cushing, Christopher Lee, Lorna Heilbron, George Benson
D: Freddie Francis
W: Peter Spenceley, Jonathan Rumbold

Creepshow
A: Hal Holbrook, Adrienne Barbeau, Viveca Lindfors, E.G. Marshall, Stephen King, Leslie Nielsen, Carry Nye, Fritz Weaver, Ted Danson, Ed Harris, John Amplas
D: George Romero
W: Stephen King

Creepshow 2
A: Lois Chiles, George Kennedy, Dorothy Lamour, Tom Savini, Domenick John, Holt McCallany, Page Hannah
D: Michael Gornick
W: George Romero

Cronos
A: Federico Luppi, Ron Perlman, Claudio Brook, Tamara Shanath
D: Guillermo del Toro
W: Guillermo del Toro

Cropsey
A: Joshua Zeman, Barbara Brancaccio, Bill Ellis
D: Joshua Zeman, Barbara Brancaccio
W: Joshua Zeman

Crow, The
A: Brandon Lee, Ernie Hudson, Michael Wincott, David Patrick Kelly, Rochelle Davis, Sofia Shinas, Bai Ling
D: Alex Proyas
W: David J. Schow, John Shirley

Crow, City of Angels
A: Vincent Perez, Mia Kirschner, Iggy Pop, Richard Brooks, Ian Dury
D: Tim Pope
W: David S. Goyer

Cry of the Banshee
A: Vincent Price, Elisabeth Bergner, Essy Persson, Hugh Griffith
D: Gordon Hessler
W: Christopher Wicking, Tim Kelly

Cry Wolf
A: Jared Padalecki, Lindy Booth, Julian Morris, Jon Bon Jovi, Sandra McCoy, Kristy Wu, Jesse Janzen, Paul James
D: Jeff Wadlow
W: Jeff Wadlow, Beau Bauman

Cube
A: Nicole de Boer, David Hewlett, Maurice Dean Wint, Andrew Miller, Julian Richings, Wayne Robson, Nicky Guadagni
D: Vincenzo Natali
W: Vincenzo Natali, Andre Bijelic, Graeme Manson

Curse of Frankenstein
A: Peter Cushing, Christopher Lee, Hazel Court, Robert Urquhart, Valerie Gaunt, Noel Hood
D: Terence Fisher
W: Jimmy Sangster

Curse of the Demon
A: Dana Andrews, Peggy Cummings, Niall MacGinnis, Maurice Dehham
D: Jacques Tourneur
W: Charles Bennett, Hal E. Chester

Curse of the Komodo
A: Tim Abell, Melissa Brasselle, William Langlois
D: Jim Wynorski
W: Steve Latshaw

Curse of the Werewolf
A: Oliver Reed, Clifford Evans, Yvonne Romain, Catherine Feller, Anthony Dawson, Michael Ripper, Peter Sallis
D: Terence Fisher
W: Anthony John, Elder Hinds

Cursed
A: Christina Ricci, Portia de Rossi, Jesse Eisenberg
D: Wes Craven
W: Kevin Williamson

Dagon
A: Ezra Godden, Francisco Rabal, Raquel Merano, Macarena Gomez, Uxia Blanco, Brandan Price, Birgit Bofarull
D: Stuart Gordon
W: Dennis Paoli

Damien: Omen II
A: William Holden, Lee Grant, Lew Ayres, Robert Foxworth, Sylvia Sidney, Lance Henriksen, Jonathan Scott-Taylor, Nicholas Pryor, Allan Arbus, Meshach Taylor
D: Don Taylor
W: Mike Hodges

Dario Argento's Trauma
A: Christopher Rydell, Asia Argento, Laura Johnson, James Russo, Brad Dourif, Frederic Forest, Piper Laurie
D: Dario Argento
W: T.E.D. Klein, Dario Argento

Dark, The (1993)
A: Brion James, Jaimz Woolvett, Cynthia Belliveau, Stephen McHattie, Dennis O'Connor, Neve Campbell
D: Craig Pryce
W: Robert Cooper

Dark, The (2005)
A: Sophie Stuckey, Maria Bello, Sean Bean
D: John Fawcett
W: Stephen Massicotte

Dark Angel: The Ascent
A: Charlotte Stewart, Angela Featherstone, Daniel Markel, Michael C. Mahon
D: Linda Hassani
W: Matthew Bright

Dark City
A: Kiefer Sutherland, Rufus Sewell, Jennifer Connelly, William Hurt, Richard O'Brian, Bruce Spence, Ian Richardson
D: Alex Proyas
W: Alex Proyas, Lem Dobbs, David S. Goyer

Dark Half
A: Timothy Hutton, Amy Madigan, Michael Rooker, Julie Harris, Robert Joy, Kent Broadhurst, Beth Grant, Rutanya Alda, Royal Dano
D: George Romero
W: George Romero

Dark Mirror
A: Lisa Vidal, Joshua Pelegrin, David Chisum, Lupe Ontiveros, Christine Lakin, David Farkas, John Newton, Jim Storm
D: Pablo Proenza
W: Pablo Proenza, Matthew Reynolds

Dark Secret of Harvest Home
A: Bette Davis, Rosanna Arquette, David Ackroyd, Rene Auberjonois, Michael O'Keefe, Joanna Miles
D: Leo Penn
W: Jennifer Miles, Jack Guss

Dark Shadows
A: Johnny Depp, Michelle Pfeiffer, Eva Green, Helena Bonham Carter, Jackie Earle Haley, Jonny Lee Miller, Bella Heathcote, Gulliver McGrath, Bella Heathcote, Christopher Lee, Ivan Kaye
D: Tim Burton
W: Seth Grahame-Smith

Dark Water
A: John C. Reilly, Ariel Gade, Jennifer Connelly, Tim Roth, Pete Postlethwaite, Ariel Gade, Perla Haney-Jardine
D: Walter Salles
W: Rafael Yglesias

Darkman
A: Liam Neeson, Frances McDormand, Larry Drake, Colin Friels
D: Sam Raimi
W: Sam Raimi, Ivan Raimi, Daniel Goldin, Joshua Goldin, Chuck Pfarrer

Darkman II: The Return of Durant
A: Arnold Vosloo, Larry Drake, Kim Delaney
D: Bradford May
W: Steven McKay, Chuck Pfarrer

Darkness
A: Anna Paquin, Lena Olin, Iain Glen, Giancarlo Giannini, Fele Martinez, Stephan Enquist
D: Jaume Belaguero
W: Jaume Belaguero, Fernando de Felipe

Darkness Falls
A: Emma Caulfield, Lee Cormie, Chaney Kley, Grant Piro
D: Jonathan Liebesman
W: John Fasano, James Vanderbilt, Joe Harris

Daughters of Darkness
A: Delphine Seyrig, John Karlen, Daniele Ouimet, Andrea Rau
D: Harry Kumel
W: Harry Kumel, Pierre Drouot, Jean Ferry

Dawn of the Dead (1978)
A: David Emge, Ken Foree, Gaylen Ross, Scott Reiniger, David Crawford, Tom Savini
D: George Romero
W: George Romero

Dawn of the Dead (2004)
A: Sarah Polley, Mekhi Phifer, Ving Rhames
D: Zack Snyder
W: James Gunn

Day of the Beast
A: Armando De Razza, Alex Angulo, Santiago Segura
D: Alex de la Iglesia
W: Alex de la Iglesia, Jorge Guerricaechevarria

Day of the Dead (1978)
A: Lori Cardille, Terry Alexander, Joe Pilato
D: George Romero
W: George Romero

Day of the Dead (2008)
A: Mena Suvari, Michael Welch, Nick Cannon, AnnaLynne McCord, Stark Sands
D: Steve Miner
W: Jeffrey Reddick

Day Watch
A: Mariya Poroshina, Konstantin Khabenskiy, Vladimir Menshov
D: Timur Bekmambetov
W: Timur Bekmambetov

Daybreakers
A: Ethan Hawke, Willem Dafoe, Sam Neill, Michael Dorman, Claudia Karvan, Vince Colosimo, Isabel Lucas
D: Michael Spierig, Peter Spierig
W: Michael Spierig, Peter Spierig

Dead Alive
A: Timothy Balme, Elizabeth Moody, Diana Penalver, Ian Watkin, Brenda Kendall, Stuart Devenie
D: Peter Jackson
W: Peter Jackson

Dead and Buried
A: James Farantino, Jack Albertson, Melody Anderson, Lisa Blount, Bill Quinn, Robert Englund, Barry Corbin, Lisa Marie
D: Gary Sherman
W: Dan O'Bannon, Ronald Shusett

Dead Man's Eyes/Pillow of Death
A: Acquanetta, J. Edward Bromberg, Lon Chaney Jr., Paul Kelly, George Meeker
D: Wallace Fox, Reginald Le Borg
W: George Bricker, Dwight V. Babcock

Dead Ringers
A: Jeremy Irons, Genevieve Bujold, Heidi van Palleske, Barbara Gordon
D: David Cronenberg
W: David Cronenberg

Dead Silence
A: Ryan Kwanten, Amber Valletta, Donnie Wahlberg,
D: James Wan
W: Leigh Whannell

Dead Snow
A: Jeppe Laursen, Jenny Skavlan, Charlotte Frogner
D: Tommy Wirkola
W: Tommy Wirkola, Stig Frode Henriksen

Dead Weight
A: Mary Lindberg, Michelle Courvai, Joe Bellnap, Aaron Christensen, Sam Lenz, Jess Ader, Matty Field, Jake Martin, Steve Herson
D: Adam Bartlett, John Pata
W: Adam Bartlett, John Pata

Dead Zone
A: Christopher Walken, Brooke Adams, Tom Skerritt, Martin Sheen, Herbert Lom, Anthony Zerbe, Colleen Dewhurst
D: David Cronenberg
W: Jeffrey Boam

Deadly Blessing
A: Maren Jensen, Susan Buckner, Sharon Stone, Ernest Borgnine, Jeff East, Lisa Hartman Black, Lois Nettleton, Michael Berryman
D: Wes Craven
W: Wes Craven, Glenn Benest, Matthew Barr

Deadly Friend
A: Matthew Laborteaux, Kristy Swanson, Michael Sharrett, Anne Ramsey
D: Wes Craven
W: Bruce Joel Rubin

Death Bed
A: Tanya Dempsey, Brave Matthews, Joe Estevez
D: Danny Draven
W: John Strysik

Death by Invitation
A: Shelby Livingston, Aaron Phillips, Norman Page
D: Ken Friedman
W: Ken Friedman

Deep Rising
A: Treat Williams, Anthony Heald, Famke Janssen, Kevin J. O'Connor, Anthony Heald, Wes Studi, Jason Flemyng
D: Stephen Sommers
W: Stephen Sommers

Demon Hunter
A: George Ellis, Erin Fleming, Marianne Gordon
D: Massey Cramer
W: Bob Corley

Demon in My View
A: Anthony Perkins, Sophie Ward, Stratford Johns
D: Petra Haffter
W: Petra Haffter

Demon Seed
A: Julie Christie, Fritz Weaver, Gerrit Graham, Lisa Lu
D: Donald Cammell
W: Robert Jaffe, Roger O. Hirson

Demons of the Mind
A: Michael Hordern, Patrick Magee, Yvonne Mitchell, Paul Jones, Gillian Hills, Shane Briant
D: Peter Sykes
W: Christopher Wicking

Deranged
A: Roberts Blossom, Cosette Lee, Robert Warner, Marcia Diamond, Brian Sneagle
D: Jeff Gillen, Alan Ormsby
W: Jeff Gillen, Alan Ormsby

Descent, The
A: Natalie Mendoza, Shauna Macdonald, Alex Reid

D: Neil Marshall
W: Neil Marshall

Devil
A: Chris Messina, Bokeem Woodbine, Caroline Dhavernas
D: John Erick Dowdle
W: Brian Nelson

Devil Doll (1936)
A: Lionel Barrymore, Maureen O'Sullivan, Frank Lawton, Rafaella Ottiano
D: Tod Browning
W: Tod Browning, Erich Von Stroheim, Guy Endore, Garrett Fort

Devil Doll (1964)
A: Bryant Holiday, William Sylvester, Yvonne Romain
D: Lindsay Shonteff
W: Lance Z. Hargreaves, George Barclay

Devil's Advocate
A: Al Pacino, Keanu Reeves, Charlize Theron, Judith Ivey, Craig T. Nelson, Jeffrey Jones, Connie Neilsen, Heather Mattarazzo, Delroy Lindo
D: Taylor Hackford
W: Tony Gilroy, Jonathan Lemkin

Devil's Backbone
A: Marisa Paredes, Federico Luppi, Eduardo Noriega
D: Guillermo del Toro
W: Guillermo del Toro, Antonio Trashorras, David Munoz

Devil's Bride
A: Christopher Lee, Charles Gray, Nike Arrighi, Leon Greene, Patrick Mower
D: Terence Fisher
W: Richard Matheson

Devil's Rain
A: Ernest Borgnine, Ida Lupino, William Shatner, Eddie Albert, Keenan Wynn, John Travolta, Tom Skerritt
D: Robert Fuest
W: James Ashton, Gabe Essoe, Gerald Hopman

Devil's Rejects
A: Bill Moseley, Sid Haig, Sheri Moon Zombie, William Forsythe, Ken Foree, Matthew McGrory, Leslie Easterbrook
D: Rob Zombie
W: Rob Zombie

Dial Help
A: Charlotte Lewis, Marcello Modugno, Mattia Sbragia
D: Ruggero Deodato
W: Ruggero Deodato

Die, Darkman, Die
A: Arnold Vosloo, Jeff Fahey, Darlanne Fluegel
D: Bradford May
W: Mike Werb

Die, Monster, Die
A: Boris Karloff, Nick Adams, Suzan Farmer, Patrick Magee, Freda Jackson
D: Daniel Haller
W: Jerry Sohl

Disturbing Behavior
A: Katie Holmes, James Marsden, Nick Stahl, William Sadleer, Bruce Greenwood, Steve Raislback, Tobias Mehler, Ethan Embry, Susan Hogan, Terry David Mulligan
D: David Nutter
W: Scott Rosenberg

Dr. Giggles
A: Larry Drake, Holly Marie Combs, Glenn Quinn, Keith Diamond, Cliff DeYoung
D: Manny Coto
W: Manny Coto, Graeme Whifler

Dr. Jekyll and Mr. Hyde (1920)
A: John Barrymore, Martha Mansfield, Brandon Hurst, Nita Naldi
D: John S. Robertson
W: Clara Beranger

Dr. Jekyll and Mr. Hyde (1931)
A: Frederic Marsh, Miriam Hopkins, Halliwell Hobbes, Rose Hobart
D: Rouben Mamoulian
W: Samuel Hoffenstein, Percy Heath

Dr. Jekyll and Mr. Hyde (1941)
A: Spencer Tracy, Ingrid Bergman, Lana Turner, Donald Crisp, Ian Hunter
D: Victor Fleming
W: John Lee Mahin

Dr. Jekyll and Ms. Hyde (1995)
A: Timothy Daly, Sean Young, Lysette Anthony, Stephen Tobolowsky, Harvey Fierstein, Polly Bergen
D: David F. Price
W: William Davies, William Osborne, Tim John, Oliver Butcher

Dr. Phibes Rises Again
A: Vincent Price, Robert Quarry, Peter Cushing, Beryl Reid, Hugh Griffith, Terry-Thomas, Fiona Lewis
D: Robert Fuest
W: Robert Fuest, Robert Blees

Doctor X
A: Lionel Atwill, Fay Wray, Lee Tracy, Preston Foster
D: Michael Curtiz
W: Earl Baldwin, Robert Tasker

Dog Soldiers
A: Sean Pertwee, Emma Cleasby, Kevin McKidd
D: Neil Marshall
W: Neil Marshall

Dolores Claiborne
A: Kathy Bates, Jennifer Jason Leigh, Christopher Plummer, Judy Parfitt, David Strathhairn, John C. Reilly
D: Taylor Hackford
W: Tony Gilroy

Dominion
A: Stellan Skarsgard, Gabriel Mann, Clara Bellar
D: Paul Schrader
W: William Wisher Jr., Caleb Carr

Donnie Darko
A: Jake Gyllenhaal, Mary McDonnell, Jena Malone, Holmes Osborne, Maggie Gyllenhaal, Daveigh Chase, James Duval, Patrick Swayze
D: Richard Kelly
W: Richard Kelly

Donovan's Brain
A: Lew Ayres, Gene Evans, Nancy Davis, Steve Brodie, Lisa Howard, Victor Sutherland
D: Felix E. Feist
W: Felix E. Feist

Don't Be Afraid of the Dark
A: Katie Holmes, Guy Pearce, Bailee Madison, Jack Thompson
D: Troy Nixey
W: Guillermo del Toro, Matthew Robbins

Don't Look Back
A: Sophie Marceau, Andrea Di Stefano, Monica Bellucci
D: Marina de Van
W: Marina de Van

Don't Look Now
A: Donald Sutherland, Julie Christie, Hilary Mason, Cielia Matania
D: Nicolas Roeg
W: Chris Bryant, Allan Scott

Dorian Gray
A: Colin Firth, Rebecca Hall, Ben Barnes, Ben Chaplin, Fiona Shaw, Pip Torrens, Michael Culkin, Emilia Fox, Nathan Rosen, Jeff Lipman, Douglas Henshall, Rachel Hurd-Wood, Johnny Harris
D: Oliver Parker
W: Toby Finlay

Dracula (1931)
A: Bela Lugosi, David Manners, Dwight Frye, Helen Chandler, Edward Van Sloan, Frances Dade, Herbert Bunston
D: Tod Browning
W: Garrett Fort

Dracula (Spanish language)
A: Carlos Villarias, Lupita Tovar, Eduardo Arozamena, Pablo Alvarez Rubio, Barry Norton, Carmen Cuerrero
D: George Melford
W: Garrett Fort

Dracula (1974)
A: Jack Palance, Simon Ward, Fiona Lewis, Nigel Davenport, Pamela Brown, Penelope Horner
D: Dan Curtis
W: Richard Matheson

Dracula (1979)
A: Frank Langella, Laurence Olivier, Kate Nelligan, Donald Pleasance, Janine Duvitsky, Trevor Eve, Tony Haygarth
D: John Badham
W: W.D. Richter

Dracula 2000
A: Gerard Butler, Justine Waddell, Jonny Lee Miller, Christopher Plummer, Jennifer Esposito, Colleen Fitzpatrick, Omar Epps, Sean Patrick Thomas, Danny Masterson
D: Patrick Lussier
W: Joel Soisson

Dracula II: Ascension
A: Jennifer Kroll, Craig Sheffer, Jason Scott Lee, Diane Neal, Khary Paton, Jason London, Chris Hunter, Brande Roderick
D: Patrick Lussier
W: Joel Soisson, Pattrick Lussier

Dracula III: Legacy
A: Diane Neal, Jason Scott Lee, Stephen Billington, Rutger Hauer, JasonLondon, Ilinca Goia, George Grigore
D: Patrick Lussier
W: Patrick Lussier, Joel Soisson

Dracula, A.D. 1972
A: Christopher Lee, Peter Cushing, Christopher Neame, Stephanie Beacham, Michael Coles, Caroline Munro
D: Alan Gibson
W: Don Houghton

Dracula: Dead and Loving It
A: Leslie Nielsen, Mel Brooks, Peter MacNicol, Lysette Anthony, Amy Yasbeck, Steven Weber, Harvey Korman, Anne Bancroft
D: Mel Brooks
W: Mel Brooks, Rudy DeLuca, Steve Haberman

Dracula, Prince of Darkness
A: Christopher Lee, Barbara Shelley, Andrew Kier, Francis Matthews, Suzan Farmer
D: Terrence Fisher
W: John Sansom, John Elder

Dracula's Daughter
A: Gloria Holden, Otto Kruger, Marguerite Churchill, Irving Pichel, Edward Van Sloan, Nan Grey, Hedda Hopper
D: Lambert Hillyer
W: Garrett Fort

Drag Me to Hell
A: Alison Lohman, Ruth Livier, Justin Long, Lorna Raver, David Paymer, Dileep Rao, Adriana Barraza, Chelcie Ross, Reggie Lee, Molly Cheek, Bojana Novakovic
D: Sam Raimi
W: Sam Raimi, Ivan Raimi

Dragon Wars: D-War
A: Amanda Brooks, Jason Behr, Robert Forster, Robert Forster, Craig Robinson, Aimee Garcia, Chris Mulkey
D: Hyung-rae Shim
W: Hyung-rae Shim

Dreamcatcher
A: Morgan Freeman, Jason Lee, Thomas Jane, Damian Lewis, Timothy Olyphant, Tom Sizemore, Donnie Wahlberg, Reece Thompson, Giacomo Baessato, Joel Palmer
D: Lawrence Kasdan
W: William Goldman, Lawrence Kasdan

Dressed to Kill
A: Angie Dickenson, Michael Caine, Nancy Allen, Keith Gordon, Dennis Franz, David Marguiles, Brandon Maggart
D: Brian DePalma
W: Brian DePalma

Drive Angry
A: Nicolas Cage, Amber Heard, William Fichtner, Billy Burke, David Morse, Christa Campbell, Todd Farmer
D: Patrick Lussier
W: Patrick Lussier, Todd Farmer

Duel
A: Dennis Weaver, Lucille Benson, Eddie Firestone, Cary Loftin
D: Steven Spielberg
W: Richard Matheson

Dunwich Horror
A: Sandra Dee, Dean Stockwell, Lloyd Bochner, Ed Begley Sr., Sam Jaffe, Joanna Moore, Talia Shire
D: David Haller
W: Curtis Hanson, Henry Rosenbaum, Ronald Silkovsky

Dust Devil
A: Robert John Burke, Chelsea Field, Zakes Mokae, Rufus Swart, John Matshikiza
D: Richard Stanley
W: Richard Stanley

Dylan Dog: Dead of Night
A: Sam Huntington, Brandon Routh, Anita Briem, Taye Diggs
D: Kevin Munroe
W: Thomas Dean Donnelly, Joshua Oppenheimer

Earth vs. the Spider
A: Edward Kemmer, June Kennedy, Gene Persson, Gene Roth
D: Bert I. Gordon
W: Laszlo Gorog, George Worthington Yates

Eaten Alive
A: Neville Brand, Mel Ferrer, Carolyn Jones, Marilyn Burns, Stuart Whitman, Robert Englund, William Finley, Roberta Collins, Kyle Richardson
D: Tobe Hooper
W: Marti Rustam, Alvin L. Fast, Kim Henkel

Ed Wood
A: Johnny Depp, Sarah Jessica Parker, Martin Landau, Bill Murray, Jim Myers, Patricia Arquette, Jeffrey Jones, Lisa Marie, Vincent D'Onofrio
D: Tim Burton
W: Scott Alexander, Larry Karaszewski

Eden Lake
A: Michael Fassbender, Kelly Reilly, Tara Ellis
D: James Watkins
W: James Watkins

Edison Frankenstein
A: Charles Ogle, Augustus Phillips, Mary Fuller
D: Searle Dawley
W: Searle Dawley

Edward Sissorhands
A: Johnny Depp, Winona Ryder, Dianne Wiest, Vincent Price, Anthony Michael Hall, Alan Arkin, Kathy Baker, Conchata Ferrell
D: Tim Burton
W: Tim Burton, Caroline Thompson

Eight Legged Freaks
A: David Arquette, Scott Terra, Kari Wuhrer, Scarlett Johansson, Rick Overton, Doug E. Doug, Leon Rippy
D: Ellory Elkayem
W: Ellory Elkayem

Embrace of the Vampire
A: Alyssa Milano, Martin Kemp, Harrison Pruett, Charlotte Lewis, Jordan Ladd, Rachel True, Jennifer Tilly
D: Anne Goursaud
W: Halle Eaton, Nicole Coady, Rick Bitzelberger

Emerald Jungle
A: Robert Kerman, Janet Agren, Mel Ferrer, Luciano Martino
D: Umberto Lenzi
W: Umberto Lenzi

End of Days
A: Arnold Schwarzenegger, Gabriel Byrne, Robin Tunney, Kevin Pollak, Derrick O'Connor, CCH Pounder
D: Peter Hyams
W: Andrew W. Marlowe

End of the Line
A: Ilona Elkin, Neil Napier, Nicolas Wright, Tim Rozon, Emily Shelton, John Vamvas, Danny Blanco Hall, Joan McBride, Nina Fillis
D: Maurice Devereaux
W: Maurice Devereaux

Evil, The
A: Richard Crenna, Joanna Pettet, Andrew Prine, Victor Buono, Cassie Yates, George O'Hanlon Jr., Mary Louise Weller
D: Gus Trikonis
W: Donald G. Thompson

Evil Dead
A: Bruce Campbell, Ellen Sandweiss, Betsy Baker, Hal Delrich, Sarah York
D: Sam Raimi
W: Sam Raimi

Evil Dead 2
A: Bruce Campbell, Sarah Berry, Dan Hicks, Kassie Wesley, Theodore (Ted) Raimi

D: Sam Raimi
W: Sam Raimi, Scott Spiegel

Evil of Frankenstein
A: Peter Cushing, Duncan Lamont, Peter Woodthorpe, Sandor Eles, Kiwi Kingston, Katy Wild
D: Freddie Francis
W: Anthony John, Elder Hines

eXistenZ
A: Jude Law, Ian Holm, Jennifer Jason Leigh, Willem Dafoe, Don McKellar
D: David Cronenberg
W: David Cronenberg

Exorcism of Emily Rose, The
A: Laura Linney, Tom Wilkinson, Shohreh Aghdashloo, Campbell Scott, Jennifer Carpenter, Colm Feore, Joshua Close, Duncan Fraser, Kenneth Welsh
D: Scott Derrickson
W: Scott Derrickson, Paul Harris Boardman

Exorcist, The
A: Ellen Burstyn, Linda Blair, Jason Miller, Max Von Sydow, Jack McGowran, Lee J. Cobb, Kitty Winn
D: William Friedkin
W: William Peter Blatty

Exorcist II
A: Richard Burton, Linda Blair, Louise Fletcher, Kitty Winn, James Earl Jones, Ned Beatty, Max Von Sydow, Paul Henreid
D: John Boorman
W: William Goodhart

Exorcist III
A: George C. Scott, Ed Flanders, Jason Miller, Nicol Williamson, Scott Wilson, Brad Dourif, Nancy Fish, Viveca Lindfors, Patrick Ewing, Fabio
D: William Peter Blatty
W: William Peter Blatty

Exorcist: The Beginning, The
A: Izabella Scorupco, Stellan Skarsgard, James D'Arcy, Remy Sweeney, Andrew French, Julian Wadham, Ralph Brown, James Bellamy
D: Renny Harlin
W: Alexi Hawley

Eye, The
A: Jessica Alba, Parker Posey, Alessandro Nivola, Rade Serbedzija, Fernanda Romero, Obba Babatunde, Danny Mora, Rachel Ticotin, Chloe Grace Moretz
D: David Moreau, Xavier Palud
W: Sebastian Gutierrez

Faculty, The
A: Jordana Brewster, Laura Harris, Clea DuVall, Josh Hartnett, Shawn Hatosy, Salma Hayek, Famke Janssen, Piper Laurie, Bebe Neuwirth, Robert Patrick, Christopher McDonald, Jon Stewart, usher Raymond
D: Robert Rodriguez
W: Kevin Williamson

Fade to Black
A: Dennis Christopher, Tim Thomerson, Linda Kerridge, Mickey Rourke, Melinda Fee, Gwynne Gilford
D: Vernon Zimmerman
W: Vernon Zimmerman

Fall of the House of Usher
A: Vincent Price, Myrna Fahey, Mark Damon, Harry Ellerbe
D: Roger Corman
W: Richard Matheson

Fascination
A: Franca Mai, Brigitte Lahai, Jean-Marie Lemaire, Fanny Magier, Muriel Montosse, Alain Plumey
D: Jean Rollin
W: Jean Rollin

Feardotcom
A: Stephen Dorff, Natascha McElhone, Stephen Rea, Udo Kier, Jeffrey Combs, Amelia Curtis, Nigel Terry, Michael Sarrazin, Gesine Cukrowski
D: William Malone
W: Josephine Coyle

Fearless Vampire Killers; or, Pardon Me, But Your Teeth Are in My Neck
A: Jack MacGowran, Roman Polanski, Alfie Bass, Sharon Tate, Jessie Robbins, Ferdinand "Ferdy" Mayne, Iain Quarrier, Fiona Lewis
D: Roman Polanski
W: Gerard Brach, Roman Polanski

Feast
A: Krista Allen, Navi Rawat, Balthazar Getty
D: John Gulager
W: Marcus Dunstan, Patrick Melton

Fellini Satyricon
A: Martin Potter, Capucine, Hiran Keller, Salvo Randone, Max Born
D: Federico Fellini
W: Federico Fellini

Fido
A: Billy Connolly, Kesun Loder, Carrie-Anne Moss, Alexia Fast, Tiffany Lyndall-Knight, Jennifer Clement, Aaron Brown, Brandon Olds, Tim Blake Nelson, Sonja Bennett
D: Andrew Currie
W: Andrew Currie, Robert Chomiak, Dennis Heaton

Fiend without a Face
A: Marshall Thompson, Terry Kilburn, Kynaston Reeves, Stanley Maxted, Terry Kilburn, Peter Madden, Gil Winfield, Meadows White
D: Arthur Crabtree
W: Herbert J. Leder

Final Destination
A: Devon Sawa, Ali Larter, Kerr Smith, Kristen Cloke, Daniel Roebuck, Roger Guenveur Smith, Seann William Scott, Tony Todd, Amanda Detmer, Brendan Fehr, Lisa Marie Caruk, Christine Chatelain, Forbes Angus
D: James Wong
W: James Wong, Glen Morgan, Jeffrey Reddick

Final Destination 2
A: A. J. Cook, Tony Todd, Ali Larter, Jonathan Cherry, Keegan Connor tracy, Terrence Carson, Lynda Boyd, James Kirk, David Paetkau, Justina Machado
D: David R. Ellis
W: J. Mackye Gruber, Eric Bress

Final Destination 3
A: Mary Elizabeth Winstead, Ryan Merriman, Kris Lemche, Alexz Johnson, Sam Easton, Jesse Moss, Gina Holden, Texas Battle, Chelan Simmons, Amanda Crew, Crystal Lowe
D: James Wong
W: James Wong, Glen Morgan

Final Destination 3D
A: Nick Zano, Krista Allen, Andrew Fiscella, Bobby Campo, Haley Webb, Shantel VanSanten, Mykelti Williamson
D: David R. Ellis
W: Eric Bress

Final Destination 5
A: Emma Bell, Nicholas D'Agosto, Arlen Escarpeta, Miles Fisher, Ellen Wroe, Jacqueline MacInnes Wood, P. J. Byrne, David Koechner, Tony Todd, Courtney B. Vance
D: Steven Quale
W: Eric Heisserer

Firestarter
A: David Keith, Drew Barrymore, Freddie Jones, Martin Sheen, George C. Scott, Heather Locklear, Louise Fletcher, Moses Gunn, Art Carney, Antonio Fargas, Drew Snyder
D: Mark Lester
W: Stanley Mann

Flatliners
A: Kiefer Sutherland, Kevin Bacon, Julia Roberts, William Baldwin
D: Joel Schumacher
W: Peter Filardi

Fly, The (1958)
A: Vincent Price, David Hedison, Herbert Marshall, Patricia Owens
D: Kurt Neumann
W: James Clavell

Fly, The (1986)
A: Jeff Goldblum, Geena Davis, John Getz, Joy Boushel, Les Carlson
D: David Cronenberg
W: David Cronenberg, Charles Edward Pogue

Fly II, The (1989)
A: Eric Stoltz, Daphne Zuniga, Lee Richardson, John Getz, Frank C. Turner, Garry Chalk, Ann Marie Lee, Saffron Henderson, Harley Cross
D: Chris Walas
W: Mick Garris, Jim Wheat, Ken Wheat, Frank Darabont

Fog, The (1980)
A: Hal Holbrook, Adrienne Barbeau, Jamie Lee Curtis, Janet Leigh, John Houseman, Tom Atkins
D: John Carpenter
W: John Carpenter, Debra Hill

Fog, The (2005)
A: Tom Welling, Selma Blair, Maggie Grace, Kenneth Welsh, DeRay Davis, Cole Heppel
D: Rupert Wainwright
W: John Carpenter, Cooper Layne, Debra Hill

Forgotten Ones, The
A: Kristy McNichol, Terry O'Quinn, Blair Parker, Elisabeth Brooks
D: Phillip Badger
W: James Mathers

Forsaken, The
A: Kerr Smith, Brendan Fehr, Izabella Miko
D: J. S. Cardone
W: J. S. Cardone

Four Flies on Grey Velvet
A: Michael Brandon, Jean-Pierre Marielle, Mimsy Farmer, Bud Spencer
D: Dario Argento
W: Dario Argento

1408
A: John Cusack, Samuel L. Jackson, Mary McCormack, Tony Shalhoub, Len Cariou, Jasmine Jessica Anthony
D: Mikael Hafstroem
W: Matt Greenberg, Scott Alexander, Larry Karaszewski

Fragile
A: Calista Flockhart, Richard Roxburgh, Elena Anaya, Gemma Jones, Yasmin Murphy, Colin McFarlane, Michael Pennington, Daniel Ortiz, Susie Trayling
D: Jaume Balaguero
W: Jaume Balaguero, Jordi Galceran

Frailty
A: Bill Paxton, Matthew McConaughey, Powers Boothe, Matt O'Leary, Jeremy Sumpter, Luke Askew
D: Bill Paxton
W: Brent Hanley

Frankenhooker
A: James Lorinz, Patty Mullen, Charlotte J. Helmkamp, Louise Lasser, Shirley Stoler
D: Frank Henenlotter
W: Frank Henenlotter, Robert Martin

Frankenstein (1910)
A: Mary Fuller, Charles Ogle, Augustus Phillips
D: J. Searle Dawley
W: J. Searle Dawley

Frankenstein (1931)
A: Boris Karloff, Colin Clive, Mae Clark, John Boles, Dwight Frye, Edward Van Sloan, Frederick Kerr, Lionel Belman
D: James Whale
W: Francis Edwards Faragoh, Garrett Fort, John Balderston, Robert Florey

Frankenstein Created Woman
A: Peter Cushing, Susan Denberg, Thorley Walters, Robert Morris, Duncan Lamont, Peter Blythe, Alan McNaughton, Peter Madden
D: Terence Fisher
W: Anthony John, Elder Hines

Frankenstein Meets the Wolfman
A: Lon Chaney Jr., Bela Lugosi, Patric Knowles, Lionel Atwil, Maria Ouspenskaya, Ilona Massey, Dwight Frye
D: Roy William Neill
W: Curt Siodmak

Frankenstein Must Be Destroyed
A: Peter Cushing, Veronica Carlson, Freddie Jones, Maxine Audley, Simon Ward, Thorley Walters, George Pravda, Colette O'Neill
D: Terence Fisher
W: Bert Batt

Frankenstein Unbound
A: John Hurt, Raul Julia, Bridget Fonda, Jason Patric, Michael Hutchence, Catherine Rabett
D: Roger Corman
W: Roger Corman, F.X. Feeney

Freaks
A: Wallace Ford, Olga Baclanova, Leila Hyams, Roscoe Ates, Harry Earles, Henry Victor, Daisy Earles, Rose Dione, Daisy Hilton, Violet Hilton
D: Tod Browning
W: Al Boasberg, Willis Goldbeck, Leon Gordon, Edgar Allen Woolf

Freakshow
A: Gunnar Hansen, Veronica Carlson, Brian D. Kelly, Shannon Michelle Parsons
D: William Cooke, Paul Talbot
W: William Cooke, Paul Talbot

Freddy versus Jason
A: Robert Englund, Ken Kirzinger, Kelly Rowland, Jason Ritter, Monica Keena, Chris Marquette, Brendan Fletcher, Katharine Isabelle, Kyle Labine, Lochlyn Munro
D: Ronny Yu
W: Damian Shannon, Mark Swift

Freddy's Dead: The Final Nightmare
A: Robert Englund, Lisa Zane, Shon Greenblatt, Leslie Deane, Ricky Dean Logan, Brecklin Majer, Yaphet Kotto, Roseanne, Johnny Depp, Alice Cooper, Tom Arnold
D: Rachel Talalay
W: Michael De Luca

Friday the 13th (1980)
A: Betsy Palmer, Adrienne King, Harry Crosby, Laurie Bartram, Mark Nelson, Kevin Bacon, Jeannine Taylor
D: Sean Cunningham
W: Victor Miller

Friday the 13th (2009)
A: Amanda Righetti, Derek Mears, Jared Padalecki, Danielle Panabaker, Travis Van Winkle, Aaron Yoo
D: Marcus Nispel
W: Damian Shannon, Mark Swift

Friday the 13th Part II
A: Amy Steel, John Furey, Adrienne King, Betsy Palmer, Kirsten Baker
D: Steve Miner
W: Ron Kurz

Friday the 13th Part III
A: Dana Kimmell, Paul Kratka, Richard Booker, Catherine Parks
D: Steve Miner
W: Martin Kitrosser

Friday the 13th Part IV
A: Erich Anderson, Judie Aronson, Kimberly Beck, Peter Barton, Tom Everett, Corey Feldman
D: Joseph Zito
W: Barney Cohen

Friday the 13th Part V
A: John Shepherd, Melanie Kinnaman, Shavar Ross, Richard Young, Juliette Cummings, Corey Feldman
D: Danny Steinmann
W: Danny Steinmann

Friday the 13th Part VI
A: Thom Matthews, Jennifer Cooke, David Kagen, Kerry Noonan, Renee Jones
D: Tom McLoughlin
W: Tom McLoughlin

Friday the 13th Part VII
A: Lar Park Lincoln, Kevin Blair, Susan Blu, Terry Kiser, Kane Hodder
D: John Carl Buechler
W: Daryl Heney

Friday the 13th Part VIII
A: Jensen Daggett, Scott Reeves, Peter Mark Richman, Kane Hodder
D: Rob Hedden
W: Rob Hedden

Fright Night (1985)
A: William Ragsdale, Chris Sarandon, Amanda Bearse, Roddy McDowall, Stephen Geoffreys
D: Tom Holland
W: Tom Holland

Fright Night (2011)
A: Colin Farrell, Anton Yelchin, David Tennant, Toni Collette, Imogen Poots, Chistopher Mintz-Plasse, Dave Franco
D: Craig Gillespie
W: Marti Noxon

Fright Night Part 2 (1988)
A: Roddy McDowall, William Ragsdale, Traci Lind, Julie Carmen, Jonathan Gries

D: Tommy Lee Wallace
W: Tommy Lee Wallace, Tim Metcalfe, Miguel Tejada-Flores

Frighteners, The
A: Michael J. Fox, Trini Alvardo, Peter Dobson, Dee Wallace Stone, John Astin, Jeffrey Combs, Troy Evans, Chi McBride, Jake Busey, R. Lee Ermey, Jim Fyfe
D: Peter Jackson
W: Peter Jackson, Frances Walsh

From Beyond
A: Jeffrey Combs, Barbara Crampton, Ted Sorel, Ken Foree, Carolyn Purdy-Gordon, Bunny Summers, Bruce McGuire
D: Stuart Gordon
W: Dennie Baoli, Brian Yuzna

From Dusk 'til Dawn
A: George Clooney, Quentin Tarantino, Harvey Kietel, Juliette Lewis, Ernest Liu, Fred Williamson, Richard "Cheech" Marin, Salma Hayek, Michael Parks, Tom Savini, Kelly Preston, John Saxon, Danny Trejo
D: Robert Rodriguez
W: Quentin Tarantino

From Hell
A: Johnny Depp, Heather Graham, Ian Holm, Robert Coltrane, Ian Richardson, Jason Flemyng, Katrin Cartlidge, Susan Lynch, Paul Rhys, Lesley Sharp, Terence Harvey
D: Albert Hughes, Allen Hughes
W: Terry Hayes, Rafael Yglesias

Frontiere(s)
A: Karina Testa, Patrick Ligardes, Aurelien Wiik, Estelle Lefebure, Maud Forget, David Saracino
D: Xavier Gens
W: Xavier Gens

Funhouse, The
A: Elizabeth Berridge, Shawn Carson, Cooper Huckabee, Largo Woodruff, Sylvia Miles, Miles Chapin, Kevin Conway, William Finley, Wayne Doba
D: Tobe Hooper
W: Larry Block

Funny Games (1997)
A: Susanne Lothar, Ulriche Muehe, Arno Frisch, Frank Giering, Stefan Clapczynski, Doris Kunstmann, Christoph Bantzer
D: Michael Haneke
W: Michael Haneke

Funny Games (2007)
A: Tim Roth, Naomi Watts, Michael Pitt, Brady Corbet, Devon Gearhart, Boyd Gaines, Siobhan Fallon
D: Michael Haneke
W: Michael Haneke

Fury, The
A: Kirk Douglas, John Cassavetes, Carrie Snodgrass, Andrew Stevens, Amy Irving, Charles Durning, Carol Rossen, Rutanya Alda, Daryl Hannah, Dennis Franz, James Belushi
D: Brian DePalma
W: John Farris

Galaxy of Terror
A: Erin Moran, Edward Albert, Ray Walston, Grace Zabriskie, Zalman King, Taaffe O'Connell, Robert Englund
D: B.D. Clark
W: B.D. Clark, Mark Siegler

Gamara, Guardian of the Universe
A: Tsuyoshi Ihara, Akira Onodera, Shinobu Nakayama, Avako Fujitani, Yukihiro Hotaru, Hatsunori Hasegawa, Hirotora Honda
D: Shusuke Kaneko, Matt Greenfield
W: Kazunori Iro

Gate, The
A: Christa Denton, Stephen Dorff, Louis Tripp, Kelly Rowan, Jennifer Irwin
D: Tibor Takas
W: Michael Nankin

Gate II: The Trespassers
A: Louis Tripp, Simon Reynolds, Pamela Segall, James Villemaire, Neil Munro
D: Tibor Takas
W: Michael Nankin

Gathering, The
A: Christina Ricci, Stephen Dillane, Ioan Gruffudd, Kerry Fox, Simon Russell Beale, Harry Forrester, Jessica Mann, Peter McNamara, Mark Bagnall, Clare Bloomer
D: Brian Gilbert
W: Anthony Horowitz

Generation X-Tinct
A: Michael Passion, Lonnie Jackson, Suzanne Labatte
D: Michele Pacitto
W: Michele Pacitto

George Romero's Diary of the Dead
A: Michelle Morgan, Joshua Close, Shawn Roberts, Amy Lalonde, Joe Dinicol, Scott Wentworth, Philip Riccio, Chris Violette, Tatiana Maslany
D: George A. Romero
W: George A. Romero

Ghost Breakers
A: Bob Hope, Paulette Goddard, Richard Carlson, Paul Lukas, Willie Best, Pedro de Cordoba, Anthony Quinn
D: George Marshall
W: Walter DeLeon

Ghost Galleon
A: Maria Perschy, Jack Taylor, Barbara Rey
D: Amando de Ossorio
W: Amando de Ossorio

Ghost of Frankenstein
A: Cedrick Hardwicke, Lon Chaney Jr., Ralph Bellamy, Doris Lloyd, Barton Yarborough
D: Erle C. Kenton
W: Scott Darling

Ghost Rider
A: Nicolas Cage, Sam Elliott, Eva Mendes, Peter Fonda, Matt Long, Raquel Alessi, Donal Logue
D: Mark Steven Johnson
W: Mark Steven Johnson

Ghost Ship
A: Julianna Margulies, Ron Eldard, Gabriel Byrne, Isaiah Washington, Alex Dimitriades, Karl Urban, Emily Browning, Francesca Rettondini
D: Steve Beck
W: Mark Hanlon, John Pogue

Ghost Story
A: Fred Astaire, Melvyn Douglas, Douglas Fairbanks Jr., John Houseman, Craig Wasson, Alice Krige, Patricia Neal
D: John Irvin
W: Lawrence D. Cohen

Ghostbusters
A: Bill Murray, Dan Aykroyd, Harold Ramis, Rick Moranis, Sigourney Weaver, Annie Potts, Ernie Hudson, William Atherton, David Margulies, Steven Tash
D: Ivan Reitman
W: Dan Aykroyd, Harold Ramis

Ghostbusters II
A: Bill Murray, Dan Aykroyd, Sigourney Weaver, Harold Ramis, Rick Moranis, Ernie Hudson, Peter MacNicol, David Margulies, Wilhelm von Homburg, Harris Yulin, Annie Potts, Ben Stein, Richard "Cheech" Marin, Brian Doyle-Murray, Janet Margolin
D: Ivan Reitman
W: Dan Aykroyd, Harold Ramis

Ghosts of Mars
A: Natasha Henstridge, Ice Cube, Pam Grier, Jason Statham, Clea DuVall, Joanna Cassidy, Richard Cetrone, Liam Waite
D: John Carpenter
W: John Carpenter, Larry Sulkis

Ghoul, The
A: Boris Karloff, Cedric Hardwick, Ernest Thesiger, Dorothy Hyson, Ralph Richardson, Anthony Bushell, Kathleen Harrison, Harold Huth
D: Hayes Hunter
W: Roland Pertwee, John Hastings Turner, Rupert Downing

Giant Spider Invasion
A: Steve Brodie, Barbara Hale, Leslie Parrish, Robert Easton, Alan Hale Jr., Dianne Lee Hart, Bill Williams, Christianne Schmidtmer
D: Bill Rebane
W: Bill Rebane, Richard L. Huff, Robert Easton

Ginger Snaps
A: Emily Perkins, Katharine Isabelle, Kris Lemche, Kris Lemche, Mimi Rogers, Jesse Moss, Danielle Hampton, John Bourgeois, Peter Keleghan, Christopher Redman, Jimmy MacInnis
D: John Fawcett
W: Karen Walton

Ginger Snaps Back: The Beginning
A: Emily Perkins, Katharine Isabelle, Nathaniel Arcand, J. R. Bourne, Hugh Dillon, Adrien Dorval, Brendan Fletcher, David La Haye, Tom McCamus
D: Grant Harvey
W: Christina Ray, Stephen Massicotte

God Told Me To
A: Tony LoBianco, Deborah Raffin, Sylvia Sidney, Sandy Dennis, Richard Lynch, Sam Levene, Andy Kaufman
D: Larry Cohen
W: Larry Cohen

Godsend
A: Robert De Niro, Greg Kinnear, Rebecca Romijn, Cameron Bright
D: Nick Hamm
W: Mark Bomback

Gojira (Godzilla)
A: Takashi Shimura, Akihiko Hirata, Akira Tadarada
D: Ishiro Honda
W: Ishiro Honda

Godzilla
A: Matthew Broderick, Jean Reno, Maria Pitillo, Hank Azaria, Kevin Dunn, Harry Shearer, Arabella Field
D: Roland Emmerich
W: Dean Devlin, Roland Emmerich

Golem, The
A: Paul Wegener, Albert Steinruck, Ernst Deutsch, Lyda Salmonava, Otto Gebuehr
D: Carl Boese, Paul Wegener
W: Henrik Galeen, Paul Wegener

Gorgon, The
A: Peter Cushing, Christopher Lee, Richard Pasco, Barbara Shelley, Michael Goodliffe, Patrick Troughton, Prudence Hyman
D: Terence Fisher
W: John Gilling

Gothic
A: Julian Sands, Gabriel Byrne, Timothy Spall, Natasha Richardson, Myrian Cyr
D: Ken Russell
W: Stephen Volk

Gothika
A: Halle Berry, Robert Downey Jr., Penelope Cruz, Charles S. Dutton, John Carroll Lynch, Bernard Hill, Dorian Harewood, Kathleen Mackey, Andrea Sheldon
D: Mathieu Kassovitz
W: Sebastian Gutierrez

Graveyard Shift
A: Silvio Oliviero, Helen Papas, Cliff Stoker
D: Gerard Ciccoritti
W: Gerard Ciccoritti

Gremlins
A: Zach Galligan, Phoebe Cates, Hoyt Axton, Polly Holliday, Frances Lee McCain, Keye Luke, Dick Miller, Corey Feldman, Judge Reinhold, Glynn Turman, Scott Brady, Jackie Joseph
D: Joe Dante
W: Chris Columbus

Gremlins 2: The New Batch
A: Zach Galligan, Phoebe Cates, John Glover, Christopher Lee, Robert Prosky, Robert Picardo, Haviland Morris, Dick Miller, Jackie Joseph, Keye Luke, Belinda Balaski, Paul Bartel, Kenneth Tobey, John Astin, Henry Gibson, Leonard Maltin, Hulk Hogan. Cameos: Jerry Goldsmith
D: Joe Dante
W: Charles Haas

Grindhouse
A: Kurt Russell, Bruce Willis, Rose McGowan, Danny Trejo, Cheech Marin, Freddy Rodriguez, Josh Brolin, Marley Shelton, Jeff Fahey, Michael Biehn, Rebel Rodriguez, Naveen Andrews, Julio Oscar Mechoso, Stacy Ferguson, Nicky Katt, Hung Nguyen
D: Robert Rodriquez, Eli Roth, Quentin Tarantino, Edgar Wright, Rob Zombie
W: Robert Rodriquez, Rob Zombie, Edgar Wright, Jeff Rendell, Eli Roth, Quentin Tarantino, Rob Cotteril, John Davies, Jason Eisener

Grudge, The
A: Sarah Michelle Gellar, Jason Behr, Clea DuVall, William Mapother, KaDee Strickland, Grace Zabriskie, Bill Pullman, Rosa Blasi, Ted Raiml
D: Takashi Shimizu
W: Stephen Susco

Habitat
A: Alice Krige, Balthazar Getty, Tcheky Karyo, Kenneth Welsh
D: Renee Daadler
W: Renee Daadler

Halloween (1978)
A: Jamie Lee Curtis, Donald Pleasance, Nancy Loomis, P.J. Soles, Charles Cyphers
D: John Carpenter
W: John Carpenter, Debra Hill

Halloween (2007)
A: Malcolm McDowell, Scout Taylor-Compton, Tyler Mane, Daeg Faerch, Sheri Moon Zombie, William Forsythe, Danielle Harris, Kristina Klebe, Skyler Gisondo, Danny Trejo, Hanna Hall
D: Rob Zombie
W: Rob Zombie

Halloween II (1981)
A: Jamie Lee Curtis, Donald Pleasance, Jeffrey Kramer, Charles Cyphers, Lance Guest
D: Rick Rosenthal
W: John Carpenter, Debra Hill

Halloween II (2009)
A: Malcolm McDowell, Scout Taylor-Compton, Tyler Mane, Sheri Moon Zombie, Chase Wright Vanek, Dayton Callie, Richard Brake, Brad Dourif
D: Rob Zombie
W: Rob Zombie

Halloween 3: Season of the Witch
A: Tom Atkins, Stacey Nelkin, Dan O'Herlihy, Ralph Strait, Michael Currie
D: Tommy Lee Wallace
W: Tommy Lee Wallace

Halloween 4: The Return of Michael Myers
A: Donald Pleasance, Ellie Cornell, Danielle Harris, Michael Pataki, George P. Wilbur, Kathleen Kinmont
D: Dwight Little
W: Alan B. McElroy

Halloween 5: The Revenge of Michael Myers
A: Donald Pleasance, Ellie Cornell, Danielle Harris, Don Shanks, Betty Carvalho
D: Dominique Othenin-Girard
W: Dominique Othenin-Girard, Shem Bitterman, Michael Jacobs

Halloween H20: Twenty Years Later
A: Donald Pleasance, Mitchell Ryan, Marianna Hagan, Leo Geter, George P. Wilbur, Kim Darby
D: Joe Chappelle
W: Daniel Farrands

Halloween: Resurrection
A: Jamie Lee Curtis, Brad Loree, Busta Rhymes, Bianca Kajilich, Sean Patrick Thomas, Daisy McCrackin, katee Sackhoff, Luke Kirby, Thomas Ian Nicholas
D: Rick Rosenthal
W: Larry Brand, Sean Hood

Hand, The
A: Michael Caine, Andrea Marcovicci, Annie McEnroe, Bruce McGill, Viveca Lindfors, Oliver Stone
D: Oliver Stone
W: Oliver Stone

Hands of Orloc
A: Mel Ferrer, Christopher Lee, Felix Aylmer, Basic Sydney, Donald Wolfit, Donald Pleasance
D: Edmond T. Greville
W: Edmond T. Greville, John Baines, Donald Taylor

Hands of the Ripper
A: Eric Porter, Angharad Rees, Jane Merrow, Keith Bell
D: Peter Sasdy
W: L.W. Davidson

Hanging Woman
A: Stan Cooper, Vickie Nesbitt, Marcella Wright, Paul Naschy, Dianik Zurakowska
D: Jose Luis Merino
W: Jose Luis Merino

Hannibal
A: Anthony Hopkins, Julianne Moore, Gary Oldman, Ray Liotta, Francesca Neri, Hazelle Goodman
D: Ridley Scott
W: David Mamet, Steven Zaillian

Hannibal Rising
A: Gaspard Ulliel, Rhys Ifans, Li Gong, helena-Lia Tachovska, Richard Leaf, Dominic West, Rhys Ifans, Richard Brake
D: Peter Webber
W: Thomas Harris

Harvest, The
A: Miguel Ferrer, Leilani Sarelle Ferrer, Harvey Fierstein, Anthony Denison, Tim Thomerson, Matt Clark, Henry Silva
D: David Marconi
W: David Marconi

Haunted
A: Aidan Quinn, Kate Beckinsale, Anthony Andrews, Alex Lowe, Anna Massey, Geraldine Somerville, Victoria Shalet, John Gielgud
D: Lewis Gilbert
W: Lewis Gilbert, Bob Kellett, Tim Prager

Haunted Summer
A: Alice Krige, Eric Stoltz, Philip Anglim, Laura Dern, Alex Winter
D: Ivan Passer
W: Lewis John Carlino

Haunting, The (1963)
A: Julie Harris, Claire Bloom, Russ Tamblyn, Richard Johnson, Fay Compton, Rosalie Crutchley, Lois Maxwell, Valentine Dyall, Diane Clare
D: Robert Wise
W: Nelson Gidding

Haunting, The (1999)
A: Liam Neeson, Catherine Zeta-Jones, Owen Wilson, Bruce Dern, Lili Taylor, Marian Seldes, Alix Koromzay, Todd Field, Virginia Madsen, Michael Cavanaugh
D: Jan de Bont
W: David Self

Haunting in Connecticut
A: Virginia Madsen, Martin Donovan, Elias Koteas, Kyle Gallner, Amanda Crew, Sophi Knight, Ty Wood
D: Peter Cornwell
W: Adam Simon, Tim Metcalfe

Haunting of Molly Hartley, The
A: haley Bennett, Jake Weber, Chace Crawford, Shannon Woodward, AnnaLynne McCord, Marin Hinkle, Nina Siemaszko, Shanna Collins
D: Mickey Liddell
W: John Travis, Rebecca Sonnenshine

He Knows You're Alone
A: Don Scardino, Caitlin (Kathleen Heaney) O'Heaney, Tom Rolfing, Paul Gleason, Elizabeth Kemp, Tom Hanks, Patsy Pease, Lewis Alt, James Rebhorn, Joseph Leon, James Carroll
D: Armand Mastroianni
W: Scott Parker

Heartless
A: Jim Sturgess, Luke Treadaway, Clemence Poesy, Justin Salinger, Noel Clarke, Fraser Ayres, Ruth Sheen, Timothy Spall
D: Philip Ridley
W: Philip Ridley

Hell Night
A: Linda Blair, Vincent Van Patten, Kevin Brophy, Peter Barton, Jenny Newmann
D: Tom De Simone
W: Randy Feldman

Hellbound: Hellraiser 2
A: Ashley Laurence, Clare Higgins, Kenneth Cranham, Imogen Boorman, William Hope, Oliver Smith, Sean Chapman, Doug Bradley
D: Tony Randel
W: Peter Atkins

Hellboy
A: Ron Perlman, Selma Blair, Doug Jones, John Hurt, Doug Jones, Rupert Evans, karel roden, Jeffrey Tambor, Brian Steele, Biddy Hodson
D: Guillermo del Toro
W: Guillermo del Toro

Hellboy II: The Golden Army
A: Ron Perlman, Selma Blair, Doug Jones, John Alexander, Seth MacFarlane, Anna Walton, Jeffrey Tambor, John Hurt, James Dodd, Luke Goss
D: Guillermo del Toro
W: Guillermo del Toro

Hello, Mary Lou: Prom Night 2
A: Michael Ironside, Wendy Lyon, Justin Louis, Lisa Schrage, Richard Monette
D: Bruce Bittman
W: Ron Oliver

Hellraiser
A: Andrew (Andy) Robinson, Clare Higgins, Ashley Laurence, Sean Chapman, Oliver Smith, Robert Hines, Doug Bradley, Nicholas Vince
D: Clive Barker
W: Clive Barker

Hellraiser 3
A: Doug Bradley, Terry Farrell, Kevin Bernhardt, Paula Marshall, Ken Carpenter, Ashley Laurence
D: Anthony Hickox
W: Peter Atkins

Henry: Portrait of a Serial Killer
A: Michael Rooker, Tom Towles, Tracy Arnold
D: John McNaughton
W: John McNaughton

Hide and Seek
A: Robert De Niro, Dakota Fanning, Famke Janssen, Amy Irving, Elisabeth Shue, Dylan Baker
D: John Polson
W: Ari Schlossberg

Hideous Sun Demon
A: Robert Clarke, Patricia Manning, Nan Peterson, Patrick Whyte, Peter Similuk. Fred La Porta, Robert Garry
D: Robert Clarke
W: Doane R. Hoag, E.S. Seeley Jr.

High Tension
A: Cecile De France, Philippe Nahon, Maiwenn, Franck Khalfoun, Oana Pellea, Andrei Finti, Marco Claudiu Pascu
D: Alexandre Aja
W: Alexandre Aja, Gregory Levasseur

Hills Have Eyes, The (1977)
A: Susan Lanier, Robert Houston, Martin Speer, Dee Wallace Stone, Russ Grieve, John Steadman, James Whitworth, Michael Berryman, Virginia Vincent, Lance Gordon, Janus Blythe
D: Wes Craven
W: Wes Craven

Hills Have Eyes, The (2006)
A: Ted Levine, Dan Byrd, Kathleen Quinlan, Dan Byrd, Emilie de Ravin, Billy Drago, Robert Joy, Ted Levine, Desmond Askew, Michael Bailey Smith, Laura Ortiz, Ezra Buzzington
D: Alexandra Aja
W: Alexandra Aja

Hills Have Eyes II, The (2007)
A: Daniella Alonso, Jacob Vargas, Michael Bailey, Lee Thompson Young, Daniella Alonso, Jacob Vargas, Reshad Strik, Ben Crowley, Derek Mears, Michael Bailey Smith
D: Martin Weisz
W: Wes Craven, Jonathan Craven

Hills Have Eyes Part II, The (1985)
A: Michael Berryman, Kevin Blair, John (Joe Bob Briggs) Bloom, Janus Blythe, John Laughlin, Tamara Stafford, Peter Frechette
D: Wes Craven
W: Wes Craven

Hitcher, The
A: Rutger Hauer, C. Thoms Howell, Jennifer Jason Leigh, Jeffrey DeMunn, John M. Jackson, Billy Green Bush
D: Robert Harmon
W: Eric Red

Hole, The
A: Keira Knightley, Thora Birch, Desmond Harrington, Daniel Brocklebank, Embeth Davidtz
D: Nick Hamm
W: Ben Court, Caroline Ip

Hollow Man
A: Kevin Bacon, Josh Brolin, Elisabeth Shue, Kim Dickens, Joey Slotnick, Greg Grunberg, Mary Randle, William Devane, Margot Rose
D: Paul Verhoeven
W: Andrew W. Marlowe

Horror Chamber of Dr. Faustus, The
A: Alida Valli, Pierre Brasseur, Edith Scob, Francois Guerin
D: Georges Franju
W: Jean Readon, Pierre Boileau

Horror Express
A: Christopher Lee, Peter Cushing, Telly Savalas, Alberto De Mendoza, Sylvia Tortosa, Julio Pena, Ange; Del Pozo, Helga Line, Jorge Rigaud, Jose Jaspe
D: Gene Martin
W: Julian Zimet, Arnaud d'Usseau

Horror Hotel
A: Christopher Lee, Patricia Jessel, Betta St. John, Dennis Lotis, Venetia Stevenson, Valentine Dyall
D: John Llewellyn Moxey
W: George Baxt

Horror of Dracula
A: Peter Cushing, Christopher Lee, Michael Gough, Melissa Stribling, Carol Marsh, John Van Eyssen, Valerie Gaunt, Charles Lloyd Pack, Miles Malleson
D: Terence Fisher
W: Jimmy Sangster

Horror of Frankenstein
A: Ralph Bates, Kate O'Mara, Dennis Price, David Prowse, Veronica Carlson, Joan Rice
D: Jimmy Sangster
W: Jimmy Sangster

Host, The
A: Kang-ho Song, Hie-bong Byeon, Hae-il Park, Doona Bae, Ah-sung-Ko, Dal-su Oh, Dong-ho Lee, Jae-eung, Lee
D: Joon-ho Bong
W: Joon-ho Bong, Won-jun Ha, Chul-hyun Baek

Hostel
A: Jay Hernandez, Derek Richardson, Eythor Gudjonsson, Barbara Nedeljakova
D: Eli Roth
W: Eli Roth

Hostel: Part II
A: Lauren German, Heather Matarazzo, Bijou Phillips, Roger Bart, Vera Jordanova, Richard Burgi, Jay Hernandez, Milan Knazko, Jordan Ladd
D: Eli Roth
W: Eli Roth

Hostel: Part III
A: Kip Pardue, John Hensley, Brian Hallisay, Chris Coy, Sarah Habel, Thomas Kretschmann, Skyler Stone, Nickola Shreli, Zulay Henao
D: Scott Spiegel
W: Michael D. Weiss

Hour of the Wolf
A: Max Von Sydow, Liv Ullmann, Ingrid Thulin, Erland Josephson, Gertrud Fridh, Gudrun Brost, Georg Rydeberg, Naima Wifstrand, Bertil Anderberg, Ulf Johansson
D: Ingmar Bergman
W: Ingmar Bergman

House
A: William Katt, George Wendt, Richard Moll, Kay Lenz, Michael Ensign, Mary Stavin, Susan French
D: Steve Miner
W: Ethan Wiley

House II: The Second Story
A: John Ratzenberger, Arye Gross, Royal Dano, Bill Maher, Jonathan Stark, Lar Park Lincloln, Amy Yasbeck, Devin Devasquez
D: Ethan Wiley
W: Ethan Wiley

House of Dark Shadows
A: Jonathan Frid, Joan Bennett, Grayson Hall, Kathryn Leigh Scott, Roger Davis, Nancy Barrett, John Karlen, Thayer David, Louis Edmonds
D: Dan Curtis
W: Sam Hall, Gordon Russell

House of Dracula
A: Lon Chaney Jr., Martha O'Driscoll, John Carradine, Lionel Atwill, Onslow Stevens, Glenn Strange, Jane Adams, Ludwig Stossel
D: Erle C. Kenton
W: Edward T. Lowe

House of Frankenstein
A: Boris Karloff, J. Carrol Naish, Lon Chaney Jr., John Carradine, Elena Verduga, Anne Gwyeen, Lionel Atwill, Peter Coe, George Zucco, Glen Strange, Sig Rumann
D: Erle C. Kenton
W: Edward T. Lowe

House of 1,000 Corpses
A: Sid Haig, Bill Moseley, Karen Black, William Bassett, Chad Bannon, Erin Daniels, Joe Dobbs III, Judith Drake, Gregg Gibbs, Waltin Goggins, Ken Johnson, Jennifer Jostyn, Walton Goggins, Irwin Keyes
D: Rob Zombie
W: Rob Zombie

House of the Dead
A: Jonathan Cherry, Tyron Leitso, Clint Howard, Ona Grauer, Ellie Cornell, Will Sanderson, Enuka Okuma, Sonya Salomaa, Kira Clavell, Michael Eklund, David Palffy
D: Uwe Boll
W: Dave Parker, Mark A. Altman

House of the Devil
A: Jocelin Donahue, Mary Woronov, Tom Noonan, A. J. Bowen, Greta Gerwig, Dee Wallace, Brenda Cooney, Mary B McCann, Danielle Noe, John Speredakos
D: Ti West
W: Ti West

House of Wax (1953)
A: Vincent Price, Frank Lovejoy, Carolyn Jones, Phyllis Kirk, Paul Cavanaugh, Charles Bronson, Paul Picerni
D: Andre de Toth
W: Crane Wilbur

House of Wax (2005)
A: Chad Michael Murray, Paris Hilton, Elisha Cuthbert, Brian Van Holt, Elisha Cuthbert, Jared Padalecki, Jon Abrahams, Robert Richard, Dragicia debert, Thomas Adamson, Murray smith, Sam Harkness
D: Jaume Collet-Serra
W: Chad Hayes

House on Haunted Hill (1958)
A: Vincent Price, Carol Ohmart, Richard Long, Alan Marshal, Carolyn Craig, Elisha Cook Jr.
D: William Castle
W: Robb White

House on Haunted Hill (1999)
A: Geoffrey Rush, Taye Diggs, Famke Janssen, Peter Gallagher, Chris Kattan, Ali Larter, Bridgette Wilson-Sampras, jeffrey Combs, Max Perlich, Dick Beebe
D: William Malone
W: Dick Beebe

House on Sorority Row
A: Eileen Davidson, Kate McNeil, Robin Melody, Lois Kelso Hunt, Christopher Lawrence, Janis Zido
D: Mark Rosman
W: Mark Rosman

House on Straw Hill
A: Udo Kier, Linda Hayden, Fiona Richmond, Karl Howman, Patsy Smart
D: James Kenelm Clark
W: James Kenelm Clark

House That Vanished, The
A: Andrea Allan, Karl Lanchburg, Judy Matheson, Maggie Walker, Alex Leppard
D: Joseph (Jose Ramon) Larras
W: Derek Fod

Howling, The
A: Dee Wallace Stone, Patrick Macnee, Dennis Dugan, Christopher Stone, Belinda Balaski, Kevin McCarthy, John Carradine, Slim Pickens, Elisabeth Brooks, Robert Picardo, Dick Miller, Kenneth Tobey. Cameos: John Sayles, Roger Corman
D: Joe Dante
W: John Sayles, Terence H. Winkless

Howling II: Your Sister Is a Werewolf
A: Sybil Danning, Christopher Lee, Annie McEnroe, Marsha Hunt, Reb Brown, Ferdinand "Ferdy" Mayne, Judd Omen, Jimmy Naill
D: Philippe Mora
W: Gary Brandner, Robert Sarner

Howling III: The Marsupials
A: Barry Otto, Imogen Annesley, Dashy Blahova, Max Fairchild

D: Philippe Mora
W: Gary Brandner, Philippe Mora

Howling IV: The Original Nightmare
A: Romy Windsor, Michael T. Weiss, Anthony Hamilton
D: John Hough
W: Gary Brandner, Clive Turner

Howling: New Moon Rising
A: Clive Turner, John Ramsden, Ernest Kester, Elizabeth She, Jacqueline Armitage, Romy Windsor
D: Clive Turner
W: Clive Turner

Human Centipede [First Sequence]
A: Dieter Laser, Ashley C. Williams, Ashlynn Yennie
D: Tom Six
W: Tom Six

Human Centipede [Full Sequence]
A: Ashlynn Yennie, Maddi Black, Laurence R. Harvey, Emma Lock, Georgia Goodrick, Daniel Jude Gennis, Dan Burman, Lee Nicholas Harris, Lucas Hansen, Dominic Borrelli, Kandace Caine
D: Tom Six
W: Tom Six

Humanoids from the Deep (1980)
A: Doug McClure, Ann Turkel, Vic Morrow, Cindy Weintraub, Anthony Penya
D: Barbara Peeters
W: Frank Arnold, Frederick James

Humanoids from the Deep (1997)
A: Robert Carradine, Emma Samms, Mark Rolston
D: Jeff Yonis
W: Martin B. Cohen, Jeff Yonis

Hunchback of Norte Dame (1923)
A: Lon Chaney Sr., Patsy Ruth Miller, Norman Kerry, Ernest Torrence, Kate Lester, Brandon Hurst
D: Wallace Worley
W: Edward T. Lowe

Hunchback of Notre Dame (1939)
A: Charles Laughton, Maureen O'Hara, Edmond O'Brien, Cedric Hardwick, Thomas Mitchell, George Zucco, Alan Marshal, Walter Hampden, Harry Davenport, Curt Bois, George Tobias, Rod La Ricque
D: William Dieterle
W: Sonya Levien, Bruno Frank

Hunchback of Notre Dame (1957)
A: Anthony Quinn, Gina Lollobrigida, Alain Cuny, Jean Danet, Robert Hirsch, Jean Dissier
D: Jean Delannoy
W: Jacques Prevert, Jean Aurenche

Hunchback of Notre Dame (1982)
A: Anthony Hopkins, Derek Jacobi, Lesley-Anne Down, John Gielgud, Tim Pigott-Smith, Rosalie Crutchley, Robert Powell
D: Michael Tuchner
W: John Gay

Hunger, The
A: Catherine Deneuve, David Bowie, Susan Sartandon, Cliff DeYoung, Ann Maguson, Dan Hedaya, Willen Dafoe, Beth Ehlers
D: Tony Scott
W: Michael Thomas, Ian Davis

Hush, Hush, Sweet Charlotte
A: Bette Davis, Olivia de Havilland, Joseph Cotten, Agnes Moorehead, Mary Astor, Bruce Dern, Cecil Kellaway, Victor Buono
D: Robert Aldrich
W: Lukas Heller, Henry Farrell

I Am Legend
A: Will Smith, Alice Braga, Charlie Tahan, Willow Smith, Zoe Neville
D: Francis Lawrence
W: Mark Protosevich, Akiva Goldsman

I Dismember Mama
A: Zooey Hall, Joanne Moore Jordan, Gerg Mullavey, Marlene Tracy, Geri Reischi, Marlene Tracy
D: Paul Leder
W: William W. Norton Sr.

I Know What You Did Last Summer
A: Jennifer Love Hewitt, Sarah Michelle Gellar, Ryan Phillippe, Freddie Prinze Jr., Muse Watson, Anne Heche, Bridgette Wilson, Johnny Galecki, Dan Albright
D: Jim Gillespie
W: Kevin Williamson

I Sell the Dead
A: Ron Perlman, Dominic Monaghan, Larry Fessenden, Angus Scrimm, Brenda Cooney, John Speredako, Eileen Colgan, Daniel Manche
D: Glenn McQuaid
W: Glenn McQuaid

I Spit on Your Grave (1978)
A: Camielle Keaton, Eron Tabor, Richard Pace, Anthony Nichols, Gunter Kleeman
D: Mier Zarchi
W: Mier Zarchi

I Spit on Your Grave (2010)
A: Sarah Butler, Andrew Howard, Jeff Branson, Daniel Franzese, Rodney Eastman, Chad Lindberg
D: Steven R. Monroe
W: Stuart Morse

I Still Know What You Did Last Summer
A: Jennifer Love Hewitt, Freddie Prinze Jr., Brandy Norwood, Mekhi Phifer, Muse Watson, Matthew Settle, Bill Cobbs, Jeffrey Combs, Jennifer Esposito, John Hawkes
D: Dianny Cannon
W: Trey Callaway

I Walked with a Zombie
A: Frances Dee, Tom Conway, James Ellison, Christine Gordon, Edith Barrett, Darby Jones, Sir Lancelot
D: Jacques Tourneur
W: Curt Siodmak, Ardel Wray

I Was a Teenage Frankenstein
A: Gary Conway, Whit Bissell, Robert Burton, Phyllis Coates, George Lynn
D: Herbert L. Strock
W: Aben Kandel

I Was a Teenage Werewolf
A: Michael Landon, Yvonne Lime, Whit Bissell, Tony Marshall, Dawn Richard, Barney Phillips
D: Gene Fowler Jr.
W: Ralph Thornton

Identity
A: John Cusack, Amanda Peet, Ray Liotta, John Hawkes, Clea DuVall, John C. McGinley, Alfred Monley, William Lee Scott, Jake Busey, Pruitt Taylor Vince, Rebecca De Mornay
D: James Mangold
W: Michael Cooney

Idle Hands
A: Seth Green, Jessica Alba, Devon Sawa, Elden Henson, Vivica A. Fox, Christopher Hart, Katie Wright, Jack Noseworthy, Sean Whalen
D: Rodman Flender
W: Terri Hughes, Ron Milbauer

I'm Dangerous Tonight
A: Madchen Amick, Corey Parker, R. Lee Ermey, Mary Frann, Dee Wallace Stone, Anthony Perkins, Natalie Schafer, William Berger
D: Tobe Hooper
W: Alice Wilson

In the Mouth of Madness
A: Sam Neill, Juergen Prochnow, Julie Carmen, Charlton Heston, David Warner, John Glover, Bernie Casey, Peter Jason, Frances Bay
D: John Carpenter
W: Michael De Luca

Incredible Shrinking Man, The
A: Grant Williams, Randy Stuart, April Kent, Paul Langton, Raymond Bailey, William Schllert, Frank Scanell, Billy Curtis
D: Jack Arnold
W: Richard Matheson

Indestructible Man
A: Lon Chaney Jr., Marian Carr, Max Casey, Adams Showalter
D: Jack Pollexfen
W: Vy Russell, Sue Dwiggins

Infestation
A: Chris Marquette, Brooke Nevin, Kinsey Packard, Wesley Thompson, E. Quincy Sloan, Linda Park, Jim Cody Williams, Deborah Geffner, Bru Muller
D: Kyle Rankin
W: Kyle Rankin

Innkeepers, The
A: Sara Paxton, Pat Healy, Kelly McGillis, Alison Bartlett, Jake Ryan, Lena Dunham
D: Ti West
W: Ti West

Innocent Blood
A: Anne Parillaud, Anthony LaPaglia, Robert Loggia, David Proval, Don Rickles, Rocco Sisto, Kim Coates, Chazz Palminteri, Angela Bassett, Tom Savini, Frank Oz, Forrest J. Ackerman, Sam Raimi, Dario Argento, Linnea Quigley
D: John Landis
W: Michael Wolk

Inside
A: Beatrice Dalle, Nathalie Roussel, Alysson Paradis, Francois-Regis Marchasson, Jean-Baptiste Tabourin
D: Alexandre Bustillo, Julien Maury
W: Alexandre Bustillo

Interview with the Vampire: The Vampire Chronicles
A: Tom Cruise, Brad Pitt, Kirsten Dunst, Christian Slater, Antonio Banderas, Stephen Rea, Domiziana Giordano
D: Neil Jordan
W: Anne Rice

Invasion, The
A: Nicole Kidman, Daniel Craig, Jeremy Northam, Jeffrey Wright, Jackson Bond, Veronica Cartwright, Josef Sommer, Celia Weston, Roger Rees
D: Oliver Hirschbiegel, James McTeigue
W: David Kajganich

Invasion of the Body Snatchers (1956)
A: Kevin McCarthy, Dana Wynter, Carolyn Jones, King Donovan, Larry Gates, Jean Willes, Whitt Bissell, Sam Peckinpah, Donald Siegel
D: Donald Siegel
W: Daniel Mainwaring, Sam Peckinpah

Invasion of the Body Snatchers (1978)
A: Donald Sutherland, Brooke Adams, Veronica Cartwright, Leonard Nimoy, Jeff Goldblum. Kevin McCarthy, Donald Siegel, Art Hindle, Robert Duvall
D: Philip Kaufman
W: W.D. Richter

Invisible Man, The
A: Claude Rains, Gloria Stuart, Dudley Digges, William Harrigan, Una O'Connor, E.E. Clive, Dwight Frye, Henry Travers, Holmes Herbert, John Carradine, Walter Brennan
D: James Whale
W: R.C. Sherriff

Invisible Man Returns, The
A: Cedric Hardwicke, Vincent Price, John Sutton, Nan Gray
D: Joe May
W: Lester Cole, Curt Siodmak

Invisible Man's Revenge, The
A: John Hall, John Carradine, Gale Sondergaard, Lester Matthews, Evelyn Ankers, Alan Curtis, Leon Errol, Doris Lloyd
D: Ford Beebe
W: Bertram Millhauser

Island of Dr. Moreau (1977)
A: Burt Lancaster, Michael York, Nigel Davenport, Barbara Carrera, Richard Basehart, Nick Cravat
D: Don Taylor
W: John Herman Shaner, Al Ramrus

Island of Dr. Moreau (1996)
A: Marlon Brando, David Thewlis, Fairuza Balk, Marco Hofschneider, Temuera Morrison, Ron Perlman
D: John Frankenheimer
W: Richard Stanley, Ron Hutchinson

Island of Lost Souls
A: Charles Laughton, Bela Lugosi, Richard Arlen, Leila Hyams, Kathleen Burke, Stanley Fields, Robert F. (Bob) Kortman, Arthur Hohl. Cameos Alan Ladd, Randolph Scott, Buster Crabbe
D: Erle C. Kenton
W: Philip Wylie, Waldemar Young

Isle of the Dead
A: Boris Karloff, Ellen Drew, Marc Cramer, Katherine Emery, Helen Thimig, Alan Napier, Jason Robards Sr.
D: Mark Robson
W: Josef Mischel, Ardel Wray

It!
A: Roddy McDowell, Paul Maxwell, Jill Haworth, Noel Trevarthen, Ernest Clark, Ian McCulloch
D: Herbert J. Leder
W: Herbert J. Leder

It's Alive (1974)
A: John P. Ryan, Sharon Farrell, Andrew Duggan, Guy Stockwell, James Dixon, Michael Ansara
D: Larry Cohen
W: Larry Cohen

It's Alive (2008)
A: Bijou Phillips, James Murray, Raphael Coleman, Owen Teale, Jack Ellis, Ty Glaser, Ioan Karamfilov, Oliver Coopersmith, Skye Bennett, Arkie Reece
D: Josef Rusnak
W: Larry Cohen, Paul Sopocy, James Portolese

It's Alive 2: It Lives Again
A: Frederick Forrest, Kathleen Lloyd, John P. Ryan, Andrew Duggan, John Marley, Eddie Constantine
D: Larry Cohen
W: Larry Cohen

It's Alive III: Island of the Alive
A: Michael Moriarty, Karen Black, Laurene Landon, Gerrit Graham, James Dixon, Neal Israel, MacDonald Carey
D: Larry Cohen
W: Larry Cohen

Jack Be Nimble
A: Alexis Arquette, Sarah Kennedy, Bruno Lawrence
D: Garth Maxwell
W: Garth Maxwell

Jack-O
A: Linnea Quigley, Ryan Latshaw, Cameron Mitchell, John Carradine, Dawn Wildsmith, Brinke Stevens
D: Steve Latshaw
W: Brad Linaweaver

Jack's Back
A: James Spader, Cynthia Gibb, Rod Loomis, Rex Ryon, Robert Picardo, Jim Haynie, Chris Mulkey, Danitza Kingsley, Wendell Wright
D: Rowdy Herrington
W: Rowdy Herrington

Jacob's Ladder
A: Tim Robbins, Elizabeth Pena, Danny Aiello, Matt Craven, Pruitt Taylor Vince, Jason Alexander, Patricia Kalember, Eriq La Salle, Ving Rhames, Macaulay Culkin
D: Adrian Lyne
W: Bruce Joel Rubin

Jason Goes to Hell
A: John D. LeMay, Kane Hodder, Kari Keegan, Steven Williams, Steven Culp, Rusty Schimmer, Erin Gray, Leslie Jordan, Billy Green Bush
D: Adam Marcus
W: Dean Lorey, Jay Huguely

Jason X
A: Kane Hodder, Jeff Geddis, Lexa Doig, David Cronenberg, Jonathan Potts, Lisa Ryder, Markus Parilo, Dov Tiefenbach, Chuck Campbell, Boyd Banks
D: James Isaac
W: Todd Farmer

Jaws
A: Roy Scheider, Robert Shaw, Richard Dreyfuss, Lorraine Gary, Murray Hamilton, Carl Gottlieb. Cameos
A: Peter Benchley
D: Steven Spielberg
W: Carl Gottlieb, Peter Benchley

Jaws 2
A: Roy Scheider, Lorraine Gary, Murray Hamilton, Joseph Mascolo, Jeffrey Kramer, Collin Wilcox
D: Jeannot Szwarc
W: Carl Gottlieb, Howard Sackler

Jaws 3
A: Dennis Quaid, Bess Armstrong, Louis Gossett Jr., Simon McCorkindale, Lea Thompson, John Putch
D: Joe Alves
W: Richard Matheson, Carl Gottlieb

Jaws: The Revenge
A: Lorraine Gary, Michael Caine, Lance Guest, Mario Van Peebles, Karen Young, Judith Barsi, Mitchell Anderson
D: Joseph Sargent
W: Michael De Guzman

Jeepers Creepers
A: Justin Long, Gina Philips, Jonathan Breck, Patricka Belcher, Brandon Smith
D: Victor Salva
W: Victor Salva

Jekyll and Hyde
A: Michael Caine, Cheryl Ladd, Joss Ackland, Ronald Pickup, Kim Thomson, Lionel Jeffries, Kevin McNally
D: David Wickes
W: David Wickes

Jennifer's Boy
A: Megan Fox, Adam Brody, Amanda Seyfried, Johnny Simmons, Sal Cortez, Ryan Levine, Juan Riedinger
D: Karyn Kusama
W: Diablo Cody

John Carpenter's Vampires
A: James Woods, Sheryl Lee, Daniel Baldwin, Maximilian Schell, Thomas Ian Griffith, Tim Guinee, Mark Boone Jr.
D: John Carpenter
W: Don Jakoby

Jugular Wine: A Vampire Odyssey
A: Shaun Irons, Rachelle Parker, Gordon Capps, Aki Aleong, Henry Rollins, Stan Lee, Frank Miller, Michael Colyar, Lisa Malkiewicz
D: Blair Murphy
W: Blair Murphy

Jurassic Park
A: Sam Neill, Laura Dern, Jeff Goldblum, Richard Attenborough, Bob Peck, Martin Ferrero, B.D. Wong, Joseph Mazzello, Ariana Richards, Samuel L. Jackson, Wayne Knight
D: Steven Spielberg
W: David Koepp, Michael Crichton

Jurassic Park III
A: Sam Neill, William H. Macy, Tea Leoni, Laura Dern, Trevor Morgan, Michael Jeter, Alessandro Nivola, John Diehl, Bruce A. Young, Taylor Nichols, Mark harelik, Julio Oscar Mechoso
D: Joe Johnston
W: Peter Buchman, Jim Taylor, Alexander Payne

Keep, The
A: Scott Glenn, Alberta Watson, Juergen Prochnow, Robert Prosky, Gabriel Byrne, IanMcKellen
D: Michael Mann
W: Michael Mann, Dennis Lynton Clark

Kill List
A: Neil Maskell, MyAnna Buring, Harry Simpson, Michael Smiley, Emma Fryer
D: Ben Wheatley
W: Ben Wheatley

King Kong (1933)
A: Fay Wray, Bruce Cabot, Robert Armstrong, Frank Reicher, Noble Johnson, Sam Hardy, James Flavin
D: Ernest B. Schoedsack, Merian C. Cooper
W: James A. Creelman, Ruth Rose, Edgar Wallace

King Kong (1976)
A: Jeff Bridges, Charles Grodin, Jessica Lange, Rene Auberjonois, John Randloph, Ed Lauter, Jack O'Halloroan, Dennis Fimple, John Agar, Rick Baker
D: John Guillermin
W: Lorenzo Semple Jr.

King Kong (2005)
A: Naomi Watts, Jack Black, Adrien Brody, Thomas Kretschmann, Colin Hanks, Andy Serkis, Evan Parke, Jamie Bell, Lobo Chan, John Sumner
D: Peter Jackson
W: Fran Walsh, Philippa Boyens, Peter Jackson

King Kong Lives
A: Brian Kerwin, Linda Hamilton, John Ashton, Peter Michael Goetz
D: John Guillermin
W: Steven Pressfield, Ronald Shusett

Kingdom of the Spiders
A: William Shatner, Tiffany Bolling, Woody Strode
D: John Cardos
W: Alan Caillou, Richard Robinson

Kiss Me Kill Me
A: Carroll Baker, George Eastman, Isabelle DeFunes, Ely Gallo
D: Corrado Farina
W: Corrado Farina

Kiss of the Vampire
A: Glifford Evans, Noel Willman, Edward De Souza, Jennifer Daniel, Barry Warren, Jacqueline Wallis, Peter Madden, Isobel Black, Vera Cook, Olga Dickie
D: Don Sharp
W: Anthony John Elder Hinds

Labyrinth
A: David Bowie, Jennifer Connelly, Toby Froud, Shelley Thompson, Dave Goelz, Karen Prell, Steve Whitmire
D: Jim Henson
W: Jim Henson, Terry Jones

Lady Frankenstein
A: Joseph Cotten, Rosabela (Sara Bay) Neri, Mickey Hargitay, Paul Muller, Herbert Fux, Renate Kasche, Ada Pometti
D: Mel Welles
W: Edward Di Lorenzo

Lair of the White Worm
A: Amanda Donohoe, Sammi Davis, Catherine Oxenberg, Hugh Grant, Peter Capaldi, Stratford Johns, Paul Brooke, Christopher Gable
D: Ken Russell
W: Ken Russell

Lake Placid
A: Bill Pullman, Bridget Fonda, Oliver Platt, Betty White, Brendan Gleeson, David Lewis, Tim Dixon, Natassia Malthe, Mariska Hargitay
D: Steve Miner
W: David E. Kelley

Land of the Dead
A: John Leguizamo, Dennis Hopper, Simon Baker, Asia Argento, Eugene Clark, Joanne Boland, Robert Joy, Tony Nappo, Jennifer Baxter
D: George A. Romero
W: George A. Romero

Last Broadcast, The
A: David Beard, Lance Weiler, Stefan Avalos, Jim Seward, Rein Clabbers, Michele Pulaski, Tom Brunt, Mark Rublee, A. D. Roso, Dale Worstall, Vann K. Weller, Sam Wells
D: Stefan Avalos, Lance Weiler
W: Stefan Avalos, Lance Weiler

Last Days of Planet Earth
A: Tetsuro Tamba, So Yamamura, Takashi Shimura
D: Toshio Masuda
W: Tsutomu "Ben" Goto

Last Exorcism, The
A: Patrick Fabian, Ashley Bell, Iris Bahr, Louis Herthum, Tony Bentley, Shanna Forrestall, Caleb Landry Jones, John Wright Jr.
D: Daniel Stamm
W: Huck Botko, Andrew Gurland

Last Horror Movie
A: Kevin Howarth, Mark Stevenson, Antonia Beamish, Christabel Muir, Jonathan Coote, Joe Hurley, Rita Davies, Namie Langthorne, John Berlyne, Mandy Gordon
D: Julian Richards
W: James Handel

Last House on the Left (1972)
A: David Hess, Lucy Grantham, Sandra Cassel, Mark Sheffler, Fred J. Lincoln, Jeramie Rain, Gaylord St. James, Cynthia Carr, Ada Washington, Martin Kove
D: Wes Craven
W: Wes Craven

Last House on the Left (2009)
A: Monica Potter, Garret Dillahunt, Tony Goldwyn, Joshua Cox, Michael Bowen, Aaron Paul, Sara Paxton, Martha MacIsaac, Spencer Treat Clark
D: Dennis Iliadis
W: Adam Alleca, Carl Ellsworth

Last Man on Earth, The
A: Vincent Price, Emma Danieli, Franca Bettoia
D: Dbaldo Ragona, Sidney Salkow
W: William F. Leicester, Richard Matheson, Furio Monetti, Ubaldo Ragona

Lawnmower Man
A: Jeff Fahey, Pierce Brosnan, Jenny Wright, Mark Bringleson, Geoffrey Lewis, Jeremy Slate
D: Brett Leonard
W: Brett Leonard, Gimel Everett

Leatherface
A: Texas Chainsaw Massacre 3
A: Kate Hodge, William Butler, Ken Foree, Tom Hudson, R.A. Mihailoff
D: Jeff Burr
W: David J. Schow

Legend of Hell House ('73)
A: Roddy Macdowell, Pamela Franklin, Clive Revill, Gayle Hunnicutt, Peter Bowles, Roland Culver, Michael Gough
D: John Hough
W: Richard Matheson

Legend of the Werewolf
A: Peter Cushing, Hugh Griffith, Ron Moody, David Rintoul, Lynn Dalby, Stefan Gryff, Renee Houston, Norman Mitchell, Marjorie Yates, Roy Castle
D: Freddie Francis
W: Anthony John Elder Hines

Lemora: A Child's Tale of the Supernatural
A: Leslie Gilb, Cheryl "Rainbeaux" Smith, William Whitton, Steve Johnson, Hy Pyke, Maxine Ballantyne, Parker West, Richard Blackburn
D: Richard Blackburn
W: Robert Fern, Richard Blackburn

Leopard Man
A: Jean Brooks, Isabel Jewell, James Bell, Margaret Landry, Dennis O'Keefe, Margo, Rita (Paula) Corday, Abner Biberman
D: Jacques Tourneur
W: Ardel Wray

Let Me In
A: Kodi Smit-McPhee, Richard Jenkins, Chloe Grace Moretz, Cara Buono, Sasha Barrese, Elias Koteas, Dylan Kenin, Chris Browning, Ritchie Coster, Dylan Minnette
D: Matt Reeves
W: Matt Reeves, John Ajvide Lindqvist

Let the Right One In
A: Kare Hedebrant, Lina Leandersson, Per Ragnar, Karin Bergquist, Henrik Dahl, Ika Nord, Peter Carlberg
D: Tomas Alfredson
W: John Ajvide Lindqvist

Leviathan
A: Peter Weller, Ernie Hudson, Hector Elizondo, Amanda Pays, Richard Crenna, Daniel Stern, Lisa Eilbacher, Michael Carmine, Meg Foster
D: George P. Cosmatos
W: David Peoples, Jeb Stuart

Lifeforce
A: Steve Railsback, Peter Firth, Frank Finlay, Patrick Stewart, Mathilda May
D: Tobe Hooper
W: Dan O'Bannon, Don Jakoby

Lifespan
A: Klaus Kinski, Hiram Keller, Tina Aumont
D: Alexander Whitelaw
W: Judith Rascoe, Alva Ruben

Link
A: Elisabeth Shue, Terence Stamp, Steven Pinner, Richard Garnett
D: Richard Franklin
W: Everett DeRoche

Lisa and the Devil
A: Telly Savalas, Elke Sommerr, Sylva Koscina, Robert Alda, Alessio Orano, Gabriele Tinti, Alida Valli
D: Mario Bava
W: Mario Bava, Afred Leone

Listen
A: Brooke Langton, Sarah Buxton, Gordon Currie, Andy Romano, Joel Wyner
D: Gavin Wilding
W: Jonas Quastel, Michael Bafaro

Little Shop of Horrors (1960)
A: Jackie Joseph, Jonathan Haze, Mel Welles, Jack Nicholson, Dick Miller, Myrtle Vail
D: Roger Corman
W: Charles B. Griffith

Little Shop of Horrors (1986)
A: Rick Moranis, Ellen Greenem Vincent Gardenia, Steve Martin, James Belushi, Christopher Guest, Bill Murray, John Candy, Tisha Campbell, Tichina Arnold, Michelle Weeks
D: Frank Oz
W: Howard Ashman

Living Death
A: Kristy Swanson, Greg Bryk, Joshua Peace, Kelsey Matheson, Mark Hickox, Vik Sahay, Neil Foster, Jennifer Waiser
D: Erin Berry
W: Chrisopher Warre Smets, Erin Berry

Lodger: A Story of the London Fog, The (1926)
A: Ivor Novello, Marie Ault, Arthur Chesney, Malcolm Keen, Alfred Hitchcock
D: Alfred Hitchcock
W: Alfred Hitchcock, Eliot Stannard

Lodger: A Story of the London Fog, The (1944)
A: Laird Cregar, Merle Oberon, George Sanders, George Sanders, Cedric Hardwicke, Sara Allgood, Aubrey Mather, Queenie Leonard, Helena Rowley, David Clyd, Doris Lloyd
D: John Brahm
W: Barre Lyndon

Lost Boys, The
A: Jason Patric, Keifer Sutherland, Corey Haim, Jami Gertz, Dianne Wiest, Corey Feldman, Barnard Hughes, Edward Herrmann, Billy Wirth, Jamison Newlander, Brooke McCarter, Alex Winter
D: Joel Schumacher
W: Jeffrey Boam, Janice Fischer, James Jeremias

Lost Continent
A: Eric Porter, Hildegarde Knef, Suzanna Leigh, Tony Beckley, Nigel Stock, Neil McCallym, Ben Carruthers, Jimmy Hnaley, Dana Gillespie
D: Michael Carreras
W: Michael Nash

Lost Highway
A: Bill Pullman, Patricia Arquette, Balthazar Getty, Robert Loggia, Robert Blake, Gary Busey, Jack Nance, Richard Pryor, Natasha Gregson Wagner, Lisa Boyle, Michael Massee, Jack Kehler, Henry Rollins, Gene Ross, Scott Coffey
D: David Lynch
W: David Lynch, Barry Gifford

Lost Skeleton of Cadavra, The
A: Larry Blamire, Fay Masterson, Brian Howe, Andrew Parks, Susan McConnell, Jennifer Blaire, Dan Conroy
D: Larry Blamire
W: Larry Blamire

Lost Souls
A: Winona Ryder, John Hurt, Sarah Wynter, Ben Chaplin, Philip Baker Hall, Elias Koteas, Brian Reddy, John Beasley, John Diehl
D: Janusz Kaminski
W: Pierce Gardner

Lost World: Jurassic Park II
A: Jeff Goldblum, Julianne Moore, Vince Vaugh, Arliss Howard, Pete Postlewaite, Peter Stormare, Vanessa Lee Chester, Richard Schiff
D: Steven Spielberg
W: David Koepp

Lucinda's Spell
A: Jon Jacobs, Shana Betz, Christina Fulton, Leon Herbert, J. C. Brandy, John El, Alix Koromzay, Fatt Natt, Brother Randy, Judy Garwood, Ajax Davis
D: Jon Jacobs
W: Jon Jacobs

Lust for a Vampire
A: Ralph Bates, Barbara Jefford, Suzanna Leigh, Michael Johnson, Yutte Stensgaard, Pippa Steele, Helen Christie, David Healy, Mike Raven
D: Jimmy Sangster
W: Tudor Gates

Luther the Geek
A: Edward Terry, Joan Roth, J. Jerome Clarke, Tom Mills, Stacey Haiduk
D: Carlton J. Albright
W: Whitey Styles

M
A: Peter Lorre, Ellen Widmann, Inge Landgut, Gustav Grundgens, Otto Wernicke, Ernest Stahl-Nachbaur, Franz Stein, Theodore Loos, Fritz Gnass, Fritz Odemar, Paul Kemp, Theo Lingen, Georg Rydlof Blummer
D: Fritz Lang
W: Fritz Lang, Thea von Harbou

Mad Doctor of Blood Island
A: John Ashley, Ronald Remy, Alicia Alonzo, Alfonso Carvajal, Angelique Pettyjohn
D: Gerardo De Leon
W: Reuben Canoy

Mad Love
A: Peter Lorre, Colin Clive, Frances Drake, Ted Healy, Edward Brophy, Sara Haden, Henry Kolker
D: Karl Freund
W: P.J. Wolfson, John L. Balderston, Guy Endore

Magic
A: Anthony Hopkins, Ann-Margret, Burgess Meredith, Ed Lauter, Jerry Houser, David Ogden Stiers, Lillian Randolph
D: Richard Attenborough
W: William Goldman

Manhunter
A: William L. Petersen, Kim Griest, Joan Allen, Brian Cox, Dennis Farina, Stephen Lang, Tom Noonan
D: Michael Mann
W: Michael Mann

Maniac
A: Joe Spinell, Caroline Munro, Gail Lawrence, Kelly Piper, Tom Savini, Rita Montone, Hyla Marrow
D: William Lustig
W: C.A. Rosenberg

Maniac Cop
A: Tom Atkins Bruce Campbell, Laurene Landon, Richard Roundtree, William Smith, Robert Z'Dar, Sheree North, Sam Raimi
D: William Lustig
W: Larry Cohen

Maniac Cop 2
A: Robert Davi, Claudia Christian, Michael Lerner, Bruce Campbell, Laurene Langdon, Robert Z'Dar, Clarence Williams III, Leo Rossi
D: William Lustig
W: Larry Cohen

Maniac Cop 3: Badge of Silence
A: Robert Z'Dar, Robert Davi, Gretchen Becker, Paul Gleason, Doug Savant, Caitlin Dulany, Jackie Earl Haley, Robert Forster
D: William Lustig
W: Larry Cohen

Manitou
A: Susan Strasberg, Tony Curtis, Stella Stevens, Ann Southern, Burgess Meredith, Michael Ansara, Jon Cedar, Paul Mantee, Lurene Tuttle, Jeanette Nolan
D: William Girdler
W: William Girdler, Tom Pope

Manmade Monster
A: Lon Chaney Jr., Lionel Atwill, Anne Nagel, Frank Albertson, Samuel S. Hinds
D: George Waggner
W: Joseph West

Man-Thing
A: Jack Thompson, Steve Bastoni, Matthew Le Nevez, Rawiri Paratene, Steve Bastoni, Alex O'Loughlin, Robert Mammone, Patrick Thompson, William Zappa, John Batchelor, Ian Bliss, Brett Leonard
D: Brett Leonard
W: Hans Rodionoff

Mark of the Vampire
A: Lionel Barrymore, Bela Lugosi, Elizabeth Allan, Lionel Atwill, Jean Hersholt, Donald Meek, Caroll Borland
D: Tod Browning
W: Tod Browning, Guy Endore, Bernard Schubert

Martin
A: John Amplas, Lincoln Maazel, Christine Forrest, Elayne Nadeau, Tom Savini, Sarah Venable, George Romero, Fran Middleton
D: George Romero
W: George Romero

Mary Reilly
A: Julia Roberts, John Malkovich, George Cole, Michael Gambon, Kathy Staff, Glenn Close, Michael Sheen, Henry Goodman, Ciaran Hinds, Sasha Hanav
D: Stephen Frears
W: Christopher Hampton

Mary Shelley's Frankenstein
A: Kenneth Branagh, Robert De Niro, Helena Bonham Carter, Tom Hulce, Aidan Quinn, John Cleese, Ian Holm, Richard Briers, Robert Hardy, Cherie Lunghi, Celia Imrie
D: Kenneth Branagh
W: Frank Darabont, Steph Lady

Masque of the Red Death (1964)
A: Vincent Price, Hazel Court, Jane Asher, Patrick Magee, David Weston, Nigel Green, Julian Burton, Skip Martin
D: Roger Corman
W: Charles Beaumont

Masque of the Red Death (1989)
A: Patrick Macnee, Jeffery Osterhage, Adrian Paul, Tracy Reiner, Maria Ford, Clare Hoak
D: Larry Brand
W: Larry Brand, Daryl Haney

Mausoleum
A: Marjoe Gortner, Bobbie Bresee, Norman Burton, LaWanda Page, Shari Mann, Julie Christy Murray, Laura Hippe, Maurice Sherbanee
D: Michael Dugan
W: Robert Madero, Robert Barich

May
A: Angela Bettis, Jeremy Sisto, Anna Faris, James Duval, Kevin Gage, Nichole Hiltz, Chandler Riley Hecht, Merle Kennedy
D: Lucky McKee
W: Lucky McKee

Mega-Python versus Gatoroid
A: Deborah Gibson, Tiffany, A Martinez, Kevin M. Horton, Carey Van Dyke, Kathryn Joosten
D: Mary Lambert
W: Naomi L. Selfman

Messengers, The
A: Dylan McDermott, Penelope Ann Miller, John Corbett, Kristen Stewart, Evan Turner, Theodore Turner, William B. Davis, Brent Briscoe, Jodelle Ferland
D: Oxide Pang Chun, Danny Pang
W: Mark Wheaton

Midnight Meat Train, The
A: Vinnie Jones, Brooke Shields, Bradley Cooper, Leslie Bibb, Vinnie Jones, Peter Jacobson, Ted Raimi, Roger Bart, Barbara Eve Harris, Stephanie Mace, Nora, Quinton "Rampage" Jackson
D: Ryuhei Kitamura
W: Jeff Buhler

Mighty Peking Man
A: Danny Lee, Evelyne Kraft, Feng Ku, Wei Tu Lin, Norman Chu, Hang-Sheng Wu, Theodore Thomas, Steve Nicholson, Yaho Hsiao, Ping Chen
D: Meng Hua Ho
W: Kuang Ni

Milo
A: Jennifer Jostyn, Antonio Fargas, Paula Cale, Richard Portnow, Vincent Schiavelli, Asher Metchik, Maya McLaughlin, Walter Olkewicz
D: Pascal Franchot
W: Craig Mitchell

Mimic
A: Jeremy Northam, Mira Sorvino, Josh Brolin, Charles S. Dutton, Giancarlo Giannini, F. Murray Abraham
D: Guillermo del Toro
W: John Sayles, Steven Soderbergh, Matthew Robbins

Mirror, Mirror
A: Karen Black, Rainbow Harvest, Kristin Datillo, Ricky Pauli Goldin, Yvonne de Carlo, William Sanderson, Charlie Spradling, Ann Hearn, Stephen Tobolowsky
D: Marina Sargenti
W: Marina Sargenti

Mirror, Mirror 2: Raven Dance
A: Tracy Wells, Roddy McDowell, Sally Kellerman, Veronica Cartwright, William Sanderson, Lois Nettleton
D: Jimmy Lifton
W: Jimmy Lifton, Virginia Perfili

Mirror, Mirror 3: The Voyeur
A: Billy Drago, Monique Parent, David Naughton, Mark Ruffalo, Elizabeth Baldwin, Richard Cansino
D: Rachel Gordon, Virginia Perfili
W: Steve Tymon

Mirrors
A: Kiefer Sutherland, Paula Patton, Amy Smart, Cameron Boyce, Erica Gluck, Mary Beth Peil, John Shrapnel
D: Alexandre Aja
W: Alexandre Aja, Gregory Levasseur

Misery
A: James Caan, Kathy Bates, Lauren Bacall, Richard Farnsworth, Frances Sternhagen, Graham Jarvis
D: Rob Reiner
W: William Goldman

Mist, The
A: Thomas Jane, Laurie Holden, Marcia Gay Harden, William Sadler, Andre Braugher, Toby Jones, Frances Sternhagen, Jeffrey DeMunn, Alexa Davalos, Chris Owen
D: Frank Darabont
W: Frank Darabont

Mr. Stitch
A: Rutger Hauer, Wil Wheaton, Nia Peeples, Taylor Negron, Ron Perlman, Michael Harris. Cameos
A: Tom Savini
D: Roger Roberts Avery
W: Roger Roberts Avery

Modern Vampires
A: Rod Steiger, Natasha Gregson Wagner, Casper Van Dien, Craig Ferguson, Kim Cattrall, Natasha Lyonne, Udo Kier, Gabriel Casseus, Robert Pastorelli
D: Richard Elfman
W: Matthew Bright

Monkey Shines: An Experiment in Fear
A: Jason Beghe, John Pankow, Kate McNeil, Christine Forrest, Stephen Root, Joyce Van Patten, Stanley Tucci, Janine Turner
D: George Romero
W: George Romero

Monolith Monsters, The
A: Grant Williams, Lola Albright, Les Tremayne, Phil Harvey, Trevor Bardette
D: John Sherwood
W: Norman Jolley, Robert M. Fresco

Monster on the Campus
A: Arthur Franz, Joanna Moore, Judson Pratt, Troy Donahue, Phil Harvey, Nancy Walters, Whit Bissell, Ross Elliott, Alexander Lockwood, Helen Westcott
D: Jack Arnold
W: David Duncan

Motel Hell
A: Rory Calhoun, Nancy Parsons, Paul Linke, Nina Axelrod, Wolfman Jack, Elaine Joyce, Dick Curtis, Rosanne Katon, Monique St. Pierre
D: Kevin Connor
W: Robert Jaffe, Steven-Charles Jaffe

Mothman Prophecies, The
A: Richard Gere, David Eigenberg, Laura Linney, Debra Messing, Tom Stoviak, Ron Emanuel, Bob Tracey, Yvonne Erickson, Will Patton, Lucinda Jenney, Laura Linney
D: Mark Pellington
W: Richard Hatem

Mulholland Dr.
A: Naomi Watts, Laura Harring, Justin Theroux, Ann Miller, Dan Hedaya, Brent Briscoe, Robert Forster, Katharine Towne, Lee Grant, Scott Coffey, Billy Ray Cyrus, Chad Everett
D: David Lynch
W: David Lynch

Mummy, The (1932)
A: Boris Karloff, ZitaJohann, David Manners, Edward Van Sloan, Arthur Byron, Bramwell Fletcher, Noble Johnson, Leonard Mudie, Henry Victor
D: Karl Freund
W: John L. Balderston

Mummy, The (1959)
A: Peter Cushing, Christopher Lee, Felix Aylmer, Yvonne Furneaux, Eddie Byrne, Raymond Huntley, George Pastell, Michael Ripper, John Stuart
D: Terence Fisher
W: Jimmy Sangster

Mummy's Curse, The
A: Lon Chaney Jr., Peter Coe, Virginia Christine, Kay Harding, Dennis Moore, Martin Kosleck, Kurt Katch
D: Leslie Goodwins
W: Bernard Schubert

Mummy's Ghost, The
A: Lon Chaney Jr., John Carradine, Ramsay Ames, Robert Lowrey, Barton MacLane, George Zucco
D: Reginald LeBorg
W: Griffin Jay, Henry Sucher

Mummy's Hand, The
A: Dick Foran, Wallace Ford, Peggy Moran, Cecil Kellaway, George Zucco, Tom Tyler, Eduardo Ciannelli, Charles Trowbridge
D: Christy Cabanne
W: Griffin Jay, Maxwell Shane

Mummy's Tomb, The
A: Lon Chaney Jr., Dick Foran, John Hubbard, Elyse Knox, George Zucco, Wallace Ford, Turhan Bey
D: Harold Young
W: Griffin Jay, Henry Sucher

Murder Weapon
A: Linnea Quigley, Karen Russell, Lyle Waggoner
D: Dave DeCoteau
W: Ross A. Perron

My Bloody Valentine (1981)
A: Paul Kelman, Lori Hallier, Neil Affleck, Keith Knight, Alf Humphreys, Cynthia Dale, Terry Waterland, Peter Cowper, Don Franks, Jack Van Evera
D: George Mihalka
W: John Beaird

My Bloody Valentine (2009)
A: Jensen Ackles, Jaime King, Kerr Smith, Edi Gathegi, Betsy Rue, Kevin Tighe, Megan Boone, Tom Atkins
D: Patrick Lussier
W: Todd Farmer, Zane Smith

My Soul to Take
A: Max Thieriot, Denzel Whitaker, John Magaro, Zena Gray, Paulina Olszynski, Jeremy Chu, Nick Lashaway, Emily Meade, Raul Esparza
D: Wes Craven
W: Wes Craven

Mystery of the Wax Museum
A: Lionel Atwill, Fay Wray, Glenda Farrell, Frank McHugh, Allen Vincent, Holmes Herbert
D: Michael Curtiz
W: Carl Erikson Don Mullaly

Naked Lunch
A: Peter Weller, Judy Davis, Ian Holm, Julian Sands, Roy Scheider, Monique Mercure, Nicholas Campbell, Michael Zelniker, Robert A. Silverman, Joseph Scorsiani
D: David Cronenberg
W: David Cronenberg

Nature of the Beast
A: Eric Roberts, Lance Henriksen, Brion James
D: Victor Salva
W: Victor Salva

Near Dark
A: Adrian Pasdar, Jenny Wright, Bill Paxton, Jenette Goldstein, Lance Henriksen, Tim Thomerson, Joshua Miller
D: Kathryn Bigelow
W: Kathryn Bigelow, Eric Red

Needful Things
A: Ed Harris, Bonnie Bedelia, Max Von Sydow, Amanda Plummer, J.T. Walsh
D: Fraser Heston
W: Fraser Heston

Nest, The
A: Robert Lansing, Lisa Langlois, Franc Luz, Terri Treas, Stephen Davies, Diana Bellamy, Nancy Morgan
D: Terence Winkless
W: Robert King

Netherworld
A: Michael C. Bendetti, Denise Gentile, Anjanette Comer. Holly Floria, Robert Burr, Robert Sampson
D: David Schmoeller
W: Billy Chicago

New Moon
A: Robert Pattinson, Kristen Stewart, Taylor Lautner, Billy Burke, Michael Welch, Anna Kendrick, Justin Chon, Christian Serratos, Christina Jastrzembska, Jackson Rathbone, Russell Roberts
D: Chris Weitz
W: Melissa Rosenberg

Night Angel
A: Isa Anderson, Linda Ashby, Ebbra Feuer, Helen Martin, Karen Black, Doug Jones, Gary Hudson, Sam Hemmings
D: Dominique Othenin-Girard
W: Joe Augustyn

Night Junkies
A: Giles Alderson, Beverley Eve, Lucy Bowen, Katia Winter, Matt Tully, Jonny Coyne, Daniel Kobbina, Lauren Adams, Rene Zagger
D: Lawrence Pearce
W: Lawrence Pearce

Night of the Comet
A: Catherine Mary Stewart, Kelli Maroney, Robert Beltran, Geoffrey Lewis, Mary Woronov, Sharon Farrell, Michael Bowen
D: Thom Eberhardt
W: Thom Eberhardt

Night of the Creeps
A: Jason Lively, Jill Whitlow, Tom Atkins, Steve Marshall, Wally Taylor, Bruce Solomon, Kenneth Tobey, Dick Miller
D: Fred Dekker
W: Fred Dekker

Night of the Lepus
A: Stuart Whitman, Janet Leigh, Rory Calhoun, DeForest Kelly, Paul Fix, Minnie Fullerton
D: William Claxton
W: Don Holliday, Gene R. Kearney

Night of the Living Dead (1968)
A: Judith O'Dea, Duane Jones, Karl Hardman, Marilyn Eastman, Keith Wayne, Judith Ridley, Russell Streiner, George Kosana, Bill "Chilly Billy" Cardille
D: George Romero
W: John A. Russo

Night of the Living Dead (1990)
A: Tony Todd, Tom Towles, Patricia Tallman, McKee Anderson, Katie Finneran, William Butler, Bill Moseley, Heather Mazur
D: Tom Savini
W: George A. Romero

Night Stalker, The
A: Darren McGavin, Carol Lynley, Simon Oakland, Ralph Meeker, Claude Akins, Kent Smith, Larry Linville, Barry Atwater
D: John Llewellyn Moxey
W: Richard Matheson

Night Strangler, The
A: Darren McGavin, Jo Ann Pflug, Simon Oakland, Wally Cox, Margaret Hamilton, John Carradine, Al Lewis, Nina Wayne, Scott Brady
D: Dan Curtis
W: Richard Matheson

Night Watch
A: Konstantin Khabenskiy, Mariya Poroshina, Vladimir Menshov, Galina Tyunina, Yuriy Kutsenko, Aleksey Chadov, Valeriy Zolotukhin
D: Timur Bekmambetov
W: Timur Bekmambetov, Laeta Kalogridis

Nightcomers
A: Marlon Brando, Stephanie Beacham, Thora Hird, Harry Andrews, Christopher Ellis, Verna Harvey, Anna Palk
D: Michael Winner
W: Michael Hastings

Nightmare
A: Jennie Linden, David Knight, Moira Redmond, Brenda Bruce
D: Freddie Francis
W: Jimmy Sangster

Nightmare before Christmas
A: V:Danny Elfman, Chris Sarandon, Catherine O'Hara, William Hickey, Ken Page, Ed Ivory, Paul Reubens, Glenn Shadix
D: Henry Selick
W: Caroline Thompson

Nightmare on Elm Street, A (1984)
A: John Saxon, Heather Langenkamp, Ronee Blakley, Robert Englund, Amanda Wyss, Nick Corri, Johnny Depp, Charles Fleischer
D: Wes Craven
W: Wes Craven

Nightmare on Elm Street, A (2010)
A: Jackie Earle Haley, Kyle Gallner, Rooney Mara, Thomas Dekker, Clancy Brown, Kellan Lutz, Connie Britton, Lia D. Mortensen, Julianna Damm
D: Samuel Bayer
W: Wesley Strick, Eric Heisserer

Nightmare on Elm Street Part 2: Freddy's Nightmare
A: Mark Patton, Hope Lange, Clu Gulager, Robert Englund, Kim Myers, Robert Rusler, Marshall Bell, Sydney Walsh
D: Jack Sholder
W: David Caskin

Nightmare on Elm Street 3: Dream Warriors, A
A: Patricia Arquette, Robert Englund, Heather Langenkamp, Craig Wasson, Laurence "Larry" Fishburne, Priscilla Pointer, John Saxon, Brooke Bundy, Jennifer Rubin, Rodney Eastman, Nan Martin, Dick Cavett, Zsa Zsa Gabor
D: Chuck Russell
W: Chuck Russell, Bruce Wagner, Wes Craven, Frank Darabont

Nightmare on Elm Street 4: The Dream Master, A
A: Robert Englund, Rodney Eastman, Danny Hassel, Andras Jones, Tuesday Night, Lisa Wilcox, Ken Sagoes, Toy Newkirk, Brooke Theiss, Brooke Bundy
D: Renny Harlin
W: Brian Helgeland, Scott Pierce

Nightmare on Elm Street: The Dream Child, A
A: Robert Englund, Lisa Wilcox, Kelly Jo Minter, Danny Hassel, Erika Anderson, Nicholas Mele, Beatrice Boepple, Christopher Ellis
D: Stephen Hopkins
W: Leslie Bohem

Nightscare
A: Craig Fairbass, Elizabeth Hurley, Keith Allen, Jesse Birdsall, Craig Kelly
D: Vadim Jean

W: Vadim Jean

Nightwing
A: Nick Mancuso, David Warner, Kathryn Harrold, Strother Martin, Stephen Macht, Pat Corley, Charles Hallahan, Ben Piazza, George Clutesi
D: Arthur Hiller
W: Steve Shagan, Bud Shrake, Martin Cruz Smith

Ninth Gate, The
A: Johnny Depp, Frank Langella, Lena Olin, James Russo, Allen Garfield, Barbara Jefford, Emmanuelle Seigner, Jack Taylor
D: Roman Polanski
W: John Brownjohn, Enrique Urbizu, Roman Polanski

Nosferatu (1922)
A: Max Schreck, Alexander Granach, Gustav von Wagenheim, Greta Schroeder, John Gottowt, Ruth Landshoff, G.H. Schnell
D: F.W. Murnau
W: Henrik Galeen

Nosferatu (1979)
A: Klaus Kinski, Isabelle Adjani, Bruno Ganz, Roland Topor, Walter Ladengast
D: Werner Herzog
W: Werner Herzog

Not Like Us
A: Joanna Pacula, Annabelle Gurwitch, Peter Onorati, Morgan Englund, Rainer Grant
D: Dave Payne
W: Daniella Purcelli

Not of This Earth (1988)
A: Traci Lords, Arthur Roberts, Lenny Juliano, Rebecca Perle, Ace Mask, Roger Lodge
D: Jim Wynorski
W: Jim Wynorski, R.J. Robertson

Not of This Earth (1996)
A: Michael York, Elizabeth Barondes, Richard Belzer, Parker Stevenson
D: Terence H. Winkless
W: Charles Philip Moore

Oblong Box, The
A: Vincent Price, Christopher Lee, Alastair Williamson, Hilary Dwyer, Peter Arne, Harry Baird, Carl Rigg, Sally Geeson, Maxxwell Shaw
D: Gordon Hessler
W: Lawrence Huntington

Of Unknown Origin
A: Peter Weller, Jennifer Dale, Lawrence Dane, Kenneth Welsh, Louis Del Grande, Shannon Tweed
D: George Cosmatos
W: Brian Taggert

Old Dark House, The
A: Boris Karloff, Melvyn Douglas, Charles Laughton, Gloria Stuart, Ernest Thesiger, Raymond Massey, Lillian Bond, Eva Moore, Brember Wills, John Dudgeon
D: James Whale
W: Benn W. Levy, R.C. Sherriff

Omega Man, The
A: Charlton Heston, Anthony Zerbe, Rosalind Cash, Paul Koslo, Eric Laneuville, Lincoln Kilpatrick
D: Boris Sagal
W: John Corrington, Joyce J. Corrington

Omen, The (1976)
A: Gergory Peck, Lee Remick, Harvey Stephens, Billie Whitelaw, David Warner, Holly Palance, Robert Rietty, Patrick Troughton, Martin Benson, Leo McKern, Richard Donner
D: Richard Donner
W: David Seltzer

Omen, The (2006)
A: Liev Schreiber, Julia Stiles, Seamus Davey-Fitzpatrick, Bohumil Svarc, Predrag Bjelac, Carlo Sabatini, Giovanni Lombardo, Marshall Cupp
D: John Moore
W: David Seltzer

Omen III: The Final Conflict
A: Sam Neill, Rossano Brazzi, Don Gordon, Lisa Harrow, Barnaby Holm, Leueen Willoughby, Robert Arden, Mason Adams
D: Graham Baker
W: Andrew Birkin

Omen IV: The Awakening
A: Faye Grant, Michael Lerner, Michael Woods, Madison Mason, Jim Byrnes, Ann Hearn, Don S. Davis, Asia Vieira, Joy Coghill, Megan Leitch, David Cameron, Duncan Fraser, susan Chapple, Dana Still
D: Jorge Montesi, Dominique Othenin-Girard
W: Brian Taggert

One Missed Call (2003)
A: Ko Shibasaki, Shin-ich Tsutsumi, Kazue Fukiishi, Atsushi Ida, Anna Nagata, Mariko Tsutsui
D: Takashi Miike
W: Minako Daira

One Missed Call (2008)
A: Edward Burns, Shannyn Sossamon, Margaret Cho, Ana Claudia, Ray Wise, Johnny Lewis, Azura Skye, Rhoda Griffis
D: Eric Valette
W: Andrew Klavan

Opera
A: Christina Marsillach, Ian Charleson, Urbano Barberini, William McNamara, Antonella Vitale, Babara Cupisti, Coralina Cataldi Tassoni, Daria Nicolodi
D: Dario Argento
W: Dario Argento, Franco Ferrini

Orphan, The
A: Vera Farmiga, Peter Sarsgaard, Isabelle Furhman, CCH Pounder, Margo Martindale, Karel Roden, Rosemary Dunsmore, Genelle Williams, Lorry Ayers, Jamie Young, Brendan Wall

D: Jaume Collet-Serra
W: David Johnson

Other, The
A: Martin Udvarnoky, Chris Udvarnoky, Uta Hagen, Diana Muldaur, Norma Connolly, Victor French, John Ritter, Loretta Leversee, Lou Frizzell
D: Robert Mulligan
W: Tom Tryon

Others, The
A: Nicole Kidman, Christopher Eccleston, Fionnula Flanagan, Alakina Mann, James Bentley, Eric Sykes, Renee Asherson, Elaine Cassidy
D: Alejandro Amenabar
W: Alejandro Amenabar

Pale Blood
A: George Chakiris, Wings Hauser, Pamela Ludwig, Diana Frank, Darcy Demoss, Earl Garnes
D: V.V. Dachin Hsu
W: V.V. Dachin Hsu, Takashi Matsuoka

Pan's Labyrinth
A: Ivana Baquero, Ariadna Gil, Sergi Lopez, Doug Jones, Maribel Verdu, Alex Angulo, manolo Solo, Cesar Vea, Roger Casamajor
D: Guillermo del Toro
W: Guillermo del Toro

Paranoiac
A: Oliver Reed, Janette Scott, Alex Davion, Liliane Brousse, Sheila Burell, Maurice Denham
D: Freddie Francis
W: Jimmy Sangster

Paranormal Activity
A: Katie Featherston, Michah Sloat, Mark Fredrichs, Amber Armstrong
D: Oren Peli
W: Oren Peli

Paranormal Activity 2
A: Katie Featherston, Micah Sloat, Molly Ephraim, Brian Boland, David Bierend, Sprague Grayden, Vivis Colombetti
D: Tod Williams
W: Michael R. Perry, Christopher Landon

Paranormal Activity 3
A: Christopher Nicholas Smith, Jessica Tyler Brown, Chloe Csengery, Lauren Bittner, Hallie Foote, Dustin Ingram, Johanna Braddy, Brian Boland, Katie Featherston, Sprague Grayden
D: Henry Joost, Arial Schulman
W: Christopher Landon

Parasomnia
A: Dylan Purcell, Jeffrey Combs, Patrick Kilpatrick, Timothy Bottoms, Cherilyn Wilson, Brennan Bailey, Dov Tiefenbach, Kathryn Leigh Scott
D: William Malone
W: William Malone

Parents
A: Randy Quaid, Mary Beth Hurt, Bryan Madorsky, Sandy Dennis, Kathryn Grody, Deborah Rush, Graham Jarvis, Juno Mills-Cockrell
D: Bob Balaban
W: Christopher Hawthorne

Passion of the Christ
A: Jim Caviezel, Monica Bellucci, Maia Morgenstern, Christo Jivkov, Francesco De Vito, Monica Bellucci, Luca Lionello, Toni Bertorelli, Hristo Shopov, Claudia Gerini, Giacinto Ferro, Fabio Sartor, Aleksander Mincer
D: Mel Gibson
W: Mel Gibson, Benedict Fitzgerald

Peeping Tom
A: Karl-Heinz Boehm, Moira Shearer, Anna Massey, Maxine Audley, Esmond Knight, Shirley Anne Field, Brenda Bruce, Pamela Green, Jack Watson, Nigel Davenport, Susan Travers, Veronica Hurst, Martin Miller, Miles Malleson, Michael Powell
D: Michael Powell
W: Leo Marks

People under the Stairs
A: Everett McGill, Wendy Robie, Brandon Adams, Ving Rhames, A.J. Langer, Sean Whalen, Kelly Jo Minter
D: Wes Craven
W: Wes Craven

Pet Sematary
A: Dale Midkiff, Fred Gwynne, Denise Crosby, Blaze Berdahl, Brad Greenquist, Miko Hguhes, Stephen King
D: Mary Lambert
W: Stephen King

Pet Sematary II
A: Anthony Edwards, Edward Furlong, Clancy Brown, Jared Rushton, Darlanne Fluegel, Lisa Waltz, Jason McGuire, Sarah Trigger
D: Mary Lambert
W: Richard Outten

Phantasm
A: Michael Baldwin, Bill Thornbury, Reggie Bannister, Kathy Lester, Terrie Kalbus, Ken Jones, Angus Scrimm
D: Don Coscarelli
W: Don Coscarelli

Phamtasm II
A: James LeGros, Reggie Bannister, Angus Scrimm, Paula Irvine, Samantha Phillips, Ken Tigar
D: Don Coscarelli
W: Don Coscarelli

Phantasm III: Lord of the Dead
A: Reggie Bannister, A. Michael Baldwin, Bill Thornbury, Gloria Henry, Angus Scrimm
D: Don Coscarelli
W: Don Coscarelli

Phantom of the Opera (1925)
A: Lon Chaney Sr., Norman Kerry, Mary Philbin, Gibson Gowland, Arthur Edmund Carewe, Snitz Edwards

D: Rupert Julian
W: Elliot J. Clawson, Raymond Schrock

Phantom of the Opera (1943)
A: Nelson Eddy, Susanna Foster, Claude Rains, Edgar Barrier, Leo Carillo, Hume Cronym, J. Edward Bromberg
D: Arthur Lubin
W: Samuel Hoffenstein

Phantom of the Opera (1962)
A: Herbert Lom, Heather Sears, Michael Gough
D: Terence Fisher
W: Anthony Hinds

Phantom of the Opera (1989)
A: Robert Englund, Jill Schoelen, Alex Hyde-White, Bill Nighy, Terence Harvey, Stephanie Lawrence
D: Dwight Little
W: Duke Sandefur

Phantom of the Opera (1998)
A: Julian Sands, Andrea Di Stefano, Asia Argento, Nadia Rinaldi, Coralina Cataldi-Tassoni, Istvan Bubic
D: Dario Argento
W: Gerard Brach, Dario Argento

Phantoms
A: Peter O'Toole, Ben Affleck, Clifton Powell, Rose McGowan, Joanna Going, Liev Schreiber, Nicky Katt
D: Joe Chappelle
W: Dean R. Koontz

Phenomena
A: Jennifer Connelly, Donald Pleasance, Daria Nicoldi, Eleanora Giorgi
D: Dario Argento
W: Dario Argento, Franco Ferrini

Picture of Dorian Gray, The
A: Hurd Hatfield, George Sanders, Donna Reed, Angela Lansbury, Peter Lawford, Lowell Gilmore, Miles Mander
D: Albert Lewin
W: Albert Lewin

Pin
A: Cyndy Preston, David Hewlett, Terry O'Quinn, Bronwen Mantel, Helene Udy, Patricia Collins, Steven Bednarski, Katie Shingler, Jacob Tierney, Michelle Anderson
D: Sandor Stern
W: Sandor Stern

Piranha (1978)
A: Bradford Dillman, Heather Menzies, Kevin McCarthy, Keenan Wynn, Barbara Steele, Dick Miller, Paul Bartel, John Sayles
D: Joe Dante
W: John Sayles

Piranha (1995)
A: Alexandra Paul, William Katt, Soleil Moon Frye, Monte Markham, Darlene Carr, James Karen, Lincoln Kilpatrick
D: Scott Levy
W: John Sayles

Piranha (2010)
A: Richard Dreyfuss, Ving Rhames, Christopher Lloyd, Elisabeth Shue, Jerry O'Connell, Steven R. McQueen
D: Alexandre Aja
W: Pete Goldfinger, Josh Stolberg

Piranha II: The Spawning
A: Tricia O'Neil, Steve Marachuk, Lance Henriksen, Ricky Paul
D: James Cameron
W: H.A. Milton

Pit and the Pendulum, The (1961)
A: Vincent Price, John Kerr, Barbara Steele, Luana Anders, Antony Carbone
D: Roger Corman
W: Richard Matheson

Pit and the Pendulum, The (1991)
A: Lance Henriksen, Rona De Ricci, Jonathan Fuller, Jeffrey Combs, Tom Towles, Stephen Lee, Francey Bay, Oliver Reed
D: Stuart Gordon
W: Dennis Paoli

Plague of the Zombies
A: Andre Morell, John Carson, Diane Clare, Alex Davion, Jacqueline Pearce, Brook Williams, Michael Ripper, Marcus Hammond, Roy Royston
D: John Gilling
W: Peter Bryan, John Elder

Plan 9 from Outer Space
A: Bela Lugosi, Tor Johnson, Lyle Talbot, Vampira, Gregory Walcott, Tom George, Duryea Keen, Dudley Manlove, Conrad Brooks, Edward Wood Jr.
D: Edward Wood Jr.
W: Edward Wood Jr.

Poltergeist
A: JoBeth Williams, Craig T. Nelson, Beatrice Straight, Heather O'Rourke, Zelda Rubenstein, Dominique Dunne, Oliver Robbins, Richard Lawson, James Karen, Michael McManus
D: Tobe Hooper
W: Steven Spielberg, Michael Grais, Mark Victor

Poltergeist II: The Other Side
A: Craig T. Nelson, JoBeth Williams, Heather O'Rourke, Will Sampson, Julian Beck, Geraldine Fitzgerald, Oliver Robbins, Zelda Rubenstein
D: Brian Gibson
W: Mark Victor, Michael Grais

Poltergeist III
A: Tom Skerritt, Nancy Allen, Heather O'Rourke, Lara Flynn Boyle, Zelda Rubenstein
D: Gary Sherman
W: Gary Sherman, Brian Taggert

Pontypool
A: Stephen McHattie, Lisa Houle, Georgina Reilly, Rick Roberts, Hrant Alianak, Beatriz Yuste, Tony Burgess, Boyd Banks, Hannah Fleming, Rachel Burns, Daniel Fathers,
D: Bruce McDonald
W: Tony Burgess

Premature Burial
A: Ray Milland, Richard Ney, Hazel Court, Heather Angel, Alan Napier, John Dierkes, Dick Miller
D: Roger Corman
W: Charles Beaumont, Ray Russell

Priest
A: Paul Bettany, Maggie Q, Cam Gigandet, Christopher Plummer, Karl Urban, Lily Collins, Brad Dourif, Stephen Moyer, Alan Dale
D: Scott Charles Stewart
W: Cory Goodman

Primeval
A: Dominic Purcell, Orlando Jones, Brooke Langton, Juergen Prochnow, Gideon Emery
D: Michael Katleman
W: John D. Brancato, Michael Ferris

Prince of Darkness
A: Donald Pleasance, Lisa Blount, Victor Wong, Jameson Parker, Dennis Dun, Susan Blanchard, Anne Howard, Ken Wright, Dirk Blocker
D: John Carpenter
W: John Carpenter

Prisoner
A: Julian McMahon, Elias Koteas, Dagmara Dominczyk, Tom Guiry
D: David Alford, Robert Archer Lynn
W: David Alford, Robert Archer Lynn

Prom Night (1980)
A: Jamie Lee Curtis, Leslie Nielsen, Casey Stevens, Eddie Benton, Antoinette Bower, Michael Tough, Pita Oliver
D: Paul Lynch
W: William Gray

Prom Night III
A: Tim Conlon, Cyndy Preston, Courtney Taylor, David Stratton, Dylan Neal, Jeremy Ratchford
D: Ron Oliver
W: Ron Oliver

Prom Night IV: Deliver Us from Evil
A: Nikki DeBoer, Alden Kane, Joy Tanner, Alle Ghadban, James Carver
D: Clay Borris
W: Richard Beattie

Prometheus
A: Michael Fassbender, Noomi Rapace, Logan Marshall-Green, Charlize Theron, Idris Elba, Guy Pearce, Sean Harris, Emun Elliott, Rafe Spall, Kate Dickie, Benedict Wong
D: Ridley Scott
W: Jon Spaihts, Damon Lindelof

Prophecy, The (1995)
A: Christopher Walken, Eric Stoltz, Elias Koteas, Virginia Madsen, Amanda Plummer, Viggo Mortensen
D: Gregory Widen
W: Gregory Widen

Prophecy II, The
A: Christopher Walken, Russell Wong, Eric Roberts, Jennifer Beals, Bruce Abbott, Brittany Murphy, Steve Hynter, Glenn Danzig
D: Greg Spence
W: Greg Spence, Matt Greenberg

Psycho (1960)
A: Anthony Perkins, Janet Leigh, Vera Miles, John Gavin, John McIntire, Martin Balsam, Simon Oakland, Ted Knight, John Anderson, Frank Albertson, Patricia Hitchcock
D: Alfred Hitchcock
W: Joseph Stefano

Psycho (1998)
A: Vince Vaughn, Julianne Moore, Anne Heche, William H. Macy, Viggo Mortensen, Robert Forster, Anne Haney, Chad Everett, Philip Baker Hall, Rita Wilson
D: Gus Van Sant
W: Joseph Stefano

Psycho II
A: Claudia Bryar, Anthony Perkins, Vera Miles, Meg Tilly, Robert Loggia, Dennis Franz
D: Richard Franklin
W: Tom Holland

Psycho III
A: Anthony Perkins, Diana Scarwid, Jeff Fahey, Roberta Maxwell, Robert Alan Browne, Hugh Gillin, Lee Garlington
D: Anthony Perkins
W: Charles Edward Pogue

Psycho IV: The Beginning
A: Anthony Perkins, Henry Thomas, Olivia Hussey, CCH Pounder, Warren Frost, Donna Mitchell
D: Mick Garris
W: Joseph Stefano

Psycho Beach Party
A: Lauren Ambrose, Thomas Gibson, Nicholas Brendon, Kimberly Davies, Matt Keeslar, Beth Broderick, Charles Busch, Danni Wheeler, Amy Adams, Kathleen Robertson
D: Robert Lee King
W: Charles Busch

Pumpkinhead
A: Lance Henriksen, John DiAquino, Kerry Remsen, Matthew Hurley, Jeff East, Kimberly Ross, Cynthia Bain, Joel Hoffman, Florence Schauffler, Buck Flower, Tom Woodruff Jr.
D: Stan Winston
W: Gary Gerani, Mark Patrick Carducci

Pumpkinhead II: Blood Wings
A: Ami Dolenz, Andrew Robinson, Kane Hodder, R.A. Mijailoff, Linnea Quigley, Steve Kanaly, Caren Kaye, Gloria Hendry, Soleil Moon Frye, Mark McCracken, Roger Clinton
D: Jeff Burr
W: Ivan Chachornia, Constantin Chachornia

Queen of the Damned
A: Aaliyah, Stuart Townsend, Marguerite Moreau, Vincent Perez, Lena Olin, Paul McGann, Claudia Black, Christian Manon, Matthew Newton, Bruce Spence
D: Michael Rymer
W: Scott Abbott, Michael Petroni

Rabid
A: Marilyn Chambers, Frank Moore, Joe Silver, Howard Ryshpan, Patricia Gage, Susan Roman
D: David Cronenberg
W: David Cronenberg

Raisins de Mort, Les
A: Marie-Georges Pascal, Jean Pierre Bouyou, Christian Meunier, Brigitte Lahai, Serge Marquand, Felix Marten
D: Jean Rollin
W: Jean Rollin

Rapture, The
A: Mimi Rogers, David Duchovny, Patrick Baucau, Will Patton
D: Michael Tolkin
W: Michael Tolkin

Rasputin, the Mad Monk
A: Christopher Lee, Barbara Shelley, Richard Pasco, Francis Matthews, Suzan Farmer, Nicholas Pennell, Renee Asherson, Derek Francis
D: Don Sharp
W: John Elder

Raven, The (1935)
A: Boris Karloff, Bela Lugosi, Irene Ware, Lester Matthews, Samuel S. Hinds
D: Lew (Louis Friedlander) Landers
W: David Boehm, Jim Tully

Raven, The (1963)
A: Vincent Price, Boris Karloff, Peter Lorre, Jack Nicholson, Hazel Court, Olive Sturgess
D: Roger Corman
W: Richard Matheson

Ravenous
A: Guy Pearce, David Arquette, Robert Carlyle, Jeremy Davies, John Spencer, Jeffrey Jones, Stephen Spinella, Neal McDonough
D: Antonia Bird
W: Ted Griffin

Re-Animator
A: Jeffrey Combs, Bruce Abbott, Barbara Crampton, David Gale, Robert Sampson, Gerry Black, Carolyn Purdy-Gordon
D: Stuart Gordon
W: Stuart Gordon, Dennis Paoli, William J. Norris

Reaping, The
A: Hilary Swank, AnnaSophia Robb, David Morrissey, Idris Elba, Stephen Rea, John McConnell, William Ragsdale, David Jensen, Yvonne Landry, Samuel Garland, Myles Cleveland, Andrea Frankle
D: Stephen Hopkins
W: Carey Hayes, Chad Hayes

[REC]
A: Ferran Terraza, Manuela Velasco, Jorge-Yaman Serrano, Carlos Vicente, Martha Carbonell, Vicente Gil, David Vert, Pablo Rosso
D: Jaume Balaguero, Paco Plaza
W: Jaume Balaguero, Paco Plaza

Red Dragon
A: Anthony Hopkins, Edward Norton, Ralph Fiennes, Harvey Keitel, Emily Watson, Mary-Louise Parker, Philip Seymour Hoffman
D: Brett Ratner
W: Ted Tally

Red House, The
A: Edward G. Robinson, Judith Anderson, Lon McCallister, Roy Calhoun, Julie London, Allene Roberts
D: Delmer Daves
W: Delmer Daves, Albert Maltz

Red Riding Hood
A: Amanda Seyfried, Lukas Haas, Gary Oldman, Billy Burke, Max Irons, Shiloh Fernandez, Virginia Madsen, Julie Christie, Shauna Kain, Michael Hogan
D: Catherine Hardwicke
W: David Johnson

Relic, The
A: Penelope Ann Miller, Tom Sizemore, Linda Hunt, James Whitmore, Clayton Rohner, Thomas Ryan, Lewis Van Bergen, Chi Muoi Lo, Robert Lesser
D: Peter Hyams
W: Amy Holden Jones, John Raffo, Rick Jaffa, Amanda Silver

Repulsion
A: Catherine Deneuve, Ian Hendry, John Fraser, Yvonne Furneaux
D: Roman Polanski
W: Roman Polanski, Gerard Brach

Resident Evil
A: Milla Jovovich, Michelle Rodriguez, Colin Salmon, James Purefoy, Martin Crewes, Eric Mabius
D: Paul W. S. Anderson
W: Paul W. S. Anderson

Resident Evil: Afterlife
A: Milla Jovovich, Wentworth Miller, Ali Larter, Kim Coates, Shawn Roberts, Sergio Peris-Mencheta, Spencer Locke, Boris Kodjoe, Sienna Guillory, Kacey Barnfield, Fulvio Cecere, Norman Yeung
D: Paul W. S. Anderson
W: Paul W. S. Anderson

Resident Evil: Apocalypse
A: Milla Jovovich, Sienna Guillory, Eric Mabius, Oded Fehr, Thomas Kretschmann, Sophie Vavasseur, Razaaq Adoti, Mike Epps, Jared Harris, Matthew G. Taylor, Sandrine Holt, Zack Ward, Iain Glen
D: Alexander Witt
W: Paul W. S. Anderson

Resident Evil: Extinction
A: Milla Jovovich, Ali Larter, Oded Fehr, Ashanti, Iain Glen, Christopher Egan, Spencer Locke, Linden Ashby, Matthew Marsden, Jason O'Mara, Mike Epps, Joe Hursley
D: Russell Mulcahy
W: Paul W. S. Anderson

Resident Evil: Retribution
A: Milla Jovovich, Sienna Guillory, Michelle Rodriguez, Aryana Engineer, Boris Kodjoe, Bingbing Li, Johann Urb, Kevin Durand, Robin Kasyanov, Ofilio Portillo, Oded Fehr, Colin Salmon, Shawn Roberts
D: Paul W. S. Anderson
W: Paul W. S. Anderson

Resurrected, The
A: John Terry, Jane Sibbett, Chris Sarandon, Robert Romanus
D: Dan O'Bannon
W: H.P. Lovecraft, Brent V. Friedman

Return of Dr. X, The
A: Wayne Morris, Humphrey Bogart, Rosemary Lane, Dennis (Stanley Morner) Morgan, John Litel, Lya Lys, Huntz Hall
D: Vincent Sherman
W: Lee Katz

Return of the Blind Dead
A: Tony Kendall, Esther Roy, Frank Blake, Gernando Sancho, Lone Fleming, Loreta Rovar, Jose Canalejas
D: Armando de Ossorio
W: Armando de Ossorio

Return of the Fly
A: Vincent Price, Brett Halsey, John Sutton, Dan Seymour, David Frankham, Danielle De Metz, Ed Wolff
D: Edward L. Bernds
W: Edward L. Bernds, Brydon Baker

Return of the Living Dead
A: Clu Gulager, James Karen, Lennea Quigley, Don Calfa, Jewel Shepard, Beverly Randolph, Miguel Nunez, Brian Peck
D: Dan O'Bannon
W: Dan O'Bannon

Return of the Living Dead Part II
A: Dana Ashbrook, Marsha Dietlein, Philip Bruns, James Karen, Thom Mathews, Suzanne Snyder, Michael Kenworthy, Thor Van Lingen
D: Ken Wiederhorn
W: Ken Wiederhorn

Return of the Living Dead Part III
A: Mindy Clark, J. Trevor Edmond, Kent McCord, Basil Wallace, Fabio Urena
D: Brian Yuzna
W: John Penny

Return of the Vampire
A: Bela Lugosi, Nina Foch, Miles Mander, Matt Willis, Frieda Inescort, Roland Varno, Gilbert Emery, Ottola Nesmith
D: Lew (Louis Friedlander) Landers
W: Griffin Jay

Return to House on Haunted Hill
A: Amanda Righetti, Cerina Vincent, Erik Palladino, Andrew Lee Potts, Tom Riley, Steven Pacey, Jeffrey Combs, Gil Kolirin, Andrew Pleavin, Calita Rainford, Charles Venn
D: Victor Garcia
W: William Massa

Return to Salem's Lot
A: Michael Moriarty, Ricky Addison Reed, Samuel Fuller, Andrew Duggan, Evelyn Keyes, Jill Gatsby, June Havoc, Ronee Blakley, James Dixon, David Holbrook
D: Larry Cohen
W: Larry Cohen, James Dixon

Revamped
A: Jeff Rector, Christa Campbell, Martin Kove, Tane McClure, Alana Curry, Fred Williamson, Victor Lundin, Sam J. Jones, Billy Drago
D: Jeff Rector
W: Antonio Olivas, Jeff Rector

Revenge of the Creature
A: John Agar, Lori Nelson, John Bromfield, John Wood, Nestor Paiva, Clint Eastwood, Robert B. Williams, Grandon Rhodes
D: Jack Arnold
W: Martin Berkeley

Riding the Bullet
A: David Arquette, Jonathan Jackson, Barbara Hershey, Cliff Robertson, Erika Christensen, Barry W. Levy, Peter LeCroix, Jackson Warris, Jeffrey Ballard
D: Mick Garris
W: Mick Garris

Ring, The
A: Naomi Watts, Martin Henderson, Brian Cox, David Dorfman, Jane Alexander, Lindsay Frost, Rachael bella, Daveigh Chase, Amber Tamblyn, Shannon Cochran
D: Gore Verbinski
W: Ehren Kruger

Ring Two, The
A: Naomi Watts, David Dorfman, Sissy Spacek, Simon Baker, Elizabeth Perkins, Gary Cole, Ryan Merriman, Emily VanCamp, Kelly Overton
D: Hideo Nakata
W: Ehren Kruger

Rise: Blood Hunter
A: Lucy Liu, Michael Chiklis, Carla Gugino, Cameron Richardson, Robert Forster, Allan Rich, Samanth Shelton, Kevin Wheatley, Margo Harshman, Cameron Goodman, Holt McCallany
D: Sebastian Gutierrez
W: Sebastian Gutierrez

Rite, The
A: Anthony Hopkins, Colin O'Donoghue, Ciaran Hinds, Rutger Hauer, Alice Braga, Toby Jones, Marta Gastini, Arianna Veronesi, Maria Grazia Cucinotta
D: Mikael Hafstroem
W: Michael Petroni

Rocky Horror Picture Show, The
A: Tim Curry, Susan Sarandon, Barry Bostwick, Little Nell, Richard O'Brien, Patricia Quinn, Jonathan Adams, Peter Hinwood, Meat Loaf
D: Jim Sharman
W: Jim Sharman, Richard O'Brien

Rodan
A: Kenji Sahara, Yumi Shirakawa, Akihiko Hirata, Akio Kobori, Yasuko Nakata
D: Ishiro Honda
W: David Duncan, Takeshi Kimura

Rogue
A: Sam Worthington, Michael Vartan, Radha Mitchell, Stephen Curry, Caroline Brazier, John Jarratt, Heather Mitchell, Geoff Morrell, Robert Taylor, Mia Wasikowska, Barry Otto, Damien Richardson
D: Greg Mclean
W: Greg Mclean

Rosemary's Baby
A: Mia Farrow, John Cassavetes, Ruth Gordon, Sidney Blackmer, Maurice Evans, Patsy Eklly, Elisha Cook Jr., Charles Grodin, William Castle, Ralph Bellamy
D: Roman Polanski
W: Roman Polanski

Ruins, The
A: Shawn Ashmore, Jena Malone, Jonathan Tucker, Laura Ramsey, Joe Anderson, Sergio Calderon, Dimitri Baveas
D: Carter Smith
W: Scott B. Smith

Salem's Lot (1979)
A: David Soul, James Mason, Lance Kerwin, Bonnie Bedelia, Lew Ayres, Ed Flanders, Elisha Cook Jr., Reggie Nadler, Fred Willard, Kenneth McMillan, Marie Windsor
D: Tobe Hooper
W: Paul Monash

'Salem's Lot (2004)
A: Rob Lowe, Donald Sutherland, Andre Braugher, Rutger Hauer, Samantha Mathis, Dan Byrd, Robert Mammone, James Cromwell, Robert Gibb, Andy Anderson
D: Michael Salomon
W: Peter Filardi

Santa Sangre
A: Axel Jodorowsky, Sabrina Dennison, Guy Stockwell, Blanca Guerra, Thelma Tixou, Adan Jodorowsky, Faviola Tapia, Jesus Juarez
D: Alejandro Jodorowsky
W: Robert Leoni, Claudio Argento, Alejandro Jodorowsky

Saw
A: Cary Elwes, Danny Glover, Leigh Whannell, Tobin Bell, Ken Leung, Shawnee Smith, Michael Emerson, Paul Gutrecht, Mike Butters, Dina Meyer, Makenzie Vega, Monica Potter, Ned Bellamy, Avner Garbi, Alexandra Bokyun Chun
D: James Wan
W: Leigh Whannell

Saw II
A: Tobin Bell, Donnie Wahlberg, Beverley Mitchell, Franky G, Erik Knudsen, Glenn Plummer, Emmanuelle Vaugier, Tim Burd, Beverley Mitchell, Lyriq Bent, Dina Meyer, Noam Jenkins, Tony Nappo
D: Darren Lynn Bousman
W: Leigh Whannell, Darren Lynn Bousman

Saw III
A: Tobin Bell, Shawnee Smith, Angus Macfadyen, Lyriq Bent, Barry Flatman, Mpho Koaho, Dina Meyer, Bahar Soomekh
D: Darren Lynn Bousman
W: Leigh Whannell

Saw IV
A: Tobin Bell, Scott Patterson, Costas Mandylor, Angus Macfayden, Betsy Russell, Lyriq Bent, Athena Karkanis, Simon Reynolds, Louis Ferreira, Donnie Wahlberg, Bahar Soomekh
D: Darren Lynn Bousman
W: Patrick Melton, Marcus Dunstan

Saw V
A: Tobin Bell, Scott Patterson, Costas Mandylor, Costas Mandylor, Meagan Good, Betsy Russell, Julie Benz, Mark Rolston, Carlo Rota, Greg Bryk, Joris Jarsky, Laura Gordon, Mike Butters
D: David Hackl
W: Patrick Melton, Marcus Dunstan

Saw VI
A: Tobin Bell, Costas Mandylor, Mark Rolston, Betsy Russell, Shawnee Smith, Peter Outerbridge, Athena Karkanis, Samantha Lemole, Tanedra Howard, Marty Moreau, Shawn Ahmed, Janelle Hutchison
D: Kevin Greutert
W: Patrick Melton, Marcus Dunstan

Saw: The Final Chapter
A: Tobin Bell, Costas Mandylor, Betsy Russell, Cary Elwes, Sean Patrick Flanery, Gina Holden, Chad Donella, Dean Armstrong, Gina Holden, Naomi Snieckus, Rebecca Marshall
D: Kevin Greutert
W: Patrick Melton, Marcus Dunstan

Scalpel
A: Robert Lansing, Judith Chapman, Alren Dean Snyder, Sandy Martin, Davod Scarroll
D: John Grissmer
W: John Grissmer

Scanners
A: Stephen Lack, Jennifer O'Neill, Patrick McGoohan, Lawrence Dane, Michael Ironside, Robert A. Silverman
D: David Cronenberg
W: David Cronenberg

Scary Movie
A: Jon Abrahams, Anna Faris, Marlon Wayans, Carmen Electra, Dave Sheridan, Frank B. Moore, Karen Kruper, Rick Ducommun, Regina Hall, Sharon Elizabeth, Lochlyn Munro, Shawn Wayans, Dan Joffre, David L. Lander, Babe Dolan, Kendall Saunders, Tanja Reichert, Kurt Fuller, Kelly Coffield Park
D: Keenan Ivory Wayans
W: Marlon Wayans, Shawn Wayans, Budy Johnson, Phil Beauman, Jason Friedberg, Aaron Seltzer

Scream
A: Drew Barrymore, Neve Campbell, Courtney Cox, David Arquette, Skeet Ulrich, Rose McGowan, Henry Winkler, Liev Schreiber, W. Earl Brown, Jamie Kennedy, Lawrence Hecht, Wes Craven, Linda Blair
D: Wes Craven
W: Kevin Williamson

Scream 2
A: Courtney Cox, Neve Campbell, Jerr O'Connell, David Arquette, Jada Pinkett, Jamie Kennedy, Liev Schreiber, Sarah Michelle Gellar, Laurie Metcalf, Elise Neal, Lewis Arquette, Duane Martin, Omar Epps, David Warner, Tori Spelling
D: Wes Craven
W: Kevin Williamson

Scream 3
A: David Arquette, Courteney Cox, Neve Campbell, Patrick Warburton, Liev Schreiber, Kelly Rutherford, Roger Jackson, Beth Toussaint, Lance Henriksen, Scott Foley, Deon Richmond, Matt Keeslar, Jenny McCarthy, Emily Mortimer, Parker Posey, Lawrence Hecht, Kevin Smith
D: Wes Craven
W: Ehren Kruger

Scre4m
A: Courtney Cox, David Arquette, Neve Campbell, Roger Jackson, Dane Farwell, Lucy Hale, Shenae Grimes, Anna Paquin, Kristen Bell, Aimee Teegarden, Britt Robertson, Alison Brie, Hayden Panettiere, Emma Roberts, Marielle Jaffe, Erik Knudsen, Marley Shelton
D: Wes Craven
W: Kevin Williamson

Scream and Scream Again
A: Vincent Price, Christopher Lee, Peter Cushing, Judy Huxtable, Alfred Marks, Anthony Newlands, Uta Levka, Judi Bloom, Yette Stensgaard
D: Gordon Hessler
W: Christopher Wicking

Screaming Mimi
A: Gypsy Rose Lee, Anita Ekberg, Philip Carey, Harry Townes, Linda Cherney, Romney Brent, Alan Gifford, Oliver McGowan, Vaughn Taylor, Stephen Ellsworth, Frank J. Scannell
D: Gerd Oswald
W: Robert Blees

Season of the Witch
A: Jan White, Ray Laine, Bill Thunhurst, Joedda McClain, Virginia Greenwald, Ann Muffly, Neil Fisher, Esther Lapidus, Dan Mallinger, Ken Peters
D: George Romero
W: George Romero

Secret Window
A: Johnny Depp, John Turturro, Maria Bello, Timothy Hutton, Charles S. Dutton, Len Cariou, Joan Heney
D: David Koepp
W: David Koepp

Seed of Chucky
A: Jennifer Tilly, John Waters, Brad Dourif, Billy Boyd, Hannah Spearritt, Steve West, Redman
D: Don Mancini
W: Don Mancini

Seizure
A: Jonathan Frid, Herve Villechaize, Christina Pickles, Martine Beswick, Joseph Sirola, Troy Donohue, Mary Woronov, Anne Meacham
D: Oliver Stone
W: Oliver Stone, Edward Andrew Mann

Sentinel, The
A: Chris Sarandon, Christina Raines, Ava Gardner, Jose Ferrer, Sylvia Miles, John Carradine, Burgess Meredith, Tom Berenger, Beverly D'Angelo, Jeff Goldblum, Arthur Kennedy, Deborah Raffin, Eli Wallach, Christopher Walken
D: Michael Winner
W: Michael Winner, Jeffrey Konvitz

Serpent and the Rainbow, The
A: Bill Pullman, Cathy Tyson, Zakes Mokae, Paul Winfield, Conrad Roberts, Badja Djola, Theresa Merritt, Brent Jennings, Michael Gough
D: Wes Craven
W: Richard Maxwell, A.R. Simoun

Session 9
A: David Caruso, Stephen Gevedon, Paul Guilfoyle, Josh Lucas, Peter Mullan, Brendan Sexton III
D: Brad Anderson
W: Brad Anderson, Stephen Gevedon

Se7en
A: Brad Pitt, Morgan Freeman, Gwyneth Paltrow, Kevin Spacey, R. Lee Ermey, Richard Roundtree, John C. McGinley, Julie Araskog, Reg E. Cathey, Peter Crombie
D: David Fincher
W: Andrew Kevin Walker

Seventh Sign, The
A: Demi Moore, Juergen Prochnow, Michael Biehn, John Heard, Peter Friedman, Manny Jacobs, John Taylor, Lee Garlington, Akosua Busia
D: Carl Schultz
W: W.W. Wicket

Severance
A: Danny Dyer, Tim McInnerny, Laura Harris, Toby Stephens, Claudie Blakley, Andy Nyman, Babou Ceesay, David Gilliam, Juli Drajko, Judit Viktor
D: Christopher Smith
W: Christopher Smith, James Moran

Sh! The Octopus
A: Hugh Herbert, Allen Jenkins, Marcia Ralston, John Eldredge, George Rosener, Brandon Tyrian, Margaret Irving, Eric Stanley, Elspeth Dudgeon
D: William C. McGann
W: George Bricker

Shadow of the Vampire
A: John Malkovich, Willem Dafoe, Udo Kier, Cary Elwes, Catherine McCormack, Eddie Izzard, Nicholas Elliott, Aden Gillett, Ronan Vibert
D: E. Elias Merhige
W: Steven Katz

Shaun of the Dead
A: Simon Pegg, Nick Frost, Kate Ashfield, Nicola Cunningham, Dylan Moran, Lucy Davis
D: Edgar Wright
W: Edgar Wright, Simon Pegg

Shining, The (1980)
A: Jack Nicholson, Shelley Duvall, Danny Lloyd, Scatman Crothers, Joe Turkel, Barry Nelson, Philip Stone, Lia Beldam, Billie Gibson, Barry Dennan, David Baxt, Lisa Burns, Alison Coleridge, Kate Phelps, Anne Jackson, Tony Burton
D: Stanley Kubrick
W: Stanley Kubrick, Diane Johnson

Shining, The (1997)
A: Steven Weber, Rebecca De Mornay, Courland Mead, Wil Horneff
D: Mick Garris
W: Stephen King

Shock Waves
A: Peter Cushing, Brooke Adams, John Carradine, Luke Halpin, Jack Davidson, Fred Buch
D: Ken Wiederhorn
W: Ken Wiederhorn, John Kent Harrison

Shocker
A: Michael Murphy, Peter Berg, Cami Cooper, Mitch Pileggi, Richard Price, Timothy Leary, Heather Langenkamp, Theodore (Ted) Raimi, Richard Brooks, Sam Scarber
D: Wes Craven
W: Wes Craven

Silence of the Lambs
A: Jodie Foster, Anthony Hopkins, Scott Glenn, Ted Levine, Brooke Smith, Charles Napier, Roger Corman, Anthony Heald, Diane Baker, Chris Isaak
D: Jonathan Demme
W. Ted Tally

Silent Hill
A: Radha Mitchell, Laurie Holden, Sean Bean, Kim Coates, Deborah Kara Unger, Tanya Allen, Alice Krige, Jodelle Ferland
D: Christophe Gans
W: Roger Avary

Silent Scream, The
A: Rebecca Balding, Cameron Mitchell, Avery Schreiber, Barbara Steele, Steve Doubet, Brad Reardon, Yvonne De Carlo
D: Denny Harris
W: Wallace C. Bennett, Jim Wheat, Ken Wheat

Silver Bullet
A: Corey Haim, Gary Busey, Megan Follows, Everett McGill, Robin Groves, Leon Russom, Terry O'Quinn, Bill Smitrovich, Kent Broadhurst, Lawrence Tierney
D: Daniel Attias
W: Stephen King

Simon, King of the Witches
A: Andrew Prine, Brenda Scott, George Paulsin, Norman Burton, Ultra Violet
D: Bruce Kessler
W: Robert Phippeny

Sixth Sense, The
A: Haley Joel Osment, Bruce Willis, Toni Collette, Olivia Williams, Trevor Morgan, Donnie Wahlberg
D: M. Night Shyamalan
W: M. Night Shyamalan

Skeleton Key, The
A: Kate Hudson, Peter Sarsgaard, John Hurt, Joy Bryant, Gena Rowlands, Joy Bryant, Maxine Barnett
D: Iain Softley
W: Ehren Kruger

Sleepless
A: Max von Sydow, Stefano Dionisi, Chiara Caselli, Roberto Zibetti, Gabriele Lavia, Rossella Falk, Paolo Maria Scalondro, Roberto Acconmero, Barbara Lerici
D: Dario Argento
W: Dario Argento, Franco Ferrini, Carlo Lucarelli

Sleepy Hollow
A: Johnny Depp, Christina Ricci, Miranda Richardson, Christopher Walken, Ian McDiarmid, Casper Van Dien, Michael Gambon, Richard Griffiths, Michael Gough
D: Tim Burton
W: Andrew Kevin Walker, Kevin Yagher

Slither
A: Nathan Fillion, Elizabeth Banks, Michael Rooker, Don Thompson, Tania Saulnier, Michael Rooker, Haig Sutherland, Jennifer Copping, Brenda James

D: James Gunn
W: James Gunn

Slumber Party Massacre
A: Michele Michaels, Robin Stille, Andre Honore, Michael Villela, Debra Deliso, Gina Mari, Brinke Stevens, Jean Vargas, Rigg Kennedy
D: Amy Holden Jones
W: Rita Mae Brown

Snakes on a Plane
A: Samuel L. Jackson, Julianna Margulies, Nathan Phillips, Flex Alexander, Rachel Blanchard, Kenan Thompson, Lin Shaye, Bruce James, Sunny Mabrey, Casey Dubois, Keith Dallas, Daniel Hogarth
D: David R. Ellis
W: John Heffernan, Sebastian Gutierrez

Snow White: A Tale of Terror
A: Sigourney Weaver, Sam Neill, Monica Keena, Gil Bellows, Taryn Davis
D: Michael Cohn
W: Thomas Szollosi, Deborah Serra

Sole Survivor
A: Anita Skinner, Kurt Johnson, Caren Larkey, Brinke Stevens, Leon Robinson
D: Thom Eberhardt
W: Thom Eberhardt

Something Wicked This Way Comes
A: Jason Robards Jr., Jonathan Pryce, Diane Ladd, Pam Grier, Richard Davalos, James Stacy, Royal Dano, Vidal Peterson, Shawn Carson
D: Jack Clayton
W: Ray Bradbury

Sometimes They Come Back
A: Tim Matheson, Brooke Adams, Robert Rusler, William Sanderson
D: Tom McLoughlin
W: Lawrence Konner, Mark Rosenthal

Sometimes They Come Back ... Again
A: Michael Gross, Hilary Swank, Alexis Arquette, Jennifer Elise Cox
D: Adam Grossman
W: Adam Grossman

Son of Dracula
A: Lon Chaney Jr., Evelyn Ankers, Frank Craven, Robert Paige, Louise Allbritton, J. Edward Bromberg, Samuel S. Hinds
D: Robert Siodmak
W: Eric Taylor

Son of Frankenstein
A: Basil Rathbone, Bela Lugosi, Boris Karloff, Lionel Atwill, Josephine Hutchinson, Donnie Dunagan, Emma Dunn, Edgar Norton, Lawrence Grant, Lionel Barrymore
D: Rowland V. Lee
W: Willis Cooper

Sorority Row
A: Briana Evigan, Carrie Fisher, Rumer Willis, Teri Andrez, Adam Berry, Robert Belushi, Jamie Chung, Leah Pipes, Audrina Patridge, Matt O'Leary, Julian Morris
D: Stewart Hendler
W: Josh Stolberg, Pete Goldfinger

Soul Survivors
A: Wes Bentley, Melissa Sagemiller, Casey Affleck, Luke Wilson, Eliza Dushku, Angela Featherstone, Allen Hamilton
D: Stephen Carpenter
W: Stephen Carpenter

Species
A: Ben Kingsley, Michael Madsen, Alfred Molina, Forest Whitaker, Marg Helgenberg, Natasha Hentsridge
D: Roger Donaldson
W: Dennis Feldman

Specters
A: Donald Pleasance, John Pepper, Erna Schurer, Katrine Michelsen
D: Marcello Avallone
W: Marcello Avallone, Andrea Purgatori, Dardano Sacchetti, Maurizio Tedesco

Spider Baby
A: Lon Chaney Jr., Mantan Moreland, Carol Ohmart, Sig Haig, Beverly Washburn, Jill Banner, Quinn Redeker, Mary Mitchell
D: Jack Hill
W: Jack Hill

Splice
A: Adrien Brody, Sarah Polley, Delphine Chaneac, Brandon McGibbon, Abigail Chu, David Hewlett, Simona Maicanescu
D: Vincenzo Natali
W: Vincenzo Natali, Antoinette Terry Bryant, Doug Taylor

Splinter
A: Shea Whigham, Jill Wagner, Paulo Costanzo, Rachel Kerbs, Laurel Whitsett, Charles Baker
D: Toby Wilkins
W: Ian Shorr, Kai Barry, Toby Wilkins

Spontaneous Combustion
A: Brad Dourif, Jon Cypher, Melinda Dillon, Cynthia Bain, William Prince, Dey Young, Dick Butkus, John Landis
D: Tobe Hooper
W: Tobe Hooper

Stendahl Syndrome, The
A: Asia Argento, Thomas Kretschmann, Marco Leonardi, julien Lambroschini, paolo Bonacelli, Luigi Diberti, John Quentin
D: Dario Argento
W: Dario Argento

Stepfather, The (1987)
A: Terry O'Quinn, Shelley Hack, Jill Schoelen, Stephen Shellan, Charles Lanyer, Stephen E. Miller
D: Joseph Ruben
W: Donald E. Westlake

Stepfather, The (2009)
A: Penn Badgley, Dylan Walsh, Sela Ward, Amber Heard, Paige Turco, Sherry Stringfield, Jon Tenney, Marcuis Harris, Braeden Lemasters, Deirdre Lovejoy, Nancy Linehan Charles, Blue Deckert, Jason Wiles
D: Nelson McCormick
W: J. S. Cardone, Donald E. Westlake

Stepfather II (1989)
A: Terry O'Quinn, Meg Foster, Caroline Williams, Jonathan Brandis, Henry Brown, Mitchell Laurance
D: Jeff Burr
W: John P. Auerbacj

Stepford Wives
A: Katherine Ross, Paula Prentiss, Peter Masterson, Nanette Newman, Patrick O'Neal, Tina Louise, Dee Wallace Stone, William Prince, Mary Stuart Masterson, Carol Rossen
D: Bryan Forbes
W: William Goldman

Stephen King's It
A: Tim Reid, Richard Thomas, John Ritter, Annette O'Toole, Richard Masur, Dennis Christopher, Harry Anderson, Olivia Hussey, Tim Curry, Jonathan Brandis, Michael Cole
D: Tommy Lee Wallace
W: Stephen King

Stephen King's Night Flier
A: Michael H. Moss, Miquel Ferrer, Julie Entwisle
D: Mark Pavia
W: Mark Pavia, Jack O'Donnell

Stephen King's Sleepwalkers
A: Brian Krause, Madchen Amick, Alice Krige, Jim Haynie, Cindy Pickett, Lyman Ward, Ron Perlman, Stephen King, Tobe Hooper, John Landis, Dan Martin
D: Mick Garris
W: Stephen King

Stephen King's The Stand
A: Jamey Sheridan, Ruby Dee, Gary Sinese, Molly Ringwald, Miquel Ferrer, Laura San Giacomo, Rob Lowe, Adam Storke, Matt Frewer, Corin "Corky" Nemec, Ray Walston, Bill Fagerbakke, Ossie Davis, Shawnee Smith, Rick Aviles, John (Joe Bob Briggs) Bloom, Bill Fagerbakke, Kareem Abdul-Jabbar
D: Mick Garris
W: Stephen King

Stephen King's The Tommyknockers
A: Jimmy Smits, Marg Helgenberger, Joanna Cassidy, E.G. Marshall, Traci Lords, John Ashton, Allyce Beasley, Cliff DeYoung, Robert Carradine, Leon Woods, Paul McIver
D: John Power
W: Lawrence D. Cohen

Stigmata
A: Patricia Arquette, Jonathan Pryce, Gabriel Byrne, Nia Long, Rade Serbedzija, Thomas Kopache, Enrico Colantoni, Dick Latessa, Portia de Rossi
D: Rupert Wainwright
W: Tom Lazarus, Rick Ramage

Stir of Echoes
A: Kevin Bacon, Zachary David Cope, Kathryn Erbe, Illeana Douglas, Kevin Dunn, Conor O'Farrell, Lusia Strus, Stephen Eugene Walker, Larry Neumann Jr., Mary Kay Cook, Jennifer Morrison
D: David Koepp
W: David Koepp

Storm Warning
A: Nadia Fares, Robert Taylor, David Lyons, John Brumpton, Jonathan Oldham, Mathew Wilkinson
D: Jamie Blanks
W: Everett De Roche

Stormswept
A: Julie Hughes, Melissa Moore, Kathleen Kinmont, Justin Carroll, Lorissa McComas, Ed Wasser, Kim Kopf, Hunt Scarritt
D: David Marsh
W: David Marsh

Strait-Jacket
A: Joan Crawford, Leif Erickson, Diane Baker, George Kennedy, Howard St. John, Rochelle Hudson, Edith Atwater, Lee Majors
D: William Castle
W: Robert Bloch

Strange Behavior
A: Michael Murphy, Louise Fletcher, Dan Shor, Fiona Lewis, Arthur Dignam, Marc McClure, Scott Brady, Dey Young, Charles Lane
D: Michael Laughlin
W: Michael Laughlin, Bill Condon

Strange Door
A: Charles Laughton, Boris Karloff, Paul Cavanagh, Sally Forrest, Richard Stapley, Michael Pate, Alan Napier
D: Joseph Pevney
W: Jerry Sackheim

Strangeland
A: Kevin Gage, Elizabeth Pena, Dee Snider, Robert Englund, Brett Harrelson, Linda Cardellini, Tucker Smallwood, Ivonne Coll, Amy Smart
D: John Pieplow
W: Dee Snider

Strangers, The
A: Liv Tyler, Scott Speedman, Gemma Ward
D: Bryan Bertino
W: Bryan Bertino

Subspecies
A: Laura Tate, Michael Watson, Anders Hove, Michelle McBride, Irina Movila, Angus Scrimm
D: TedNicolaou
W: Charles Band, Jackson Barr

Summer of Fear
A: Linda Blair, Lee Purcell, Jeremy Slate, Carol Lawrence, MacDonald Carey, Jeff McCracken, Jeff East, Fran Drescher
D: Wes Craven
W: Glenn Benest

Supernova
A: James Spader, Robin Tunney, Peter Facinelli, Angela Bassett, Lou Diamond Phillips, Wilson Cruz
D: Walter Hill, Franci Ford Coppola, jack Sholder
W: David C. Wilson

Surgeon, The
A: Isabel Glasser, James Remar, Sean Haberle, Charles Dance, Peter Boyle, Malcolm McDowell, Charles Bailey-Gates, Gregory West, Mother Love
D: Carl Schenkel
W: Patrick Cirillo

Survival of the Dead
A: Alan Van Sprang, Kenneth Welsh, Kathleen Munroe
D: George A. Romero
W: George A. Romero

Suspiria
A: Jessica Harper, Joan Bennett, Alida Valli, Udo Kier, Stefania Casini, Flavio Bucci, Barbara Magnolfi, Rudolf Schuendler
D: Dario Argento
W: Dario Argento, Daria Nicolodi

Take Shelter
A: Michael Shannon, Jessica Chastain, Shea Whigham, Tova Stewart, Katy Mixon, Natasha Randall, Robert Longstreet, Scott Knisley, Ron Kennard
D: Jeff Nichols
W: Jeff Nichols

Tale of Two Sisters, A
A: Kap-su Kim, Jung-ah Yum, Su-jeong Lim, Geun-Young Moon
D: Jee-woon Kim
W: Jee-woon Kim

Tales from the Crypt: Demon Knight
A: Billy Zane, William Sadler, Jada Pinkett, Brenda Bakke, CCH Pounder, Dick Miller, Thomas Haden Church, John Schuck, Gary Farmer, Charles Fleischer
D: Ernest R. Dickerson
W: Ethan Reiff, Cyrus, Voris, Mark Bishop

Tales from the Crypt: Bordello of Blood
A: Dennis Miller, Angie Everhart, Chris Sarandon, Corey Feldman, Erika Eleniak
D: Gilbert Adler
W: Gilbert Adler, A.L. Katz

Tales from the Darkside: The Movie
A: Deborah Harry, Christian Slater, David Johansen, William Hickey, James Remar, Rae Dawn Chong, Julianne Moore, Robert Klein, Steve Buscemi, Matthew Lawrence
D: John Harrison
W: George Romero, Michael McDowell

Tarantula
A: John Agar, Mara Corday, Leo G. Carroll, Raymond Bailey, Edwin Rand, Ross Elliott, Nestor Paiva, Hank Patterson, Bert Holland, Steve Darrell
D: Jack Arnold
W: Robert M. Fresco, Martin Berkeley

Targets
A: Boris Karloff, James Brown, Tim O'Kelly, Peter Bogdonovich, Mary Jackson, Sandy Baron, Monte Landis, Mike Farrell, Nancy Hsueh, Arthur Peterson, Tanya Morgan
D: Peter Bogdonovich
W: Peter Bogdonovich

Taste the Blood of Dracula
A: Christopher Lee, Ralph Bates, Geoffrey Keen, Gwen Watford, Linda Hayden, John Carson, Peter Sallis, Isla Blair, Martin Jarvis, Roy Kinnear, Anthony Higgins, Anthony Corlan, Michael Ripper
D: Peter Sasdy
W: Anthony Hinds

Temptress
A: Kim Delaney, Chris Sarandon, Corbin Bernsen, Dee Wallace Stone, Jessica Walter, Ben Cross
D: Lawrence Lanoff
W: Melissa Mitchell

Tenebre
A: Anthony (Tony) Franciosa, John Saxon, Daria Nicolodi, Giuliano Gemma, Christian Borromeo, Mirella D'Angelo, Veronica Lario, Ania Pieroni, Carola Stagnaro, John Steiner, Lara Wendell
D: Dario Argento
W: Dario Argento

Terror, The
A: Boris Karloff, Jack Nicholson, SandraKnight, Dick Miller, Dorothy Neumann, Jonathan Haze
D: Roger Corman, Jack Hill, Francis Ford Coppola, Money Hellman, Dennis Jacob, Jack Nicholson
W: Leo Gordon, Jack Hill

Terror at Red Wolf Inn
A: Linda Gillin, Arthur Space, John Neilson, Mary Jackson, Janet Wood, Margaret Avery
D: Bud Townsend
W: Allen Actor

Terror Train
A: Jamie Lee Curtis, Ben Johnson, Hart Bochner, David Copperfield, Vanity, Howard Busgang, Michael Shanks, Amanda Tapping, Troy Kennedy Martin, Anthony Sherwood, Timothy Webber
D: Roger Spottiswoode
W: T.Y. Drake

Texas Chainsaw Massacre (1974)
A: Marilyn Burns, Allen Danziger, Paul A. Partain, William Vail, Teri McMinn, Edwin Neal, Jim Siedow, Gunnar Hansen, John Dugan, Jerry Lorenz
D: Tobe Hooper
W: Tobe Hooper

Texas Chainsaw Massacre (2003)
A: Jessica Biel, Jonathan Tucker, Andrew Bryniarski, Erica Leerhsen, Mike Vogel, Eric Balfour, David Dorfman, R. Lee Erney
D: Marcus Nispel
W: Scott Kosar

Texas Chainsaw Massacre: The Beginning
A: Jordana Brewster, Matt Bomer, Diora Baird, Taylor Handley, R. Lee Erney, Andrew Bryniarski, Lee Tergesen, Terrence Evans, Marietta Marich
D: Jonathan Liebesman
W: Sheldon Turner

Texas Chainsaw Massacre 2
A: Dennis Hopper, Caroline Williams, Bill Johnson, Jim Siedow, Bill Moseley, Lou Perry
D: Tobe Hooper
W: L.M. Kit Carson

Texas Chainsaw Massacre 4: The Next Generation
A: The Next Generation
A: Renee Zellweger, Matthew McConaughey, Tony Perenski, Robert Jacks, Lisa Newmyer
D: Kim Henkel
W: Kim Henkel

Theatre of Blood
A: Vincent Price, Diana Rigg, Ian Hendry, Robert Morley, Dennis Price, Diana Dors, Milo O'Shea, Harry Andrews, Coral Browne, Robert Coote, Jack Hawkins, Michael Hordern, Arthur Lowe
D: Douglas Hickox
W: Anthony Greville-Bell

Them!
A: James Whitmore, Edmund Gwenn, Fess Parker, James Arness, Onslow Stevens, Jack Perrin, Joan Weldon, Sean McClory, Sandy Descher, Dub Taylor, William Schallert, LeonardNimoy
D: Gordon Douglas
W: Ted Sherdeman

They
A: Laura Regan, Marc Blucas, Ethan Embry, Dagmara Dominczyk, Jon Abrahams, Jessica Amlee, Peter LaCrois, Jonathan Cherry, Mark Hildreth, Desiree Zurowski, Alexander Gould
D: Robert Harmon
W: Brendan Hood

They Came from Within
A: Paul Hampton, Joe Silver, Lynn Lowry, Barbara Steele, Susan Petrie, Allan Magicovsky
D: David Cronenberg
W: David Cronenberg

They Live
A: Roddy Piper, Meg Foster, Keith David, George "Buck" Flower, Peter Jason
D: John Carpenter
W: John Carpenter

Thing (from another World), The (1951)
A: James Arness, Kenneth Tobey, Margaret Sheridan, Dewey Martin, Robert Cornthwaite
D: Christian Nyby, Howard Hawks
W: Charles Lederer, Ben Hecht

Thing, The (1982)
A: Kurt Russell, Wilford Brimley, T.K. Carter, Richard Masur, Keith David, Richard Dysart, David Clennon, Donald Moffatt, Thomas G. Waites, Charles Hallahan
D: John Carpenter
W: Bill Lancaster

Thing, The (2011)
A: Joel Edgerton, Mary Elizabeth Winstead, Ulrich Thomsen, Kim Bubbs, Trond Espen Seim, Paul Braunstein, Adewale Akinnuoye-Agbaje, Eric Christian Olsen, Jorgen Langhelle, Jan Gunnar Roise, Stig Henrik Hoff, Kristofer Hivju, Jo Adrian Haavind, Carsten Bjornlund
D: Matthijs van Jeijningen Jr.
W: Eric Heisserer

Thirst
A: Kang-ho Song, Ok-bin Kim, Hae-suk Kim, Ha-kyun Shin, In-hwan Park, Sal-su Oh, Young-chang Song, Mercedes Cabral, Eriq Ebouaney
D: Chan-wook Park
W: Chan-wook Park, Seo-Gyeong Jeong

Thirteen Ghosts
A: Tony Shaloub, Shannon Elizabeth, Empeth Davidtz, Matthew Lillard, Alec Roberts, JR Bourne, Rah Digga, F. Murray Abraham, Matthew Harrison
D: Steve Beck
W: Benjamin Carr, Richard D'Ovidio

30 Days of Night
A: Josh Hartnett, Melissa George, Danny Huston, Ben Foster, Mark Rendall, Mark Boone Jr., Joel Tobeck, Megan Franich, Manu Bennet, Amber Sainsbury, Elizabeth Hawthorne, Craig Hall, Nathaniel Lees
D: David Slade
W: Steve Niles, Stuart Beattie

301/302
A: Eun-Jim Bang, Sin-Hye Hwang, Chu-Ryun Kim
D: Chul-Soo Park
W: Chul-Soo Park

Thrill of the Vampire
A: Michel Delahaye, Dominique, Jean Durand, Sandra Julien, Nicole Nancel, Jacques Robiolles, Kuelan Herce, Marie-Pierre Tricot
D: Jean Rollin
W: Jean Rollin

Tim Burton's Corpse Bride
A: Johnny Depp, Helena Bonham Carter, Emily Watson, Christopher Lee, Tracey Ullman, Albert Finney, Danny Elfman, Paul Whitehouse, Michael Gough, Richard E. Grant, Jane Horrocks, Enn Reitel, Deep Roy
D: Tim Burton, Mike Johnson
W: John August, Caroline Thompson, Pamela Pettler

Tingler, The
A: Vincent Price, Darryl Hickman, Judith Evelyn, Philip Coolidge, Patricia Cutts, Pamela Lincoln
D: William Castle
W: Robb White

To Sleep with a Vampire
A: Scott Valentine, Charlie Spradling, Richard Zobel, Ingrid Vold, Stephanie Hardy
D: Adam Friedman
W: Patricia Harrington

To the Devil a Daughter
A: Richard Widmark, Christopher Lee, Natassia Kinski, Honor Blackman, Denholm Elliott, Michael Goodliffe
D: Peter Sykes
W: Christopher Wicking

Tombs of the Blind Dead
A: Caesar Burner, Lone Fleming, Helen Harp, Joseph Thelman, Rufino Ingles, Maria Silva
D: Armando de Ossorio
W: Armando de Ossorio

Torso
A: Suzy Kendall, Tina Aumont, Luc Merenda, John Richardson, Roberto Bisacco, Ernesto Colli, Angela Covello, Carla Brait, Conchita Airoldi
D: Sergio Martino
W: Sergio Martino, Ernesto Gastaldi

Torture Chamber of Baron Blood
A: Joseph Cotten, Elke Sommer, Masimo Girotti, Rada Rassimov, Antonio Cantafora
D: Mario Bava
W: Vincent Fotre, William Bairn

Tourist Trap
A: Tanya Roberts, Chuck Connors, Robin Sherwood, Jocelyn Jones, Jon Van Ness, Dawn Jeffory, Keith McDermott
D: David Schmoeller
W: David Schmoeller

Town That Dreaded Sundown, The
A: Ben Johnson, Andrew Prine, Dawn Wells, Jimmy Clem, Charles B. Pirece
D: Charles B. Pierce
W: Earl E. Smith

Transmutations
A: Denholm Elliott, Steven Berkoff, Miranda Richardson, Nicola Cowper, Larry Lamb, Art Malik, Ingrid Pitt, Irina Brook, Paul Brown
D: George Pavlou
W: Clive Barker, James Caplin

Trauma
A: Colin Firth, Naomie Harris, Dorothy Duffy, Sean Harris, Alison David, Martin Hancock, Tommy Flanagan, Paul Rattigan, Liam Reilly
D: Marc Evans
W: Richard Smith

Tremors
A: Kevin Bacon, Fred Ward, Finn Carter, Michael Gross, Reba McIntire, Bibi Besch, Bobby Jacoby, Charlotte Stewart, Victor Wong, Tony Generos, Ariana Richards
D: Ron Underwood
W: S.S. Wilson, Brent Maddox

Tremors 2: Aftershocks
A: Fred Ward, Michael Gross, Helen Shaver, Christopher Gartin, Marcelo Tubert
D: S.S. Wilson
W: S.S. Wilson, Brent Maddox

Tremors 3: Back to Perfection
A: Michael Gross, Susan Chuang, Shawn Christian, Ariana Richards, Charlotte Stewart, Tony Genaro, Robert Jayne, John Pappas, Barry Livingston
D: Brent Maddock
W: John Whelpley

Trick or Treat
A: Tony Fields, Marc Price, Ozzy Osbourne, Gene Simmons, Elaine Joyce, Glenn Morgan, Lisa Orgolini, Doug Savant
D: Charles Martin Smith
W: Joes Soisson, Michael S. Murphy, Rhet Topham

Trick 'R Treat
A: Anna Paquin, Brian Cox, Dylan Baker, Rochelle Aytes, Quinn Lord, Lauren Lee Smith, Moneca Delain, Tahmoh Penikett, Brett Kelly, Samm Todd, Jean-Luc Bilodeau, Britt McKillip, Leslie Bibb, Connor Christopher Levins, James Wilson
D: Michael Dougherty
W: Michael Dougherty

Trilogy of Terror
A: Karen Black, Robert Burton, John Darlen, Gergory Harrison, George Gaynes, James Storm, Kathryn Reynolds, Tracy Curtis
D: Dan Curtis
W: Richard Matheson

Trilogy of Terror II
A: Lysette Anthony, Richard Fitzpatrick, Geraint Wun Davies, Matt Clark, Geoffrey Lewis, Blake Heron
D: Dan Curtis
W: Dan Curtis, William F. Nolan, Richard Matheson

Troll
A: Noah Hathaway, Gary Sandy, Anne Lockhart, Sonny Bono, Shelley Hack, June Lockhart, Michael Moriarty, Lennifer Beck, Phil Fondacaro, Bard Hall, Julia Lewis-Dreyfus
D: John Carl Buechler
W: Ed Naha

Troll 2
A: Michael Stephenson, George Hardy, Margo Prey, Jason Steadman, Darren Ewing, Jason Wright, Robert Ormsby, Connie Young, Deborah Reed
D: Claudio Fragasso
W: Rossella Drudi, Claudio Fragasso

Trollhunter
A: Otto Jespersen, Robert Stoltenberg, Knut Naerum, Tomas Alf Larsen, Ermila Berg-Domaas, Hans Morten Hansen
D: Andre Ovredal
W: Andre Ovredal

Tucker & Dale versus Evil
A: Tyler Labine, Alan Tudyk, Katrina Bowden, Jesse Moss, Philip Granger, Christi Laing, Chelan Simmons, Brandon Jay McLaren, Alex Arsenault, Adam Beauchesne, Joseph Allan Sutherland
D: Eli Craig
W: Eli Craig, Morgan Jurgenson

Turistas
A: Josh Duhamel, Olivia Wilde, Melissa George, Max Brown, Beau Garrett, Desmond Askew, Miguel Lunardi, Agles Steib
D: John Stockwell
W: Michael Ross

28 Days Later
A: Cillian Murphy, Naomie Harris, Christopher Eccleston, Alex Palmer, Bindu De Stoppani, Jukka Hiltunen, Toby Sedgwick, Noah Huntley, Christopher Dunne, Emma Hitching
D: Danny Boyle
W: Alex Garland

28 Weeks Later
A: Jeremy Renner, Rose Byrne, Robert Carlyle, Harold Perrineau, Catherine McCormack, Imogen Poots, Idris Elba, Mackintosh Muggleton, Emily Beecham, Garfield Morgan, Shahid Ahmed
D: Juan Carlos Fresnadillo
W: Rowan Joffe, Juan Carlos Fresnadillo, Enrique Lopez Lavigne, Jesus Olmo

Twentynine Palms
A: David Wissak, Yekaterina Golubeva
D: Bruno Dumont
W: Brumo Dumont

Twilight
A: Kristen Stewart, Robert Pattinson, Billy Burke, Sarah Clarke, Matt Bushell, Gil Birmingham, Taylor Lautner, Justin Chon, Gregory Tyree Boyce, Michael Welch, Anna Kendrick, Kellan Lutz, Nikki Reed, Christian Serratos
D: Catherine Hardwicke
W: Melissa Rosenberg

Twilight Saga: Breaking Dawn—Part 1
A: Kristen Stewart, Robert Pattinson, Taylor Lautner, Billy Burke, Gil Birmingham, Sarah Clarke, Ty Olsson, Ashley Greene, Jackson Rathbone, Peter Facinelli, Elizabeth Reaser, Nikki Reed, Kellan Lutz
D: Bill Condon
W: Melissa Rosenberg

Twilight Saga: Breaking Dawn—Part 2
A: Kristen Stewart, Robert Pattinson, Taylor Lautner, Billy Burke, Peter Facinelli, Elizabeth Reaser, Nikki Reed, Kellan Lutz, Jackson Rathbone, Chaske Spencer, Mackenzie Foy, Jamie Campbell Bower, Maggie Grace, Christopher Heyerdahl
D: Bill Condon
W: Melissa Rosenberg

Twilight Saga: Eclipse
A: Kristen Stewart, Robert Pattinson, Taylor Lautner, Billy Burke, Anna Kendrick, Christian Serratos, Michael Welch, Justin Chon, Ashley Greene, Paul Jarrett, Iris Quinn, Sarah Clarke, Peter Facinelli
D: David Slade
W: Melissa Rosenberg

Twins of Evil
A: Madeleine Collinson, Mary Collinson, Peter Cushing, Kathleen Byron, Dennis Price, Damien Thomas, David Warbeck, Katya Wyeth, Maggie Wright, Luan Peters, Kristen Lindholm, Judy Matheson
D: John Hough
W: Tudor Gates

Two Evil Eyes
A: Adrienne Barbeau, Ramy Zada, Harvey Kietel, Madeleine Potter, Bingo O'Malley, E.G. Marshall, John Amos, Sally Kirkland, Kim Hunter, Martin Balsam, Tom Atkins
D: George Romero, Dario Argento
W: George Romero, Dario Argento, Franco Ferrini

Two Faces of Dr. Jekyll
A: Paul Massie, Dawn Addams, Christopher Lee, David Kossoff, Francis De Wolff, Oliver Reed, Norma Marla, Terry Quinn
D: Terence Fisher
W: Wolf Mankowitz

2000 Maniacs
A: Thomas Wood, Connie Mason, Jeffrey Allen, Ben Moore, Gary Bakeman, Jerome Eden, Shelby Livingston, Michael Korb, Yvonne Gilbert, Mark Douglas, Linda Cochran, Vincent Santo, Andy Wilson
D: Hershell Gordon Lewis
W: Hershell Gordon Lewis

2001 Maniacs
A: Robert Englund, Lin Shaye, Giuseppe Andrews, Jay Gillespie, Marla Malcolm, Dylan Edrington, Matthew Carey, Peter Stomare, Gina Marie Heekin, Brian Gross, Mushond Lee, Bianca Smith, Brendan McCarthy, Adam Robitel, Christa Campbell, Wendy Kremer, Cristin Michele, Kodi Kitchen, Ryan Fleming
D: Tim Sullivan
W: Tim Sullivan, Chris Kobin

Un Chien Andalou
A: Pierre Batcheff, Simone Marevil, Jaime Miravilles, Luis Bunuel, Salvador Dali
D: Luis Bunuel, Salvador Dali
W: Luis Bunuel, Salvador Dali

Unborn, The
A: Gary Oldman, Odette Annable, Cam Gigandet, Meagan Good, Jane Alexander, Atticus Shaffer, James Remar, Carla Gugino, C. S. Lee, Idris Elba
D: David S. Goyer
W: David S. Goyer

Undead
A: Felicity Mason, Rob Jenkins, Mungo McKay, Dirk Hunger, Noel Sheridan, Robyn Moore, Robert Jozinovic, Lisa Cunningham, Emma Randall, Steve Grieg, Gaynor Wensley, Eleanor Stillman
D: Michael Spierig, Peter Spierig
W: Michael Spierig, Peter Spierig

Underworld
A: Kate Beckinsale, Scott Speedman, Shane Brolly, Bill Nighy, sophia Myles, Robbie Gee, Wentworth Miller, Zita Gorog, Kevin Grevioux, Erwin Leder
D: Len Wiseman
W: Danny McBride

Underworld: Awakening
A: Kate Beckinsale, Michael Ealy, India Eisley, Stephen Rea, Theo James, Sandrine Holt, Charles Dance, Kris holden-Ried, Jacob Blair
D: Mans Marlind, Bjorn Stein
W: Len Wiseman, John Hlavin, J. Michael Straczynski, Allison Burnett

Underworld: Evolution
A: Kate Beckinsale, Scott Speedman, Bill Nighy, Tony Curran, Derek Jacobi, Steven Mackintosh, Shane Brolly, Brian Steele, Zita Gorog
D: Len Wiseman
W: Danny McBride

Underworld: Rise of the Lycans
A: Michael Sheen, Rhona Mitra, Bill Nighy, Steven Mackintosh, Kevin Grevioux, David Aston
D: Patrick Tatopoulos
W: Danny McBride, Dirk Blackman, Howard McCain

Unearthed
A: Emmanuelle Vaugier, Luke Goss, Beau Garrett, Charles Q. Murphy, Tommy Dewey, M. C. Gainey, Miranda Bailey, Tonantzin Carmelo, Russell Means, Whitney Able
D: Matthew Leutwyler
W: Matthew Leutwyler

Uninvited, The (1944)
A: Ray Milland, Ruth Hussey, Donald Crisp, Cornelia Otis Skinner, Gail Russell, Alan Napier, Dorothy Stickney
D: Lewis Allen
W: Dodie Smith

Uninvited, The (2009)
A: Emily Browning, Arielle Kebbel, Elizabeth Banks, David Strathaim, Kevin McNulty, Jesse Moss, Maya Massar, Dean Paul Gibson, Don S. Davis, Danny Bristol, Matthew Bristol, Lex Burnham
D: Charles Guard, Thomas Guard
W: Craig Rosenberg, Doug Miro, Carlo Bernard

Unnameable, The
A: Charles King, Mark Kinsey Stephenson, Alexandra Durrell, Laura Albert, Eben Ham, Blane Wheatley, Mark Parra, Kartin Alexandre
D: Jean-Paul Ouellette
W: Jean-Paul Ouellette

Unnameable II: The Statement of Randolph Carter
A: Statement of Randolph Carter
A: Mark Kinsey Stephenson, John Rhys-Davies, David Warner,Julie Strain, Maria Ford, Charles Klausmeyer
D: Jean-Paul Ouellette
W: Jean-Paul Ouellette

Untold Story, The
A: Anthony Wong, Danny Lee
D: Herman Yau
W: Kam-Fai Law

Urban Ghost Story
A: Jason Connery, Stephanie Buttle, Heather Ann Foster, Nicola Stapleton, James Cosmo, Elizabeth Berrington, Billy Boyd, Andreas Wisniewski, Siri Neal
D: Genevieve Jolliffe
W: Genevieve Jolliffe, Chris Jones

Urban Legend
A: Jared Leto, Rebecca Gayheart, Alicia Witt, Robert Englund, Michael Rosenbaum, Loretta Devine, Joshua Jackson, Tara Reid, John Neville, Natasha Gregson Wagner, Danielle Harris, Julian Richings
D: Jamie Blanks
W: Silvio Horta

Vacancy
A: Kate Beckinsale, Frank Whaley, Luke Wilson, Scott G. Anderson
D: Nimrod Antal
W: Mark L. Smith

Vamp
A: Grace Jones, Chris Makepeace, Robert Rusier, Gedde Watanabe, Sandy Baron, Dedee Pfeiffer, Billy Drago, Lisa Lyons
D: Richard Wenk
W: Richard Wenk

Vampire Bat
A: Lionel Atwill, Melvyn Douglas, Dwight Frye, Maude Eburne, George E. Stone
D: Frank Strayer
W: Edward T. Lowe

Vampire Circus
A: Adrienne Corri, Laurence Payne, Thorley Walters, John Moulder-Brown, Lynn Frederick, Elizabeth Seal, Anthony Corlan, Richard Owens, Domini Blythe, David Prowse
D: Robert W. Young
W: Judson Kinberg

Vampire in Brooklyn
A: Eddie Murphy, Angela Bassett, Kadeem Hardison, Allen Payne, Zakes Mokae, John Witherspoon
D: Wes Craven
W: Charles Murphy, Christopher Parker, Michael Lucker

Vampire Lovers
A: Ingrid Pitt, Pippa Steele, Madeleine Smith, Peter Cushing, George Cole, Dawn Addams, Kate O'Mara, Ferdinand "Ferdy" Mayne, Douglas Wilmer, Harvey Hall
D: Roy Ward Baker
W: Tudor Gates

Vampire's Kiss
A: Nicolas Cage, Elizabeth Ashley, Jennifer Beals, Maria Conchita Alonso, Kasi Lemmons, Bob Lujan, David Hyde Pierce
D: Robert Bierman
W: Joe Minion

Vampyr
A: Julian West, Sybille Schmitz, Henriette Gerard, Maurice Schutz, Rena Mandel, Jan Hieronimko, Albert Bras
D: Carl Theodor Dreyer
W: Carl Theodor Dreyer, Christen Jul

Vampyres
A: Marianne Morris, Anulka, Murray Brown, Brian Deacon, Sally Faulkner, Michael Byrne, Karl Lanchbury, Bessie Love, Elliott Sullivan
D: Joseph (Jose Ramon) Larraz
W: Diane Daubeney

Videodrome
A: James Woods, Deborah Harry, Sonja Smits, Peter Dvorsky, Jack Creley
D: David Cronenberg
W: David Cronenberg

Virus
A: Jamie Lee Curtis, William Baldwin, Donald Sutherland, Joanna Pacula, Marshall Bell, Sherman Augustus, Cliff Curtis, Julio Oscar Mechoso
D: John Bruno
W: Chuck Pfarrer, Dennis Feldman

Wait until Dark
A: Audrey Hepburn, Alan Arkin, Richard Crenna, Efram Zimbalist Jr., Jack Weston
D: Terence Young
W: Robert B. Carrington

Walking Dead, The
A: Boris Karloff, Ricardo Cortez, Edmund Gwen, Marguerite Churchill, Warren Hull, Barton MacLane, Henry O'Neill, Joseph King, Addison Richards, Paul Harvey
D: Michael Curtiz
W: Ewart Adamson, Lillie Hayward, Robert D. Andrews, Peter Milne

Warlock
A: Richard E. Grant, Julian Sands, Lori Singer, Mary Woronov, Richard Kuss, Kevin O'Brien, Anna Levine, Allan Miller, David Carpenter
D: Steve Miner
W: David Twohy

Warlock: Armageddon
A: Julian Sands, Chris Young, Paula Marshall, Steve Kahan, Charles Hallahan, R.G. Armstrong, Bruce Glover, Zach Galligan, Dawn Ann Billings, Joanna Pacula
D: Anthony Hickox
W: Kevin Rock, Sam Bernard

Wasp Woman, The (1959)
A: Susan Cabot, Fred Eisley, Barboura Morris, Michael Marks, William Roerick, Frank Gerstle, Bruno Ve Sota, Frank Wolff
D: Roger Corman
W: Leo Gordon

Wasp Woman, The (1996)
A: Jennifer Rubin, Daniel J. Travanti, Maria Ford
D: Jim Wynorski
W: Kinta Zertuche

Wax Mask
A: Robert Hossein, Romina Mondello, Riccardo Serventi Longhi, Valery Valmond, Umberto Balli, Gabriella Giorgelli
D: Sergio Stivaletti
W: Lucio Fulci, Daniele Stroppa

Wendigo
A: Patricia Clarkson, Jake Weber, Erik Per Sullivan, John Speredakos
D: Larry Fessenden
W: Larry Fessenden

Werewolf of London
A: Henry Hull, Warner Oland, Valerie Hobson, Lester Matthews, Spring Byington, Lawrence Grant, Zeffie Tilbury
D: Stuart Walker
W: Robert Harris, John Colton

Werewolf of Washington
A: Dean Stockwell, Biff McGuire, Clifton James, Jane House, Beeson Carroll, Michael Dunn
D: Milton Moses Ginsberg
W: Milton Moses Ginsberg

Wes Craven's New Nightmare
A: Robert Englund, Heather Langenkamp, Miko Hughes, David Newsom, Tracy Middendorf, Fran Bennett, John Saxon, Wes Craven, Robert Shaye, Sara Risher, Marianne Maddalena
D: Wes Craven
W: Wes Craven

What Ever Happened to Baby Jane?
A: Bette Davis, Joan Crawford, Victor Buono, Anna Lee, B.D. Merrill, Maidie Norman
D: Robert Aldrich
W: Lukas Heller

What Lies Beneath
A: Harrison Ford, Michelle Pfeiffer, Katharine Towne, Miranda Otto, James Remar, Victoria Bidewell, Diana Scarwid

D: Robert Zemeckis
W: Clark Gregg

When a Stranger Calls (1979)
A: Carol Kane, Charles Durning, Colleen Dewhurst, Rachel Roberts, Rutanya Alda, Carmen Argenziano, Kirsten Larkin, Ron O'Neal, Tony Beckley
D: Fred Walton
W: Fred Walton

When a Stranger Calls (2006)
A: Camilla Belle, Tommy Flanagan, Katie Cassidy, Clark Gregg, Brian Geraghty
D: Simon West
W: Jake Wade Wall

When a Stranger Calls Back
A: Carol Kane, Charles Durning, Jill Schoelen, Gene Lythgow, Karen Austin
D: Fred Walton
W: Fred Walton

White Zombie
A: Bela Lugosi, Madge Bellamy, John Harron, Joseph Cawthorn, Robert Frazer, Brandon Hurst, George Burr Macannan, John Peters, Dan Crimmins, Clarence Muse
D: Victor Halperin
W: Garnett Weston

Wicker Man, The (1975)
A: Edward Woodward, Christopher Lee, Britt Ekland, Diane Cliento, Ingrid Pitt, Lindsay Kemp, Irene Sunters, Walter Carr, Geraldine Cowper, Lesley Mackie
D: Robin Hardy
W: Anthony Shaffer

Wicker Man, The (2006)
A: Nicolas Cage, Ellen Burstyn, Leelee Sobieski, Kate Beahan, Frances Conroy, Molly Parker, Diane Delano
D: Neil LaBute
W: Neil LaBute

Wicker Tree, The
A: Brittania Nicol, Henry Garrett, Graham McTavish, Christopher Lee, Honeysuckle Weeks, Clive Russell, David Plimmer, Jacqueline Leonard, Leslie Mackie, Prue Clark
D: Robin Hardy
W: Robin Hardy

Willard (1971)
A: Bruce Davison, Ernest Borgnine, Elsa Lanchester, Sondra Locke, Michael Dante, J. Pat O'Malley
D: Daniel Mann
W: Gilbert Ralston

Willard (2003)
A: Crispin Glover, R. Lee Ermey, Laura Harring, Jackie Burroughs, David Parker, Laara Sadiq, Ashlyn Gere, William S. Taylor, Edward Horn, Gus Lynch, Ty Olsson
D: Glen Morgan
W: Glen Morgan

Wind Chill
A: Emily Blunt, Ashton Holmes, Martin Donovan, Ned Bellamy, Chelan Simmons, Donny James Lucas
D: Gregory Jacobs
W: Joe Gangemi, Steven Katz

Witchboard
A: Todd Allen, Tawny Kitaen, Stephen Nichols, Kathleen Wilhoite, Burke Byrnes, Rose Maris, James W. Quinn, Judy Tatum, Gloria Hayes, J.P. Luebsen, Susan Nickerson
D: Kevin S. Tenney
W: Kevin S. Tenney

Witchboard II
A: Ami Dolenz, Laraine Newman, Timothy Gibbs, John Gatins, Julie Michaels, Marvin Kaplan
D: Kevin S. Tenney
W: Kevin S. Tenney

Witchboard: The Possession
A: David Nerman, Locky Lambert, Cedric Smith, Donna Sarrasin
D: Peter Svatek
W: Kevin S. Tenney

Witchcraft
A: Anat "Topol" Barzilai, Gary Sloan, Lee Kisman, Deborah Scott
D: Robert Spera
W: Jody Savin

Witchcraft through the Ages
A: Maren Pedersen, Clara Pontoppidan, Oscar Stribolt, Benjamin Christiensen, Tora Teje, Elith Pio, Karen Winther, Emmy Schonfeld, John Andersen
D: Benjamin Christiensen
W: Benjamin Christiensen

Witches, The
A: Anjelica Huston, Mai Zetterling, Jasen Fisher, Rowan Atkinson, Bill Paterson, Brenda Blethyn, Jane Horrocks, Anne Lambton, Charlie Potter
D: Nicolas Roeg
W: Allan Scott

Witches of Eastwick, The
A: Jack Nicholson, Cher, Susan Sarandon, Michelle Pfeiffer, Veronica Cartwright, Richard Jenkins, Keith Joakum, Carel Struycken
D: George Miller
W: Michael Cristofer

Witching, The
A: Orson Welles, Pamela Franklin, Michael Ontkean, Lee Purcell, Lisa James, Harvey Jason, Terry Quinn
D: Bert I. Gordon
W: Bert I. Gordon, Gail March

Wizard of Gore, The (1970)
A: Ray Sager, Judy Cler, Wayne Ratay, Phil Lauenson, Jim Rau, Don Alexander, Monika Blackwell, Corinne Kirkin
D: Herschell Gordon Lewis
W: Allen Kahn

Wizard of Gore, The (2007)
A: Kip Pardue, Bijou Phillips, Crispin Glover, Jeffrey Combs, Joshua John Miller, Brad Dourif, Garz Chan, Tim Chiou, Evan Seinfeld
D: Jeremy Kasten
W: Zach Chassler

Wolf
A: Jack Nicholson, Michelle Pfeiffer, James Spader, Kate Nelligan, Christopher Plummer, Richard Jenkins, Om Purl, Eileen Atkins, David Hyde Pierce, Ron Rifkin, Prunella Scales
D: Mike Nichols
W: Wesley Strick, Jim Harrison

Wolf Creek
A: Nathan Phillips, Cassandra Magrath, Kestie Morassi, John Jarratt
D: Greg Mclean
W: Greg Mclean

Wolf Man, The (1941)
A: Lon Chaney Jr., Claude Rains, Maria Ouspenskaya, Ralph Bellamy, Bela Lugosi, Warren William, Patric Knowles, Evalyn Ankers
D: George Waggner
W: Curt Siodmak

Wolfen
A: Albert Finney, Gregory Hines, Tom Noonan, Diane Venora, Edward James Olmos, Dick O'Neill, Dehl Berti, Peter Michael Goetz, Sam Gray, Ralph Bell
D: Michael Wadleigh
W: Michael Wadleigh, David Eyre

Wolfman (2010)
A: Benicio del Toro, Anthony Hopkins, Emily Blunt, simon Merrells, Gemma Whelan, Nicholas Day, Art Malik, Cristina Contes, Asa Butterfield, Mario Marin-Borquez
D: Joe Johnston
W: Andrew Kevin Walker, David Self

Woman in Black, The
A: Daniel Radcliffe, Ciaran Hinds, Janet McTeer, Sophie Stuckey, Roger Allam, Lucy May Barker, Shaun Dooley, Mary Stockley, Alexia Osborne, Daniel Cerqueira, Liz White, Victor McGuire, Alfie Field, William Tobin
D: James Watkins
W: Jane Goldman

Woods, The
A: Lauren Birkell, Agnes Bruckner, Jane Gilchrist, Emma Campbell, Bruce Campbell, Patricia Clarkson, Catherine Colvey, Marcia Bennett, Rachel Nichols, Kathleen Mackey, Cary Lawrence, Colleen Williams
D: Lucky McKee
W: David Ross

Wraith, The
A: Charlie Sheen, Nick Cassavetes, Sherilyn Fenn, Randy Quaid, Matthew Barry, Clint Howard, Griffin O'Neal
D: Mike Marvin
W: Mike Marvin

Wrong Turn
A: Jeremy Sisto, Eliza Dushku, Emmanuelle Chriqui, Desmond Harrington, Kevin Zegers, Linda Booth, Julian Richings, Garry Robbins, Ted Clark, One-Eye, Yvonne Gaudry, Joel Harris
D: Rob Schmidt
W: Alan B. McElroy

Young Frankenstein
A: Peter Boyle, Gene Wilder, Marty Feldman, Madeline Kahn, Cloris Leachman, Teri Garr, Kenneth Mars, Richard Haydn, Gene Hackman
D: Mel Brooks
W: Mel Brooks, Gene Wilder

Zeder (Voices from the Beyond)
A: Gabriele Lavia, Paola Tanziani, Anne Canovas, Cesare Barbetti, Bob Tonelli, Ferdinando Orlandi, Enea Ferrairio, John Stacy
D: Pupi Avati
W: Pupi Avati, Maurizio Costanzo, Antonio Avati

Zombie
A: Tisa Farrow, Ian McCullough, Richard Johnson, Al Cliver, Auretta Gay, Olga Karlatos, Stefania D'Amario, Ugo Bologna, Monica Zanchi
D: Lucio Fulci
W: Elisa Briganti

Zombie Lake
A: Howard Vernon, Pierre Escourrou, Anouchka, Anthony Mayans, Nadine Pascale, Jean Rollin
D: J.A. Laser, Jean Rollin
W: A.L. Mariaux, Julian Esteban

Zombie Strippers
A: Robert Englund, Jenna Jameson, Roxy Saint, Whitney Anderson, Penny Drake, Jennifer Holland, Shamron Moore, Jeannette Sousa
D: Jay Lee
W: Jay Lee

Zombieland
A: Woody Harrelson, Jesse Eisenberg, Emma Stone, Abigail Breslin
D: Ruben Fleischer
W: Paul Wernick, Rhett Reese

INDEX

Notes: boldface page numbers refer to the main entry of a movie; (ill.) indicates photos and illustrations.

B

G

M

N

O

P

Q

R